Violence

Violence

A Micro-sociological Theory

Randall Collins

PRINCETON UNIVERSITY PRESS

PRINCETON AND OXFORD

Copyright © 2008 by Princeton University Press
Published by Princeton University Press, 41 William Street, Princeton, New Jersey 08540
In the United Kingdom: Princeton University Press, 3 Market Place, Woodstock, Oxfordshire
OX20 1SY

Library of Congress Cataloging-in-Publication Data
Collins, Randall, 1941–
Violence : a micro-sociological theory / Randall Collins.
    p.   cm.
Includes bibliographical references and index.
ISBN-13: 978-0-691-13313-3 (hardcover : alk. paper)
ISBN-10: 0-691-13313-1 (hardcover : alk. paper)
1. Violence—United States. 2. Violence—United States—Psychological aspects. I. Title.
HM1121.C64   2008
303.60973—dc22   2007015426

British Library Cataloging-in-Publication Data is available

This book has been composed in Sabon

Printed on acid-free paper. ∞

press.princeton.edu

Printed in the United States of America

10 9 8 7 6 5

ISBN-13: 978-0-691-14322-4

Contents

Illustrations and Tables

Illustrations

Tables

Acknowledgments

I AM INDEBTED to the following for advice, comments, or information: Jack Katz, Elijah Anderson, Larry Sherman, Anthony King, Curtis Jackson-Jacobs, Georgi Derlugian, David Grazian, Marc Sageman, Tom Scheff, Eric Dunning, Johan Goudsblom, Johan Heilbron, Murray Milner, Robin Wagner-Pacifici, Katherine Newman, Dan Chambliss, Jerry M. Lewis, Geoffrey Alpert, Jens Ludwig, Meredith Rossner, Wes Skogan, Lode Walgrave, Ian O'Donnell, Nikki Jones, Peter Moskos, Alice Goffman, Deanna Wilkinson, Maren McConnell-Collins, Ken Donow, Jon Olesberg, Jon Turner, Rae Lesser Blumberg, Anthony Oberschall, Rose Cheney, Irma Elo, Patricia Maloney, Mollie Rubin, Clark McCauley, Judith McConnell, Heather Strang, Stefan Klusemann, Donald Levine, Robert Emerson, Jeff Goodwin, Richard Trembley, and Anthony McConnell-Collins. I thank also colloquium participants at the universities of Amsterdam, Cambridge, Copenhagen, Galway, University College Dublin, Notre Dame, Princeton, Kent State, UCLA, and at the International Institution for the Sociology of Law at Onati, Spain; officers of the San Diego and Philadelphia Police Departments, California Highway Patrol, New Jersey State Police, and the Irish Garda; and members of my classes in social conflict at University of California Riverside and University of Pennsylvania. I owe special thanks to Danielle Kane, who provided invaluable research assistance. The Solomon Asch Center for Study of Ethnopolitical Conflict has provided a stimulating environment for discussions of multiple aspects of conflict, as have the Jerry Lee Center for Criminology and the Department of Criminology at the University of Pennsylvania.

Violence

CHAPTER 1

The Micro-sociology of Violent Confrontations

THERE IS A VAST ARRAY of types of violence. It is short and episodic as a slap in the face; or massive and organized as a war. It can be passionate and angry as a quarrel; or callous and impersonal as the bureaucratic administration of gas chambers. It is happy as drunken carousing, fearful as soldiers in combat, vicious as a torturer. It can be furtive and hidden as a rape-murder, or public as a ritual execution. It is programmed entertainment in the form of sporting contests, the plot tension of drama, the action of action-adventure, the staple shocker of the news edition. It is horrible and heroic, disgusting and exciting, the most condemned and glorified of human acts.

This vast array can be explained by a relatively compact theory. A few main processes, in combination and in differing degrees of intensity, give the conditions for when and how the various forms of violence occur.

Two moves will set up the analysis. First, put the interaction in the center of the analysis, not the individual, the social background, the culture, or even the motivation: that is to say, look for the characteristics of violent situations. That means looking for data that gets us as close as possible into the dynamics of situations. Second, compare across different kinds of violence. We need to break down the usual categories—homicides in one research specialty, war in another, child abuse in another, police violence yet elsewhere—and look for the situations that occur within them. Not that all situations are the same; we want to compare the range of variation in situations, which affects the kind and amount of violence that emerges. This will turn the wide variety of violence into a methodological advantage, giving clues to the circumstances that explain when and in what manner violence unfolds.

VIOLENT SITUATIONS

Not violent individuals, but violent situations—this is what a micro-sociological theory is about. We seek the contours of situations, which shape the emotions and acts of the individuals who step inside them. It is a false lead to look for types of violent individuals, constant across situations. A huge amount of research has not yielded very strong results here. Young men, yes, are most likely to be perpetrators of many kinds of violence. But not all young men are violent. And middle-aged men, children, and women are violent too, in the appropriate situations. Similarly with background variables such as poverty, race, and origins in divorce or single-parent families. Though there are some statistical correlations between these variables and certain kinds of violence, these fall short of predicting most violence in at least three aspects:

First, most young men, poor people, black people, or children of divorce do not become murderers, rapists, batterers, or armed robbers; and there are a certain number of affluent persons, white people, or products of conventional families who do. Similarly, the much asserted explanation that violent offenders are typically past victims of child abuse accounts for only a minority of the cases.[1]

Second, such analysis conveys a plausible picture of the etiology of violence only because it restricts the dependent variable to particular categories of illegal or highly stigmatized violence; it does not hold up well when we broaden out to all kinds of violence. Poverty, family strain, child abuse, and the like do not account for police violence or for which soldiers do the most killing in combat, for who runs gas chambers or commits ethnic cleansing. No one has shown that being abused as a child is likely to make someone a cowboy cop, a carousing drunk, or a decorated war hero. No doubt there are readers who will bridle at the suggestion; for them, violence naturally falls into hermetically sealed sections, and "bad" social conditions should be responsible for "bad" violence, whereas "good" violence—which is not seen as violence at all, when it is carried out by authorized state agents—is not subject to analysis since it is part of normal social order. In this way of thinking, there is an intermediate category of innocuous or "naughty" violence (i.e., carousing that gets out of hand), or violence that is committed by "good" persons; this is explained, or explained away, by another set of moral categories. Such distinctions are a good example of conventional social categories getting in the way of sociological analysis. If we zero in on the situation of interaction—the angry boyfriend with the crying baby, the armed robber squeezing the trigger on the holdup victim, the cop beating up the suspect—we can see patterns of confrontation, tension, and emotional flow, which are at the heart of the situation where violence is carried out. This is another way of seeing that the background conditions—poverty, race, childhood experiences—are a long way from what is crucial to the dynamics of the violent situation.

Third, even those persons who are violent, are violent only a small part of the time. Consider what we mean when we say that a person is violent, or "very violent." We have in mind someone who is a convicted murderer, or has committed a string of murders; who has been in many fights, slashed people with a knife, or battered them with fists. But if we consider that everyday life unfolds in a chain of situations, minute by minute, most of the time there is very little violence. This is apparent from ethnographic observations, even in statistically very violent neighborhoods. A homicide rate of ten deaths per 100,000 persons (the rate in the United States peaking in 1990) is a fairly high rate, but it means that 99,990 out of 100,000 persons do not get murdered in a year; and 97,000 of them (again, taking the peak rate) are not assaulted even in minor incidents. And these violent incidents are spread out over a year; the chances of murder or assault happening to a particular person at any particular moment on a particular day during that year are very small. This applies even to those persons who actually do commit one or more murders, assaults, armed robberies, or rapes (or for that matter, cops who beat up suspects) during the course of the year. Even those persons who statistically commit a lot of crime scarcely do so at a rate of more than once a week or so; the most notorious massacres in schools, workplaces, or public places, carried out by lone individuals, have killed as many as twenty-five persons, but generally within a single episodes (Hickey 2002; Newman et al. 2004). The most sustained violent persons are serial killers, who average between six and thirteen victims over a period of years; but these are extremely rare (about one victim per five million population), and even these repeat killers go months between killings, waiting for just the right situation to strike (Hickey 2002: 12–13, 241–42). Another kind of rare cluster of violence, crime sprees, may continue for a period of days, in a chain of events linked closely by emotions and circumstances so as to comprise a tunnel of violence. Leaving these extended sequences of violence aside for the moment, I want to underline the conclusion: even people that we think of as very violent—because they have been violent in more than one situation, or spectacularly violent on some occasion—are violent only in very particular situations.[2] Even the toughest hoodlums are off duty some of the time. Most of the time, the most dangerous, most violent persons are not doing anything violent. Even for these people, the dynamics of situations are crucial in explaining what violence they actually do.

MICRO-EVIDENCE: SITUATIONAL RECORDINGS, RECONSTRUCTIONS, AND OBSERVATIONS

Surveys of individuals orient our theories to the characteristics of individuals, packaged in the terms of standard sociological variables. To move to a sociological theory, not of violent individuals, but of violent situations, we must emphasize a different way of collecting and analyzing data. We need direct observation of violent interaction to capture the process of violence as it actually is performed. Our theories are constrained by having been based upon statistics assembled after the fact, packaged by the criminal justice system, or upon interviews with convicted prisoners or other participants. Victim surveys are a step in the right direction, but they remain limited, not only by the issue of to what extent victims are telling the truth, but also by the problem that persons are generally not good observers of the details and contexts of dramatic events. Our ordinary discourse does not provide the language in which to describe micro-interaction well; instead, it offers a set of clichés and myths that predetermine what people will say. This is true also of military violence, riots, sports violence, or even ordinary quarrels; when participants talk about violent situations, they tend to give a very truncated, and by their own lights, idealized version of what went on.

A new era has emerged in recent decades as it has become possible to study violence as recorded on video tape from security systems, police recordings, and news and amateur video photographers. When ordinary observers see such recordings, they are usually shocked. A riot eventually followed the publicity given to a video recording, taken by an amateur with a new camcorder, of the Rodney King arrest in Los Angeles in 1991. Events are always interpreted in terms of prevailing ideological categories; the concepts easily at hand were those of a racially motivated beating. But what was so shocking about the Rodney King video was not its racial aspect; it was the beating itself, which did not look at all like what we think violence is supposed to look like. Visual evidence shows us something about violence that we are not prepared to see. The pattern looks much the same in a wide range of incidents, in many different ethnic combinations within and across ethnic group lines (we will examine some of these in chapters 2 and 3). Racism may contribute to building up some situations of violence, but it is one lead-in condition among others, and neither a necessary nor a sufficient condition; the situation of violence itself has a dynamics that is more pervasive than racism.

Violence as it actually becomes visible in real-life situations is about the intertwining of human emotions of fear, anger, and excitement, in ways that run right against the conventional morality of normal situations. It is just this shocking and unexpected quality of violence, as it actually appears in the cold eye of the camera, that gives a clue to the emotional dynamics at the center of a micro-situational theory of violence.

We live in an era in which our ability to see what happens in real-life situations is far greater than ever before. We owe this new vision to a combination of technology and sociological method. The ethnomethodologists of the 1960s and 1970s took off as an intellectual movement in tandem with the use of newly portable cassette tape recorders; this made it possible to record at least the audio part of real-life social interactions, and to play it back repeatedly, slowing it down and subjecting it to analysis in a way that had been barely possible with fleeting observations in real time, giving rise to the field of conversation analysis (Sacks, Schegloff, and Jefferson 1974; Schegloff 1992). As video recording devices became more portable and ubiquitous, it has been possible to look at other aspects of micro-behavior, including bodily rhythms, postures, and expressions of emotion. Thus it is not surprising that the period from about 1980 onward has been the golden age for the sociology of emotions (Katz 1999, among many others).

It is not literally true that a picture is worth a thousand words. Most people will not see what is in a picture, or will see it through the most readily available visual clichés. It takes training and an analytical vocabulary to talk about what is in a picture, and to know what to look for. A picture is worth a thousand words only for those who already have internalized an adequate vocabulary. This is particularly so when we have to train ourselves to see micro-details: the movements of some facial muscles rather than others that distinguish a false smile from a spontaneous one; the movements that display fear, tension, and other emotions; the smoothness of rhythmic coordination and the hitches that indicate disattunement and conflict; the patterns in which one person or another seizes the initiative and imposes a rhythm upon others. The methods of visual and auditory recording now available open up the potential to see a vast new landscape of human interaction; but our ability to see goes in tandem with the expansion of our theories of what processes are out there to be seen.

This is so also in the micro-sociology of violence. The video revolution has made available much more information about what happens in violent situations than ever before. But real-life recording conditions are not like Hollywood film studios; lighting and composition are far from ideal, and the camera angles and distance may not be just the ones a micro-sociologist would prefer. We need to disengage ourselves from the conventions of dramatically satisfying film (including TV commercials) where the camera cuts to a new angle every few seconds at the most, and a great deal of editing has gone on to juxtapose an interesting and engaging sequence. A micro-sociologist can spot the difference between raw observational recording and artistically or editorially processed film, usually within seconds. Raw conflict is not very engaging, for all sorts of reasons; as micro-sociologists, we are not in it for entertainment.

Other approaches besides live video have opened up the landscape of violence as it really happens. Still photography has gotten better throughout the past century and a half; cameras have become more portable, and lenses and lighting devices have made it possible to capture scenes that previously would have been limited to static posed shots in relatively sheltered conditions. Professional photographers have become more intrepid, particularly in riots, demonstrations, and war zones; the number of photographers killed has gone up drastically in the past ten years, far above any previous period.[3] This too is an opportunity for micro-sociologists, although the aforementioned caveats again apply. Still photos are often better than videos for capturing the emotional aspects of violent interaction. When we analyze a video of a conflict sequence (or indeed any video of interaction), we may slow it down to segments of micro-seconds (frame-by-frame in older camera film) to pull out just those details of bodily posture, facial expression, and sequence of micro-movements. In depictions of riots, which I use extensively in this work, still photos dramatically show the division between the active few on the violent front and the supporting mass of demonstrators. The danger is in assuming one can read the still photo without sociological sensibilities. Highly artistic or ideological photographers are less useful here than routine news photographers; some photos of demonstrations or combat have an artistic or political message that governs the whole composition; we need to look from a different vantage point to get at the micro-sociological aspects of conflict.

An intellectual stance on what to look for has gone along with technological advances, and sometimes preceded them. The military historian John Keegan (1976) set out to reconstruct battles from the ground up, investigating what must actually have happened as each segment of troops rushed forward or fell down; as horses, men, and vehicles got tangled in traffic jams; as weapons were wielded skillfully, accidentally, or not at all. Other military analysts have found out how many guns were loaded when recovered from dead troops on battlefields; and historical battles have been reconstructed with laser beams. What we have learned about soldiers in combat has opened the door for understanding violent situations in general. The emotional relationships between soldiers and their comrades, and between them and their equally human enemies, provided one of the first clues to how violent situations unfold.[4]

In our ordinary compartmentalized way of viewing things, it is a leap from military history to reconstructions of police violence, but the methodological and theoretical parallels are strong. We can understand the occasions on which police are violent by techniques such as video recordings and through methods of reconstructing events, such as ballistics analysis of the trajectories of bullets, how many hit intended and unintended targets, and how many missed entirely. Old-fashioned ethnographies have helped too; ride-alongs by sociologists in police cars, dating to the 1960s, preceded some of these technological advances and provided some key theoretical components. Technologies by themselves rarely provide real insight; it is their combination with analytical viewpoints that is crucial.

To summarize, there are at least three methods for getting at situational details of violent interactions: recordings, reconstructions, and observations. They are most useful when used in combination.

Technologies of recording real-life conflict are useful for a series of reasons: they can provide us details that we otherwise wouldn't see at all, that we were not prepared to look at, or did not know were there; they can give us a more analytical stance, more detached from the everyday perceptual gestalts and the clichés of conventional language for talking about violence; they enable us to look at a situation over and over, getting beyond the initial shock (or jadedness, prurient interest, and the like) so that we can bring our theoretical minds to bear, and to make discoveries or test theories.

Reconstructions are important because violent situations are relatively rare, and for many incidents we would most like to understand, there were no recording devices available at the time. We are not as much in the dark as we once thought we were: as we have gotten better at situational analysis, and (coming from another angle) as new techniques keep on being developed for analyzing physical clues left on the ground, it has been possible to reconstruct many violent scenes. A wide range of reconstructions is useful to us, including historical events, because they give us theoretical leverage for finding both the commonalities and the dimensions of variation among violent situations.

Finally, there is human observation. This can be old-fashioned ethnography, especially the participant observation version in which the sociologist (or anthropologist, psychologist, or sophisticated journalist) gets inside the scene with his or her senses sharpened, looking for telling details. A variant is equally old-fashioned self-observation, reports on what oneself experienced as a participant. In the field of violence, much of what we have learned comes from reports by ex-soldiers, ex-criminals, or indeed not so "ex" persons, who are reflective enough to talk about fights they have seen or been in. There is also much of value here in reports from victims of violence, although this has not been much exploited by sociologists, beyond bare statistical counts of how often certain kinds of victimization occurs. Moreover, as we gain a better theoretical understanding of what are the important micro-details of violent confrontations, we become better at interrogating our own experience, and better at asking retrospective observers for the kind of details we would like to know about their encounters with violence. By providing a vocabulary, we make our informants often quite good reporters of details they otherwise gloss over.

The three kinds of situational evidence fit together. They complement each other not only ethodologically but also substantively. They all reveal a common situational dynamic. That is what this book is about.

COMPARING SITUATIONS ACROSS TYPES OF VIOLENCE

To develop a theory of the dynamics of violence requires another shift: to work across research specialties, rather than be confined within them. The center of this approach is to compare different kinds of violence in a common theoretical framework. Is this not to compare apples and oranges, or at best merely to taxonomize? This is a point that cannot be decided a priori. Once we look, we find that violence is an array of processes that all follow from a common situational feature of violent confrontations.

I will state the point cryptically here: violence is a set of pathways around confrontational tension and fear. Despite their bluster, and even in situations of apparently uncontrollable anger, people are tense and often fearful in the immediate threat of violence—including their own violence; this is the emotional dynamic that determines what they will do if fighting actually breaks out. Whether indeed that will happen depends on a series of conditions or turning-points that shape the tension and fear in particular directions, reorganizing the emotions as an interactional process involving everyone present: the antagonists, audience, and even ostensibly disengaged bystanders.

How do we know this? The theoretical point has developed from accumulating information on a variety of violent situations. The first breakthrough came from the study of military combat. Fear, wild firing, hitting soldiers on one's own side, freezing up: these were features noted by officers analyzing the behavior of frontline troops in battle, beginning with the nineteenth-century French officer Ardant du Picq, who collected questionnaires from combat officers. S.L.A. Marshall got closer to the immediate action in his World War II post-battle interviews with soldiers themselves. In the 1970s, the picture of battle behavior was systematized in historical reconstructions by Keegan and others. By the 1990s, the military psychologist Dave Grossman synthesized a theory of combat centered on the management of fear. An even more pronounced pattern of alternating fearful and aggressive behavior is seen in ethnographic films made in the 1960s of fighting among tribal societies. Comparing across different kinds of military violence leads to a theoretical insight: armies vary in their performance because of the kind of organization used to control fear among their troops. Generalizing the point, we can say that all types of violence fit a small number of patterns for circumventing the barrier of tension and fear that rises up whenever people come into antagonistic confrontation.

The military model also fits police violence during arrests and handling prisoners. Police and military confrontations lead to atrocities by the same path: the sequence of emotional events that, in chapter 3, I call "forward panic." Crowd violence or riot also resembles military violence in some central mechanisms; much of the time confrontation is largely bluster and gesture but leads to little real harm; what is fateful are sudden breaks in the solidarity of one side, which spreads them out into an open field of small groups, where a superior number from one side can isolate and beat up an individual or two separate from their comrades. These are all very ugly forms of violence when we actually see them in detail; indeed, the disparity between their idealized self-image and their atrocious reality is one more situational feature they have in common.

These various forms of violence are subtypes within one of the main pathways around confrontational tension and fear: find a weak victim to attack. Domestic violence is harder for outside observers to study directly, and recordings are virtually nonexistent; we rely here on interview reconstructions, which are limited by being largely confined to reports from just one participant. Nevertheless, working through a large body of evidence, I conclude that the major forms of domestic violence resemble the type of military and police situation that fits under the rubric of "attacking the weak." The nastiest version of this happens when the confrontational tension builds high, followed by a sudden collapse so that an opponent who initially seems threatening or frustrating turns out to be helpless, unleashing in the other a transformation of fear and tension into ferocious attack. There are also more institutionalized forms of attacking the weak, repetitive patterns in which one or both sides become accustomed to acting out the roles of strong and weak in a situational drama. These include bullying and also the kinds performed by specialists in criminal violence, muggers and holdup artists, who have perfected their skills at finding the right kinds of victims in the right kinds of situations; their success depends upon battening upon confrontational tension itself. Comparisons across disparate forms of violence thus uncover similar mechanisms of emotional interaction.

In another large set of situations, a very different pathway circumvents situational tension and fear. Instead of finding a weak victim, the focus of emotional attention is on the audience before whom the fight is performed. These fights differ greatly from the attacking-the-situationally-weak kind of pathway, because the fighters attend much more to their audience than to each other; as we shall see from evidence presented in chapter 6, the stance of the audience has an overwhelming effect on whether and how much violence is carried out. Such fights are typically stylized and limited, although what happens within those limits may be bloody enough or indeed deadly; in one major variant, violence is socially organized as fair fights, limited to certain kinds of appropriately matched opponents. Here again the social structures promoting and controlling such fights best become visible by comparing across situations. These include personal fights as observed on streets or places of entertainment; fighting as a form of carousing fun; children's ordinary scuffling and mock-violence; dueling; martial arts and other fighting schools; and sports violence among both players and fans. This set of situations might be regarded as violence for fun and honor, in contrast to the truly nasty forms of violence noted earlier, which depend upon finding a situationally weak victim. Nevertheless, as we look into the micro-realities of fighting for fun and honor, we find they too remain shaped by confrontational tension and fear; people are still for the most part not good at violence, and what they manage to do depends on how attuned they are with an audience that gives them emotional dominance over an opponent.

FIGHT MYTHS

The most common pathway around confrontational tension and fear is a very short one, leading no further: people do not get beyond the emotional tensions of the confrontation, but confine themselves to bluster, or to finding face-saving or sometimes humiliating ways of backing down. When violence does break out, it is usually incompetent, because tension and fear remain during the performance.

One reason that real violence looks so ugly is because we have been exposed to so much mythical violence. That we actually see it unfolding before our eyes in films and on television makes us feel that this is what real violence is like. Contemporary film style of grabbing the viewers' attention with bloody injuries and brutal aggressiveness may give many people the sense that entertainment violence is, if anything, too realistic. Nothing could be farther from the truth. The conventions of portraying violence almost always miss the most important dynamics of violence: that it starts from confrontational tension and fear, that most of the time it is bluster, and that the circumstances that allow this tension to be overcome lead to violence that is more ugly than entertaining. The entertainment media are not the only sources of pervasive distortions of the reality of fighting; the verbal conventions of bragging and threat, and of telling stories about fights we have seen, all contribute to making violence a modern-day mythology.

A particularly silly myth is that fights are contagious. This is a staple of old film comedies and melodramas. One person punches another in a crowded bar or restaurant; the waiter topples over with a tray, outraging another patron, and in the next frames everyone is hitting everyone around them. This fighting of all against all, I am quite certain, has never occurred as a serious matter in real life. The typical response of bystanders when a fight breaks out in a crowded place is to back away to a safe distance and watch. Polite middle-class crowds react with more unease or horror, shrinking away as far as possible without showing overt panic; I have witnessed this, for instance, when a couple of homeless men got into a scuffle on the sidewalk outside a downtown theater while the audience was outside during intermission. The punch-throwing was brief, followed by the usual hostile muttering and gesturing; the well-dressed middle-class people kept their wary distance in hushed unease. In boisterous working-class or youth scenes, the crowd generally will make a space for the individuals to fight; it sometimes cheers and shouts encouragement from a safe distance. But if the level of anger is high among the principals, onlookers tend to shrink back vocally as well as physically.[5] Even more so with fights in sparsely populated public places: bystanders keep their distance.

What one does not see is a contagion of belligerence, everyone starting to fight with everyone else. People are not on a hair trigger of aggressiveness, ready to be released by the slightest catalyst. The Hobbesian image of humans, judging from the most common evidence, is empirically wrong. Fighting, and indeed most overt expressions of conflict, most typically call out fear or at least wariness.

The exception to non-contagiousness is when the crowd is already divided into antagonistic group identities. If a fight breaks out between individuals from opposing groups, others from their side may join in, and the fight will expand. This is one typical scenario by which crowds of rival football supporters (so-called football hooligans, especially British) begin their violence; it is also an instigator of ethnic violence and other kinds of what Tilly (2003) calls "boundary activation" of collective identities. This is not war of all against all; the inaptly named "free-for-all" may look chaotic and unstructured to outsiders, but it is indeed quite strongly organized. This organization is what enables individuals to overcome the pervasive fear that keeps most of them from fighting; if it were not socially well organized, wide-participation fighting would not be possible.

Even in these instances, we should be wary of assuming that all confrontations of individuals belonging to hostile groups lead to mass participation. Football hooligans in a strange town, encountering the local supporters, may shout insults, threaten, even skirmish a little, running forward and then back into the safety of their side; but in many instances they do not get into a full-scale "aggro." The catalytic moment does not always happen; the participants on both sides are often content to find excuses, especially when they are overmatched, or even just equally divided; the confrontation they are looking for, they decide, is still in the future. Such mini-confrontations play a considerable part in the ongoing lore of the group; it is what they like to talk about, what their conversational rituals center on in their drinking gatherings, as they reinterpret the

Figure 1.1 Bystanders keep back from fight (New York City, 1950). Elliott Erwitt/ Magnum Photos.

events of the past hours or days; the standoff is often blown up into a battle, or taken as a sign of the other side's cowardice in backing down from their toughness (King 2001; Eric Dunning, personal communication March 2001). Groups that engage in some fighting build up mythologies around themselves, exaggerating the amount of fighting and their performance in it, and downplaying their own tendencies to back away from most fights.

Another apparent exception to the non-contagiousness of fighting is the friendly free-for-all such as pillow fights or food fights. Pillow fights at a festive occasion such as a children's sleep-over typically have an all-against-all character; this both promotes and enhances a mood of hilarity, implying that the situation is very unusual, framed as an exceptionally

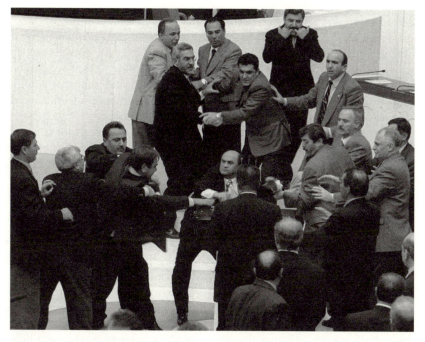

Figure 1.2 Turkish members of parliament fight while colleagues hold each other back (2001). Reuters.

good joke. The multi-sidedness of the pillow fight is more of a participation-spreader, bringing everyone into the collective fun. In this respect, friendly pillow fights are like New Year's or other carnival celebrations, which involve throwing streamers and blowing noise-makers indiscriminately at other people. The same goes for bathers playfully splashing water at each other in a swimming pool—by my observations, this occurs in the early moments, as soon as a group of acquaintances has entered the pool, that is, entered the festive space. Nevertheless, if the play turns at all rough, it falls into a two-sided pattern. Pillow fights taking place as a form of entertainment in prison cells, for example, often escalate by putting books or other hard objects inside the pillow cases, and these turn into ganging up on the weakest victim, the one most prone to break down (O'Donnell and Edgar 1998a: 271). During food fights in institutional dining halls, people throw food around more or less randomly, without looking at targets; they throw it up in the air, generally in the direction of persons at distant seats, or better yet, distant tables. In these settings, food fights have both the character of spontaneous self-entertainment, but also a revolt against authority in total institutions. Food fights are also observed in popular lunch-time groups in American high schools, but here it is less a free-for-all and more often a form of boy-girl flirting or playful activity among friends, the same persons who engage in food sharing as a sign of intimacy (Milner 2004: chap. 3). The upshot is that we can be pretty sure, when we see a fight in the all-vs.-all mode, that this is only play-violence, not serious; the emotional tone is not confrontational tension-fear, and everyone can sense when it is or isn't.

A second myth is that fights are long. In Hollywood films (not to mention Hong Kong kung-fu films and similar action adventure films the world over), fist fights as well as gunfights go on for many minutes. Fighters are resilient, taking many blows and coming back to dish them out; crashing over tables, knocking down shelves of bottles, bouncing off walls, falling over balconies and down stairs and hillsides, in and out of cars and other speeding vehicles. Shooting involves much resolute stalking, running from cover to cover, sometimes daringly outflanking the opponent, but never retreating; on the other side, the evil-doers keep coming back, sneakily and warily if not by sheer pugnacity and ferociousness. In the 1981 film *Raiders of the Lost Ark*, the hero trades punches with a beefy villain for four minutes; then he immediately jumps on a horse to chase and board a speeding truck in another fight sequence, lasting eight and a half minutes. During the course of these sequences, the hero kills or knocks out fifteen of the enemy, plus another seven civilian bystanders. Dramatic time of course is not real time; but whereas most film and stage dramas compress real time to gloss over the dull and routine moments of ordinary life, they expand fighting time by many times over. The illusion is further bolstered by fights staged as entertainment. Boxing matches typically are planned for a series of three-minute rounds, up to a maximum of thirty or forty-five minutes of fighting (in the nineteenth century sometimes much longer); but these are deliberately controlled by social and physical supports and constraints so as to make most matches produce many minutes of more or less continuous fighting. Even here, referees generally have to prod boxers to stop stalling or tying each other up by clinching. It takes continuous social pressure to keep a fight going. Such fighting is an entirely artificial construction; it is an entertaining spectacle precisely because of its extreme departure from ordinary reality.

In reality, most serious fights on the individual or small-group level are extremely short. If we cut out the preliminaries and the aftermath, with their insults, noise, and gesturing, and look only at the violence, it is often remarkably brief. The actual gunfight at the O.K. Corral in Tombstone, Arizona, in 1881 took less than thirty seconds (see reprint of *Tombstone Epitaph*, Oct. 1881); the 1957 movie version took seven minutes. Crimes involving the use of guns almost never take the form of gunfights between sides both armed and firing at each other. The vast majority of murders and assaults with deadly weapons consist of one or more armed persons briefly attacking an unarmed person. Since the latter half of the twentieth century, gang fights, drug turf battles, or reputational confrontations, as in violence-prone areas such as inner-city racial ghettos, often involve guns. But they are usually not gun-battles, but very brief episodes, usually with only one side firing.

Fist fights are also generally brief. Many bar-room brawls and street fights are one-punch affairs. The lore of such fighting is that whoever gets in the first punch generally wins. Why should this be so? Consider the alternatives. A two-sided, relatively evenly matched fight could hypothetically go on for some time. But evenly matched scuffling is likely to be unsatisfying when, as is usually the case, neither does much damage, or nothing happens that counts as a dramatic blow producing dominance. Fighters in such situations settle for demonstrating their willingness to fight, and then truncating the actual fighting by letting it degenerate into gesturing and name-calling. Another common occurrence is that one of the fighters hurts himself, such as by breaking his hand in throwing a punch.[6] Injuries of this sort are often regarded as fair grounds for ending the fight. A key issue then is when a fight is considered to be over. Far from seeking long-term, knock-down drag-out fights of the Hollywood film or boxing match type, ordinary belligerents are satisfied for fights to be short dramatic episodes, minimizing the period when they are actually fighting. They are willing to give or take a hurt during that period, and then use the hurt as a resolution for the fight, at least for the time being.

A fight of this sort may be part of a series of violent confrontations; for example, a short fight in a bar may lead to one of the participants leaving, getting a gun, and returning to shoot the winner of the first fight. But this is typically two short episodes of micro-confrontation. Individuals' anger and feelings of being involved in a conflict are not coextensive with their peak capacity actually to carry out violence.

Fights with knives and other cutting weapons also tend to be brief. For the most part, these are situations of flashing knives at each other but letting the confrontation turn into a standoff; where serious injury is done, a quick blow is struck, and the fight is thereby regarded as at an end. Thus another staple of entertainment lore regarding an earlier historical period, the extended swordfight as choreographed in films and plays, was probably for the most part mythical. In early modern Europe, if someone actually succeeded in killing the other, or inflicting serious injury (cases likely to come to the notice of authorities), it was usually described as an ambush, or a group attack on an individual (Spierenburg 1994). This would be the equivalent of the one-punch, sucker-punch bar fight.

There are two important classes of exceptions. Exceptions to a generalization are valuable because they enable us to refine the explanation.

Where individual or small-group fights are prolonged beyond a few moments, it is typically because either (a) the fight is highly circumscribed, so that it is not really "serious," or it is clearly understood that there are safeguards to limit the fighting; or (b) the type of exception described by the expression "hitting a man when he is down" (although the victim may well be a woman or a child), where in effect there is no real fight but a massacre or punishment.

The typical exception of type (a) has the structure of the boxing match, or even more so, sparring practice for such a match. European aristocrats in the seventeenth and eighteenth centuries spent much time in fencing lessons; nineteenth-century German university students belonged to dueling fraternities, fighting matches that ended not so much in victory as in getting a scar on one's face as a mark of honor. These are controlled forms of fighting and could be extended for as long as fifteen minutes (Twain 1880/1977: 29–31); not only is the extent of injury generally quite limited, but also the confrontational mood is dampened; these are not angry encounters, but even a form of solidarity.

Just how narrow is this exception becomes apparent when we compare practicing for duels with the duels themselves (for further detail, see chap. 6). Most pistol duels were literally one-shot fights—that is, one shot was planned to be fired by each side. The moment of danger, though real, was brief; if both survived, honor could be considered satisfied. Duels had the same structure as modern fights: typically very brief, within a few seconds of actual violence; preceded by a build-up period of ritual exchange of insults; and terminated by mutual agreement as the result of the conflict, whether by explicit tradition or implicitly.

The same pattern appears in Japan during the Tokugawa era (seventeenth and eighteenth centuries). Samurai were ideally expected to defend their honor with a fight to the death, and could be quite touchy about insults in public places (Ikegami 1995, personal communication). Indeed, samurai went out of their way to make insults very easy, since an accidental knocking of sword scabbards in passing was taken as an affront. One side effect—or perhaps it was the main effect, motivating the practice— was that samurai went about clutching their scabbards, one on each side, the mark and privilege of the samurai rank being to wear two swords. This kept them constantly focused on their emblem of social identity as fighters, even as it prevented most outbursts from occurring. If a fight broke out, it happened on the spot, without the apparatus of challenges, seconds, and advance scheduling found in European duels. Samurai thus tended to be in a constant state of threat and gesture rather than actual fighting. According to the professional lore of the sword instructors, deadly fights should be very brief, consisting of a sudden decisive stroke; in reality, most fighters were probably not this accomplished, although the ideology may have justified the brevity of actual fights. Vastly more time was spent in samurai schools, practicing fighting in controlled ways that obviated injury as well as angry emotion; indeed, such schools tended toward formal exercises of movements aimed at imaginary opponents— like the *katas*, which make up much of the activity of martial arts schools in karate.

The most famous case of a samurai avenging an insult was the so-called forty-seven *ronin*, in 1702. One high-ranking samurai was insulted by another over a matter of etiquette in the shogun's palace; he drew his sword and wounded the insulter, but was quickly disarmed by other attendants. This was not a duel, since the insulter did not draw a weapon; it was not highly effective, since the man was not killed. The incident was apparently very brief, resulting in a few slashes. The attacker was condemned for drawing his sword in the palace, and required to commit *seppuku*. The forty-seven retainers (*ronin*) eventually avenged the death of their master, again not by dueling, but by a military assault on the house of the original insulter, killing a number of guards and the samurai lord, who did not defend himself. None of the forty-seven was killed in the attack, indicating that they had overwhelming force, the typical pattern of a strong force ganging up on a weaker one. Even the aftermath did not match the heroic code. The court ruled that avenging honor was not an excuse in this case, but the forty-seven *ronin* were allowed to commit *seppuku* as an honorable way to die. Ideally, this was supposed to consist of cutting open one's bowels with a short knife across the stomach; the agony then would be cut short by being beheaded by a man standing behind the seated samurai. In reality, the forty-seven committed "fan *seppuku*"—instead of a knife they held a fan with which they gestured a stomach slash, whereupon they were beheaded (Ikegami 1995). It was in fact an execution by beheading, mitigated by the formalities of ritual suicide, which was how the event was publicly announced and received. Japanese samurai movies, continuing an earlier genre of stories, are as mythical as Hollywood westerns.

Another variant on the pattern of prolonged protected fights comes into focus when we examine children's fights. Fighting among children is the most common form of violence in the family; it is far more common than spousal violence or child abuse (see chapter 4). But children are rarely injured in these fights; in part because children, especially when small, have little capacity to hurt each other in these scuffles. More importantly, children pick their occasions for such scuffles, generally when parents or caretakers are nearby, so that if the fight escalates, they can call for help and end the fight. An example from my ethnographic notes:

Somerville, Mass. December 1994. Family in working-class neighborhood, getting into car on Sunday morning. Father sitting at wheel, warming up car; two boys (about ages 8 and 10) playing around behind car (in alley where it's parked, outside house), with a little girl (about 3 or 4); mother (woman around 30) coming out of house last. Little girl is getting into back seat from left side of 4-door car; smaller boy bumps her with the door and she starts to cry, whereupon bigger boy hits younger boy, "look what you did!" Mother comes out at just this time; father ignores it. Mother now hurriedly tries to make the boys get into car. They evade her, going behind car and start running around and swiping at each other. Bigger boy has a soft drink sitting on trunk; smaller boy spills it onto ground. Bigger boy now hits him hard and makes him cry. Mother intervenes, threatens the bigger boy, who runs away from her. She turns and puts the smaller boy into the car from the left rear side. The bigger boy now comes and tries to pull him out: "That's my seat!" Father turns around from front seat and half-heartedly tries to pull one of the boys off. The mother, who starts out hurried but fairly quiet, starts screaming, and pulls the bigger boy out of the car. The bigger boy now appeals to his father, says he's forgotten something in the house. He goes into house. Now mother demands smaller boy to move over to other side of car; he resists, she finally pulls him out and forces him to move over, protesting that he's the victim of his older brother. Older boy comes back; same sequence of fighting over back seat, but briefer; finally all get into car (older boy in left back) and car leaves.

In this sense, children act like adults, except that the latter have developed means of bringing fights to an end on their own, whereas children rely on outsiders to do it for them.[7] Similarly, fights that break out in schools commonly occur in the presence of a teacher, or where a teacher will likely come quickly to break it up; in prisons, most fights occur in the presence of guards (Edgar and O'Donnell 1998). This is a mechanism by which fights are kept short.

Exception (b) consists in longer violence that may take place in instances where there is overwhelming disparity in force between the two sides, a group gives an isolated enemy a prolonged beating, or a strong individual beats on a weaker. The lesson suggested by this exception is that it is the fighting confrontation rather than violence per se that is hard to sustain for very long: the tension of a one-on-one fight or evenly matched small groups, trading blow for blow, shot for shot; but if one side gets the other down or in an unprotected position, the tension is resolved and violence can proceed.

Real fights are generally short; participants do not appear to have reserves of motivation that carry them into a prolonged violent struggle with another individual. Fights are kept short because participants are good at finding stopping points that they regard as dramatically appropriate. Fights can take longer when they are deliberately staged as not serious, not part of the ground-zero real world. Violent episodes can be longer and more drawn out if they are controlled, restrained both in their likelihood of injury and in their atmosphere of hostility; practice-fighting is thus much lengthier than real fights. Even angry fights tend to happen in places where they can be broken up.

Another entertainment myth is the smiling, joking killer or bad guy. It is extremely rare that killers, robbers, or fighters are in a laughing good humor, or even display sardonic wit.[8] The laughing villain image comes across so well precisely because it is unrealistic, giving a coded message that the villainous deeds are not real, but encapsulated within an entertainment frame; hence it is a favored stereotype for cartoons and comic/fantasy melodrama, and introduces just such a comic tinge into allegedly serious drama. The image enables the viewer to take the entertainment-audience attitude, not the horrified attitude that would occur with real violence. Once again, entertainment violence manages to present violence so that its key feature—confrontational tension and fear—is covered up.

VIOLENT SITUATIONS ARE SHAPED BY AN EMOTIONAL FIELD OF TENSION AND FEAR

My aim is a general theory of violence as situational process. Violent situations are shaped by an emotional field of tension and fear. Any successful violence must overcome this tension and fear. One way this is done is by turning the emotional tension into emotional energy, usually by one side of the confrontation at the expense of the other. Successful violence battens on confrontational tension/fear as one side appropriates the emotional rhythm as dominator and the other gets caught in it as victim. But only small numbers of persons can do this. This is a structural property of situational fields, not a property of individuals.

As I have argued in a previous book, *Interaction Ritual Chains* (Collins 2004), emotional energy (which I abbreviate as EE) is a variable outcome of all interactional situations, most of which are not violent. EE varies with the degree that the people present become entrained in each other's emotions and bodily rhythms, and caught up in a common focus of attention. These are positive experiences when all participants feel solidarity and intersubjectivity. In these successful interaction rituals, individuals come away with feelings of strength, confidence, and enthusiasm for whatever the group was doing: these feelings are what I call emotional energy. Conversely, if the interaction fails to produce entrainment for certain individuals (or if they are subordinated or excluded by others), they

lose EE, and come away feeling depressed, lacking in initiative, and alienated from the group's concerns.

Violent interactions are difficult because they go against the grain of
normal interaction rituals. The tendency to become entrained in each other's rhythms and emotions means that when the interaction is at cross
purposes—an antagonistic interaction—people experience a pervasive
feeling of tension. This is what I call confrontational tension; at higher
levels of intensity, it shades over into fear. For this reason, violence is
difficult to carry out, not easy. Those individuals who are good at violence
are those who have found a way to circumvent confrontational tension/
fear, by turning the emotional situation to their own advantage and to the
disadvantage of their opponent.

It is the features of situations that determine what kinds of violence will
or will not happen, and when and how. This means that what happens
further back, before people arrive in a situation of confrontation, is not
the key factor as to whether they will fight, nor how they will fight if the
situation moves in that direction; nor indeed who will win and what kind
of damage gets done.

ALTERNATIVE THEORETICAL APPROACHES

Most existing explanations of violence fall into the category of background explanations: factors outside the situation that lead up to and
cause the observed violence. Some background conditions may be necessary or at least strongly predisposing, but they certainly are not sufficient;
situational conditions are always necessary, and sometimes they are sufficient, giving violence a much more emergent quality than any other kind
of human behavior. As already noted, conditions such as being subjected
to poverty, racial discrimination, family disorganization, abuse, and stress
are far from determining whether violence will happen or not. This is also
true for the venerable psychological hypothesis that frustration leads to
aggression, where frustration may be far in the background but also could
be quite proximate.

My objection across the board is that such explanations assume violence is easy once the motivation exists. Micro-situational evidence, to
the contrary, shows that violence is hard. No matter how motivated someone may be, if the situation does not unfold so that confrontational ten-
sion/fear is overcome, violence will not proceed. Conflict, even quite
overtly expressed conflict, is not the same as violence, and taking the last
step is not at all automatic. This holds as well for a frustration that crops
up immediately in the situation: someone may become angry at the frustration and at the person held responsible for it, but that still is not enough

to proceed to violence. Many, probably most, frustrated persons swallow their anger, or let it go with bluster and bluff.

It might seem a natural step to form a multi-level theory, combining background and situational conditions. This may eventually turn out to be a good way to proceed. But there is much to be understood before taking that step. Most background theories of violence are concerned with criminal violence in a narrow sense. But there is a lot of violence that is not well understood in terms of background conditions at all: for example, the violence committed by the small proportions of soldiers who are effective fighters, and by rioters, police, athletes and fans, duelists and other elites, carousers and entertainment audiences. Often these violent persons come from the opposite sorts of background as those alleged to be crucial for criminal violence; and these forms of violence have patterns of situational emergence in which emotional dynamics of the group are overwhelmingly apparent. My preferred strategy is to push as far as possible with a situational approach; eventually we may be in a position to work backward and incorporate some background conditions; but I am not yet convinced that is going to be as important as we have usually believed. Here it may be more useful to reverse the gestalt completely, and concentrate on the foreground to the exclusion of all else.

Opportunity and social control theories give a situational emphasis that is surely on the right track. These theories downplay background motives. Generally they assume that motives for violence are widespread; or that motives for transgressions may be situationally emergent. Routine activities theory (Cohen and Felson 1979; Felson 1994; Meier and Miethe 1993; Osgood et al. 1996), the most prominent version of an opportunity approach, is a theory of crime generally, which is not necessarily violent. In a typical case, the reason a group of youths steal a car may simply be that they found one with the keys left in. Such opportunity explanations leave a much wider gulf to be jumped when the crime is a violent one. The formula for crime is a coincidence in time and space of a motivated offender, an accessible victim, and the absence of social control agents who could deter the crime. The emphasis in routine activities theory is on variations in the latter two conditions, which are held to explain shifts in crime rates apart from any shift in motivating conditions (like the background conditions discussed earlier). What such research has shown is mainly that work and carousing patterns (such as those that involve being out late at night), together with demographic concentrations of particular kinds of persons in particular neighborhoods, affect victimization rates. Since this is an interactive model of several variables, there need not be any change in criminal motivation to account for changes in crime rates; and indeed criminals' motivations need not be very strong if the opportunities are particularly easy. Although the approach is situational, the analysis mainly focuses on macro-level comparisons. Thus it does not get closely into the process by which violence takes place. The incompleteness of opportunity theory is that it assumes violence is easy; if an opportunity presents itself and no authorities are around to prevent violence, then it pops out automatically. But violence is not easy, and situational patterns of incipient, threatened violence are a barrier that has to be gotten around. The micro-situational mechanism still has to be supplied.

A similar limitation exists with Donald Black's (1998) theory of the behavior of law. The theory is valid as far as it goes, but where it goes is an explanation of how conflict is managed once it breaks out; varying amounts of formal legal intervention are determined by repetitive, trans-situational features of the social structure: the hierarchical distance among the parties to the dispute, and their degree of intimacy. It is an important theoretical advance to see that moralizing about violence is a variable that can be explained by the participants' and the social control-lers' locations in social space. But the theory still assumes that violence is easy; its focus is on what happens after violence breaks out, on the societal reaction. It is true, for example, that much violence is self-help, the escala-tion of ongoing conflicts among persons known to each other, and that the very intimacy of the relationship deters formal intervention by police and legal authorities. But self-help violence still needs to be situationally constructed; it still needs to get past the barrier of confrontational tension and fear. This is not easy; and there is not as much self-help violence as might be expected from the numbers of persons who have motives to help themselves against local antagonists (described, for example, in unpub-lished research by Robert Emerson, UCLA, on roommate quarrels).

A similar problem exists with more macro explanations of violence, which includes theorizing violence as resistance. Resistance theories frame violence as a local response to subordinate location in large-scale social structure; usually this is class location in the capitalist economy, some-times abstracted more generally into a structure of domination that in-cludes race and gender.[9] The micro thesis again applies: resistance theory assumes that violence is easy, that all it takes is a motive. But resistance violence is just as hard as any other kind of violence. When resistance violence occurs—or at least violence that plausibly can be construed as such, because it occurs in the lower class or a racial ghetto—it is by going along with situational dynamics and constraints. These are the same pat-terns found elsewhere: small numbers of violent specialists, getting their energy from the unviolent part of the group, requiring the support of audiences, and battening on the emotionally weak. Micro-situational con-ditions favor attacking victims inside the community of the oppressed, much more than its ostensible class oppressors. Resistance theory often has a twisted quality: as an interpretation put forward by altruistic outsiders bending over backward to be sympathetic, it heroizes and justifies violent predators who perform most of their violence against the members of their own oppressed group.

Even in those instances where violence is most explicitly resistance, as in ghetto uprisings under slogans of rebellion against racial injustice, the violence is almost all local, and most of the destruction is in one's own neighborhood. The rhetoric of the uprising is one thing, the actual violence is another; the attacks are local because this is the situationally easiest way. When an ideologically aroused group invades someone else's neighborhood, it is less likely to be vertical resistance to the overarching social order, but rather a lateral assault on some other ethnic group, thus forfeiting the moral legitimacy of being seen as resistance by altruistic onlookers from higher social classes.

Cultural explanations of violence are almost always macro explanations; a wide-ranging, trans-situational culture is assumed to be the (necessary, and implicitly even sufficient) explanation of why the violence takes place. There is the same flaw here, from the point of view of micro-situational analysis, as in resistance theories, even when the explanation is turned around. Some theories regard violence, not as resistance, but as imposition from above, disciplining and deterring resisters in the name of upholding the cultural order. Thus a culture of racism, homophobia, or machismo is offered as an explanation of attacks on minorities, women, and other victims. This kind of interpretation at least is on stronger empirical grounds than resistance interpretations, since such attackers usually vocally state their prejudices during their attack, whereas the alleged resisters usually do not. But the interpretation suffers from failing to look closely at the dynamics of micro-situations; the great majority of them involve bluster and bluff, substituting verbal insult for actual violence, and sometimes (given additional conditions) using the energy of bluster to carry over into actual violence. It is not at all clear that the insulting expressions used in these situations represent long-held beliefs and deep-seated motivations for action. I will discuss this in greater detail in chapter 8, in regard to the ritual insults used by sports fans and soccer hooligans. There is micro-sociological evidence that racism and homophobia are situationally constructed too. The fact that these words are nouns misleads us into reifying what are actually fluctuating and temporally situated processes.

A similar line of argument applies to "culture of violence" explanations in criminology. Here there is more ethnographic grounding, less imposition of a political interpretation upon the data. But the fact that we can observe distinct groups of persons (such as young men in poverty zones) who talk in a favorable way about violence does not mean that this talk carries over automatically into violent behavior. Violence is hard, not easy. Virtually no cultural discourse admits this; neither perpetrators nor pro-violence groups, nor victims, nor altruistic or righteous observers-from-a-distance. Everyone thinks violence is easy to perform, whether one brags about it, fears it, or hopes to eliminate it. But the micro-situational realities of talking about violence fall into ritual patterns of bluster and bluff, and these rituals provide an ideology that covers up the real nature of violence—that it is hard to perform, that most people are not good at it, including those who are doing the bragging and swaggering. There are cultures of violence in the sense of distinctive networks who circulate this kind of violent talk; but we need to get beyond taking them at their word.

Macro-cultural approaches to violence become vacuous when they reach the concept of "symbolic violence." This helps us not at all to explain real violence, but muddies the analytical task. Physical violence has a clear core referent, which we can study using micro-situational observations. We are in a very different conceptual universe, when Bourdieu writes of schooling requirements as symbolic violence, and in general invokes the entire arena of symbolic possessions as "the gentle, invisible form of violence, which is never recognized as such, and is not so much undergone as chosen, the violence of credit, confidence, obligation, personal loyalty, hospitality, gifts, gratitude, piety. . . . [S]ymbolic violence is the gentle, hidden form which violence takes when overt violence is impossible" (Bourdieu 1972/1977: 192, 195). This is a merely rhetorical usage, a way of dramatizing the argument that school achievement, cultural tastes, and ritual practices are part of a self-reproducing structure of stratification, which the author wants to impress on his audience is morally illegitimate. But the dynamics of school requirements and cultural stratification are not at all similar to the dynamics of physically violent confrontations. The latter is a micro-situational process revolving around emotions of fear, tension, and forward panic, with strong elements of emergence; Bourdieu's "symbolic violence," to the contrary, is smooth, tension-free, non-confrontational, highly repetitive, and without situational contingencies.[10]

Of course, any core concept has its borderline areas. It is not useful to insist that violence must fit an exact preconceived definition. When people aim blows or weapons at each other, there is a period of buildup and anticipation, and these periods are worth studying even when they do not lead to actual violence. As we know, blows and projectiles often miss their targets; sometimes they are not very much intended to hit; sometimes they hit someone unintentionally. Where do we draw the boundaries? Are threats a form of violence? Clearly they are close enough to it that we have to put them into the model of situational dynamics. And this is so even though there is a good deal of cursing which does not lead to violence. By the same token, we will study the situational dynamics of quarreling, and of fearful, tense, and hostile emotions generally. The methodological rule should be to let the research process find its own borders. By this criterion, rhetorical pseudo-explanations get ruled out because they do not connect.

"Symbolic violence" is mere theoretical word play; to take it literally would be to grossly misunderstand the nature of real violence. Symbolic violence is easy; real violence is hard. The former goes with the flow of situational interaction, making use of the normal propensities for interaction rituals. The latter goes against the interactional grain; it is because the threat of real violence runs counter to the basic mechanisms of emotional entrainment and interactional solidarity that violent situations are so difficult. It is precisely this tension that produces confrontational tension and fear, the chief feature of micro-situational interaction on which pivot all the features of violence when it does occur.

HISTORICAL EVOLUTION OF SOCIAL TECHNIQUES FOR CONTROLLING CONFRONTATIONAL TENSION

Finally, a few words about a prominent research program that has a very explicit theory of violence, evolutionary psychology. This theory extrapolates from a general theory about evolutionary genetics to specific human behaviors including homicide, fighting, and rape (Daly and Wilson 1988; Thornhill and Palmer 2000). The theory makes much of the empirical patterns that young men of peak reproductive ages perform most violence, and that the instigation of violence is often sexual jealousy or masculine posturing. Violence is interpreted as an evolutionary selected propensity for males to struggle over reproductive dominance.

One cannot rule out a priori the possibility that there are genetic components of human behavior. But a wide range of empirical comparisons lead to the conclusion that the genetic component, if it exists, is small, and is overwhelmed by social conditions. For one thing, violence is not confined to young men of reproductive age. The most common type of violence in the family, for example, is not between adult sexual partners; this is outweighed by parent/child violence, typically in the form of severe corporal punishment; and that in turn is less frequent than violence among children (see chapter 4). Violence among children is not very severe, for reasons that we will consider, including the tendency for violence that is restricted and regulated by outsiders (in this case, adults) to be chronic rather than severe. This poses a puzzle for evolutionary theory; children scuffling starts at quite young ages, and often involves aggression by little girls, which is gradually restricted as they get older (Trembley 2004). In sheer quantity, the greatest frequency of incidents of violence occurs at non-reproductive ages, and is not exclusively intra-male. Evolutionary psychologists may overlook this kind of violence because it is not very severe, and doesn't get recorded in the official crime statistics; nevertheless a comprehensive theory should account for all sorts and all levels of intensity of violence. Micro-situational theory does quite well in incorporating data on children; as we shall see, scuffling among small children shows the same two patterns that are at the center of adult violence: the situationally strong ganging up on the weak and fearful, and staged, limited fights. The pattern is structural rather than individual; taking children out of the group and putting in others rearranges the pattern of dominance, and shifts who plays the roles of bully and victim (Montagner et al. 1988).

Evolutionary psychology is also vulnerable on its main turf, the propensity of young men to be involved in serious violence. It is not difficult to construct alternative explanations of why young men are violent, based on social conditions. Of any age group, they have the most ambiguous status in society; physical strength and violence is the one resource in which they have superiority, whereas they rank low in economic position, deference, and organizational power. The point I want to stress again is my micro-sociological refrain: evolutionary theory assumes that violence is easy—provided that the genes are primed for it—whereas in fact violence is hard, even for young men. Indeed, the majority of our micro-evidence is about the failures of violence among young men.

Large sectors of the intellectual world today dismiss evolutionary theory: partly in response to its perceived insensitivity to cultural and interactional patterns; partly out of long-standing intellectual antagonism between interpretive and positivistic approaches, between *Geisteswissenschaft* and *Naturwissenschaft*. Although my intellectual alliances are largely with the interpretive camp, nevertheless I want to cross over to evolutionist terrain and suggest that evolutionary psychology has made two serious mistakes, on its own terms.

The first mistake is about what has genetically evolved. The evolutionary orthodoxy of today holds that humans have evolved to be egotistical gene propagators, and that males have evolved the biological hard-wiring to be aggressive in order to propagate their genes in preference to some other male's genes. I suggest a very different interpretation of what is the main evolutionary heritage on the biological level. As I have argued elsewhere (Collins 2004: 227–28, in the context of explaining human eroticism), humans have evolved to have particularly high sensitivities to the micro-interactional signals given off by other humans. Humans are hard-wired to get caught in a mutual focus of intersubjective attention, and to resonate emotions from one body to another in common rhythms. This is an evolved biological propensity; humans get situationally caught up in the momentary nuances of each other's nervous and endocrinological systems in a way that makes them prone to create interaction rituals and thus to keep up face-to-face solidarity. I am making more than the banal point that humans have evolved with large brains and a capacity for learning culture. We have evolved to be hyper-attuned to each other emotionally, and hence to be especially susceptible to the dynamics of interactional situations.

The evolution of human egotism, then, is far from primary; it emerges only in special circumstances, for the most part rather late in human history (see Collins 2004, chap. 9, "Individualism and Inwardness as Social Products"). All this has a direct effect on human violence, although rather the opposite of the premises of evolutionary psychology. Humans are hard-wired for interactional entrainment and solidarity; and this is what makes violence so difficult. Confrontational tension and fear, as I will explain in greater detail, is not merely an individual's selfish fear of bodily harm; it is a tension that directly contravenes the tendency for entrainment in each other's emotions when there is a common focus of attention. We have evolved, on the physiological level, in such a way that fighting encounters a deep interactional obstacle, because of the way our neurological hard-wiring makes us act in the immediate presence of other human beings. Confrontational tension/fear is the evolutionary price we pay for civilization.

Humans have the capacity to be angry and to mobilize bodily energies to be forceful and aggressive. These, too, have physiological bases; they are universal in all societies (Ekman and Friesen 1975), and are found among most small children.[11] The capacity for anger is explained in evolutionary psychology as a means of mobilizing bodily effort to overcome an obstacle (Frijda 1986: 19). But when the obstacle is another human being, the hard-wired capacity for anger and aggression meets an even stronger form of hard-wiring: the propensity to become caught up in a shared focus of attention and the emotional rhythms of other people. How do we know the propensity for interactional entrainment is stronger than mobilized aggression? Because the micro-situational evidence, reviewed throughout this book, shows the most frequent tendency is to stop short of open violence; and when violence does emerge, it happens in an interactional process that is oriented in detail to overcoming the confrontational tension, while continuing to leave traces of it.

That is not to say that humans cannot be in conflict. They often have conflicting interests, and they often express their antagonism toward opponents. But this antagonism is expressed for the most part against other persons (or better yet, vaguely indicated groups) who are at a distance, preferably out of sight and hearing. It is the immediately situational confrontation that brings up an overwhelming tension; for face-to-face violence to occur, there must be some situational way around this emotional field.

Here I will introduce a second feature of evolution that is relevant to the construction of human violence. Now we are concerned not with biological evolution of the physical hard-wiring of human bodies, but with human institutions, which can also be seen as evolving over time, with some institutions being selected for survival and others selected out. If humans beings have evolved on the physiological level to be full of confrontational tension when they encounter another human in an antagonistic mode, the development of violence in human history must be due to the social evolution of techniques for overcoming confrontational tension/fear.

Historical comparisons show that social organization is a huge component in determining the amount of violence that takes place. The history of armies is the history of organizational techniques for keeping men fighting, or at least not running away, even though they are afraid. In tribal societies, battles are short, mostly skirmishes among a few hundred men or less, intermittently for a few hours, usually ending when a single victim is killed or seriously wounded. Without social organization to keep soldiers together in ranks, they dart back and forth across a skirmish line, a few men at a time, running away if they are in enemy terrain for more than a few seconds. The structure is analogous to today's gangs who carry on vendettas in the form of reciprocal drive-by attacks, firing at the opposing group from a passing car: when one group meets the other en masse, they generally bluster and insult but contrive to evade an open clash. The comparison shows that evolution of social technique for promoting violence is not just a matter of historical time; groups within modern societies are in the same structural condition as small primitive tribes, without the organizational apparatus for compelling troops to stay in a combat situation.[12]

More complex social organization in ancient Greece, Rome, and China brought larger numbers (sometimes on the order of tens of thousands) and more disciplined troops into battle and could keep them in combat as long as a day. One day was also the normal length of battles in medieval Europe. By the time of the Napoleonic wars, armies were sometimes on the order of hundreds of thousands of men, and battles lasted as long as three days. In the world wars of the twentieth century, battles were sustained as long as six months or more (e.g., Verdun, Stalingrad), backed up by a massive bureaucratic apparatus. In all historical periods, most of the troops were young men around peak reproductive age, but what determines the amount of killing done is the kind of social organization. Struggle for reproductive fitness does nothing in explaining the variance. What has evolved have been the organizational techniques for keeping soldiers in line where they could do some damage (or at least to stand up to long-distance weapons that would do damage to them). These techniques have evolved through such devices as the close-ranked phalanx;

parade-ground drilled troops surrounded by an officer corps concerned with keeping them in line; the politicized appeals and morale-building techniques of modern mass armies; bureaucratic methods for entrapping individuals in an inescapable organization; as well as coercive specialists like military police whose job is to keep soldiers from running away (Keegan [1976] may be read as a comparison of such techniques across several historical periods; see also McNeill [1982, 1995]).

Military organization is the easiest place to trace the social techniques for overcoming our biological propensity not to be violent. There are other spheres of violence where techniques have evolved, such as the evolution of dueling, martial arts and other fighting schools, and of sports fans' collective behavior routines. The development of football hooligans in twentieth-century Britain, for example, may be seen as the evolution of techniques beginning with participation in the staged excitement of sports contests, then emancipating the excitement away from the game itself so that an elite of specialists can promote their own form of "riot on demand." These themes will be taken up in later chapters.

The old-fashioned usage of "evolutionary" to mean progress does not fit well with the historical pattern of violence; if there is a historical pattern, it is that the capacity for violence has increased with the level of social organization. Violence is not primordial, and civilization does not tame it; the opposite is much nearer the truth. But there is an aspect of evolutionary theory in a technical sense that is relevant here. Its conclusions are not comforting ones. In Norbert Elias's terms, the pattern can be as much "decivilizing" as it is a "civilizing process."[13] I am not wedded to an evolutionary conceptual vocabulary; I am more inclined to see historical sequences in terms of a Weberian theory of multi-dimensional changes in the social organization of power (on this, the most comprehensive formulation is Mann [1986, 1993, 2005]). Techniques for carrying out violence must always be fitted to the task of overcoming confrontational tension/fear; however extensive these organizations are at the macro and meso level, their effectiveness is always tested at the micro level. What the evolutionary perspective does for us here is chiefly to remind ourselves of a very long-run perspective; it is the biological hardwiring of human beings to have so much emotional difficulty at face-to-face violence that has set the problem which the development of social techniques has tended to solve. Fortunately for human welfare, the problem to a large degree still resists solution.

Sources

The book is theoretically organized but strongly oriented toward the data. It aims to depict violence at as close range as possible. I have pressed into service every source of information that has been accessible to me. I have tried to exploit visual records wherever possible. Video recordings of fights are chiefly accessible for police, sports, and crowd violence. Video is occasionally useful on contemporary warfare; more revealing is anthropological film of tribal war. Still photos have turned out to be even more useful than video tape, since they can catch emotion and show the details of bodies in space. I insert photos in the text as much as possible within practical constraints. Some of my generalizations draw on my entire photo collections of particular kinds of violence.

Another major source is observation. I have made use of my own observations wherever there was something to gleaned from them. Some of these were deliberately gathered, when I was in violent zones at dangerous times (living in certain parts of East Coast cities has facilitated this), or by police ride-alongs; others have come from being alert, ready to drop into a sociological mode and to look carefully and make notes when something comes up. This is not as melodramatic as one might think; I am interested in conflict situations at low levels as well as high, and it is of interest to see how people handle confrontations, most of which do not in fact escalate all the way to violence, let alone extreme violence.[14]

On some topics in this book, I have made extensive use of student reports. These are retrospective accounts of situations that my students have observed. I have primed them by instructing what to pay attention to: emotions, body postures, the details of timing. I asked them to describe a conflict they have seen up close, which did not have to be violent; the corpus includes quarrels and abortive fights, an important part of the range of situational dynamics. Given that these students are largely from middle-class backgrounds (although widely ranging in ethnicity and country of origin), the kinds of violence they report tend to be limited to carousing, entertainment, and sports settings, with a certain amount of domestic conflict, and some descriptions of demonstrations and riots. Obviously such data cannot be used to count the statistical frequency of various kinds of violence; but they are very revealing on the relationship among different features of situations, which is what I am after.

I have interviewed persons who have observed or been involved in violence in various ways: police officers in several countries, ex-soldiers, youth scene musicians, bouncers, judges, and criminals. Throughout my emphasis has been on what they have observed, less upon how they interpret or explain what they see (although one can hardly exclude that). Interviewing has ranged from highly structured (but open-ended) questioning, to informal discussion; where it has been fruitful, I have engaged in lengthy and repeated discussions. It has been particularly useful to ask for observational detail from other ethnographic researchers, who have told me things that go beyond their published reports—not because they were holding anything back, but because I have pushed for material from a new angle of relevance. I have also gotten some detailed accounts of various kinds of violence from court sources. My years of participation in various martial arts schools has also been a source of information.

News reports figure largely on some topics. These vary a great deal in the situational detail they provide; but since violence, especially in its more elaborate forms, is a relatively rare event, there is often no substitute for news accounts. They are especially useful where they report follow-up information in police cases such as ballistics reports. There are also some long stories (such as on riots) available on the Internet, which give much more detail than the truncated news dispatches. Television news reports are usually more cryptic and more commentary-laden, hence less useful, except where they provide videos. The main exception here is on sports violence. I have used my own observations of televised games for analysis of player and fans violence. American sports are so record-oriented that one can often go from a cryptic news story of a fight to reconstruct much of the context: for example, how the players and teams were doing in the competition leading up to the fight. I have also been able to check certain features such as how frequently players are hit by pitches in relation to when these lead to fights.

Previously published materials are woven into the analysis throughout the book. Some of these are from other researchers; especially valuable are the ethnographers of violence (Elijah Anderson, Anthony King, Bill Buford, Curtis Jackson-Jacobs, Nikki Jones, and others), and those who study the milieux in which certain kinds of violence occur (David Grazian on entertainment scenes; Murray Milner on high school status systems). I am particularly indebted to researchers like Jack Katz who have pioneered in bringing together all the close-up data from various angles. A number of these colleagues (Katz, Milner, Grazian) use collective ethnographies—observational reports from a number of observers collected either retrospectively, or from observers sent out to cover particular scenes. This approach has not been much discussed in the methodological literature, but it has many advantages and deserves wider consideration.

I draw on published interviews (such as with criminals, in or out of jail), as well as biographical and autobiographical accounts of participants in violence (especially military violence). Historians have been useful where they give micro-observational details from their sources.

Literary sources are also sometimes useful. One needs to proceed with care here, since literary accounts of violence are a major source of the mythology that obscures our understanding. This is especially true of film drama, which with tiny exceptions are extremely unreliable depictions of violence. Some literary accounts, chiefly in the naturalistic style of the early twentieth century, are useful for detail on warfare and on fights, and for the micro-dynamics that lead up to fights, or for the carousing scenes that are their background. A few writers, like Tolstoy, Hemingway, and Fitzgerald, were micro-sociologists before the occupation was invented. Older literature such as Homer and Shakespeare, mythology-propagating in other respects, nevertheless is sometimes useful for describing the ritualism surrounding violence in particular historical periods if not the process of violence itself.

Quantitative data is also used here where relevant. It has been useful (though hard to get) on certain aspects of police violence; and military reconstructions have been at the heart of the academic awakening of how violence really happens, including counts of soldiers firing, hits, ammunition expended, and casualties. A few demonstrations and their casualties (such as the 1970 Kent State national guard killings) have been reconstructed in detail; and I have drawn on data on looting, arrests, and time-patterns of the spread and severity of riots.

Throughout I follow the rule to make my own interpretations of the data. This often means detaching them from the reporter's or the previous analyst's concern for what is important, and from their framework of understanding. One might say that sociology is to a large extent the art of reframing other people's observations. Where the observations are those of previous sociologists and the reframing is strongly overlapping, we can speak of cumulative theoretical progress.

My sources are very heterogeneous. This is as it should be. We need as many angles of vision as possible to bear on the phenomenon. Methodological purity is a big stumbling block to understanding, particularly for something as hard to get at as violence. Obviously, the micro-sociological study of violence can be done better in the future than as I have done here; for now, it is the direction of movement that counts.

PREVIEW

Chapter 2 lays out the basic model: violent situations are full of confrontational tension and fear. Hence, most violence is bluster and standoff, with little actually happening, or incompetent performance with mostly ancillary and unintended damage. For real harm to be inflicted on the enemy, there must be pathways around confrontational tension/fear; what these are is mapped out in the following chapters.

Chapter 3 describes a special kind of dynamic sequence when a tense confrontation is suddenly resolved in favor of one side, which takes overwhelming superiority. The result is what I call a forward panic. Many famous atrocities (including many in the headline news) come about in this way.

Chapters 4 and 5 examine the pathways around confrontational tension/fear that consist in attacking a weak victim. Here we look at the situational dynamics of domestic violence, bullying, mugging, and hold-ups. Some of these are more institutionalized than others, going on repetitively over time. Forward panic, treated in the previous chapter, is also a variant on attacking the weak, although at the other end of the continuum, where the weakness is emergent and the suddenness of the emotional shift is the key to the ferocity of the attack. All these forms of attacking the weak show a key feature of successful violence: picking a target that is emotionally weak, which is more important than being physically weak.

So far, these chapters deal with violence that is ugly and morally despicable, once we see it close up. The second part of the book covers a different set of pathways around confrontational tension/fear. Here the violence is honorable, happy, ebullient, or at least in an in-between zone where it is socially excused and covertly encouraged. Chapter 6 deals with fighting that is deliberately staged for an audience; the same features that make it limited and protected also tend to elevate its practitioners into the sphere of an honored elite. Even here, confrontational tension/fear remains and shapes the violence, like the return of the repressed.

Chapter 7 considers various ways that happy occasions of celebration, carousing, and entertainment can give rise to violence; as well as how some kinds of unhappy violence, such as riots, can take on a carousing tone.

Chapter 8 explains how the structure of sports as dramatic pseudo-violence gives rise to real violence at predictable moments among players and fans. I consider also the conditions under which fans' violence spills over outside the sports arena, and even becomes autonomous of it: the "B-team" promoting itself to equal or superior status to the "A-team" in the emotional dramatics of sporting action.

Chapter 9 looks at how fights do or do not start. I focus in on the micro-dynamics of bluster and bluff, and examine how these may be institutionalized as a preferred style in the inner-city code of the street.

Chapters 10 and 11 consider who wins and loses fights as a process of micro-situational domination. Success in violence is stratification of an emotional field, parallel to the "law of small numbers" that shapes creativity in intellectual and artistic fields; all these are variants on seizing emotional dominance over limited niches in an attention space. Those who become the violent elite—"elite," of course, in a structural sense, which may be morally despised as well as adulated—get their emotional dominance from all the other persons in the field. They batten emotionally on their victims, drawing their success from the same process that makes their opponents fail; and they capture the emotional energies of lesser members of the supporting cast and audience.

There is at least this much of a sociological silver lining. Violence has very strong structural limits, by its very nature as the product of an emotional field. The same features that make a minority of persons successfully violent makes the rest of us unviolent. What we can make of this pattern constructively for the future remains to be seen.

THE COMPLEMENTARITY OF MICRO AND MACRO THEORIES

Since we social scientists tend to be polemical, and to act as if our own theoretical approach is the only correct one, I would like to go on record as saying that micro-sociological theory is not the whole of sociology. Researchers have successfully studied large-scale structures—networks, markets, organizations, and states and their interplay in the world arena—without looking at micro-details. We have cumulated some useful theories about these meso and macro structures, and I am not suggesting that sociologists should throw these aside to concentrate only on face-to-face situations. The issue isn't ontological—what is real and what isn't—but pragmatic: what works and what doesn't. In the particular area of violence research, perhaps more than any other topic, we have misunderstood the most basic micro-interactional pattern. We have assumed that violence is easy for individuals to carry out, so we skip the micro level as unproblematic and turn to conditions in the meso background or the macro organization or overarching culture.

This turns out to be a pragmatic mistake. Violence is not easy, and the key stumbling blocks and turning points are at the micro level. That does not mean that meso and macro conditions don't exist, or that they cannot be usefully integrated into a more comprehensive theory, once we get the micro mechanisms right.

This book may strike many readers as altogether too micro. It cuts out preceding motivations, background conditions, and long-term consequences of violence. It also omits the way in which violence is produced by larger social structures than the immediate situation, such as by militaries or politics. I agree. But in order to focus closely on the micro-dynamics of violence, it is necessary here to bracket the rest. This book is the first of a two-volume series. The second expands the frame to what has been left out. Among other things, it considers what we know about institutionalized violence, or rather, that which is repetitive, structured, and thus organized into meso- and macro-organizations that provide a regular flow of resources for specialists in violence. It will consider such topics as war and geopolitics, as well as torture and the many contexts and varieties of rape.

This expansion of the topic of violence pushes across several conceptual and empirical boundaries. The topic of large-scale and long-term structures for producing violence borders on the theory of conflict generally; this is a larger topic, since conflict is often not violent. The two are connected by a process of escalation and counter-escalation, which I will broaden to include the crucial but less often considered theory of de-escalation. The second volume will focus on conflict—violent and unviolent alike—as a process swelling up and ebbing away in time. It will attempt to map out the time-laws of when and how conflict occurs at some moments and not in others. This will make time-process a key feature of violence in its own right, apart from other conditions that promote violence; the occurrence of violent events depends on its timing in relation to other such events, as well as in the internal flow of timing in micro-incidents. This may take us some further distance toward understanding violence as a relatively rare event, underdetermined by background conditions.

The appropriate relationship of micro- and macro-sociology is not to reduce one to the other, but to coordinate the two levels of analysis where it leads to some useful result. Violence is one area where doing so is crucial. Despite the shift in scale, there is a thread connecting both volumes. This is the theory of the interactional processes of emotional fields, laid out for micro slices of time and space in the present book, and for larger slices in the following one.

In what follows, I will use the male pronouns "he," "his," and "him" deliberately to refer to males. There are similarities between males and females in their behavior in violent situations, but the now-conventional expression "he or she" would be highly misleading for this topic. I will discuss female-on-female violence and male/female violence separately and explicitly.

PART ONE

The Dirty Secrets of Violence

CHAPTER 2

Confrontational Tension and Incompetent Violence

From my ethnographic notes:

> *Somerville, Mass. (a working-class area of Boston) Oct. 1994, ca.
> 11:30 p.m. weekday.* I'm walking along the street and see a flashy car
> pull up at the curb in a business district, in front of a warehouse/busi-
> ness. Young white guy in his 20s in short jacket gets out, slamming
> the door. I keep on walking. Farther down the street (on the opposite
> sidewalk, the right side as I turn around to look back up the street) is
> another young white guy. He starts pulling bottles out of the garbage
> (on the street for next morning collection) and smashing them on the
> sidewalk. He's angry, pacing around. He spots the guy across the street,
> about 40 yards or so back. Yells: "Joey! [OBSCENITIES]" and some-
> thing like: "I'm going to get you Joey!" He rushes into the middle of
> the street (main traffic street, rather wide, no traffic at all at this hour),
> where the other guy comes rushing to meet him from the left side. (Ap-
> parently they've been waiting for each other.) At the same time, a third
> guy comes running out from up the street, 50 yards or so back, on the
> right side I think. The two allies (Joey and friend) attack the bottle-
> smasher. They take a few swings at each other; I don't think any
> punches are landed. Bottle-smasher starts yelling: "Hey, fair fight, fair
> fight! No two against one! One against one!" They recede back up the
> street from where I'm standing. For a couple of minutes the shouting
> continues, quiets down; then breaks out again. Finally I leave (after
> about 5 minutes, watching from 50 yards away; another passerby, a
> woman stands near me to watch; the fighters don't pay attention to us).
> It's not clear that they actually landed any punches at all.

The fighters start off making a show of being tough, angry, belligerent—
breaking bottles, slamming doors, yelling obscenities. They throw a couple of punches, which miss. Very quickly they find an excuse to stop fighting; not only the one who is outnumbered, but also the ones who have
the advantage seem to accept the excuse. The aftermath consists in making angry noises for a while.

BRAVE, COMPETENT, AND EVENLY MATCHED?

The prevailing mythology about fights may be summed up in the formula
that the fighters are brave, competent, and evenly matched. In entertain-

ment and in the tropes of ordinary discourse, belligerents are usually distinguished in moral terms, as heroes and villains, the honorable and the culpable; but the bad guy is a good strong fighter, otherwise the drama is spoiled, and the story does not cast such a good light on its protagonist. Sports, which are entertainments organized to have the structure of dramatically satisfying conflicts, are usually devised so that the competition is evenly matched. In fictionalized confrontations, unmatched forces are appropriate only if the hero wins out against superior strength; this is, of course, easier to achieve in fiction than in real life.

The reality is almost entirely the opposite. Fighters are mostly fearful and incompetent in their exercise of violence; when they are evenly matched, they tend to be particularly incompetent. It is when the strong attack the weak that most violence is successful.

The pattern is well illustrated in an ethnographic film, *Dead Birds*, depicting tribal warfare in highland New Guinea (Garner 1962). The fighters consist of all the adult males of two neighboring tribes, several hundred on each side. They meet at their traditional fighting ground on the border between their territories. The film shows a dozen or so fighters in the forefront, with an individual or two darting forward to shoot an arrow at the enemy side; when this happens, the other side falls back. The battle has a rhythmic pattern of waves, rushing forward and then back, as if there were a magnetic force that keeps even the bravest fighters from going far beyond the dividing line; as if the courage of attack were a force that expends itself as the individual penetrates deeper into enemy territory, even a few yards, and the relapse backward is matched by a surge of courage by the enemy coming forward. Most of the arrows miss. Most wounds are in the buttocks or back, incurred when running away. There appear to be relatively few wounds during a day's fighting, something on the order of 1 or 2 percent of the participants. Fighting goes on repetitively over a period of days, until someone is killed or injured severely enough to be expected to die of wounds.

When one person is killed, the fighting stops; the body is taken back to the village for the funeral ceremony, and the killing side carries out their own celebration. This period of celebration is implicitly a truce; the frontier does not have to be guarded and everyone can attend their own ceremonies. There are additional ways in which the amount of fighting is restricted: the fighters are willing to call off the fighting when the weather gets bad, or when the rain will ruin their war decorations; they take breaks during the battle to eat and discuss how they have performed—typically with much bragging and exaggeration.

Tribal warfare of this sort has the structure of a vendetta; generally one victim is killed at a time, and each victim must be avenged, thus setting up future battles. Any member of the opposing group is a suitable victim. In *Dead Birds*, a raiding party of the enemy crosses into tribal territory and kills a small boy in an outlying field. Full-scale battle confrontations between the entire adult forces of each side generally are standoffs, ballet-like semblances of warfare but quite incompetent in killing the enemy; an attack on isolated and weak members of the tribe are more effective. The pattern holds generally in tribal warfare (Divale 1973; Keeley 1996). In addition to full-scale battle confrontations, tribes also engage in raiding, attempting to surprise a village, especially when the fighting men are away; or they may engage in ambushes. When tribal fighters have the advantage over defenseless enemies, they often massacre them. Keeley gives numerous examples from warfare of North American Indian tribes attacking both Indian and white European settlements. The biggest incidents of violence happen where opposing sides are very unmatched in strength.[1]

If the dramatic image of fighters is so inaccurate, how does it survive? In part because entertainment violence, including its sports version, is contrived to stage a dramatically satisfying image. The same is so in the conversations of everyday life, which are little stagings of dramas in which one tells stories about oneself or other persons; the appeal of conversation is in being attention-getting and entertaining, not in being strictly true. These are reasons why individuals generally lack the vocabulary with which to describe fights accurately; for fights they have been in themselves, there is overwhelming incentive to fall into the stereotypes of depicting oneself as brave, competent, and matched with a strong enemy; and there is no virtue in winning over a fearful, incompetent enemy—and much less in running away from such an enemy. To be sure, there is a form of rhetoric that insults the enemy by calling him cowardly; what this usually means is that the enemy's attack was successful because it was unexpected, sneaky, and not a fair fight; or it is a morale-building boast that we will win when we meet him head-on. Soldiers who have been in combat and had direct contact with the enemy tend to depict him as courageous; it is enemies on more distant combat zones who are not respected; and soldiers in rear areas, and even more so civilians at home, who express a low regard for the enemy (Stouffer et al. 1949: 158–65). In fact, behavior in combat, as in other kinds of fights, is generally quite fearful, and so the frontline soldiers are also perpetrating a myth about the enemy as well as themselves. That is why we need to use direct evidence of how humans behave in conflict situations, not relying on what they say about it.

THE CENTRAL REALITY: CONFRONTATIONAL TENSION

I began this chapter with a description of a fight between Boston tough guys that did not come to much. The simplest interpretation is that the fighters get into a state of fear or at least high tension as soon as the

Figure 2.1 Tension/fear in military combat. One man fires, eleven take cover. Palestinian policemen firing back at Israelis near Gaza (October 2000). Reuters.

confrontation comes to the point of violence. I will call this tension/fear; it is a collective interactional mood that characterizes the violent encounter on all sides, and that shapes the behavior of all its participants in several typical ways.

The emotional pattern comes out when we see what combat actually looks like and attempt to analyze its nonverbal expressions. Figures 2.1 and 2.2 show men under fire; some of their actions might be called courageous. Even so, their postures and facial expressions are crouched and fearful; even the most active firers are tense and strained. In figure 2.3, a SWAT team (Special Weapons and Tactics—i.e., a police unit specially formed for military-like attack operations) is moving in on a lone gunman holding hostages. They have him outnumbered and outgunned, but their postures are creeping, slow, cautious, as if pushing their unwilling bodies forward by sheer will.

Figure 2.4 shows facial expressions close up. A group of boys in the Palestinian *intifada* are throwing stones at an Israeli tank. They are not actually being shot at, and their action is essentially bravado; but they are all in the grip of the emotions of confrontation. The boy in the front

Figure 2.2 Tension in face and body postures: Palestinian gunmen battle Israeli soldiers (2002). AP/World Wide Photos.

shows the classic signs of fear: brows raised and drawn together, wrinkles arching across center of forehead, upper eyelids raised, low eyelids tensed, mouth open with lips slightly tensed (Ekman and Friesen 1975: 63). The boy throwing a rock has a similar expression on his face; courage is acting even when afraid, not the absence of fear. The others are crouching or cowering in various degrees of tension.

Whatever happens in a fight situation is shaped by tension/fear: how the violence is carried out, which is to say, for the most part, incompetently; the length of fighting; and the tendency to avoid fighting once it becomes an imminent threat, and to find ways of ending it or avoid participating in it. How tension/fear is managed also determines when and to what extent violence is successfully unleashed, and against whom.

TENSION/FEAR AND NON-PERFORMANCE IN MILITARY COMBAT

The most extensive evidence on fear and its effects has been gathered on the performance of soldiers in combat. S.L.A. Marshall (1947), the chief combat historian for the U.S. Army in the central Pacific in 1943 and in Europe in 1944–45, interviewed troops immediately after battle. Marshall

Figure 2.3 Police SWAT team moves in cautiously upon a single gunman holding hostages in restaurant (Berkeley, California, 1990). AP/World Wide Photos.

concluded that typically only 15 percent of frontline troops fired their guns in combat, reaching at most 25 percent in the most effective units.

> When (a commander of infantry) engages the enemy not more than one quarter of his men will ever strike a real blow unless they are compelled by almost overpowering circumstances or unless all junior leaders constantly "ride herd" on troops with the specific mission of increasing their fire. The 25 percent estimate stands even for well-trained and campaign-seasoned troops. I mean that 75% per cent will not fire *or will not persist in* firing against the enemy and his works. These men may face the danger but they will not fight. (1947: 50, emphasis added)

> We found that on an average not more than 15 percent of the men had actually fired at the enemy positions . . . the figure did not rise above 20 to 25% of the total for any action. . . . Most of the actions had taken place under conditions of ground and maneuver where it would have been possible for at least 80 percent of the men to fire, and where nearly all hands, at one time or another, were operating within satisfactory firing distance of enemy works. Scarcely one of the actions had been a casual affair. The greater number had been decisive local actions in which the operations of a company had had critical effect upon the fortunes of some larger body and in which the company itself

Figure 2.4 Fear in faces and body postures of Palestinian boys, a few of whom are throwing rocks at an Israeli tank. Boy in the front shows the classic signs of fear: brows raised and drawn together, wrinkles arching across center of forehead, upper eyelids raised, lower eyelids tensed, mouth open with lips slightly tensed (2002). Reuters.

had been hard-pressed. In most cases the company had achieved a substantial success. In some cases, it had been driven back and locally defeated by enemy fire. (1947: 54)

In an average experienced infantry company in an average stern day's action, the number engaging with any and all weapons was approximately 15 per cent of total strength. In the most aggressive infantry companies, under the most intense local pressure, the figure rarely rose above 25 per cent of total strength from the opening to the close of action. . . . Moreover, the man did not have to maintain fire to be counted among the active firers. If he had so much as fired a rifle once or twice, though not aiming it anything in particular, or lobbed a grenade roughly in the direction of the enemy, he was scored on the positive side. . . . Terrain, the tactical situation, and even the nature of the enemy and the accuracy of his fire appeared to have almost no bearing on the ratio of active firers to non-firers. Nor did the element of battle experience through three or four campaigns produce any such radical changes as might be expected. The results appeared to indicate that the ceiling was fixed by some constant which was inherent in the nature of troops or perhaps in our failure to understand that nature sufficiently to apply the proper correctives. (1947: 56–57)

The firing ratio would increase if an officer was directly beside an infantryman demanding that he fire; but as Marshall noted, most NCOs (Non-Commissioned Officers) "cannot for long move up and down a fire line booting his men until they use their weapons" (1947: 57–58). Not only is he likely to be killed constantly moving about, but he is more likely to be trying to fire his own weapon to beat back the enemy, and "supporting and encouraging the relatively few willing spirits who are sustaining the action."

In Marshall's picture, a small portion of troops, on both sides, are doing all the fighting. (I will refer to this as the SLAM effect, after S.L.A. Marshall's nickname, taken from his initials.) Even they are not necessarily effective; most of their weapons miss. What are the others doing? In varying degrees, they are incapacitated by the combat situation. Here is one closeup example, from the American troops who entered Peking during the Boxer Rebellion in 1900:

> One Chinese soldier darted behind a fence and was pumping away at us as fast as he could load. A man from the Fourteenth Infantry pointed him out to Upham, yelling "There he is! Shoot him! Shoot him!" I asked him why he didn't do a little shooting himself. The man did not reply but kept jumping up and down, yelling "Shoot him!" (Preston 2000: 243–44)

Upham fired and hit the Chinese soldier on his third shot.

Sometimes soldiers run away. This is usually very noticeable and considered very dishonorable, unless the whole body of troops retreats in a panic, in which case individual soldiers are likely to be excused. Full-scale panic retreats can be important in decisive battles, but they are not the most common form of incapacitating fear in battle. Running away on one's own gets one labeled a coward, but other types of fear are generally condoned by fellow soldiers; running away, especially without the accompaniment of others, is the action accepted as emblematic of dishonorable fear; but all disgrace is concentrated on this one action, allowing other manifestations of fear to remain honorable or at least unremarked upon.

Not uncommon is loss of control of one's sphincters, urinating or shitting in one's pants (Holmes 1985: 205; Stouffer et al. 1949 vol. 2, Dollard 1944; Grossman 1995: 69–70). American figures in World War II were 5 to 6 percent, up to a high of 20 percent in some combat divisions. Soiling oneself is also described for British and German troops, and for U.S. troops in Vietnam. Nor does this seem to be distinctively modern squeamishness; Pizarro's soldiers urinated in fear before capturing the Inca emperor (Miller 2000: 302). War is a dirty business in more ways than one. Other physiological reactions include violent pounding of the heart (reported by almost 70 percent of soldiers), as well as trembling, cold sweat, weakness, and vomiting.

Some soldiers attempt to burrow into the ground, covering their faces and heads; or cover themselves with blankets or sleeping bags (Holmes 1985: 266–68). This behavior can occur out in the open, in the midst of crucial periods of combat, where there is no prospect of being unnoticed by the enemy. It is a paralysis of terror, and sometimes troops in this condition are unable even to surrender, much less fight back, and are killed where they lie. It does not appear to be merely modern Western softness; instances are recorded for German, French, Japanese, Viet Cong, American, Argentine, and Israeli soldiers, and for participants in medieval and early modern combat (Holmes 1985: 267).

Marshall's figure of 15 to 25 percent of American troops in World War II doing all the firing has been controversial. The main criticism has been methodological: that Marshall did not engage in systematic interviews asking every soldier explicitly if he fired (Spiller 1988; Smoler 1989). Some World War II combat commanders (typically high-ranking officers) dismissed his figures as absurd; other veterans supported his conclusions on non-firing in combat (Moore 1945; Kelly 1946; Glenn 2000a: 5–6, 2000b: 1–2, 134–36). A German officer wrote that there were numerous non-shooters in the German infantry but that "their percentage is unknown" (Kissel 1956). An Australian officer endorsed Marshall's general position as to the German army in World War II and British Commonwealth troops in Korea, noting in the latter case that 40 to 50 percent of troops might not return fire when under attack (Langtry 1958). A British army comparison of the difference between training trials and actual combat results found it was consistent with Marshall's estimate of 15 percent firing participation (Rowland 1986).

The different accounts may be reconciled by positing a combination of conditions: (a) observers from different military vantage-points had their biases in how they constructed their accounts of battle performance; (b) we should make more refined distinctions as to how often and in what manner soldiers fired in combat; and (c) the proportions of highly active firers, non-firers, and those in-between changed historically between different wars as military organization changed.

We would expect that higher-ranking officers would be least likely to perceive the problem. In all organizations, those at the highest ranks are least likely to have accurate information on what is going on at the lowest level of practical action; in addition, the higher the rank, the more the person identifies with the formal frontstage ideals of the organization and is likely to talk in official rhetoric. Frontline combat soldiers of the lower ranks would have a different viewpoint. Yet another bias comes from the contrast between detailed observation of what is happening in each micro-situation, and summary accounts of an ideal-typical version of performance; the latter would tend to be more idealized toward a favorable image, and we would expect that this bias would grow with time as the actual memories of combat experience become more distant. In these respects, SLAM's method of interviewing the entire combat group immediately after combat, asking each one what he had done and observed (Marshall 1982: 1), is still among our best data.[2] Particularly valuable was Marshall's method of bringing all the soldiers together, like a focus group, and questioning them without considerations of rank, probing until a full and consistent reconstruction was made.

As we see in the preceding quotes, Marshall hedges his figures in various ways, suggesting that in some circumstances, for brief periods, the figure rises above 25 percent. It seems clear that Marshall is not presenting a statistical argument, but was summarizing his judgment—as one of the first to look into the question up close, which he did during a period of more than two years in combat zones, interviewing approximately 400 infantry companies—that a large majority of combat soldiers did little or no firing.

Marshall's impression, imprecise as it may sometimes be, is borne out by his detailed descriptions of particular individual combats. One instance is the defense by a battalion (at full strength, this should be 600 to 1,000 men) against an all-night attack by Japanese troops in the Gilbert Islands, November 1943. The Japanese attack failed, with heavy casualties. "Most of the killing took place at less than a ten-yard interval. . . . Every position was ringed with enemy dead." On the American side, "approximately half of the occupants of the forward foxholes were either killed or wounded." Marshall summarizes his findings as follows:

> We began the investigation to determine how many of our men had fought with their weapons. It was an exhaustive search, man by man and gun crew by gun crew, each man being asked exactly what he had done. Yet making allowances for the dead, we could identify only thirty-six men as having fired at the enemy with all weapons. The majority were heavy weapons men. The really active firers were usually in small groups working together. There were some men in the positions directly under attack who did not fire at all or attempt to use a weapon even when the position was being overrun. (Marshall 1947: 55–56)

This is a remarkably small percentage: 36 men (of those still alive at the end) had done all the firing, out of a total of 600 or more. Even if there were only two companies on the front foxholes, and half of them were killed or incapacitated, the firing ratio is about 36/200, or 18 percent.[3]

Marshall's characterization of predominantly incompetent performance, qualitatively if not quantitatively, has been supported by the principal scholars of combat. The first to inquire specifically into combat behavior, Colonel Charles Ardant du Picq (1903/1999), distributed questionnaires to French army officers in the 1860s, who reported a tendency for soldiers to fire wildly in the air. John Keegan (1976), who led the movement by modern historians to reconstruct actual battlefield behavior, described the combat zone as a place of terror rather than heroic aggression, including medieval battles, the Napoleonic wars, and World War I. In eighteenth- and early nineteenth-century massed firing formations, NCOs were typically stationed just behind the firing line, often pressing their swords horizontally against the back of soldiers to force them to hold their position (Keegan 1976: 179–85, 282, 330–31). In the world wars, all major armies had battle police, typically picked from among the biggest and most imposing men, whose job was to keep soldiers from running from the front. The pre-Soviet Russian army used mounted Cossacks for that task, giving them a purpose well past the period when horses had become an anachronistic vulnerability against modern firepower. A similar use of cavalry was advocated by a general during the Thirty Years' War (1618–48), along with cutting off one's own lines of retreat to give cowards no options, and detailing troops to shoot those who retreated (Miller 2000: 131). Griffith (1989) finds a similar pervasiveness of fear and firing incompetence in the American Civil War. Holmes (1985) and Grossman (1995) document it extensively for twentieth-century wars, and uphold Marshall's position after reviewing the evidence against it. Dyer (1985) estimated the volume of fire in Japanese and German armies as similar to those in Allied forces, concluding that the level of non-firing was similar in all armies.

How much of this battle fear can be attributed to soldiers who are conscripts unused to military life, or to the shock of first battle experience? Ulysses S. Grant (1885/1990: 231–32, 1005) describes the first day of the battle of Shiloh in April 1862, in which raw troops, who had just arrived at the battle zone and just been issued their weapons, broke under Confederate attack and fled in panic; some four to five thousand (approximately one entire division of the five divisions initially engaged on the Union side) ended up cowering below the riverbank that was the rear of the Federal position. Grant remarks that he had about a dozen officers arrested for cowardice.

Nevertheless, the difference between "green" troops and "seasoned veterans" is not large. Studies on Allied soldiers in World War II suggested that soldiers reached their maximum efficiency at around ten to thirty days of combat experience; if they stayed in combat continuously thereafter, they became jittery and hyper-reactive, and after fifty days reached emotional exhaustion (Swank and Marchand 1946; Holmes 1985: 214–22). With intermittent rest periods away from combat, it was suggested that incapacitating behavior might generally be postponed to "200 to 240 aggregate combat days" (Holmes 1985: 215). Officers, too, experienced a breakdown in effectiveness, even when they suppressed signs of fear (or perhaps because of the strain of doing so), usually around a year of combat; among their symptoms were passiveness, slow-wittedness, apathy as well as shirking.[4] The effect of combat experience is not just "hardening" but also "softening" through psychological and physical strain. In confirmation, among British divisions in the Normandy campaign in 1944, the performance of the veteran units was much worse than those who had never been in combat (Holmes 1985: 222).

Indeed, "hardened" troops subjected to long-term battering may go to extremes in their unwillingness to fight. Mutinies break out late in campaigns, and among veterans. Keegan (1976: 275–77) offers a general explanation: when an army has taken 100 percent casualties—everyone from the original troop strength has been killed or seriously wounded, so that there is a clear sense that everyone is a replacement—the soldiers regard themselves as good as dead, and refuse to fight further. Mutinies in World War I occurred among all the armies that had been long in action, or had taken accumulated casualties of that scale: the French in May and July 1917; Russian in July and September 1917; Italian in November 1917; British in September 1917 and March 1918; Austrian and Hungarian in May 1918; Germans were the latest to mutiny, in October 1918, although they had been sustained by victories through most of the war. The American army was the main exception, but it had been in combat in any considerable numbers for less than six months (Gilbert 1994: 319, 324–43, 349, 355, 360, 397, 421–22, 429, 461–62, 481–85, 493–98).

The effects of tension and fear on combat performance vary historically depending on what armies do to control the fear. Marshall's estimate of a minority of fighters, somewhere around a quarter of troops who actively fire their guns in combat, holds up well for the world wars of the twentieth century and for similar wars of the nineteenth century. But the estimated firing ratio for American troops in the Korean war rose to 55 percent (documented by Marshall himself); and in the Vietnam war, 80 to 95 percent, at least for the best troops (Grossman 1995: 35; Glenn 2000a: 4, 212–13). Armies have changed over the years in their organization during combat, as well as in training and recruitment. Historically earlier parade-ground formations of massed infantry firing together in ranks tended to have high firing rates, but their problem was the opposite: wild over-firing with poor aim and much in the way of friendly fire casualties. The open skirmish formations of twentieth-century wars, designed to reduce the target for machine-gun fire, eliminated the tight organizational control and put soldiers maximally on their own on the battlefield; this left them most susceptible to confrontational tension/fear, without the countervailing effects of strong social support. Recognizing this problem in response to Marshall's findings, the U.S. Army, after the Korean war, redesigned training and combat organization to promote firing and keep up social cohesion in the combat unit. Here is a rare instance where a social science finding has been used as a basis of social change. Traditional firing-range practice was replaced by realistic combat situations in which soldiers are conditioned to fire automatically at suddenly appearing targets (Grossman 1995: 257–60). Recruitment too had its effects: the draftee armies of the world wars performed with a lower level of firing than volunteer enlisted armies (as we will see from Glenn's [2000a] evidence). Thus the soldiers whom SLAM observed in World War II were those who, on all counts, would likely have had the poorest overall combat performance.

The effects of this change in training methods, as well as their limits, can be seen in Glenn's (2000b: 37–39, 159–61) survey of Vietnam combat veterans. Only 3 percent of the troops reported that they themselves ever had an episode where they did not fire in a combat situation where they should have fired; in other words, the self-reported firing rate was 97 percent. When asked whether they had ever seen another soldier who failed to fire under such circumstances, however, about 50 percent said they had witnessed this one or more times. Fear was cited by 80 percent of the troops as the reason for others' non-firing.

We have a range of figures: 97 percent firing from self-reports (an egotistical bias); 50 percent non-firing occasionally, as observed by others; 83 percent estimated by other soldiers to fire when necessary. Are these figures too high? The surveys have some likely biases: they were retrospective, made between fifteen and twenty-two years after these soldiers had been in combat, and they lumped specific situations together into a generalized memory. There is an upward bias in the sample toward higher ranks, which would lead to a more idealized picture. And the sample was weighted toward the more gung-ho, combat-seeking troops, more of a sample of the best fighters, rather than of the average fighters.[5]

Glenn's data (2000b: 162–63) can be recalculated to give the distribution of soldiers' firing behavior, by their own report. Relatively few of them reported that they rarely fired their guns (those who estimated firing between 0 and 15 percent of the times in which they were engaged with the enemy in a life-threatening situation); but there is considerable variation in whether they reported themselves as virtually always firing (in 85 to 100 percent of such situations), or in-between, sometimes firing, sometimes not.

TABLE 2.1
Frequency of firing in life-threatening enemy confrontations

	Fired			
	Rarely	Sometimes	Virtually always	N
Non-weapons roles[a]	23%	54%	23%	43
Combat enlisted men	12%	48%	40%	73
NCOs	4%	42%	52%	69
Helicopter crews	10%	14%	76%	28
Machine-gunners	0	14%	86%	7
All infantry	9%	45%	46%	181[b]

[a]These are soldiers whose primary task was other than to use direct-fire weapons, including administrative duties, artillery, engineers, etc., but who did come into enemy engagement and had small arms that they could have used.

[b]This line is calculated from Glenn (2000b: 162) and excludes artillery, aviation, administration, and others; hence, it is not a total of the above categories.

The group of high-firers is about 40 percent of the ordinary combat troops. This is higher than Marshall's World War II figures; improved training and organizational methods succeeded in raising the rate. Combat officers—squad leaders and platoon sergeants—were higher (52 percent); this is in keeping with surveys in Korea in which the aggressiveness of enlisted men is related to their rank (Glenn 2000b: 140). Those who operated crew-served weapons (helicopters and machine-gunners) were especially likely to be in the high-firing group (76 to 84 percent)—again, consistent with Marshall's observations. Finally, we can note as a comparison group, that troops that were not especially organized to fire weapons in combat—administrative or other auxiliary service troops who came under fire and had weapons with which to respond—were much more like SLAM's estimates: 23 percent were high-firers when the occasion arose. They also cast light on what may be the probable distribution of SLAM's relative non-firers: about a quarter rarely fired at all, finding ways to avoid combat entirely; another half occasionally took part. And overall, it appears that—except for those special weapons crews, who consisted almost entirely of high-firers—roughly half of all the soldiers were in this middle group, sometimes joining in, sometimes not. Given the existence of deliberate efforts in training and combat organization in the post-SLAM army to keep up firing rates, it is noteworthy that there still is a division between a highly aggressive elite and the mass of the ordinary soldiers. In this respect they are like workers in factories and other manual

TABLE 2.2
Percentage of troops firing in combat photos

	All photos	No. of troops in photos	Photos where at least 1 is firing	No. in photos
Vietnam	18%	342	46%	133
Other twentieth-century wars	7–13%[a]	338–640[a]	31%	146
Iraq	8–14%[b]	63–103[b]	28–50%[b]	10–50[b]

[a] One photo shows a Russian infantry attack in World War I, in which no one in a massed battalion of 300 appears to be firing. The higher firing percentage is based on excluding this photo.

[b] One photo shows a Marine Corps platoon of forty men in a tight firing line. My estimate of how many are firing may be inaccurate. Excluding this photo gives 8 percent firing for all photos, 28 percent firing for photos in which at least one person is firing.

labor: most will do enough to give an appearance of keeping up the average rate of work (Roy 1952).

An alternative to surveying soldiers is to use photos and make our own counts of how many troops are firing.[6]

Photo evidence generally backs up the pattern of relatively low combat firing. Taking all the combat photos together, we find the firing rates are very much in SLAM's low range—13 to 18 percent (and possibly as low as 7 to 8 percent if we allow single photos of large numbers of troops to skew the averages). If we take a more restrictive standard—where at least one person in the photo is firing—we get top firing rates of 46 to 50 percent. These are for American troops in Vietnam and Iraq, after new training methods had taken hold; troops of many nations in earlier wars, and paramilitaries in recent years, are lower, but still at the top of SLAM's range. On the whole, the top of the range is still only about half or less of the troops firing when we would most expect them to do so. SLAM was more right than wrong. And there appear to be limits on how much military organization can do about it.

The problem of tension/fear is what fighting organizations, of whatever kind, have to deal with; the nature of the organization and its performance is shaped by what devices it adopts to deal with it. One of these methods is to take individual initiative away from the soldier, by putting troops in massed formations acting in concert. In the West, there have been two periods of such massed formations: in the ancient Mediterranean, these were phalanxes of men with spears or pikes; such pike formations were revived and continued in late medieval and early modern Europe, up through the early gun-powder period of the seventeenth century. Phalanxes were typically superior to undisciplined bodies of troops that relied on individual valor of heroic fighters who darted forward from the larger mass of supporters, rather like the skirmishers in *Dead Birds*. Roman legions usually defeated larger armies of Gauls or Germans;[7] this would have resulted not only from the advantage of greater discipline in the phalanx in promoting confidence and a firm defense, but the fact that the berserkers or other individual heroes who faced them were a small proportion of the tribal forces. Using SLAM ratios, the aggressive fighters in the tribal armies would have been numerically weaker than the Romans who actually used their arms. As Marshall, McNeill, and others have noted, the use of arms is highest in closely coordinated groups, and with group-operated weapons. The proportion effectively using their spears or swords in a Roman combat formation did not have to be especially high for it to outweigh that of a typical tribal army.

When phalanxes fought other phalanxes (the Greek city-state wars, the Roman Punic and civil wars) the amount of tension/fear seemed to be about the same on both sides. Ancient authors (Thucydides Book 5: para. 71) noticed the tendency of a phalanx to crowd toward the right by trying to shelter increasingly under the shield of the man on that side. The phalanx formation operated primarily to keep men in line and prevent their running away; battles were generally pushing matches, in which relatively little damage was done, unless one side broke formation. And even then, in Greek city-state warfare it was not customary to pursue a broken and fleeing phalanx, and casualties were generally limited to about 15 percent at worst (Keegan 1993: 248–51).

From the seventeenth to the mid-nineteenth century, close-order drill was the preferred formation for European armies. In part this was an effort to speed up, by mass drill, the reloading of firearms, which had to take place after every shot; in part, to keep down self-inflicted casualties by firing together on command; and in part, given the relative inaccuracy of fire, to concentrate its effect by a simultaneous volley. As noted, parade-ground formations also had an organizational advantage in keeping soldiers from running away; and as a mode of discipline, they were no doubt attractive to officers in an era when armies were escalating in size, from on the order of several thousand men in medieval battles to formations that reached hundreds of thousands in the Napoleonic wars. But the firing ratio in parade-ground formations was far from maximal. In American Civil War battles, 90 percent of muzzle-loading muskets collected after the battle of Gettysburg were found loaded, and half of those were multiply loaded, with two or more rounds on top of one another in the barrel (Grossman 1995: 21–22); this implies that at least half the troops, at the moment they were hit or threw away their arms, had been repeatedly going through the motions of loading, but without actually firing, time after time. As we see later, casualties produced by these mass-formation troops were not high, and that could be attributed partly to non-firing, partly to inaccurate firing.

Parade-ground battle formations started going out of style in the mid-nineteenth century, as breech-loading rifles, and then machine-guns, brought a much higher aggregate level of fire to the battlefield, and made mass infantry formations too vulnerable as targets; these formations had survived for over two hundred years, be it noted, because they were not so very dangerous to each other. Battles now were fought in dispersed formation, soldiers strung out across a long line, avoiding bunching, and seeking cover on their own initiative. Nevertheless, close-order marching drill has remained a staple of military training, and of non-combat, home-front and peacetime army life. It is rationalized as a necessary means of establishing discipline, the automatic obedience to authority that will enable a soldier to perform well under the stresses of combat. By extrapolation, even in an era of SLAM-inspired sophistication about combat fear and low firing ratio, close-order drill can be promoted as a solution precisely to the motivational problem shown in Marshall's and similar studies. But in fact robot-like obedience does not promote effective firing in combat; Marshall noted (1947: 60–61) that the minority of combat firers often contains soldiers who are otherwise unamenable to discipline, who perform badly in barracks drills, and often are in the guardhouse for violations of authority. Thus it appears likely that even in the era of mass-formation firing, parade drill was not really a means of making troops effective in combat; it was even then largely a ritual of peacetime discipline, a symbolic effort to display an image of the army impressive to outsiders and, indeed, to itself. Marching and drill could get the troops into combat; but it could not make them effective fighters. It continues as an initiation ritual for new soldiers, and a symbolic marker between them and civilians in an era when it is irrelevant to the conditions of combat.

A higher firing ratio (and more generally across history, a higher frequency of using one's weapons) is the result of a number of conditions. (Many of these are summarized in Grossman 1995.)

1. Group-operated weapons: teams of soldiers manning machine-guns, bazookas or rocket launchers, mortars, and other weapons where part of the team feeds ammunition or provides ancillary services.

2. Greater distance from the enemy: artillery has a high firing rate; snipers firing at long distance with telescopes have a high rate;

infantry firing in close combat has a low rate; and use of weapons in hand-to-hand combat is very low.

3. A stronger command hierarchy: superior officers on the spot who directly order soldiers to fire. This was easier to achieve in mass formations and in very small groups; relatively difficult in dispersed battlefield conditions of modern fighting.

4. Psychologically realistic training: not parade-ground drill, nor target practice, but simulation of the chaos and tension of battlefield conditions, with exercises that make firing at suddenly appearing threats an automatic reflex.

All of these are ways of counteracting the tension/fear of violent confrontation. Group-operated weapons rely on solidarity at the most micro level; the effective combat team is one in which the soldiers are paying attention to each other more than to the enemy. Group-operated weapons are important, then, not so much because of the specific technology but because they facilitate a mood of solidarity; there is some evidence that just getting going at firing is a catalyst, and that soldiers in these weapons teams switched from one weapon to another as the fighting went on.[8] Over and above the fire-power they provide, group-operated weapons facilitate troops falling into an interaction ritual with each other, entraining their bodies into a collective enterprise and a common rhythm; just as in non-conflictual rituals, emotional entrainment and mutual focus of attention creates a cocoon of local solidarity and emotional energy, the confidence and enthusiasm to fire even when others succumb to the debilitating tension of combat.

Such rituals can be deliberately inculcated in training. British troops at the turn of the twenty-first century trained with special emphasis on keeping up a continuous chain of communication—by voice or predesignated gestures—from one man to the next during combat and thus to use social cohesion to promote appropriate firing (King 2005). The infantry squad was trained to move and fire in an alternating rhythm with each other, in effect turning individual weapons into group-operated weapons.

Distance from the enemy cuts down just those cues that make the confrontation fearful. Command authority, by itself alone, is probably the least effective. Command authority may operate as a way of reestablishing group attention; there are numerous instances where a panic retreat is quickly stopped by officers issuing firm orders, and conversely where a group of men in retreat become uncontrollably afraid when officers are vacillating or are themselves panicked (Holmes 1985). And finally, realistic combat-style training was instituted out of a conscious effort to give men an automatic response of firing in confrontational situations.

Yet the effectiveness of these conditions themselves varies: group solidarity may be high but instead of promoting firing, it may encourage soldiers to resist or ignore higher command. To these we must add a fifth source of variation: even across these conditions, a minority of soldiers do most of the active fighting. The theoretical problem is to account for the distribution of these individuals; that is, to bring all of these into a deeper explanation of how the situation of fear and tension gets resolved into a minority who ride the wave of fear, and a majority who are swept along by it.

LOW FIGHTING COMPETENCE

Whether soldiers fire their guns or not—or otherwise use their weapons—they still do not appear to be very effective with them. A high firing ratio is not the same as high effectiveness in hitting the target. The minority of effective soldiers may thus be much lower than 15 to 25 percent; and firing levels of 80 percent or more indicated for the Vietnam war in fact turn out not to be more effective than previous war performance.

In the musket era, contemporary estimates ranged from one hit for 500 rounds fired, up to one hit per 2,000 or 3,000; modern reconstructions suggest a 5 percent maximum for that period. Smoothbore muskets were not very accurate at long range. But the Prussian army in the late 1700s firing at targets representing the size of an enemy formation showed "40 percent hits at 150 yards, and 60 percent hits at 75 yards;" but in battle their firing at very close range of thirty yards resulted in less than 3 percent hits (Grossman 1995: 10; Keegan and Holmes 1985). The high point could be somewhat better; an elite unit of British marksmen in the Napoleonic wars fought an engagement in which they fired volleys totaling 1,890 rounds and caused 430 casualties, a hit rate of about 23 percent; they were in stationary position receiving a French attack, and fired volleys between 115 and 30 yards (Holmes 1985: 167–68). But this was exceptional; most troops of the Napoleonic and Civil War era firing at an exposed formation, typically at the close distance of thirty yards, would hit "only one or two men per minute," by a unit containing between two hundred and one thousand men. Griffith (1989) comments: "Casualties mounted because the contest went on so long, not because the fire was particularly deadly."

The breech-loading rifles of the late nineteenth century were technically better weapons but their main effect was to increase the number of rounds fired per period of time, not to improve the ratio of hits. A battle in the Franco-Prussian war of 1870 saw the Germans fire 80,000 rounds to hit 400 Frenchmen, and the latter firing 48,000 rounds to hit 404 Germans;

hit ratios were one per 200 and one per 119 rounds respectively. American troops in a battle on the western plains in 1876 fired 252 bullets for every Indian casualty. An abundance of easy targets at point-blank range would improve the hit ratio but not give a high level of reliability. In South Africa in 1879, a British unit of 140 men was nearly overwhelmed by three thousand Zulus, and fired over twenty thousand rounds in repulsing the attack; but Zulu casualty rates were at most one per thirteen rounds fired.[9] In World War I battles in which rifle firing was predominant, typical hit ratios were one per twenty-seven rounds fired. In the Vietnam war, where American soldiers were equipped with automatic weapons, estimates were on the order of fifty thousand bullets fired per enemy killed (Grossman 1995: 9–12; Holmes 1985: 167–72). One almost ritualistic procedure was the so-called mad moment when a unit settled down into a battlefield position, soldiers would empty their weapons with firing all around the perimeter (Daughterty and Mattson 2001: 116–17). In short, as weapons became better, overall efficiency remained low; better weapons allowed a greater volume of wild and inaccurate shooting.[10] In World War II, more than half of soldiers believed that they have never killed anyone (Holmes 1985: 376). This is no doubt true; indeed, most of those who claim they have killed were probably exaggerating.

A few individuals have been highly accurate combat shooters. Chief among these are snipers, but these have been a very small proportion of troops, and individuals firing with great accuracy are not how most casualties in battle are inflicted. In the modern era, casualties were caused primarily by artillery fired at long distance. In the musket era of parade-ground formations, cannon operating closer to the battle line generally accounted for more than 50 percent of the casualties; the most successful generals, including Gustavus Adolphus in the seventeenth century and Napoleon at the turn of the nineteenth, emphasized small mobile field-pieces spread throughout combat units that could be fired at close range, especially with grapeshot that gave a machine-gun–like effect (Grossman 1995: 11; 154). In World War I, artillery caused almost 60 percent of British casualties, bullets about 40 percent; in World War II, artillery and aerial bombs caused about 75 percent, bullets less than 10 percent. In Korea, shells and mortars caused about 60 percent of American casualties, while small arms caused 3 percent of deaths and 27 percent of wounds (Holmes 1985: 210). This does not mean that artillery is particularly cost-effective for the volume of fire. On one day in 1916, for example, the British fired 224,000 shells and killed six thousand Germans (a ratio of one hit for thirty-seven shells fired); the Western Front of World War I was the apex for sheer volume of artillery fire, but comparable ratios of shells to casualties are found for World War II and smaller wars of the late twentieth century (Holmes 1985: 170–71).

How are we to interpret this pattern? As Grossman documents, artillery achieve a higher level of firing than riflemen and frontline troops generally; the sheer distance from the enemy, and especially being shielded from personally seeing the men one is trying to kill, increases the level of performance. Additionally, artillery are group-operated weapons; local small-group solidarity and emotional entrainment keeps men on the job, keeping up a regular rate of fire. Artillery thus overcomes the SLAM problem of a low firing rate. Even so, high firing rates are not the same as highly accurate rates; in the fog of battle, firing often misses. And even when it hits its target, enemy soldiers are often protected by defensive positions. Fighting is intrinsically inefficient, all the way around. Distance weapons have become more important in causing casualties chiefly because the logistics of warfare have improved so that huge amounts of firepower can be brought to the battlefield, and fire can be sustained for a long enough period so that the casualties mount up even with a low ratio of effectiveness. The tension/fear of combat is almost completely debilitating at close range, and in the individual use of small arms; at longer range, tension/fear is overcome, but something like it remains in a degree. As long as both sides remain engaged, damage is done by keeping up a chronic condition of low-efficiency firing, rather than an acute moment of all-out destruction.[11]

FRIENDLY FIRE AND BYSTANDER HITS

All evidence points to the fact that fighting takes place in a condition of tension and fear. Most fighters close up to the enemy take little or no belligerent action; when pressed by strong organizational controls, or supported by small group ties, they engage in firing, and some small proportion of fighters become aggressive participants. But most of these firers, reluctant and enthusiastic alike, are quite incompetent at it. They often fire wildly about them. As a result, it should not be surprising that they often hit troops on their own side. In the late twentieth century, this became publicized as "friendly fire"—fire by the "friendlies" rather than by the enemy.

Friendly fire appears to have existed in all armies of all historical periods, and indeed in all fight situations. In the era of mass formations, where there was more organizational pressure to fire, a troop of soldiers marching into combat might shoot off their guns in a mutual contagion of excitement. A nineteenth-century French officer speaks of soldiers becoming "drunk on rifle fire," and Ardant du Picq, as well as German officers, describes troops firing from the hip without taking aim, and mostly firing wildly in the air (Holmes 1985: 173). This "panic-firing" or "nervous firing" as nineteenth-century military writers referred to it, tends to take place at such distance from the enemy that it is just wasting ammunition, contravening the "fire-discipline" demanded by their officers. The collective mood of troops entering combat might be more aptly described as symbolic of combat. It is essentially a blustering gesture from a psychologically safe distance, at considerable remove from the real confrontation when firing becomes considerably harder.[12] Thus they overcome the SLAM problem to a degree, but not the incompetence problem; and they create another problem, the tendency to injure each other. "Marshal Saint-Cyr estimated that one-quarter of French infantry casualties during the Napoleonic period were caused by men in the front rank being accidentally shot by those behind them" (Holmes 1985: 173).

Despite the fact that the close-order formation was drilled explicitly, and indeed in part designed, to prevent firing within one's own ranks, when battle broke out, this discipline tended to disintegrate.[13] Similar problems apparently afflicted the older phalanx formations: they could keep a semblance of concerted threat when they held long spears that extended far to the front, but when men came into close combat and began to swing about with swords and clubs, they not only were often ineffective against the enemy, but must have inflicted wounds on themselves. Among the most famous of such casualties was the Persian king Cambyses in 522 B.C., wounded by his own sword (Holmes 1985: 190). It is the same in modern times. In 1936, the most popular anarchist leader in the Spanish Civil War, Buenaventura Durruti, was killed by his own companion when his machine pistol caught on a car door (Beevor 1999: 200).

The problem continues in the very different formations of modern warfare, with troops spread out along a firing line. Holmes (1985: 189–92) gives numerous examples: artillery firing on their own troops in World War I (killing 75,000 French soldiers alone); bombers bombing their own positions in World War II; troops attacking allied positions because of failing to recognize them. Sentries and pickets firing on apparent strangers have killed many of their own officers, in French, Prussian, British, and other armies. The death of the Confederate general Stonewall Jackson at the end of the victorious battle of Chancellorsville in 1863, shot by his own sentries who did not recognize him, was only one of many such incidents.

Keegan (1976: 311 to 13) estimates that 15 to 25 percent of battle casualties are from accident. In the era of mechanized warfare, these increasingly occur from traffic or heavy equipment accidents: being run over by tanks or trucks, being crushed by artillery or other large weapons while moving them around. In theaters of difficult movement, such as the British front in Burma 1942–43, non-battle injuries outnumbered battle injuries by five to one (Holmes 1985: 191). Attempts to supply troops by air have resulted in deaths, as when ground forces had crates of food dropped on their heads. It is not so much ironic as appropriate that General Patton, famed for speedy tank movement, should have been killed in an auto crash soon after the end of World War II. Military aircraft are much more prone to traffic problems than civilian aviation; over and above enemy fire, an additional 20 percent of U.S. planes were lost in Korea by accidents (Gurney 1958: 273). The shift to high-mobility helicopter transport has brought its corresponding form of transport casualties. In the Afghanistan war of 2001–02, a large proportion of casualties were from helicopter accidents. In the Iraq war from March 2003 to August 2005, 19 percent of American troop deaths were by accidents (*Philadelphia Inquirer,* Aug. 11, 2005; from iCasualties.org). Tension infects not just the soldiers using their own weapons, to the potential harm of those nearest to them, but also the larger-scale organizational environment, where the war consists in moving large and dangerous material objects in ways that often lead to collisions with humans in the tension-ridden situation.[14]

My analysis thus far has drawn largely upon military combat, but the patterns apply generally to all violent conflicts. The category of friendly fire, and a near extension that we may call bystander hits, which the military calls "collateral damage," is prominent in small-scale civilian conflicts as well.

A major form of gang fighting, at least on the West Coast, is drive-by shootings, in which members of one gang in a car shoot at a gathering of an opposing gang (Sanders 1994). Often these are weddings, parties, or other festive gatherings, since they are the kind of occasions where a gang knows targets can be found. Usually just one shot is fired into the group, while the car speeds away. Since these are vendetta shootings, any member of the group, male or female, can be an appropriate victim. Generally gang members themselves are not hit, although their friends and families are. Such drive-by shootings may hit a totally unrelated bystander, including a child or other especially helpless victim.

The apparently high proportion of gang-vendetta shootings that hit bystanders, and the low proportion that hit fighting members of the opposing gang, seems perversely unjust. However, it fits a well-established pattern in another area: in disasters, those most likely to die are children and old people, while able-bodied young males are most likely to survive (Bourque et al. 2006). A fight situation resembles a disaster scene in that the most nimble and alert are most likely to evade the dangers, while the most helpless are most likely to succumb—in this case, to remain oblivious or immobile in the line of fire.

The same is true in small group and individual fights, with and without weapons. In the high-tension situation of the fight, members of a group are likely to swing wildly, and are likely to hit members of their own side, especially if they are packed close together.

From a student report: A group of fifteen teenage boys came into a high school locker room to confront one boy who had been in a dispute with two of them. The observer noted the tension on all sides: the target sweated, trembled, and attempted to hide; the attackers were bodily tense, breathing heavily, and continually encouraged each other as if to work up their courage. When they saw their target's fear, they rushed at him, punched and knocked him down, and kicked him on the ground. Since the beating occurred in the narrow space of the locker room, several punches hit the attackers themselves; one had a finger broken when he tripped and was stepped on; another was bruised on the arm. Bystanders who gathered to watch the fight were unable to keep a safe distance, and one of them was accidentally punched in the face. Total casualties included the victim, two attackers (both from friendly fire), and one bystander.

From another student report: A group of seventeen members of a teenage gang set out in four cars to find the house of a member of an opposing gang. From the outset there was confusion: a lengthy discussion over who would ride in which car, as well as numerous wrong turns in traveling to the target's house. When they arrived, there was further hesitation about what to do; no one knocked on the door. After ten minutes, the victim's older brother, a twenty-eight-year-old man, came out and said that he was not at home. After a thirty-second argument through the car window, the most aggressive of the gang members jumped out and started a scuffle. As soon as the man was knocked down, the rest of the gang left the cars and rushed to join in stomping him on the ground. At this juncture the gang was reduced to fourteen, since three of them, as the altercation began, jumped into two of the cars and drove off, leaving the rest with only two cars. The majority of the gang were too busy to notice, since they were crowding each other to get an opportunity to kick the man on the ground; at least two of the attackers punched each other in the mêlée. In about two minutes, a group of two men and two women, older family members of the twenty-eight-year old, came out of the house and began to throw bottles and rocks at the cars. This unexpected source of resistance panicked the attackers, who attempted to crowd back into the two remaining cars. This seemed to embolden the bottle-throwers, who, although showing fear on their faces, pressed their attack on the retreating side, who were tumbling over each other attempting to get into the cars. One driver had to get out and change seats, unable to drive because his hands were too badly bruised from repeatedly punching the first victim. The disorganized retreat left the last car, packed with eight gang members, stranded for three minutes, while the locals continually pelted them from a distance, smashing in all the windows on one side of the car. Finally they made their escape. The observer noted that after they were safely back on their home territory, they described the events in a manner that left out all the disreputable details of their performance, instead bragging about how they had won the fight.

Fist fights generally involve wild swinging, and bystanders are often hit, unless there is sufficient warning for them to back away quickly to a safe distance. This is not always possible in a crowded place. There is no systematic data that would enable us to tell how often particular kinds of fights lead to bystander hits. Judging from all sources from which I have compiled fight descriptions, it appears that in a substantial minority of fights there are bystander hits. The exception is the class of fights in which a fight is planned and organized as a spectacle. These will be treated later as "fair fights" in chapter 6. That is to say, unless fights are specially organized so that they are restricted—with an explicit, high-priority concern to avoid friendly fire—the pervasive incompetence produced by the tension of conflict leads to some substantial chance of bystander injury.

Police violence resembles other kinds of violence in this respect as well as in most others. Police shoot-outs with criminal suspects often involve friendly-fire casualties. One such case involved a chase of a man wanted for murder, who was traced to a motel room (information supplied by supervisor of a state police force). Ten officers surrounded the door in a rough semi-circle; when the suspect emerged, he brandished a TV remote control as if it were a weapon, and was shot by the officers. The man apparently wanted to be killed rather than be captured; the colloquial term for this is "suicide by cop." Thus, in this case, all bullets were fired by police. What is relevant here is that the ten officers wounded one of their own side; ballistics tests showed that many rounds went wild into the walls and ceiling; only eight of the twenty-eight bullets fired hit the suspect.

In 1998, sixty of 760,000 U.S. police officers were killed on duty; 10 percent by their own guns—that is, by friendly fire. In 2001, omitting the seventy-one officers killed at the World Trade Center, seventy officers were killed in action (mostly by firearms), plus another seventy-eight died in accidents (largely vehicle crashes); altogether eight were killed by their own weapons or were accidentally shot: a friendly-fire ratio of 11 percent (*Los Angeles Times*, July 26, 1999; FBI report, Dec. 3, 2002).

Police fire also hits bystanders. The pattern here is not too different from gang shootings, especially when shooting is made difficult by speeding cars.

Bystander injuries also occur in police auto chases (Alpert and Dunham 1990; see further discussion in chapter 3). The sociological point here is not to allocate blame but to point out the pattern: conflict situations involving vehicles are much like combat situations where moving military

equipment across space in high-tension situations while rapidly outma-
neuvering the enemy is a priority.

Here again entertainment depiction of violence creates a severe distortion. A staple of action-adventure films is the auto chase scene. This normally depicts a great deal of accidental damage to property, and climaxes
with a spectacular crash, usually depicted in a lighthearted or humorous
mode. Bodily injury or death of the principals to a movie chase is rarely
shown; at most the bad guy's car disappears in flames. Bystander injuries
are never depicted.

Bystander hits are a feature of military combat wherever there are civilians present. It is particularly likely in urban fighting, where civilians have
not been able to leave, and thus has occurred in traditional and modern
sieges; as well as in guerrilla warfare, where fighters deliberately hide
among the civilian population. To fight at all in a heavily populated area
is bound to produce non-combatant casualties, whatever care is taken to
avoid them, short of not firing at all.

Technological improvements hypothetically might reduce bystander
hits; by the turn of the twenty-first century, these included computer controlled firing, remote radar and satellite sensing, and highly accurate navi-
gational systems for bombs and missiles, as well as improvements in
sighting and sensing systems for ground weapons and small arms. Nevertheless, the experience of early twenty-first-century wars continues to
show problems of bystander hits and friendly fire.[15] These patterns suggest
that the root problem is not the technology, but the fog or tension of
combat itself. The weapon, no matter how technically reliable, is always
controlled by humans who pick out targets or at least set the criteria for
firing at them—however automatically these are carried out. Given that
combat is a matter of defensive evasions, deceptions, and maneuverings,
picking a target is intrinsically difficult to judge accurately. Thus it is not
unlikely that an Afghani wedding party would be taken for al-Qaeda
troops, especially when the sensing apparatus is in outer space; or that a
hospital can be regarded as a disguise for a weapons dump. Devastating
firepower motivates opponents to hide where they can, including in civilian installations or close to them; knowing this, attackers with high-tech
distance weapons are motivated to interpret targets broadly rather than
narrowly. Combat creates a mood in which targets are chosen in a belligerent haze. There is nothing in the record of technological improvements,
which have already gone through many generations, to suggest that these
factors will cease to be important.

As combat casualties go down, friendly-fire casualties go up. In the
Afghanistan war during 2001–02, the proportion of friendly-fire and accidental casualties was 63 percent.[16] In wars fought with one-sided technological superiority, casualties inflicted by enemies on high-tech troops tend

to be low; these troops typically fire from a distance and have high mobility and evacuation capacity, thus deadly casualties are especially likely to be low as combat wounds are more easily tended. Friendly fire, and especially the borderline self-inflicted casualties of traffic accidents, account for a higher proportion of deaths, both because enemy casualties make up a smaller proportion and because the high-tech mobility of the army, especially battle helicopters and other intrinsically dangerous machinery, is more heavily relied upon. The increasing power of munitions also poses a risk for anyone who is around them, especially troops who move and store them. In the Iraq war 2003–05, a considerable proportion of deaths from accident were from munitions accidents.

It was in this context of dwindling combat casualties in U.S. actions during the 1990s that the news media discovered the phenomenon of friendly fire. When casualties occur in incidents of one or a few men at a time spread over many weeks, events such as a single pilot being shot down, or a single CIA operative being killed while interrogating prisoners, get a large amount of media attention; this would not have been possible in previous wars where casualties were so common that most were necessarily anonymous. Under this type of publicity, friendly-fire accidents receive great scrutiny, whereas they would have been hidden under the massive casualties of World War II. Investigations and apportioning of blame for friendly fire, however, are not likely to bring about a decline in its incidence, since it is structurally built into violent conflict situations. Like political scandals, these kinds of controversies are repetitive, and investigations, outcries, and punishments do not make them go away.[17]

Friendly fire and bystander hits are offshoots of the basic character of fight situations: tension/fear and resulting incompetence. This is a version of haste makes waste, considering that fighting puts a premium upon hasty action at the moment that violence is going on. What is sometimes called the fog of combat can also be described as a psychological condition of tunnel vision. Fighting takes up the complete attention of those who are engaged in it; it overwhelms the senses and focuses the mind so that all else fades into invisibility. It is hard enough to maintain an effective focus on the enemy; temporary obliviousness to whoever else might be in the fighting zone is inevitable. This is true of angry men engaged in a cursing and gesturing match, oblivious to the consternation of bystanders; police officers who expect their blaring sirens, loud squawk boxes, fast driving, and other gestures of designating a crime scene to take precedence over all other normal human concerns;[18] and soldiers in battle putting everything on the battlefield at their disposal, whether to occupy houses or to blow them up.

This self-centeredness of fight situations affects even the fighting elite: those who are in SLAM's elite of firers, and the smaller-still elite of those who fire accurately. In one famous case, the Ruby Ridge standoff in 1992, a police sniper with a telescopic sight hit not the man who was the object of the stake-out in his mountain cabin, but his wife who came to the window carrying a child (Whitcomb 2001: 241–311; Kopel and Blackman 1997: 32–38). This is a case of a bystander hit. It is not an instance of technical incompetence; sharp-shooters are unlike everyone else in being extremely accurate at hitting human targets. In this case, the kill ratio was one bullet, one kill. The sniper simply misidentified the target coming into the window where he expected his man to be. Fighting limits attention; in that tunnel of confrontational tension, damage is often done, in ways that are only loosely connected with what was consciously intended outside the tunnel.

Joy of Combat: Under What Conditions?

Fighting is shaped by tension and fear. But some proportion of individuals, in some situations, enjoy fighting. How do we account for this minority? Better yet, what light does such an investigation cast on the variable processes that produce violent action?

An extreme position, taken by some authors, is that men typically like combat. This is an explicitly gendered argument; males, whether because of macho culture or genetics, are fighters and killers and get pleasure out of these actions. The most extreme interpretation is that killing is a sexually pleasurable drive (Bourke 1999).

Evidence for this argument needs to distinguish the kinds of situations in which men (and in some instances, women) express feelings of joy about combat. One type is pre-battle elation. Bourke (1999: 274) quotes a World War I British chaplain who describes his own, and his troops' "strange and fearsome delight at being at last up 'really' up against it." This is a case of feelings prior to these men's first battle, still in the phase of rhetoric. Ulysses S. Grant (1885/1990: 178) similarly describes troops in November 1861 in his first Civil War command, who were so eager for battle that he felt he could not maintain discipline if he did not find an engagement for them to fight.

Related to this type is the bloodthirsty rhetoric expressed at a distance from the front. Given the size of the logistics and support train for twentieth- and twenty-first-century armies, a considerable proportion of troops are in no position actually to fire at the enemy, and in relatively little danger of receiving fire; but they often carry weapons and have been trained to use them, and so they have some plausible self-description as fighting soldiers.[19] Soldiers in rear areas express more hatred of the enemy, and more ferocious attitudes toward them, than frontline troops (Stouffer et al. 1949: 158–65). Whereas combat soldiers are more likely to treat prisoners well—once the danger point has been passed when they are actually being captured, often sharing food and water with them—rear-area troops tend to treat prisoners more callously, or even brutally (Holmes 1985: 368–78, 382). Continuing the progression, civilians at home are more likely to express violent rhetorical hatred against the enemy and blood-thirsty joy in killing them (Bourke 1999: 144–53). Given the relatively high proportion of women on the civilian homefront, there is reason to doubt that gender per se, rather than situational differences, accounts for differences in ferociousness.

The farther from the front, the more rhetorical ferociousness is expressed, and rhetorical enthusiasm for the whole fighting enterprise. This fits the general pattern of all fights: surrounded by bluster and gesture up until the actual fight situation, when the emotion shifts drastically and tension/fear takes over (documented in Holmes 1985: 75–8, citing many observers). The proportion of empty rhetoric expands with each step toward the rear; war is successively more idealized, the enemy successively more dehumanized, attitudes toward killing successively more callous, and the whole affair more like the cheering of sports fans.

Rarer is joy in actual combat. Here we need to be very precise about just what is being experienced. Given SLAM's low firing ratio, this is not necessarily the experience of firing one's weapon; nor, given low effectiveness, the experience of hitting the enemy. Thus Bourke (1999: 21) quotes a British World War II pilot who liked the sound of firing bullets: "What a thrill!" As Marshall and others have noted, soldiers typically find the most enjoyable part of military training is firing guns on the range; but this is quite different from the feelings of hitting an enemy.

Finally, we come to expression of positive emotions about killing an enemy. Bourke (1999) presents quotations culled from letters, diaries, and reminiscences of Anglophone soldiers—British, Canadian, Australian, American—in the two world wars, Korea, and Vietnam. She gives twenty-eight such cases. Only four of Bourke's cases describe something like sexual pleasure in killing; another nine describe the exhilaration or frenzy of close-up killing, where the enemy can be actually seen. The latter generally look like the special situation that, in chapter 3, I will describe as a "forward panic." The rest of the cases—half or more—are instances of distant killing, sharpshooting by former animal hunters, or victories by fighter pilots. But as we shall see in chapter 11, snipers and ace pilots are the most unusual of all fighters, competent where most others are not, because of their special emotional techniques for overcoming confrontational tension. Carefully examined, much of what Bourke interprets as joy of killing are expressions of pride or relief in successful performance—the majority of pilots shoot down no enemy planes, and those who do are treated as a special elite.

Within the relatively small proportion of soldiers who kill in combat, there are a variety of emotions: cold and businesslike; pride in one's competence; elation at a job well done; hatred, frenzy, feelings of revenge for deaths on one's own side; positive pleasure. It is difficult to tell what proportions of soldiers feel which of these emotions; more importantly for theoretical explanation, we need to seek out the circumstances in which they feel them. Positive emotions should also be balanced with negative emotions to killing, such as the following example from the Boxer Rebellion:

> [A British marine] had shot and bayoneted a man early in the siege, driving the bayonet in up to the hilt in the man's chest and then discharging the entire contents of his magazine. Now, badly traumatized, he lay thrashing about, shrieking hour after hour "How it splashes! How it splashes!" (Preston 2000: 213)

THE CONTINUUM OF TENSION/FEAR AND COMBAT PERFORMANCE

There are a variety of ways that soldiers behave in combat. This is best seen as a continuum of degrees and kinds of tension and fear, with different degrees of incompetence or competence in resulting performance. At one end is frozen incapacity, burrowing into the ground or childishly hiding from sight of the enemy. Next is panic retreat. Next comes shitting and pissing in one's pants, physical manifestations of fear but not necessarily stopping one from at least going through the motions of fighting. This part of the continuum also includes lagging back from the front line, seeking excuses to do something other than move forward, drifting away (Holmes 1985: 229). Then comes moving forward but not firing; not firing but helping those who are firing, such as by giving them ammunition or reloading for them; then firing one's weapons but incompetently, missing the enemy. Finally, at the high end, there is accurate and well-timed firing, and other aggressive maneuvers in combat. We have as yet no clear evidence as to what the emotions are at the high end of competent violence. Is it simply no overt expression of fear; more rarely, complete lack of subjective or covert fear? A relatively small number of men report no fear in battle (Holmes 1985: 204). Is it at this end of the continuum that we will find exhilaration, enjoyment of battle? And still more extreme, enjoyment of killing? Although there are folk theories about this, it remains to be shown: is competent violence hot or cold?

Let us turn to the photographic evidence again. Using the combat photos from the sources listed earlier in note 6 it is possible to judge the emotions of 290 soldiers from visible faces and body postures.[20] The distribution of emotions is as follows:

Strong fear: 18 percent
Mild fear, apprehension, worry: 12 percent
Stunned, exhausted, sad, anguished, pained: 7 percent
Yelling, shouting orders, calling for help: 2 percent
Tense, wary: 21 percent
Alert, concentrated, serious, making effort: 11 percent
Neutral, calm, impassive, relaxed: 26 percent
Anger: 6 percent
Joy, smiling: 0.3 percent

About a third of the soldiers (30 percent) show either strong or mild fear. Another third (32 percent) are in the middle ground of tension and concentration. A quarter (26 percent) are calm and neutral. One might conjecture that the last group would be the most competent in combat, but they are just as likely to be among non-firers as those who are firing their weapons.

A small group (7 percent) are stunned or incapacitated. These are chiefly the wounded and dying, plus prisoners and subjects of torture. Some of those about to be executed show fear, but fear is more common among non-wounded soldiers. In one famous photo (Howe 2002: 26) a Saigon police official executes a captured Viet Cong with a pistol; the victim shows a blend of fear and shock, but the strongest expression of horror is on the face of another policeman looking on. The executioner's face is impassive, as is generally the case with photos of interrogators.

Joy in the moment of combat is almost nonexistent. Only one photo shows a member of a mortar crew smiling—and this is a distance weapon, not directly confrontational. The complete photo collections include another fifteen photos of soldiers smiling, all of them outside of combat situations. Most of them are in moments of victory—showing off weapons captured from the enemy, or the time when peace is declared. Smiles are most common among fighter pilots elated at returning to base with their victory totals establishing their ranking as aces; some are depicted smiling in front of their planes (found also in Toliver and Constable 1997). In one photo, the first American ace in Vietnam recounts his air battle to a circle of smiling shipmates, although the pilot himself, caught up in his story, has an expression of anger and aggression (Daugherty and Mattson 2001: 508).

Perhaps most surprising is the rarity of expressions of anger in combat. Only 6 percent of the soldiers show this. And most of the anger is not in the form of striking out at the enemy. There are a couple of instances where machine gunners fire with a hard-set anger mouth. Anger is more often shown by prisoners (especially in Vietnam) and victims of torture if they are not stunned; sometimes their anger blends with fear. Wounded soldiers are mostly stunned, sometimes mildly fearful; anger comes out more in the faces of buddies and medics who are tending to them, especially when calling for help—usually in a blend with sadness or fear. Torturers themselves do not look angry, although several photos show angry expressions on soldiers who are dragging prisoners into captivity—here anger blends with muscular effort to overcome resistance. Anger in fact seems to occur mostly in moments of intense effort. We see this in the expressions of officers calling out orders in the heat of combat. Two of the strongest anger faces are of U.S. security guards in a tussle with a panicked crowd attempting to board a plane evacuating Saigon during its fall to the enemy; the guards are straining their muscles to clear the door so the plane can take off, and one of them punches a civilian (Daugherty and Mattson 2001: 556). The most intense expression of anger in the book of 850 Vietnam war photos is not in the war zone at all, but of a peace demonstrator in the United States (Daugherty and Mattson 2001: 184).

This gives us a clue to the rather disjointed relationship between anger and violence. Competent use of weapons is for the most part not angry. Anger is effective only in situations where sheer muscular force is at issue, and then more in the effort to exert compliance than to cause actual harm to an opponent. Anger comes out where there is little or no confrontational fear: in controlled situations where the opponent is already subdued, or in completely symbolic confrontations where there is no fighting but opinions are expressed or vented.[21] Ironically, there is probably more anger in civilian life than in actual combat.

To ask whether the basic human propensity is fear, or pleasure in killing, or something else, is the wrong way to go about producing an explanation. Better to proceed on the assumption that all humans are basically alike and that situational dynamics over very specific periods of time determine where individual fighters will be on the continuum. The very same soldiers who minutes earlier were in a frenzy of killing a helpless enemy, or exulting over victory, can be sharing rations with surrendered prisoners (Holmes 1985: 370–71); an hour before that, they could be in a phase of high tension, non-firing, and half-paralysis. Not violent individuals, but violent situations; and also, not fearful individuals but fearful positions in situations. And thus across the board.

CONFRONTATIONAL TENSION IN POLICING AND NON-MILITARY FIGHTING

The same kinds of patterns that demonstrate the importance of tension/fear in military combat are present in virtually all other kinds of fighting. The main exception is where violence is encapsulated and restricted so that it makes a recognizably artificial situation, such as the dueling and entertainment violence that we will deal with in chapters 6, 7, and 8. Other than this, "serious" violence is basically the same everywhere. We see this in the case of police violence: the relatively small proportion of police who fire their guns or physically beat suspects; the extent to which police who do fire do so wildly, missing targets, causing casualties by friendly fire or bystander fire; instances of overkill and forward panic.

The same is true for gang fights: the prevalence of drive-bys and other kinds of hit-and-run attacks; violence against outnumbered enemies, especially those who are caught alone or in very small numbers in enemy territory. In contrast are the standoffs, gesturing, and blustering that occur when gangs encounter each other in full force.

Similarly again in riots, including ethnic riots. As we shall see, crowd violence is almost always carried out by a small proportion of persons at the front, throwing stones, taunting the enemy, burning or smashing enemy property. The behavior of most people in riots shows tension and fear, manifested in great caution, and frequently in running toward safety at signs of counter-attack from the other side. The "elite" of crowd fighters, those at the front, also generally shows some manifestations of fear or at least high degrees of tension. We generally see a pattern of running forward and back, exactly like the film evidence of tribal warfare. Crowd fighters—rioters—pick their targets carefully, attacking where they have a few of the enemy quite outnumbered, or helpless and unable to fight back. Where enemies make a strong showing, or where police or other authorities display clear willingness to use force, the rioters almost always retreat, at least in that immediate locality.[22] Figure 2.5 shows the obverse of this situation: the U.S. soldier has the gun and the body armor, but it is the unarmed Iraqi crowd that is advancing on him with hostile gestures, while he backs away from the confrontation. In the collective mood of such confrontational situations, the momentum of retreat and attack are reciprocally entwined.

Individual fights, as we have seen, are structured by tension and fear. In most fights among the relatively evenly matched, there is much bluster, little action, and that action demonstrates little competence. Where violence does take place it occurs by the strong attacking the weak—those with much greater numbers attacking isolated victims, the heavily armed attacking the unarmed, the bigger and more muscular beating the smaller. And such fights often show incompetence by missing targets, with civilian versions of friendly fire and bystander hits. These also happen in fights with fists and other crude weapons.

We have little systematic evidence, comparable to non-firing and hit rates in military combat, for ineffectiveness in civilian fights. Scattered data on police shoot-outs are the closest to this, and these resemble the military pattern. We have no data on how many drive-by shootings miss

Figure 2.5 Soldier backs up, unarmed crowd advances (Baghdad, October 2004). AP/World Wide Photos.

their targets and how many hit the wrong person. Sanders (1994: 67, 75) indicates that not all gang members like to go hunting for rival members, and that of those in the car, usually only one shoots; and so the firing ratio in drive-bys is probably one in four persons or less. Since the point of the car attack is to keep the confrontation as brief as possible, there is a very low rate of sustained fire. The most extensive data on gang shootings is Wilkinson's (2003) study of violent offenders in black and Hispanic poverty areas in New York, which asked them to describe various kinds of violent incidents they had been involved in. Of 151 incidents in which guns were present, they were fired 71 percent of the time; when they were fired, someone was injured 67 percent of the time (calculated from Wilkinson 2003: 128–30, 216). When someone was hit, 36 percent of the time it was a bystander rather than one of the principals, indicating a high level of friendly fire.[23]

Comparison of civilian and military violence casts light on another point. Tension/fear is one explanation for low firing ratios among soldiers, and for relatively incompetent performance in hitting enemy targets. But other reasons may be involved: One is that on the modern battlefield, soldiers are dispersed and take cover, so that the battlefield looks empty;[24] thus lack of visible targets may be responsible for some of the non-firing or ineffective firing. But Marshall himself discounts this, by showing non-firing also in situations of close combat; and historically there are similar patterns in premodern massed firing. More importantly, in sustained warfare, soldiers are often deprived of sleep; they are physically worn down, by exposure to the elements, sometimes by lack of food, sometimes by the noise and emotional battering of enemy fire over a long period of time (Holmes 1985: 115–25; Grossman 1995: 67–73). Under these conditions, soldiers may fall into a dull, zombie-like state where they do not fire, or do not fire accurately. But civilians in violent situations tend to act similarly to soldiers—a low proportion of active participation, a considerable amount of ineffective violence—even though their targets are clear, and they are not subject to prolonged sleep-deprivation, physical stresses, or long-term debilitation. This suggests the tension/fear in the situation of violent confrontation itself determines violent performance, irrespective of the special difficulties of military combat.

No doubt there are a proportion of civilians who are on the higher end of the continuum of fighting performance: some of them are not afraid of violent confrontations; others channel tension into an onslaught; some enjoy the violence, abortive or successful. Some are "cowboy cops" disproportionately involved in shooting or beating suspects; some guards are sadistic as a matter of routine; some children are bullies. But they are a minority of persons and, more importantly for a theory of situational action, a minority of situations. As in the case of soldiers reporting their feelings about combat, we need to be careful to distinguish to what extent these reports are general expressions of feelings about fights at various distances, and how much of this talk is bluster, bragging, or covering up actual fighting performance. In big-city black ghettos, fighting is sometimes regarded as "show time" (Anderson 1999), but this may be more the feelings of onlookers of well-staged fights than of the fighters themselves. Nevertheless, there are a minority of cases where effective violence does emerge; our pathway to understanding this is through understanding how some positions in situations enable some individuals to take advantage of the tension/fear and transform it into violence against others.

FEAR OF WHAT?

What kind of fear do most people have in violent situations? Most obviously, it would seem they are afraid of being killed or injured. Soldiers who see their fellows, or enemies, torn by shells, pieces of bodies blown apart, or the agony of the wounded with bloody gashes or organs protruding, are understandably loathe to have this happen to themselves. This is consonant with the pattern that most people try to stay away from sources of physical danger: soldiers hanging back from the front line, rioters keeping a safe distance, gangs speeding away from a drive-by. It also fits the pattern that fighting is most chronic and prolonged where it is protected, so that injuries are slight: we will see in chapter 8 that violence is most common in the kinds of athletics where players are most heavily padded against injury. And the social category that has the highest incidence of violence is among children, where the ability to injure is slight.[25]

But this explanation encounters several paradoxes. One is that under some social circumstances, persons willingly undergo not only severe danger but actually welcome pain and injury. Initiation rites, which usually involve some degree of discomfort and humiliation, are sometimes very painful. North American tribal coming-of-age initiations for warriors included not only painful ordeals but also body slashings; captives who performed well under torture were honored and might be adopted into the tribe. Some gang initiations involve having to fight a bigger person and receive a considerable beating (Anderson 1999: 86–87); the Japanese Yakuza (organized crime) ritual involves the mutilation of cutting off a finger (Whiting 1999: 131–32). Scars, black eyes, and bandages can be marks of pride for athletes in violent sports and for youthful males generally. These are, to be sure, limited situations, where the violence is expected to have a clear termination point, and in many cases physical injury is not so severe as injuries in all-out fights. But the pain and injury may also be quite severe in ritualized situations, as in ritual suicide such as Japanese *seppuku*.

Undergoing pain and injury can be successfully ritualized when they occur at the focus of social attention that conveys a strong sense of membership in an exclusive group. It becomes what Durkheim (1912/1964) called the *negative cult*: voluntarily to undertake pain that most ordinary persons shun puts one in an elite group. But the key to this ritual status is undergoing suffering, not inflicting it on others. Thus a large proportion of soldiers in combat risk pain, mutilation, or death, even though many of them do little else while they are in the combat zone than just be there; it is easier to put up with injury and death than it is to inflict it. It is often said that fear of dishonor, fear of letting the group down, overcomes fear of injury in fighting. But this kind of social fear seems to be stronger in overcoming fear of injury and death, than in overcoming the tension that gets in the way of performing effectively in combat. Fear of injury and death tend to be biggest at the outset, indeed before first going into battle (Shalit 1988); once soldiers have gotten used to seeing dead or mutilated bodies, they become somewhat inured to them; although, as we have seen, their fighting performance does not improve very much, indicating that the larger tension is still there.

A related problem is that the circumstances that cause the most fear are not necessarily those that are objectively the most dangerous. Artillery shells and mortars, as we have seen, cause by far the most casualties—and the soldiers themselves generally know that (Holmes 1985: 209–10)—but the greatest difficulty in combat performance is in confronting small-arms fire at the forward edge of the combat zone. Some surveys show relatively high fear of being killed by bayonet and knife, events rare to the point of fantasy but indicating the quality of soldiers' imagery about what they feel is in front of them. Nor do persons in highly dangerous situations all show the signs of incapacitating fear that affects frontline troops (Grossman 1995: 55–64): navy personnel are subject to the same dangers as army soldiers of being blown apart by enemy shells—the largest source of ground combat casualties—in addition to prospects of drowning, but data on long-term breakdown from combat stress—which is one measure of combat fear—shows much lower rates of breakdown for sailors in combat zones. Similarly for civilians under bombardment, including long-term blitzes such as the German attack on England, or the Allied bombings of German cities; casualties included being burned alive or sustaining extreme bodily mutilations resulting from burns. Nevertheless, civilian psychiatric casualties were low in these areas compared to army troops.

Several refined comparisons are revealing of the precise source of tension/fear. Prisoners of war under fire or aerial bombardment had no increase in psychiatric casualties; whereas their guards apparently underwent increased tension, since their psychiatric rates went up (Grossman 1995: 57–58; Gabriel 1986, 1987). That is to say, the guards were still in a combat mode, perhaps because they were confronted with enemies under their own eyes, at the same time they were struggling to maintain control over them; whereas the stance of the POWs was merely to endure. Grossman (1995: 60–61) also points out that reconnaissance patrols behind enemy lines, although extremely dangerous, do not lead to psychiatric casualties. The reason, Grossman argues, is that such patrols are attempting to gather information by stealth and, above all, to avoid attacking the enemy. And combat officers, although in most wars they have had physical casualty rates considerably higher than their men, have had a much lower rate of psychiatric casualties (Grossman 1995: 64). Here we see that the source of strain is neither fear of death and injury, nor aversion to killing in principle, since officers are in charge of directing their men toward killing, and indeed pressing them to overcome their fear and incompetence. What is different, and what seems to buffer them from tension/fear, is that they personally do not have to do the killing. The same goes for non-firers, who often perform other useful tasks on the battlefield, such as helping load ammunition into the firers' guns (Grossman 1995: 15). This shows they are often willing to expose themselves to as much danger as the firers. It isn't even that they are opposed to killing; they just can't bring themselves to do it themselves.

Medics in ground combat are subject to the same sorts of dangers as infantry troops; yet their rate of combat fatigue is much lower (Grossman 1995: 62–64, 335). Their peak performances are apparently more common: medics received a high and increasing proportion of medals of honor in the American wars of the twentieth century, evidence of their high level of bravery (Miller 2000: 121–24). And their level of routine performance in combat is higher; we do not hear of non-performance among medics comparable to non-firing rates, although soldiers on the battlefield might be expected to complain if medics shirked in helping the wounded. Yet medics are those who most consistently witness the painful and mutilating effects of enemy fire. This indicates that they have a social mechanism for distancing themselves from fear of bodily injury, and even more importantly, from the more basic source of tension/fear in combat. Their focus is not on confrontation with the enemy; not on killing, but on life-saving. They reverse the normal gestalt for viewing injuries, seeing them in a different frame: this is what sends them into action.[26]

Yet another indication that fear of injury is not the only source of fight tension is the fact that there are indications of fear even among those who have the upper hand, who are in little or no danger of being injured. Interviews with gunmen, and with their victims, indicate that the stickup situation is one of high tension; the "street-wise" person in high-crime areas knows that to survive a stickup one should avoid making the gunman snap over the edge from tension to shooting. Especially significant is to avoid looking the gunman in the eye—not merely in the sense of identifying him, but to avoid the confrontational stare that gives a sense of hostile challenge (Anderson 1999: 127).[27] Thus even in non-stickup situations in the violent street zone, a challenging eye-to-eye confrontation may well provoke a fight.

This suggests that the tension of the confrontation itself is the most central feature. Grossman (1995) argues that it is fear of killing. In an earlier interpretation of the military evidence, Marshall suggested that the standards of civilized behavior, deeply engrained by civilian experience, create a blockage against trying to kill people, even if they are enemies who are trying to kill oneself. But this cultural-inhibition model does not adequately explain the range of cultural settings in which tension/fear inhibits fighting performance. Tribal warfare also shows a low level of effectiveness and high degree of fear behavior on the front line; the performance of combat troops is similar across all periods of history, including societies whose cultures endorse extreme ferociousness toward enemies. And within the same societies and armies, the degree to which fear inhibits violent behavior is highly situational: those who withhold using their weapons, or use them badly in pitched confrontations, can be quite ferocious in situations of massacring enemies in ambushes or captives in a besieged city. Tension/fear seems universal across cultures, both those that claim to be ferocious and those that claim to be peaceful; and so are circumstances where tension/fear is overcome to generate violence. And even in modern Western cultures, where cultural socialization against violence exists, one may participate as audience in witnessing and encouraging considerable ferocity and harm (as we shall see in detail in chapter 6). The same persons who are enthusiastic about violence as members of an audience show very strong limits when in a confrontation, face to face, with one's antagonist.

Is it, then, a primordial dislike of killing? On this interpretation, human beings are genetically hard-wired with an antipathy to killing each other. This inhibition is not so strong that it cannot be overcome by other strong social forces; but when this happens, humans feel badly and express manifestations of their discomfort in physical and psychological symptoms. Grossman (1995) argues that soldiers who have been conditioned to kill pay the price subjectively in post-combat stress and breakdown.

But this line of argument goes too far. After all, humans do kill and injure each other, in various kinds of situations that we can specify. And these social arrangements often justify the killing to those who take part, so that they feel no neurotic consequences. Later chapters will present some of these structures in which killing and injuring others is morally neutralized or even morally favorable. In the *Dead Birds* film, we witness a celebration after an enemy has been killed; the feelings expressed are not guilt but joy and enthusiasm.

There is a confrontational tension that arises in all situations of potential violence. It is not merely fear of killing, since we see it in instances where the attackers intend only to beat someone up, or, indeed, where they are only threatening to engage in angry argument. Threatening to kill someone, or confronting someone who threatens to kill or severely injure oneself, is only a part of this larger confrontational tension. The ability of human beings to carry out violence against another person depends not only on the social pressure and support in the background that pushes them into this situation, and that will reward them after they have gotten through the situation, but also on the social characteristics of the confrontation itself. Grossman (1995: 97–110) shows that the degree of willingness to fire at an enemy depends on the physical distance from that person. Operators of bombers, long-distance ballistic missiles, and artillery achieve the highest rates of fire, and have the highest willingness to kill the enemy; for them, the target is most depersonalized, even though they may well have an explicit cognition of the human casualties they are causing. This is similar to the higher degree of rhetorical ferociousness found in the rear combat areas and at home, compared to soldiers at the front. I would interpret this to mean that tension is inhibiting their conflict behavior so little, not because they are unaware of their human targets, but because they are not in a bodily face-to-face situation with them.

Difficulty in carrying out violent actions increases as the social situation becomes more closely focused. Firing guns or other missiles at a distance of hundreds of yards is easier than firing close-range. When the latter does happen, the shots often go wild; we see graphic evidence of this in police shootings, where officers often miss at ten feet or less, even though they are accurate shooters on target ranges at many times that distance (Klinger 2004; Artwohl and Christensen 1997). Still closer is killing with edged weapons: spears, swords, bayonets, knives—or with clubs or other blunt instruments. In ancient and medieval warfare, there appears to have been a high degree of incompetence in the use of these weapons, judging from battlefield casualty ratios: most such killing occurred in a forward panic, which, as we shall examine shortly, occurs when the tension is taken off. Most use of swords and knives has been by slashing, even though a forward thrust directly into the enemy's body produces a much deadlier wound (Grossman 1995: 110–32). Modern evidence is more detailed: bayonet killing is extremely rare, making up well below 1 percent of wounds inflicted at Waterloo and the Somme (Keegan 1977: 268–69). In trench warfare (mainly in World War I), troops successfully storming a trench preferred to throw in grenades, which kept them at a somewhat greater distance and out of sight of the men they were killing; troops with fixed bayonets tended to reverse their rifles and use them as clubs; some troops (notably the Germans) preferred to use their trench shovels as clubs (Holmes 1985: 379). There appears to be a special difficulty in confronting another person face to face and sticking him with a knife-edged blade. When knife attacks are used, as in commando warfare, by far the preferred method of killing is from behind, as if to avoid seeing the eyes of the man being killed (Grossman 1995: 129). This is also the case with recorded knife attacks in historical data; in early modern Amsterdam, most knife attacks were from the rear or the side, rarely directly head on (Spierenburg 1994). This fits as well the procedures of executions; the executioner, whether ceremonially beheading a condemned person with an axe or sword, or a gangland or terroristic police agent shooting a victim in the back of the head, virtually always stands behind the victim, avoiding face-to-face confrontation. Similarly, kidnap victims are more likely to be executed if they are hooded (Grossman 1995: 128). This is the interactional significance of blindfolding the person standing before a firing squad, as much for the benefit of the firers as of the victim.

The special difficulties of killing victims face to face comes out graphically in evidence on German military police who performed mass shootings in the Holocaust (Browning 1992). Their victims were almost entirely helpless and passive, and the soldiers generally accepted the ideological atmosphere of Nazi anti-Semitism and war propaganda, as well as up-holding military solidarity within their own ranks. Nevertheless the great majority found these killings to be revolting, and even after considerable acclimation, highly depressing. Psychological revulsion to killing was es-pecially strong when soldiers had close contact with their victims, most of whom they shot point-blank in the back of the head while made to lie prone on the ground. Even at this range, soldiers frequently missed (62–65). A remarkable instance of bodily revulsion to overwhelming ideology is a committed Nazi officer who developed a psychosomatic illness (stom-ach colitis) that prevented him from accompanying his troops in person on their killing missions (pp. 114–20). He recovered from his illness when he was transferred to regular frontline duty, where shooting was done at a distance, and he distinguished himself in action.

Disfunctioning bowels are found in situations of high tension and fear, occurring in confrontations ranging from soldiers who shit their pants in combat, to burglars who give away their presence to the police by the smell they leave.[28] Thus the expressions "intestinal fortitude" and having the "guts" or the "stomach" for fighting are not merely metaphorical, but also point to a deep bodily revulsion from violence that must be overcome by those who are successful at it.

Antagonistic confrontation itself, as distinct from violence, has its own tension. People tend to avoid confrontation even in merely verbal conflict: people are much more likely to express negative and hostile statements about persons who are not immediately present, than to express such statements to persons who are in conversation with them. Conversation analysis of tape-recorded talk in natural settings shows a strong propen-sity to agreement (Boden, 1990; Heritage 1984).[29] Hence conflict is ex-pressed largely at a distance, toward persons who are absent. Hence when conflict has to come down to the immediate micro-situation, there are great difficulties in carrying out conflict, and especially violence.

Compare what we know about human interaction from the other side, normal interaction rather than violence. The basic tendency is for persons to become caught up in a mutual focus of attention, and to become en-trained in each other's bodily rhythms and emotional tones (evidence for this pattern is summarized in Collins 2004). These processes are uncon-scious and automatic. They are also highly attractive; the most pleasur-able kinds of human activity are where persons become caught in a pro-nounced micro-interactional rhythm: a smoothly flowing conversation to the beat of a common intonational punctuation; shared laughter; crowd enthusiasm; mutual sexual arousal. Ordinarily these processes constitute an interaction ritual bringing feelings of intersubjectivity and moral soli-darity, at least for the present moment. Face-to-face conflict is difficult above all because it violates this shared consciousness and bodily-emotional entrainment. Violent interaction is all the more difficult because winning a fight depends on upsetting the enemy's rhythms, breaking through his mode of entrainment and imposing one's own action.

There is a palpable barrier to getting into a violent confrontation. It goes against one's physiological hard-wiring, the human propensity to become caught up in the micro-interactional rituals of solidarity. One needs to cut out all one's sensitivity to cues of human-to-human ritual solidarity, to concentrate instead on taking advantage of the other's weaknesses. Soldiers approaching the combat zone are moving into a region where they feel, in their own bodies, the sense that the enemy is nearer, that they will get close to this kind of confrontation. Up to that point, they are interacting almost exclusively with each other, with friends or normal interactants, and the content of what they say to each other, and what feelings that they have and express, can contain a great deal of negatives about the enemy—who, after all, is not *here*. The micro-situational reality of the home front or the rear staging areas is all *us*, even as its talk refers to the enemy as a symbolic object defining the outer boundaries of the group. Coming nearer the front, one's attention shifts more and more to the enemy as a real social presence. As this happens, there is increasing difficulty in firing, even in orienting oneself to the enemy by one's own physical posture. We see this in the soldiers of World War I going "over the top" into no-man's land: all photos show them leaning forward, as if into a stiff wind; this is not a physical wind, but the gradient of approaching the enemy steadily from a distance. The courage of World War I soldiers was not so much in firing weapons, but in going forward against heavy fire. It was not so much courage to kill, as courage to be killed.

We have seen that officers generally show less fear in combat than the men they command. On the micro-interactional level, officers do not experience nearly so much confrontational entrainment. Officers focus their attention—and their eyes—on interacting with their own men, trying to keep up a positive flow of coordinated entrainment on their own side; they are not focused on the enemy per se, whereas the men actually attempting to use their weapons bear the brunt of the confrontational tension.

This is why eyes are so important in violent confrontations. Soldiers paralyzed in terror avert their eyes, just as they make childish-magical gestures to avoid being seen. Battle victors hate to see the eyes of the enemy they are killing. In ordinary life, staring contests are hard to maintain more than a few seconds, and often more than fragments of seconds (Mazur et al. 1980). Eye-to-eye confrontations, however truncated, between holdup man and victim, appear to be unbearable for the gunman to sustain.

Pushing forward to this barrier, invisible but palpably and bodily felt, some minority of combatants (on a minority of occasions) go through the barrier. Often it happens with a sudden rush, as if pushing through a glass wall, then falling wildly onto the other side: the other side where there is forward panic, and all the tension now goes into attack. For some fighters, the barrier becomes lowered in a more permanent way or at least for an extended period of time; they are in the subjective fighting zone, where they do the firing, take the initiative, sometimes even fire well. These are the violent elite. We will examine them in more detail in chapter 8; but we can say that they too are shaped by the barrier of tension/fear that is the emotional structure of a combat situation, quite literally emotions as spread out over a region in space. Some, the cold or cool ones, are those who perceive the tension/fear of other persons from a detached distance; their success comes from their detached relationship to the tension/fear. Others, the hot and frenzied ones, are battening on the fear in the others, less consciously but by a kind of asymmetrical entrainment, fear on one side drawing out frenzied attack on the other.

The battlefield is often described as the "fog of combat." This pervasive confusion, haste, and difficulty in coordination operates on many levels: organizational, communicative, logistical, and literally visual. I have argued that its biggest component is the tension of breaking through normal interactional solidarity. It also involves other component fears: fear of killing other people as well as fear of injury and mutilation and death to oneself. These fears concatenate into a larger feeling of tension. One or another of these specific fears can be calmed or reduced to a level where it has moderate or slight effects on performance; this is especially the case with fear of one's own injury or death, which seems to be the easiest fear to overcome, with the help of social support or under social pressure. Fear of killing others also can be overcome, especially by transforming the collective tension of combat into moments of entrainment in aggression. That is why I hold that the deepest emotion is the tension of conflict itself, which shapes the behavior of fighters even at the moments when they overcome the aspect of fear that impels them to shrink back or run away.

The fog of combat is an emotional fog. Sometimes it is dull, sleepy, trance-like; some soldiers describe combat as like moving in a dream. Some feel it as time slowed down, or time speeded up, in either case as a disruption of the ordinary rhythms of social life (Holmes 1985: 156–57; Bourke 1999: 208–9; similar patterns from police shootings are reported in Klinger 2004; Artwohl and Christensen 1997). And since our emotions and thoughts are shaped from the outside in by ongoing interactions, to be in the combat zone where ordinary processes of entrainment and mutual focus of attention are severely disrupted, is necessarily to experience a different rhythm and tone, for the most part a disrupted rhythm. Sometimes the emotional fog is so thick that it reaches emotional chaos or paralysis; sometimes it is merely a light mist, within which combatants move with some degree of effectiveness.

The fog of combat is a metaphor for confrontational tension. That tension encompasses the various kinds of fear, which have real objects that the fighters can pay attention to: the safety of their own bodies; the enemy whom one doesn't want to see, or doesn't want to see killed; sometimes we can add fear of ridicule, fear of being punished by one's own officers, fear of letting one's side down, fear of being labeled a coward; and among officers, fear of making mistakes that will cost the lives of one's men. In non-military fighting, the list of fears is generally shorter. But all kinds of violent confrontations have the same basic tension; and persons in those situations react in much the same range of ways to those tensions, and are shaped by those tensions. The fundamental tension is not fear of an external object; it is a struggle of opposing action tendencies within oneself.

The basic tension can be called non-solidarity entrainment. It comes from trying to act against another person, and thus against one's own propensities to fall into solidarity with that person, to get into a common rhythm and common cognitive universe. It is all the harder because the violent situation has its own entrainment and focus: there is focus on the fighting itself, on the situation as a violent one, and sometimes an emotional entrainment in which the hostility, anger, and excitement of each side gets the other more angry and excited. But these elements of shared consciousness and entrainment make it all the harder to act in that situation in a way that each can effectively carry out violence; antagonists have gone some way toward being caught up in collective solidarity, a Durkheimian collective effervescence, but simultaneously have to radically shift direction, so that each is the other's cognitive alien, and each tries to impose a rhythm of dominance and an emotion of fear on the other.

This is the tension of the confrontational zone. Much of the time the tension is too strong: individuals cannot approach the confrontational zone closely, being content to fling words or sometimes missiles from a distance; or they approach it only briefly and then are driven away from it by their own bodies, emotions, and nervous systems. If fighters are organized or forced so as to remain in the confrontational zone, they are for the most part not very effective; and staying there takes its toll on them in the form of combat fatigue or breakdown.

There is another way in which the tension is resolved. Kept long enough in a situation of high tension, torqued up bodily and emotionally, humans in conflict sometimes have an opportunity for falling out of the tension zone, not away from the enemy but toward him or her. This is the situation of forward panic, the most dangerous of all social situations.

CHAPTER 3

Forward Panic

In April 1996, two southern California deputy sheriffs chased a pickup truck crowded with Mexican illegal immigrants. The truck had driven around a checkpoint north of the border, refusing to stop then or later as the patrol car followed it at speeds over 100 miles per hour. During the chase, weaving through freeway traffic, occupants of the truck threw debris at the police car and attempted to ram other cars to divert their pursuers' attention. After almost an hour and having gone eighty miles, the truck drove off the side of the road, and most of its twenty-one occupants climbed out and ran into a plant nursery. The deputies caught up with only two, a woman who had trouble getting the front door of the truck cab open and a man who stayed to help her; these the furious officers beat with their nightsticks. One deputy clubbed the man on the back and shoulders six times, continuing while he fell to the ground. As the woman emerged from the cab, the deputy hit her twice on the back and pulled her to the ground by her hair, as the other deputy hit her once with his baton. The beating lasted about fifteen seconds (*Los Angeles Times*, April 2, 1996). A television news helicopter had been following the last part of the chase, and its cameras taped the beating. When these tapes were shown on the air, there was a public outcry; the officers were brought to trial, a federal investigation was launched into the racial aspect of the incident, and the twenty-one illegal aliens, including the driver, were offered amnesty and admission into the United States.

The incident has the character of a forward panic. This is likely the most frequent kind of police atrocity, and perhaps of police violence generally. The basic structure of this kind of interaction—an onrushing flow of events in time—can be found very widely in civilian and military life. Marine Lt. Philip Caputo gives a military example from the Vietnam war:

> A helicopter assault on a hot landing zone creates emotional pressures far more intense than a conventional ground assault. It is the enclosed space, the noise, the speed, and, above all, the sense of total helplessness. There is a certain excitement to it the first time, but after that it is one of the more unpleasant experiences offered by modern war. On the ground, an infantryman has some control over his destiny, or at least the illusion of it. In a helicopter under fire, he hasn't even the illusion. Confronted by the indifferent forces of gravity, ballistics, and machinery, he is himself pulled in several directions at once by the range

Figure 3.1 A,B After 100 mph chase, a patrolman catches and beats the last of a truckload of illegal immigrants, who is too weak to escape (California, April 1996). AP/World Wide Photos.

of extreme, conflicting emotions. Claustrophobia plagues him in the small space: the sense of being trapped and powerless in a machine is unbearable, and yet he has to bear it. Bearing it, he begins to feel a blind fury toward the forces that have made him powerless, but he has to control his fury until he is out of the helicopter and on the ground again. He yearns to be on the ground, but the desire is countered by the danger he knows is there. Yet, he is also attracted by the danger, for he knows he can overcome his fear only by facing it. His blind rage then begins to focus on the men who are the source of the danger—and of his fear. It concentrates inside him, and through some chemistry is transformed into a fierce resolve to fight until the danger ceases to exist. But this resolve, which is sometimes called courage, cannot be separated from the fear that has aroused it. Its very measure is the measure of that fear. It is, in fact, a powerful urge not to be afraid anymore, to rid himself of fear by eliminating the source of it. This inner, emotional war produces a tension almost sexual in its intensity. It is too painful to endure for long. All a soldier can think about is the moment when he can escape his impotent confinement and release this tension. All other considerations, the rights and wrongs of what he is doing, the chances for victory or defeat in the battle, the battle's purpose or lack of it, become so absurd as to be less than irrelevant. Nothing matters except the final, critical instant when he leaps out into the violent catharsis he both seeks and dreads. (Caputo, 1977: 277–78)

A forward panic starts with tension and fear in a conflict situation. This is the normal condition of violent conflict, but here the tension is prolonged and built up; it has a dramatic shape of increasing tension, striving toward a climax. The police car aims to catch up with the speeding truck; the helicopter maneuvers through the fire zone to the landing. There is a shift from relatively passive—waiting, holding back until one is in a position to bring the conflict to a head—to be fully active. When the opportunity finally arrives, the tension/fear comes out in an emotional rush. Ardant du Picq, observing the pattern repeatedly in military battles, called it "flight to the front" (1903/1999: 88–89). It resembles a panic, and indeed the physiological components are similar; instead of running away, caught up in a mood in which running and fear feed each other as specified in the James-Lange theory of emotion, the fighters rush forward, toward the enemy. Running forward or backward, in either case they are in an overpowering emotional rhythm, carrying them on to actions that they would normally not approve of in calm, reflective moments.

The emotional sequence is described in detail by Caputo in a second incident: First he is full of enthusiasm leading a patrol. His mood switches when three of his advance men locate enemy soldiers unaware of their presence, in a village immediately across a river. Caputo now feels signs of extreme excitement: "My heartbeat sounded like a kettle-drum pounding in a tunnel." In part this is suppression of the anticipated attack, since he is trying to keep quiet in order to crawl back in the jungle to call up more of his men for the attack. When firing breaks out, he momentarily burrows into the ground. "The experience of being under fire is like suffocating; the air suddenly becomes as lethal as a poison gas."

Then comes an emotional switch:

An eerie sense of calm came over me. My mind was working with a speed and clarity I would have found remarkable if I had had the time to reflect upon it. . . . The whole plan of attack flashed through my mind in a matter of seconds. At the same time my body was tensing itself to spring. Quite separate from my thoughts or will, it was concentrating itself to make a rush for the tree line. And that intense concentration of physical energy was born of fear. I could not remain in the hollow for longer than a few more seconds. After that, the Viet Cong would range in on me, a stationary target in an exposed position. I had to move, to face and overcome the danger. . . . Without a command from my conscious mind, I lunged into the woods and crashed down the trail, [calling for reinforcements].

When these arrive, he feels elated. The entire group, now some thirty strong, begins firing, overpowering the enemy. Caputo was now "shouting myself hoarse to control the platoon's fire. The marines were in a frenzy, pouring volley after volley into the village, some yelling unintelligibly, some screaming obscenities. . . . A bullet smacked the earth between us and we went rolling over and came rolling back up again, me laughing hysterically." As enemy fire fades away, and reports come in by radio that the Viet Cong are retreating, Caputo tries to find a way to get his platoon across the deep river to finish them off. "The platoon became as excited as a predator that sees the back of its fleeing prey. . . . I could feel the whole line wanting to charge across the river" (249–53). But there turns out to be no way to get across, and Caputo has trouble coming down from his emotional high. "I could not come down from the high produced by the action. The firefight was over, except for a few desultory exchanges, but I did not want it to be over." He then deliberately exposes himself to draw enemy fire so that a sniper can be located—"walking back and forth and feeling as invulnerable as an Indian wearing his ghost shirt." When nothing happens, he begins shouting and firing wildly, and when his own troops begin to laugh at him, he laughs uncontrollably too. Eventually he calms down (254–55).

The whole incident is a version of forward panic, truncated at the end because the target has disappeared. The undertone throughout is tension/fear, transmuted at times into detachment, clarity, flickers of panic/suffocation; there are moments of elation, when something works out. When the fear disappears at the end, he goes into a frenzy, trying to find one last victim.

A third incident described by Caputo brings out just how far fighters may go when caught up in that emotional zone. Caputo's troops, after being pinned down by enemy fire, advance through a village believed to have been an enemy base:

> The noise of the battle was constant and maddening, as maddening as the barbed hedges and the heat of the fire raging just behind us.
>
> Then it happened. The platoon exploded. It was a collective emotional detonation of men who had been pushed to the extremity of endurance. I lost control of them and even of myself. Desperate to get to the hill, we rampaged through the rest of the village, whooping like savages, torching thatch huts, tossing grenades into the cement houses we could not burn. In our frenzy, we crashed through the hedgerows without feeling the stabs of the thorns. We did not feel anything. We were past feeling anything for ourselves, let alone for others. We shut our ears to the cries and pleas of the villagers. One elderly man ran up to me, and, grabbing me by the front of my shirt, asked, "*Tai Sao? Tai Sao?*" Why? Why?
>
> "Get out of the goddamned way," I said, pulling his hands off. I took hold of his shirt and flung him down hard, feeling as if I were watching myself in a movie. . . . Most of the platoon had no idea of what they were doing. One marine ran up to a hut, set it ablaze, ran on, turned around, dashed through the flames and rescued a civilian inside, then ran on to set fire to the next hut. We passed through the village like a wind; by the time we started up Hill 52, there was nothing left of Ha Na but a long swath of smoldering ashes, charred tree trunks, their leaves burned off, and heaps of shattered concrete. Of all the ugly sights I saw in Vietnam, that was one of the ugliest: the sudden disintegration of my platoon from a group of disciplined soldiers into an incendiary mob.
>
> The platoon snapped out of its madness almost immediately. Our heads cleared as soon as we escaped from the village into the clear air at the top of the hill. . . . The change in us, from disciplined soldiers to unrestrained savages and back to soldiers, had been so swift and profound as to lend a dreamlike quality to the last part of the battle. Despite the evidence to the contrary, some of us had a difficult time believing that we were the ones who had caused all that destruction. (Caputo, 1977: 287–89)

The soldiers go into the emotional tunnel of violent attack, then come back out of it at the end. In the village where they expected resistance, they find no fighting men but only helpless villagers, whom they treat brutally. The soldiers feel detached from themselves—which is to say, their cognitive image of themselves—and in the aftermath treat their own behavior as if it were a separate reality.

Caputo's description of burning the village resembles the more famous case of My Lai, on March 16, 1968. It was the most intense period of the Vietnam war, during the Tet offensive, which had begun six weeks earlier, when Viet Cong and North Vietnamese troops temporarily captured several large cities and put American forces on the defensive. The My Lai incident occurred during the counter-offensive aimed at driving the enemy back out of its conquests. A U.S. Army company made a helicopter landing on an area long believed to be a Viet Cong stronghold, expecting heavy resistance. The company leading the assault had never been in battle, although it had taken casualties from mines and booby traps. It turned out that there were no enemy forces to be found in My Lai. The lead platoon went on a rampage, burning the buildings, and killing three to four hundred Vietnamese civilians, most of them women and children, military-age men having fled the village (Summers 1995: 140–41). The platoon commander, Lt. Calley, enthusiastically led the killing. When the massacre was brought to official attention after a year's delay, it was an enormous public scandal.

Despite the conclusions of the official inquiry to the contrary, incidents of this type were fairly common in the Vietnam war, differing only in how extensive the killing of civilians, and how much this was embellished with mutilation and rape (Gibson 1986: 133–51, 202–3; Turse and Nelson 2006; www.latimes.com/vietnam). At a minimum, these were orgies of destruction, vandalism on an extreme scale. Given the character of guerrilla war, the conditions for a forward panic are frequent: a period of prolonged tension/fear, with a hidden enemy and strong suspicions that the normal surroundings and civilian population are a cover for sudden attacks; forward-advancing operations in this danger zone, building up frustration and anticipation at finally catching the enemy, and triggering moments when the enemy seems to have been caught; a frenzied rush of destruction. Regular armies fighting guerrillas take most of their casualties when they are caught off guard; when they actually catch up with the guerrillas, the disparity in arms usually makes for an easy victory. It is the ease of beating a long-sought enemy that makes for the transformation of tension/fear into the frenzied attack of forward panic. All the more so when the enemy turns out not to be there at all, but only some helpless victims who are associated with the enemy side: the women and old men at My Lai; the woman in the speeding pickup truck in Los Angeles.

Most incidents of police violence that create public scandals have the character of forward panic. The Rodney King beating in Los Angeles, 1991, is an archetypal instance (www.law.umke.edu/ faculty/projects/ftrial/lapd). Police chased a speeding car at up to 115 miles an hour for eight miles on a freeway and city streets; radio calls for backup brought twenty-one officers by the end of the chase, when King was cornered behind an apartment house. A famous amateur video recorded the last three and a half minutes of the arrest. Patrol officers were in a mood of excitement and tension from the high-speed chase, enhanced by anger at King's refusal to obey their sirens and pull off, and determination to win the race and bring him to submission. On emerging from the car, it turned out there were two young black men: one a passenger who submitted to arrest; the other King, a big, muscular man, whom the officers interpreted was likely an ex-convict, judging from his "prison body" of a weight-lifter; they also thought he was high on the drug PCP. The chase was not yet over. King was uncooperative to his arrest, creating a brief moment of counter-attack by rushing at one of the officers; at this point he was knocked down by four officers using night clubs and a taser (a device sending high-voltage electric shock). Beating with the clubs continued for another eighty seconds—the part captured on the video—until King was completely trussed up, and the police prepared to move out their vehicles. The most active officer—the one who had been knocked down by King—hit him over forty-five times with his stick.[1]

Among the sidelights that captured public attention, and made the atrocity seem particularly egregious, was evidence of the emotional tone of the police officers during and after the beating. Although twenty-one officers were present, only four took part in the beating; the others stood around in a circle, backing up the principals and yelling encouragement. Recordings of police radios after the beating also showed elation: "We really did some hitting . . . it was gorillas in the mist"—an allusion to a then-popular movie about African gorillas. At the hospital where King was taken for his injuries, the attending police officer, full of good humor, kidded King about his job at the Dodger baseball stadium with such words as "We really hit some home runs out there tonight, didn't we?" This is the same sort of elation that Caputo described when combat went well, and in the aftermath of an enthusiastic high.

Confrontational Tension and Release: Hot Rush, Piling on, Overkill

Let us consider the emotional sequence in detail. First comes a buildup of tension, which is released into a frenzied attack when the situation makes it easy to do so. The previous chapter concluded that this is a tension/fear peculiar to conflict in immediate confrontation with other human beings. This confrontational tension builds up as persons in conflict come close to each other, and not merely because that is the point at which one might

Figure 3.2 Rodney King beaten by four policemen after high-speed chase (Los Angeles, March 1991). Getty Images.

be hurt; it is at the point that one has to face the other person down, to put him or her under one's violent control against their resistance.

The tension can build up from various components. Police officers in a high-speed chase have some feelings of the danger of fast-moving vehicles, especially when potentially dodging other vehicles and obstacles; their tension can also be partly excitement, partly frustration at not yet catching one's target. For police officers, this is an exacerbated version of their normal situation when dealing with civilians, and especially civilian suspects: their effort always to control the interactional situation (Rubinstein 1973). The resistance of a civilian to letting the officer control the situation brings about a confrontational tension, raising the possibility of the officer using both official authority and informal pressure to gain command. As Rubinstein shows from ethnographic observation, police try to position their bodies to control anyone they stop for questioning; their nonverbal maneuvering ranges from putting themselves in a position to disarm individuals of weapons or overpower them, to brushing against them in casual searches. At minimum, police exercise more subtle control by aggressive use of eyes in observing the other person in a prolonged and deliberate fashion contrary to normal civilities of interpersonal looking and eye contact. Thus the police in a chase are experiencing a prolonged situation of being frustrated in what they normally expect to carry out in any interaction.

The tensions that produce a forward panic can also be observed in individual fights. A good source is biographical material on Ty Cobb, who was involved in many fights that are well documented, due to his fame as the top baseball player of his day. In May 1912, Cobb jumped into the stands to attack a fan who had been jeering him. The incident happened in New York, where Cobb's Detroit team was visiting. In an earlier incident, Cobb had collided with a New York player at third base, during Cobb's typically aggressive base-running; the two players shoved each other, and fans threw debris from the stands. Four days later, a fan sitting near the dugout kept up a steady flow of loud insults directed at Cobb. In the fourth inning—after about an hour—Cobb took action. "Leaping a railing, (Cobb) trampled fans to get at the tormentor, sitting a dozen rows up in the stands. He battered Lueker's head with at least a full dozen punches, knocked him down, and with his spikes kicked the helpless man in the lower body. . . . (The spectator) had no fingers on one hand, only two fingers on the other. . . . (having) lost them in an industrial accident. . . . Fans scattered with shouts of, 'He has no hands!' Witnesses said they heard Cobb retort, 'I don't care if he has no legs!' " (Stump 1994: 206–7).

The beating he inflicted was typical of Cobb's violent rages: once he started, he continued, even after getting his opponent down. The fight was clearly won at the outset, but it went on for a flurry of punches and then kicking the now-vanquished body on the ground. In this case, the disparity of power is underlined, since it turns out that the jeering fan was physically handicapped.[2] In the midst of his rage, this did not faze Cobb at all; in the course of a forward panic, any evidence of the weakness of a victim does not matter, even when the perpetrator is explicitly aware of it.

The tension in this case has several components: in the immediate foreground, Cobb's antagonistic relationship with the New York players and their fans, which had been at a high level for four days. The incident is embedded in a larger pattern: Cobb was successful as a player precisely because of his extremely aggressive style of play; in the previous year he had set the record for stolen bases, and had hit .420—one of the highest averages of the modern era of record-keeping; and his 1912 season, then underway, would result in an unprecedented two years in a row of hitting over .400 (this time .410).[3] Some individuals use their ability to work themselves into a high level of confrontational tension as a means of dominating others. Once they get into a high level of arousal, however, they can no longer control themselves; thus Cobb beating up a spectator—and others like him—well past the point at which the fight was won.

The various kinds of tension/fear that come out in a rush of violence have often been described as an adrenalin rush. Soldiers in combat and its immediate aftermath, like police officers at the end of a vehicle chase or an arrest, can be seen as unable to control their adrenalin (Artwohl and Christensen 1997; Klinger 2004; Grossman 2004). But forward panic is not simply a physiological process; what a person will do while in a condition of adrenalin arousal is shaped in various directions and into varying actions, depending on situational conditions. After a near-miss of a traffic accident, a driver may go through an episode of uncontrollable bodily trembling; during the moment when you have to pull the wheel sharply, the body is tensed for action; only when the time for action has passed and there is nothing more to be done does the full effect of the arousal work itself out. Some persons respond to a crisis, just after it is resolved, by bursting into tears. The emotion one feels upon reaching a difficult goal, such as the release from tension that occurs upon scaling a mountain peak,[4] is not generally a violent one. Reactions such as anger, or a violent attack on a now-helpless victim, occur only in particular kinds of situational sequences.[5]

What kind of emotion is occurring during a forward panic itself? Most obviously, anger in its extreme forms: rage or fury. The connotation of these latter terms, and especially of the term "frenzy," is that the anger is overriding and compelling. But we also see other kinds of emotions in these situations of uncontrolled violence: One may be hysterical laughter, described at several points in Caputo's Vietnam incidents. These occur during the height of the fighting itself, where it is highly contagious: Caputo rolls on the ground with a companion escaping a bullet; later, when he is wildly daring a sniper, his bravado makes his troops laugh, which sets him off into more uncontrollable laughter. In a different context, tapes of the mass murders by two students at Columbine High School in Littleton, Colorado, in April 1999 show the killers laughing hysterically during the shooting. Laughter and shared good humor also may continue in the period after the end of a forward panic. In the aftermath of the Rodney King beating, the arresting officers are in high spirits; one reason why their behavior seems so shocking is that they cannot keep from expressing their mood, by humorous messages over the police radio and by remarks at the hospital where King is taken for his injuries.

Often there is a mood of elation, both during the violence and sometimes afterward. Caputo alternates between feeling tense, fearful, and angry, and feeling superlatively happy. These mixed emotions are not well described by conventional labels. The composite mood of a forward panic comes from the transformation of tension/fear into aggressive frenzy, usually centered on rage. Troops in close combat have historically made a great deal of noise, a mixture of jeering, cursing, roaring, or whooping

(Keegan 1976; Holmes 1985; Caputo 1977 mentions this in each of his episodes; see non-military examples in the section on bluster in chapter 9). At the moment of victory, these noises can shade over into a note of elation, sometimes of hysterical laughter, something between cheering for oneself and the sheer energetic expression of one's forward-moving action. There do not seem to be many silent forward panics; it is a climax of noise as well as of violence. This mixture of aggressive energy, anger, and ebullient cheering often carries over into the situation just after the conflict. A forward panic, after all, is a total victory, at least locally and on the physical and emotional level, and calls for celebration.[6]

The emotion of a forward panic, whatever its mixture, has two key characteristics. First, it is a hot emotion, a situation of being highly aroused, steamed up. It comes on in a rush, explosively; and it takes time to calm down. It contrasts with a far more unusual type of violence, cold or detached violence found among specialists such as snipers and hitmen, that we will consider in chapters 10 and 11; and also with half-hearted, fearful violence of the kind we have considered in chapter 2. Second, it is an emotion that is rhythmic and strongly entraining. Individuals in the throes of a forward panic keep repeating their aggressive actions: the illegal migrants are clubbed again and again by the highway patrol; Rodney King is repeatedly hit; Caputo's marines torch one hut after another, even though they already know there is nothing there; Cobb keeps kicking his man on the ground. The emotion is flowing in self-reinforcing waves. The individual gets caught up in his or her own rhythm;[7] Cobb is acting alone, although in the background he is accustomed to setting the rhythm of action in a baseball game, and responding to the repeated—and therefore rhythmic—jeering of the fan is part of what he becomes entrained in at the moment.

More often the process is group entrainment in a collective emotion. The soldiers get each other whooping, cursing, sometimes hysterically laughing, while they are also firing—as we know, largely inaccurately, but the bam!bam!bam!bam! of the guns is also part of the rhythm they are caught up in. As noted, both of the two killers in Columbine High School were laughing hysterically throughout the killing; it appears also that they stayed together throughout the episode, even though, from a strictly utilitarian viewpoint, they would have been more effective at killing more people if they had split up and covered different places. Being together allowed each one's mood to feed off the other's, and this kept them locked into their mood of frenzy and hysterical elation. One can question, of course, whether the emotion was truly one of elation: it surely must have been mixed with a feeling that they themselves were going to die, as they soon committed suicide, and would have faced dire punishments if they had survived. But that is just the crucial point about the emotions felt during a forward panic: all the components that come out during the hot rush of a successful, unopposed attack are cycling back upon themselves: anger, release from tension/fear, elation, hysterical laughter, sheer noisiness as itself a form of aggression—all of these are generating a social atmosphere in which persons keep on doing what they are doing, over and over, though it may make no sense even as aggression.[8]

A forward panic is violence that for the time being is unstoppable. It is overkill, the overuse of force far beyond what would have been needed to bring about the victory. Persons who have fallen off the point of tension into a forward panic situation have gone down into a tunnel and cannot stop their momentum. They fire far more bullets than they need; they not only kill but destroy everything in sight; they throw more punches and kicks; they attack dead bodies. Relative to what kind of conflict it is— after all, Cobb does not kill his man—there is far more violence than the violent situation itself would seem to call for. If there is a group involved, typically there is a pattern of ganging up; everyone wants to get in a punch or a kick at the fallen victim; in sports, this would be called piling on.

A forward panic always has the look of an atrocity. It is patently unfair: the strong against the weak; the armed against the unarmed (or the disarmed); the crowd against the individual or tiny grouplet. A forward panic is a very ugly-looking event, even when the victim is not badly injured. It is the moral look of it which is so offensive. When someone is in fact killed or maimed, it is the way it is done that makes it an atrocity.

ATROCITIES OF WAR

Forward panics are common in warfare. The most obvious instance is the tendency for troops to kill enemy soldiers who are trying to surrender. This was especially well documented for trench warfare in World War I. Troops of all sides, when they reached the enemy dugouts in a dominant position, were likely to shoot the men who emerged to surrender. The German soldier Ernst Jünger saw this as an emotional momentum: "A man cannot change his feelings again during the last rush with a veil of blood before his eyes. He does not want to take prisoners but to kill" (quoted in Holmes 1985: 381). Holmes generalized, "No soldier who fights until his enemy is at close small-arms range, in any war, has more than perhaps a fifty-fifty chance of being granted quarter" (Holmes 1985: 382, also 381–88; Keegan 1976: 48–51, 277–78, 322). The pattern also was documented widely in World War II, on the part of American, British, German, Russian, Japanese, Chinese, and other troops, and against all of these as victims.

Some of this killing of surrenderers has had a deliberate component, motivated by unwillingness to take on the practical burden of shepherding prisoners back to rear areas, and giving them the requisite supplies; sometimes it was a matter of being suspicious of whether the surrenderers might suddenly and treacherously turn belligerent again. Sometimes the hot emotions involved have been revenge for previous losses. But a considerable proportion of such killings are results of the situational momentum itself. We know this where the surrenderers, once safely past the danger moment, are treated in a comradely fashion by their captors, indeed generally better than they will be treated later by rear area troops (Holmes 1985: 382). And there are instances where troops go into a momentarily uncontrollable rage. S.L.A. Marshall gives an example of U.S. troops in Normandy in June 1944, during a period when their battalion had been under heavy German fire for three days, unable to evacuate their casualties, and suffering from shortage of water. A platoon under Lt. Millsaps broke under enemy machine gunfire and ran away in a panic retreat, until the officers finally beat them back into action with physical violence:

> At last they charged the enemy, closing within hand-grappling distance. The slaughter began with grenade, bayonet, and bullet. Some of the patrol were killed and some wounded. But all now acted as if oblivious to danger. The slaughter once started could not be stopped. Millsaps tried to regain control but his men paid no heed. Having slaughtered every German in sight, they ran on into the barns of the French farmhouses where they killed the hogs, cows, and sheep. The orgy ended when the last beast was dead." (Marshall 1947: 183)

These troops had been under great pressure, including from their own officers. Quite literally, they began with a panic retreat, which an hour later turned into a forward panic. At the end, they were so charged with emotion that they could not stop, even slaughtering the livestock—much like Lt. Caputo in his Vietnam battle looking for more enemies to kill. The spillover of forward panic into killing animals, although bizarre, also has its parallels.[9] According to one observer, "[D]uring the 1953 riot in Kano, northern Nigeria [between Ibo and Hausa tribes] . . . mutilations, castrations, and burnings of bodies occurred. Periodically, the police were able to separate the combatants. During these intervals, there were several instances in which armed Ibo participants danced in 'crocodile' formation and others in which they slaughtered with their hatchets nearby horses, donkeys, and goats" (Horowitz 2001: 116).

Similar patterns are found in ancient warfare. At the end of the decisive battle of Thapsus (in modern Tunisia) in 46 B.C., when Julius Caesar's army routed the forces of his rival in the civil wars for control of Rome, the defeated legions attempted to surrender; under the military politics of

Figure 3.3 A, B Killing surrenderers: Afrikaner resistance fighters, already wounded, are killed after a failed attack (South Africa, 1994). Reuters.

that time, these legions would have been added to Caesar's forces, and thus it was a rational policy for him to accept their surrender. But Caesar's "veterans were inflamed with anger and resentment . . . and so all these soldiers of Scipio's, although pleading to surrender unconditionally to Caesar, were slaughtered down to the last man under Caesar's very eyes as he begged his men to spare them" (Caesar, *Civil War*, 234–35). The victorious troops had been marching and counter-marching in the semi-desert for three months and enduring enemy skirmishing while trying to bring them to a full-scale battle; when they finally got the decisive battle they had been waiting for, they were so charged up by their victory that they went on to kill unpopular officers in their own army, while Caesar himself was unable to protect them.

A variant, common in ancient and medieval warfare, was for a massacre of inhabitants to take place at the end of a siege. Sometimes this was done as a matter of deliberate policy, to frighten inhabitants of other towns to surrender without a siege. In medieval Europe, the custom was for the attacking army to pause once a breach had been made in the walls, calling on the garrison to surrender; if they refused, they would be killed "without giving quarter" when the battle ended (Holmes 1985: 388; Wagner-Pacifi 2005). But such a slaughter, once begun, was not easily confined to the soldiers. Cromwell's parliamentary army, attacking the Catholic royalist stronghold of Drogheda, Ireland, in 1649, slaughtered not only the defenders but also most of the civilian population as well, 4,000 persons altogether. In 337 B.C., Alexander's Macedonian forces captured the Greek city of Thebes when, after a battle outside the walls, the Thebans, retreating in panic, were unable to close the gates behind them. Some Thebans were in the peace party, which had been willing to placate the Macedonians: but the victorious forces made no distinctions: soldiers and civilians alike were massacred, many of them pursued into the surrounding countryside as they tried to escape (Keegan 1987: 73).

The most notorious modern instance of this pattern occurred at Nanking in December 1937 (Chang 1997). Japanese forces had been advancing rapidly southward through China since war broke out in July 1937, until finally meeting strong resistance in a battle at Shanghai, prolonged between August and November. Having at last won this battle, they were now in a position to take the Chinese capital, Nanking, by moving up river 150 miles against the disorganized Chinese troops. This they did, entering the city on December 13. From the Japanese point of view, this was a decisive victory, giving them control of China, and thus putting them in a jubilant mood. There were, however, ninety thousand Chinese troops surrendered in the city, and another two hundred thousand Chinese troops in the surrounding area, having retreated in disorder from their defeat at Shanghai. Japanese forces on the spot numbered only fifty thousand, but were well armed, organized, and emotionally dominant, as against their much larger number of disorganized and demoralized enemy. The commanding general, concerned about both the logistics and the practical difficulties of guarding prisoners outnumbering his own forces by a factor of between 2:1 and 6:1, gave the order to kill all prisoners. Once the killing began, it became unstoppable. On the rationale that many Chinese soldiers had discarded their weapons and uniforms and were hiding in the civilian population, the Japanese began to kill all fighting-age males.

The situation quickly escalated out of control of the Japanese commanders. Eventually, about three hundred thousand persons were killed, about half of the population of Nanking that had not fled the city. Killing such a large number of persons, as a practical matter, is not easy, nor is the disposing of their bodies. Initially, some of the Japanese troops were reluctant to engage in the slaughter of unresisting persons; they were prodded by lower-ranking officers, who were generally the most enthusiastic actors in the massacre, and by the pressure of their fellows who had joined in. Eventually, it appears, many or most of the Japanese troops were caught up in the mood of destruction.[10] Officers initially tried traditional Japanese-style executions with swords, but this was too inefficient; it was superceded by firing on victims at the edge of mass graves or riverbanks, and bayonet practice on live targets. As the slaughter stretched out over many days, the Japanese soldiers began to liven the task with killing games: contests among young officers to see how many they could kill; tortures; placing bodies of Chinese victims in grotesque postures; mutilations and collections of severed body parts.

Once the order to kill prisoners had been given, the Japanese commanders had no more control over their troops. There was no immediate military threat to distract them and call them back to duty. They entered the situational zone that sociologists of collective behavior call a "moral holiday," like rioters on a looting rampage, in which moral constraints are suspended, and no one restrains anyone else from violating normal civilized practices.[11] Once the Chinese population became targets for more-or-less universal killing, all lesser taboos fell away too. The Japanese began to rape young Chinese women, then older ones. Sporadic raping was historically a common occurrence among victorious troops in most armies until very recent times, when some twentieth-century armies began to institutionalize stricter organizational controls. And it fitted official Japanese policy to take women of conquered populations as forced prostitutes or sex slaves. But the rapes went beyond these more-or-less institutionalized practices, which generally leave sexually desirable women alive. Instead, rapes were assimilated to the general mood of killing, and even taking on its atmosphere of mutilation, torture, and grotesque killing games. Photos in Chang (1997) show Chinese women killed while bound in pornographic poses or with a bayonet thrust in the vagina. These are similar to other photos taken of severed heads of Chinese soldiers, for instance with cigarettes in their mouths: sardonic juxtapositions expressing a mood of violent mockery.

On top of this came looting. This too is a normal practice, at least to a small extent, in all wars (Holmes 1985: 353–55). In Nanking, the looting spread out of control to a general destruction of property, a mood of deliberate vandalism. Eventually most of the city was burned. Like the killing and the forced sex, the looting and destruction may have started with a component of practical self-interest, but it spread out of control to the point where it was non-utilitarian even to the selfish purposes of the Japanese army, destroying the very spoils of victory. The moral holiday, once breaking through the membrane of normal social life—and even the normal life of an army—became a grotesque carnival, a celebration of destruction. The mood in this case lasted unusually long: it was at its most intense in the first week, from December 13 to 19, and finally began to peter out in early January 1938, three weeks after it had started.

The rape of Nanking, although a highly emotional process, was not an uncontrollable frenzy—or rather, frenzy is never asocial, oblivious to all but one's inner urges. Japanese soldiers did not go berserk, lashing out in all directions; they did not shoot each other, and they generally respected their own hierarchy, although disregarding higher officers who did not go along with their orgy of destruction. They generally respected the bounds of the "International Zone," the section of the colonial city where Europeans lived, and where some Chinese fled for shelter; there were some incursions into the zone in search of women to rape, but these were sometimes repelled by the protests of European civilians. A local German official, wearing his Nazi insignia, was especially effective in overawing Japanese soldiers and rescuing Chinese.[12] These exceptions demonstrate that the Japanese soldiers' moral holiday had its implicit boundaries; it was a frenzy of destruction, but a targeted and delineated frenzy. This pattern too is general. A forward panic and similar moods of onrushing, uncontrollable violence is like roaring down a tunnel; but the tunnel has a place in social space, with a beginning and an ending in time, as well as walls that define its territory as a place for moral holiday.[13]

CAVEAT: THE MULTIPLE CAUSATION OF ATROCITIES

Not all atrocities are the result of forward panics. Counting this as (1), three other sources are: (2) deliberate orders from high military or political authorities to massacre a population (e.g., out of racial/ethnic, religious, or ideological animosity; or to dispose of POWs); (3) scorched earth policy to deprive the enemy of resources; or predatory living off the land by troops, which destroys the means of livelihood of civilians; usually this also involves some direct violence against civilians in the process of dispossessing them of food and shelter; and (4) exemplary punishment or terroristic retaliation to attempt to overawe resistance.

Examples of (2) are massacres during the sixteenth- and seventeenth-century European wars of religion (Cameron 1991: 372–85); the killing of Jews, communists, and other targets of Nazi ideology on the eastern front in World War II (Bartov 1991; Fein 1979); and the massacres of Tutsis and moderate Hutus in Rwanda in 1994 (Human Rights Watch 1999). Examples of (3) include a great deal of premodern warfare, as well as colonial wars of expansion, British anti-guerrilla tactics in the Boer war, and again the behavior of the Wehrmacht during the invasion of the Soviet Union (Keeley 1996; Mann 2005; Bartov 1991). Examples of (4) are the practices of Nazi troops in retaliating against partisans in conquered territories by massacring entire village populations (Bartov 1991; Browning 1992); and practices on both sides in the Spanish Civil War (Beevor 1999).

Recognizing these multiple causal paths means that not all atrocities can be explained in the same way; our analysis must move forward from prior conditions and processes toward the outcome, not backward from outcomes and with the assumption that there is only one pathway to get there. In forward panic, the pathway is a rapid emotional flow during a discrete local episode, beginning with the tension of the fight itself, transformed into a sudden rush of frenzied overkill in an atmosphere of hysterical entrainment. It is like an altered state of consciousness, from which the perpetrators often emerge at the end as if returning from an alien self. The other three pathways, in contrast, are much less local and situational, more embedded in recurrent institutions and macro hierarchies; these latter types of atrocities come about from deliberate decisions, made in advance and passed along chains of command or in widespread groups. Their emotions are flatter, more callous; the consciousness of the perpetrators is more filled with justifying ideologies or rationalizations, and has less of the sense of an episodic break with normalcy that characterizes forward panics. All these varieties are ideal types, and in some instances they might overlap. In the Nanking massacres, the initiating event was the Japanese commander's order to kill the Chinese prisoners, out of practical considerations of guarding such large numbers; this in turn unleashed a moral holiday, emotionally fueled by the tension of the Japanese troops in their prior campaign, now confronted with the total collapse of resistance from their enemy. The frenzy of destruction went beyond any rational scorched earth policy or exemplary terror, and is best seen as an unusually prolonged forward panic.

After the defeat of Japan in World War II, the Tokyo War Crimes Trial found the commanding general of all Japanese forces in central China guilty of the Nanking massacres, along with the prime minister, and condemned them to death. The general who actually issued the order to kill all prisoners, and the staff officer who formulated it, were not prosecuted (Chang 1997: 40, 172–76). After the My Lai massacre in Vietnam came to light, the general in charge of the division was reduced in rank and censured for not investigating the atrocity properly; the brigade commander, along with the company commander Capt. Medina, Lt. Calley, and two dozen other officers and NCOs were brought to trial; only Calley was found guilty (Anderson 1998; Bilton and Sim 1992). The usual legal and political reaction to military atrocity typically focuses on the highest-ranking officers or government officials; the assumption is that the crucial causal factor is in the chain of command, whether for giving direct orders, or for setting an encouraging or permissive atmosphere, or for not exerting sufficient control, or for covering up. What gets overlooked is the emotional dynamics of the local situation, as if the perpetrators themselves—virtually all low-ranking fighters—were mere passive conduits of orders from above. This is not to say there may not also be organizational complicity of the kinds listed above; but these are not a sufficient explanation of what happens. The order of the Japanese general at Nanking to kill all the military prisoners was a catalyst, but the conditions for a forward panic were also present. The same is true for Capt. Medina, under whose overall command was Lt. Calley's platoon, and who made an inflammatory speech to his troops the night before. Nevertheless, it was only one platoon (about twenty-five to thirty men) of the three taking part in the assault who carried out the massacre—the platoon that first entered the village, while the others were held in reserve or sent to nearby targets. The local emotional contagion was the critical element, the sine qua non of the atrocity.[14]

And so is the case with explanations that emphasize other long-term characteristics of the perpetrators. Scheff (2006: 161–82) argues that the chief explanatory condition was the hypermasculine personality of Lt. Calley himself: an individual who experienced repeated failure throughout his school and work career, including scornful treatment in the army by his commanding officer. In the light of Scheff's theory of unacknowledged shame turning into anger, Calley was an emotionally frozen individual without social bonds who released his repressed anger into a murderous outburst, ordering troops to kill defenseless civilians, and killing many of them himself. It should be noted, though, that Calley's platoon had perpetrated a good deal of violence on civilians in prior patrol operations (as did many other American units), but had never unleashed a concerted massacre; the local situation of tension buildup and the sudden let-down of discovering there were no Viet Cong soldiers in the village was the temporal scenario that this massacre had in common with most others.

We see this yet again with explanations of military atrocities that emphasize cultural scorn, prejudice, or racism directed against the enemy
population. Such attitudes are widespread, and are intensified in the polarization of war situations; yet it is only in specific scenarios that massacres are carried out. Authors like Chang (1997) and Bartov (1991) attribute atrocities largely to the ideology of the perpetrators; but forward
panics occur in a wide range of situations, many of which lack any long-
term ideology; and ideology alone without situational conditions does not
produce forward panic. And the forward panic dynamic may be combined with other causal patterns, which may expand the atrocity, both in
time, and in the kinds of violence carried out.[15] Minus additional conditions, the forward panic may be relatively brief and contained; soldiers
may be killed but not mutilated; women may be raped but not subsequently killed; a criminal suspect may be beaten severely, or less so. These
distinctions may not seem very relevant in the public emotional reaction
to any particular atrocity, which is already bad enough, but they make a
large difference in the damage done.

ASYMMETRICAL ENTRAINMENT OF FORWARD PANIC AND PARALYZED VICTIMS

Detailed examination of the Nanking case gives insight into another feature of the dynamics of such massacres. The Chinese troops greatly outnumbered the Japanese troops on the scene; once it became apparent they
were being slaughtered, why didn't the Chinese fight back? Although they
generally lacked weapons, they could have mounted some resistance and
at least have gone down fighting, or possibly overpowered small groups
of Japanese. In fact, the Japanese soldiers themselves quickly acquired an
attitude of contempt for the Chinese soldiers for passively going to their
deaths. This attitude enhanced the feeling of dehumanization, making it
easier for the Japanese to carry out the killing.

A forward panic arises in an atmosphere of total domination. Initially
this comes about for military reasons: one side moves forward in a successful attack, the other disintegrates and is unable to resist. The emotional tunnel, the mood of slaughter, opens up through recognition of that
situation, not so much rational and cognitive as emotional and collective
in the broadest possible sense. The emotional mood is interactional; it is
shared on both sides. The domination is emotional even more than physical; the victorious side feels ebullient, charged up; the losing side feels
despairing, helpless, frozen, suffocated. These emotions circulate and reinforce each other: in a pair of feedback loops within each body of troops,
the victors pumping each other up into the frenzy of destruction and the

losers demoralizing each other; and in a third loop connecting the two loops, the victors feed off of the demoralization of the losers, and the losers are emotionally battered still further by the dominants. It is a process of asymmetrical entrainment; the winner becomes entrained in its own rhythm of attack, among other reasons, because its moves are reinforced by the moves of the losers. It is a process found, on a much lower level of violence, in the micro-interactional processes of victory and defeat in sports, and in domination in the subtleties of interaction in everyday life (Collins 2004: 121–25). The contemptuous striking out, the cruel jokes of the winners, are sustained by the cringing despair and dull passivity of their victims. The forward panic of one side is fed by the panic paralysis of the other side. It is something like a bullying child growing more and more infuriated at the cringing of a cat he is torturing.

This paralysis of the defeated has been widely documented. At the battle of Granicus in 334 B.C., the Macedonians trapped the Persians' mercenary infantry in the midst of a general panic retreat of the Persian army. Keegan quotes an ancient historian: " 'They stood,' said Arrian, 'rather rooted to the spot by the unexpected catastrophe than from serious resolution.' " Keegan goes on to generalize, "That is a phenomenon reported time and again from battlefields: the rabbit-like paralysis of soldiers in the face of a predator's unanticipated onslaught. They were shortly surrounded and hacked down on the spot" (1987: 80–81). Over two millennia later, the pattern is displayed when Yugoslav partisans killed unarmed German prisoners in 1944: "[L]ike most prisoners, the Germans were as if paralysed, and didn't defend themselves or try to flee" (Keegan 1993: 54).

There is an element of passivity in atrocities of virtually all kinds. It has often been questioned why the Jews did not fight back against the Holocaust, why they did not at least make a last stand instead of being led mechanically into the gas chambers. It is the same pattern we see with the defeated Chinese in Nanking; later, when we consider deadly ethnic riots in India and many other places, we see again that victims are almost entirely passive, caught in an emotional paralysis that precludes significant resistance. The victims do not fight back at that moment in time—although they might have at some previous moment, in some other interactional situation—because they are trapped in a collective emotional atmosphere.[16]

In team sports the metaphor is used of one team gaining the momentum, the other team losing it. This is the situation in atrocities and violent domination in general—the victor imposing momentum on the loser. Here the conflict is much more extreme, but there is a similar mechanism of asymmetrical entrainment in a common emotional definition of the situation. In atrocities, this mechanism is not the mood of sports victory or defeat, but ebullient killers feeding off the hopeless passivity of those who are being killed, and the victims caught in helpless shock and depression by the emotional dominance of those who kill them. This seems irrational, against all self-interest of the victims. Nevertheless, it is a factual pattern that characterizes virtually all major atrocities. Here, the social science phrase "blaming the victim" does not help us to understand what is going on. It is not simply that the victim could, rationally, have behaved differently and thereby made it much more difficult for the attacker. The nature of conflict is not one of making independent, rational decisions—verbal sequences clearly going though their minds. Persons might make such decisions before the contact actually begins. Once locked in confrontation, they are caught up in a shared emotional field. There is contagion of emotion not only among persons on the same side of the conflict, but a contagion between the two antagonistic sides. It is the form of this emotional contagion above all that determines whether they will fight and how intensely, whether it will be a standoff, and who will win. At extremes, this emotional field turns into a dominance of mind and body by one side that produces atrocities. The hot rush and overkill of the victors is part of the same interactional mood as the stunned passivity of the victims; both are constitutive of each other. This cannot be explained by characteristics of the individuals themselves, but calls for a theory of violent interaction itself.

As yet, we are assembling evidence of a pattern. The explanation will deepen in later chapters, as we probe the micro-interactional mechanisms.

FORWARD PANICS AND ONE-SIDED CASUALTIES IN DECISIVE BATTLES

Atrocities of this kind, when the dynamic is allowed to build over an extended period of time, are truly horrifying. But some degree of atrocity is not uncommon in fighting, because decisive war victories generally have come about when conditions arose culminating in a forward panic.

A good example is the battle of Agincourt in 1415. The English army of 6,000 or 7,000 troops, mostly archers, defeated a French army of about 25,000, mostly heavy-armored knights, some fighting on horseback, others dismounted. The French lost about 6,000 dead, the English a few hundred wounded and small numbers of dead (Keegan 1976: 82–114). How was this possible? How did a smaller army beat a larger one, and suffer proportionately far fewer casualties? The secret of the size of armies, in an era of hand-to-hand combat, was that large numbers counted only if they could actually be brought up close to the enemy where they could strike at him. The English chose their position in a meadow a few hundred yards wide between two woods. The much larger French forces attacked into this funnel; their front line could be at most about as numerous as the front line of the English, even though a much larger group crowded behind them. The initial French attack of armored knights on horseback almost broke the English line; it was stopped only because French horses ran onto the row of sharpened stakes that the English had driven into the ground as a defense.

> The charge, momentarily terrifying for the English, [by] French men-at-arms, twice their height from the ground, and moving at ten or fifteen miles an hour on steel-shod and grotesquely caparisoned war-horses, had stopped only a few feet distant. . . . And as they rode off, the archers, with all the violent anger that comes with release from sudden danger, bent their bows and sent fresh flights of arrows after them, bringing down more horses and maddening others in uncontrolled flight. (Keegan 1976: 96)

The horses, less well armored than their riders, who were covered almost entirely with steel sheet metal, were more likely to have been hurt, as well as panicked. As Keegan (93) notes, the sound of arrows clanking on the armor must have been a weird cacophony, having mainly a psychological rather than physical effect; the strained atmosphere would have been increased by wounded horses screaming in pain. As the French cavalry momentarily recoiled, they crashed into their onrushing troops behind them, creating a massive traffic jam. Heavily armored soldiers fell down and were unable to rise due to the weight of sixty or seventy pounds of armor, and by the tripping of soldiers falling on each other. Wounded horses thrashed about, trampling soldiers and worsening the crush.

At this point, the English rushed forward. This was a literal forward panic; the archers just minutes before had cowered behind their sharpened stakes as the French cavalry bore down on them. One moment they are terrified by the imposing French knights advancing in a furious rush; the next moment they see their enemies helplessly tangled and lying on the ground. The archers rush forward to catch them while they are down, stabbing them with daggers through the chinks in their armor, chopping and clubbing them to death with axes and mallets used for driving stakes. The reserve lines of French troops, coming up to join the mêlée, became embroiled in the traffic jam; those who could free themselves retreated to a safe distance, where they stood disheartened for several hours without renewing the battle.

On first reading of the disparity in casualties between winners and losers in decisive battles, one is inclined to attribute the numbers to propagandistic exaggeration. But the pattern is found quite generally, and accepted by realistic modern historians who make great efforts to estimate troop numbers from logistical necessities. The disparity in casualties is explained by a combination of two patterns: First, in most battles there are relatively few casualties; this follows from the fact that soldiers are under great tension/fear and consequently are incapable of doing much damage. In an ordinary battle in the era before field artillery, without a decisive breakthrough, casualties were usually around 5 percent.[17] Second, the great majority of casualties in decisive battles occurred at the end of the battle, when one side has broken up into a disorganized retreat, and the other side jumps on them as helpless victims of a forward panic. Thus, at Agincourt, the English outkilled the French by a ratio of more than 20:1, virtually all of the French casualties coming in the traffic jam or mêlée. It is noteworthy, too, that in this case the surviving French troops, still greatly outnumbering the English, were demoralized and unable to follow up with a counter-attack. This shows that the mood of victory and defeat in battle is not simply a matter of numbers, but of emotion-laden perceptions. If the normal level of casualties is on the order of 5 percent, it is tremendously shocking to take 6,000 casualties out of 25,000 troops—something like 25 percent of one's side—in a short period of time. This is experienced as a disaster that numbs—more or less literally paralyzes—those who survive it.

There are numerous similar examples. The worst defeat of an ancient Roman army happened at Cannae in 216 b.c., when Carthaginian forces commanded by Hannibal maneuvered the Romans into being surrounded, disorganized, and demoralized, ending with some 50,000–70,000 of 75,000 Romans slaughtered. Since the Carthaginians lost 4,500 of 36,000, mostly in the early going, it is apparent that virtually all the casualties took place in the phase of battle where the defeated were putting up no resistance (Keegan 1993: 271). Ardant du Picq (1903/1999: 19–29) used Cannae as the basis for formulating his principle that most casualties occur when one side has broken down and has lost the advantage in morale to the other.

Alexander's decisive victories over the Persians all had the same form: huge numbers of Persians (40,000 at Granicus versus 45,000 Greeks, but the former outnumbered the Greeks in cavalry 20,000 to 5,000; about 160,000 at Issus versus 40,000; 150,000 or more at Gaugamela versus 50,000) standing in defensive formation against relatively smaller and more compact bodies of Macedonian troops; the former strung out in long lines, far too wide for all to engage the enemy, and generally further encumbered by a static defense, which kept them from swinging around to attack the Greek rear. In each case, Alexander's most aggressive troops, his personal cavalry attacking in a wedge headed by himself, picked out a vulnerable spot, generally near the command post of the Persians. Here, despite the overall advantage in numbers of the defenders, the immediate ratios were equal, and the momentum went to the attackers. Keegan (1987: 78–79) conjectures that the Macedonians had already half won the battle through a species of psychological warfare, inferring that the Persians took up defensive positions because they were afraid of them.

Alexander did everything possible to increase that fear by encouraging aggressive posturing by his army, and keeping the enemy on edge waiting for the attack. Quite possibly he looked for the moment when the Persian line wavered—since horses have emotions too, this could have been seen by their quavering—and launched his attack at just that time and place.[18] In each of the three great battles—Granicus near the edge of the Persian territory in Asia Minor; Issus, where the Persians attempted to keep Alexander out of the Fertile Crescent; and Gaugamela, where Darius stood to defend his capital at Babylon—the Greeks broke up the Persian line, forcing the commander to flee and setting off a disorderly panic retreat throughout the entire army. The losses were extremely one-sided in each case: about 50 percent of the Persians at Granicus, perhaps even greater losses at the other two battles; the Macedonians' biggest loss was 130 men—a fraction of 1 percent (Keegan 1987: 25–27, 79–87).

A key feature of these battles is that they were decisive. Since this becomes known only after the fact, we need to consider what makes the difference in the processes leading up to decisive vis-à-vis non-decisive battles. Julius Caesar was very conscious of the difference, and his long-term strategy during the Civil Wars was aimed at bringing about a decisive battle. What was a non-decisive battle? Fighting between phalanxes of infantry tended to be a shoving match, with relatively few casualties unless one side broke apart; thus many battles of the Greek city-state era were nondecisive (and the small city-states, which rarely took new territory, may have been content to have them so). Another type of non-decisive battling was skirmishing among cavalry or light-armed, rapidly moving troops, or between such troops and the more ponderous heavy-armed phalanxes. Unless the fast-moving troops got the infantry disorganized, or caught it by surprise or on the march, the result was typically that the horsemen or other skirmishers would retreat without much damage to either side. When Caesar was seeking to bring about a full-scale battle in North Africa in 46 B.C., his legions were often harassed on the march by Numidian tribal horsemen and light-armed runners; but "if no more than 3 or 4 of Caesar's veteran soldiers faced about and threw their spears with all their might at the Numidians who were bothering them, more than 2000 of them took flight as one man; then wheeling their horses round at random they would form up in line again, follow at a distance, and hurl their javelins at the legionaries" (Caesar, *Civil War*, 226–27). In a day's march of this kind, Caesar lost ten wounded, while inflicting three hundred casualties on the enemy. The Numidians were practicing a style of fighting adopted from tribal warfare, repeatedly rushing forward and deliberately retreating, avoiding a full-scale confrontation.

A decisive battle required a full-scale, set-piece battle between the main forces of both armies, lined up in formation on level ground. Such a battle was repeatedly offered by either Caesar or his opponents, but infrequently accepted; one side might line up on a hillside where they had the advantage of fighting downhill; or one side might be bluffing, making a display of their forces, while waiting for the other to run out of water or supplies. Thus one part of making a battle decisive was that both sides had to agree that they would fight such a battle. Alexander in his campaigns against the Persians avoided night attacks or sudden moves that might give the enemy the excuse of being caught off guard; he aimed at creating the propaganda of having won a clear victory that would bring resistance to an end (Keegan 1987: 85–86). In the same way, Caesar maneuvered, in each of his campaigns—that is, a year's fighting season in a particular geographical theater of operations—to bring the campaign to an end with a battle that would conclude that part of the war and bring political dominance over that region.

Having brought about the battle, the aim was to maneuver so as to create a panic retreat in one part of the enemy's forces, which would spread to the rest of the army and turn into a situation of forward panic. In 48 B.C., after campaigning in Greece and the lower Balkan peninsula for seven months, Caesar fought a full-scale battle against his rival Pompey at Pharsalus (Caesar, *Civil War*, 123–30). Caesar had 22,000 men, of which he lost about 1,200 (5 percent); Pompey had 45,000, but lost 15,000 (33 percent) in the battle, with another 24,000 (most of the remaining 30,000) surrendering. Pompey's advantage in numbers had no effect because they could not all be brought into contact with the enemy; as was typical in such battles, a decisive movement on one part of the battlefield set the emotional tone and direction of action for the rest. The battle began with Caesar's line attacking straight ahead; initially with little effect, typical of phalanx-on-phalanx, except to clog that part of the battlefield. The turning point came when Pompey's cavalry attacked the left wing of Caesar's line, winning a local victory and attracting Pompey's light-armored troops, the archers and slingers who made up the long-distance missile-throwers, to rush forward on that side. At this point Caesar sent a reserve force to counter-attack; this was successful—a disciplined phalanx with its hedge of spears could always beat cavalry, which in this case had become disorganized by their own charge—and now Pompey's cavalry ran away in a panic, sweeping rearward and off the battlefield. Worse yet, the several thousand archers and slingers were left exposed and were all killed. The local scene on the left wing was thus a classic forward panic: after a period of tension and momentary defeat, Caesar's troops sweep forward in a killing frenzy against a now-helpless target, continuing onward to find new victims in the main body of Pompey's infantry, who are now becoming disorganized from the flight of their own cavalry, and are encircled from behind. The result is a general panic retreat, with defeated soldiers throwing away their weapons, and a considerable proportion of them cut down in a defenseless position.

The battle of Thapsus, which brought to an end the campaign in north Africa in 46 B.C., was simpler. Caesar's army had been marching about Tunisia attempting to make Scipio's forces leave their garrisons and fortified camps and fight a set-piece battle. He finally achieved this by making Scipio attempt to relieve the siege of a major city. One section of Scipio's troops were visibly fearful, as they kept running in and out of the gates of their camp, wavering whether to give battle; on seeing this, Caesar's troops (already lined up for action) could not restrain themselves and rushed forward to attack. Panic retreat became general, resulting in the uncontrollable slaughter that I have described previously. Scipio's army lost 5,000 of about 30,000 or 40,000; Caesar's lost 50 of about 35,000 (Caesar, *Civil War*, 231–35). The disparity, and above all the breakdown in organization, was enough to bring the entire phase of war to an end.

Panic was not confined to humans; Scipio's war-elephants became terrified by a hail of arrows and slingers' stones, and began rampaging through their own ranks, trampling many of their own men. An incident with the elephants brings this far-off battle to life: "An elephant on the left wing was wounded, and maddened with pain had attacked an unarmed camp-follower; the animal put its foot on him, then knelt on him with all its weight, and as it was crushing him to death, waving its trunk in the air with a mighty trumpeting, the soldier (from one of Caesar's legions) could not endure the sight and felt bound to confront the animal. When the elephant saw him coming with his sword raised to strike, it left the corpse, wound its trunk round the soldier, and lifted him right off the ground. The soldier, being the kind of man who thought that in a dangerous situation like this determination was required, kept hacking as hard as he could with his sword at the trunk in which he was wrapped, and caused the beast such pain that it threw him aside and with tremendous noise and flurry rejoined the other elephants" (Caesar, *Civil War*, 234). The elephant acts remarkably like a human: frightened by the aggressors, it finds a weak target to attack and goes into a kind of piling on. The legionary acts quite remarkably for the time, since a camp-follower could not have been much higher-ranking than a slave or a despised ethnic, but the elephant's attack strikes the soldier as so atrocious that he goes into his own counter-attack—and even though the elephant's victim is now dead. And the elephant, finally beaten by the superior power of human weapons—or the strength of the human emotional rush—ends by retreating to the solidarity of the other elephants.

Caesar's own army at times was on the receiving end of a forward panic. In Greece in 48 B.C., a month before his victory at Pharsalus, Caesar had been carrying out a form of trench warfare in the open field, trying to pin Pompey's troops down by constructing fortifications around him, who in turn dug counter-fortifications, something like moves in the Japanese game of "Go." A battle broke out on one of these construction sites, during which Caesar's advancing cavalry became panicked at being trapped in the enemy fortifications, and in their rush to escape set off a panic among nearby infantry, many of whom crushed each other to death by jumping down into the ditches on top of each other—a version of the traffic jam at Agincourt. "There was such confusion, panic and flight all around that although Caesar seized the standards of his fleeing men and ordered them to halt ... others in their fear even threw away the standards and not a single man halted" (Caesar, *Civil War* 113–14). Caesar lost about 1,000 men, about 6 percent of his total forces, and more seriously, about 15 percent of his officers; most of the latter were apparently trampled in trying to hold back the flight. What likely kept this panic from destroying Caesar's entire army was that his troops were spread out along a long line of fortifications, so that the local event was contained; and his enemy did not press the advantage quickly, giving Caesar opportunity to regroup. It was, however, regarded by all as a defeat, leading Caesar to withdraw from the entire battlefield.

A variant on forward panic is the post-victory letdown. When the enemy is easily overcome or a position is taken without expected resistance, soldiers tend to lapse into a mode of celebration. "Tension is the normal state of mind and body in combat," says Marshall (1947: 194). "When the tension suddenly relaxes through the winning of a first objective, troops are apt to be pervaded by a sense of extreme well-being and there is apt to ensue laxness in all its forms and with all its dangers." A relatively innocuous example is Grant's first Civil War battle, at Belmont, Missouri, in November 1861, where his troops easily panicked the Confederates into retreat, and then spent the next hours celebrating enthusiastically in the captured camp. When the Confederates brought in reinforcements to counter-attack, it was only with difficultly that Grant got his troops back into sufficient order to retreat safely (Grant 1885/1990: 178–85). Battles sometimes turn decisive because of a two-step pattern, in which an initial victory on one part of the field so disintegrates the victorious forces that the entire army is left vulnerable to a disciplined counter-attack in the second phase.

Just this pattern characterized the battle of Naseby in the English civil war in 1645, in which the parliamentary forces achieved their biggest victory over the royalists. Both sides began with their infantry in the middle of the line, consisting of musketeers and pikesmen, and cavalry on the flanks. Seen from the parliamentary point of view, Prince Rupert's royal cavalry attacks on the left wing, dominating the momentum and routing the parliamentary cavalry. Meanwhile in the middle, the royalist infantry advances uphill on a mild slope, slowly in order to keep massed in line; since the parliamentary volleys don't have much effect—the usual ineffectiveness of combat firing, especially in the musket era—the advance reaches close quarters, at which the royalists push the parliamentarians slowly back in severe fighting. Parliament does well only on the right flank, where Cromwell's cavalry attacks and defeats the royal cavalry on that side of the field. Thus far the battle looks symmetrical: a royalist advance on the left wins and drives through the rear area; royalist advance in the middle is eventually stopped; a parliamentary advance on the right wins and drives through toward rear area (from Naseby battlefield historical markers).

The crucial difference occurs because the royal cavalry on the left becomes disorganized in victory; in a frenzy of celebration, the horsemen continue through to the rear to sack the baggage train. They have ridden right off the battlefield, losing all formation, and play no more part in the battle, which is still going on and now entering its crucial second phase. In contrast, Cromwell's cavalry on the right, less flamboyant but better disciplined, maintains order, or manages to regroup after its victory over the royal cavalry on that wing, turns and encircles the royal infantry, driving them into a helpless position in the center. The result is a surrender, followed by widespread killing of prisoners and the ignominious flight of the king, who had been watching from a nearby hilltop. In a sense, this victory indicates a shift to modern organization of warfare. Although the troop numbers were relatively small—around ten thousand on each side—the parliamentary units are well enough organized so that a second phase of action can be carried out after the first phase was finished; whereas the royalists, winning initially in a burst of forward panic, have only one move to make, and no counter to the second move.

Forward panics were most decisive in warfare before the firearms era, when troop numbers were relatively small compared to modern armies; battle formations packed human (and animal) bodies tightly together; and troops had to get within hand-weapons range to do much damage. There are other ways besides forward panic that heavy casualties can occur, especially through artillery fire and long-distance bombardment. The crucial point is that although massive killing sometimes happens in modern battles without a forward panic, such battles are rarely decisive.[19] They are not the same kind of clear-cut dramatic event, which on all sides is regarded as a catastrophe bringing a war or campaign to an end. For the most part, these are bloody standoffs, like most of the months-long battles of the western front in World War I.

Forward panics have generally been reduced to a detail inside a large-scale modern war. But the pattern remains relevant today. Civilian fighting is very similar to ancient battles, or even to tribal warfare, as we see in the case of gang fights, ethnic riots, and police violence. If guns are used in these kinds of fights, it is almost always at close range, in the forward panic/overkill pattern, and casualties in any given incident are heavily one-sided. Under optimistic scenarios, mobilization of large armies may become infrequent; but the fighting of ethnic groups, crowds, and police, as well as smaller-scale civilian fights, and anti-guerrilla warfare, leave us squarely in the pattern where forward panics prevail.

ATROCITIES OF PEACE

In the normal routines of life inside the modern state, a monopoly on violence is claimed by the state, while all others are expected to "keep the peace"; state agents themselves are enjoined to keep their authorized violence to the minimum necessary. But these ideals frequently clash with the micro-situational dynamics of forward panic. The resulting atrocities have existed throughout the history of policing, but they have become objects of tremendous public scandal since the 1990s, when the details of incidents have become much better known through ballistics tests, video recordings, and the buildup of news attention and political reaction to police violence.

In a famous case in New York City in February 1999, an African street vendor, Amadou Diallo, was followed into an apartment house hallway by four undercover policemen. The police were a special detail, part of a city-wide program of looking aggressively for street criminals; in effect, they were something like anti-guerrilla soldiers on patrol, suspicious of everyone in the civilian population. In this case, the police were looking for a neighborhood rapist, whose description resembled that of Diallo. Apparently frightened by their appearance, Diallo made a sudden move back into the building, which the officers interpreted as a furtive sign of guilty flight—or they were just caught up in the pattern of chasing whatever runs away; they rushed forward and interpreted Diallo's next gesture as pulling out a weapon—although it turned out he was reaching for his wallet for identification. All four policemen fired, a total of forty-one bullets, of which nineteen hit their target. This tremendous overkill was the central point of outrage in the news media and the popular protests that ensued. But consider another point: the policemen fired at a distance of less than seven feet, but half of their bullets missed.[20] This situation has all the marks of a forward panic: tension/fear by the police, a sudden retreat of the apparent enemy, a triggering gesture of apparent resistance, a hot rush of attack, more ferocious than accurate. The police are entrained in their own firing, unable to stop.

Compare a case that has a somewhat different buildup but much the same outcome. In Riverside, California, in December 1998, a young black woman returning from a party had a car breakdown at 2 A.M. (*Los Angeles Times*, Jan. 2, 1999; *San Diego Union*, Dec. 30, 1998; *USA Today*, Jan. 21, 1999). Believing herself (with some justification) to be in a dangerous neighborhood, she stopped at a gas station, locked herself in the car, and used her cell phone to call her family for help. Family members arrived, but the woman had gone to sleep, under the influence of alcohol and drugs, and they were unable to awaken her. They in turn called the police. Because of her feeling of danger, the woman sleeping in the car had placed a handgun on the car seat next to her. The police, accordingly, approached the car with their guns drawn, and after unsuccessfully attempting to waken her, broke the car window. In the following seconds, the four policemen fired twenty-seven bullets (as indicated by cartridges found at the scene), hitting her with twelve of them. The incident has overtones of absurdity—being killed by one's own rescuers; what was most shocking to both the family and the public was the sheer amount of firing unleashed. Reaction to the news was outrage in the local black community, demonstrations against the police, and investigations launched by political authorities. Here again the elements of forward panic are clear: tension/fear, a sudden trigger, wild firing, overkill.

Numerous incidents show a similar pattern. In Los Angeles, March 1998, a drunken thirty-nine-year-old white man was shot 106 times by police. He had been sitting on a freeway ramp for an hour, then led police cars in a low-speed chase at twenty miles an hour to another location, where he got out of his car, and waved what turned out to be an air pistol, at times pointing it at his head as if to commit suicide (*Los Angeles Times*, July 26, 1999). The large number of bullets fired were due to the very large number of police cars that had accumulated during the long standoff. During this period, police radio dispatchers spread erroneous reports that a man had been firing at police helicopters and at deputies on the ground. The sheer number of police called in from different jurisdictions no doubt built up confusion and magnified the sense of threat. Some of the police bullets hit apartment houses two blocks away. Here we see both wild, inaccurate, and bystander-threatening fire, as well as the tendency for rumors to become more inflammatory as the links in the chain grow longer.

After two days of anti-war demonstrations at Kent State University in May 1970, National Guard troops killed four students and wounded nine others. Demonstrators had burned the campus army ROTC building, and were taunting the guardsmen, with some students throwing rocks. In a sudden thirteen-second burst, the guardsmen fired sixty-one shots. One of those killed was a student not in the demonstration but passing near-by on her way to class. The rate of casualties to shots fired was thirteen of sixty-one, about 20 percent, the typical pattern of wild and inaccurate fire (Hensley and Lewis 1978).

Wild firing is not confined to police. In a bank robbery in February 1997 in Los Angeles, two robbers wearing body armor, apparently emboldened in thinking they were invulnerable, engaged in a fifty-six-minute shootout with police. The robbers fired 1,100 rounds from automatic weapons; two hundred police fired a proportionate number of bullets in return. Eleven officers and six bystanders were wounded, some by friendly fire. The two robbers were killed; one was shot twenty-nine times. Police reportedly shooed away paramedics and let the robber bleed to death while holding a gun at his head (*Los Angeles Times*, March 1, 1997; *San Diego Union*, Feb. 20, 2000). Both sides engaged in tremendous overfiring, most of it inaccurate; about 1 percent of the bullets hit someone.

Further cases could be added. My point, however, is not statistical frequency, but the pattern found in such cases. Most famous cases are no doubt those that are forward panic atrocities; thus we tend to sample on the dependent variable, and miss those circumstances in which a police arrest or other confrontation did not build up to a forward panic. I shall deal with this in subsequent chapters, especially in chapter 9, where we look at interactions that do not proceed to violence.

Most of the political outrage at these cases in the 1990s and thereafter have seen them as manifestations of racism. The outrageous behavior—usually focusing on the overkill, the repeated and non-utilitarian acts of violence—is what draws attention to these cases. If one bullet were fired, or one punch thrown, it seems likely that the cases would not have attracted as much attention. Once we have publicly defined the cases as outrages, we are quick to attribute as cause the skin color of the police and their victims. But the dynamics of forward panic are central. Racism may sometimes be involved; but it is a contingent factor, which sometimes sets up the initial situation. In the Diallo shooting, the police were operating in a black neighborhood that they took as a general sign of danger; their stereotyping of Diallo was what created the tension and the sudden chase into the hallway. But the wild firing and overkill is the mechanism of forward panic, which exists very widely and is not confined to racial boundaries. Similarly in the Riverside case, the perception of a dangerous black neighborhood (shared by the victim herself), and the fact that she is perceived as part of it, is what sets up the police outburst. We see this again by comparing the various fights that Ty Cobb had during his life (Stump 1994). Cobb was straightforwardly a racist, in a way that few people were in the late twentieth century; as a Southerner in the North around the 1910s, he felt affronted whenever a black person refused to defer to him. Several of his ferocious assaults occurred against black service personnel in a hotel, butcher shop, or stadium. But Cobb's fights with white persons, which were even more frequent than with blacks, had the same pattern, culminating in pounding and kicking the defeated opponent on the ground. We also find cases of white-on-white forward panic in police shootings, such as the apparent suicide on the Los Angeles overpass, the students at Kent State, and the bank robbers in body armor.

We see the dynamics of forward panic both across and within a wide variety of ethnic groups, graphically illustrated in photos. A rather small street boy (probably around nine to twelve years old), who has been caught stealing in an open-air market in Kenya in 1992, is being stepped on and beaten by two adult men, while a crowd of at least fifteen men in the background watch. In an all-white instance, a Greek Cypriot in Cyprus in August 1996, part of a demonstration that had entered the Turkish zone to protest Turkish occupation, becomes separated from his compatriots, and is now a lone individual knocked to the ground while four men swing long sticks at him and another nine rush up to join in the attack. Photos of crowd violence, which I will consider more systematically later, show much the same pattern across many contexts and ethnic combinations.

Racial prejudice can be the initial factor that builds tension and sets off a forward panic, and thus the perception of an atrocity. But forward panic has its own dynamics and operates independently of racism. As noted, forward panic is one process that may play into a multi-causal situation. The upshot is not a comforting one; if racism did not exist, police violence and similar atrocities would still occur. Racial antagonism is not the only way that the initial tension of confrontation can build up; where it is involved, it often is superimposed on the more general mechanism of tension/fear.

CROWD VIOLENCE

Forward panic is frequently involved in violence perpetrated by crowds (although not in the case of carousing crowds). Tell-tale signs are in the massive disproportion of strength between the crowd and its victims, the rhythmic entrainment in the act of violence itself, the piling on, and the overkill. But we cannot infer a forward panic merely from the results; we need evidence of a pattern developing in time, the buildup of tension/fear and the shift to sudden weakness of the victim that opens the dark tunnel down into which people collectively fall.

Ethnic riots usually show just this pattern. There are, of course, structural conditions in the background, more long-term in nature, which affect whether ethnic groups have an antagonistic relationship.[21] But ethnic antagonisms do not always or even for the most part lead to murderous

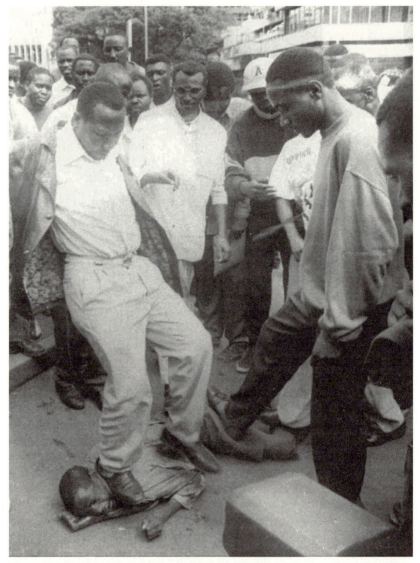

Figure 3.4 Kenya market thief stomped by two men while crowd watches (Nairobi, 1996). AP/World Wide Photos.

riots; and even among ethnic groups where riots sometimes occur, they do not occur every day but on very special occasions.

An ethnic riot is a sequence of events with a rising dramatic intensity, monopolizing attention and impelling participation. The plot of this drama, in the largest sense, is always the same: upon the background of

Figure 3.5 Group attack on fallen victim: Turkish versus Greek Cypriots (1996). Reuters.

a longer-standing trouble (consider this the prologue to Act I), a precipi-tating event occurs, something that one ethnic group takes as a provoca-tion from another group (Act I). Next comes a period of lull, a mood of ominous quiet, the calm before the storm (Act II). Then the outburst of ethnic violence, the riot claiming its victims, almost always in one-sided atrocity (Act III). There can be further acts in the drama, generally in the form of repetitions of Act III, along with occasional counter-actions by the opposing group, and interventions by the authorities with greater or lesser success. What I want to focus on here is Act II and the beginning of Act III, since this is where the pattern of the forward panic is found.

The lull before the storm is a period in which an ethnic group gathers itself together to create a response to the precipitating event, something that it comes to regard as a provocation. The period of lull usually lasts less than two days, although occasionally up to a week (Horowitz 2001: 89–93). It is a period of ominous calm, ominous because the prevailing emotion is a widespread feeling of tension. In retrospect, we can label the tension a sense of foreboding of what is going to happen, an anticipated and preliminary tension for the fight that is about to happen. But it also is tension centered on fear of the enemy. The precipitating event, in the immediate background, evokes fear: for example, the enemy has just won an election that will result in the permanent exclusion of our ethnic group from power, or has just marched (or has announced a plan to march) in a massive procession in a show of force through our territory, or has subjugated our compatriots and will soon attack the rest of us (Horowitz 2001: 268–323).

The lull is a period of rumor; it is quiet because talk is being carried out backstage, out of public sight, which is to say out of sight of the enemy and the authorities. But it is an abnormal quiet; people stay off the streets where they would ordinarily be; they avoid their normal pursuits and pleasures. The mood is contagious; the very abnormality of the public scene makes everyone nervous, wary, and careful even if they are no enthusiasts for prospective violence. A mass public mood is established; even those at its fringes become aware of it, and that increases the sense of importance among those who are at its core. It is a widespread contagious excitement, not boisterous and shouted and therefore not yet ebullient as it will eventually become, but full of fear and tension.

Rumor has several effects. It looks backward in time and outward at the enemy, painting them ever more deeply in the colors of malice and evil. Rumor enhances fear and tension. In part it does this by the process of exaggeration. If the target group has already gathered for a demonstration or procession, rumor claims that violence has already happened; if they have not gathered, rumor describes impending atrocities (Horowitz 2001: 79–80). Rumors play up ritualistic offenses, attacks on sacred religious places, stories of sexual mutilation, such as castrating men or cutting off women's breasts.[22] As stories circulate, belief in them grows stronger; they cannot be shaken by official denials; no account that disagrees with the rumor is taken as authoritative. The cognition is thus more effect than cause of the group's behavior; its rumor-mongering is an emotional contagion of drawing in on itself. The content of the rumor is just like a Durkheimian symbol, an identity-marker of the mobilized group. To credit the rumor is to show oneself a member of the group; to question the rumor is to place one's membership in question; to reject it is to put yourself outside and in opposition to the group. Thus there is another reason why the period of lull takes time: it is a period in which real interactional work is carried out, counting up the bandwagon, issuing subtle and eventually entirely nonsubtle threats against those who oppose the group. Attacks on peacemakers and multi-ethnic cosmopolitans are the business of the day, and these are usually the first targets in an escalating atrocity (Kaldor 1999; Coward 2004; Horowitz 2001). And this is another feature that makes the lull a period of growing tension.

Rumor also begins to look forward, first in wondering what will happen next; in fear of what the enemy will do; and increasingly in a plan to do something to preempt, to stop the enemy before they can commit great evil upon us. Rumor-mongering becomes planning, shifting from atrocitymongering to premonitions that something is to be done, it will be done, people are gathering, some of them you may know yourself, someone can tell you where it will happen. Rumor is not merely cognition, but action; it is the action of spreading connections among people, getting them focused on a common point of attention, and in the process getting them focused upon themselves as a group. The rumoring process itself makes people feel they are taking part in a larger current, something larger than themselves; and therefore something strong, something that can be victorious if it takes action. The rumor-spreading phase, when it is successful, which is to say when it creates a bandwagon effect with large numbers joining in, is a process of mobilization.

The buildup of tension is equivalent to the first stage of a forward panic. An ethnic riot is a larger-scale tension-and-release pattern than a small-scale fight or police action or even military action in the midst of a battle; it takes more time and spreads over more people. It takes more time because it is a collective process in which people try to bring as many allies as possible into the action. It can be regarded as a meso-level tension-and-release pattern; more spread out on the side of the tension, but sometimes in the time period of release too, although the moment of transition is the same falling into the mouth of the tunnel that we have seen before.

The onrushing release of tension into mob violence is heavily one-sided. Horowitz (2001: 385–86) estimates that 85–95 percent of deaths in ethnic riots are on one side. This implies that the victims do not fight back, even though in another situation and location[23] the attack may have gone successfully in the opposite direction. The pattern is again like that of forward panic: the surge of violence against almost entirely helpless victims; and the victims are not only militarily defenseless in that immediate location and situation, but are emotionally passive, incapable of mounting a counter-attack.[24]

The moment of the attack itself often becomes a mood of high excitement and even fun. Torture and mutilation may be performed in a mood of hilarious, "malevolent frivolity" (Horowitz 2001: 114). In the immediate post-riot period, there is an absence of remorse, defining the incident as what Horowitz (366) calls "the moral mass murder." The two features—grotesque enjoyment and display of cruelty, and the lack of moral culpability afterward—are especially loathsome to outsider observers; but together they give a clue to the underlying process. As Lt. Caputo writes about the aftermath of a Vietnam war atrocity/forward panic, there was "a dreamlike quality to the last part of the battle . . . (so that) some of us had a difficult time believing that we were the ones who had caused all that destruction" (Caputo, 1977: 289).

Perpetrators of this kind of violence have been in a hermetically sealed zone of socially shared emotion, a special reality that not only overpowers all other moral sentiments at the moment, but cannot be penetrated by memory or moral judgment from outside even in retrospect. This sealed emotional enclave, what I have referred to as going down into the tunnel, also explains the peculiar mood of exaltation that is felt while inside it. Hilarity and frivolity in the most extreme cruelty are part of the feeling of being in a special reality, in a zone that is cut off from ordinary morality; the very sense of the break from what preceded is part of the sense of exaltation that comes out looking like diabolical good humor. It is doubtful whether this mood carries over—doubtful that perpetrators of these horrors can remember them in the same mood of a hilarious good time; like the dream-world, it is hermetically sealed from later recollection.

Mob violence of this kind is a version of piling on a temporarily weak victim. The emphasis here should be on temporarily. The starting point of the ethnic hostility, and the precipitating incident, typically is perception of a strong enemy; the threatening quality of the enemy is what begins the process of fear and tension. Horowitz (2001: 135–93) marshals evidence to show that ethnic rioters do not pick ethnic groups as targets simply because they are weak; they do not displace their frustration from economic or other problems onto a conveniently weak scapegoat. To the contrary: there is no correlation with the economic success of target groups, either as superiors targeted by jealousy, or inferiors easy to despise.[25] Targets of ethnic violence are perceived as strong, aggressive, and imminently threatening. But they are attackable because they are found in a local situation where they can be safely attacked (Horowitz 2001: 220–21, 384–94). That means choosing a neighborhood or business district where the enemy is not mobilized—often the non-culpable, more peaceful cousins of those who mounted the provocation; a region that is nearby the staging area of the attacking group, easily accessible and also allowing easy retreat in case of resistance or government intervention. A favorite site is to attack targets in areas of mixed ethnicity, where the attackers have a strong majority.[26] Attackers are good, too, at monitoring the authorities, seeking signs of their tacit approval or judging their past performance of slackness or inefficiency in putting down a riot. Attackers look for their window in time and space, and exploit it. In this respect they are like armies, seeking local superiority; in both cases, the launching of a successful attack typically has the character of a forward panic.

The seeking out of weak targets is one of the activities in the period of lull. Along with rumor, the action begins to be mobilized; small groups of activists, feeling themselves empowered by the gathering community that will soon spring into action, start to reconnoiter, to find the targets they will attack. Houses where the enemy live, shops that they own, are noted and marked out by signs or spots of paint. This kind of activity, along with the ability of attackers to calculate realistically on the behavior of the police and of their victims, tends to support the side in the debate between theorists who see violence as rational pursuit of interests, as against those who see it as emotional and expressive. But people always act with a combination of rational calculation and socially based emotion. A forward panic is a zone in time where the emotional impulses are overwhelming, above all because they are shared by everyone: by one's supporters and fellow attackers, and in a reciprocal way, by the passive victims. A forward panic is a period of roaring down into a tunnel. But there can be considerable foresight and calculation in finding the mouth of the tunnel.[27] It is the same with army and police forward panics; during the period of tension buildup, there is much rational calculation of practical action that leads to the brink of confrontation. Forward panics, when they happen, have the look of being out of control, so far out of the zone of normal behavior that they look archetypally irrational. Yet normal action and normal calculation is what leads to the opening of the tunnel.

DEMONSTRATORS AND CROWD-CONTROL FORCES

The forward panic pattern is also characteristic of violence that occurs during organized demonstrations, both on the side of the demonstrators and on the side of police or military forces marshaled to control them. Demonstrations often mass large numbers of persons. But when violence breaks out, in the vast majority of instances the serious damage does not occur in a head-on collision of two masses. Like evenly matched armies, demonstrators and their official opponents generally get into standoffs, taunting one another (in the modern situation of police crowd control, the taunting typically occurs on at first only on one side, as the authorities stand in more fixed bureaucratically controlled order) (figures 3.6 and 3.7).

Crowds of demonstrators and crowd-control forces very much resemble armies in the era of phalanx formations, and their fighting, when it breaks out, typically looks like the shoving matches that characterized most phalanx fighting. Thus in some photos we see mild violence occurring when both demonstrators and crowd-control forces keep their organized lines intact while they physically clash. In such cases, police use their batons to strike randomly at demonstrators who push into their police line (or are pushed, or even inadvertently stumble into contact); this is like a version of the phalanx-mêlée, and tends to cause relatively little damage, for the same reasons that phalanxes are not capable of very much serious fighting as long as the lines stay together. One way in which this comes about is where the police maneuver demonstrators into an enclosed space, such as cutting off their escape in all directions from an

Figure 3.6 Standoff between crowd-control forces and aggressive edge of protesters (Serbia, 2000). AP/World Wide Photos.

intersection or plaza. This forces the demonstrators into a crush, at the perimeter of which police can club individual demonstrators as they try to escape. An example is the May Day demonstrations in London (depicted in photographs in the *Daily Mail* and the [London] *Times*, May 2, 2001). Most of the demonstrators look frightened and crushed; a few individuals kick or punch at the police lines, while the police strike out with batons. The press did not depict the police behavior as an atrocity. This sort of crowd violence, although painful to the individuals who get beaten, and an unpleasant crush as well as a frightening experience for others, does not look very spectacular in the eyes of journalists and observers, and does not usually get much publicity. In part this is because forward panics do not get going as long as the crowds stay massed on both sides; the situation is not set up for the sustained, emotional rush of attack that has such an ugly look.

Another relatively rare but spectacular pathway from standoff to violence results in more casualties because the authorities, much more heavily armed than the demonstrators, open fire with guns or other weapons. A famous historical instance in the Russian Revolution happened in Petersburg in July 1917 at a big march under communist leadership against the resumption of participation in the world war. Figure 3.8 shows the moment that troops suddenly fired on the marchers; we see some of the crowd scattered in all directions away from the fire, some have fallen, while most of the crowd huddles against the buildings. The armed forces undergo a for-

Figure 3.7 Two rock-throwers in front of crowd of demonstrators; rear part of crowd is turned away from action (Genoa, July 2001). AP/World Wide Photos.

ward panic of their own; the tension of a protest is suddenly broken by firing that may start with just one soldier and then is rapidly taken up in a wave of shooting that sweeps up all of them. Unlike demonstrations where the lines stay intact, these are very dramatic events, sometimes historical turning points. It is the panicky breakup that conveys this impression, since it is easily construed either as a massive victory or a massive atrocity. In

Figure 3.8 Crowd breaks up as soldiers fire machine-guns (Petrograd, July 1917).

the Petersburg "July days," the momentum of the rebellion was broken, and by the next day a crackdown on dissidents was successfully enforced, driving the communists into hiding (Trotsky 1930: chapter 25). Or the press and public can interpret a similar pattern of one-sided breakdown as an atrocity calling for massive counter-mobilization. A turning point in the civil rights movement occurred in Selma, Alabama, on March 7, 1965, when police attacked civil rights marchers with clubs and dogs, injuring sixty-seven of six hundred marchers (Gilbert 2000: 323). Publicity galvanized Congress and the president to pass a voting rights act as sympathy swung irretrievably against the segregationists.

Yet the dramatic effect is not based simply on the number of casualties. In Petersburg, the casualties were not large: about six or seven killed and twenty wounded; if the crowd was ten thousand or more, less than 0.3 percent. At Selma, no one was killed, and injuries amounted to about 10–11 percent of the demonstrators. In military terms, these were light casualties, not significant for the material strength of the opposition. What was important for the momentum swing was the dramatic image of one side being emotionally terrorized by the other. In demonstrations, violence provides the *coup de théâtre*. But the violence must be dramatically clear-cut, susceptible to one of two kinds of interpretations: soldiers fired and dispersed the unruly crowd, preserving order; or authorities attacked peaceful marchers, causing indiscriminate carnage. In either case, it is the image of the crowd breaking up in terror that becomes the socially propagated reality, not the actual casualties.[28]

But most common of all forms of crowd violence is yet another pattern, where both sides act in a non-heroic way. Here the sordid details do not make good theater and do not lend themselves to clear-cut political interpretations. The most typical way in which serious harm is done by either side is because the mass formations have broken up into small groups, the overall confrontation turning into a series of small confrontations. This generally happens in two phases. First, the demonstrators break up into little clusters. Sometimes these are little roving squads of violent activists, throwing stones or other projectiles. For example, figure 3.9 shows a demonstration in September 2002 in Buenos Aires during a presidential crisis, where a cluster of six men are running forward on a street littered with cobblestones. The three most militant are without shirts, in the act of throwing rocks, while two follow them in support, and another one slightly to the side (possibly not connected with this cluster) is in a posture of shrinking back. An opposing cluster of about ten helmeted police are visible running up behind them about twenty yards away; while a few spectators—perhaps less militant members of the original demonstration—are scattered in the distance.

So far, these little clusters are likely to perform the usual incompetent violence, making a show of bravado, but mostly missing their targets or occasionally hitting someone (not necessarily the one aimed at) by accident. They become truly dangerous when their maneuvering through the streets results in little local situations of overwhelming advantage. Now a group of police finds itself beating a single demonstrator, or a group of demonstrators beating a single policeman or soldier. Demonstrators wreak serious violence only when they get a few cops or soldiers isolated from the mass in something like a four to one or eight to one ratio; the single representative of authority may still be armed, but is unwilling to use his weapons, caught in the passivity that befalls victims of a much larger and more energized group bearing down on him in a forward panic. These mini-crowds become active where they catch an enemy in a vulnerable position, cut off from support and surrounded, unable to decide which way to face, so he ends up covering his head, crouching or falling to the ground, whereupon the captors rain down a series of kicks and blows, sometimes with metal bars and other weapons. A photo (not shown) from the overthrow of the Serbian dictator Milosevic in Belgrade in October 2000 shows four men lunging at a single riot policeman who attempts to cover his head with his arms, making no attempt to reach for his holstered pistol; while two of his assailants attempt to trip or tackle him, and several swing at him with stick and tire irons (*Daily Telegraph*, Oct. 6, 2000).

Police violence versus demonstrators is a mirror image of the above: the orderly march or picket line of demonstrators breaks up into little pockets, typically when they are running away from a police charge. Little

Figure 3.9 Cluster of rock-throwers in Argentina demonstration (2002). AP/World Wide Photos.

clumps of police gather around a single demonstrator, beating him or her with nightsticks. This is depicted in a photo (not shown) of a demonstration of unemployed workers in Buenos Aires in July 2002 (*The Australian*, June 28, 2002). The demonstrators are running from a police charge; many cower against walls along the sidewalk, while in the street it is those who have fallen to the ground, presumably by stumbling in the chase, who are being beaten by police armed with batons.

These mini-confrontations are destructive because each little encounter becomes the denouement of a forward panic: First, a period of tension, building up during the massed confrontation; the emotions are initially just anticipation, waiting for something to happen; or in case of police, simmering outrage at the affront to their authority; these can be mixed with fear, which grows when violence erupts, even in small amounts, and also when the crush of bodies becomes more intense. Serious violence starts with a sudden break that galvanizes both sides into rapid action. The precipitant of violence is at those locations where tension is followed by a perceived weakness of what had moments before been a massed enemy. Typically this comes from the problem of moving bodies rapidly in a crowd, which breaks its orderly lines; sometimes it is literally a traffic jam, like the battle of Agincourt, with demonstrators—or police—tripped up and fallen on the ground. It is precisely the fallen ones, those who are not agile enough to get out of the way or to keep in a defensible posture with their compatriots, who become the object of attack.[29]

These processes are illustrated by a description of a May Day demonstration of radical worker organizations in Berlin, in the late 1990s (Stefan Klusemann, unpublished paper, Univ. of Pennsylvania, 2002). About seven hundred demonstrators marched on a route guarded by mass ranks of about twenty-five hundred policemen; both sides kept up a high level of noise, amounting to auditory assault: the demonstrators blaring speeches and music from loudspeakers mounted on cars, as well as singing and beating drums; the police countered with sirens and repeating orders by their own loudspeakers. When the demonstration reached its traditional ending point—a small plaza surrounded by narrow streets—massed walls of police closed in, pressing the demonstrators to disperse by standing shoulder to shoulder brandishing shields and clubs. The tension was broken when one demonstrator ran at high speed across the plaza, thereby setting off a rush in the crowd to escape. In other words, some of the demonstrators went into a panic retreat, at which moment the police line surged forward to chase them. Police swung their sticks at demonstrators running by them, and rushed forward in little groups of three or four hitting those whom they caught, threatening and repeatedly striking those who fell to the ground.

Some of the demonstrators, in return, having reached the shelter of the smaller streets, stopped to pick up cobblestones to throw at the police. The very advance of the police, now chasing little groups of demonstrators instead of funneling a solid line of marchers, had broken up the police line. In some places across the fighting front, police had gotten isolated in ones or twos, becoming locally outnumbered by demonstrators, who would attack them in groups of four or more. When caught in this position, the police would go on the defensive, cowering behind their shields. As larger numbers of police approached within about thirty meters, the demonstrators who had been boldly attacking would scatter and run; some of these would become isolated and attacked in turn by groups of three or four police, who would push a lone individual to the ground, sitting on him and hitting him with their batons while arresting him (these

were little series of Rodney King–type incidents). This went on reciprocally, wherever demonstrators or police had local superiority of numbers
to attack a weak victim. Since on the whole the police had greater cohesion and better armament, they ended up inflicting more violence, while
taking just enough harm of their own to incite them to attack vociferously
where they could.

Forward panics are typical in situations where a group has overwhelming local superiority in numbers and strength, following a situation in
which a confrontation among organized crowds has built up tension. The
large-scale standoff provides the tension; the breaking up into little pockets provides the sudden release. This is the most typical scenario where
serious injury is done. Very commonly photos of this kind of crowd event
show a group attacking a single individual, who is usually down on the
ground and unable to defend him or herself. Examples include numerous
incidents photographed or described during the riots in Los Angeles and
elsewhere in 1992, following the acquittal verdict in the Rodney King
beating trial, showing individuals—white or Asian—being attacked by
groups of young black men (Reuters photos, May 1, 1992). Similar patterns are found around the world, in many different ethnic combinations.[30] What is constant is the ratio: usually in clusters of three or four
on one.

This seems to be the archetypal ratio. Most members of crowds (like
most soldiers) are only background participants, and the small fighting elite
is ineffective in equal confrontations with their counterparts on the other
side. Hence, most instances of effective violence boil down just to them,
when they can find isolated victims—at a ratio of about four to one.

THE CROWD MULTIPLIER

Forward panic–like patterns can be found in conflicts as small as one-on-
one encounters; this typically happens, as we shall see in the next chapter,
where the overwhelming advantage of aggressor over victim comes from
big differences in size and strength, such as adults versus children. The
most blatant cases of forward panic, however, are in groups, where the
advantage is the big group against the isolated individual, or the armed
force against the unarmed or temporarily disarmed one. The size of the
group present—the sheer number of bodies at the scene—increases the
tendency for forward panic. Thus most instances of police atrocities—
overkill, prolonged beatings—occur where there is a considerable group
of officers involved. The Rodney King beating took place with twenty-
one officers in on the arrest; it is quite likely that it would not have hap-

pened, or not to the same extent of prolonged violence, if there were only a couple of officers present.

The Rodney King beating, in fact, was over-determined by a concatenation of causes, all associated with police violence. Police violence is more frequent when the suspect resists, and especially when he tries to escape (Worden 1996; Geller and Toch 1996; Alpert and Dunham 2004). It is also more frequent following a car chase, apart from resistance. (These patterns are borne out also by the illegal immigrant car chase at the beginning of the chapter). Alpert and Dunham (1990: 28–39, 97; and my recalculations) found that in various jurisdictions, 18 to 30 percent of vehicles in car chases escape; thus apart from the tension of high-speed driving, and anger at defiance of authority, police have a genuine feeling of uncertainty about the outcome. In 23 to 30 percent of car chases there is an accident with property damage. In 10 to 17 percent of the chases, there is bodily injury, although usually minor (this figure would be 12 to 24 percent of the cases where the pursued car does not get away). In one-third of these cases, the injury happens after the chase stops: that is to say, the injury is not caused by a vehicle accident, but by violence. Another study found that 46 to 53 percent of vehicular chases of fleeing suspects ended with police use of force, and 11 to 14 percent with excessive force (Alpert and Dunham 2004: 24).

Causally, the Rodney King case was one of triple jeopardy: resistance to arrest, high-speed car chase, and an additional pattern. This is the bystander effect: the more police involved in an arrest (and indeed the more bystanders of any kind), the more likelihood of police violence (Worden 1996; Mastrofski, Snipes, and Supina, 1996). Group size has this effect not because there are more persons who take part in the attack, since the crowd typically has a rather small spearhead, or violent elite, a relatively small number of activists no matter what the size of the total group; of the twenty-one officers present, four did all the beating of Rodney King.[31] Instead, the crowd acts to amplify the emotion: to make the tension stronger and to intensify the flow of action after it is released. The multiplier effect has been documented by a number of studies of ethnic violence and other political crowds, as well as other kinds of mob action (these and the following are summarized and cited in Horowitz [2001: 116–17]). "Experimental studies confirm that collectivities aggress more severely, sharply, and rapidly than do individuals. . . . Larger lynch mobs committed more atrocities than smaller ones did" (Mullen 1986).

Psychologists are prone to explain these effects by the notion of de-individuation, the loss of individual identity in the larger group and, with it, any individual sense of responsibility. This is overstated, since persons generally are recruited into active crowds by networks of acquaintances, and most individuals take part as members of small groups within the crowd, where they retain a clear sense of their own identities (McPhail 1991). I would place greater emphasis on the emotional process building up in time, the entrainment in emotional rhythms from one body to another; the prime attractions and pleasures of social interaction of all kinds come from entrainment in a strongly rhythmic bodily/emotional pattern. Humans are highly susceptible to such entrainment; during the period of buildup of tension, one might say that sharing the tension is the price one pays for the feeling of solidarity with the group, even as the process of folding everyone into the group mood ratchets tension still higher. And the outburst into collective violence, and especially in the rhythmic, repetitive pattern that constitutes the overkill and the atrocity, is so compelling to its participants because it constitutes an extremely high degree of solidarity.

This entrainment in a zone of heightened reality is all the more attractive because violence breaks with ordinary reality; the violence is the occasion for getting into that special zone of experience. This happens in situations that are not, strictly speaking, forward panics, where there is little prior buildup of tension, or at least of the kind of tension that builds from fear. Such situations tend to have a mood of celebration, which outsiders find morally grotesque. Thus, in cases of threatened suicide, "large crowds are more likely to taunt and urge the victim to jump than smaller crowds are" (Horowitz 2001: 117, citing Mann 1981).

A case that combines elements of sheer bystander enthusiasm and fight escalation is the following, which took place in Oakland, California, in August 1993. The dispute began when a nineteen-year-old black woman, Stacey Lee, angrily tried to drive away a thirty-one-year-old woman, Deborah Williams (also black), from her apartment building hall where she had seen Williams smoking crack:

> Williams refused, and a fight ensued. Lee quickly got the upper hand, punching Williams and striking her with a piece of metal bed frame. Neighbors finally separated the two, and Williams fled. Lee then went into her apartment, grabbed a kitchen knife from her sink and took up the chase. . . . Bleeding and staggering, Williams attempted to take refuge in a liquor store. But witnesses said the store owner slammed and locked the door in her face. . . . Minutes later, Williams was trapped by a group of (about fifteen) young adults, mostly men, who had been gathered on a street corner. They knocked her down and yelled insults at her. Curled in a fetal position over the grate of a storm drain, she was stomped, kicked and struck with a wine bottle on the head. . . .
>
> Detectives say Williams would likely have lived if not for the crowd . . . who tripped and corralled her, then encouraged Lee with shouts of "Kill her!" and "Beat her ass!" Lee initially told detectives the crowd's exhor-

tations had no effect on her behavior, noting that she was "already mad." Now, she contends that the cheers drove her to straddle Williams and stab her in the side. (*Los Angeles Times*, Aug. 30, 1993)

Likely the mood in which the bystanders entered the fight was one of amusement at seeing two women fight, a rarer occasion than male-on-male fights, and thus something of a spectacle and perhaps also a vicarious erotic thrill. Initially, the bystanders were probably just trying to keep one fighter from getting away, so that the spectacle could be prolonged; this may well have been set off as the liquor store owner slammed the door on her, creating what to the crowd looked like a pathetic-comic chase. But their behavior soon escalated into their own version of forward panic or at least entrainment, since once they had the woman knocked down, they kept on beating her. The initial fight has elements of forward panic, too, with the victor in the fight—Lee—frustrated because the fight had first been broken up, on the very doorstep of her own turf. The two forward panic entrainments flowed together—the young woman's and the street crowd's—and the atrocity was the result.

A similar dynamic is visible in an incident in Milwaukee, Wisconsin, in October 2002, in which a thirty-six-year-old black man was beaten to death by a group of children and teenagers ranging in age from ten to eighteen. The man was a shabby, disheveled figure, homeless and usually inebriated, a weak target:

> [A]bout 16 to 20 young men prodded a 10-year-old to throw an egg at Young. The egg hit the man in the shoulder, and he started chasing the boy [brief threat]. But a 14-year-old got between the two, and Young punched him, knocking out a tooth [threat becomes injury, from what is regarded as a weak and despised person]. Several of the youths then banded together to attack Young. They chased him onto the porch of a house and pummeled him, leaving blood splattered from floor to ceiling [prolonged beating]. Young managed briefly to escape into the house, but the mob dragged him back outside and beat him until police responded to a neighbor's 911 call. (AP News report, October 1, 2002)

Here the pattern is buildup of taunting, in expectation of aggressive fun; brief counter-attack, creating momentary tension increase; panicked retreat by weak victim, which leads to entrainment of mob in chase mode, enhanced by crowd multiplier.

Such dynamics can happen with the "good guys" too. In a southern California beach community, a fifty-eight-year-old woman had her purse snatched by two teenage boys while loading groceries into her car in a parking lot. "She called out for help and began running after the boys. A store employee and a bystander followed, and along the way a water-delivery man and others joined the pursuit." The crowd built up to about fifty people, mostly men, who formed a perimeter and scoured the neighborhood in cars, on bicycles, and on foot, and eventually captured two boys, ages sixteen and seventeen, hiding in the bushes in a backyard. Participants acted with great esprit de corps, proud of themselves for pitching in as a community. But here's the rub: "An unidentified man on a bicycle became so involved in the manhunt that officers had to restrain him when the arrests were made" (*San Diego Union Tribune*, March 23, 1994). In short, the enthusiasm of good-doers, in protecting a woman, became an emotional rush, and when the target was finally captured, at least one participant did not want to stop the attack.[32] Here, it is easy to label the heroes and the villains; yet the dynamic of solidarity is much the same in any conflict group, making it heroic in its own eyes, no matter how much its violence may be viewed by outsiders as an atrocity.

Alternatives to Forward Panic

Forward panic underlies many of the most spectacular forms of violence, both the big victories in morally sanitized situations like warfare, and the worst atrocities in situations where we are forced to see too clearly what is happening—whether by modern honesty or modern recording technology—or in situations where the moral dispensation is lacking. Forward panic is theoretically central, too, because it follows so directly from our theoretical baseline of conflict. Conflict situations are first and foremost full of tension and fear; and it is this tension/fear that is released into forward panic, bringing about the engrossment in a rhythm of repetitive, temporarily uncontrolled attacks on a helpless victim, the piling on and overkill that so shocks outside observers and attracts the label of atrocity. The spectacular character of forward panic makes it tempting to see it everywhere. But forward panic is only one pathway from the starting point of tension/fear in conflictual confrontations. Forward panic is set in motion only if the tension is suddenly released, if the apparent threat and strength of the opponent rapidly turns into weakness; there must be a space in that situation into which to rush forward instead of running away, a vacuum into which the encounter is precipitated. If that vacuum does not open up, the situation flows in a different direction.

Quite often, the tension is not released, because there is no sign of disproportionate weakness on one side; many conflictual situations—indeed most, if we count all the banal incipient conflicts—become standoffs, with much posturing but petering out with little damage done. Sometimes, in rather rare situations, the violence is not hot but cold; instead of a hot emotional rush (or indeed hot harmless posturing), there is cool execution of a calculated plan of violent action; the rarity of such cold violence puts it at the apex of the stratification of violence as a hierarchy of competent performance, and we will consider it in that perspective in chapter 11. Yet another pathway is where fights are socially staged so that they will be fair fights; the pattern is so much the opposite of normal conflict, with its tension and its resulting (if unacknowledged) preference for unfair fights and weak victims, that we shall need to look for special circumstances that insulate and support this artificial form of fighting. There are other versions of unfair fights, too, besides forward panic: patterns where there is no sudden shift from tension to victim weakness, but an institutionalized situation of violent dominance, bullying, or scapegoating; and other patterns where social enclaves pop up that are not tense but joyous, zones of carousing and celebration that create places for violence that is protected emotionally as well as politically. These alternatives will be taken up in the following chapters.

CHAPTER 4

Attacking the Weak: I. Domestic Abuse

Reconstructed from forensic evidence:

> A female babysitter is giving a one-year-old child a bath while the parents are away. The child resists, squirms, and cries. The babysitter tries harder to control the child; as they struggle, she turns up the rush of water into the tub—the hot water faucet—and pushes the child's hand under the spigot. The child screams louder, which increases the babysitter's determination to keep the child in the water. The child is eventually scalded, and hospitalized with second-degree burns (from California court files).

This is a case of forward panic. The woman did not set out to harm the child. There is an escalated struggle over control; the child resists, going into a paroxysm of rage and pain; the adult increases her own efforts. At the same time that she is winning the battle—by sheer physical coercion of forcing the child to stay in the water—she is entrained in the victim's mood of shrieks, anger, and tensed muscles. Both parties to the conflict are out of control; since one is very much weaker than the other, the tension of the struggle turns into the hot rush and vicious overkill of forward panic. Recall the marines coming out of the Vietnamese village they have just burned (chapter 3); child abusers, too, often come out of their scenario of violence like wakening from a dream, amazed at what they have done.

THE EMOTIONAL DEFINITION OF THE SITUATION

If tension/fear is the dominant emotion in confrontations of imminent violence, how does anyone do any damage? Much of the time, they do not; they shy away from the fight, find excuses not to join in the action, satisfy themselves with bluster and pretence. For violence to take place, the persons involved must find a pathway around confrontational tension/fear. The most prominent of such pathways is attacking a weak victim.

What makes the weak vulnerable is not merely that they cannot fight back, and cannot hurt the aggressor; it is not so much fear of being killed or hurt that generates the tension/fear of confrontation, but a tension or fear of the clash and strain in the micro-interactional process. The "fear" in the encounter is the tension of breaking the fundamental solidarity ritual, the propensity to mutual entrainment. A violent conflict in its first moments, and until dominance is established, is an interaction ritual that has a very strong mutual focus of attention, but the rhythms attempted by the two sides are very much disattuned. The struggle to establish attunement to one's own pattern, to impose one's rhythm and direction against the effort of the opponent to evade this attunement or to establish their own initiative upon oneself, is at the micro-interactional core of the confrontational tension.

In this sense, "fear" may be a misnomer; certainly it does not capture the whole sense of what is going on. What makes a victim "weak" is situational, an interactional stance; the fact that the victim cannot defend him or herself is important chiefly because it allows the aggressor to take the initiative and control the process and direction of mutual entrainment. Successful aggression is action no longer at cross-purposes, but action that becomes coordinated; aggressor and victim get into a particular kind of entrainment, where one takes the leading role and the other responds to it. We shall see this with particular clarity in the interactional details of bullying and holdups, where the aggressor attempts to seize control of the situation, to make it a one-sided flow, and to avoid at all costs a two-sided conflictual process; and this is over and above the possibility of turning the tables and getting hurt oneself. In domestic abuse, too, we see this micro-process of taking on the role of the victim. Domestic abuse is often described as an effort for control; and that is correct, even in a much wider and more generic sense than feminist theory's emphasis on male control of females. Abusers get carried away on a freight train of emotional momentum, often leading to atrocities; and this happens because of the way in which the struggle to get through the confrontational tension flows into a particularly vicious form of entrainment between the momentarily resistant, now weak victim and the momentarily struggling but ascendant abuser, now thoroughly dominant. Dominance is a matter of seizing control of the emotional definition of the situation.

BACKGROUND AND FOREGROUND EXPLANATIONS

Background conditions generally have demonstrable but weak relationships to violence. Poverty and social discrimination are widely found concomitants of some kinds of violence. Background explanations are weak because first, many kinds of violence are not confined to, or even especially characteristic of, lower classes and discriminated minorities. This is the case with bullying, carousing and entertainment violence; staged fair fights such as dueling; military and police violence; social movement violence; and terrorism. Second, for the kinds of violence that are more prevalent in unprivileged groups, not everyone in those groups is violent; the majority of poor and discriminated persons are not robbers, street fighters, or domestic abusers. The modest correlation with background variables leaves actual violence under-determined. Third, under-determination is even greater, since those persons that are sometimes violent are not violent all the time. Just where and when they will become violent depends on situational circumstances, above all, on conditions that overcome the tension/fear of confrontation and channel it into domination. Poor and discriminated persons need pathways around these obstacles to violence, as much as anyone else.

Being a prior victim of abuse is yet another background condition; although often asserted as an explanation of violence, it has the same shortcomings. A considerable body of evidence supports the point that persons who were victims of child abuse tend later in their lives to become themselves perpetrators—not only of abuse but also other crimes of violence (and other forms of social deviance). But the pattern is quite under-determined. The majority of victims of abuse do not go on to commit violence. Children who are abused or neglected (which adds a wider, nonviolent background condition) are arrested for a juvenile or adult crime of violence at a rate of 18 percent; but this is only marginally higher than the arrest rate for a matched control group, 14 percent (a ratio of 1.3 to 1).[1] Reversing the question, it has not been established that a high percentage (let alone a majority) of those who commit various kinds of violence were previously abused.

Certainly this is not going to work as an explanation of violence all across the spectrum: prior abuse has not been shown (nor is it likely to be shown) to explain which soldiers are in the combat high-performing 15 percent, which are the cowboy cops, which are the rock-throwing demonstrators, and who participate in fraternity hazing, in duels and other staged fair fights, and in carousing and entertainment violence. It might be the case that in one specific sphere, being a domestic abuser is positively correlated with prior victimization of just this kind. But it is still the case that the majority of perpetrators of domestic abuse were not themselves prior victims.[2] There are other pathways to domestic abuse than having been abused.[3] Again, remote background conditions are only weak predictors; whatever the long-term propensities there might be for turning the tables, or perhaps just for using a technique that one has learned by hard experience in childhood, these cannot be unleashed unless there are currently existing situational conditions that overcome tension/fear. The pathway to abuse has to go through one of the pathways that all violence has to take.

ABUSING THE EXCEPTIONALLY WEAK: TIME-PATTERNS FROM NORMALCY TO ATROCITY

There are a variety of relationships in domestic violence. One spouse can attack another; adults can beat up children, but also vice versa; the adults involved could be parents, but also stepparents, casual boyfriends of a parent, or babysitters. There is also elder abuse of aged parents by grown children, and similar patterns of abuse by elder-care workers. And finally, the most common form of family violence occurs among siblings (Gelles 1977). We should keep this variety of domestic violence in mind in considering whether a general theoretical argument is adequate.

The usual suspects for causing domestic violence are poverty, stress, life-transitions, and social isolation (Straus, Gelles, and Steinmetz 1988; Gelles and Straus 1988; Starr 1988; Straus 1990; Giles-Sim 1983; Stets 1992; Cazenave and Straus 1979; Gelles and Cornell 1990; Bishop and Leadbeater 1999). But most persons in these situations are not violent; it takes a further situational process to create actual incidents of violence.

We can gain a clue by examining some of the most horrendous situations. Victims of abuse are especially likely to be handicapped or chronically ill (Lau and Kosberg 1979; Pillemer and Finkelhor 1988; Sprey and Mathews 1989; Garbarino and Gilliam 1980). This is a pattern both of child abuse and elder abuse, and of other adult victims as well. Abuse of these exceptionally helpless persons seems especially vicious, yet its perpetrators are rather average human beings caught up in a distinctive temporal dynamic. Handicaps and illness call for sympathy, a socially highly esteemed quality. But altruism is an ideal that is easiest to put into performance for a short period of time; initial crises of illness and other emergencies call out a surge of emotion, thus an intensified ritualism and heightened solidarity. If these are intimate relationships, the solidarity takes the form of a high commitment to love the needy person.

Over time, nevertheless, the problems of caring for a helpless person become routine. At the same time that the caregiver gets reduced emotional energy from playing the altruistic role (the burn-out that is typical in the helping professions), there is a heightened sense of power struggle. The very fact that the caregiver is committed to being altruistic gives the patient a weapon over him or her. As in other forms of love relationships, the principle of least interest holds: the person who loves most is at a disadvantage to the person who loves less. Thus although the healthy adult caregiver physically has all the power, the helpless child or elder has an emotional weapon in recognizing and taking advantage of the caretaker's commitment, whether that commitment comes from the caregiver's religious or altruistic belief, sense of duty, or personal love bond.[4] The general pattern of conflict applies: unequal resources lead to conflict, particularly when there are two different kinds of resources, and the disparity is not recognized overtly. This is, of course, just what an altruistic, loving ideal does: it denies fundamental inequality, at the same time that it acts upon a practical problem based on inequality in resources.

The result can be the building up of anger and resentment on both sides. The caretaker in turn comes to feel pressured: in part because these demands take away from other life activities; and, most importantly in building up the conditions for abuse, because of a growing feeling that he or she is being controlled. The patient may invest energy into this struggle out of sheer boredom, by virtue of immobility and helplessness lacking anything else to do; better a painful and annoying pastime than no pastime at all. Struggling with the caretaker to get attention is one way of getting social contact that is otherwise lacking.

Such a caretaking relationship takes on an increasingly nasty tone. The caregiver may try to break away momentarily, win some of the little contests of will by not giving in to demands, or not immediately responding; the patient replies by increasing whining, calling for aid, or perhaps dramatic displays of distress. Through emotional/physiological feedback effects, such a patient can make him or herself more ill by emotional distress or just by displays of it. Played out repetitively, these scenarios bring rising distrust, both sides suspicious of the motives and sincerity of the other: the patient suspicious of the avowed altruism of the caretaker whose aid is given in an annoyed or hostile tone; statements in the vein of "look at all I've done for you," given with justifiable pride and justifiable exasperation, nevertheless feed into the interactional tone by putting more negative emotions in circulation. Both sides may attempt to guilt trip the other. Sometimes this works, evoking momentary compliance, but it is also felt as a power move, a form of control, creating resentment and reciprocal countermoves.

These patterns are best documented in studies of elder abuse, primarily in home situations, although there may be similar patterns in nursing homes. Much of this research has concentrated on the stress felt by the caregiver, especially when she (the majority of caregivers are female) has full-time responsibilities for care, without others to help her (Steinmetz 1993; Philips 1983). Spreading the caregiving around to several persons, from the point of view of the patients, also increases network ties, and thus reduces their social isolation; thus the social weakness of the patient is reduced at the same time that stress on the caregiver is reduced. There is considerable evidence that the elder's degree of dependency increases the chances of abuse (Fulmer and O'Malley 1987; Fulmer and Ashley 1989). But it is not the health of the patient per se that makes one a victim; Pillemer (1993) summarizes evidence that there is no important difference in health and functional status of abused and nonabused elders. What seems to be going on is a building up of a pattern of conflict, with moves and counter-attacks on both sides. Pillemer (1993) notes that abusive caregivers are more likely to be financially dependent on the elder person; thus there are resources on both sides, the elder withholding or manipulating their control over money, the younger feeling additionally frustrated by these control moves compounding the normal stresses of being tied up in caregiving.

Most caregivers do not become abusive, or at least not seriously abusive. Many caregivers worry about their own feelings and fear that they will become violent, but most of them do not; and there are few discernable background differences between them (Pillemer and Suitor 1992). Situational processes seem to make much of the difference.

The temporal process is crucial. A typical scenario may take the following form: a patient gets into a power struggle with a caretaker, starting with minor disputes over promptness of response and the extent to which demands are taken seriously. Over time, the caretaker escalates against annoyances that are felt to be increasingly unjustified, and the patient becomes increasingly uncooperative or demanding. This makes the job harder for the caretaker, both physically and emotionally; the patient's main weapons are to act more sick, or make more of a mess with bodily functions and eating; to an unsympathetic eye, the patient becomes more and more unattractive, less worthy an object for altruism. The same physical behavior, when experienced initially or in an emergency situation, is a challenge that altruism proudly rises to meet; but the process of escalating conflict leads to polarization of viewpoints, and it becomes seen increasingly in a more negative light.

From this struggle of wills, carried out with tactics of services performed grudgingly and of problems created and demands escalated, the situation may proceed to physical abuse. Here the severity of disability—which may indeed be growing through feedback loops of the conflict itself—can increase the psychological polarization, giving an emotional justification to physical abuse. Usually other conditions need to coincide for this to happen, notably a sealed-off location so that the caretaker can fall back on physical force with impunity. The situation may well be living hell for the abused person; emotionally it may have the quality of an enclosed hell for the abuser as well.

Abuse of crying babies has a similar dynamic. The immediate precursor is usually the baby crying persistently. It may be because the child is sick or colicky; or because of an ongoing struggle over control with the caretaker; demanding attention may take the form of multi-sided rivalries, such as between siblings for the parent's attention; or between adult partners for attention, thereby taking attention away from the child. These factors interact and cumulate; and they can combine further with other conditions such as the parents being frustrated with other immediate life events. Thus there are many scenarios reported in the clinical literature (e.g., Stith, Williams, and Rosen 1990; Hutchings 1988; Thorman 1980) of parents who are unemployed or working at difficult jobs, mothers who are harried by caretaking several children without respite, blowing up at a crying baby and hitting or shaking it so hard that it is killed or injured.

Abusive violence does not occur at the child's first cry; there is a time-pattern in which crying builds up, and efforts to quiet it down are unsuccessful. This involves two time components: a long-term pattern, in which the child has many episodes of lengthy, unresolvable crying, so that the present episode is seen as "here we go again," another episode of foreseeable frustration all around; and a short-term pattern, the amount of time that the child has been crying persistently, and how deeply entrained she or he is in the sobbing and shrieking. We have little evidence on what length of these two components makes for the greatest danger-point of abuse; a conjecture is on the order of half a dozen or more past episodes, and an immediate situation of fifteen minutes or more of crying and attempting to make the child stop crying.

These time-patterns may vary with the kinds of background factors affecting the parents (conditions of social stress, isolation, and availability of various control resources); but it seems likely that some time-buildup, in the long-run and immediate short-run situation, is necessary no matter what those background conditions are; greater stressors, isolation, and lack of resources other than coercion may shorten these time-conditions, but surely not to extremely brief ones. One pattern often observed, for instance, is where a boyfriend is visiting a woman (usually for sex), and her child (or children) are whiny, sick, or crying. This is very likely a conflict over attention (although surreptitious and not overtly perceived as such); so there is an ongoing battle for at least some minutes or hours. The boyfriend who eventually slaps the child into a brutal injury, or throws the crying baby against a wall, is not simply acting out a momentary frustration, or even in conjunction with a long series of stressors and a pattern of inability to deal with frustration. This is a time-scenario of conflict, a battle of wills that has gone through a number of phases of escalation. The visiting boyfriend may be on a shorter fuse than the birth father, and being on drugs can also shorten the fuse, but there is still a time-pattern, steps that have to be escalated through before there is resort to overwhelming force against the physically weak.[5]

Crying is a conflictual interaction. It is a weapon of the weak, and can be a dangerous weapon to use, but a weapon nevertheless. The link between weakness, indeed the extreme weakness of physical debility, and victimhood is mediated by a time-process of conflict in which one side's moves are entirely communicative and emotional. These are hard to ignore, because they are among the most interpersonally entraining of all forms of emotional expression. Crying brings asymmetrical entrainment (unlike symmetrically entraining emotions that both sides share, such as joy/laughter, sadness, and sometimes fear and anger). Crying is getting wrought up, bodily engaged in one's own rhythms in the process of making sounds. As Katz (1999: 229–73) shows by micro-detailed analysis of video and audio recording, the crying child becomes absorbed in making a repetitive whining sound; it is like singing a song that draws all her attention into a cocoon, sheltered inside her own body, only just aware of the body of the caretaker impinging outside her shell. The caretaker (in this case, a nursery school aide) is caught in the same rhythm of body movements: though she is trying to distract the child's attention onto another activity and make her stop crying, her own movements are synchronized with the child's up-and-down wailing song that is the whining sound. The two bodies are entrained; in this case (and in many others), the caretaker makes it a benevolent entrainment, if not unmixed with frustration at the difficulty in making the child stop crying. In this instance, there is relatively little conflict, because the child is in synchrony with the teacher, and the adult gives in for the most part. A struggle over entrainment, built up on both sides into exasperation, perhaps also such emotions as fear, anger, and guilt over one's own behavior, is found in the conflictual response to crying that builds up into violence.

All the various kinds of abuse—child, spouse, elder—involve a time-process in which conflict builds up emotional entrainment. Knowing the time-patterns would be helpful for practical measures in training to prevent violence; it could give conscious awareness of the maximal danger zones.

THREE PATHWAYS: NORMAL LIMITED CONFLICT, SEVERE FORWARD PANIC, AND TERRORISTIC TORTURE REGIME

It has been proposed that there are two kinds of family violence: one Johnson (1995) calls "common couple violence," which is fairly frequent, not very severe, and practiced rather equally (in modern America) by both males and females. The second is violence used for purposes of control; Johnson calls it "intimate terrorism," involving serious physical injury or an ongoing atmosphere of threats; perpetrators are chiefly males, their victims chiefly females. We will see that severe violence further divides into two causal pathways: forward panics and terroristic torture regimes.

In spousal violence and other partner conflict, the mild version takes the form of routine quarrels, raised voices, and heated expressions, escalating to slapping, shoving, and grabbing. As measured by conventional scales of family conflict tactics, women report using these forms of violence on their partners roughly as often as vice versa (Sugarman and Hotaling 1989; Johnson and Ferraro 2000; Kimmel 2002). Here the escalation of violence is controlled and limited; such conflicts are almost a version of protected fair fights. They are protected by staying within an understood range of escalation. Injury rates are low (about 3 percent; Stets and Straus 1990); the level of severity does not rise over time, implying it is routinized, something that happens repeatedly without destroying the relationship.

This kind of violence also implies a balance of power between the partners. Neither is a weak victim; given the prevalence of tension/fear in violent encounters, and general incompetence of violence, neither is in a position to do much damage. The serious imbalance that generates a forward panic does not exist, and all-out violent frenzies do not occur. Not to say that individuals in these disputes may not become outraged, giving vent to emotions, shouting, shrieking, and crying; but that shows that emotions obey social constraints and are channeled by interactional patterns. Venting of emotion can go along with slapping, throwing and breaking household things, but nevertheless it can stay in a limited range as far as doing damage to the partner. In quarrels of this sort, the participants (especially women) do not report feeling afraid (O'Leary 2000). The fight does not get to the zone where attempts are unleashed to seriously hurt or even to deeply challenge the other; it feels protected, and may be an accepted routine, even a form of excitement and entertainment.

This limited violence is more frequent among young couples, especially during the dating/courtship period (Stets 1992; Stets and Pirog-Good 1990; O'Leary 2000; Kimmel 2002). Such incidents are typically rather mild, involving only pushing, grabbing, and slapping, and are rather gender symmetrical. One reason for this is that couples are testing out power relations (Blood and Wolfe 1960); they make moves for dominance in small matters (who gets how much precedence in telling the other what to do, controlling the conversation, setting the situational mood, choosing social activities) that are contested, giving rise to heightened emotions and mild escalation. Dating violence, during the process of courtship commitment, is interpreted by many women as a sign of love (Henton et al. 1983); as if the process of negotiating control is a mark of increasing commitment. During the courtship period, sexual attractiveness of both partners is likely to be at its height; and since this is early career stage, male advantage in income is not yet high; women's sexual bargaining power tends to set them in a fair balance of power with their prospective partners. This is one reason why considerable routine quarreling exists at this age in the form of restricted, gender-symmetrical violence.

Both short-term gender-symmetrical violence and long-term male-dominated severe violence must go through situational buildups. Like violence of any kind, these can break out only if they can find some way around confrontational tension/fear. The difference between common couple violence and severe relationship violence must be that the former kind of confrontation is channeled into protected, limited violence; whereas the latter develops into the pattern of situational tension and sudden release that leads to the violent overkill of forward panic, or to ongoing torture.

Common couple fights go through a few mutually acceptable moves, an escalation just so far and not farther. These disputes have a scripted ending. The first outburst of violence usually ends the episode; once the violence establishes the dramatic peak, the tacitly agreed-upon limit, the fight stops. The blowup often clears the air; the participants recognize that to go further would be to threaten the relationship, the balance of power that they have worked out. The scene ends; often with some standardized dramatic gesture, leaving in a huff, slamming the door, followed by a cooling-off period, and either to ignoring the incident in upcoming encounters, or to apologies and reconciliations.

Here it is useful to turn to a comparison of parent/child violence, since it also divides into normal limited violence and severe, forward panic–like abuse. This comparison shows that the cause is not gender per se, but the situational time-dynamics that limit or fail to limit violent escalation.

Low-level violence against children is common. It is especially common for American parents to spank, slap, or hit their small children; some studies show that 85 percent of two- to three-year-olds, and 95 percent of four- to five-year-olds are hit during the year, with frequency rates of 2.5 incidents per week (Dietz 2000; Straus 1994; Holden et al. 1995). Indeed this is so ubiquitous that parental ideology makes no difference—those who say they are opposed to corporal punishment nevertheless use it as much as parents who endorse it as a mode of control (Straus and Donnelly 1994: 208). This implies that immediate situational dynamics bring out the use of violence over small children. This makes sense, if we consider that material controls (such as allowances) are not applicable to small children; and that the more complex ritual/emotional forms of control do not work for children who have not yet learned to speak, or to internalize symbols in inner thinking.[6] This leaves coercion as the most immediately available form of control.

Mild violence against children arises out of the same range of situations as does common, limited spousal violence. It is also rather gender symmetrical, in the sense that both male and female parents/caretakers use it on children; and in the situation where it is most common—on small children—it tends to be used fairly symmetrically against both boys and girls (given the 85 to 95 percent rates for at least some incidences); although there are some indications that girls receive less severe corporal punishment than boys (Jouriles and Norwood 1995). Most studies find that women more frequently use routine violence against small children than men do, although this is doubtless because they spend more time around children (Dietz 2000: 1531; Straus and Donnelly 1999).

At the level of more severe violence, it is typically males who physically abuse teenagers, whereas females are the most frequent abusers of small children (Garbarino and Gilliam 1980; Gelles 1977). This is consistent with the pattern that the stronger attack the weaker; older children, particularly in their teenage years, become too big for females typically to manhandle them (unless the teenager is ritually and emotionally cowed into putting up with it). In the most severe violence on children, infant homicides, mothers' boyfriends and other non-biological parents are virtually the stereotyped offenders in public estimation. But, in fact, women kill their own babies at a higher rate than anyone else does, typically as a way of disposing with an unwanted birth.[7] Here I am not concerned with analyzing the motives but just to point out that the pattern is consistent with opportunities involving sharp differences in strength and vulnerability.

It is not, on the face of it, a male dominance pattern; men do not use corporal punishment (or for that matter severe abuse) upon girls to a greater degree than upon boys; in the case of teenagers, fathers tend not to punish their daughters corporally (although mothers sometimes do) (Straus and Donnelly 2001).[8] The upshot is that common corporal punishment, or coercive control of children, does not fit the pattern of males using violence to control females. Females use it too, sometimes to control males, sometimes to control females;[9] and there are some indications that adult males use it less against female children. We could describe this as fitting the same pattern as limited spousal violence; both types show that both sexes use violence, when it is the most readily available resource, apposite to the situation; and both sexes receive violence, with some bias, in this case, toward more use against males. Moreover, in the case of severe violence against children, here too there is gender symmetry, according to opportunity.

The difference between common disciplinary violence and severe child abuse is not a matter of which one is a struggle for control; they are both struggles for control. What distinguishes them is that the latter, just like spousal abuse, is much more escalated, and it involves much tighter linkage from one incident to the next. Normal child disciplinary disputes, like common spousal fights, are isolated from one another and soon forgotten; severe abuse in either kind of relationship has a continuing dramatic buildup. The one is like a series of short stories; the other is like a Kafka novel or a Shakespearean tragedy.

Consider three incidents of domestic violence. The first, presented at the beginning of the chapter, is the babysitter who scalded the child's hand. This case is short and episodic, with no apparent background, a sudden forward panic.

The second is recounted by a ten-year-old girl:

One day about two months ago my mom and dad got into a fight. First, my mom and I came home from the mall. We had a really nice time there. But, when we came home our nice time got to be terrible. I knew they were going to get into a fight, so I went into my bedroom and did my homework. I knew he was going to talk to her about something, but I didn't know what. Then I heard my mom start screaming and I went to the door and asked what was wrong. My dad said, "Oh, nothing is wrong. Go do your homework." But I knew something was wrong so I went and prayed to God. My dad was really mean that night. . . . Then I heard my mom scream something but I didn't understand what she said because my dad covered her mouth with his hand. Afterward she told me she said call the cops. Anyway, I went back to the door by the bedroom and told my mom I needed help on my homework, but I didn't. I just wanted my mom to come out of the bedroom because I was afraid. Then they both came out. And I hugged my mom and went to bed. Then my dad started to strangle my mom. So I went out and told my dad to stop. He told me to go back to the bedroom and go to sleep. So I did. . . . Then I heard my mom screaming. So I went back into the living room and he was kicking my mom. He wouldn't stop, he kept kicking her in the arm and legs. I told him to stop. He told me to go back to bed but I said, No! Then he took his guitar and was gonna hit her over the head. But I went on top of my mother. He told me to get off. But I said, No! So he put down the guitar, then he got her ice for her arm. Then I went to sleep crying. The next morning I didn't go to school and she didn't go to work. Then he called up the house and talked to her for a while. He threatened to kill her. So we left to go to the shelter. (Stith et al. 1990: 38–39)

The conflict progresses through a series of stages: (1) Emotional tension: the child knows there will be an argument (implying this has happened before), but the topic is not obvious. (2) The argument begins, and the woman starts screaming. (3) The woman screams to call the cops for aid, and the man stops her from screaming by covering her mouth with his hand—apparently the first physical contact. (4) After a break caused by the child attempting to intervene or distract the participants—she intervenes between each of the stages she describes—the man tries to strangle the woman: apparently she is still screaming, and this is a progressive step from hands over mouth to throat. (5) Next he kicks her repeatedly in arms and legs (apparently she is knocked to the ground). (6) Finally he raises a guitar as a weapon to hit her over the head. Here the child manages to stop the fight by physically interposing her body; and the scene winds down in a minor move by the man to make amends as he brings ice for the woman's bruises. (7) Next day, the quarrel resumes by telephone, escalating further to a death threat.

The fight takes many hours: from late afternoon when mother and daughter arrive home, until bedtime and later. The tension builds from step to step, as a series of new tactics, levels of coercion, and finally weapons are brought in by the man. It is difficult to tell how much the woman's behavior and tone changes, except for heightened screaming from steps (1) to (3); at any rate, her continued screaming keeps him entrained in the struggle. Unlike normal quarrels, the escalation doesn't stop; even severe violence itself isn't enough. There is a search for new moves to make, attempts to dramatize his seriousness: hand over mouth, strangling, kicking her fallen body (but on the limbs, not vital parts), using a weapon to her head (although a light weapon, a guitar), which also shows he is ready to destroy his own property. Nevertheless his anger is very focused; although the daughter repeatedly intervenes, he never hits her, or apparently even threatens her; and she succeeds in bringing the episode to an end by physically putting her body in the way where he would have to strike through her to get at the woman. He is entrained in his own anger and in his wife's resistance, but this is a tunnel, and he is nevertheless aware of the walls of the tunnel, and does not encroach on them. In fact, the child's intervention breaks his emotional entrainment, and his mood changes.

This incident shows a micro-situational pattern of short-run escalation and entrainment. It is a forward panic, with frenzied overkill in the later stages, after a period of strong confrontational tension turns into all-out domination. In the third case, we see another kind of scenario besides the hot emotional rush of forward panics: colder, repetitive, terroristic routine of violent domination.

Barbara had been living with her boyfriend Bill for twelve years. The pattern always followed the same sequence.

> The abuse repeatedly occurred when Bill had been drinking, and was always preceded by Bill's declaration that Barbara didn't love him and was going to leave him. Her solution was to try to reassure him of her love and her loyalty. As she became more affectionate and solicitous, the battering would start. Bill would call her names, insults would escalate to physical shovings or holdings to demonstrate superior power by Bill. This would be followed by Barbara expressing sorrow, and continued attempts of reassurance. . . . More recently, the threats of

abuse were accompanied by the presence of a large hunting knife. The knife had been held at Barbara's throat, and Bill had pricked her chest with it on more than one occasion. (Stith et al. 1990: 62)

The pattern is to attack the weak, indeed precisely as she demonstrates her weakness, the attacker becomes entrained in her yielding. As she gives way, physically and emotionally, he presses forward. This is not simply a matter of the man assuring himself he has control; there is no indication in this case (at any rate in the materials reported) that he is making up for an initial loss of control. The situational dynamic (which seems to go on for at least a half an hour, perhaps several hours) is pulling them deeper and deeper into the pattern of abuse. It is like a long drawn-out forward panic in its later phase, except there is no apparent beginning in confrontational tension and no sudden collapse; it is the reciprocal entrainment of the cringing victim (in this case, emotionally cringing in subservience) and the repetitive attacking that we find in troops committing an atrocity against helpless foes. It is a broken record of the worst kind—the needle caught in the groove of an old-fashioned vinyl record so the same segment of the tune is played again and again. The emotional tone is low and maudlin rather than heated and strident. It does not appear to be stress-related, but rather an institutionalized game that he plays with her, a ritual in which he sets all the rhythms.

The woman is playing the victim role all too well, and this is part of the micro-interactional feedback that keeps the dominator entrained in his aggression. In this case, there is striking evidence that this is so. After her therapist convinces Barbara that the pattern is not going to change in the future, she takes action.

Barbara entered the next therapy session with a huge smile. She reported to the therapist that Bill had again begun to accuse her of not loving him and she had recognized the first stage of yet another abusive episode. She had been riding in the car with Bill at the time, holding a large carry-out cola. Barbara reported to the therapist that she took the cola and "dumped it into Bill's lap." "I was damned if I was going to play that game again, and I told him so." Barbara reported that Bill was so shocked that they focused on her behavior rather than continuing the typical abusive pattern. (Stith et al. 1990: 62)

It is too simple an answer to advise women in such relationships not to play the victim role. Sometimes this works, sometimes it doesn't. Women who fight back risk escalation to more severe violence; leaving can lead to another kind of escalation, including stalking by the obsessed male, sometimes a buildup in the conflict of wills to the point of murder (Tjaden and Thoennes 2000; Kimmel 2002: 1350–53). This is the same ambiguity in robberies: as we see later, resisting rather than playing the victim increases the chances that the robbery will be unsuccessful, but it also increases the chances that the victim will get hurt.

Entrainment of victim with aggressor is a central micro-process that gives abusive episodes their situational momentum. The key point in time must be some feature of the escalation chain, perhaps where repetitions become established. We still lack information on how such sequences get started, a problem arising from sampling on the dependent variable in the detailed case studies that alone can reveal dynamic patterns. Research to ferret this out would be of great practical value.

Negotiating Interactional Techniques of Violence and Victimhood

There seems to be considerable indeterminism in my argument. Background conditions—stress, life transitions, isolation—do not necessarily lead to severe violence, or any violence at all. And so it is with the situational sequences that I have described; particular forms of these are well documented in the case-study literature, but these are sampling on the dependent variable, investigating where an atrocious outcome has occurred. I have given scenarios by which handicapped persons, like crying babies, get into a polarizing conflict in which the other is dehumanized and time-patterns culminate in atrocities; but most crying babies, handicapped persons, and elders are not severely abused, because things do not go that far. Corporal punishment of children is very widespread and most of it does not escalate to extremes; nor do most ordinary couple quarrels.

We cannot get out of this methodological problem simply by avoiding sampling on the dependent variable by going back to large N comparative studies; these are too much limited not only by a narrow range of standard variables, but also by being unable to pick out the processual dynamics. What makes a difference between the mild cases of conflict and those that escalate to violence and serious abuse depends on processual turning points. We can turn this variety to our analytical advantage if we compare situationally across: *unviolent domestic conflict*; *limited and balanced fights*; and two kinds of severe violence, hot *forward panics* and cold *terroristic torture-regimes*.

What are the differences in micro-mechanisms among these? They are variants on the mutual focus/emotional entrainment model that encompasses all interaction. Let us take up again the most contentious point. I have argued that people are not good at violence; the big barrier that any violence must find a way around is confrontational tension/fear. This is what they are chiefly afraid of—not the fear of being hurt, fear of sanctions from the larger society, fear of being punished.

This may seem inherently implausible. What can be easier than big persons beating up small ones, strong beating up weak, armed killing the unarmed? But ask yourself: can *you* do it? Specifically and concretely, *whom* could you hit, or commit another form of violence upon? For that matter, whom can you raise your voice with, or engage in other conflict tactics with? (Or *when* could you do this, at some particular time in your life?) Perhaps the specific scenarios involve a spouse, a sibling, an acquaintance, one's child, or certain situations and scenes involving strangers. In each case that one can concretely visualize, I submit that a process of negotiation went on, which led up to that kind of violence being allowed; and this negotiation is a matter of managing the situational tension of conflict, not primarily a matter of fear of punishment or retaliation.

This process of negotiating one's way into a violent relationship is illustrated by the following:

> Jennie was married soon after her graduation from college. Her husband, Ralph, graduated from law school the previous year and was beginning a promising practice with a prominent attorney. In the second year of the marriage, Ralph began to become highly critical of Jennie. In public situations, he went out of his way to embarrass her with comments about her lack of intelligence. When they returned home from a visit with friends, he would criticize her behavior, saying she was pushy, aggressive, and unfeminine. During these times, Jennie remained quiet. She seldom took a stand against her husband, accepted his criticism, and agreed to try to please him by changing her behavior.
>
> In the second year of the marriage, Ralph's psychological and verbal attacks on Jennie became more severe. Again, Jennie retreated. The verbal attacks became more frequent, and eventually, Ralph ended these verbal tirades with a physical attack on Jennie. The attacks always came late at night. They were usually followed by Ralph insisting on having sexual relations as a way of resolving the problem. (Thorman 1980: 139)

It appears that the husband's occupational status is rising relative to his wife's; in this social class, their socializing is likely to be with the man's professional associates (Kanter 1977), and thus it is when she is in the presence of his professional peers that he belittles her, and it is in regard to what he perceives as her faulty self-presentation in these situations that he begins to engage in tirades at home. He is becoming relatively stronger socially, and she is coming to accept that relationship. Then he escalates his power advantage, as the momentum of verbal tirades flows into physical violence.

A sociological interpretation of the overall pattern is that within the first two years of their marriage, the man has discovered that he is in an improving position on the interactional market relative to his wife; since he apparently does not want to leave his wife, or seek additional partners, he uses his implicit market power to demand greater subservience from his wife in their own personal and sexual relationships. Blau's (1964) principle applies here: the person with a weaker exchange position can compensate by subservience. His initial criticisms of her indicate recognition that she does not match his status, and that he wants to be with someone who matches his life-style self-presentation; the criticism becomes a pathway toward affirming her situationally passive, weak position. In effect, they are trying out how their bargaining resources will be turned into ongoing roles: he is learning techniques of building his emotional momentum as dominator, she is learning to be a victim.

I have argued that all violence must find a pathway around the barrier of confrontational tension/fear. Here I add a second point: the specific character of the violence is a particular kind of transformation of confrontational tension/fear. And this is a situational process, going on over time, as particular pairs of individuals (at least in the case of domestic abuse) develop a pathway together in which both work through the tension/fear and channel it into a particular scenario of violence. The pathway is simultaneously a way in which individuals develop techniques of conflict, techniques of using their resources to control the other, techniques of being violent but also of being subject to violence. Obviously some of these "techniques" are not in the interest of the individual who thereby has violence performed upon them, but they are two-sided, interactional accomplishments nevertheless. They are roles that both sides learn to play, and to play with each other.

In the case of forward panic, the process consists in self-reinforcing loops of entrainment, between attacker and victim, and self-entrainment on the part of the attacker. Mutual asymmetrical entrainment is found at the climax of a military forward panic; the defeated soldiers going into a despairing, frozen, passive state, while their attackers seem goaded into a frenzy of killing that involves a feeling of disgust at their passive victims. In domestic violence, too, there is often this pattern of the passive, helpless victim whose ostentatious helplessness, or ineffectual resistance, seems to pull the aggressor into still more paroxysms of overkill (as in the case described earlier, the man who kept looking for new ways to attack his wife, finally attempting to brain her with his guitar). Here again are subpathways: One is that the victim's cringing makes the aggressor disgusted and increasingly angry; it is a self-perpetuating loop since the aggressor feels drawn into continuing the attack just because of his anger at the other's cringing. The effect is that attacker and victim are tied together in the moment of violence, the two organisms sending out bodily and emotional signals that are passing through each other and further enhancing what they are doing: more cringing by one, more anger and attacking by the other.

The following example gives the subjective viewpoint or account of an attacker, not in a domestic case but analogous on this particular point: Two young black men kidnap an old white woman in her camper.

> When she came back to the camper, we pulled a knife on her and told her to start driving. She said, "I'll do anything you want, but please don't hurt me." . . . After she parked the camper, she started crying and slobbering. "Please don't hurt me, please don't hurt me. I'm sorry, please . . ." I knew the old stinking bitch was only lying. Seeing her slobber like that only made me madder and hate her even more.
>
> I jumped out of the camper, grabbed her by the shoulders and threw her out of the cab. She landed face first in the dirt. She got up on her hands and knees and started yelling, "Help, police, help police, help." I said, "Shut up you old stinking bitch," and kicked her in the stomach as hard as I could and knocked all the wind out of that old bag. She rolled up in a ball in the mud gasping for her breath, and I kicked her again which straightened her out like a stick. I tried to lift her up by the clothes, but she was so muddy that she slipped out of my hands, so I grabbed her by the hair. James said, "Would you look at her ugly old face." After I looked at it, I got so mad, I smacked and backhanded her about twenty times. Then I threw her against the camper and she slumped down on the ground. James opened a can of pop and asked her, "Do you want some pop?" She said, "No, I only want you to let me go." I said, "I'm not going to let you go, you stinking old bitch, I'm going to kill you." I grabbed her by the hair again and slammed her head back and forth against the side of the truck until blood started running out from her hair and over her ears. Then I dropped her on the ground, kicked her over into the mudpuddle and left her for dead. We got into her camper and drove off. (Athens 1989: 3)

We see not only attacker-victim entrainment, but self-entrainment of the attacker in his own action and emotion.[10] Emotionally aroused behavior, full of effort, has its own bodily tensions and rhythms; like a runner getting caught up in a running rhythm, the attacker also gets into feeding on himself (to stick to the male case here); he is "on a roll," he has momentum. It too is an emotional trance, a hormonal rush; like eating salted nuts, it sustains itself as a period of appetite, feeling both good and feeling like a compulsion, a train he is riding that he neither can nor wants to get off. This component is self-entrainment, insofar as it does not depend upon feedback from the victim; it is one's own rhythms and the emotional energy they give off that keep the cycle going.

Consider now the difference between forward panic and a cold, deliberate pattern of torturing the victim. The latter often involves psychological pressures, threatening the victim over a period of hours, playing upon her hopes of appeasing the aggressor, even though he is never satisfied with the appeasement and just uses it as another step toward eventual violence (e.g., the man with the hunting knife). The pace here is slow rather than a sudden rush; the emotional tone of the aggressor is relatively cool rather than hot and hysterical. Forward panic has a dramatic profile of buildup to high tension, including the tension of standoff or struggle, and then sudden collapse into the rush of aggressor overkill. A terrorist torture regime is more like a suspense thriller; it does not build on sudden confrontations and incidents, but seems much more deeply premeditated by the aggressor; if not a conscious calculation, at least it is a routine in which the aggressor picks on his victim, looking for petty issues and occasions, or even starting up without ostensible provocation of any sort.

Here what is lacking, compared to the forward panic, is the entire first phase, the tension buildup that is released into the sudden rush of forward panic. Nevertheless, partner torture has something of the character of the latter part of a forward panic, the same loops of entrainment between victim and aggressor in the process of the violence itself; and a loop of self-entrainment within the aggressor. One might describe a torture relationship as a truncated forward panic, in which the torturer has found a different pathway that leads to the forward panic outcome. The tension and energy that is driving the forward panic does not come from the immediately prior confrontation, as in the case of a military battle or police chase, or indeed a heated domestic argument, but it is charged up from the immediate process of dominating the victim. The long drawn-out psychological phase of torture is precisely a battle of imposing one will on another, played in the game of soliciting appeasement but then rejecting it as insufficient, an endless-in-principle tantalizing that the torturer controls. It is a way he can get the confrontational tension and use it to motivate his own violence; it is a deliberate method (at least on a nonverbal level of awareness) of how to get oneself into a pleasurable situation of entrainment with the victim, and the high of self-entrainment that goes with it. The torturer has learned a skill, a rather complex interactional technique, for getting an end-condition of emotional feedbacks—rather like creating a drug high—out of one's own body and via the intermediary of another body. However horrible, it is a form of knowledge, a way of feeling comfortable in the zone of being a habitual abuser of some other person, much like an addict feels comfortable in the zone of his drug addiction.

We have launched into this micro-analysis of the gruesome details of abusive violence in order to locate the kinds of turning points, or situational sequences over time that bring it about. We want to see how some persons go down that tunnel, while others, who may have the same background or even foreground characteristics, do not. My argument is that the forms of abusive violence involve several kinds of entrainment, and that it is these entrainment loops that become learned, negotiated, or built up. This is a tacit bargaining process, a process of feeling one another out, discovering one's strengths and weaknesses; it involves making use of one's resources (coercive power, material resources, emotional rituals, interactional market opportunities) *as they can be brought to bear on the immediate situation.* It is not raw resources alone that matter here; they have to be brought into action so that they work in controlling one's partner. There is skill involved in this, techniques that are acquired, or fail to be acquired.

These techniques or skills thus include, from the side of the aggressor, knowing how to get oneself into a position where one can feed on entrainment with one's victim; similarly, into a position where one can feed on self-entrainment—like going off on a jag of anger that builds on itself. Usually these are relationally specific accomplishments, specific to particular couples or families or groups; for if one person is going to get his emotional kicks by putting himself more and more deeply into a zone where he is getting high on his own bodily anger, the others around him must have negotiated a *modus vivendi* that has allowed him to do so. This involves a chain of processes over time, taking smaller steps that lead to further steps, like an army gradually taking ground before it begins its main assault.

There are both short-term techniques (like the entrainment with self and with victim that occurs in violent action), and also long-term techniques, techniques of how to maneuver down that slope to get to that point. Conversely, there must be techniques, implicit and unreflective though they may be, by which some persons (apparently a big majority) resist moving far on that slope. These include the techniques that are developed in what we have been calling common couple violence, techniques by which resources get balanced and conflicts are stopped, to go thus far and no farther.

On the side of the victim, there is a similar and parallel process of learning, for all that they are procedures that have terrible consequences for oneself. One learns how to become a victim. This occurs both in the short run, at the violent end of the process, and in the long run of moving down the slope. One learns how to fall into resolutions to confrontations that put one successively on the defensive, increasingly passive, increasingly allowing the tension/fear of confrontation to transfer energy to the aggres-

sor and take it away from the victim. Humans are emotionally programmed for solidarity rituals, for maintaining mutual focus and emotional entrainment; if someone else is setting the pattern of the focus and
the tone and rhythm, one has a tendency to go along with it just to avoid
the tension of a dispute. Often this takes place just at the level of avoiding
momentary unpleasantness. It is a bad bargain, since current ritual solidarity, keeping up the Goffmanian surface of interaction for the present,
may come at the cost of a much worse bargain later on. Nevertheless, we
may reasonably describe this as learning techniques for keeping up the
situation in the least disturbed manner for the present moment. Victims
learn specific scenarios, complementary to the roles played by their aggressors; some learn the role of the victim in episodic blowups of forward
panics; others learn the role of the victim of slow torture, repeatedly appeasing someone whose role is to make appeasement itself a game of tantalizing suspense and betrayal.

In this sense, the indeterminacy of background variables in predicting
domestic violence, as well as the indeterminacy of going down any of the
particular pathways, is not methodological or philosophical, but real. It
is an indeterminacy in the world, since it is a matter of how individuals
actually work out a chain of interaction rituals. What happens depends
on the skills that each person in a particular ongoing relationship acquires. For an act of abusive violence to take place, two (or more) chains
of learning techniques must coincide: The aggressor must have learned
the techniques that will work on this particular person; some of these
involve high degrees of self-entrainment in being worked up in confrontation and violence; others are skills of how to get one's own energies entrained in the reaction of another person to one's own violence.

On the other side, the victim must have learned the techniques of how
to get along with the aggressor, keeping the relationship going and subtly
encouraging him in his techniques of aggression. At the violent end, there
are two branches to this pathway: One is where the victim has learned
some devices for confrontation, but not the techniques that lead to limiting fights at the level of common, power-balanced episodes; this is the
pathway that leads to heightened tensions, then forward panic blowups.
The other pathway leads to slow insidious appeasement and terroristic
torture regime; here the victim has learned to get very small ritual payoffs
while at the cost of falling passively into the role of being tortured.

There may be other pathways. But all involve the coincidence of two
lines of learning: a learning of abusive skills on the part of the aggressor,
and a learning of victim roles, or at least a failure to learn violence limitation skills, on the side of the victim. These two roles will come out very
clearly in the case of bullying, which takes a combination of a skilled

bully and a skilled victim—although the latter's skill may also take the form of being in many ways socially skill-less.

This is depressing, but it also is hopeful. Background resources are not the only thing that counts; situational management skills can compensate for resources. Skill at situational techniques may forestall fights, or balance them off and end them quickly when they get going. On the other side, one may learn the skills to dominate, even if one lacks other resources. In this sense, it may not simply be males compensating for lost economic or other positions who use violence; violence is not brute force alone, but where successful it is a skill at picking and maneuvering victims into playing one of the victim roles.

CHAPTER 5

Attacking the Weak: II. Bullying, Mugging, and Holdups

THE MOST FREQUENT KIND of attacking the weak is probably bullying. This is most common among children, and declines with age except in total institutions that in effect treat their inmates like children. I will deal here also with muggings and holdups, which make a typical sequence for growing up into a life of crime. All together, these go from easy to hard forms of violence; in each case, the perpetrators have to learn how to make them easy to perform.

An unusually full micro-description of the social context of bullying is given in Montagner et al. (1988). This is a study of French daycare centers, where the children are very young—from three to thirty-six months, and kindergartens (ages two to six years)—and their behavior is recorded on videotape. The children fall into five main types (see figure 5.1).

1. Popular dominants: these children are sociable, but also threatening and appeasing. Always interacting with other children, they are happy and playful, but also compete with others. They take other children's toys away from them, but then give them back: as if just to show they can do it, as if starting little disputes just for fun. After they win they are friendly.

2. Sociable and appeasing: children who are friendly but noncompetitive; when another child tries to take a toy from them, they give it up. These children's network ties are with the popular dominants (1).

3. Aggressive: children who are constantly competing with other children and trying to dominate them; they take their toys away from them, make them cry, keep the toys just to show they possess them, and toss them away when other children no longer try to get them. These little bullies associate chiefly with each other, in little bully gangs. They do not aggress against the sociable dominants (1), however, or their complaisant pals (2); the dominants win any disputes with the bullies.

4. Fearful victims: these children are timid and cry easily. They are the favorite targets of the bullies (3). They are also followers; to the

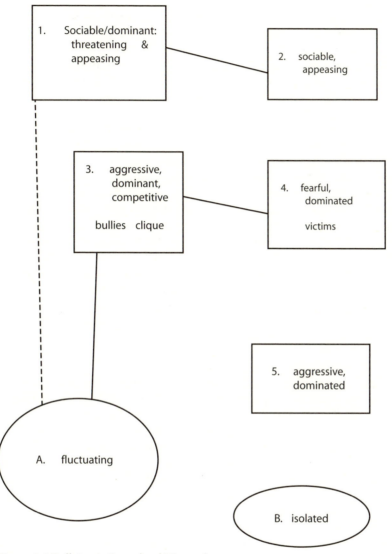

Figure 5.1 Bullying in Pre-school Networks

extent that they play with or near other children, it is the bullies that they follow.

5. Aggressive and dominated. These children are generally dominated, but they become intermittently aggressive. They are typically network isolates.

In addition to these five stable types, there are two others: (A) fluctuating personalities, going through all of the aforementioned types; their network ties are usually in associating with (3), the bullies. (B) Isolated: these children are non-sociable, non-aggressive, and non-appeasing; they have nothing to do with the others. Typically these are the youngest children, but may maintain their personality style until age three or four at which point they fall into one of the stable types.

The bullies resemble the dominant children in that both are competitive and dominating, and they also attempt to be connected to others; they differ in that the dominants are also more friendly, and they use their aggressiveness chiefly as a ritual for establishing membership for those who will play with them in a subordinate capacity. The bullies are in the middle ranks of the status system. They are not part of the network of the dominants and their followers; they create their own network, both among themselves, and with the fearful victims who rank at the bottom. One might ask why the fearful don't associate with the dominant stars instead of with the bullies; the answer may be that those who do associate with the dominants become less fearful, and the bullies are left with those who remain easy targets; another possibility is that the dominants, being sociometric stars, already are surrounded by many children and thus there is more competition to be near them; hence those who don't make it into this circle through its implicit sociability competition hang around with their tormenters, a social contact *faute de mieux*. Finally, we might query the status of (5), dominated but intermittently aggressive children: these are low in the hierarchy, with weak network ties, but they also refuse to put up with being targets all the time. One thinks of teenagers in the high school system who reject the entire status system and become rebels, weirdos, adherents of intellectual or culturally distinctive styles.

Bullying is most usefully conceptualized as an ongoing social tie of repetitive dominance and subordination. It is not a one-shot incident, but an expectable, locally institutionalized pattern. Such ongoing relationships include mocking and jeering someone as the habitual butt of jokes; exclusion from sociability; stealing (including taking toys from young children, later taking their clothes, food, or money); and beating. Bullying is typically found in schools and in prisons; in the latter, the range of institutionalized dominant/subordinate relationships can include one-sided homosexual relations commanding anal sex.

Bullying resembles the type of domestic abuse that is ongoing torment and torture. The micro-interactional mechanism similarly involves the bully's pleasure in frightening the victim, keeping him/her in suspense, enjoying the victim's palpable humiliation, indeed more of this than actual violence. Bullying differs from domestic abuse by being embedded in a more complex social hierarchy. Bullies have a recognized position in the status hierarchy of a community: they are not part of the elite, but rank in a middle or ambiguous position.

In the classic novel of the British boarding school, *Tom Brown's School Days* (Hughes 1857/1994), the bully, Flashman, is not part of the school elite: he is not one of the school athletes, who are described (as in Montagner) as brave, dominant, but also leaderly in their concern for the school's ideals and the welfare of the group. Flashman is big, rough, a carouser who joins ostentatiously in all the occasions of uproar and fun; he and the other bullies are part of the gambling and drinking set, but find their special niche in leading the fun against the younger boys. They terrify the smaller boys in the dormitories at curfew, tossing them into the air in a blanket, something of a playful ordeal in a spirit of good humored fun, but taking special pleasure in hitting them against the ceiling or dropping them on the floor. The bullies also appropriate their food, money allowances, and gifts from home; and subject them to a regimen of kicking, cuffing, throwing things, and cursing at them.

This is a description of the 1830s, but similar patterns are reported for British boarding schools from the late 1960s through the early 1990s. Boys' rituals included hanging their victims upside-down from windows; girls' bullying was more psychological.

> The most prevalent sort of bullying was "verbal abuse;" there was a certain amount of physical bullying, though initiation ceremonies such as "bog-washing," in which boys' heads were pushed down lavatory basins, and "divisional scrubs," in which they were blackened with boot polish, were said to be "part of the folklore of the past." Most parents were perfectly satisfied with the school and some believed "bullying and teasing were a good preparation for later life." One former pupil said his residence house was "the worst house for sprog-bashing [beating up the new boys or younger children], a nightly occurrence that left me having panic attacks at 9 p.m. every night [after leaving]. . . ." Once the pecking order was established you were stuck, it seems. You know the kind of thing—possessions "borrowed," opinions ridiculed, excluded from just about everything. (Duffell 2000: 186, 188)

The more extreme practices of bullying—stealing and physical violence—are more often found among boys than girls. The female equivalent is to be verbally aggressive, making catty and snide remarks, more than overt public jeering and insulting, which is chiefly a male province. Although both boys and girls pass around some of the same items of discourse (e.g., degrading nicknames, humiliating stories), girls are less likely to be in the forefront of an active crowd jeering a victim to their face, and are more active in malicious gossiping and spreading rumors.

Both boys and girls use relational aggression: telling someone they are not a friend, excluding them from groups, giving the silent treatment (Prinstein and Cillessen 2003). Girls chiefly bully (in this verbal and covert way) other girls, while boys bully (especially in the more overt forms) other boys (but also girls, in the earlier grades) (Pelligrini and Long 2002; Olweus 1993: 15). As they get older, bullying becomes finely tuned to gender-segregated status hierarchies. Girls verbally bully others chiefly in terms of their low status in the sexual attractiveness/dating market; boys physically bully others chiefly for their perceived low standing in physical aggression, which in practice means their self-presentation as confident bluster.

There is considerable evidence that bullying victims—in playschools, elementary and secondary schools, prisons and army camps—are those who are socially isolated, unpopular, shyer, less confident (Olweus 1993; Farrington 1993; Ostvik and Rudmin 2001; Nansel et al. 2001). Bullied children also are more likely to have been emotionally and physically maltreated by parents (Duncan 1999b); this is not a pattern of the previously abused becoming abusers, cycling from bottom to top in the next round, but rather continuing one's low position from one arena to the next. Children who start out with low EE from home become victims in school. Bullies are similar in some respects to their victims. Both bullies and victims are outside the popular group and tend to be rejected by other children; both have high anxiety and depression, although that of the victims are even higher than that of their oppressors (Connolly and O'Moore 2003; Boulton and Smith 1994; Rican 1995; Kaltiala-Heino et al. 2000). Observations of preschoolers at home and at preschool show that children who have younger siblings are more dominant in both places than children without younger siblings (Berndt and Bulleit 1985). Again we see that high aggression in one arena carries over into another; conversely, lack of opportunity to practice skills of being dominant at home puts children at a disadvantage (especially the only child) when they go into the larger arena of the school, where they are likely to become targets.

Some studies show a process of mobility or cycling from role of victim to bully; Haynie et al. (2001) found one-half of all middle school bullies had been victims;[1] and those who were combination bullies/victims scored the lowest on psychosocial and behavioral measures. There is a hierarchy of maladjustment: bullies/victims at the bottom; next pure victims; then pure bullies; best adjusted on all measures were children not involved in bullying in any respect. This kind of result probably indicates that the category of "bullies" was construed as including both those who dominate others and those who fight back episodically and unsuccessfully (no. 5 in figure 5.1, aggressive and dominated, and/or A, fluctuating) in Montagner's networks. Thus some studies (Espelage and Holt 2001) report that bullies have the same number of friends as non-bullies; these are probably the true bullies, the middle class of the system. Bullies have larger networks than their victims (on evidence from early adolescents), but detailed analysis shows that they are connected largely with assistants in bullying, and with "reinforcers" of bullying—children who join in by jeering and sympathetically observing (Salmivalli et al. 1997). In another study, 75 percent of bullies named other bullies as their friends (Espelage and Holt 2001). All this is consistent with Montagner's network patterns. Victims spent significantly more time alone (Salmivalli et al. 1997). Bullies had high social and physical self-concepts, although low self-concepts in other areas (such as intelligence); adolescents who had low social and physical self-concepts, or indeed low self-concepts in all areas, were the most victimized (Salmivalli 1998). Bullies are among the gregarious kids; ability to make friends easily is negatively related to being bullied and positively related to bullying (Nansel et al. 2001). Bullies have social skills that they use in a manipulative and domineering way (Smith and Brain 2000).

Bullies are a phenomenon of the middle, in almost every respect. As individuals, bullies are in the middle of status hierarchies, lording it over those below, not really accepted into the high-status hierarchy above. Institutionally, bullying happens most often in middle schools; a longitudinal study following children from fifth through seventh grades found that bullying increased at the transition to middle school, as children attempted to establish their position in a new social environment (Pellegrini and Long 2002)—indeed, moving from being the oldest kids in the elementary school of grades one through six, to the youngest and least prestigious kids in middle school of grades seven through eight or seven through nine. Studies of high schools (Milner 2004) show a peak of bullying behavior in the first year.

Aggressive children are perceived by others as popular, but they are not generally well liked—tenth graders can see that they are sociably active and well-connected, but personally they do not want to be around them (Prinstein and Cillessen 2003; also Eder, Evans, and Parker 1995). When kids perceive someone using overt aggression (directly threatening, hitting, kicking, pushing, or teasing and name-calling) in an instrumental fashion—"to get what they want," they tend to see him or her as highly popular; when they perceive someone being aggressive because of being hurt or in a bad mood, they regarded this person as especially unpopular, as well as someone one personally wants to avoid. Both patterns fit with Montagner's types: the top dogs are masters of aggressive tactics, but use them in a controlled fashion, taking the initiative rather than responding by being upset; those who fight back in reaction to their low standing only reinforce their low status. There is a whole range of aggressive styles, and the two we have just noted are at the top and bottom respectively; again bullies come in the middle.

Bullying overlaps with the normal processes of constructing status at all levels in the contemporary American high school. These are well described in Milner (2004) and Merten (1997), the basis for the following. The top of the hierarchy are the "popular" elite, those who dominate sociability. Membership depends upon being fashionably dressed in whatever are the latest of shifting styles, as well as upon being good-looking, and thus high-ranking in the sexual market; family wealth is helpful for being fashionable; and athletes, who occupy the most widely visible focus of attention, also are generally considered part of the elite (the two wings are sometimes referred to as "preps" and "jocks"). Most importantly, this is the network where there is the highest emotional energy, the most action, the most fun, the most collective effervescence. Articulate members of the elite would deny that membership is based only on clothes or money, or on sexiness (which may well be more blatant in lower-ranking crowds). The elite are those who dominate the center of attention, because they are where the most fun is happening; they host and attend the best parties off school grounds; during the school day, they dominate the common gathering places, especially the lunch room, where the pecking order is most clearly manifested in who sits with whom, and which tables have the liveliest conversation and most laughter. To be isolated is to be farthest from any center of sociability; and this establishes the lowest end of the hierarchy. Within a closed system of awareness, being isolated is not just to be left alone, but to attract attention of a negative sort.

There are a number of middle-status groups, which can vary considerably in large pluralistic schools. There is a fringe of the popular group, those who are moderately sociable or who have network contacts (friendships or siblings and other relatives) with some of them, and thus can be present at some of their gatherings. There are alternative groups with their distinctive cultures: musicians who take part in band or choir; drama clubs who dress in black and take an avant-garde stance; a variety of counter-culture groups often based on bizarre dress and whose ritual rallying point is a particular form of popular music. Intellectuals and studious kids are generally denigrated as "nerds" (old-fashioned terms: "grinds," "wonks"). Working-class and rural students are usually distinctive enclaves, looked down upon by the popular and upper-middle-class students (as "shit-kickers," "hoods," "greasers," etc.); some of these may organize their own gangs, violent or quasi-violent. Racial and ethnic minorities may form enclaves or cut across several of these groups. There is also a large group of average kids, not especially noticeable in any respect.

Low status is marked in several ways: as being unfashionable in dress (which may be deliberate alternate clothing cults, or just lack of following current fashions); this is the most obvious marker and most often re-marked upon. But the central feature is being socially inept; that is, not fun, playful, skilled at the techniques for being in the sociable action. Since sociability, the skills for having lively fun together, is the standard around which the status system is constructed, those who most conspicu-ously lack this skill are boundary markers, representing just what the ground cuts itself off from. In Durkheimian terms, they are negative sa-cred objects; in religious and political systems, they call forth righteous anger and punishment; in a sociability-oriented, fun-oriented status sys-tem, they call forth righteous (i.e., completely unsympathetic and vindic-tive) scorn expressed in a mood of happy jeering.

A great deal of what goes on in such a status system looks like forms of bullying, but it is not bullying in the full sense of the term (an enduring exploitative relationship of dominance and subordination between spe-cialized bullies and specialized victims). The more extreme forms of bul-lying—threats, physical violence, stealing—are not much part of the sys-tem. On the other hand, throughout the hierarchy from top through middle to bottom, there are ongoing practices that also are found in bul-lying: exclusion; malicious gossip and mockery out of presence of the target ("behind their backs"); rejection to their face; and face insults and jeering. It would be confusing to refer to the entire high school status system as a multi-level system of bullying; but these milder bullying tactics are constitutive of much of the main hierarchy:

1. Individuals' rank depends upon whom they associate with, and hence on whom they do not associate with. There is much sorting into categories, which are given collective labels and reputations, especially upon the entry of a new cohort (the ninth or tenth grade in high school, the seventh grade in middle school). Hence there is much incentive for particular kids to cut loose from their friendships with elementary school or neighborhood kids, if the latter are being placed in an undesirable category. Kids who want to move up are motivated to demonstrate their distance and superiority to these encumbering ties by criticizing and rejecting them, and this causes them to use negative stereotypes about them. Hence there is much feeling of bitterness about two-facedness, superficiality, and oppor-tunism of friendships.

2. Talking about others in ways that puts them down is a chief form of entertainment. Since status is based on having fun, being humor-ous and lively, the most convenient source of entertaining conversa-tional material is to make jokes at other students' expense: to tell embarrassing stories about them, criticize their clothes, taste, sexual failures, and social faux pas. The collective effervescence of sociabil-

ity in this self-conscious community is fed to a large extent by recycling accounts of the low-status behavior of one's fellows. This is not entirely directed downward, however, since students can also create a lively and entertaining gossip about the foibles of their own group members, and about the elite higher than themselves. This creates further (and justified) complaints about back-biting one's own friends.

3. Overt jeering can be a collective activity when low-status persons invade the territory where high-status persons are gathered; those who enter their special part of the lunch room, or their after-school hangout, are likely to be spotted and given an unpleasant welcome.

None of this is bullying insofar as it is an ongoing round of criticism within the middle and upper ranks of the popularity hierarchy, in which many persons are both mockers and mocked. But full-scale bullying can occur within the system, and indeed is promoted by this atmosphere. It has two forms: collective bullying of perennial scapegoats, and specialized bullies who prey on the especially weak. Collective bullying especially consists in mass jeering at scapegoats, not only making them the butt of humor out of their presence, but deriding them in public. Such mob action can escalate into pranks and physical violence; for instance, locking an unpopular a boy in his hall locker, or taking away his pants, or stealing his clothes or lunch. Generally these actions are carried out in a mood of ebullient good humor, regarded as pranks, good fun; the victim does not usually see it this way, but the status system boundaries prevent those above from empathy with his point of view. (It appears to be generally boys who are recipients of the most extreme overt forms of bullying.)

Individual specialized bullies can emerge in this situation as well. They may start as those who take the lead in collective jeering (we might call them "jeer-leaders") and in violent pranks; in this respect they are like the small number of the violent elite who do most of the violent action in mobs (described in chapter 10). But the bullying 5 to 10 percent are not the elite of the status system, but only of its lower middle class, its tough sergeants or prison guards on the front line of dealing with the lowest level below. Specialized bullies become committed to this role; they develop skills at it, a symbiotic relationship with victims whom they are especially good at baiting and tormenting. In this respect they converge with the kind of domestic abusers who practice psychological as well as physical torture on victims whom they have cultivated into long-standing relationships. Once established, bullying relationships tend to persist for several years (Olweus 1993: 28).

Figure 5.2 The Faces of Bullying and Playing the Victim. In lieu of good micro-situational pictures of school or prison bullying, the following may be illustrative. Philippine guerrilla leader poses with two American missionaries whom his group has kidnapped and is holding for ransom. Note the two kinds of false smiles: the bully has a domineering grin; the victims display forced smiles, "miserable smiles" in Ekman's (1978) terms. A third American captive was beheaded. After a year of captivity, the male missionary was killed and the woman wounded during a shoot-out between the guerrillas and the army (2002). Reuters.

THE CONTINUUM OF TOTAL INSTITUTIONS

Bullying thrives in a distinctive structural setting: total institutions. These are closed communities, cut off from the surrounding world, in which most or all aspects of life are carried on in common (Goffman 1961). Thus they are closed reputational systems, in which social identities are known by all and prestige hierarchy is inescapable and pervasive in the activities of daily life. In this respect, organizations exist on a continuum of totalness; we expect the most severe bullying in the most total of institutions, with lesser amounts in partial approximations—as in high schools where children go home at night, as compared to boarding schools. Schools where most sociable activities are centered on the school (e.g., in conjunction with school sports and dances) are more total than those where leisure activities take place in specialized networks. Moreover, the students can make their school more of a closed system, precisely because they exclude their parents and homes from any connection with it: they refuse to tell parents what is happening, are ashamed to be seen with them by other students, and cut off their ties (at least while they are at school) with friends from their neighborhood (Milner 2004). These practices make the high school a goldfish bowl, an artificial total institution.[2]

A total institution is conducive to bullying in several ways. There is no escape; the weak can't get away from their tormenters, and the latter have easily accessible victims. It is a situation of high information, so that weaknesses, once revealed, are widely broadcast. It also has conditions for high ritual density, and thus for reification of membership symbols, and emotionally compelling ritual punishments for violations of group standards. And there is a limited center of attention, creating both high focus upon "where the action is," and implicitly a high degree of competition to be in that limited center; consequently, a stronger sense of exclusion and draining of emotional energy for those who fail to be in that center.

One other crucial feature of a total institution is the division between staff and inmates: teachers vis-à-vis students, officers vis-à-vis military trainees, guards vis-à-vis prisoners, camp counselors vis-à-vis summer campers. Despite the large divisions of rank and practices of dominance within the inmate populations, they have one feature of identity in common: they are all students or prisoners; this group solidarity is enforced by the ubiquitous code against calling on staff for help, or reporting anything about another inmate. The worst punishments in prisons are reserved for "snitches" or "grasses" (in British slang). One way to gain at least a small amount of status in a total institution is to demonstrate one's loyalty, by not reporting misbehavior at one's own expense. This leaves the inmate group to be self-policing and self-stratifying, often by criteria at odds with that of the staff.

Hierarchy among inmates is generally a matter of the strong over the weak, the socially central over the peripheral. Often it is the older and more experienced members of the institution over new arrivals. Here we should distinguish between bullying, as a long-term relationship, and hazing, an initiation rite that, once passed, allows one to become a member. Hazing is generally part of the institutional tradition where there is a regular calendrical intake of cohorts, and especially where the oldest cohorts graduate or move out, thus guaranteeing upward mobility over time. The other structural feature for hazing is high ritual density in the group, with a strong sense of boundaries and hence of symbolic and moral differences between insiders and outsiders. Thus quasi-total institutions, such as fraternities, which make up totally encompassing situations for collective living, sociability, and entertainment (members going outside only to attend classes, to the extent they do), have ritual hazing that involves humiliation and sometimes physical punishment. Hazing in such groups is usually carried out in an atmosphere of fun and hilarity, at least on the part of the perpetrators, helping to legitimate it. The same kind of structural locations that promote hazing have ritual carousing and ritual vandalism. In the early twentieth century, when American colleges were more sharply segregated from normal life, restricted to all-male student bodies, Monday-through-Saturday extensive class schedules, dormitory regulations, and dining room hours, they also had traditions involving ritualized violence. These included collective rites of passage such as freshman/sophomore battles on a given day of the year (usually at the beginning or end of the term) (Horowitz 1987). Here again is the typical pattern of hazing: the group that has been hazed in the previous cohort takes the lead in hazing the next group. In this respect, hazing parallels bullying, insofar as bullies are the middle class of the hierarchy, not the elite. In schools, at least (but not in prisons), cohort initiation rites can act as a substitute for bullying; since it is collectively practiced, and the victims are a collectivity rather than individuals, there is an aspect of solidarity within the cohort and a lack of the individual and permanent subordination that makes up bullying. Collective bullying can be a substitute for, and a structural barrier against, individual bullying. However, if there are also further subgroups within the school, these set the framework of differential prestige within which further individual bullying can take place.

The staff of a total institution sometimes encourages inmate hierarchy, even officially recognizes and supports it (Lloyd-Smith and Davies 1995). British elite boarding schools traditionally turned over routine discipline and ceremonial leadership of dormitories to older boys; each younger boy was assigned as petty servant to those in the top form (i.e., what Americans call "grade"), for carrying his books, fetching things, cleaning his study, etc., a practice known as "fagging" (from which the derisory term for homosexual later evolved). This official hierarchy provided a context for bullying, which took normal practice to an extreme (Hughes 1857/1994). Although only the top-form boys and school-appointed student officials had the right to assign younger students as "fags," big boys in the intermediate forms could usurp authority and informally demand fagging services. The official hierarchy from the teachers and top boys on down were aware of this, but they took the stance that the boys should manage their own affairs and not tell tales to official channels. The pattern by which the school officially delegated authority to those next lower down tended to be repeated at further levels, including by usurpation.

Bullying violence was also encouraged by official practices of ceremonial corporal punishment: a student might be boxed in the ear by the headmaster annoyed at repeated poor performance in reciting and translating Latin lines (the chief form of educational exercise); students who broke serious rules could be flogged with a cane, in a public demonstration before the entire school or dormitory group, again delegated to the boy-officials to carry out.

The school also set an atmosphere in which rough games were regarded as manly and fun. Rugby School, the subject of Hughes's description, was the place where the brand of football by that name originated, and was the leader in encouraging sports as part of the school routine. Fun in the form of mock fights existed at all levels; the younger boys were not merely victims, but engaged in collective games such as throwing slippers at each other at bedtime or on arising; the bullies were also described as throwing shoes with more serious intent to hurt, and protectors against bullies used the same weapons. This does not mean simply that bullying cycled to new victims, but that some violence was regarded as legitimate, because of being egalitarian or fun.

The school became organized into sub-hierarchies beneath the stronger boys of the upper forms. Hughes (1857/1994) describes three kinds of patronage relations. Some younger boys "toady" to the bullies, flattering them, offering them services, and insinuating themselves into the hierarchy by acting as go-betweens, seeking out targets to perform fagging services and carrying tales about victims and rebellions. Beginning as a toady was regarded as a way to work one's way up to becoming a bully as one grew bigger. Other boys are described as "pets," who are especially good-looking and delicate (perhaps a beginning of homosexual affairs); these are protected by high-ranking upper-form boys, not bullies but members of the sociable elite, who might choose them as their fags but give them light duties and keep them away from having to perform onerous fagging for others. And some of the earnest moral boys of the school took on the role of protector to weak, shy, or artistic younger boys, sometimes at the instigation of higher authorities or family connections. In reality, the three types might blend together; Hughes describes the hero of his book, who is a good patron, together with his friends, beating up a "toady" who intrudes in his own sphere of protection, using tactics not so different from those bullies used on their victims. The pervasive creation of sub-hierarchies based on violence and protection might make all varieties distinguished by insiders look somewhat similar to a disinterested outsider.

The situation in prisons is more complex. Although there is considerable violence and other exploitation among inmates, much of this is not bullying, or is ambiguous enough so that inmates themselves are unclear whether to call it bullying (O'Donnell and Edgar 1998b). Prisons generally have an underground economy: buying or trading illicit goods smuggled in, including drugs; legitimate possessions (such as phone cards, personal items, and cigarettes), which may be borrowed, also stolen; on the borderline of these practices are forced loans. As an unregulated economy, inmates use violence to settle claims and collect debts, but also to steal from each other. The percentage of inmates involved in violence, either as perpetrators or as victims, is larger than the percentage involved in ongoing, one-on-one exploitative bullying relationships. Moreover, those who bully others in the strict sense may be motivated by the material and utilitarian aspect of prison life with its economy of scarcity, in contrast to school bullying, which is largely a matter of prestige and dominance of the enclosed emotional atmosphere. Prison bullying does involve the same range of techniques—exclusion, jeering, stealing, and beating. Jeering is often used in other ways too, as a form of entertainment among prisoners; and such trading of insults also leads to fighting, but not always to a bullying hierarchy, since the fights may fend off further insults. Amidst all these other kinds of violence and struggle, bullying exists too; and it has the typical pattern of victimizing the weak.

Characteristics and behaviors of victims contribute to their victimization, in prison as elsewhere; but the specific kind of weakness that makes up vulnerability to bullying must be distinguished from other conditions of prison life (Edgar and O'Donnell 1998). Taking part in utilitarian activities like trading commodities in the illegal economy, or merely borrowing and lending, can lead to fights. The routine time-space ecology of activities can put one at risk (Cohen and Felsen 1979) in places like showers and toilets, as well as intake and visitor areas where victims are accessible to aggressors and out of the protection of authorities. And some fights are victim precipitated: the loser is the one who started the fight; a key predictor of being assaulted is having assaulted others. The strongest indicator of being bullied thus is not so much assault, threats, and insults—which are most often two-sided—but being subject to robbery in the common areas, forced loans, cell theft, and exclusion—such as not being allowed a turn at telephones, TV, or game equipment. Dominant individuals are not subjected to any of the latter, although they can be insulted and assaulted (O'Donnell and Edgar 1999).[3]

Being vulnerable in one way tends to make one vulnerable in other ways (O'Donnell and Edgar 1999). Vulnerability to bullying is not just a matter of appearance and physical weakness. Besides being small and weak, vulnerability includes low intelligence or little education; having few possessions; and lack of previous prison experience. Other vulnerabilities come from style and behavior: acting quiet, timid, or anxious; trying to avoid contact with other prisoners; staying close to staff. In short, all the ways of being low-status in the inmate scheme of things, or in almost any other status system as well, make one vulnerable.

Low status alone is not enough to generate a bullying relationship; it is developed as an interactional process. Insults are often the first stage. This is in part a test to see how the recipient will respond. Insults can also damage the person's reputation, circulate as slanderous rumors, resulting in isolation and exclusion, and thus a further step toward social weakness; the result is both lack of potential backup or intervention from third parties in fights, and loss of emotional energy so that one is less capable of fighting, or fighting well, fighting with spirit. On the other hand, insulting is a very routine activity in prisons.[4] It is insults that are not answered, either by ritually appropriate insults or other moves, or by escalation, that open the way to a reputation for vulnerability. Showing fear or lack of self-esteem to defend what are perceived to be one's interests, according to prison standards, opens a door to further attack.

Especially devastating is crying:

> There were four of us in one dorm. One come off his visit with some cannabis. He shared it out. We started pillow fighting. He showed he was the weakest. All three of us set on him. We had books stuffed in pillows. It turned nasty and we were punching him. It started as a joke, but it got serious. My friend held him down on the bed and I put a pillow over his head and held it. And he was crying and we started hitting him. I said, "If you don't stop crying we will do it for real." I put the pillow back on and held it longer. My friend got a broomstick and put it up his boxer shorts. If he had done something to resist it would have ended right there. If he had tried to stand up for himself, then things might have been different. But he just stayed still and the other boy shoved it up his arsehole. I don't know why we did it. In the dorms, people get bored and look for entertainment and fun. Unfortunately, it is the weak who are the entertainment." (O'Donnell and Edgar, 1998a: 271)

This incident has the character of ebullient carousing, in which the victim-to-be takes part at first by sharing his drugs; as he shows increasing weakness, the attacks on him escalate; the others become entrained, in something like the conclusion of a forward panic, but with the special character of disgust at someone who violates the group standard of membership, a stance of macho toughness.

Responding to insults and challenges is often a turning point. An otherwise weak individual can raise his status by taking part in what is virtually a ritual of passage:

> I was in the box waiting for my legal visit. We were all reading newspapers. A friend from the street saw a girl in the paper and said she looked

like my missus. A guy grabbed the paper and said, "I know your missus. Everyone's had her." I told him to fuck off. And he kicked seven kinds of shit out of me. I was sitting down and he hammered into me, punching, kicking, hitting. I was all cut up and bruised. Then, a couple of weeks later, waiting to go to court this bully came up to me. He demanded cigarettes. I said, "Fuck off, I'm not giving you any. If you want to take me on, without your gang, let's do it now." Bully said, "If we do, you know you'll lose." I said, "I know, but I'm not giving you anything." He said, "You're all right." Later he came up with his gang; asked how things went in court. He said it again, "You're all right." Then he walked away." (Edgar and O'Donnell 1998: 644)

In the British prison culture, severe attacks and pervasive scorn are viewed as justifiable ways of dealing with informers and sexual offenders (O'Donnell and Edgar 1998a). Often prisoners become labeled as sex offenders inaccurately, and starting such rumors is a way of beginning a bullying process, since it makes its targets ostracized and thus cuts them off from allies who can deter attack. Bullying the allegedly sexually deviant in prisons illustrates a larger pattern of bullying in institutions. An ideology of cultural inferiority is created in order to justify bullying the weak. In the case of British prisons, it is alleged sexual offenses; in American public schools, it is often accusations of homosexuality (for the most part inaccurate).[5] In boarding schools (including those British schools in which homosexuality itself was practiced) , the ideology takes a different form. In all cases, a cultural hierarchy is manufactured, which in turn serves as an excuse for attacking the smaller and weaker, which otherwise would be rather dishonorable.

The violent or nonviolent culture of the group per se is not a determining factor for bullying (although it may affect the kind of bullying tactics used). Thus it is not a result of social class. Boarding schools have the most bullying, since they are the most total institutions. Japanese public schools have been described as highly conducive to bullying; their official structure is very authoritarian, hierarchical, and regimented; at the same time, activities are very group-oriented (Yoneyama and Naito 2003). They have high ritual density, which brings strong emphasis upon inner solidarity and external boundaries; combined with internal hierarchy, this breeds enforced conformity. Bullying attacks are especially severe on new transfers; it is unclear if these are initiation rites or whether the bullied are eventually accepted. Japan generally has very low violence rates, with very high collective controls and strong group memberships. Hence its violence occurs structurally just where one would expect it, at the borders of membership into highly ritualized groups.

As American children move from elementary to secondary school, bullying becomes more collective, more concentrated on a small number of low-status victims, and also more verbal and psychological than physical. Children in the early teen years enter larger schools and a larger context of status comparison; the beginning of the sexual marketplace imposes a prestige system in which everyone becomes publicly ranked, and thus gives an ideological justification in terms of which bullying can be carried out. This is the peak for collective bullying. Older teenagers, especially in the last year at high school, are looking ahead to other contexts of education and career, and have more network contacts outside the school, which frees them from the local hierarchy that is the context for bullying. Colleges are more open and heterogeneous in activities and networks; and this reduces bullying, either by replacing it with institutionalized cohort relations and hazing rituals, or by dissipating the sense of a collective focus of attention. The degree of bullying is related to the extent to which the school resembles a total institution.

In American public schools, bullying—at least in the collective form of ostracism and jeering—appears to be more prevalent in small-town and suburban communities than in big cities. Such schools have more bullying because they are further along the continuum toward total institutions than urban schools, particularly where urban students commute long distances in a city, and where students participate in more cultural activities apart from the school. This is counter-intuitive in that we associate school violence with inner-city, ethnic minority schools. But bullying and gangs—the typical form of organization of violence in areas of poverty and ethnic segregation—are structurally antithetical. Gangs channel violence into horizontal conflicts, between one gang and another; internally they lack stratification, externally they differentiate only between gang members and the non-belonging masses. The latter may be targets of attack and exploitation by gang members (stealing their lunches, clothes, and money), but this is not their chief form of action. The classic places for bullying—British boarding schools—were very vertically oriented, class-conscious without and within, but they lacked gangs and were very far from a culture of violence except in bullying relationships. Gangs engender cycles of violence among themselves, but the schools and communities where they are located are not the places where most bullying occurs, nor mass retaliations against bullying. Even where there is bullying by gang members of non-members who have no gang to protect them, kids who are bullied could clearly identify the gang as the culprit, not the school, and thus would choose a different object of retaliation.[6]

Violent gang members may seem like bullies, in the sense of predatory tough guys, to those outside the group; but within the gang, there are no regularized relationships of bullies and bullying-victims (Jankowski 1991; Anderson 1999). The violent elite character of the gang itself within the larger community precludes having bullying-victims within its ranks. Gangs often practice rituals of hazing, and fighting a bigger member, or allowing oneself to be beaten up by the group, is used as a rite of recruitment. But hazing, as is generally the case, is a passage into an elite group, and hence there is no bullying once fully accepted. In the same way, we should distinguish attacks on the weak that a gang may carry out, from long-term bullying relations; thus, in American ethnic neighborhoods, young men who visit from another neighborhood (perhaps because they have relatives there) may be violently attacked by a large group; but such incidents are not the repetitive, exploitative hierarchy of dominance and subordination between individually known bullies and known victims.

We should doubt the prevalence of the often-asserted pattern of bullying-victims going on to become bullies in their own right. Bullying-victims sometimes retaliate, but the retaliations we know about, such as spectacular mass school killings, are similar neither in form nor in quantity to the original bullying. Bullying is an ongoing relationship, a torment by its very continuity and implacability; mass shootings are brief events, without a personal relationship of dominance. Estimates of bullying in schools are generally around 5 to 15 percent of school children as victims, 7 to 17 percent as bullies (Olweus 1993; Duffell 2000; Nansel et al. 2001); the amount of retaliation is proportionately miniscule; the vast majority of schools (over 99 percent) are without killings, and indeed without serious violence (Kimmel and Mahler 2003); this means that the great majority of bullying-victims do no more than dream of revenge. It is conceivable that bullying-victims might turn the tables and become practitioners of jeering, exclusion, stealing, and picking on particular individuals; but this would involve a huge reversal in the status hierarchy of the school. What studies there are of mobility between strata in middle schools or high schools show very little upward mobility from the bottom, and very little downward mobility from the top group, although some shifting among groups in the middle (Milner 2004; Franzoi et al. 1994).[7] Those surveys, which show that 2 to 3 percent report both bullying others and being victims of bullying (Haynie et al. 2001) may well be using the term in an imprecise manner, to indicate any verbal aggression, social exclusion, or violence, without taking into account the repetitive ongoing relationship that is at the social and psychological core of bullying.

Victims of bullying do not usually go on to become bullies, in part because they follow another pathway: this may well be a source of libertarians. Persons who most dislike the experience of total institutions are often the persons who upon release (or graduation) become principled anti-authoritarians. In American schools, at least, such students are disproportionately from the intellectual or artistic side, out of tune with the partying socialites and jocks (Milner 2004); and these two large clumps of students tend to correlate, respectively, with adult attitudes that are anti-authoritarian, on one side, and conformist/authoritarian on the other. On the individual level, bullying does not perpetuate itself by a cycle of reversal; its determinants are in the institutional context.

Muggings and Holdups

Muggings and holdups are the most immediately situational forms of attacking the weak, since there is the least history of interaction between attacker and victim, and the least amount of time to settle into reciprocal roles. Such attacks also differ from the kinds that we have been considering since they are outside the institutional context of families and total institutions, out in the public world of strangers. They are in the realm of what Goffman called "behavior in public places." These characteristics bring out especially clearly the situational features of managing collective emotional energy in violent conflict.

Under this rubric is a range of actions, from aggressive begging and purse-snatching at the borderline of unviolent behavior, with street holdups and armed robberies that escalate into serious violence at the other end. These attacks fall into a rough order, from those involving the least face confrontation, to those in which dominating the intersubjective encounter becomes the main object of the attack.

At the low end, the most shying away from confrontation occurs in purse-snatching, especially if it is carried out by driving by on a vehicle such as a motorbike. Not much more confrontation exists in rolling drunks or drugged-out persons; here the "jack-roller" (to use an early twentieth-century term, classically documented by Shaw 1930/1966) picks targets who are completely intoxicated and preferably unconscious, not drunks who are in the phase of energetically staggering around. The attacker thereby avoids not only physical retaliation, but any communicative interaction with another conscious human being. A slightly higher level of mugging is "yoking," grabbing a victim from behind, pinning their arms and thus simultaneously immobilizing them, catching them by surprise by coming up out of their field of vision, and avoiding having to look them in the face. One might argue that this is in order to avoid being recognized, but there is also an avoidance of confrontational tension/fear; as we have seen in the case of close military combat, and in execution-killings, seeing the victim's eyes is a deterrent to attack.[8]

Muggers are typically young; the majority are under twenty-one, and the most confrontation-avoiding versions are carried out by the youngest (often in their early teens) (Pratt 1980; Shaw 1930/1966). There is a career hierarchy as young muggers work their way up to more face-confronting styles. Typically mugging is carried out in groups of two, but in about 20 percent of cases (in Britain and the United States) it occurs in groups of four or more. When there is more than one victim (i.e., a little group is the target), the muggers are always a bigger number. In one case, at 10:30 on a Sunday night near the dormitory area of an urban university, six teenage boys attacked two college boys, but then ran away when confronted by one plain-clothes security guard, who chased them (*Daily Pennsylvanian*, Feb. 2, 2004). The passive or frightened posture of the student victims made them vulnerable, but the aggressive stance of the security guard quickly turned the momentum of fear in the other direction.

Interviews with muggers show that their chief concern is with selecting a weak victim, and with managing their own fear (Lejeune 1977; Lejeune and Alex 1973). In the preconfrontation stage, muggers reassure themselves by thinking of past successful muggings that they have carried out; they also derive a feeling of bravado from bragging and blustering in the presence of a group of peers—in effect, carrying over the emotional effervescence of their support group into their own energy to offset fear as they strike out as a small "crew." In the phase of actual confrontation, the mugger manages fear by choosing weak victims, especially those of the respectable, well-mannered higher classes, whom he expects to offer no resistance.[9] When all goes well, the mugger enjoys a feeling of power, as well as whatever money or goods are taken; often he further justifies himself by describing his attack as retribution for past injustices of race or class (Lejeune 1977; Jankowski 1991).

Holdups—that is, using a weapon—involve a higher degree of confrontation (Katz 1988: 169–94; Luckenbill 1981). For one thing, the victim must be made to see the weapon, and to acknowledge that he or she knows it is there and that there is expectation of its being used if compliance is not forthcoming; so it is intrinsically a more interactive communicative situation. Armed robbers nevertheless attempt to multiply their advantages, not trusting merely in their superior armament. Street robbers prefer to pick victims who are elderly, physically unimposing, or smaller and weaker than themselves. An armed robber (as well as a very aggressive unarmed mugger) plays up his threatening appearance by posture, show of muscles, and may further dramatize himself by style of dress. His aim is to shock the victim and thereby gain situational dominance.

Robbers load the dice still further by seeking out moments of contextual weakness. Stickups on the street occur chiefly at late night, between 10 p.m. and 5 a.m. (Katz 1988: 170; Pratt 1980), in part because this is when intoxicated carousers are out, but also because streets are largely deserted and an isolated victim or small group can be most easily found. Again, the utilitarian aspect—lack of witnesses—may be less important than the feeling the robber has of operating on his own territory—in this case, a time territory; he owns the late night, and victims often feel uneasy about being out in this alien time-terrain. Conversely, daylight street stickups in the presence of lively foot-traffic are rare in part because the atmosphere is a different one; passersby feel more at ease and appear less like weak victims, and the confrontational tension/fear of the robber is heightened because he is out of his element. On the other hand, robbers who hold up offices such as banks and commercial targets such as jewelry stores like to pick hours when there are few customers around (and thus avoid robbing during the noon hour) (Morrison and O'Donnell 1994).

Stickup artists employ still further tactics to get the jump on a victim. They may play the "Murphy game" (a recognizable technique that has its own name in American criminal tradition), in which the victim is some- one who is venturing into the realm of illegal activities, such as seeking prostitutes or buying drugs (Katz 1988: 170). Thus he is less likely to call on the police for aid; moreover, he is caught in a situational disadvantage: he is taking a stance of furtiveness in the first place, putting some degree of trust in the underground characters he deals with and putting himself in a position of dependence on them; they can threaten to denounce him, and at the same time lead him on in the name of deceptive moves that they must make together to avoid detection.[10]

Another ploy, used in the opposite circumstances where the victim is seemingly accorded higher social status, is to play on his or her altruistic accessibility (Katz 1988: 174). An ostensibly and indeed ostentatiously poor person and/or discriminated minority initiates contact with a stranger and asks for money, or perhaps only for directions or conversa- tion; the situational aggressor refuses to relinquish contact, thereby lur- ing him/her into a scene where they are isolated as well as passive, having ceded up the interactional initiative to the other. Once in this situation, armed robbery may follow; sometimes no weapon is used or even bran- dished if the victim is sufficiently entrained in the situation and gives in to persistent importuning for more and more money. The middle-class white person may well feel a sense of danger and of being led against his or her will, but the situational momentum is against them, because they are conscious of the implied charge of class snobbery or racism that they face if they do not treat the situation in the most favorable light; they are forced into keeping up a frontstage performance of polite nor- malcy although any degree of sophistication would indicate it is far from being such.[11]

Figure 5.3 Situational dominance in a street confrontation (New York, 1997). Credit: Ovie Carter.

Getting the jump on a victim is often a matter of fine interactional timing. The robber springs a gun on a store-owner just at the moment when he is not expecting it, such as when he is closing up the store. Again, this is not merely a utilitarian consideration (he has more cash at that time), because the timing can be very refined indeed: the robber chooses just the moment when the owner is turned around to lock his door, or stepping outside before he has had a chance to scan the field of vision,[12] or otherwise in a transitional moment between one scene and another.

Getting the jump on a victim is taking a micro-situational advantage, establishing the rhythm in favor of the robber and taking it out of the hands of the victim; and this happens over and above the brandishing of a weapon, and may even take its place (the weapon being only implied). Getting the jump means getting control of the emotional momentum, taking the initiative, in such a way that the entire situation flows in favor of the aggressor and puts the victim in a feeling of going along with the inevitable.

The robber is on the lookout for signs of fear in a victim, and acts to take advantage of these. He battens on fear, and on all those emotional dynamics that are similar to it. Sometimes this can even result in turning the tables against the police:

> My friend and I were punching the safe when a real young cop came in with his gun drawn and said, "You're under arrest; put your hands up." The first thing I thought was here is ten years and I don't want to do any more fucking time. I decided then that I wasn't going to give myself up. The cop walked up closer to us and I thought about getting his gun away from him, but I wondered where his partner was. He looked nervous, scared. I thought in the back of my mind that he would not use the gun, but I didn't care either. Then I figured he didn't have any partner and thought about hitting him. I had to get out of the situation. When he got right up to us, I hit him with the hammer [and in fact killed him]. (Athens 1980: 24)

Here the contrast between the experienced ex-con and the nervous rookie cop leads to a switch in situational dominance; the robber strikes just after he interprets the cop's fear as due in part to his being alone—whereas there are two robbers, who thus generate greater solidarity in the social situation.

The following case is a rape that momentarily disguises itself as a robbery, to throw the woman off guard. A young black man has gone to a white middle-class urban neighborhood looking for a target:

> I got a good look at this middle-aged white broad walking around some apartments, and I said to myself, "I'm going to get that pussy and enjoy it."
> I followed her up to the entrance of an apartment building. She used a key to get into the main door, and I had to get to it fast before it shut. I barely got to the door in time, but I waited a few seconds before I walked in since I didn't want her to see me. When I went in, I heard her going up the stairs and I followed her. As soon as I got to the top of the stairs, I spotted her walking down the hallway, and I crept up

behind her. When she opened the door to her apartment, I put my hands over her mouth, pushed her through the door and said, "Don't make a sound." Then I shut the door behind me and said, "If you make one fucking sound, I'll kill your ass."

I didn't want her to panic too soon, so I threw her off base and said, "Do you have any money?" She said, "All I have is the $10 in my church envelope." I said, "Well, give it here." She took the envelope out of her purse and handed it to me. Then I said, "Take your coat off." I took a long look at her and thought, "I'm going to drive this broad all night long."

I grabbed her by the shoulders and threw her on the floor. She started yelling. "What are you doing, what are you doing?" I figured that I better let her know that I meant business, so I jumped right on her ass and started smashing her in the face and saying, "Shut up, shut up." As soon as she did, I stopped hitting her. Then I pulled her dress up above her waist and reached for her meat, and she started screaming "Stop, stop, stop" and stomped the floor with her feet. I just thought, "I have got to shut her ass up fast before somebody hears her," and then I really cut loose on her with lefts and rights and said, "Shut up, shut up, before I beat you to death." Finally she shut the fuck up, and I pulled her dress back up, tore her panties off her legs and. . . ." (Athens 1980: 23–24)

The rapist aims for stealth and surprise. It did not seem necessary for him first to ask the victim for money, since he was going to beat her up sooner or later to make her submit and be quiet, but he regarded this as a way to "throw her off base" and gain a bit more advantage before she was aware a rape was going to commence.

The technique of violent predators is a miniaturized, micro-situational version of an army's tactics. A military unit usually wins an engagement not by smashing against the enemy's strongest forces, but by finding a local advantage, a place where the enemy has fewer forces concentrated; or by hitting a spot where the enemy easily becomes disorganized because it is caught by surprise, or in the midst of some other activity where it is not prepared to fight. Holdup tactics are the same, except that instead of making an organization lose coherence and initiative, the holdup artist makes an individual body lose its ability to act on its own terms.

The armed robber aims to acquire dominance by means of threat, but the threat may escalate to violence and murder if there is resistance from the victim. This brings the dominance contest to the fore; as Katz argues, the robber who is committed to his identity as a "hard man" or "badass" is now playing for the largest stakes in his personal universe. After killing a resisting victim, he may not even take all his or her money (Katz 1988:

186–87). The same goes for unarmed muggers who are physically much stronger than their victims, and use display of muscular power as their chief tool of domination; if there is resistance, he cannot back down since his fundamental skill is in question. Such a mugger at times provokes the victim in order to justify inflicting injury, since he can then blame the victim for the violence (Lejeune 1977). Such cases imply that the confrontational robber is proud of his skill, his technique for dominance, and gets pleasure from exercising it to the hilt.

It is instructive to compare episodes where resistance is successful, or does not result in escalation to serious injury. In this account, a man needs money to buy drugs, and considers various places to rob:

> Finally a cleaner's flashed in my mind. I figured that it would be the best hit since there would be enough money and only old ladies worked there. I put on my sunglasses, grabbed my .45, took off the safety clip, and headed for the cleaner's. I walked in the place, pulled out my pistol, and pointed it at the old lady behind the counter. I said, "This is a hold-up, I don't want to shoot you, so give me all the money out of that cash register fast." She walked over to the cash register, but then just stopped and said, "I'm not going to give you this money" and stepped on a button on the floor.
>
> I told myself I was going to get that money. I leaned over the counter and put the barrel of the pistol in her face and said, "Lady, now I'm going to kill you." But just as I was going to pull the trigger, she opened the cash register drawer and said, "You can get the money yourself." I then told her to get away from the cash register, and she did. After I grabbed all the paper money, she smiled and said, "I guess I don't know much about you youngsters these days." I looked at her for a moment and thought that she was just a nice old batty grandmother. Then I split fast." (Athens 1980: 33)

In effect, the old woman tests the robber by bluntly refusing him; when he raises the threat level, she makes a compromise move: verbally she sticks to her guns, she does not give him the money, but tells him to take it himself. Her next comment, "I guess I don't know much about you youngsters these days," conveys that she is aware they were testing each other. They even leave on a mildly solidaristic note, having figured this out about each other, with her smile and his attribution that she is like a grandmother.

The last instance is another rapist, in the parking lot of a shopping center while people are doing their Christmas shopping:

> I wanted to find a broad with a nice full ass walking alone to her car. I figured that I'd jump into her car with her and then make her drive out

to a deserted area nearby that I knew about. I was watching people going to their cars when I spotted this broad with a nice face and big hips and a fat round ass walking by herself. She looked like an easy rip-off, so I started following her and snuck up right behind her. When she stuck her keys in the car door, I grabbed her by the arm, flashed my knife in her face and said, "Get into your car and don't make any noise." She just stood there like she was in a complete daze. So I let go of her arm and grabbed her car keys and opened the car door myself. I told her to get in because we were going for a ride, but she just started screaming her ass off. First I decided to force her into the car, and I grabbed onto her again, but she kept on screaming and started getting away from me. I figured that other people were probably seeing by now what was happening, so I thought I had better get the hell out of there fast before I got busted. Then I booked it, and she ran off toward the stores screaming." (Athens 1980: 35–36)

The crucial moment is the woman's initial reaction, which is to be completely stunned, "in a complete daze." As yet she is neither resisting nor complying; since the rapist needs to get her to drive away with him, her opting out of the situation, by total psychological withdrawal if only momentarily, makes him lose the initiative. Then she takes control of the situation, no doubt without much calculation, when her daze gives way to uncontrollable screaming; unlike the other women victims in the cases we reviewed earlier, she does not make any articulate statements, but merely shrieks continuously; she seems entrained in her own screaming, and thus impervious to perceiving any threats. The rapist has not dominated the intersubjectivity of the situation; and is psychologically forced to retreat.

A number of holdups do not come off, because the victim resists. There are indications that in about half the cases where the robber encounters physical resistance, or just determined rejection of the robbery frame, the robber abandons the effort (Luckenbill 1981). But chances of injuries go up: in a Chicago study of robberies with guns, 78 percent of resisting victims were injured, compared to 7 percent of those who did not resist (Block 1977). There are other reasons why robberies abort, especially inside offices that have security glass or high counters, where clerks can retreat or duck out of sight (Morrison and O'Donnell 1994). These "hardened targets," however, are not invariably safe from robbery; it all depends on what transpires in the brief moments when the robber attempts to establish emotional dominance over the situation.

One might think that a gun used against an unarmed person would provide overwhelming threat. Nevertheless, robbers who have guns do not always use them, or shoot effectively; and the gun may be chiefly a matter of threat, even of pretense or bluff. This comes out particularly clearly in a study by Morrison and O'Donnell (1994) of some eleven thousand armed robberies in London, along with interviews with two hundred imprisoned robbers. Guns were not often fired; this happened in only 4 percent of the robberies. Moreover, of the forty-five occasions where shots were fired, in a third of the cases bullets were fired into the ground or the air or ceiling, usually at the beginning of the robbery when there was some hesitance about complying with the robber's demands. In thirteen (i.e., a little less than 30 percent) of these cases, shots were fired at the victims or at guards or bystanders, but only five persons were actually hit by bullets—an accuracy rate of 38 percent. All this is rather comparable to military performance, as we recall from chapter 2 (and, indeed, police performance; cops and robbers are on a pretty even basis).

This is not to say that robbery victims do not get injured with at least moderate frequency: in the English data, about 7 percent of armed robbery victims were hurt; but of these incidents, the vast majority—94 percent—were caused by something other than gun-shots. Most common was the use of the firearm as a bludgeon—pistol whipping or beating with the butt of a sawed-off shotgun (28 percent). Almost as many injuries (24 percent) came from kicking or punching. Another common source of injuries was use of some other weapon, such as a bat, hammer, or knife; many of those who carried guns also carried these other weapons. Considering that all the robbers in the sample carried guns (or as we shall shortly see, presented themselves as carrying guns), it is notable that the guns were not much used for shooting, or even seriously threatening to shoot; they were used to present a definition of the situation—this is a stickup, this is a gun. There is a quality of symbolic violence about forcing someone to submit to a gun, by shoving the gun at them, even hitting them with it, but not firing it. Similarly, in Luckenbill's (1981) data, 22 percent of the time the armed robbery began by hitting the victim, causing injury as a mode of intimidation: violence as a way of seizing the definition of the situation.

Moreover, in the London robberies, the chances of injury went up the more robbers were involved. A single robber acting alone rarely produced an injury, but this went up to 25 percent when there was a gang of three or more robbing a security van (armored car carrying cash), and to 50 percent for gangs of four or more robbing jewelry stores. A similar pattern was found in Australian data (Kapardis 1988): the bigger the team of robbers, the more chance for injuries. (And as we have seen in chapter 3, the same is true for the number of cops.) This is very much like the audience effect that we will see in chapter 6: bigger fighting groups create their own emotional zone, pump each other up with enthusiasm, and produce more serious violence than one-on-one fights.

A notable feature of the London study is that robbers could be divided into three groups: those who carried real guns; those who carried replicas—fake guns that could not be fired, although they looked like guns; and those who bluffed by indicating an object in a bag or pocket that they said (or stated in a note) was a gun. Real gun-carrying robbers, as we have seen, did not shoot their guns very much, and rarely hit anyone with a bullet. But interviews showed they were strongly attached to their guns, regarding them as a sign of their seriousness. Gun-carrying robbers were by far the most professional and dedicated of the armed robbers; they identified themselves with criminal careers, and expected to continue after they got out of prison. They did considerable advance planning for their robberies, carefully choosing and observing targets, wore disguises and developed elaborate escape plans. These robbers almost always worked in groups (82 percent)—by contrast, 46 percent of the fake-gun robbers had accomplices, and only 16 percent of the bluffers did. This meant, in part, that gun-carrying robbers were more ensconced in criminal networks; it also meant that they had more social support in their identities as robbers. And this social support, this group emotional atmosphere, carried over to the robbery itself; thus they were most likely to be pumped up by the situation, ready to establish domination. Hence the greater likelihood of violence: tough guys performing before an audience of other tough guys. The guns they carried are chiefly to be regarded as marks of group identity; not that they have no other uses, but their major effect is upon the confidence and aggressiveness of their carriers.

Robbers who used fake guns were less serious in their criminal identities; some indeed expressed the point that the inauthenticity of their gun made the episode only a play: "I'm only a small time thief—I'm not a gangster. . . . For me, the seriousness was taken out of it because the gun was not real." Another said, "I would play a part for that 20 minutes. . . . assume an identity not my own." And another, "Once you are in there, you turn into a robot. You know what you have to do and you just do it" (Morrison and O'Donnell 1994: 72–73). These fake-gun robbers also expected to make less money out of each robbery, and had lower confidence in their success—many expected to be caught before long, unlike the gun-carrying professionals. Just as the gun-carriers appeared to get confidence, or emotional energy, from their guns and all that went with them, the pretenders were not much energized by the weapons that they knew were not real. They must have hoped their Goffmanian show would be real for the audience of robbery victims—and indeed much of the time it was—but it was not real for the performers. Thus, unlike the professionals, they rarely described any emotional enjoyment in robbing; half of them said they felt bodily sick or faint. One stated, "I think I was more frightened than the girl behind the counter." Another, "I avoided eye contact because I was embarrassed about what I was doing" (Morrison and O'Donnell 1994: 73).[13]

Still further out on the continuum were the bluffers. These were individuals in a criminal career mode as well, insofar as they had a long series of previous arrests (although usually not for robbery); but they were at the loose ends of the criminal world, unattached individuals, with little skills or connections. Their robberies were usually decided on the spur of the moment, when feeling an urgent need for money for gambling or drugs; they did little advance planning, tended not to wear disguises or to have an escape plan. Bluffers overwhelmingly (95 percent) regarded themselves as failures in their criminal careers. "I'm not a very good thief and I've got nothing to show for it. I'm in a mess" (Morrison and O'Donnell 1994: 77). They usually picked the easiest targets, especially building societies (savings and loan offices), where the clerks were women and easy to intimidate.

Bluffers further reduced the confrontational aspects of robbery by making their demands by a written note (two-thirds used notes, compared to one-tenth of other robbers). Robbers were not very confident about this: "I didn't expect it to work. I thought the cashier would laugh and I would have to leave with nothing" (Morrison and O'Donnell 1994: 78). In fact, they may have used the note because their emotional energy was so low that they didn't trust their voice to make a convincing statement; even their verbal intimidation was a fake. Robbers who carried real guns, on the other hand, always displayed them. If the gun is not so much a utilitarian threat as a symbol of seriousness, both for the victim and even more for the robber, displaying the gun is the crucial ritual act; it is this above all else that gives robbers their emotional energy. Lacking this, the robber does not feel real: "I view it as very petty and no big deal—not a lot different from snatching a purse" (Morrison and O'Donnell 1994: 78).

The crux of being an armed robber is skill at interactional techniques for establishing situational domination. Individuals who continue crime move up through a career hierarchy, from the relatively low-confrontational forms of mugging to high-confrontational forms; this is not merely a career progression toward robbing larger amounts of money, since this may not be true (especially in relation to the money needs of young teenagers vis-à-vis adults). It is a progression in sophistication in how to manage attacks on the weak, indeed how to produce weakness by playing on the rhythms of normal social interaction and making the other person's confrontational tension/fear work to one's own advantage.[14] It should not be surprising that individuals who have developed these skills are proud of them, and regard them as important for their own sake.

Katz (1988: 195–236) points out that persisting in stickups is not in itself a very rational choice, if one is concerned only with material ends. Not only do career armed robbers tend to get caught or killed eventually, but even if they sometimes rob fairly large amounts of money, they usually dissipate it quickly in an ostentatiously hedonistic lifestyle. Katz interprets this as a commitment to being in the "action" scene, the world of gambling, drugs, commercial sex, and of bragging and showing off one's criminal exploits; carrying on robberies is itself as much a part of the "action" as spending the money. There is also an element of gaming in the techniques of confronting victims: getting the jump on them, using techniques of conning them before springing the stickup on them; it is a pleasure in controlling situational realities, the ability to make other people believe that one thing is happening, then shocking them into recognizing that they have been misled and now they will pay yet another price, in situational humiliation.

It can be a dangerous game; in part because there is always the chance someone will fight back, and the robber will have to escalate; there is also the chance that he will not be able to dominate, that his technique will fail—an even more serious psychological challenge. In the background, no doubt, there is also the confrontational tension/fear of all violence-threatening situations; the mature armed robber is at some distance from the fear-management techniques of the young mugger, but there is fear in the faces of robbers in the photos available from closed-circuit video cameras in banks, at ATMs, and other places.

The technique of the mature robber incorporates all this; he has learned how to take the tension of the situation, including his own fears, and turn it into an additional element of excitement. This is analogous to the way in which some persons increase their sexual thrills by carrying out erotic encounters in situations where they risk being caught by observers.[15] It is the same attraction Katz (1988) describes for girls and young women shoplifting; it is playing with the Goffmanian presentational practices of normal everyday life, and the dangers of getting caught if one fails to manipulate them properly, that is the emotional payoff. In comparison to this, the material gains are of little weight.

The interaction ritual mechanism that shapes everyday encounters is an emotion transformer; it takes initiating emotions, and, where conditions for mutual cognitive focus and interbodily entrainment are present, intensifies them and transforms them into emotional energy. The robber's technique is that he has learned how to work a special kind of one-sided dominance ritual in which he gets to make others fearful, weak, and passive, while he gets the emotional energy. Courting danger and dealing with his own fears is just an additional way of raising the voltage, adding another emotional tension to the mix that will become transformed into a still higher level of emotional energy. If indeed, as I have argued, humans seek out the highest source of emotional energy in their interactional opportunities, the armed robber has found a source for very intense EE spikes. He has learned how to get himself emotionally high on an extreme kind of situational dominance. An English armed robber summed up his robberies: "I really enjoyed them—it was better than drugs—a real buzz" (Morrison and O'Donnell 1994: 55). It is a technique in the same sense that Howard Becker (1953) described as the crucial step in becoming a marijuana user. At the top of the career hierarchy of confrontational criminals, the armed robber is an addict of situational dominance, a prisoner of his own interactional skill.

BATTENING ON INTERACTIONAL WEAKNESS

Domestic abuse, bullying, mugging, and holdups do not just come naturally. They are not merely frustrated reactions to stress, deprivation, or having been a prior recipient of such violence in the past. They are techniques that individuals have learned; better put, they are interactional styles that have been negotiated over a chain of encounters. This is easiest to do if the encounters are always with the same persons, so that both sides can learn their parts; that is why abuse is most common in families, where there is intimate familiarity allowing for all sorts of mutual adjustments (positive ones as well, one hopes); and why bullying is the specific form of attacking the weak that occurs in total institutions with their inescapability and their rigid status systems. Mugging and robbing are the most difficult, because they are practiced on a changing cast of victims, and the techniques of being successful at these involve forcing the individual into the victim role very swiftly without prior rehearsal; even here there is a truncated history, as the attacker may spend a few seconds in setting up the victim before he or she is propelled through the trap-door into full-scale victimhood (as in the case of the rapist who pretends at first to be only after the woman's money). This is a reason why muggers are rarer than abusers and bullies, and armed robbers are the rarest of all.

There is a constant rank ordering in frequency of crime victimization (the following figures come from 1972 to 2000, Bureau of Justice Statistics; www.ojp.usdoj.gov/bjs, updated August 2003):

burglary: ranges from peak of about 110 per 1,000 population over age 12, down to low of 35 per 1,000.

simple assault: (without weapons and with no or minor injuries): peak 30 per 1,000, low 15 per 1,000.

aggravated assault: (with weapons whether or not injury, or without weapons but with serious injury): peak 12 per 1,000, low 6 per 1,000.

robbery: peak 8 per 1,000, low 2 per 1,000. [The category "robbery" here includes both muggings and armed robberies, since it does not distinguish whether weapons were used and whether there was a face confrontation.]

homicide: peak 10 per 100,000, low 5 per 100,000 [i.e., peak .001 per 1,000, low .0005 per 1,000].

What we see is that the crime that involves no social presence at all—burglary (similarly auto theft, apart from carjacking)—is by far the most frequent; confrontational violence is rarer the more force is used, with homicides the most exceptional of all.

Victimization rates for domestic abuse and for bullying are much higher than all but the most anonymous property crime:

severe abuse occurs among 2–4 percent (i.e., 20–40 per 1,000) of children (Straus and Gelles 1986).

serious bullying is inflicted upon 5–6 percent of pupils in British boarding schools (Duffell 2000: 186), and 5–9 percent in public middle schools (Olweus 1993)—50–90 per 1,000; American estimates range up to 15 percent (Nansel et al. 2001)—150 per 1,000, with outliers at 25 percent or even 50 percent, although using very loose definitions of bullying.

Severe partner violence occurs at a rate of about 6 percent of domestic couples per year—60 per 1,000.

Common couple violence at about 16 percent (Straus and Gelles 1986; Kimmel 2002)—160 per 1,000; this figure is at a level well above even the most common forms of unviolent crime.

Elder abuse has been estimated at 10 percent for those living with family members (Lau and Kosberg 1979).

Highest of all, 50 percent of teenagers are *physically coerced by parents*;

80 percent of children *attack their siblings*;

physical punishment is inflicted on 85–95 percent of small children by parents (Dietz 2000; Gelles 1977; Straus and Donnelly 1994).

For those who need help with the arithmetic, these numbers translate into 500 per 1,000, 800 per 1,000, and 850–950 per 1,000—a long way from the armed robbery rate of 2–8 per 1,000.

It also follows that whatever genetic or physiological factors may exist that predispose particular individuals toward violent crime, such an individual cannot become a successful mugger, robber, or indeed even a bully or abuser, without going through a career of learning interactional techniques. This has not been studied in much detail; but it would be useful to know what would happen when a person with a very short fuse—a genetic predisposition to react angrily by striking out at others—carries this out for the first time. Does he (assuming males for the moment) become a successful bully? He would also have to learn how to find bullying-victims; he will not find them among the sociable-leader type of children in Montagner's playroom; and without some sociable skills of his own, he will not make it into the middle of the playroom status hierarchy where bullies are located, but become an isolate, and thus unable to join in any collective forms of attacking others. He might grow up to become a lonely serial killer, but not most of the other kinds of violent practitioner—and in fact he would be unable to handle the clandestine tactics and normal cover that characterizes most serial killers (Hickey 2002). Again, if his short fuse is not supplemented by other sociable techniques, he is not likely to find sexual partners and to get into a domestic situation; a woman that he does find may be quickly repelled by the violence, in the absence of the more subtle or insidious techniques by which an abusive interaction simultaneously trains an ongoingly available victim. And since mugging is usually learned in small teams, and the more difficult forms of confrontational robbery come after apprenticeship in the easier forms, this individual with the hypothetical genetic short fuse would likely not become much of a criminal predator either.

Perhaps (some researchers think undoubtedly) there are such individuals out there in the population; if so, they have been walking around with their genetic short fuses for many years, and have committed some proportion of the violence on which we have records. But what we know of such violent actions—as best we have been able to get up close to them, beyond the merely statistical reports, and to look at the situational processes—is that they are committed in social patterns, not by isolated individuals with short fuses; however short their fuses, it is in social situations and relationships of the kind we have been describing that they manifest themselves. It also follows that they must fit into the prevailing pattern of confrontational tension/fear, cowardice, and incompetence in violence, and hence in choosing weak victims to attack, if they are going to successfully attack anyone. Bodies with genetic short fuses (however many there may be) are not merely walking time-bombs; they have to learn interactional techniques just like everyone else. Paradoxically, if their fuses are too short, they may never learn enough of the techniques to be successful at violence. It might mean that those who are much more normal may be better at learning those techniques.

Those who successfully attack the weak—domestic abusers, bullies, violent robbers—have learned that weakness is not merely a physical condition. It is not simply a matter of some persons being smaller or less muscular than others. Victims are generally weak in a social sense: ongoingly, as low-status persons, social isolates, those who have swallowed their humiliation and adapted themselves to their tormenters, or who fight against them in ineffective ways that provoke without deterring. In particular situations of confrontation, they are situationally weak; someone else has gotten the jump on them, manipulated their sense of reality, taken away their initiative, subjected them to an emotional entrainment from outside.

The common denominator running through all these patterns and occasions of victimhood is loss of emotional energy. Ongoing conditions put them in the stratum of those who have little EE, and are obvious targets for those who get most of their EE from violence or its threat and are seeking for easy victims on which to batten. In immediate situations, too, a victim is someone who suffers a sudden loss of EE; perhaps there may be no long-term pattern, but just being in the wrong place at the wrong time, where someone who has learned the techniques of getting the situational jump puts their skill into practice. Either way, victimizers batten on fear; they batten on those low in EE. Something like the vampires of mythology, the blood of their victims is what sustains them; but it is not because they are healthy living creatures that the vampire gets the blood he needs to stay alive; it is because they are socially weak that he gets into their veins. The metaphor is both gruesome and inexact. It is an interactional symbiosis; the specialist in violence has found a niche where he can batten on interactional weakness.

PART TWO

Cleaned-up and Staged Violence

CHAPTER 6

Staging Fair Fights

Word was going around the high school Friday afternoon there would be a fight. At a nearby park, 3 o'clock: two well-known seniors, Dawson and Rashad, would find out who was the bigger man. A crowd of one hundred was gathered fifteen minutes early, eager with anticipation. After five minutes, Dawson appeared. He paced about rhythmically; the crowd could not stand still. An observer reported his own hands were shaking as he realized he was about to see a *real* fight.

Then Rashad appeared at the far end of the park, flanked by two followers, moving quickly. Rashad appeared calmer than Dawson, not angry but purposeful and determined. Dawson was jumping around with excitement. Rashad never changed his brisk pace, never took his eyes off his target as he marched into the horseshoe ring of spectators. When their eyes met, the observer sensed a glimmer of fear in Dawson, and he seemed to freeze. Rashad walked straight up to him and without opposition landed a punch to his jaw.

The crowd, hushed until now, erupted; mostly all younger and smaller than the two fighters, they shoved to get close to the action. Some were silent, some shrieked, all were wide-eyed. Rashad landed one punch after another as Dawson staggered backward. He went down on his back and Rashad straddled him, punching him in the face in a steady rhythm. The crowd formed a tight circle around them, their heads bobbing with the action; the observer described himself and others as in a trance.

Finally someone from outside the circle broke in and tore Rashad off. The crowd came out of its trance; some buried their faces in their hands, some threw up, a few were in tears. Dawson was lying bloody and disfigured. Eventually he stood up, and the two shook hands; Dawson patted Rashad on the back, conceding defeat (adapted from Phillips 2002).

Rashad seizes the emotional momentum in every respect. He makes the best entrance: last to arrive, while the others await him; his opponent comes alone, Rashad is flanked by his sidekicks, although the latter stay strictly out of the fight. He establishes a rhythm as he marches up from the distance, imposes it on his excited but jumpy opponent; from the moment their eyes meet, he has established dominance. His opponent never lands a blow, never even effectively wards one off. His entire glory, as it turns out, is just to be in the fight; in the aftermath, he is happy to acknowledge kinship with his conqueror—after all, he was the one who fought him. The crowd is entrained, first by one fighter, then by the other; at first, it is nervous and jumpy in anticipation with Dawson; then it is entranced by Rashad's rhythmic steps and blows.

The fight, though brutal, is regulated and restricted. Nothing but fists are used; there are no weapons, no kicking, gouging, or hair-pulling; all the blows are to the front of the upper body and face, face-forward to the attacker. The audience too is well-behaved, in the mood of the situation: no one makes a move to intervene (the observer later remarks on his post-fight feelings of guilt for this); the exception comes at the conclusion, when someone who is not in the inner circle of entranced spectators breaks up the fight; but this is accepted by all, since something was needed to bring the rhythmic pounding to an end. And the ending calls on conventional rituals of solidarity: animosity is gone; the fighters shake hands and indicate marks of respect in their now-confirmed status of victor and defeated.

Both are heroes; that is, they are status notables. Their fight has rearranged their ranking relative to each other, but also reaffirms that they are in the small elite in the center of public attention.

Of theoretical interest is how the micro-details of imposing rhythmic entrainment determines who wins. But here I want to concentrate on a more basic point: how this kind of procedure, a staged fair fight, overcomes normal confrontational tension/fear and allows violence to proceed.

Hero versus Hero

The original referent of "hero" is just such an individual who takes part in violent contests while submitting himself to social rules. These rules are explicitly agreed upon beforehand; sometimes they take the form of a test that the hero must pass, as in mythological stories of ordeals that the hero must undergo to win a treasure, marry a king's daughter, or found a kingdom. Such ordeals may be fanciful and romanticized distortions of real-life procedures. More to the purpose here is the fight of hero versus hero in single combat. Whatever the literary distortions, such fights undoubtedly happened, indeed, were the preferred form of violence in some historical periods.

Consider the following, from the *Iliad*, the oldest canonical work of literature of the European tradition (ca. 750 B.C.). The very first event of the first day of battle described in the poem, before anything else happens, is a duel. The Trojan prince, Paris, stands in front of the army of his city and its allies, and calls out the leaders of the Greeks to send someone to meet him in single combat. The one who answers him is Menelaos. This is appropriate, since the war was started by Paris abducting Helen, Menelaos's wife. Paris and Menelaos agree that whoever wins the duel, gets the woman and thereby settles the dispute; the war will be over and the two sides will swear to be friends. Not only they personally, but both armies swear the oath. The aged king of Troy, Priam, comes out and officiates at the ritual sacrifice, calling on the gods to enforce the oath. The ritual does not end here. Menelaos and Paris draw lots for who will have first turn to throw a spear at the other.

The duel commences. Paris gets the worst of it, and when he is in danger of being killed, he is spirited away by a goddess who takes the Trojan side. At every crucial point in the poem, a deity is depicted as intervening to advise a hero, or to protect or harm him. We could interpret this instance as running away from the duel; in any case the duel miscarries. The troops are still sitting down disarmed, in spectator mode, when one of the Trojans—egged on by the malevolent goddess—fires an arrow and wounds Menelaos. The narrator refers to him as a fool, presumably for violating the ritual truce; the deities often inspire irrational action, and so this could be interpreted as an emotional outburst by the losing side. Firing the arrow is regarded by the Greeks as violating the oath, and sets off full-scale battle.

The entire narrative of the *Iliad* is organized around single combats, which provide intermittent high points and build up to the climax of the drama. These alternate with battle descriptions, but the latter are neither strategic maneuvers nor clashes between organized bodies of troops; instead, in each episode a particular hero goes on a rampage and kills a large number of enemies. Those whom they kill are men of repute; Homer gives each one's name and genealogy, and for important cases, a history of his notable exploits. The winning hero is totting up his own reputational score by the significance of the secondary heroes he has killed.[1]

Thus: the first day of battle, the Greek hero Diomedes goes on a rampage through the Trojan army. Finally he is challenged by one of the chief Trojan heroes, Aineias; their single combat is not ritualized by formal oaths, but they go on at some length in shouting challenges to each other and exchanging several blows, until Aineias too is spirited away by a protective goddess. The victor exults in at least capturing Aineais's horses, since they are a famous possession and make a glorious trophy. Later in the same battle, Diomedes faces off in the mid-space between the armies with an impressive-looking Trojan hero, Glaukos; they ask each other's names and genealogies, and discover that they are "guest-friends by lineage," since their fathers had been host and visitor, exchanging ritual gifts.

So instead of fighting they make a pledge of friendship, clasp hands, and exchange valuable pieces of armor.

Finally, as the day of battle is nearing late afternoon, the gods are depicted as arranging a break for the armies: another single combat while the rest of the troops sit down and watch. Hector, the strongest Trojan hero, challenges the Greeks to send a champion against him; they agree that whoever wins will get the loser's armor, but the dead body will be given back for a decent funeral. The nine leading Greek heroes volunteer,[2] and one of them, Aias (Ajax) is chosen by lot.[3] This fight is meant to be inconclusive; unlike other fights, they exchange quite a few blows, without serious damage. As night falls, they break, separated by heralds from both sides who act as referees. Hector and Aias then give each other pieces of their clothing and weapons, as "famous gifts" to show they had fought and properly reconciled. The Greeks take this equal ending as a victory, since Hector is reputed the better fighter.

The second day of battle, the tide swings and Hector goes on a rampage through the Greek army. This is halted only when Achilles, sulking in the camp, allows his friend Patroklos to borrow his armor and join the battle. Achilles's reputation is such that this turns the tide again; Patroklos goes on a rampage through the Trojans. Finally Hector seeks him out, ignoring the rest of the battle; with the help of a god, he kills him. But this is not a fully ritualized single combat; they have made no prior agreement, and the battle now rages over Patroklos's body. Hector settles for taking Achilles' armor—which he henceforth will wear himself—and the Greeks finally recover the body.

The third and last day of battle—as far as the *Iliad* narrative is concerned—takes place as Achilles, having received new armor from the gods, returns to the fight and goes on a rampage killing Trojans. Hector knows he is overmatched, and runs away from Achilles; the respective armies draw back to watch as their chase circles the city walls. This is not a formal single combat, but Achilles forbids his allies from shooting at Hector and taking away his renown for the kill. Hector (bolstered by a god) turns to confront Achilles, and offers his usual agreement: victor gets the armor as spoils, but gives back the body for a funeral. Achilles, however, is angry at having lost his bosom friend, and refuses to make a covenant. Achilles kills Hector, and drags the body ignominiously behind his chariot back to camp. The action of the story is now over. But there is one more episode: old King Priam sorrowfully goes to the Greek camp and begs to ransom his son's body. Achilles is shamed and agrees to give the body up; and so the story ends: the great hero, the strongest fighter, has finally learned to follow the ritual proprieties.

Battles of this kind, which resolve into a series of single combats, are common in particular social formations. Celtic warriors at the time of the

Roman conquests of Europe would seek out an individual enemy; they kept records of their victories by displaying severed heads, hung from their belts. These were trophies and tokens of honor, similar to scalps or body parts taken by North American tribal warriors; for the latter, eating the heart or other organs of a famous enemy incorporated his power into the victor. The general pattern is to build one's reputation—and one's fighting confidence, or emotional ascendancy—by taking a commemorative emblem and publicizing it. In Homeric Greece, the heroes repeatedly display their single-combat trophies, exchange them as gifts, and attribute their origins—if they are especially renowned—to supernatural beings, in every respect treating them as sacred objects. In early medieval Europe, a similar reputational system is reflected in stories of magic swords that could be won only by the strongest and bravest hero, and of treasure hoards guarded by dragons and monsters that only a hero could kill. In early China, and again in periods of weak dynasties when irregular bandit-armies flourished, heroes are depicted as experts in single combat, who slaughter lesser persons with ease, and gain honor by facing off against other well-known fighters; sometimes their fights are resolved by adopting one another into a sworn brotherhood (Ross 1970; Finley 1973; Brondsted 1965; Shi and Luo 1988).

The social structure in which single combats among ritually exalted heroes occurs is one in which hierarchically disciplined military forces are absent. The Celtic warriors were explicitly undisciplined; a prestigious custom was to strip off their clothes and fight naked, impervious to the elements and displaying their contempt of bodily danger. A similar pattern of "berserkers" (named after the Norse version) is found widely in Bronze and Iron Age fighting from Mesopotamia to Scandinavia (Speidel 2002). That is to say, combat centering on emotionally charged individuals, putting themselves into a combat frenzy, exists in societies with loose military coalitions—that is, societies that have expanded beyond tribal networks, but without a firm state organization of kingship, aristocracy, or citizen armies (Searle 1988). Building up this emotional frenzy is a device for motivating combat performance, found in particular social conditions: these include the focus on individualized reputations—made possible by a small scale of warfare and by devices for broadcasting reputations on both sides of a conflict, like those we have seen among the Homeric Greeks.

Another condition is the absence of any other social organization of violence superior in dominating a battlefield. The single-combat style—whether in the extreme "berserker" variant or in a more courtly fashion—is ineffective against well-organized group force. Roman legions had little difficulty in defeating the Celts and similar warriors; simply by maintaining their massed ranks, they could shield themselves against any individual attack no matter how frenzied, and they could muster the superiority of numbers in cutting down isolated individuals. The Romans severely prohibited breaking ranks in combat; their emphasis was not on showing off individual courage and prowess, but on keeping up group discipline.[4]

The individual "hero," realistically, must have depended for success in considerable part upon terrifying an enemy—with sheer emotional force, with reputation. We see this in Homer—where Hector, known as the bravest and best of the Trojan fighters, nevertheless gives way against the reputation of Achilles;[5] and in the contemporary high school fight, where Rashad emotionally overbears Dawson from the first moment of visual contact. But where the enemy is organized to keep up its own source of emotional force, and where it is tactically concerned not with the honor of individual reputation but with applying unequal weight of effective numbers against the opponent's weakness—in such circumstances, the hero style loses its chief weapon, its emotional dominance. A man in the hero/berserker mode when confronting disciplined army organization, or modern police forces, is just a pathological individual, and a loser to boot; the same style of behavior in the situation where fighting is uncoordinated by hierarchical organization becomes heroic.

AUDIENCE SUPPORTS AND LIMITS ON VIOLENCE

The socially staged and limited character of a fight controls confrontational tension/fear, but not merely because participants are less worried about being hurt. In fact the rules may allow rather severe damage; only particular kinds of damage or tactics are ruled out. As I have argued throughout, the most important tension and fear comes not from concern for bodily pain; this is something that people endure surprisingly easily (perhaps because so often we have no choice about it, in the course of normal bodily ailments and accidents), and which a large proportion of people are able to steel themselves to face.

Agreed-upon limitations in a fair fight come about as a shared orientation, a tacit or even explicit communication between the fighters. Even when they are trying to smash one another into unconsciousness, or to kill one another, they are keeping up a level of solidarity in their mutual agreement. They are in effect constantly telling one another that they do not and will not engage in certain practices—for instance, in gouging eyes but only in pounding fists in the face. Every time they start at a given signal, and stop at a given breaking point, they are affirming that a thread of contact holds beneath all the action at cross-purposes. The fight, of course, breaks normal interactional entrainment; but a fair fight hedged round by rituals and limitations simultaneously imposes another level on which both sides are strongly entrained, strongly intersubjective. It is an overtly two-level interaction; the ritualism of the fair fight imposes an overriding level of solidarity within which the antagonism is contained and dropped to a second level of attention. It is this structure that overcomes tension/fear and allows the fight to proceed, indeed to proceed with enthusiasm.

The audience is crucial in a staged fight; it provides the support that circumvents confrontational tension/fear; and it helps enact the limits that give the fight its etiquette and make it a fair fight. The fighter's focus of awareness is on several things: on the opponent, of course, in the technical aspects of the fight, how to attack and defend against him. His focus is also on the audience, before which one must put on a good show; and hence it is also on both self and opponent together in the eyes of the audience; this adds yet another layer of mutual awareness between the fighters as to how they appear collectively, and therefore in some degree cooperatively, in the show they are putting on. The fighter's attention is shifted away from the tension/fear of confrontation and onto the social supports and pressures that encourage him to fight.

The audience cooperates or even takes the lead in the limitations of the fight: signaling the starting and stopping points, and monitoring the tactics that are agreed upon as fair. It may also take a considerable hand in the selection of who will fight, matching equals, strong versus strong instead of strong versus weak. Collective attention upon these limitations is another way in which tension/fear is overcome. The enactment of etiquette can also be a compulsion to fight. Once the machinery of dealing with an insult by a staged fight is set in motion—or closer to the event, once the audience is assembled ready for the fighting to begin—there can be overwhelming social pressure not to back out; the cost can range from ignominy to scornful attacks such as pelting the hesitant fighter, or worse. These social pressures have often been remarked, as if they are to blame for the fighting; the analytically more important point is that the audience also provides the social energy and solidarity to overcome tension/fear and make fighting possible at all. Willing fighters pump themselves on social support as much as they curb their unwillingness on the compulsion; it is one and the same pressure. A fight may start, of course, from an individual's grievance; but grievances easily get swallowed up in the dynamics of appearing before an audience (whether magnified or diminished). And grievances may be merely an excuse for taking a prominent position before an audience, as in present-day carousers looking for trouble. It is sometimes difficult to see which route is being followed, but in many respects it doesn't matter, if the audience is the crucial determinant.

A testable hypothesis: a focused audience lowers fighters' tension/fear and affects their willingness to fight at all, for how long and with what intensity. Small and unfocused groups in the surrounding situation should result in low willingness to fight. This may be a crucial factor in so-called honor confrontations; it is often difficult to tell, since news stories and police reports rarely give information about the size and attentiveness of an audience.[6] The fact that honor confrontations that escalate to violence disproportionately occur in entertainment venues and carousing situations (i.e., weekend evenings) implies that there are large numbers of people around, and that they are actively interested in witnessing fights. One might hypothesize that a fight is much less likely to happen in a near-empty bar on an off night of the week; or in a situation where the crowd is not paying attention.[7]

There is some illustrative evidence from my own observations and from the collection of student reports. One instance is a fight that does not come off: A girl waiting for a ride after school notices two teenage boys shouting at each other, but no crowd gathers around them. The other students are scattered, not assembled together but waiting for individual rides from parents, and they do not take on an active audience mode. After a few minutes, the boys themselves drift apart as if in boredom with the situation. A second case is from my own observations of the minor street altercation in Somerville, Massachusetts (described in chapter 2): the handful of spectators are distant, nearly invisible, and not very interested, and the fight soon winds down.

A third incident, which I observed in Philadelphia in January 2003, began when a white man in his twenties, riding a bicycle in the midst of evening rush-hour traffic, is lightly struck by a taxi as he weaves between the lines of cars. The man is not hurt, and his bike is not damaged (since he rides away on it at the end of the incident); but he is angry, apparently at being embarrassed by falling off his bike in front of traffic, perhaps also frightened. He berates the taxi driver, a black man of about the same size and age (apparently an African immigrant), who refuses to get out of his cab. The refusal to confront makes the bicyclist even angrier (and perhaps emboldens him). While carrying on his harangue, the man leaves the bicycle in front of the taxi, blocking it from moving; and he stands in the other lane of traffic, thereby blocking all other traffic on the one-way street. He thus accumulates an audience in the form of other drivers, who honk their horns angrily to get the traffic moving, although most of them are too far back to see what is happening. Half a dozen passersby (including myself), stand on the sidewalk at a safe distance and watch; we do not clump together or say anything to each other. The only attempt at intervening is by the driver of a delivery truck, parked just behind the taxi; he asks the bicyclist to take his bike to the sidewalk, but the latter ignores him, and the driver (a fairly big workman) shies away and does not pursue it. Finally the bicyclist resolves the incident by telling the taxi driver that he has his number and will report him to the police.

He moves his bike to the sidewalk, and traffic begins to move. However, only a few cars get past the stop light at the nearby corner before it turns red. The car that reaches the stop line is driven by a muscular American black man, who had been only a few cars back from the incident; he rolls down his window and yells angry curses at the bicyclist for holding up traffic. The bicyclist curses back, then picks up a heavy steel bicycle lock, and swinging it menacingly moves toward the man's car. The man opens his door and gets out. Then the light changes; something rapidly transpires— probably just that each slightly hesitated; the black man gets back in his car and drives away. The bicyclist gets on his bike and drives off, still in the middle of the street, defiantly weaving his way amidst slow-moving cars. The whole incident took four minutes. The confrontation is mostly bluster all the way around; it is consistent with the general principle that lack of a focused and supportive audience keeps a fight from escalating.

Yet another abortive fight with a similar interactional structure comes from Japan in 1864, even though the setting is a lawless one and the fighters are potentially deadly. A samurai (Fukuzawa 1981: 236–37) recounts walking home through the deserted streets of Edo (later Tokyo) between long rows of low wooden houses with their shutters all closed for the night:

The time had already turned an hour past midnight—a cold and clear winter night with the moon shining brightly overhead. Its silent, white beams made me feel unusually chilly for no good reason. I walked along the broad, vacant street—no one in sight, absolutely still. Yet I remembered that strolling ruffians had been appearing every night, cutting down unfortunate victims at dark corners. I tucked up the wide ends of my divided skirts in order to be ready to run at any signal and kept up a fast pace. . . .

I saw a man coming toward me. He looked gigantic in the moonlight, though now I would not swear to his stature at all. On came the giant. Nowadays there are policemen to depend upon, or we can run into someone's house for protection, but at that time no such help was to be expected. People would only bar their doors more heavily and would never think of coming out to assist a stranger calling for help.

"Now, here is a pretty pass," I thought. "I cannot run back, for the rascal would only take advantage of my weakness and chase me more surely. Perhaps I had better go ahead. And if I go ahead, I must pretend not to be afraid. I must even threaten him."

I moved out diagonally to the middle of the street from the left side where I had been walking. Then the other fellow moved out too. This gave me a shock, but now there was no retreating an inch. If he were to draw, I must draw too. As I had practiced the art of *iai*, I knew how to handle my sword.

"How shall I kill him? Well, I shall give a thrust from below."

I was perfectly determined that I was going to fight and felt ready if he showed the slightest challenge. He drew nearer. . . .

[N]ow there seemed no alternative. If the stranger were to show any offense, I must kill him. At that time there was no such thing as police or criminal court. If I were to kill an unknown man, I would simply run home, and that would be the end of it. We were about to meet.

Every step brought us nearer, and finally we were at a striking distance. He did not draw. Of course I did not draw either. And we passed each other. With this as a cue, I ran. I don't remember how fast I ran. After going a little distance, I turned to look back as I flew. The other man was running, too, in his direction. I drew a breath of relief and saw the funny side of the whole incident. . . . Neither had the least idea of killing the other, but had put up a show of boldness in fear of the other. And both ran at the same moment. . . . He must have been frightened; I certainly was."[8]

Conversely, the audience may be the central feature of the fight. Fox (1977) describes a repetitive pattern of fights in small communities of western Ireland. Disputes break out among men drinking at community dances. The assembled friends and relatives of each fighter support him by flocking around and making noise. But they also hold him back from serious bloodshed; most of the action consists in scuffles between each principal and his own handlers, in a loud bluster of "Let me at him, I'll kill him!" and efforts to restrain the fighters from carrying out their threats. The same antagonists who have loudly threatened to kill one another ignore each other when they encounter one another on following days when no audience is present. This is an extreme instance where, without the support and control of the crowds, the fighters are not able to carry on any combat at all.

The pattern is borne out by my collection of eighty-nine first-hand observations of violence-threatening confrontations, in which appropriate information is available (seventy-four are student reports, fifteen are my own observations). In seventeen cases where the crowd cheers and encourages the fight, fifteen give rise to serious fights (88 percent), and in eight of these, some of the crowd joins in the fight. In twelve cases where the crowd's expressions are mixed (mildly excited, part of crowd entertained, laughing, amused), one leads to a serious fight (8 percent), and eight result in prolonged but mild scuffles, blustering, or other extended but limited violence (67 percent); three have very brief fights (25 percent). In twenty-

TABLE 6.1
Seriousness of fight affected by audience behavior

	Violence				
	Serious fight	Prolonged/ mild	Mild/ stops	Aborts	Total
Audience					
Cheers	15 (88%)	2 (12%)			17
Mixed	1 (8%)	8 (67%)	3 (25%)		12
Neutral	9 (32%)	3 (11%)	10 (36%)	6 (21%)	28
Uneasy/fearful	1 (5%)	4 (19%)	4 (19%)	12 (57%)	21
Intervenes		1 (9%)	5 (45%)	5 (46%)	11
Total	26	18	22	23	89

one cases the crowd is silent, uneasy, embarrassed, tense, or afraid: here there is *one serious fight* (5 percent); four cases of prolonged but mild scuffles (19 percent); four brief and mild episodes of violence (e.g., one punch or slap) that end abruptly (19 percent); and in twelve cases the fight aborts (57 percent). In eleven cases the audience intervenes, mediates, or breaks up the fight: this leads to *one case of prolonged scuffling* (9 percent); five cases of brief, mild violence (45 percent); four cases where the fight aborts (46 percent). Overall, there are extremely strong parallels between the degree of encouragement or opposition by the audience, and the amount of violence that takes place.

I have saved for last the type of audience with the most variable outcomes. In twenty-eight cases the audience is neutral: that is, absent, distant, dispersed, invisible, not paying attention, or small in number compared to the belligerents. In nine of these (32 percent) there are serious fights; three prolonged scuffles or blustering quarrels (11 percent); ten mild and brief fights, stopping abruptly (36 percent); in six cases the fight aborts without any violence (21 percent). What makes the difference? Unquestionably it is the number of belligerents; of the nine serious fights, in *all but one case*, these are substantial groups (on the order of ten or fifteen on a side, with the smallest consisting of five vs. five): in two of the cases, there are demonstrators numbering in the hundreds. In almost all the other cases with neutral audiences and mild or abortive violence, the participants are few (mostly one-on-one, sometimes two or three on the defensive side; the only instance of bigger groups here is six-on-six).

TABLE 6.2
Seriousness of fight affected by size of belligerent groups (audience neutral)

	Violence				
	Serious fight	Prolonged/ mild	Mild/ stops	Aborts	Total
Size of belligerent groups					
1–3	1 (6%)	1 (6%)	10 (59%)	5 (29%)	17
5–100s	8 (73%)	2 (18%)		1 (9%)	11
Total	9	3	10	6	28

If the fight breaks out where belligerent groups are already large, these groups override any audience effects; in effect, these fighters bring along their own supportive audiences (since in fact only a proportion of the group takes a really active part in the fighting). This helps explain the few anomalies in the prior paragraphs, which I have *italicized*. In one case the audience is fearful, but a serious fight occurs nevertheless: this is a popular concert where two rival groups of skinheads invade the mosh pit from opposite sides, scattering the usual moshers; these are groups of twenty to thirty fighters, ignoring and frightening the crowd of several hundred fans. The audience does not matter when the fighting groups are large.

Thus in the total of eighty-nine cases, there are only two real anomalies. In one case (*italicized* earlier) audience intervention fails: this is the incident described in chapter 1, where two preadolescent boys scuffle in and around the car as their family attempts to leave for an outing. The other anomaly is among the cases where there is serious violence and a neutral audience, but the group is small instead of large: three young white men, cruising the deserted night-time streets of a small western town, flag down another car, and two of them beat up the driver, whom they accuse of being a drug informant to the police. Family violence does not depend on audience effects; nor apparently do ongoing personal vendettas.[9]

The audience not only influences whether a fight will be serious, mild, or abortive, but it also determines whether it is in the fair-fight mode. In establishing the point, I have begged the prior question: why does an audience take one stance or another? We are not yet in a position for an answer, but we will return to the point.

Social limits on fighting come in a package, including not only what fighters do to each other, but what the audience will and will not do to the fighters, and what the fighters can do to the audience. In a staged fair fight, the audience has in effect agreed not to intervene in the fight, at least not to any considerable extent; and the fighters do not attack the audience. There are degrees of intervention, but these are usually customary, and although their boundaries are not sharp they are self-policed by the group. Audiences normally intervene in a fair fight by cheering one side and jeering the other. As the heat of the fight builds up, the crowd may become more entrained in it, undergoing vicarious participation with one side and vilification of the other; and this may lead to violations of the limits. Just how these violations occur and are handled is revealing. Typically the worst violations occur at crucial moments of a fight; but even there the crowd is divided—a small minority of zealots may throw things at their favorite's opponent, but rarely enough to impede the action; and the majority of the crowd almost always wants the fight to proceed on its own terms.[10]

Proper etiquette is not always followed, of course, and agreed-upon limitations are sometimes transgressed. Looking at such instances is a good methodological tactic for a sociologist, for violations are always revealing of the mechanism that upholds normal conformity. Consider first the processes that are set in motion when audience/fighter boundaries are seriously violated. Small violations are dealt with by tolerance or by minor adjustments, as long as their remaining small conveys a sense that the perpetrators still have a limit: that is, they have moved the boundary, but they signal that there is still a boundary, or that the shift is only temporary. Large violations, however, are those that threaten the entire framing of the fight, and these bring a strong reaction.

An example from student report, regarding a 1997 event:

> The fight was between two high school girls, one Asian and one Latino, on the front lawn of the school. A crowd of 150 to 200 gathered to watch, with the male friends of each girl at the center of the circle cheering them on. Then a large black male from the surrounding neighborhood broke into the circle, and punched one of the Asian girl's friends, a small boy of about 5′ 4″ and 120 pounds, perhaps half the weight of his assailant.

> The fight between the girls immediately stopped and the crowd surged at the black man, pushing and punching him. He managed to break through the crowd and ran into the street, with the crowd following him. Five minutes later, several police cars pulled up, with the black man under arrest. The Asian boy was called to identify his assailant; the students crowded around to get a glimpse. There were cheers and shouts of self-congratulation: "yeah, that's him" "we got him"; fingers pointed at the captive, and a few students tried to push by the police

to throw a punch at him (no doubt feeling quite safe under the circumstances, since the officers held their ground, and soon drove off with the arrestee).

The audience tacitly agreed to stay out of the initial fight, as well as to help promote it; when the fight was interrupted by an outsider, a different mode of fighting came into operation: no longer a staged fair fight, but a moralistic group attack on the deviant outsider.[11]

A more complex example is the heavyweight prize fight between Mike Tyson and Evander Holyfield in 1997. Here, several kinds of limits are violated: the normal procedures of fair fighting between the fighters, and then the fighter/audience boundary. Tyson, who had the reputation of a thug, high in muscle and low in intelligence and sophistication, had once been considered invincible, but in recent years his career had gone downhill. Now he was losing a rematch to a fighter who had already beaten him once. During a clinch in round three, Tyson bit off a piece of Holyfield's ear. Holyfield was furious. The normal level of anger and aggression of a pumped-up prize fighter went through the roof. What did he do? He hopped around the ring, gesticulating with his raised arms, howling with anger. He did not close in on Tyson, escalating the violence into a frenzy of blows; he did not attempt to punish Tyson physically at all. He punished him in a much stronger sense: he refused to continue to fight him. He applied the ultimate sanction of a fair fight: he excluded the offender from membership. Holyfield, who had been winning the fight, gave off no sense of backing down from his opponent; he gestured toward him repeatedly, but with scorn, in high dudgeon, keeping his distance as if from someone polluted. The crowd and the officials were also indignant (*Los Angeles Times*, June 29–30, 1997; *San Diego Union Tribune*, June 29–30, 1997). The incident was instantaneously regarded as a scandal, the most serious of Tyson's scandal-ridden career (more serious, for instance, than conviction for rape).

Violation of the etiquette of fair fighting is not a matter of sheer damage done or pain inflicted. A perfectly fair fight could involve being hit in the face and eyes, resulting in blindness, brain damage, excruciatingly crushed cartilage and bone, even death. Beaten fighters take such punishment as a matter of normal risk. Having a piece of one's ear bitten off is probably a minor pain in comparison to some of these; but it is unexpected, out of bounds, a moral violation where the others are not. It is this that produces the outrage. Underneath it, the emotional dynamics may well be that confrontational tension/fear, so successfully banned even from very punishing violence by shared rituals, is now being allowed to creep back in. Thus the aftermath of the 1997 Tyson-Holyfield fight was also unusual: The crowd spilling out of the arena in a Las Vegas casino became hysterical; scuffles and rumors of gunfire (later found to be unsubstantiated) set off panicky rushes through the lobbies and gaming areas, turning over tables and hospitalizing forty persons with injuries. Police at one point drew guns and ordered people to the floor, then closed the casino and surrounding streets for several hours. The breakdown of normal order, for a time, was contagious.

The audience also sanctions a fighter who gives up, who acts blatantly cowardly, or who ends the fight without an appropriate way of taking his punishment. This is one circumstance in which the audience is considered justified in intervening in the fight: again, they are not intervening inside the frame of the fight, but intervening to punish a break in the frame. It is notable that the fighter who quits may still be stronger, and more dangerous, than the members of the audience; but on such occasions, it is unheard of for the fighter to fight back against the audience that is attacking him. He is too crestfallen to retaliate; the emotional energy of the situation has flowed away from him, and he becomes a passive victim of his collective fate.

FIGHTING SCHOOLS AND FIGHTING MANNERS

Heroes, both as icons and as real actors, are products of social structure. The micro-situational conditions include an audience, a means of keeping track of reputational rankings, and a stock of ritualized procedures for staging the fights themselves. As we have seen in the examples at the outset of this chapter, such fights are explicitly announced and scheduled; times and places are set, often including an ending time; stakes are announced, honorific tokens are recognized and agreed upon; weapons and tactics may be specified or limited. As states became better organized and penetrated into control of everyday life, staged fights become unimportant as a way of carrying out serious military conflict; but they survive in at least two forms: in the unpenetrated interstices of social life, where unofficial communities work out their own hierarchies; but also in officially recognized, highly structured types of fights, treated as exhibitions, training, or special displays of rank.

Where the society has an explicit status group stratification in the Weberian sense, such as aristocrats or gentlemen in contrast to commoners, there is often an honorific form of fighting confined to the upper-status group. The rituals of fighting are themselves status markers; those who perform them get status recognition from each other and their audiences; lower-status persons are refused participation, thereby marking the vertical boundary. When a conflict arises between higher- and lower-status persons, the lower is not accorded ritual honors in fighting, but may be peremptorily chastised by the high-ranking, or handed over to underlings to be thrashed. In the *Iliad* (Book 2), when a disrespectful commoner (Thersites) intrudes into the dispute of the Greek chiefs in council, he is summarily beaten with a staff by one of the heroes, while the others laugh. In Tokugawa Japan, a samurai had the privilege of peremptorily cutting down with his sword any commoner who affronted him; when two samurai clashed, however, they fought a ritual duel (Ikegami 1995). In nineteenth-century France, gentlemen who had been properly challenged fought with swords or pistols; but a man considered unworthy would be merely beaten with a cane, or even kicked and thrown out by the gentleman's attendants (Nye 1993: 179, 209).

Dueling and other forms of single combat have been carried out with a variety of weapons and techniques: spears, swords, knives, pistols, fists, and in other ways. These techniques and skills with weapons are typically a matter for explicit training, among the historically earliest kinds of schooling have been fight training,[12] and schools for various kinds of fighting or martial arts have continued up to the present, outside the organizational purview of more conventional forms of education. Schools for teaching fighting techniques are not just ancillary to the formalized dueling culture, but often its chief component.

Fighting and weapons schools were one of the chief places where the ritual etiquette of single combat was taught. This can be seen today in contemporary schools of martial arts (which are chiefly in the Japanese, Korean, and ultimately Chinese traditions). Pupils don a special costume; they wear colored belts or other emblems marking their rank proficiency; they give deference to others of higher rank; they ceremoniously bow while holding out their fists at entry and exit points of the fighting practice: at the front door of the exercise hall; when stepping onto or off of the exercise mat; when beginning a bout or training exercise with another pupil, they bow to each other, and again at the end of the bout.[13] The most important effects of these rituals, performed at every session and often at numerous times during it, are to set off the fighting activity as a special, sacred space, separate from the profane world outside; to limit and constrain the fighting to a specific procedure, within clearly marked beginning and ending points; and to express mutual honor and shared membership between those who ritually fight each other. The fighting techniques may be touted as quite deadly: a kick or punch is supposed to be able to break wooden boards, and to kill a human opponent; in training fights, the punches are designed to come within a tiny distance of smashing their target; and skilled fighters are supposed to evade and block these deadly attacks. The deadliness is at the same time an artificial game, kept within precise bounds.[14]

Etiquette and technique have comparable patterns in other kinds of fighting schools (Nye 1993; McAleer 1994: 119–58; Twain 1880/1977: 26–50). The rules for fighting with swords of various kinds (single cutting-edged sabers, pointed rapiers, heavier épées, etc.) included not just the techniques of how to parry defensively and maneuver around such defenses offensively, but also saluting one another before and after a fight; scoring hits and points (including the famous "touché" uttered in good sportsmanship by the man who has been touched); taking breaks and starting again; counting wounds and deciding what is an honorable amount of bloodshed. In German university dueling clubs, which flourished in the nineteenth century, students were padded up to the chin and wore protective goggles, and aimed at giving—and above all receiving— an honorable scar on the face or head. The membership emblem was not that of victor, but of ritually injured participant. Boxing and other training schools similarly taught both the actual techniques of fighting and the rules of how fights start and end. How much physical damage counted as sufficient to end a fight has varied greatly over the centuries, but the basic pattern of explicitly scheduled, explicitly rule-bounded fighting is characteristic of fighting schools everywhere, and thus of the kinds of fighting outside which these schools promote.[15]

When staged fights are seriously enacted, the code is explicitly and repeatedly announced. Such fights are almost without exception carried out before audiences; even in the past when a quasi-illegal duel was carried out in seclusion, there were always seconds—who at first were called "witnesses" (McAleer 1993: 223)—and these sometimes expanded into a considerable entourage. Participants generally stated the rules they will abide by, at the outset of the fight, or at the time when the challenge was made and accepted. This does not mean they always abided by the rules, but violation were considered more dishonorable than whatever started the quarrel in the first place (Nye 1993). The fight schools, above all, were centered on reiterating the proper etiquette; their practice fights, whatever level of competence they may involve in fighting skill, were always oriented toward following the routine of proper beginnings, endings, and deference to fellow participants.[16]

The quantitative high point in dueling was in Europe in the late nineteenth century. As we shall see in detail momentarily, some two hundred to three hundred duels a year were fought in France, and also in Italy, while in Germany perhaps a third as many. But these events were dwarfed by the popularity of dueling schools, halls, and societies. In Germany, every university had its dueling corps with several hundred members, of whom some took part in staged bouts several days a week. In France, there were dozens of fencing halls totaling thousands of members, as well as shooting societies (Nye 1993: 157–66). Paris newspapers and department stores had private fencing halls for their employees. Members worked out on a regular basis, in part to put in an appearance at a fashionable social scene. Public fencing exhibitions—called *"assaults"*—were held weekly, and elegant gentlemen would hold them as evening entertainments at their homes. Winners and losers were not declared in these bouts; the aim was a display of correctness, along with a flashy style. All told, the amount of such display fencing must have greatly exceeded the number of duels.

At times, fighting schools and exhibitions have been where virtually all of the fighting takes place. In Tokugawa Japan, samurai schools were where the Bushido code—the "way of the warrior"—was most fully developed. In the period of warfare before this era of pacification, samurai had codes that emphasized chiefly hierarchical loyalty to their masters; now as samurai became a leisured status group, they shifted to a code of personal honor (Ikegami 1995). Sword-fighting became ritualized at just the time when the centralizing state prevented their military use. Leading sword teachers became famous for their writings about the philosophy of Bushido; some infused it with Zen, others became prominent philosophers who developed a cult of Confucian "ancient learning" (Collins 1998: 350–58; Kammer 1969). By no means did all samurai discard their military identities; but the martial art that they now practiced was more a scholastic enterprise than a practical one. Samurai spent far more time at their sword academies than in fighting duels to the death.

This was also the case with the chivalric joust in Europe, an exhibition of single combat by heavily armored horsemen, charging at each other with lances along adjacent lanes of prepared track. Jousting was popular during the fourteenth through sixteenth centuries, a time when armies were becoming consolidated into mass infantries, and even horsemen fought in mêlées rather than individually (McAleer 1994: 16–18; Bloch 1961). Indeed, single combats had never made much difference in real battles, from the time of the Greek city-states onward; even the barbarian coalitions of the early Middle Ages fought in large groups; and as we have seen in chapter 3, most victories occurred because one side became tangled in its own disorganization. Chivalry was always an artificial construction, nostalgic in its ideology, but very contemporary in its social appeal: used more to legitimize the status of newly hardening lines of aristocratic rank in social relationships, rather than for fighting on the battlefield. Even private struggles over precedence were carried out not by single combats, but by private armies or entourages of followers maintained by eminent lords (Stone 1967).

This is not to say that all forms of artificial single combat were archaisms; they might be invented comparatively recently, or without drawing upon class precedents. Boxing became a favorite form of exercise among upper-middle-class males in England and the United States during the late nineteenth and early twentieth centuries (not in other countries, where older forms of dueling or fight training schools still survived). Such gentlemen were not professional competitive boxers; the latter were always identified with the lower classses.[17] Like Tokugawa samurai, gentleman boxers spent much more time in practice bouts than in public fisticuffs. Similarly again with karate, kung-fu, and other martial arts students of the twentieth century.[18] These schools, in fact, were generally not very ancient. Aikido was invented in Japan at the turn of the twentieth century; so was kendo—practice fighting with wooden swords, at the time when real swords were replaced in the Japanese army by modern guns (Draeger 1974). Fighting ceremonies become more elaborate as fighting becomes less of a practical concern.

For our analytical purposes, a chief effect of fight training schools is to overcome confrontational tension/fear. They provide a pathway around this obstacle to violence because the focus of attention is so much on other aspects than the confrontation itself: on the etiquette, the limits of time and place, the starting and stopping points. Above all, the focus is on the social membership shared by fighters by virtue of these rituals; and on the elite social standing of those who enact the ritualism. There is much micro-interactional concern for appearing properly before an audience, and thereby rising above the audience.

Confrontational tension/fear is swallowed up in two ways: first, in the larger resonance of the crowd and its elevation of the fighter (indeed, both fighters simultaneously) into the emotional center of attention. And it is swallowed up in the sense of solidarity between the fighters, precisely because they are ensconced inside the same ritualism. No doubt some tension/fear may still remain; in both the Rashad/Dawson and the fictional Achilles/Hector bouts, one side disproportionately gets the emotional energy of the situation, the other slides downhill into fear or paralysis. But even this emotional inequality is an apportioning out of the common charge of EE; and this is what gets the opponents past the initial barrier of confrontational tension in the first place and into the violence. And even if during the course of the fight one of the fighters surrenders to tension/fear as the other monopolizes the situational energy, ritual procedures at the end of the fight will pull the loser back into solidarity with the winner, and into the esteem of the audience.

In the training school, even this vestige of confrontational tension/fear is minimized. The emphasis is on the rituals of membership, and on the artificiality—the make-believe quality—of the confrontation. It becomes palpably a confrontation for the sake of experiencing the solidarity of membership and the status of fighters, a hero-elite marked off from the rest of the world by being inside the training enclave.

Displaying Risk and Manipulating Danger in Sword and Pistol Duels

Dueling was tied to fencing schools from the outset of its classic period. Individual dueling, as distinct from group brawls or vendettas, began to develop in the sixteenth century in Italy and France. By the 1590s it was becoming something of a fad in England (Kiernan 1988; Peltonen 2003; Nye 1993; McAleer 1994). The practice of dueling was spread by soldiers, especially mercenaries, but it acquired the connotation of a practice of courtiers, and thus of fashionable courtesy and manners. It was associated with the newly literate and increasingly centralizing princely courts, displacing the rural castles of feudal lords and their private armies.

The duels that take place in Shakespeare's plays thus were rather a novelty for their audience, which included the same courtiers who were taking up the new practice. Dueling was not only a staged fair fight; at first, it was quite literally staged. In *Romeo and Juliet*, the plot hinges upon a rapier duel in which Romeo kills Tybalt in revenge for killing his cousin Mercutio, thereby upsetting his love match with Tybalt's cousin; in fact this is still a transitional pattern, mixing the individual duel with the group vendetta. Once the dueling code was firmly established, death in a duel was not something anyone could or should avenge; and indeed the duel itself ended whatever insult had started it. *Romeo and Juliet* was first performed about 1593; by 1601 when *Hamlet* was presented, the rules of the duel that bring that play to an end are closer to their canonical form.[19]

Dueling was carried out with a light sword, not the heavy battle weapon; fashion turned to the needle-pointed rapier, which had no cutting edge; it was in fact a weapon useless in military combat, but it was light and easy to carry as part of one's normal upper-class attire. A rapier had no effect against armor, but in civilian life it had the potential for a deep penetrating wound to a vital organ. It signaled that one was always ready for a fight upon momentary provocation; this readiness was connected to polite social intercourse, since the rules of politeness were just those whose violation was regarded as calling for a duel. But dueling was forbidden at courts, which were attempting to impose pacification; and thus wearing a rapier was chiefly an item of self-presentation; one rarely fought on the spot, but arranged an occasion on which to fight, safely out of view of the authorities.[20] Sword duels thus became fencing matches, accompanying a vogue of upper-class fencing schools and private fencing masters, which were the above-ground and indeed the most typical manifestation of the dueling culture. The first fencing school in England was established in 1576, followed by even more fashionable schools in the 1590s, just as dueling took off (Peltonen 2003: 62).

Pistols began to supplant swords around the 1740s and 1750s, and had fully displaced them by around 1790 in England, Ireland, and America; in France and Italy, fighting with rapier or épée (its nineteenth-century version) remained fashionable down to World War I, although pistol duels also existed; in Germany a distinctive form of limited dueling, using sabers (i.e., edged rather than needle-pointed swords) was also popular, but pistols were preferred in serious cases.

The social formalities and courtesies of dueling, established during the rapier era, continued and indeed were elaborated into the pistol era. Proper etiquette included the challenge: verbal insults and rejoinders, including a formulaic "You lie!" (a charge that did not necessarily imply the telling of an untruth), and sometimes a slap on the face with one's gloves—wearing gloves being part of a gentleman's proper attire. Seconds were designated, who then conferred to arrange the time and place, choice of weapons and procedures. Seconds also served as witnesses for the proper ending: if both shots in a pistol duel missed, the principals usually declared themselves satisfied; if one was wounded, he would be tended by a doctor whom the seconds usually brought along. One might be killed, but this was not the only way the duel could end. The ritual was just as much a way of bringing a quarrel to an end, with relatively minimal bloodshed, as of displaying anger and getting "satisfaction" for an insult. In this respect, a pistol duel could be more forgiving than a sword fight, where at a minimum some wounds were required, and stopping points were not as clear and dramatic as the firing of a shot, although by the 1830s the practice emerged of ending a sword duel at the first drawing of blood.

Participating in the dueling ritual was a mark of elite status. One needed to know the proper etiquette, and (from the late 1700s onward) to have access to a set of dueling pistols. The protocol followed many points of polite society: exchanging calling cards so that one's seconds could make contact; carrying gloves; punctilious (if also sardonic) courtesy of speech. The dueling place itself was referred to as "the field of honor." Seconds must be gentlemen; and thus assembling seconds on each side was a way to ratify membership in networks of high status. Seconds served to vouch for the elite social reputation of the principals, and to control the violence and distinguish it from an unseemly brawl of the lower classes. Possibly a challenge might fail because one could not produce acceptable seconds. An extremely high-ranking person could not be challenged, in any case; a great lord would not fight with mere gentry; a general would not fight with lower officers (although he might, as in the German army, prescribe that subalterns should duel), and in fact most duels took place among the junior officers (Peltonen 2003: 83, 205; Kiernan 1988: 103; McAleer 1994: 114–17). In the early years of the United States, General Andrew Jackson could turn down a challenge from a young civilian without loss of face (Wyatt-Brown 1982: 335–36).

Duels in principle always carried the risk of death. But the statistical pattern, such as we can estimate it, shows a paradoxical character: in general, the more frequent the dueling, the less likely it was to be deadly or even injurious. In the late nineteenth century, German duels were by far the most dangerous; but even here, the fatality rate was about 20 percent; two-thirds of German duels ended in bloodshed. Most of these were pistol duels among military officers, where the frequency can be estimated at around ten to fifteen per year at the low end, up to around seventy-five per year at the high end. For France at the fin-de-siècle, the death rate never exceeded 3 percent, and in some years was 0.5 percent or below; at the high point of the 1890s, duels were being fought (usually with swords) at a rate of two hundred to three hundred per year. In Italy, from 1880 to 1900, almost 4,000 duels were recorded (almost always with swords), of which twenty ended in death: which is to say, about 200 duels a year of which one or less (0.5 percent) was fatal.[21]

In Ireland, we can trace a rise in the popularity of dueling from the early 1700s, when there were about ten to fifteen duels per decade, to about ten times as many in the 1770s, then falling off again somewhat toward 1810. Early on, when duels were rare and fought with swords, 63 to 100 percent of them ended in death, and in the remainder someone was almost always wounded. After mid-century, when pistols supplanted swords, fatalities dropped to 36 percent, declining further to 22 percent at the end of the century, and proportions wounded dropped as well. The poor aim of pistol-firing was partly responsible for the decline in casualties. But also, although it was hypothetically possible to keep on firing until someone was hit, the proportion of duels that ended after one round rose from 40 percent to 70 percent (calculated from Kelly 1995: 80–83, 118–20, 213–14).

We see a similar historical pattern elsewhere. In England, duels were just becoming institutionalized in the early 1600s; about twenty duels per year were known, and fatality rates were apparently high (Peltonen 2003: 82, 181–86; 202). By the 1660s, an elaborate etiquette of polite civility and its breaches was recognized, and challenges were frequent; but ways of evading duels proliferated as well. By the 1670s, duelists were satirized as fops doing more pretending than fighting—which is to say, when dueling, or at least challenges to duels, became widespread, procedures for limiting the damage also developed. The pattern was repeated again as sword fighting gave way to pistol dueling in the mid-eighteenth century: between 1762 and 1821, the fatality rate was 40 percent; in the years leading up to the abolition of dueling in 1840, fatalities were down to 7 percent and woundings to 17 percent (Nye 1993: 268, referring to Simpson 1988; Kiernan 1988: 143).

Over time, dueling became more and more subject to etiquette and fair play. In the early decades of the 1700s, in quasi-civilized places like Ireland, seconds might still join in the fighting; this had also been the tendency in sixteenth-century Italy and early seventeenth-century England and France, where the distinction between group vendetta and individual duel was just being established (Peltonen 2003: 179, 191, 203–4). By the late 1700s, seconds had become punctilious arbiters. In military combat at this time, the smooth-barrel musket was replaced by the rifled barrel, greatly improving target accuracy; but rifling for pistol barrels was regarded as unsporting in a dueling weapon, especially in Britain. Similarly the hair-trigger of the newer pistols was rejected as an unfair advantage (Kiernan 1988: 143). Duelists stuck to outmoded weapons; owning a pair of dueling pistols was becoming a fashionable archaism, similar to officers wearing a sword as a badge of honor in an era of mechanized combat. The very sense that the weapons were out of date also sent a message that the fight had an element of make-believe.

The same pattern may be traced in France. The number of duels rose around the time of the 1789 revolution, as the bourgeois claimed the previously aristocratic right to honorable fights. By the 1830s, with improved pistol-firing mechanisms (percussion caps having replaced older spark-producing flint-locks), fatalities were about one-third of the approximately eighty duels fought per year. In response, a dueling code was published and widely promulgated in 1837, formalizing pistol as well as sword-dueling etiquette, and providing many ways to reduce fatalities; in the following years, death rates fell to about six a year, making up 8 to 10 percent of the duels (Nye 1993: 135; McAleer 1994: 64, 248). In the Third Republic (from 1875), dueling became extremely popular as a mark of democratic participation. Politicians debating in the Assembly, and journalists trading accusations, were especially likely to settle their disputes by duels. But these men in public life had no career advantage in actually killing anyone, and in fact their duels were rather tame: during the 1880s, of 108 political duels, there were no fatalities and only eleven (10 percent) produced serious injuries; of about two hundred journalists' duels, there were two deaths (1 percent) and twelve serious injuries (6 percent). So-called private duels, mostly concerning sexual affairs, were more dangerous, but even here the casualty rates were low: 6 percent killed and 34 percent badly wounded out of a total of 85 (Nye 1993: 187–215).

How was all this managed? How, in effect, was the risk of casualties adjusted to circumstances? Seconds had a wide range of conditions to choose among. First of all, they might arrange for a settlement, declaring a misunderstanding, apology, or other extenuating circumstances. For this reason, an older and experienced second was recommended, and young hot-heads were to be avoided; one German expert seconded some fifty duels, of which only five came to actual fighting, resulting in only two serious injuries.[22] Duels might also abort for various procedural reasons; a challenge was supposed to be delivered within twenty-four hours after the alleged insult, and could be honorably disregarded if it came later; the fight itself was to take place within another forty-eight hours (usually early the next morning), and again if the deadline was missed, the fight was called off. If one of the duelists failed to appear within fifteen minutes of the set time, the other was not obliged to wait. And given the short notice, sometimes duels were fought in heavy rain, badly obscuring the aim. In places where duels were illegal, a duel could be evaded by tipping off the police. Alternatively, pistol misfires counted as a round and ended the match, unless further rounds had been agreed upon by the seconds (McAleer 1994: 49–56, 66, 84).

Aside from these contingencies, the seconds could set procedures that made the danger high or low. In pistol duels, choices involved the number of shots to be fired, and at what distance. The more rounds, of course, the more danger; one round of exchanging fire was standard. Continuing up to four rounds was considered very bloody-minded, although in one duel between German officers in 1886, twenty-seven shots were fired, giving some indication of poor aim as well as perseverance (McAleer 1994: 68; Nye 1993: 195, 207). The distance of twenty-five paces was typical in France, fifteen paces in Germany; ten paces was severe, and five paces was point-blank, even with smooth-bore pistols. On the other hand, distances were often set as far as thirty-five paces or more, especially in France—one way in which French casualty rates were kept low.[23]

The distance set also depended on the type of dueling procedure (McAleer 1994: 70–75; Nye 1993: 195, 207, 269). The most popular form was the so-called barrier duel, which began with the opponents facing each other at a distance (e.g., ten or twenty paces) behind a rectangular barrier zone, marked with stakes, usually five, ten, or fifteen paces wide. Thus they began somewhere between thirty and fifty-five yards apart; these opening distances were not very dangerous, but the duelists could increase the danger. At the start signal, they began walking toward the barrier, and could fire at will. The one who fired first could win if he hit and disabled his opponent; but if he failed to dispatch him, he would be honor-bound to stand in place, while the other had one minute to advance up to the barrier and take careful aim before he shot.

Another variant, the "signal duel," generally put the duelists closer but gave them little time to aim; they began with pistols down, until the signal was given. Within the count of three, each was required to raise his gun, aim, and fire; shooting after the count of three was considered dishonorable. Moreover, law courts in Germany (where dueling was illegal but tolerated) and in France (where it was legal as long as the rules were followed) placed great emphasis on whether the duelist who killed someone had followed the proper rules. The signal duel gave better chances of surviving by presenting a smaller target, since the duelists stood in profile to each other, and afforded some protection by their advanced arm and shoulder. In contrast, the barrier duel, although in some ways less dangerous, required the men to stand facing forward. Another way to reduce the chances of good aim was to line up back to back, and on signal, whirl and fire. More danger could be introduced in the "*visé*" (aimed) duel, which allowed both sides a set amount of time (usually sixty seconds) to aim and fire. This might turn into a prolonged stare-down, a real test of nerves; in a duel between Hungarian parliamentarians in 1893, the opponents held a bead on each other for thirty seconds without firing, then finally put their pistols down, embraced, and made up (McAleer 1994: 70).

If the seconds wanted to make sure that dangers were minimized, they might doctor the weapons, since they were in charge of loading them: they could use balls made out of quicksilver, which disintegrated in the air, or load very small balls, or reduce the charge of powder (McAleer 1994: 66–67, 189). Requiring old-fashioned smooth-bore weapons not only kept up tradition but made backstage conniving easier than with modern weapons. There was still some risk; round balls had more irregular trajectories than modern cylindrical bullets for rifled barrels, but since they were fired with lower muzzle velocity they also might lodge in the body when a modern bullet would penetrate cleanly through. Some risk always had to be present, if only in the mind of the duelists. Seconds were stage-managers of a rather Goffmanian collective presentation of self; the ritual involved a division of labor, with the principals supposed to show their ardent concern for honor and their bravery under threat, while the seconds (quite possibly without awareness by the principals) made the dangers lower than they appeared.

Sword duels also could be hedged and limited (McAleer 1994: 59–62; 185; Nye 1993: 197, 201–2, 291). In Germany, sabers might have blunt points; and in any case, the curved blade made deep rapier-like penetration unlikely. This left slashing, which generated blood and scars but generally kept it at that. No talking or taunting was allowed, and a man who fell or lost his weapon was not to be attacked until he was back in fighting position; unlike Hollywood sword-fights, there was no kicking or punching with the free hand. The preferred form was for duelists to stand close together, so that momentum of sword thrusts was limited (something like

Figure 6.1 French sword duel with large audience. Top hats are marks of fashionable society at this time (1901). The duelists, keeping their distance, wear no shirts, in order that first drawing of blood can be easily seen. Seconds stand close by to supervise the action.

clinching in a boxing match, which is also a typical tactic in modern fistfights). A certain amount of protection was possible, such as wrapping scarves around neck or mid-section. Alternatively, duelists might expose as much skin as possible, so that any spot of blood would be visible, and the duel stopped according to the rule of drawing first blood. This was particularly the case in France, where duelists sometimes might be set by their seconds to fight without shirts; or at any rate in white shirts on which the blood would stand out. French duelists generally did not wear leather gauntlets, since the most likely wounds were to the hands and wrists; these were the usual targets, and it was considered very severe (and perhaps culpable) to aim for the mid-section, or even at the tendons and big arteries of the legs. In Germany, however, heavy gauntlets were usually worn, since the duelists did not want to end with such slight wounds, and the more serious cuts were a badge of honor. The bigger the gauntlets, the more serious the duel. Dueling procedures could be calibrated rather finely to the amount of damage sought.

The point of the duel was more to demonstrate one's status-group membership than to establish dominance over one's opponent. Thus it was less important to win than to display courage; an honorable defeat was better than a dishonorable victory, indeed in terms of reputation, it might be better even than an honorable victory. The height of bravado (at least in England and France) was to let one's opponent fire first, then fire one's own pistol in the air. Dueling thus came close to a form of gambling (another pastime of elite circles, especially in the "fast set"). Some forms of pistol dueling were very much like a card game. Duelists might draw lots over who had the first shot, making the round into a successive test of nerves first for one, then for the other. A more complicated form of gambling was a version of the barrier duel, with the normal no-man's-land of ten to fifteen paces between the fighters shrunk to a single line; if the first one to fire missed, his opponent could walk up to the barrier, and if the first firer had dared to come so far forward, he would have to let the other, if he wished, shoot him point blank. It appears that relatively few took this kind of advantage; the display of bravado was generally enough to end the duel with a wasted shot. Even more explicit gambling occurred in the type of duel where the pistols were prepared by an extra pair of seconds, out of sight from the duelists, and only one loaded; the duelists then selected one pistol by lot—neither knowing if he were the one fighting with an unloaded gun (McAleer 1994: 229–30). Gambles at this high level of danger, however, were generally frowned upon; in periods where dueling was most popular, low-risk procedures were preferred.

Dueling practices became traditionalized and conservative. Weapons technologies improved, but elite duelists did not adopt them. Colt invented the revolver in 1835; it became widely known after it was adopted by the U.S. Army after the Mexican War of 1846–48 (Chambers 1984). An old-fashioned pistol had to be reloaded, a somewhat cumbrous operation, after each shot. Thus a duel of two or more rounds would require the same number of pauses, making it both suspenseful and formalistic in the extreme. A revolver would have made it possible to continue firing up to six shots, and would have produced a higher level of casualties. But this kind of repeated firing was never allowed in gentlemanly duels; if a revolver had to be used, in the absence of a traditional dueling pistol, only one bullet was loaded for each round. Cowboy gunfights, of course, were another matter; they were the famous gunfights of the revolver era, but were considered plebeian by the European dueling culture (McAleer 1994: 68, 79–80).

As pistol dueling was on its way out, lore developed around a hybrid form. The game of "Russian roulette" was a combination of dueling and gambling, displaying one's honor by willingness to risk one's life with a pistol shot. Russian roulette was a way of fighting a duel without an opponent. Both were similar in that a duel typically also involved being subject to only one or at most two shots, that most of the time would likely miss or prove non-fatal; and the chances of not hitting the one loaded cylinder in a six-shot revolver held to one's head were similarly favorable. Death-defying acts of bravado were ways of gaining status, as well as claiming the center of attention among one's aristocratic peers.[24] But in fact there is no hard documentation outside of literature of Russian roulette actually being played before the early twentieth century (www.fact-index.com/r/ru/russian_roulette). The setting always included Russian officers, but the procedures varied, and the details seem to have become distorted into a game played with that plebeian weapon, the revolver. What the legend of Russian roulette plays up is a structure underlying both it and the duel: the opponent to be overcome is always one's own fears, and doing so makes one part of a death-defying ostentatious elite.

THE DECLINE OF ELITE DUELING AND ITS REPLACEMENT BY THE GUNFIGHT

Dueling always had its opponents; not merely from the church but also from the state attempting to monopolize violence. This opposition was ineffectual during the seventeenth and eighteenth centuries, especially in countries where an aristocratic status group controlled the high offices of government; thus the same persons would officially frown upon dueling, but privately condone it or practice it. During the nineteenth century, as dueling had shifted over to gun-fighting, it became less elite, and eventually became plebeian enough to be outlawed.

What finally killed dueling, although at an uneven pace between various countries, was the process of democratization. Until the nineteenth century, dueling was the province of gentlemen, and of military officers as gentlemen ex officio if not by birth. But the increasing size of nineteenth-century armies, and the widening base of military recruitment, eroded this eliteness; initially it was the spread of the dueling culture to all officers that began to spoil it as a class distinction. Similarly with civilian duels: these expanded enormously in the late nineteenth century, especially in the French Third Republic and in the parliamentary regime of unified Italy. Politicians, and indeed any politically active citizen, now took upon himself the rights of a gentleman, including the right to defend his honor in a duel. In Germany, the expanding student population spread the practice of the dueling clubs into the bourgeoisie. At first blush this might have seemed the imposition of aristocratic, militaristic values upon the larger society; but its long-term tendency was to make dueling less elite.

The process was especially noticeable in the American South in the years before the Civil War. In contrast to the haughtiness of dueling aristocrats in Europe, white Southern males claimed democratic equality, including the right to challenge anyone as a statement of one's honor. In reaction, the wealthiest and most cultivated Southern landowners began to turn away from dueling, seeing it as merely an expression of boisterous and uncultivated plebeians (Wyatt-Brown 1982: 351).[25] Eventually, the dueling club had too many members; it lost its caché. Genteel manners now came to be defined as those of peaceful society, not violent honor.[26]

The last gasp of pistol duels in the United States was in the so-called wild West in the years between 1865 and 1900 (Kooistra 1989; Hollon 1974). Western gunfighters constituted something of a reputational elite on the frontier, romanticized as well as vilified in the press. But they were not members of the upper class, nor did they practice a genteel life-style. Whereas the older dueling culture had existed among the propertied elite, gunfighters were not the wealthy ranchers, although they often worked as a floating population of armed men in their employ.[27] There were occasional elements of etiquette in gun-fighting, and there might be staged fights at designated meeting times; but the apparatus of formal challenges, seconds, genteel firing in the air, and polite terminations was pared away. Gunfighters were more concerned with kill or be killed than with enacting an elite status membership. The most successful gunfighters were apparently those who practiced not staged fair fights but were quickest to take offense and fire on the other man on the spot; many of their recorded killings were by ambush. The gunfighter was a transitional phenomenon between the elite duelist and the modern bar-room brawler.

Western gun-fighting took place in the transitional zone where state penetration was just under way. The lack of state control and protection encouraged private forces; indeed, the private armies of cattle-ranchers, landowners, and railroad magnates involved in making violent claims and defending against them produced much more violence than the individual gunfighters (Hollon 1974). Our picture is distorted because the latter got most of the publicity and the romantic reputation, since they best fit the cultural image of the hero in single combat. Even among these famous individuals, some of the most successful were those who had worked (at some point in their careers) for government forces, as sheriffs or U.S. marshals. The most famous of the Western gunfights, the OK Corral fight in the Arizona territory in 1881, was fought not between two individual heroes in single combat, but between two organized forces: the U.S. marshal and three deputies, armed with both pistols and a shotgun; and five men belonging to the private household forces of a property-aggrandizing rancher, armed with pistols and rifles (reprint of *Tombstone Epitaph*, Oct. 1881).

Guns disappeared from twentieth-century duels or single combats; instead, where the practice of staged fair fights continued, it was with other weapons, chiefly fists and knives; conversely where guns were used, it was in non-fair fights. The ethos of staged fair fights has continued in places that are artificially closed communities with static status hierarchies, such as American high schools and other total institutions. The same structures that produce bullying of the bottom rank also produce staged fights within the elite at the top.

Here we may summarize the conditions under which occur fair fights between status notables. One subtype occurs in loose ad hoc coalitions of military units that stand in the place of states; historically these have existed when tribal units based on kinship ties were superceded by larger units of volunteer marauders, or of inter-tribal coalitions, but where no stable hierarchy of military command had crystalized.[28] Ad hoc coalitions of this sort produce the particular kind of hero represented by the berserker, the ferocious individual fighter who overawes others by his heedless aggressiveness and his reputation, vaunting his contempt for risks. Preferred fights are individual ones, not collective, since these maximize individual reputation. Moreover, the unit of organization is the personal following, or rather a series of heroes with their personal followings united into a temporary coalition (like the Greek army at Troy) not the corporate vengeance unit of the clan or gang. Hence there are individual fights among heroes, not vendettas with their structure of alternating ambushes.

An additional feature of this type of structure is a division between an aristocratic rank, and common people in the rest of the population. The heroes confine their staged fair fights to encounters with each other, and derive their highest honor from these fights.[29] Ideally, the aristocratic stratum is based on the criterion of being a fighter of high reputation, but in fact also on being a propertied elite. In reality, a propertied upper class may not be completely made up of such fighters; with hereditary property and rank transmission, and in more settled conditions, the gentry may be distinguished more for their manners (including their manners in fighting) than their particular ferociousness and effectiveness.

Here the category of berserker heroes shifts over into a category of polite gentlemanly duelists. Hence, a second sub-type of conditions for staged fair fights: where loose ad hoc coalitions are supplanted by a strong state, dueling may persist as long as there remains a rank structure of aristocratic status groups standing above commoners. Under these conditions, a dueling ethos is kept alive, especially through the existence of training schools for fighters, in which the etiquette is practiced, and which have the character of upper-class clubs. In fact, the vast majority of staged fights take place in these schools, relatively rarely as serious fights to the death as in the outside world. Staged fair fights of the dueling type disappear when the aristocrat/commoner distinction disappears, although they may peak temporarily during the transition.

The importance of the elite fighting school or club for the ethos of honorific, staged fair fights is demonstrated by comparing what happened to such schools in the twentieth century, as honorific dueling with weapons disappeared. Training schools for fighting carried over into the twentieth century and beyond, but transmuted into a new form: the gym or fitness center. The weapons dropped out, and training shifted to the physical body itself: modern gyms build muscles and endurance, although some teach specific fighting techniques such as boxing and Asian martial arts. Contemporary Americans regard this as peaceful and innocuous. In the period of the fitness movement from the 1970s onward, gyms became increasingly middle class, non-belligerent, with large proportion of female participants; these gyms have neither political nor gang connections. Gyms became places not for showing off or even for social belonging but for private self-development, a kind of shared backstage where one got oneself in shape, rather than a place for frontstage performance. But in Europe, gyms—usually gender segregated—have often been places for recruitment of paramilitaries and criminal gangs. In the 1920s, German paramilitaries were organized around athletic and exercise movements. Fitness centers were used as bases for Yugoslav ethnic cleansers in the 1990s, and as rape centers; Russian gyms in the 1990s were organizing places for criminal gangs; in India, gyms have been bases for those who act as local criminal enforcers and who periodically lend their services as shock troops in ethnic disputes (Fritzsche 1998; Kaldor 1999; Tilly 2003: 36–38; Katz 1988: 272; Mann 2005). These plebeian gyms did not operate by a code of honor, nor of individual combat, but quite the opposite.

HONOR WITHOUT FAIRNESS: VENDETTAS AS CHAINS OF UNBALANCED FIGHTS

Under modern conditions, the use of guns shifts over to not-fair fights. These fall into two further types, which together make up most modern gun violence (apart from predatory violence in the course of committing robberies and other crimes). On the one hand, there are vendettas carried out by groups; on the other, individual quarrels that escalated into shootings. The latter are often described as honor confrontations, but their distinctive dynamics are better captured if we call them leap-frog escalations.

Gun vendettas are familiar to us in the form of drive-by shootings between rival gangs and more broadly reciprocated gang violence (Sanders 1994; Jankowski 1991; Wilkinson 2003). Gangs protect their turf, which may comprise only a few neighborhood blocks, by attacking young males from outside who enter the area; in vengeance for previous attacks, or to make a statement and display their power, they make occasional incursions into a rival's turf. Vendettas are not fair fights. An episode does not take the form of a one-on-one bout in the presence of an audience that maintains procedural rules. Instead, the aim is to apply overwhelming superiority when it is one's turn to dominate (that is, when one wants to get back at the other side for a previous attack, or when on one's home turf). This unfair advantage is important in making the violence come off at all, from the point of view of overcoming confrontational tension/fear. When a gun is used, typically there are a considerable number of gang members who take part in the incursion or the ambush, even if only one of them actually fires the gun. The rest provide moral backup; they also represent the collective rather than individual character of the fight—it is not one individual taking vengeance or establishing honor upon another individual, but a group sending a message to another group. Who the particular victim is does not matter; killing a girlfriend or a child connected to the opposing group is just as meaningful as killing a major gang fighter.

Nor are vendetta episodes usually staged, in the sense of being announced in advance, agreed upon as to time and place, with rules of engagement. The essence of vendetta tactics is to catch one's opponent off guard and at a disadvantage. What makes for successful killings, and thus what keeps the vendetta going, is the reciprocal chain of one-sided advantages. Lacking the element of surprise, or overwhelming local advantage, encounters among gangs—like front-on meeting among armies—are generally standoffs, full of bluster and noise but little actual damage.

The following case shows where guns are fired largely for effect, with some rather random casualties. A group of young black men accompanied a friend to a rival housing project to see a girl:

> We was smokin' (marijuana), mindin' our own business and shit. Then the niggas from the other side come up and ask mad questions, "who this?" you know, like "who the fuck are you?" And I'm like, you know, "who the fuck are YOU?" and shit. What the hell are you, what's the problem, man, we just chillin'. So, you know, we started with the lip and shit. And one thing led to another and we was fightin' and everybody started pullin' out and we started bustin' each other, and I think nobody got hit. One person got hit from the Brownsville side, 'cause my man hit him up against the chest. I didn't get hit. So it was a lot of gunplay and shit. And we started blastin', not really paying. . . . When people blast I don't think they really aimin' at anyone, you know, a blast is just a blast. A lot of stray bullets be going everywhere, you know. I'm glad we got out of that situation. (Wilkinson 2003: 153)

The use of guns also tends to limit the amount of fighting: gang fights with guns rarely take the form of extended battles, with shots repeatedly fired by both sides. In part this is due to normal tension/fear; in part to the lack of training in the use of guns, and the frequently low quality of the weapons. In contemporary gangs, gun-buyers are often quite ignorant about guns; they are often sold poor-quality or malfunctioning weapons, and treat the gun more as a fetish than an effective weapon (Venkatesh 2006). Usually all that can be mustered is one good shot. These features all converge on keeping gun use by gangs in the form of vendettas, a chain of small-scale shootings.

Compared to staged fair fights, vendettas are drawn out in time: equal forces are not brought together at the same time and place, but there is an alternation: ideally, first one side has the unfair advantage, then the other. The whole chain might balance over time, but at any particular moment one side or the other generally feels they have been subjected to unfairness. And so they have; and so they try to shift the balance of unfairness to make it weigh against the other side. Although from the point of view of an abstract theorist, the chain may seem balanced, in the phenomenological reality of the participants, it is palpably unfair. Thus vendettas are notoriously self-perpetuating; whereas staged fair fights have the character of bringing an episode of conflict to mutually accepted conclusions. Duels end with "satisfaction" of the parties; vendetta episodes do not.

I have just given a list of general conditions for the occurrence of staged fair fights; here is a counterpart list of conditions for vendettas. Paralleling the case of individual hero fights, there are two subcases: an ancient form and its reappearance in some modern enclaves. First, vendetta-like violence occurs where there are tribal corporate units with stable, non-shifting boundaries, and relatively low internal hierarchy—what Black (1998) calls "stable agglomerations." This means that individual identities are firmly embedded in group identities; unlike the shifting ad hoc coalitions in which hero-fighters appear, every man sticks with his group (though women might move through marriage) and has little opportunity to acquire a singular reputation (or to trade on such a reputation in making deals with possible allies). Lack of internal hierarchy contributes to the reciprocating vendetta pattern because there is no command structure to force individuals to fight very seriously; generalized group pressure can bring them out to the fighting line, but most of them do so with little courage or enthusiasm; and they are quite willing to end the fighting in each episode as soon as a single victim is taken or given up. The one-shot vendetta episode thus allows maximal play for normal cowardice, while keeping up a minimal façade of courage.

Vendetta structures arising from tribal corporate units are characteristic of pre-state societies, especially those horticultural economies that have stable territories. In the second subtype, vendettas also occur in relatively modern times where bureaucratic state penetration is partial or in a condition of transition. The classic areas of vendettas have been Sicily, Calabria, Corsica, and Spain in the seventeenth to nineteenth or early twentieth centuries. The key feature is the existence of relatively self-contained peasant villages, or subsistence farmers organized chiefly by kinship ties. These need not be aboriginal, but could be formed by migrating away from state-penetrated areas: a famous example is the feud of the Hatfield and McCoy families in an extremely isolated region of West Virginia and Kentucky between 1863 and 1891 (www.matewan .com/history/timeline.htm). A similar structure underlies modern urban gang vendettas: the local territory is the city neighborhood; the gangs are not hereditary units like tribes (although there can be an element of family transmission of a tradition of membership [Horowitz 1983; Jankowsky 1991]), but they are artificially contrived to act as corporate vengeance units.[30]

Ephemeral Situational Honor and Leap-Frog Escalation to One-Gun Fights

The other type of amateur gun violence is what I will call leap-frog escalations in individual disputes. Often these are referred to as honor disputes or face contests, but the rubric does not sufficiently capture its dynamics. Typical examples are disputes that arise in bars or other public places, and escalate through a rising level of challenges and insults (Luckenbill 1977). The culmination is that one person produces a gun (in many bar fights, he leaves the bar and returns later with it) and shoots the other man. Superficially these resemble traditional honor disputes, and may take the form of single combats. Luckenbill calls them Goffmanian "character contests" or "face contests." But they differ from duels in important respects: These are not fair fights, because one person leap-frogs up the chain of escalation ahead of the other and produces a gun, and so the fighters are no longer equally matched. Rather than gunfights, we should call them one-gun fights. There is nothing like the protocol of a duel, offering choice of weapons, allowing each side to shoot one shot, and ceasing thereafter. In one-gun fights, it is not unusual for the shooter to fire multiple times. There is no discussion of formalities such as when or where to meet.[31] There are no seconds to arrange such matters, and thus also to provide social pressure to enforce the limitations of the fight period; no delays, which could have provided a cooling-off period and made the belligerents more willing to end the fight with risky gestures leading to mutual satisfaction. There is nothing but self-managed, hot-headed escalation on the spot, with the chief breaks in the actions consisting in one side leaving to procure heavier weapons.

Leap-frog escalations of this sort may be described as including an element of honor, insofar as both sides take themselves as having been insulted; but the honor is purely personal and self-centered. It is not the honor of mutually participating in a fair fight, and thereby enacting one's status as member of a well-mannered elite; it does not bind the antagonists together and raise them above the commoners. Leap-frog escalations are the kind of fighting that occurs in democratic, egalitarian settings, where there are no status-group rankings and boundaries, and in anonymous public situations where one does not even have a reputation circulated in established community networks.

Leap-frog escalations are part of what I have called "situational stratification" (Collins 2004, chap. 7): the modern public condition in which no one gives deference to anyone else as belonging to a higher-ranking category, or even recognizes such categories. In such situations, one can have only a personal reputation (e.g., as a celebrity, or an individual who is well known in a particular occupation or network); but outside that network, the only way to get deference or attention is to be situationally dominant, by being noisy, ebullient, shocking, or belligerent. I have offered the following principle (Collins 2004: 272–74): formally scheduled, publicized, and scripted rituals produce and reinforce categorical identities; informal interaction rituals, which are unscheduled and unscripted, result in personal reputations that are ephemeral, confined to the immediate situation. This fits the contrast between dueling and leap-frog escalations quite nicely. What makes a duel both elite and controlled is its scheduling, its commitment to protocol, and its expansion to a public realm consisting of the network of seconds. To carry out such procedures confirms one's gentry status. A leap-frog escalation is a hot-headed rush, improvised on the spot; although such fights may resemble each other, this is not because of adherence to a formal script; and the result is not that one enacts membership in an honored category, but merely acquires some personal reputation as a hot-head or a murderer. One might argue that the bar-room fighter becomes at least a situational elite, since he (usually he) dominates the immediate focus of attention. But even here the identity is not generally an honored one; other carousers may well look down on the brawlers as low-lifes.[32] At best, the fighter in this situation is caught up in a tunnel of his own subjectivity, engaging in situational self-aggrandizement without much social backup, manufacturing an image of oneself as honorable that is not shared by anyone else.

Even further out on the continuum of anonymity are disputes that arise in traffic; the most famous of these are called road rage, although there are similar fights that emerge from foot traffic, in which persons' own bodies (and the parcels and accoutrements they are carrying) are the vehicles that get in each other's way.[33] In some ways these traffic fights are the ultimate generalization of anonymous leap-frog escalations. They are not confined to a lower-class or working-class culture of machismo, nor to a particular ethnic group, nor are they particularly male; women and middle-class persons appear to be frequent perpetrators. Road rage is the ultimate democratization of honor; every driver (and every pedestrian) is equal to any other, and ready to take insult at having one's rights apparently violated.

As Katz (1999) and others (Tilly 2003: 151–56) have shown, escalation occurs beyond the original offense because drivers are generally oblivious to the signals that others give off asking for rectification of the offense; the fight escalates to a higher level of dispute over failure to make ritual repairs. Here again such fights may end in one-gun fights (although sometimes the vehicle itself is used as a weapon, smashing the other or pushing it off the road). These are fights over honor, but it is honor known only to occupants of each car, and indeed sometimes only to the driver, with the passengers wondering what all the fuss is about. This is a far cry from the duel: unscheduled, suddenly emergent, without protocol, without social networks as audience and control; it does not even result in any personal identity, unless one is arrested by the police—Katz notes that drivers often come out of an episode of road rage as from a dream, disowning the temporary self that had been displayed there. Not all road rage incidents end up in leap-frog violence; the vast majority of them peter out at a much lower level—as do most fights. (This is the case in note 33.)

My constant theme has been that fights are difficult. Staged fair fights are one of the chief ways of circumventing confrontational tension/fear. Duels did this by enlisting the support of an elite status group in motivating violence, but also in formalizing it to a degree that one had mainly to display one's willingness to take a risk of being killed, while that risk itself was limited by protocol. Vendettas circumvent the barrier by going back to attacking the weak, at least by maneuvering for a temporary situation of outnumbering the opponent and catching them out of their terrain or off their guard; and vendettas, with their pattern of one victim at a time, hit and run away, leave the general pattern of fear and incompetence close to the surface.

Ad hoc individual fights of the kind I have called leap-frog escalations take another pathway around: lacking social support, they revert to the unfair fight, especially by bringing in a weapon far more deadly than what the opponent possesses at that moment. There is a symbolic aspect to this as well; the man who rushes from the bar after he has come off worse in a round of insults is likely feeling the reality of his cowardice in not pursuing the fight on a bodily level. If he gets a gun, it no doubt has some of the qualities of the sacred object of what I have called the gun cult (Collins 2004: 99–101). Its ritualistic qualities, acquired in networks where cultish practices of adulating weapons give it emotional resonance, provide him with a vicarious charge of emotional energy; the man who was insulted and degraded now feels superior. His superiority depends on the knowledge (or belief) that he has a gun, and his opponent does not. It is precisely this unfairness in the possession of ritual weapons that gives him the courage to return, overcome tension/fear, and carry on the fight. Here I am asserting, as elsewhere, that the gun is not just a weapon in a practical sense; when soldiers on both sides of a battle have guns, they tend to be even more frightened and incompetent. It is the possession of ritual superiority that surmounts the barrier and unleashes the violence.

Behind the Façade of Honor and Disrespect

It is common to attribute small-scale violence among males to a code of honor. A similar case is explanation by disrespect, except the latter can be broader, including not only individual combat but also group attackers and group victims, and not necessarily in the form of a fair fight. An instance from my files involves a black neighborhood gang that attacks two black teenagers, dressed in their Sunday best, who are outsiders visiting their grandparents. The perpetrators themselves explain their behavior in a huff of righteous justification: "Who do they think they are, coming in here, disrespecting us?"

Both explanations are empathic efforts to get inside the viewpoint of the attackers. Although often overlapping, the two explanations carry some difference in tone. Codes of honor are regarded as deep-seated traditions, afforded some grudging admiration from a conservative standpoint or romantic nostalgia about the past. Explanation by disrespect has a tone of altruistic sympathy with an underdog who is put down by social prejudice and disadvantage, and who is fighting "in search of respect" (in the title of Bourgois's [1995] book).

Such efforts at empathy, although worthy as an ethical stance, distort both the structural conditions and the situational phenomenology of violence. A code of honor is not just a matter of tradition. It is the cultural ideology that is verbalized where particular social conditions are present.

Another line of explanation of fighting under a code of honor emphasizes its rationalistic elements. The argument, as formulated by Gould (2003) and Tilly (2003), holds that in the absence of a state legal system and police forces providing security, the only way to deter violence is to demonstrate two things: that one personally cannot be taken advantage of in any way; and that one has the loyalty and support of a group that would carry out revenge. Thus it is in one's interest to adhere to a code of honor, showing willingness to resort to violence at the merest slight; and scrupulously to adhere to group obligations to support one another in revenging insult and injury to one another. The first gave one a personal reputation as someone not to be messed with; the second gave the group a reputation for solidarity that made it formidable in backing up its individual members.

This explanation has a functionalist tone. In the absence of other social mechanisms for providing security, it says, an honor code arises to provide individuals with security. The argument is peculiar because the outcome it allegedly brings about is undermined by the mechanism itself. Touchiness about personal honor, and honor-bound vengeance from one's group, are supposed to bring security. But in fact societies with an honor culture are notorious for their level of violence, and even more for their pervasive atmosphere of threat and insecurity. The hypothetical alternative is difficult to quantify; we are asked to believe that without the honor code, there would be even more violence and insecurity than there is. Empirically, though, societies practicing vendettas are at the high end of the known scale of violent death (Keeley 1996). If this is the best functional alternative there is, it is none too successful. The security it provides is illusory. We might further argue that societies with honor codes are unusually violent, because they tend to escalate minor disagreements into violent ones, and to manufacture occasions for trouble where none need exist.

Another kind of empirical point also tells against the rationalistic explanation of an honor code as providing informal law and order: Many late-twentieth-century fights in countries like the United States are attributed to honor confrontations: altercations in bars, for instance, or road rage shootings. These do not occur only in places where there is no state penetration and no formal mechanisms for enforcing security, but to a large extent in places that are not at all lawless. Moreover, these are often anonymous public situations, where the individual has no reputation to uphold, since there is no mechanism for circulating such a reputation. To fire a gun into the cab of a pickup truck on an interstate highway in San Diego, after a tail-gating incident over possession of the fast lane, thereby wounding the driver and killing a seventeen-year-old girl sitting beside him (*San Diego Union*, March 8 and March 13, 2004) can be construed as an honor confrontation; but it does nothing to establish the reputation of anyone as not to be messed with; nor does it invoke the possibility of group revenge, since no group identities are displayed. The structural conditions under which honor code violence is supposed to be functional are not present, but the behavior is.

My point is that so-called honor code violence is not an avoidance process, motivated by fear and lack of security, but an aggressively proactive one, motivated by seeking elite status. It is not a way of keeping up with everyone else, a rationalistic tit-for-tat egalitarian self-help security enforcement, but an inegalitarian move to raise oneself above others. I offer two sources of evidence:

One is that many fights do not occur even where the honor code is supposed to be in place; many slights are not taken, many provocations are not interpreted as such. Gould (2003) describes societies such as nineteenth-century Corsica, where the honor culture purportedly demands that family members back each other up in murderous vendettas; but in fact his evidence (121–33) shows that the great majority of vendettas do not go beyond the most immediate links of payback; most people shirk their alleged honor obligations to get involved in an extended exchange of murders. This is in keeping with my general theme: that most people are not good at violent confrontations, and only with special circumstances are they able to carry them through.[34] This fits the pattern, too, that only a small number of persons perform virtually all of the violence; this is a practical reality, known to those who are in violent situations, and it gives rise to a sense of stratification between a violent elite (or at least a blustering, violent-appearing elite) and the majority who back down from fights. This, I submit, is what we see in situations dominated by the honor code: not that everyone lives up to the code, but that the community is palpably divided into an elite of tough guys and tough groups (whether they are called gangs, families, clans, aristocrats, etc.), and those who are subject to them (whether as commoners, followers, persons under protection, payers of protection, etc.); among Wilkinson's (2003) New York violent elite, they are called "punks" or "herbs." This stratification is a strong structural correlate of the existence of honor codes.[35]

The second source of evidence is that in honor code situations, individuals often go looking for trouble. They are not merely defending themselves against slights, peacefully minding their own business otherwise. These are precisely the scenes or recurrent situations where people are hypersensitive, and where they do things to provoke others, to drive them to the edge. The typical micro-scenario of honor confrontations revealed in contemporary ethnography is where someone uses a repertoire of half-insults, insolent gestures, and verbal games to provoke someone else into a fight. The rhetoric and the idiom is that of honor, but here the honor code is being used provocatively, not defensively; it provides an excuse for fighting while putting the onus on the other for having behaved outrageously and thus deserving the violence that follows.[36]

Wilkinson (2003: 140) gives an instance:

[W]e went to this party and sometimes I thought I was the man 'cause I smoked weed so I thought I was the man. So I used to act like a fool, profile, I used to profile hard. Going into parties, rock my shoulders, bumping people. And after the party was over I got jumped and I got stabbed twice. . . . I wasn't by myself, though. Everybody that was with me ran.

This fight was not a face confrontation; the fifteen-year-old who had done all the bumping and "profiling hard" was stabbed in the back by someone who ran up on him after the party; his companions acted ignominiously too, running away.

In another case, the interviewee recalls that his father had three handguns in the house, which his teenage sons borrowed and lent out to their friends (Wilkinson 2003: 54):

> INT: And what was the reason they was borrowing these guns, they had beef?
>
> JEROME: No. They just wanted to hold them.
>
> INT: And what happen?. . . they went out there doing stupid shit and they got caught up in the mix?
>
> JEROME: Yup. And these is the people that we grew up with and stuff, the only friends we had, the only friends we knew.
>
> INT: And they all got killed. How did that make you feel?
>
> JEROME: It had me fucked up 'cause even before we lent them the gun, it was cool. And, um, its like when, after we let them, when we let them hold it, it seemed like. . . . They changed into they world. I was what, I was in the, um, we was in the seventh grade. We used to mess with the eighth and ninth graders. It was like everybody was scared of us 'cause everybody knew we had guns.

Several respondents explicitly linked the dangerousness of a neighborhood with looking for trouble:

> INT: How would you describe your neighborhood on the terms of safety?
>
> OMAR: It's alright, it's alright, you could walk over there and ain't nobody gonna mess with you [by you, he meant the interviewer, a tough-looking young male of Hispanic origin]. Just don't act up and try to rule shit, rule the street.
>
> INT: So there is a lot of violence?
>
> OMAR: If you look for it you gonna find it. (Wilkinson 2003: 50–51)

There is no deterrence in this repertoire of provocation, no concern for providing future security. What it does accomplish is two things: it elevates (or attempts to elevate) the perpetrator as a tough guy, one of the elite; here again we see that the code of "honor" is merely a claim to be superior to other people. And it provides a scene of action—excitement, collective effervescence, situational entertainment, what in black street culture is referred to as "show time" (Anderson 1999). The street elites both make the scene and dominate the scene.

An honor code is an ideology of stratification that emerges in particular kinds of social structures; it is a justification, a moralistic cover that operates to give a veneer of legitimacy to stratification, just like any other stratification system. In this case, it is the blatant stratification of the violent over the unviolent, of groups who make toughness an organizing principle over those who are not so tough. To explain this by a mode of functionalist sociology is no better than older functionalist theories of stratification that took ideologies of domination at face value and construed them as real contributions to the collective good.

A similar line of analysis applies to "disrespect" and "seeking respect." In contemporary times, "disrespect" is a favorite excuse for attacking the weak in public situations. It is sociologically naïve to take such excuses at face value. They are an instance of the micro-interactional procedure that Goffman (1967) and others (Scott and Lyman 1968) call "accounts": a ritual repair for a violation of normal interactional flow, a category that includes not only excuses but also explanations, apologies, admissions of guilt, as well as shifting the blame to someone else. Some kinds of accounts are more insincere or self-serving than others; all we need to note is that making an excuse for being violent implies an admission that there is something that needs excusing. *Qui s'excuse, s'accuse.*

Fighting for "respect" can be a version of blaming the victim, except that the perpetrator rather than the analyst makes the self-serving diagnosis. The altruistic middle-class observer, standing outside the struggle over control which goes on in areas of youth and gang violence, is a prime audience for such justifications. Jankowski (1991: 255, 264–70) observes that gang members are well aware of sympathetic treatments in the mass media, and of the prevailing discourse among court officials and other social service professionals, and frame their justifications to fit what will make the best impression. It is possible that the lower-class slang "to diss" ("he dissed me") is a case of linguistic trickle-down from social science, in contrast to the tendency for many slang expressions to move upward from the lower class.

As in the case of fair fights staged as single combat, the broader category of fighting justified by "disrespect" aims to establish a social hierarchy. The discourse of "respect" is found above all in the realm of gangs, covering such offenses as violating a gang's territory (being in the wrong neighborhood, for whatever reason), as well as conventional challenges when encountering a member of a rival gang, or someone who is suspected of belonging to a rival gang, or merely someone who is an outsider.

One might describe gang culture as a culture of respect, or more accurately, a culture of looking for what can be called disrespect, in order to start a fight.

Just such gangs are the ones that attempt to present themselves as elites, at least in the local area where they hold sway. Katz (1988) describes them as "street elites," ruling over the common people in their neighborhood who don't belong to gangs—or rather, claiming to rule or control "what goes on around here," since in fact this is mostly posturing, and relatively little in the area is under their control. Jankowski (1991) describes gang members as "defiant individualists," persons who are too self-willed to give in to ordinary social controls; they explicitly reject the prospects of a working-class job and aim to become part of the wealthy and powerful, enjoying its luxuries and displaying the easy use of money, which is taken as an emblem of success. Their aim to be upper class, to be sure, is acted out by local standards of what is frequently a poverty area, so the luxuries come mostly in the form of drugs and sex, and deference is found mainly by lording it over local persons who are poorer and weaker, and in ritual challenges to other gangs constituting mutual validation of each other's standing. Katz (1988: 120–21) makes the telling observation that lower-class ethnic gangs choose names that are wildly self-aggrandizing: "Kings," "Pharaohs," "Viceroys," "Lords," etc. [37] They are "defiant individualists," too, in the sense that they are self-centered, attempting to impose themselves on others to the extent they can get away with it.

The tactic of picking fights by accusations of disrespect is found among individuals as well as among gangs. Katz refers to such individuals by the self-adopted vernacular as "badass" (one of a series of such terms portraying oneself as "bad," deliberately evil; the white Mafia term was "wiseguy"). One could impose a rationalistic interpretation upon such self-presentation: the belligerent stare, the cocky body-stance, the dark glasses and clothes chosen to express alienation and threat, the cultivating of a reputation as willing to hurt anyone at the slightest provocation—all these could be taken as a strategy to fend off trouble, to show that one is not to be messed with. Nevertheless, above and beyond such considerations, as Katz stresses, the chief priority of the "badass" is to display his dominance over whomever he encounters. The violent elite also wants to be in the center of illicit action, gambling, whoring, partying precisely because it is where the center of attention of counter-normal society is. As Goffman (1967) says, "where the action is" is the realm of testing one's character by being on the edge, showing one's superiority over other persons and over the banality of ordinary lifestyles precisely because one takes risks others will not take, and takes them with aplomb, showing that one is a denizen of this world and not merely a tourist in it. "When people party all night or for days on end, they don't have fun, as they might at a children's party; they are into the action" (Katz 1988: 200). Goffman's prime example of the world of action is the gambler; Goffmanian face-contests among street hoodlums are no mere utilitarian maneuvers to assure protection, but are the same kind of thing as making one's reputation as a riverboat gambler.

The world of "disrespect" fights differs from dueling and other staged fair fights in its curtailment of etiquette: the formalities of agreeing when and where to fight, how the fight is declared over, and the general tone of courtesy in following these rules, which mark the participants off as gentry. In short, what differs is precisely what makes some of the fights focus on being fair fights—the display of fairness and respect for the rules is what enacts one's claim to being in an elite group. Gang fights and tough-guy tactics also claim elite membership, but by a different pathway: not by respecting self-limiting rules but by defying them, making a spectacle of how far one is beyond the bounds of propriety. The pure tough guy is a community elite, but he does not occupy an institutionalized position; what he lacks is the apparatus for scheduled, scripted, and publicly announced rituals in which he gets dominance. He is constantly improvising, making himself a situational elite.

The places where honor confrontations occur gives a clue to the social audience they are appealing to. Street violence is almost literally in the street. In Wilkinson's date (2003: 180) 72 percent of violent events occurred on the street or corner, at a drug spot, or at a party or club (in that order); for events involving guns, 87 percent occurred in those locales. Guns were virtually never used in schools (4.3 percent), and stores, homes, sports, and parks were less likely locales. Sanders (1994: 54) similarly finds West Coast gang violence most frequently in the street, with only a tiny percentage at schools (1.1 percent) and recreation centers (1.6 percent). All this is to say that violent confrontations occur in the places that are the stages for action, the gang's own turf, or hot spots that are the action for everyone; in places where the kind of event going on is of a different sort (schools, athletics, homes) there is little violence. West Coast gangs, moreover, keep their violence segregated within their own ethnic group. Mexican-American gangs fight rivals from different barrios; when they engage in robberies, their targets are generally non-gang members who live in their own ethnic neighborhood (Sanders 1994: 123, 134). There is an element of ethnic eliteness in this self-segregation of violence; Chicano gangs tend to act as if blacks, whites, and Asians are outside of their universe of honor and retaliation, not even worth fighting.[38] In this respect it approaches the dueling culture, organized by ethnic groups instead of by social class.

TABLE 6.3
Severity of fights in scheduled and unscheduled situations

	Fight			
	Serious	*Mild*	*Aborts*	
Scheduled situation	21 (42%)	22 (44%)	7 (14%)	50
Unscheduled situation	5 (13%)	18 (46%)	16 (41%)	39
Total	26	40	23	89

We are finally in a position to answer the question that I left dangling earlier: given that audiences have a huge effect on whether a fight will be serious, mild, or abortive, how can we explain when the audience will take one stance or another? Audiences that cheer or otherwise support and encourage the combatants tend to promote serious fights;[39] mildly involved spectators tend to get prolonged if often milder fights; uneasy and fearful spectators tend to produce abortive fights or at least mild ones; and spectators who intervene make fights either abort or stay at a mild level. Neutral spectators similarly tend to see mild or abortive fights, with the exception being where the fighters are in big enough groups so that they provide their own audiences, in which case the external audience becomes irrelevant.

What makes the audience focused and favorable to the fight, or take a contrary attitude? Prior announcement of a fight draws a supportive crowd, and no doubt selects out those who are not supportive; other fights develop spontaneously, but in situations where there is prior scheduling of a gathering for the purposes of carousing, or what in the following chapter we will consider as "moral holidays." Unscheduled, unscripted confrontations in ordinary practical circumstances of daily life are much less likely to give rise to supportive audiences, and hence to carrying through a serious fight.[40] Antagonistic confrontations that occur in transportation situations generally have audiences that are concerned with their own paths, and they may well treat the fight as a cause of a traffic jam, which they want to avoid (as in the case of the bicyclist who confronted a taxi driver and became subjected to the pressure of honking cars). Crowds who are assembled merely ad hoc, because they happen to be going somewhere, are less likely to consist in sizable groups, and are highly unlikely to know who each other is. In the other direction, where the audience already has a network of relationships, their likelihood of taking a definitive stand on the fight goes up; this is all the more so where the audience has a collective identity, either long-term (e.g., as members of a high school), or situational (as participants in a carousing situation); similarly with better established group networks, identities of the fighters are known, and the crowd can cheer them on as individuals. Scheduling and social publicity about the persons involved increase the possibility of serious violence; episodic agglomerations of persons in the same place, where anonymity is high all the way around, reduce the possibility of sustained violence. And this appears to be the case, on the evidence, despite the reputation of anonymous crowds for being dangerous. But fighters need social support to overcome confrontational tension; accordingly, dense social networks are potentially more dangerous than sparse.

But this is not enough. The audience may consist of well-organized networks, but how much violence it will support depends on additional factors. Some crowds, in my data, attempted to mediate or break up fights, usually with at least moderate success against small fights; other audiences, as in the case of nineteenth-century French duels, manipulated the show so that the amount of damage was kept rather low. Some audiences promote staged fair fights; others cheer any kind of fight at all, and may join in palpably unfair fights.[41] Here the other conditions already discussed come into play; an elite status group promoting dueling, or a closed and ranked community like a high school promoting its own well-publicized hierarchy. And fighting schools, of course, turn every aspect of the fight into a scheduled encounter in a network of collective identity and known reputations; hence they can fine-tune the amount of violence to a very high degree.

THE CULTURAL PRESTIGE OF FAIR AND UNFAIR FIGHTS

We have seen throughout that the fundamental reality of violence is confrontational tension/fear. The vast majority of fights are decidedly not brave, competent, and evenly matched. How did we get the idea that this is what fights are like? Staged fair fights do exist, but only where there are conditions to support them. But even at those times, most violence is not at all fair. Leaving aside the kinds of pathways around tension/fear that I have been developing in these chapters, what other kind of violence is there? Where there is an organized structure of power, it does not seek a fair fight, but to win, and therefore to have an unfair fight. Police do not seek a fair fight, but to bring overwhelming force against any resistance. Armies attempt the same, although not always with success against opposing armies. Parents don't have fair fights with children, but seek to enforce discipline. Similarly with organized crime such as the Mafia: they are largely in the enforcement business, and hence seek maximal intimidation. The Mafia has their own notion of honor, but it is not the notion of honor in a fair fight.

Fair fights usurp the archetype of what fighting is supposed to be about, chiefly because they are the most dramatic form. They are what makes up much of the content of literature, drama, popular entertainment, as well as informal gossip about real fights. A staged fair fight, such as a duel, is full of dramatic elements: it establishes plot tension, progresses through several levels of suspense, and provides delays so that suspense can build; it focuses the audience on just what to expect, including the moments of highest drama where the greatest uncertainties are to be found—magnifying the intensity of uncertainties by making them bounded uncertainties. It makes heroes and also tragic heroes; the plot can be played on a simple level of hero beats villain, but also on a high literary level with hero taking an inner victory though an outer defeat; and thus a fair-fight story can play a moral lesson, even with religious overtones. It makes room for gallantry as well as courage and skill, and thus builds up dramatic leads, heroes in every sense of the term.[42]

The conditions that once supported the real-life version of fair fights, however, were historically specific, and are now almost entirely out of date. Even in their day, I have suggested, duels were more image and show than reality, and most of the actual practice of them was literally practice shows in training schools. Ancient berserkers and Homeric-style heroes no doubt existed, but even then the significant battles were won not by them but by relatively more organized troops that engaged in state-building conquests.

In contemporary times, one aspect of the rhetoric of fair fights continues to be used: the notion that one fights to defend honor and overcome disrespect. This too, I have suggested, is mostly self-advertisement and self-justification. Individuals who practice leap-frog escalation do not make up a socially recognized stratum; and they are not engaging in staged fair fights. The raisons d'être of gangs and organized crime practice are distinctive forms of violence, but for neither is it the staged fair fight.

For gangs, the typical pattern of violence is the vendetta. In reality, this looks a lot like cowardice, ganging up on weak or exposed victims. And it is often incompetent, in the specific sense that particular persons who are aimed at do not get hit, but rather someone else who happens to be in the rather wild line of fire. For the gang's purposes, this kind of incompetence is not necessarily a bad thing; they are engaged in collective vengeance and collective reputation-building, so it does not matter if they hit one or another member (or friend or relative) of the opposing gang. It does not even matter if it is some bystander who is hit, since this serves as a generalized attack on the other's community and shows that the rival gang is not capable of defending its territory. Even if not that, it shows that one's gang is particularly rough, bad, something to be feared.[43]

Not to say that gangs never engage in staged fair fights. These occur chiefly among their own members, as initiation rites; or as ways of settling disputes, including their own ambitions over rank within the group (Jankowski 1991: 141–48).[44] In these instances, the group acts as audience and limiter of the violence. Thus staged fair fights are put to good use, as far as the organization is concerned, in keeping up solidarity and minimizing damage to its own forces.

Organized crime, on the other hand, does not engage in staged fights at all. The Mafia eliminates most ritualism around violence itself. Its families fight to monopolize territories, but they do not fight over merely ritual and physical incursions into their communities, the way gang members do; they do not engage in challenges over "where ya from" or insult each other's insignia. In part this is because Mafia families attempt to keep up a cartel structure as a way of regularizing business; they are not interested in honor challenges for their own sake (Gambetta 1993; Katz 1988: 256–62; Bourgois 1995: 70–76; see also references in chapter 11, note 16). In part it is a difference in the tactics of fighting, and above all the preliminaries of building up to a fight. The Mafia's favorite tactic is deception: keeping up appearances of normal relationships, including friendly sociability with one's possible enemies.[45]

Mafia killings depend upon careful planning, based on knowing the routines of other players, as well as up-to-the-minute information as to where persons are at any one time. This is what makes possible the sudden attack, catching one's opponent unaware. Mafia practice of violence hinges on treachery, since it plays on ostensibly friendly or at least normal relationships in order to get close to opponents and catch them off guard. This is a distinctive way of overcoming tension/fear: the appearance of confrontation is avoided until the very last moment; thus it is not socially real for the attacker either, enabling him to make his moves with normal confidence. Mafia enforcers and hired hit-men thus appear to operate at a level of violent competence that is much higher than that of gangs, and indeed of the police.

Gangs generally cannot match Mafia competence in overcoming tension/fear and carrying out precise hits on intended targets. Their entire style of social intercourse and violent interaction is different; since gangs are primarily concerned with advertising themselves as neighborhood elites and protectors, bluster and open display is their method; the Mafia's emphasis on deceptiveness in public and on impenetrable backstage loyalties runs in a direction that gangs are not prepared to emulate. Gangs hit at opposing gangs rather indiscriminately, in practicing collective vengeance or intimidation; the Mafia target particular individuals in opposing organizations, or indeed in their own organization, when there is a disciplinary issue or power struggle. Mafia control tactics are premised on a higher level of individual accuracy in the use of violence. In their display of ritual styles of violence, the Mafia comes across as ruthless and effective, where gangs appear as hot-headed and immature.

Perhaps this explains why there has been a shift in recent decades toward a romanticization of the Mafia. Popular entertainment becomes less focused on the cowboy gunfighter, or even on the private detective, both of which are late versions of the individual hero. The classic films of these genres—*High Noon*, *The Maltese Falcon*, Clint Eastwood westerns, and others—are about the heroic individual fighter, keeping up honor at all personal cost. These are historically transitional figures, romanticized out of all proportion to their real-life representatives. This is not surprising, given that the contemporary world has little of the social structures that support the ethos of staged fair fights, which is where heroes are manufactured. A version, of course, exists in the world of sports, but explicitly staged for entertainment and thus palpably artificial.

Our chief contemporary archetype for romanticized violent reality has become the Mafia family. It fills the niche vacated by the outgoing heirs of the duelists, because it has an equally compelling dramatic form. Its structure is different but provides the same deep elements of a successful drama: plot tension and suspense. Since Mafia organization is concerned above all with monitoring each other, to maintain loyalty as well as to make possible successful deception when an enemy is to be suddenly hit, it is a world in which everyone is constantly on the watch. Gambetta (1993) notes this for Sicily: in communities where the Mafia is strong, everyone is connected with it in one way or another, watching each other's movements, ready to report on where people are. This gives Sicilian villages a tone of ominous alertness and silence. Otherwise innocuous activities take on significance, since there is no telling where a friend or a normal passer-by or worker may turn out to be a killer; or conversely where oneself may be playing one of these normal roles in order to get close to someone who is to be killed. It is a method of violence and fending off violence that plays up the Goffmanian staging of everyday life, and gives it a life-or-death significance.

There is another side of the Mafia that adds to the romanticization: beneath the layers of deception in the outer rings of organized crime networks, there are core groups; these are real families, or pseudo-families practicing fictive kinship.[46] These, too, are readily turned into entertainment, both as sentimental depictions of solidarity in extended kinship groupings that have become rarer in American life, and in satirical or serious treatments of their real family tribulations. Mafia families make for soap opera melodrama as well as for suspense thrillers. In either dimension, they turn the ordinary details of everyday life into something of significance, against the backdrop of potential eruptions of violence.[47]

Fair fights or deceptive trickery, or even the drawn-out cycles of vendettas: these provide ways of using violence as a form of dramatic entertainment, and of giving status to the persons who can carry them off. Perhaps this is a reason why not only in entertainment but also in real life, there is an attraction toward violence. Against this, the huge mass of ugly violence that we have seen in the forms of forward panics and attacking the weak fade into the background of cultural consciousness.

CHAPTER 7

Violence as Fun and Entertainment

CONFRONTATIONAL TENSION and fear make most people most of the time avoid the actual experience of violence, and act incompetently when they are in violent situations. We have been tracing a series of pathways around this obstacle, ways of circumnavigating confrontational tension/fear. There are two main routes. The first route is attacking a weak victim; this can be done in a variety of ways, the most spectacular of which is forward panic. The second route is to confine violence in a protected enclave, staged and organized so that violence is limited or at least predictably shaped, and the social tension of confrontation is displaced by a collective concern for some other aspect of the situation. This second pathway splits into subpaths. The previous chapter dealt with staged fair fights; there the key displacement is that the fighters are treated as an elite by themselves and their audience; membership in this elite community becomes the overriding situational concern, binding fighters to each other and allaying tension and fear. Nevertheless, as we have seen in duels, tension and fear persist and cause incompetent performance. The fundamental breach of interactional entrainment never goes away; like the return of the repressed, it affects the pattern of violence, even in protected enclaves. Another subpathway is the vendetta, in which violent confrontation is limited as a series of reciprocal moves spread out in time. And staged and balanced fights could break down, lacking social organization and support, into a species of attacking the weak with momentarily superior weaponry.

This chapter and the following examine yet another subpath, routinely constructed violence that is treated as a celebration, an act of collective enjoyment, and thus widely legitimated. Some of this violence may be considered staged, but these are not necessarily fair fights; and the dynamic is not that of fighters showing off their elite membership in front of an admiring crowd—the key feature that brings the concern for fairness—but mass participation by the crowd itself. Moral holidays of looting and traditionalized vandalism (such as Halloween pranks) have a tone of egalitarian saturnalia; carousing zones create a widely shared atmosphere of ebullience that violence brings to a peak. Similarly, the varieties of violence in and around sports and entertainment events develop as crowds become emotionally entrained in the staging of the show; and players are carried by the momentum of artificial conflicts into limited, if technically illegitimate, violence at dramatically appropriate moments.

These collectively constructed situations are experienced as enclaves separate from ordinary social life, artificial, not quite real; and the violence that occurs comes from shared participation of everyone in an elevated emotional atmosphere. In Durkheimian terms, this is the violence of collective effervescence and its mass solidarity. Within these artificial enclaves, just when and how does violence occur? In the midst of a wild party or in the carousing zone, a fight does not break out every moment. Even when carousers are quite drunk, as we will see, there are sharp limits on how often violence can take place. Just when violent incidents happen needs to be examined by focusing the sociological microscope more closely on the contours of the situation.

MORAL HOLIDAYS

Moral holiday is a classic concept in collective behavior. There is a temporary breakdown in normal social controls; police authorities are absent, or they are ignored or actively disrespected by the crowd. Most of the time most people follow the conventions of public behavior that Goffman describes as keeping up customary demeanor and deference; this makes the job of policing a narrow one of cracking down on isolated disturbances. But in a moral holiday the crowd as a whole is galvanized into a collective consciousness in opposition to these restraints; authorities, if present, are overwhelmed. A moral holiday comprises a free zone in time and space, an occasion and a place where the feeling prevails that everyday restraints are off; individuals feel protected by the crowd, and are encouraged in normally forbidden acts. Often there is an atmosphere of celebration, or at least exhilaration; it is a heady feeling of entering a special reality, separate and extraordinary, where there is little thought for the future and no concern for being called to account.[1]

A moral holiday can temporarily break down a variety of normal restraints: on violence; on respect for property, allowing looting, vandalism, and material destruction; but also restraints on customary demeanor, thus allowing for shouting, noise-making, and sometimes sexual display. Sometimes it is as simple as violating customary restraints on public spaces, such as standing in the street. Not everything necessarily breaks down at once, and moral holidays tend to specialize in particular kinds of violations. These antinomian actions usually go through a sequence.

The following example shows much of the gamut: In February 2002, the now-customary Mardi Gras celebration took place along Philadelphia's South Street, an enclave of counter-culture shops and bars. Auto traffic jammed the street; pedestrians overflowed the sidewalks and walked amidst the cars, despite the efforts of police barricades to keep them separate. Eventually the police gave up and stopped allowing cars onto the street. Some men carried Mardi Gras beads and offered to exchange them to women in return for flashing their breasts, but at this point few women did so. (See Shrum and Kilburn [1996] on the New Orleans version of this ritual.) In early evening the crowd was mostly under-age youths, while the adults were inside the bars drinking; as the crowd took over the street, people from the bars joined the throng. The observer saw two fist fights, one between two girls, the other between two guys (I follow the terminology of the college-age observer); each commotion attracted a rush of onlookers to the spot, the most active cheering the girls' fight and yelling obscenities, until the fight was broken up by police.

Shortly thereafter a bottle was thrown at a police van. The precedent was quickly taken up by a barrage of bottle-throwing. Glass was shattering; many spectators ran for cover. Some climbed on parked cars, overturned trash cans, and climbed up traffic lights and street signs. Young males still on the street now began aggressively accosting women, offering them beads to flash; generally frustrated by the women's response, the males became more hostile in their language and gestures. Bottle-throwing continued, along with breaking car windows and side mirrors and scratching their paint. Around midnight a line of police on horseback formed at the east end of the street and pushed the crowd westward (the direction from which most of the crowd had come, since the street ends on the east at a highway and river). Much of the crowd panicked and ran to the west; a smaller number hung back and hurled missiles at the police. In about fifteen minutes, the crowd was dispersed, leaving a street full of broken glass, trash, and damaged cars (adapted from student report).

The whole sequence took some six hours. The sheer density of the crowd (estimated at 40,000) gradually overtook normal traffic patterns, and demonstrated the ineffectiveness of the police. The crowd became an audience for staged, isolated fair fights, and objected when this form of entertainment was broken up. The first thrown bottle was a catalyst for many others; at this point the police withdrew, and the crowd settled into attacking parked cars and store windows—but not the bars, which were part of the staging of this carousing zone; and there was some merely exuberant, "crazy" behavior of scaling traffic lights and street signs. The Mardi Gras beads-for-sexual-display ritual was increasingly attempted once the free zone was fully established, but without much cooperation from the women in this scene of violence; this led to more antinomian outbursts, but generally restrained short of physical assault. Finally the police reappeared with superior force, resulting in one last flurry of concentrated resistance, which dispersed in a few minutes as the surrounding crowd disappeared.

A moral holiday is uncontrolled by authorities, but it is not a situation of sheer chaos. It is not a Hobbesian free-for-all among the members of the crowd within the zone; to the contrary, the crowd is quite strongly focused and entrained in particular kinds of behavior. The Philadelphia Mardi Gras crowd concentrated on throwing bottles and damaging cars; it did not set fires or loot shops. Some persons invoked the traditional New Orleans–style Mardi Gras theme of ritual sexual display, but even this was of a limited sort, soliciting shows of breasts and not genitals, and sexual violence was generally ruled out. Compare the New Year's celebration that I observed in Las Vegas at the break of the year 2000: the crowd built up excitement for several hours by jovially accosting strangers, and as the moment struck, cheering, hugging, kissing. Here the moral holiday was rather limited, in part by well-known traditions, in part by taking place in a carousing zone where gambling provided many with an unaccustomed plunge beyond the normal. As in the Philadelphia instance, a few young men celebrated by acts of bravado, climbing lighting fixtures, and one was electrocuted by a sign hanging over the street where the crowd was thickest. The behavior might be regarded as senseless and tragic, but sociologically it reveals another feature of moral holidays: a few members of the crowd actively take the lead in pushing for excitement; spectacular risk-taking is one way to do so.

LOOTING AND DESTRUCTION AS PARTICIPATION SUSTAINERS

Looting and destroying property is a relatively mild form of violence that arises within moral holidays when authority has broken down. More extreme violence also may happen, and this is usually what is regarded as defining a state of riot (an approximate lay term for a moral holiday). But as we shall see, what we might call violence toward property—that is, looting and other property destruction—is crucial for the large segment of the crowd who are not otherwise violent; and that segment is crucial for determining how long the moral holiday will keep going, and thus for sustaining the frame within which more serious violence can be carried out.

I will concentrate here on the kind of moral holiday in which an identifiable group defies the police on their home neighborhood or turf; and put aside for now the subtype of riot in which an ethnic or other group invades the home turf of an enemy group. The former type, colloquially referred to as a ghetto uprising or riot, and which we might call a home turf protest, has been the common version of the looting riot in the United

States since the 1960s; the latter type, the territorial incursion riot, is more typical of deadly ethnic conflict around the world (Horowitz 2001). Riots may occur within a larger context, such as the civil rights conflicts of the 1960s, or the Rodney King trial verdict in 1992; and such context provides a rhetoric for justifying the violence, and for motivating its initial outbreak. These contexts have been extensively examined (Kerner Commission 1968; Baldassare 1994; Halle and Rafter 2003); what I wish to concentrate on here is the actual sequence and process by which looting occurs once a situation of moral holiday is established.

First must come overt defiance or attack on the police, establishing the assembled crowd as a quasi-military entity at that moment, and signaling the successful raising of the regime of local normalcy. In a racially charged situation, attacks on the police may go along with attacks on members of the opposing racial group who happen to be in the area (e.g., the white trucker in a black neighborhood who was pulled out of his cab and beaten in the street at the beginning of the 1992 L.A. riot). Nevertheless, fighting with ethnic outsiders, and indeed with the police, is not the main activity that the mass of participants in a ghetto uprising takes part in. This is a reason to consider such riots separately from ethnic turf-invasion riots, which are more directly oriented toward seeking out enemy persons to attack (their property may also be attacked, but that is secondary), whereas in ghetto uprising, looting is a key feature.

Fighting with the police generally takes the form of throwing things (bottles, cement blocks, stones) at their cars; this both mobilizes a crowd and sets in motion a process of property destruction. Pelting the enemy, much more so than firing guns or using explosives, is an activity that is easy to engage in; it has a dramatic quality, full of smashing sounds, and it leaves visible signs—a litter of glass, broken and jaggedly cracked windows, crunched-in vehicles—that are both an open break with normalcy, and yet not as extreme as bloody human bodies.[2] When the first acts of driving out authority, the acts that establish a moral holiday, are dramatic physical destruction—property destruction more than human casualties—they set the pattern that leads to widening the target to whatever public or institutional property is visible.

Looting may start out targeting a particular ethnic group, but if a free zone lasts for many hours or days, there is a tendency for all stores and markets in the area to become targets. Whatever is damaged is breached as far as social restraint is concerned; a storefront that is smashed becomes an invitation to enter, whoever it may have been once regarded as belonging to. Setting fires furthers this process, since they tend to spread from specific targets (such as the hated ethnic group) to adjacent buildings, turning everything into a part of the free zone (Tilly 2003: 143–48).

Looting develops in a spontaneous form of organization similar to other aspects of crowd violence: a small elite at the front, followed by a larger group of supporters and half-committed onlookers. Hannerz (1969: 173) observed that some individuals play the part of looting leaders, who take the initiative in breaking into stores; they are even rather altruistic in the temporary community of the street crowd, not engaging in looting themselves, but moving ahead to open up places to loot so others can follow. They seem to be aware that much of the crowd will not engage in frontline violence, even against physical objects, but only will take part once someone else has taken the earlier step of establishing a free zone and a looting situation. Looting leaders are facilitators, something like non-commissioned officers in a non-hierarchic, completely voluntary, ephemeral army.

Setting fires might be regarded as an emotional expression of anger against an enemy. But it is more than that. When the riot is an uprising in one's own neighborhood, arson is rather unreasonable, since it rarely stays contained in those particular buildings identified as enemy property.[3] Nevertheless, destruction of one's own property is not unusual in particular kinds of collective events, especially carousing (I will later discuss "wild parties"). In both cases, destruction is a way of generating a center of attention and its attendant collective effervescence; there is nothing that demands attention more urgently than a fire, especially when it is close by. The phrase often repeated and quoted from black ghetto insurrections in the 1960s, "burn, baby, burn!" (and echoing threats from militant political leaders "the fire next time"), was politically inflammatory, incendiary rhetoric; the fires, too, were largely a form of rhetoric, a theatrical gesture of the most dramatic sort. Their main effect, beyond the limited destruction they caused to the enemy, was to demand attention: from the world outside, but above all from nearby residents who could now not help but take their stand, one way or the other, in the now-established moral holiday.[4]

If fires are the device for assembling people for witness to the moral holiday, looting is the device for building mass participation. Looting gives large numbers of people something to do; it is an act of defiance against authority, and thus joins them into the moral holiday. Looting is relatively risk-free, and even free of confrontational tension/fear, since looters (at least the rank-and-file, as opposed to the looting elite) do not generally confront any persons, but only property that has already been violated. It is a banal point, but insufficiently appreciated, that rioters must have something to do, otherwise the riot peters out. If the crowd stops gathering, the emotional atmosphere that sustains the moral holiday evaporates; the police can return, normalcy is established; the momentum is lost. Once stopped, the riot cannot be started again.

Riots that go on for a particularly long time, accordingly, must be those in which there is a particularly large amount of looting or property destruction, over a widespread area. Very prolonged riots—beyond the customary one to two days—occur where the geographical area of looting or destruction keeps shifting, so that new participants can be recruited, and new targets for looting and arson (and, in some cases, massacres) can take place.

For example, in 1830 English farm workers, disgruntled over layoffs and wage cuts, burned barns and farmhouses from late August through mid-December, with the bulk of the activity in the two months of October and November (Tilly 2003: 178–87). This was called the "Swing rebellion," after the mythical avenger Captain Swing; the name implied the threat of hanging enemies but in fact most violence was limited to arson, except for peak period confrontations with authorities. When deterred by organized forces, rebels moved on to the next parish, recruiting new participants and finding new targets. There was no centralized organization, and violence was confined to a few adjacent places each day. The movement began with furtive arson, and, in late November after the height of showdown, when demonstrations were overawed by the government, the movement petered out again in arson. The process illustrates that arson is easier to perform and spreads more widely than direct confrontation.[5]

Looting was central to the American mega-riots that went on for a period of four to five days: the Newark riot in June 1967; the Detroit riot in July 1967 (Kerner Commission 1968; Halle and Rafter 2003; Tilly 2003: 145–49). These had an unusually large amount of violence (twenty-six and forty-three deaths, respectively, along with 1,500 and 2,000 injured) and involved sniper-style gun battles against massive police and military forces. Here looting played its part in spreading and sustaining the rioting. The first two days of the Detroit riot consisted almost entirely of looting and burning, as police avoided intervening until troops arrived; when the troops went into action, the next two days were taken up with gunfire. Thereafter the riot petered out, while troops patrolled the area for an additional six days. Two-thirds of the 7,200 persons arrested were accused of looting. The Newark riot began more politically, following a traffic arrest of a black taxi driver, when rumors of police atrocities spread among other taxi drivers. The Newark riot diffused into nearby New Jersey cities of Plainfield, Jersey City, and Englewood (i.e., as far as twenty miles away in several directions). As a dramatic event, these were not really separate riots. Although their beginnings lagged one to three days after the beginning of the Newark riot, all came to an end on the same day. In these outlying areas, riot activity consisted largely of looting; in the core area, there was both massive looting and massive violence in fighting with police and military forces.

The 1960s American race riots followed a similar geographical pattern of diffusion as the 1830 English rural arsons. A riot in one city tended to set off riots within the following week in nearby smaller cites, with the chances of a riot declining with greater distance (Myers 1997, 2000). This was especially important for riots that were not given much national news coverage. Riots diffused in concentric circles around the initial riot, especially if the riot started in a city with a TV station. In the era before mass communications, all this would have been done by personal networks. Repeated chains of rioters, moving to nearby regions but not farther, shaped the diffusion of the 1830 Swing Rebellion; itinerants spread the news along canals and market highways, and farm workers collaborated with those in a neighboring parish, then returned home (Tilly 2003). In both periods, the rebellion was kept up by moving to new areas rather than burning and looting the same area over again.

An implication is that a burnt-out area cannot repeat riots for a considerable length of time—at least not at a high degree of severity—until it recovers so that there is something to burn and loot. Riots, like forest fires, take a number of years to recover and build up fuel (both literally and emotionally) for the next outburst. In the short run, a big riot preempts subsequent big riots in the same place; even with external precipitating conditions, only small riots are possible, if any.[6]

Mass participation in looting is a key device for making a riot last, indeed for building it up into a notable event, getting it political attention in the enemy camp or in the eyes of the wider public. The looters themselves generally lack a political ideology; politicized black civil rights activists in the 1960s riots were often disgusted with the looting and the attitude of the looters. Tilly (2003) thus categorized these riots as only marginally racial protests that degenerated into opportunistically seeking private gain.[7] But this is to omit the part that looting, along with arson, play in the dynamics of riots: looting is a mass-recruiter and a momentum-sustainer. Without it, if the riot took nothing but the form of violent confrontations against the police, the riot could easily be dealt with by police withdrawing until the crowd became bored, drifted away, and disassembled; or it could be put down by putting in overwhelming force against the inevitably small group that would actively confront it. Looters are the foot-soldiers of a riot; better put, they are the half-hearted hanging-back, the 85 percent who never fire their guns. Looting is a brilliant tactical invention—so to speak, because no one invented it—since it takes the relatively useless part of the supporters and onlookers of an insurrection and turns them into activists of sorts, keeping alive the emotional atmosphere that is where a moral holiday lives or dies.

Looters pointedly disrespect normal property rights; but a remarkable pattern is that looters generally do not loot from each other. Each loots what he or she can, but looters rarely fight over what goods they can take, nor rob one another as they carry the goods away. One sees this, for example, in a series of photos of the 1992 Los Angeles riot set off upon the announcement of not-guilty verdicts in the Rodney King beating trial. In these, as in other looting riots, looters take the postures of what Goffman calls normal "civil disattention," maintaining pedestrian traffic that attempts to keep out of each other's way, even in a somewhat crowded and frenzied situation. In part the lack of struggle among looters may be because the items that are looted are not of great value to them. In the L.A. riot photos (*Los Angeles Times*, May 12, 1992), we see, for example, a man whose arms are overflowing with packages of tissues and paper napkins from a grocery store; a small Hispanic boy with his father, exiting a sporting goods store carrying several boxes of ladies' "Thigh Master" exercise equipment; a young black man coming out of the broken window of a beauty supply shop carrying a packaged hair dryer. Interviews with looters in 1960s ghetto riots generally found their looting was non-utilitarian; some looters said later they did not need the goods or could afford to buy them; some rationalized that the stores owed them for past grievances (Dynes and Quarantelli 1968; Quarantelli and Dynes 1968, 1970; Tilly 2003: 148). The looters were engaged in an act of mass solidarity. Possessing any particular goods was not the point, hence there is a kind of "altruism" among looters that keeps them from being selfish with each other. Looting is largely Durkheimian ritualism done for the sake of the activity itself, and as a symbolic expression of membership; the objects stolen can be nearly worthless in every other respect, but they represent one's partnership in breaking the law. Post-looting interviews show a considerable number of otherwise respectable persons (married, employed, church-goers, members of what Anderson [1999] calls the decent, non-street part of the ghetto) taking part in the looting; there is a widespread emotional attraction or social magnetism of joining in the collective effervescence. The second-order problem of "who guards the guardians" in rational/utilitarian theory is strikingly absent here; if we ask, "who loots from the looters" once law and order is gone, the answer is virtually no one—the moral holiday has its own form of social solidarity. The breakdown of external authority in a moral holiday does not promote a free-for-all of unrestrained violence.[8]

The best detail available on the sequential dynamics of looting comes, not from a protest riot, but from the blackout of the electric grid in New York City for one night in July 1977 (Curvin and Porter 1979). This looting had more utilitarian aspects than others, since it did not start with an atmosphere of heightened racial antagonism, nor in an escalating confrontation with police.[9] From hour-by-hour arrest data, as well as interviews, we find three waves of looters. The first wave were professional criminals, typically men in their twenties; within the first hour of the blackout (which started at 9:30 p.m.), they broke into jewelry and electronic goods stores and took the most valuable items. The second wave consisted heavily of youth gangs looking for fun and excitement as well as plunder, appearing on the scene around 11 p.m. (They did not, however, fight with each other, but joined the moral community of the free zone.) The third wave were ordinary residents of all social classes, venturing out into the scene of action, beginning after midnight and lasting into the daylight hours of the following day until petering out in the afternoon.[10] Here curiosity turned into a magnetic attraction to take part in the looting. The third wave resembled the looters in other riots, swept up in the emotional participating, looting objects of little value to themselves. One looter, for example, took a side of beef from a grocery store, then abandoned it on the sidewalk.

A married man, employed as a salesman, and with a daughter in parochial school, reported that the urge to loot came over him in the midst of the chaos.

> "I don't know; I felt I wanted to snatch something while I was out there. . . . I happened to be on the scene when they just began to break into a store. Things started flying out, and I happened to get my hands full of the stuff. And I was standing on the corner talking, when suddenly a police car pulls up, and they got me." He was in possession of ten pairs of women's slacks and seven blouses; he told the interviewer later that he didn't intend to give them to his wife, and he wasn't sure what he was going to do with them. (Curvin and Porter 1979: 15)

This looting-riot was initiated by persons with ostensibly utilitarian motives. Nevertheless, the effect of this wave of well-calculated robbery was to create a moral holiday with many features of a community of temporary solidarity. Groups of men formed, consisting at least in part of strangers to one another, who collectively attacked the iron protective grills over the closed store fronts; ten to twenty men would mass their weight to pull down the grills, sometimes taking ten minutes or more of hard exertion, and taking rest breaks together to coordinate their next assault.

The later wave of looters, taking advantage of the breaches made by the activists who preceded them, displayed the usual pattern of non-utilitarian, symbolic-emotional participation in the looting. Aside from the property destruction, there was little violence. Looters did not fight with store owners who happened to be present; even a token show of opposition by store personnel was enough to deter most of the looters. This could be explained by the feeling (expressed by some looters) that there was no need to trouble oneself with resistance, since there were plenty of other places open to loot; but it also shows that confrontational tension/fear was strong. Antagonism to an "enemy" was not a driving force (again, very much in contrast to territorial incursion riots), even though the store-owners were mostly white and lived outside the neighborhood. The police, although highly outnumbered, were rarely assaulted, and when they made arrests met with little resistance.

The emotional atmosphere mixed exhilaration and fear. It was near-total darkness, punctuated by police cars speeding along the streets with sirens wailing, crowds rushing about, sometimes hooting and yelling; police firing guns in the air in an effort to scare off looters—this had little deterrent effect, since looters soon realized the police were not shooting to hit them. Crowds sometimes turned into pockets of frenzy, while other places were festive or amiable in mood. A twenty-one-year-old black man recalled he was out playing basketball:

> When the lights went out, everybody started screamin', you know. . . . At first really I was yelling just to be fancy, yeah, yeah, yeah, yeah. [Then someone suggested a commercial street to loot.] Everybody from all over was down there. Everybody was just walkin' and talkin'. We went into this gift shop and they just started getting shit and then they broke. . . . Excited, excitement you know; I was up. I was charged, you know, with the excitement of the moment. The lights was out, you know; we was going to see what we can do. Like, I was really charged up—We just jumped into the mood, you know? Like they say, when you're Roman, do what the Romans do. We just went crazy. (Curvin and Porter 1979: 188)

Another remarkable feature of restraint in particular kinds of looting situations is sexual. One might expect that if all rules are off, individuals would take whatever selfish pleasures they could; and in chaotic crowds, many strangers would be encountered who could be sexually victimized with impunity. Tilly (2003) characterizes many riots as starting with moral outrage against authorities or racial injustice, but turning into opportunistic pursuit of private gain under the cover of the breakdown of authority. But this is not what happens in the sexual sphere, at least not in the moral holidays of ghetto protest riots. The crowd of looters do not engage in raping or even sexually groping the women in their crowd. In the American race riots of the 1960s, and in the 1992 L.A. riot, there were virtually no indications of rapes.

There are, however, kinds of riots in which the situation is decidedly the opposite. In ethnic turf-invasion riots, there may be rather systematic rapes of women of the targeted enemy; breaking into houses of the ethnic enemy can involve both looting and raping (Horowitz 2001; Kaldor 1999). What makes the difference between riots in which sexual restraint is the norm, and those in which sexual violence is featured along with other forms of attack? Riots on one's home turf, without members of the enemy group present, place most of their energy in attacking inanimate targets; invading enemy turf to attack persons provides more occasions for rape. Another condition is that rapes occur in riots where the attackers and looters are exclusively men. In riots where women join in the looting, they do so with impunity from sexual coercion.[11] The moral holiday constricts the boundaries of the group down to an enclave of local solidarity—or indeed perhaps expands into an enclave of solidarity in what was otherwise an anomic neighborhood; the Durkheimian collective effervescence gives a sense of security for themselves, even if they are in a normally crime-ridden area. As long as they take part in the ritual activities of the group, participants are bodily safe. A moral holiday is a holiday from some morals, but it strongly institutes other morals.

THE WILD PARTY AS ELITE POTLATCH

What makes a "wild party"? This is a metaphor, of course, one of a family of metaphors including such terms as "a blast," "a blow-out," "a bash," "a riot." Persons who take the leading part acquire the reputation of "a wild and crazy guy," "hell-raiser," "devil-may-care," "a pistol," "a party animal." What these terms imply is a high level of collective effervescence, and a strong sense of antinomianism, breaking the bounds of normalcy.

The easiest way to escalate a party or festival into a memorable carousing is by destruction of property. This is something like looting in a moral holiday. It differs in that looting (at least in home-turf riots) is a form of rebellion from below against what are regarded as at least token targets of enemy groups. Material destruction at a wild party, however, is generally destroying one's own property. A wild party of this sort is an elite potlatch.

The archetype comes from the festivals of Indian tribes of the Pacific Northwest coast, an area rich in products of the sea and forest (Kan 1986; Ringel 1979). Fur-trading in the nineteenth century made these tribes wealthy by local standards. Their festivals were organized by invitations from one local chief to another, in which the host would show off his wealth by giving it away lavishly to the guests; the latter were under pressure to reciprocate by an equally lavish party. Warring clans might hold potlatches as peace ceremonies, and gestures of ritual hostility were often prominent. Competition over status display escalated; blankets, copper sheets, Western trading goods (such as sewing machines) and other treasures were not only given away but smashed up in front of the guests, or thrown into the sea, in grand gestures of disdain for mere property. Tribes were sharply stratified between aristocrats and commoners; only the aristocrats could own slaves and copper sheets. The high point of a potlatch was reached in killing slaves in a ceremonial execution. Slaves and coppers were not used for utilitarian purposes, and slaves were acquired just before the potlatch for the purpose of sacrificing them in front of one's guests. The crucial test in a reciprocal potlatch was whether the next host could sacrifice honorific possessions of equal or greater value.

In addition to these forms of violent destruction of valuable and especially status-giving property, potlatches had dancing and eating contests. Hosts tried to give the impression of an endless supply of food, and forced it on the guests, who were expected to overeat and vomit. If nobody vomited, it reflected largely upon the hosts and their hospitality.

We should envision a potlatch as a large, noisy party, full of boasting and ebullient pride. A potlatch was elite, because it could be given only by the wealthiest members of the community; and since one lost status by attending without being able to give a similar party in return, guests too had to be of high status, or at least aspire to it (a point emphasized in the classic analysis of Mauss [1925/1967]). Potlatches were competitive, and had overtones of violent threat; but fights between guests and hosts were rare, and the competition of ostentatious destruction of one's wealth held the center of attention.

Compare the behavior of wealthy Oxford students in the years around 1900–1930.[12] Their college rooms were private suites, where they were waited upon by servants; prestigious sociability among the popular men involved hosting luncheons and dinners in one's rooms, or sometimes in a hired hall. In such all-male schools, with rare opportunities to associate with young women, something like a rating-and-dating complex usually found in heterosexual courting was orchestrated by the young men themselves. It also resembled rounds of party-giving by middle-aged hostesses of the higher classes. Students vied for invitations, or for guests who had reputations as aristocratic, stylish, sophisticated, notable in athletics, or just plain lively and fun. The atmosphere was one of mildly flaunting authority, cutting classes, breaking curfews, and drinking. Social striving and rivalry must have given a feeling of ebullience to the young men who were admitted into the most sought-after gatherings; and their ritualistic dinners (which featured drinking games aimed at getting particular individuals very drunk) sometimes culminated in riotous destruction. Drunken students would build a bonfire in the center of a college quad, piling on not only stolen firewood but also college furniture; college authorities who ventured to put down the breach of order were jeered and sometimes pelted. Authorities usually confined their intervention to fines levied in the aftermath; these fines went to college treasuries, where they served to stock the wine for equally elite but more discretely private dinners by the college Fellows (i.e., the bachelor faculty residing in college).

Thus the undergraduates' flamboyant carousing was recycled into a more genteel carousing by their teachers.

In earlier centuries, university students were even wilder (Midgley 1996). Students went to town taverns for drinking and sometimes had full-scale town-and-gown fights against the locals. Students evaded the college proctors (guards hired by college authorities to enforce discipline) and sometimes fought with them. An Oxford "rag" of the 1700s involved drunken vomiting in the streets, mild vandalism, fighting, and sexual assaults of local women. Other riotous occasions arose out of countryside expeditions by unserious students, including drunken foot races with neighborhood girls in deshabillé. The riotous "bloods" or "high-livers" typically were drawn from the aristocracy, who had special privileges and immunities not shared by poorer students grinding at their studies for careers chiefly as clergymen. The hierarchy of rich and comparatively poor, of elite and modest class background, was enhanced by the situational stratification between high-spirited carousers and the duller sorts in the background. Oxford "rags," like the early-twentieth-century college bonfires, were implicitly displays of wealth and status, conspicuously flaunting an insouciant disregard for costs, conventions, and serious purposes. Young "bloods" frequently went through their allowances, contracted debts from lavish entertaining or the furnishing of their rooms, as well as from gambling, and were sent down (i.e., expelled) from college. All this was just what the lower-status students could not afford to do. Nevertheless, the lower-ranking were a necessary backdrop for the carousing elite, someone to be impressed and scorned by their escapades. By contrast, riotous carousing of this sort was not much carried on when the aristocratic elite was gathered on their private estates, where the audience consisted of servants and dependent workers and tradespeople; there needed to be an audience close enough in status, and an atmosphere of status competition, for carousing to be an effective display of contempt for ordinary proprieties. Strongly institutionalized social ranks lead to sedate and rather dull parties; it is where there is ongoing situational stratification, the sheer momentary attention-gaining of a noisy display of uninhibited fun, that carousing becomes destructive.

A current example comes from a student report on a group of American college undergraduate males who share a rented house. A big athlete, when he is drunk, starts smashing up the staircase balustrade. One of his housemates is hit by a piece of flying wood, and angrily threatens to fight. The group gathers around and turns the situation into a joke, with everyone joining in the fun of destroying the balustrade. They all have to pay the landlord for the damage, but the incident is remembered as a notable occasion.[13] This is the potlatch pattern, destroying one's own living environment.[14]

Elite-potlatch type of carousing is generally confined to property destruction. Sheer ebullience, even with the motives of status display as an antinomian elite, and inside the protection of a temporary moral holiday, remains within highly conventionalized limits. Confrontational tension/fear does its work, even here. Destroying property is usually enough to keep up the mood of excitement and boundary-breaking. How then does violence occur in carousing situations?

CAROUSING ZONES AND BOUNDARY EXCLUSION VIOLENCE

Most wild parties are not violent. But examining these parties has given us a clue to parties that are. The most successful party generates its own temporary stratification, a situational elite of those who are in the center of the action, followed by a penumbra of those who are striving to take part, and a fringe of those who are excluded. It is contested stratification around the boundaries of carousing occasions that produces much carousing violence.

There are three main pathways: authorities' intervention and ensuing counter-escalation, gate-crashing violence, and end-resisting violence.

A large proportion of fights at parties or holiday street crowds occur when police arrive, attempting to reduce the noise, force a crowd out of the street, or deter unlawful drinkers.[15] This leads to violence where the police forces are no match for the size and emotional enthusiasm of the crowd; the carousers have resources that allow them to counter-escalate against the police, and an initially small amount of police violence may be met by a much wider front of violence or at least threatening gestures. The crowd's reaction at this point, including throwing bottles and overturning cars and other forms of vandalism, is largely a form of bluster, quasi-threats of personal violence acted out without much direct confrontation. As in other riots and battles, a small number of activists can start a phase of escalation, which becomes general in part through the sheer chaos of people running about (seeking shelter, among other reasons); this in turn tends to make the police strike out indiscriminately against whoever is moving around in the carousing zone. The process escalates feelings of anger on both sides, and expands the amount of violence—although as we have seen with all fighting, it is mostly incompetent and misdirected violence. The very fact that most people live through such a situation, with a lot of excitement but not too much chance of personal damage, is one reason why big carousing scenes remain popular with their veterans; most people live to tell the tale, and find it a valuable piece of cultural capital in the conversational circuits of subsequent parties.

A carousing zone is a place where the ritualism of generating antinomian excitement prevails and may even be institutionalized. It can consist of just the place where a party is going on, or more widely a region where revelers and fun-seekers go, such as an area of bars, clubs, and possibly erotic entertainment and (at the time when it was more illicit) gambling. Carousing zones are also zones in time, open for action on a schedule such as weekend nights, or particular holidays. When it is fully in operation, a carousing zone is a pocket of emotional high pressure or collective emotional energy; attempts to interfere with carousing rituals, or even just to enter the zone (if one is an inappropriate person in the eyes of the carousers), constitute a pressure against its boundary. The carousing zone, at the height of its power (which is chiefly emotional power), fights to defend its own existence, so to speak. But carousing zones are collective enactments; like other rituals, the emotional enthusiasm of carousing exhausts itself over a period of hours (usually four to six hours, in my cases); thus carousing that can lead to enthusiastic battles if authorities intervene at its height will easily dissipate if the intervention occurs when the enthusiasm is already ebbing and people are drifting away.

A hypothesis: police are more likely to provoke violence if they try to break up a party in which the energy level is high, where people are having a good time, than if they break up a less successful party scene.

In an extreme instance, intervention turns into murder: Two New Jersey police officers investigated a complaint of noise at a roadside tavern. What they intruded upon was a celebration by two armed robbers who had just robbed a Brooklyn bookie of a large amount of money. They were drinking heavily and firing shots in horseplay. The robbers no doubt had a practical interest in escaping, but their immediate reaction was an elaborate ritual of humiliation: the officers were held at gunpoint, pistol-whipped, forced to strip to their underwear and kneel down, and finally shot in the head (*Philadelphia Inquirer*, Feb. 11, 2002). The carousing mood was being interrupted at its height; the response was itself an extension of the carousing: previous gun-play turned into further playing with guns, sadistic but ebullient. When the carousing mood had passed, the robbers acted differently. Two days later one of the robbers was killed in a shoot-out with police, and the other surrendered.

A second pathway to violence is where individuals or small groups attempt to force their way into a carousing scene but are excluded. Unlike authorities trying to break up a party, this is a case of would-be carousers trying to join in.

A group of middle-class young men are having a party in an apartment; they all know one another and are sitting down talking. Three guys arrive looking for the roommate of the party host; he isn't here, but they decide to wait. The party is no doubt rather boring and the intruders do not enter into the conversation. One of them, a Marine, asks the host for a needle to give himself a tattoo. The host refuses, saying he would not allow that in his apartment. (This suggests a cultural difference in social class; the intruder probably knew he was stirring something up, and the host resists.) The Marine persisted in asking for a needle, the host persisted in refusing; the argument escalated, with the intruder standing up and yelling that he was a Marine and demanded respect. (The incident took place in January 2002, at the time of the United States war in Afghanistan.) The host responds by standing up and replying, "Listen, it doesn't matter to me who you are, but this is my apartment and you have to leave. I don't want to fight you, just leave!" He says this in a loud voice but in a relatively flat tone, as if to stand his ground but not to escalate further.

The two stand facing each other, backs arched and chests puffed. They repeat themselves for several minutes, a typical standoff. This comes to an end when the host turns his back to sit down on the couch, breaking eye contact. The Marine, perhaps feeling frustrated in starting a fight—and also feeling a momentary advantage—punches the host in the shoulder. The sudden release of tension precipitates the violence. The host's two closest friends now jump into the action, as do the Marine's two companions; the host is pushed onto the sofa while the others engage in grappling, punching, and kicking. Not much damage is done, and there is some accidental hitting of one's own side.

Other men now pull the fighters apart. The two groups of three now confront each other again but from opposite sides of the couch, yelling their positions repeatedly: the Marine refusing to leave and the host declaring it was his apartment. Finally a young woman gets in the midst of the confrontation, tells the intruders she is tired and wants to go to bed; after many repetitions, they leave. The police had been called at the beginning of the fight, but they never arrive. (adapted from student report)

Such fights raise an analytical question, in that the party is a zone of solidarity, indeed heightened and demonstrative solidarity. Why should solidarity, a desire for friendly inclusion, lead to violence? Why go where one is not wanted, and expect to be favorably received? A display of violence is hardly calculated to make one more welcome. The key is that carousing solidarity is stratifying; the boundary sends the message of inferiority and rejection. This is so even where the partiers are of a higher social class, politer, more restrained, and less prone to violence than the lower-ranking intruders. It may not be a very good party from the latter's point of view, but they are on the outside looking in and haven't a clear sense of what they are trying to get into. Boundary-exclusion violence almost always is started by the intruder, responding to the status insult.

Exclusion from parties and carousing scenes, of course, is quite common, indeed usual. What then makes the difference in those instances where it is violently contested? High school sociable elites, as we have seen, typically have their territories—lunch tables, after-school hang-outs—and they easily defend them against less popular kids by collective jeering. Here the status hierarchy is so widely known, and the emotional energy so concentrated in the elite, that intruders are easily humiliated; most lower-ranking kids do not try to intrude, even where they are physically tougher and stronger. When it does happen, crashing parties of the popular high school crowd can lead to fights (Milner 2004: 72–73). Much gate-crashing violence occurs in anonymous scenes, where the party is large, or the intruder comes from a remote part of the social network (in the previous instance, a friend of an absent roommate).

We see the same pattern at a cast party for members of an MTV reality show. Two off-duty policemen, together with a friend, having heard about the party while in the process of providing security for the television shoot, showed up at 9:30 p.m. and began pounding on the door demanding admittance. An on-duty officer told them to disperse; whereupon words were exchanged, and the officer was punched in the face (*Philadelphia Inquirer*, May 10, 2004).

A condition for gate-crashing violence is that stratification is not clearly institutionalized or widely visible: an atmosphere of superficial egalitarianism, in which there are no class distinctions and no recognized hierarchy of group prestige. This is what motivates action-seekers, like youths on weekend evenings, to make their way into whatever party they hear is happening, and to fight when they are not admitted. The sheer absence of stratification is not sufficient; it is the absence of repetitive, institutionalized and normalized stratification, combined with the situational stratification of partying itself, the prestige of being in a scene of effervescence.

The egalitarianism in manners and in visible markers such as styles of dress, that characterizes youth culture since the late twentieth century, is one of the causes of carousing violence. Comparative data is lacking, but a hypothesis is that in earlier generations there was much less gate-crashing violence, because gate-crashing (when practiced) was much more a matter of deferential attempts at clandestine assimilation, and detection would lead to humiliation and easily enforced exclusion rather than violent expostulation by the gate-crasher. It is the egalitarianism, the sense of "I'm just as good as anybody else," that leads to righteous anger by those excluded.[16]

END-RESISTING VIOLENCE

Some violence occurs, not in order to force one's way into a carousing scene, but by refusal to let a carouse come to an end:

> I was over at my friend's place just sitting around drinking whiskey with him and another guy. This other dude came over, and we began

shooting dice for half dollars. After about an hour or so of shooting dice, I started feeling the whiskey and decided that I better be leaving. I told them that I had to go, and I picked up my dice and put them in my pocket. Then X jumped up and said, "What did you pick up those dice for?" I said, "Because I'm finished shooting, and I'm going to split." He said, "You can't quit now; you have to give me a chance to win back some of my money." I couldn't understand him coming down on me with that because I hadn't won that much money. I said, "Hey, man, I'm tired of shooting, and I've got to be somewhere now."

Then he got right up in my face and said, "You're not quitting yet, motherfucker." I said, "The hell if I'm not; I told you that I'm tired of playing." He stared at me with his eyes popping out of his head like he was crazy and said, "You dirty, no-good fucking ass punk." I knew the drunken fool wasn't in his right state of mind, and I got scared because I knew he carried a gun and didn't care what he did. I heard that he had killed a dude some time back.

I said, "Man, will you get the fuck out of my face?" But that just sent him into a rage. He started swinging his arms side to side and calling me a motherfucking punk, and he spit in my face. I called him a dirty motherfucker, and he shoved me. I figured then that he wasn't going to be wasting more time on me, and when he went into his coat I thought that he was reaching for his piece. I knew then that I had to act quick, so I pulled out my pistol and shot the crazy damn fool before he could shoot me. (Athens 1980: 30–31)

In another instance, two men become friendly with another man at a bar; after the bar closes, they are invited to his apartment to continue drinking. They buy several six packs of beer, and take a cab to his apartment. After the beer is gone, the host tells them they have to leave. The visitors are enraged—in part because they have no transportation, but also because the festive mood is abruptly closing down. They get into an argument, which escalates to a shoving match; one of the visitors hits the host with a punch, hits him over the head with a lamp, knocks him down and stomps him in the face. He is later arrested for aggravated assault (Athens 1980: 37–38).

End-resisting violence can also occur not just among hardened action-seekers and in casual anonymous settings, but among friends. Here the violence is usually more limited:

In one instance (from student report), a group of high school students on the weekend after their senior prom go to a mountain resort, where they rent six nearby houses. They spend their time with music, dancing, hot tubs, watching movies and hanging out; the mood is friendly and happy. On the last night, a group of boys in one of the houses has a toga party, with a great deal of drinking and noise-making. A group of girls four houses away, hearing a rowdy group of boys approaching from the party, lock the doors and windows to keep them out. This enrages the boys, who shout at them through the glass doors, calling them "bad friends" and "disloyal." One of the girls is outside in her car; the boys surround her, pounding on the car windows and rocking the car back and forth. One of the toga boys gets into the house, where he ceremoniously smashes the furniture, most notably two ceramic elephants from the mantel which he throws to the ground.

As the noise escalates, two other boys show up to confront the toga group and defend the girls. This leads to a renewed escalation; five of the toga boys, lead by a 6 foot 4 inch athlete, attack the two (who are much smaller) while another eight or nine toga boys cheer them on. The beating breaks off as the group rampages into the house, breaking objects and bringing the girls to tears. The toga group then leaves, still yelling, looking for more partying elsewhere. Several hours later, at about 4 a.m., the group returns and throws things against the windows for half an hour. The party winds down in a mixture of fun and anger.

Frustrated Carousing and Stirring Up Effervescence

A certain amount of fighting occurs inside carousing scenes, not so much because people are having a good time, but because the scene does not meet expectations. The external elements of festivity are present: a crowd of people, the excitement of bodies jammed in one place, loud noise from background music or just from trying to be heard over others' voices. But there is not much laughing or sense of fun; persons stuck in the crowd can be bored and keyed up at the same time. Annoyances with the jostling crowd can turn into a fight, which simultaneously releases tension and raises the level of action.

An instance from a student report: A rather average-seeming college frat party is going on. A large number of freshman boys are standing around, not talking much, filling the void with rapid drinking. Hence there is a large crowd around the beer keg, pressing to fill their cups. One of the frat boys is shoved forward by the jostling crowd, knocking into a large football player who is filling his cup and spills his beer. He pushes the frat boy back violently into the crowd, whereupon the latter bounds back and the two scuffle over the keg. Several other big fraternity boys come to their brother's aid and drag the football player outside.

A few minutes later, the athlete returns with a group of his teammates. This leads to a standoff at the front door; insults and threats go on for some minutes, finally ending when someone inside yells the police had been called and would be arriving soon. (This turned out not to be true.) After the threat had ended, all the brothers who had been involved in any degree went on at length describing their deeds, boasting and exaggerating. Everyone was talking about it. The brawl supplied the previously missing topic of conversation, creating a focus of common attention, and raising the level of collective effervescence far above the initial, rather pathetic level.

This is not to say that the individuals who started the brawl had conscious intentions of livening up the party. The initiation was random and accidental. Likely they were merely part of a large group that felt tension compounded by expectation of party action—whatever that vaguely defined entity might be—plus a sense of frustration arising from comparative boredom and frustration with the sheer physical press of the crowd. The mixture can produce pleasure in the fight—even though the usual indicators of tension/fear are still present, with the fight being brief and incompetent, the standoff easily broken up, and much more bluster than violence. The post-fight circulation of excited conversation in the crowd is actually the most important aspect, since it is what defines the fight as a pleasurable thing, not so much by explicit labeling as by casting an emotional aura over it retrospectively.

Fights often arise in situations of this sort, where the outcome is not necessarily to make the experience into a pleasurable one. Several student reports detail public festivals where large crowds of people press one another on the streets. In a street carnival in London, for instance, the crowd is so tightly packed they can barely move. Despite prior expectations of a good time, the immediate reality is that one can do nothing but shove and be shoved along with the crowd. A fight breaks out between two men, one black and one white; they are so closely locked together that they can do little damage to each other; nor can police get through to break them up, and the crowd is too packed to intervene. It appears the men are isolates, alone without supporters to join in or indeed friends to hold them back, in contrast to most members of crowds, who attend with their friends. Thus it may be that these are individuals who are especially frustrated in expectations that the carnival will bring a sharp rise in ordinary social ebullience. My collection of reports contains several instances of this sort, in which the fight makes no one happy.

Fights of this sort are sometimes cheered by spectators, who take it as a form of entertainment. In these instances, the fighters may be frustrated but the crowd benefits by taking them as a focal point for collective action as a coordinated mass of spectators; their fighting enables the crowd to turn from a mere traffic jam of small groups at cross-purposes into a larger emotional entrainment, raising their collective spirit.

In another instance (from a student report), a large audience at a street festival is waiting impatiently for a band to begin to play. They express their restlessness in outbursts of rhythmic clapping and hooting. Then they are distracted when a drunken, homeless man begins urinating in the midst of the crowd; other people push back in the crush to get away from him, as he sits in the midst of a pool of his urine. As the crowd focused on him, palpably tense, a bottle is thrown, then a shower of missiles. He starts to throw them back, making the crowd yell at him; three large men rush at him and kick him, finally throwing him aside. The music finally starts and the crowd turns its attention to the stage, suddenly happy.

There is no automatic, functional feedback loop whereby a frustrated, would-be carousing crowd can create effervescence by starting a fight; sometimes it happens that the crowd becomes focused and entertained; sometimes this fails to occur and the crowd is merely increasingly annoyed or frightened. At this point, detail is lacking as to what switches the course of action in one direction or the other. This would be a crucial extension of a processual theory of violence, since as we have seen in chapter 6, the attitude of the crowd has a strong effect upon the confinement or escalation of violence.

Paradox: Why Does Most Intoxication *Not* Lead to Violence?

Carousing and violence might appear to be linked by a simple and obvious path: drunkenness.[17] There is considerable evidence that intoxication leads to violence (e.g., Parker and Auerhahn 1998). American victim surveys show that over one-quarter of victims of criminal assault thought their assailants were under the influence of alcohol, a figure borne out by urinalysis of persons arrested for violent crimes. The pattern of alcohol use is found both in homicides and through toxicology of homicide victims, indicating that both sides of a fight are often escalated through alcohol. But there is something paradoxical in the pattern: as we shall see, the vast majority of drunken experiences do not lead to violence. We will need a situational mechanism to explain when they do.

When drunks are violent, how does this happen? Parker (1993; Parker and Rebhun 1995) proposes that contextual conditions combine with alcohol to disinhibit violence selectively.[18] The combination includes a dispute and encouragement from bystanders. Ordinarily individuals consciously decide not to use violence to solve a dispute, but alcohol disinhibits this kind of self-constraint.

Ethnographies of drunken parties give abundant examples. A student report (by a female) describes a fraternity party at a Southern college in which the steady drinking of beer led to increasingly uninhibited behavior as the evening wore on. When the young women first arrived, their hosts acted courteously, holding doors for them, attentively asking them if they would like more drinks or snacks. As the drinking progressed, the fraternity brothers' attentions became more blatant. A typical line: "Hey girl. What's your name? Linda? Linda, Linda, let-me-in-da! I'm *Dave*. You enjoying yourself? Did you get some of Pi Delta's beer? Likin' it? Want some more? You let me know if you want some more!" After his sixth drink, a student who had started out as shy cornered one of the women against a wall, removed her sweater and fondled her breasts. Women too lost their inhibitions; a friend of the reporter who began the party in the role of protectress ("Hey, Linda. You let me know if any idiot guys are bothering you!"—although this could have been a version of bluster and a claim to know her way around) eventually ended up dancing on top of a table, twirling her sweater over her head and shouting "Wahoo! Look at me!" The table broke, as did some lamps that were knocked over, lending an air of potlatch to the proceedings.

This party featured one fight, late in the evening. Two men who had paid no attention to each other previously became embroiled, apparently randomly, in an exchange of angry obscenities. "Who you callin' a wuss? You callin' me a wuss? Whatever man! YOU the wuss!" The reply was in the same vein: "YOU are the wuss. You *are!* If you aren't, then why don't you *show me* what you're made of, you little fuckface?" A circle of spectators gathered around, excitedly awaiting the action. The two men wrestled each other down to the floor, while the crowd cheered on whoever was momentarily on top. The fight went on for several minutes with neither side winning. The fighters came to a standstill, lying entangled on the floor looking exhausted. The crowd lost interest and drifted away. "Wuss," the two muttered at each other. Eventually each was picked up by a friend and helped home to clean up the bloodied noses, scrapes, and scratches.

The incidents of the party have a repetitive micro-rhythm. The brawlers mirror and repeat each other, and themselves, in their series of accusations. The background music is loud, accentuated beats of rap lyrics, more significant for punctuated exclamations ("Who be chillin' *in da house* tonight?") than for literal sense. The conversation ("Linda, Linda, let-me-in-da!") is more incantation than substance. All this is highly characteristic of drunken behavior, which progressively reduces down to the simplest aspects of interaction rituals.

Although the connection between intoxication and violence seems obvious, it is a very partial picture. A large proportion of violence is not caused by alcohol, and indeed intoxication can be antithetical to effective violence. And as we shall see shortly, in those particular kinds of circumstances where drinking is most often connected to violence, the problem of sampling on the dependent variable gives a very misleading picture.

Consider the array of kinds of violence in this book. Military violence is not necessarily connected with drunkenness; soldiers sometimes drink before battle, but it does nothing to improve their firing aim; on the whole, calmer and soberer troops are better fighters than drunken ones. Police violence occurs with emotional intoxication, not drinking. In most political and ethnic demonstrations, riots, and massacres, the participants are sober, including the leading activists; the exceptions are riots by festive, holiday crowds, but these are generally the less destructive and homicidal crowds.[19] The worst kind of mass violence, forward panics, do not depend upon intoxication.

Drinking is involved in many reports of domestic abuse; in British data, the proportion is 44 percent (Richardson et al. 2003). These reports are chiefly about drunken abuse of spouses; abuse of children, the elderly, and handicapped seem relatively unconnected with alcohol. The selective pattern suggests something closer to a carousing situation with a sexual element; this is especially apparent in the cases (in chapter 4) where a husband treats abuse as a form of amusement in private drinking situations. Some spousal abuse thus takes the form of frustrated carousing. Other forms of attacking the weak are generally without intoxication: bullying almost never is (given its institutional settings); muggings and holdups apparently hardly ever—since here the premium is upon effective violence and emotional control of the situation, qualities that intoxication tends to undermine. Some staged fair fights do occur among drinkers; challenges to duels may have been issued in these circumstances, although the duel itself was generally fought sober. Vendettas, with their trickery and careful planning, seems to be carried out mostly sober. Successful gunfighters very likely are the soberest ones; what I have called "leapfrog escalation" to one-gun fights, on the other hand, seem to occur often by escalation of drunken disputes in carousing situations.

This is congruent with the statistics; about three-quarters of ordinary criminal violence is not associated with intoxication (the obverse of the one-quarter figure cited earlier). It is in particular kinds of settings that the intoxication/violence link is found.

Consider now the problem of sampling on the dependent variable. It is easy to show that the amount of drinking is far greater than the amount of violence. In the late 1990s, 105 million persons ages twelve and over had drunk some alcohol in the past month (i.e., about 47 percent of the U.S. population); forty-five million had engaged in binge drinking (five or more drinks on one occasion; 20 percent of the population); and twelve million were heavy drinkers (five or more drinks on at least five different days in the past month; 5.5 percent of the population) (1999 National

Household Survey of Drug Abuse; U.S. Dept. of Health and Human Services, National Institute of Alcohol Abuse and Alcoholism; www.niaa.gov/databases). There were 15,500 murders in 1999, of which about four thousand are attributed to alcohol (Federal Bureau of Investigation, Uniform Crime Reports 1999; www.fbi.gov/ucr). There were about 1,474,000 reported victims of aggravated assault in 1999; 4,620,000 victims of simple assault (Bureau of Justice Statistics, Criminal Victimization 1999 ; www.ojp.usdog.gov/bjs).

If we take just the binge drinkers, assuming for simplicity that they are responsible for all the alcohol-related violence, the *chances that they will kill someone during the year is about one in eleven thousand. Serious assaults* can be pinned on 3.3 *percent of binge drinkers during the year*, and 10.3 *percent are involved in a simple assault* (i.e., a relatively harmless fight).

And given that these drinkers go on more than one binge during the year, the *chances of any particular drunken episode turning violent falls to one in 366 for serious assault (0.3 percent) and 1 in 117 episodes for simple assault (0.9 percent)*. Even if we assume all the violence is done by heavy drinkers (those who binge repeatedly during the month), most of their episodes of drinking are harmless; the *chance of any one binge resulting in a serious fight is one in 488 binges (0.2 percent); a mild fight occurs in 1 in 156 binges (0.6 percent)*.[20] Even these low ratios are unrealistically high estimates, since my calculation ignored the proportion of violence produced by people who are not drunk.

The pattern is similar in England and Wales. The British Crime Survey asked victims of violence if their attackers were intoxicated; they found 285,000 victims of drunken woundings (the equivalent of aggravated assault) and 855,000 victims of drunken common assaults (simple assault) in 1999. Data on binge drinking is available only for the 18 to 24 age group; this is the heaviest drinking group, in which 48 percent of males reported being very drunk at least once a month. That age cohort comprised 2,169,000 males, giving a total of at least 12,493,000 binge events for the year. If we make the extreme assumption that all serious and minor assaults were committed by binge drinkers in this age group, nevertheless only a minority of violent incidents are accounted for by drunkenness: 2.3 *percent of drunken episodes lead to woundings, and 6.8 percent to common assaults*. These percentages are higher than the American data; but the denominator is estimated in an extremely conservative manner. It is likely that there were many more binges, since a substantial proportion of these young men binged more than once per month, and some males younger than eighteen or older than twenty-four also binged. Thus the total number of binges could be several times higher, and the percentage of drunken incidents leading to violence correspondingly lower (calculated from 2000 British Crime Survey, Table A; Richardson et al. 2003; Budd 2003; all available at www.homeoffice.gov.uk/rds/bcs1/html and www.statistics.gov.uk).

If we go looking for drunken violence—that is, sampling on the dependent variable—we will find it. In these British studies 22 percent of the youthful binge-drinking males said that during the past year they had taken part in a group fight in a public place, as compared to 6 percent of "regular drinkers" who were less often intoxicated. (Keep in mind that the data does not say they got into a fight in these proportions on the occasions when they were drunk, but rather that they had a fight on at least one such occasion during the year.) Of the binge drinkers, 56 percent said they had gotten into a heated argument during or after drinking, and 35 percent had gotten into a fight under those circumstances (for regular drinkers, 30 percent were in heated arguments and 12 percent in fights) (Richardson et al. 2003, Tables 1 and 3). But notice that even here, only a minority were getting into fights; as I have argued elsewhere, it is a lot easier to engage in angry talk than actually to fight. Notice too that women, although they get very drunk less often than men (31 percent of young British women do this monthly), have quite low levels of fighting when drunk—only 2 percent had joined a group fight, and 11 percent had any kind of fight; but these women get into heated arguments almost as much as the men (41 percent). The step from an argument to a fight is far from automatic.

Why do so few occasions in which people are drunk lead to violence? There are at least three reasons.

First, fight situations sometimes develop, then abort. Student reports describe several versions. After midnight on a Saturday night about twenty young males are drinking beer in front of a college fraternity. Two men, built like heavy, muscular athletes, come out of a frat house, then move in opposite directions down the sidewalk until they are about ten feet apart. They stand back to back and remove their shirts. The crowd is murmuring with excitement. It is said one man accused the other of spitting at him. One or two friends gather around each one, talking in low voices. The observer saw one's face: he is biting his lip and saying nothing to those in his corner. The other man's face is not immediately visible; when the observer circles around, he is found to be crossing his arms with brows furrowed. The crowd is eager for a fight, and some of them talk excitedly about past fights they have seen and how this one would match up with them in viciousness. But after three or four minutes one man puts his shirt back on and goes back inside the frat house; the other follows shortly. The crowd murmurs unhappily for a moment and then many of them return to the house as well.

Another form of abortive fight is illustrated in a nightclub in Philadelphia frequented by college-age Korean-Americans. One young man gets into a pushing match with another; their friends hold them back, while they engage in cursing and threatening one another. One guy pulls free, throws a punch that does no damage, and is restrained again. Shortly afterward, one of the group who surrounded the puncher takes offense at an innocent inquiry made by an individual unattached to either group; again there is an exchange of insults, an offer to fight, which is broken up by friends on each side. This is the same pattern found at dances in small Irish towns (Fox 1977, described in chapter 6): the action consists almost entirely in bluster and in struggling with one's own friends, who restrain the fighters from actually doing anything.

It is difficult to know at this point what proportion of drunken disputes abort in these ways; it is surely much larger than the number of fights. There is a hazy borderline; a punch may actually be thrown, but often misses or does so little damage that it is not counted as a real fight. The lore of bar-room fights (as I heard it in the 1970s) was that most fights are one-punch fights. One would expect that many of these in-between fights do not make it into the victimization surveys. What is more important to know, and is as yet poorly understood, are the conditions and the processes that cause fights to abort.[21]

A second reason why drunkenness fails to produce violence is that heavy drinking makes one slow, ponderous, and clumsy.[22] Very drunken persons tend to lose their balance and fall down. This is one reason why fights at drunken parties tend to consist of shoving and then grappling, with both sides falling down; like wrestling matches (but carried out by persons who do not know the techniques of wrestlers) this limits the damage, since punches cannot be freely thrown. This scuffling also disguises the likely fact that the fighters lack good balance, timing, and coordination in their drunken condition. They also tend to lose audience encouragement in a few minutes, since the fight is not very spectacular and soon turns into a dull stalemate. This is the ideal type, so to speak, of a fight that stays confined to a "fair fight," one-on-one; such fights do little damage. If the fight becomes organized as a group beating on an isolated individual, they are usually in better position to keep their feet and do more damage with full-scale kicks and punches. It is not clear if this is just the result of superior numbers; or whether a group of this sort is usually reasonably sober, so they do not fall down and trip each other.

In contrast, the most serious and skilled practitioners of violence avoid alcohol and drugs when they are working; this includes military snipers (Pegler 2004: 216), professional hitmen (Fisher 2002), armed robbers (Wilkinson 2003: 202), and burglars.[23] A black teenage thug describes how he beat a long-standing opponent:

So I seen him the next weeks, right. . . . I got a couple of peoples with me. I got like three fellows with me. So the next thing, we at a party and shit. . . . I didn't drink nothing that night. Everybody started drinking the most. He gets happily drunk and everything. So the next thing you know—I got a hoodie. He couldn't see me. . . . I put on my hat, my gloves, and everything. Ran up from behind with my three boys. My two boys grabbed his arms. I just ran up through him and just cut him. Slashed him in the neck. I don't know if he lived or died. He was drunk. He thought everything was all forgotten. Little do he know in his sleep is the kiss of death. (Wilkinson 2003: 213)[24]

At a lesser level of violence, too, it may well be that the persons who get into successful fights in carousing zones are those who are relatively more sober; being less drunk would be a strong advantage if the parties are not equally matched in alcohol consumed.[25] This is a rather sophisticated tactic, perhaps not very widespread. There is a sub-subculture inside the punk culture, called "straight-edgers," young males who are militantly opposed to drinking and drugs. Their chief thrills, besides punk music itself and moshing, are fighting with other persons in the youth scene who are drunk or high. The rationale for straight-edging is to keep one's body purer, and also the recognition that sobriety makes one a better fighter.[26]

But drunks mainly fight with each other, and on the same level of drunkenness. The persons at highest risk of being victims of drunken violence have the same profile as the most frequent perpetrators—in British data, young single males who drink frequently at pubs and night clubs (Budd 2003). On the whole, the clumsiness induced by drinking probably inhibits many fights from getting going, even to mild levels of ineffectual scuffling.

Drunkenness does not easily overcome normal confrontational tension/fear. Drunks may be disinhibited enough or made belligerent enough by the carousing atmosphere and the alcohol to start a possible confrontation. But a large proportion of drunks abort the fight at that point; micro-evidence of the kind noted above shows a lot of anxiety and unwillingness to go further. Here confrontational tension/fear persists during the drunken episode. If the fight actually breaks out, usually with an audience's emotional support, tension/fear is apparently surmounted; but the amount of alcohol necessary to reach this point likely has a counter-balancing effect of making the fighters less competent, and thus limiting the fight from that direction. In this case, tension/fear is reduced but the same outcome is reached: both tension/fear and heavy drinking make fighters incompetent. This is parallel to military, police, and group fighting under the influence of tension/fear; drunken fights—where they go beyond shoving matches—generally involve a lot of wild swinging and hitting (parallel to wild and inaccurate fire), and a considerable proportion of the damage may be the equivalent of friendly fire on one's own supporters, or hitting bystanders.

THE ONE-FIGHT-PER-VENUE LIMITATION

A third cause of the relatively limited proportion of drunken episodes that are violent may be the most important. This is a situational pattern: it operates through the structure of attention and emotional charge in the group, rather than through individual motives per se. The pattern is: only one fight per gathering. In my collection of fight ethnographies, it is typical that there is only one fight at a party.[27] It captures attention for a time, building up excitement, tension, and sometimes enthusiasm in the group. Once that group has lost its interest and shifts its attention away, the spell is broken. In the emotional dynamics of the gathering, often the fight episode (including an abortive one) is enough to give the evening a dramatic structure; after the denouement of the drama, things wind down. This appears to be true of abortive fights as well, and of those instances of the "let me at him!" variety restrained by supporters. For dramatic purposes a little violence goes a long way; and crowds' emotions are easily shaped by the simple plot taken to its conclusion.

But why should a prior fight keep other individuals on the scene from fighting, who are equally drunk, uninhibited, or action-seeking? My argument is that once a fight has taken its dramatic course, other persons present are relatively de-energized from further fighting. They may be buzzed with conversation about the fight that did (or indeed did not) occur; but that is a different focus of attention, putting participants in an audience rather than in a participant mode, or in the position of satisfied braggarts if they can claim to have been connected to the fight in some way. A fight, as it were, constructs around itself a sphere of status, like the mana of the tribal notable or magician; just being close to a fight is enough to make one into an excited conversationalist, talking about how close one got to the action, and exhibiting one's inside information. There is a sort of magical contagiousness from the fighters to its primary witnesses that spreads out through a chain of listeners and gossipers, all sharing in the energy from the center of attention. A single such center of magnetic resonance is enough to define a party as a dramatic unit; and having formed once, it generally reorganizes the emotional atmosphere so that another such event cannot happen again, until the first one dissipates.

This is the ideal type. Consider now the variations and exceptions. My collection of cases includes some where one fight is chained to the next; a shoving match at a fraternity beer keg results in ejection of one partisan, who returns later with backup. Such second fights may or may not come off; my collection shows several in which it aborts or fizzles out. Either way, it is taken by the audience as all one episode, all one narrative. We do not find two such narratives holding the attention space at the same party. In other instances, a scuffle can give rise to an aftershock or peripheral wave; in the Korean-American nightclub, one near-fight is restrained, and soon after one of the secondary participants threatens to start a fight with a third party who intrudes too closely—that is, into the hot center of action around the first would-be fighter. But this too is one continuous center of attention; the episodes are close together in time, and overlap in personnel; moreover, both parts of the episode—both scenes in the play— are much the same, abortive rather than full-scale. We might hypothesize that abortive fights may be especially likely to have this kind of spill-over, since there is lingering tension after the first of such linked episodes. Yet the second episode is likely to feel rather old hat, thereby ratifying the declining energy for the fight action.

In one student ethnography, a fight breaks out in a bar, and a bystander who attempts to break it up is taken by the bouncer for one of the brawlers and is expelled, along with his friends; later the group returns to the bar and fights with the bouncers and kitchen workers. Here one fight is directly chained on the other; it is the same flow of attention and narrative of grievance.

All this is contingent upon the sheer numbers of persons assembled. In big crowd scenes (in my ethnographic collection, the Philadelphia Mardi Gras, sports victory parades, street festivals), there are sometimes reports of two or more fights with distinct casts of characters. All five of my cases of this sort happened in large crowds.[28] As a rule of thumb, we might estimate that a fight for every one thousand persons or so in a crowd is what the emotional attention space can handle. A punk rock musician, who has performed at several hundred concerts and clubs over a period of three years, and has observed many other such venues, reports that in her experience there is a maximum of one fight per venue per evening, with the following exception: It is possible to have more fights in very large crowds (on the order of 1,000s), where not everyone can see what is happening, and each fight creates its own "stage." The "venue," then, is shorthand for an attention space that is separate because of the physical ecology of the setting or limitations on visibility in a crowd.

The house parties at which fights occur, on the other hand, are medium-sized affairs, at the upper limit something on the order of fifty to two hundred bodies crammed into a space (which may be around 400 to 1,000 square feet). In these situations, one fight per evening seems plenty to give a buzz shared by the entire assemblage. But these party crowds generally consist of a considerable portion of persons who are unknown to each other (i.e., familiarity may be confined to groups of ten to thirty, or even smaller posses of visitors); the audience as a whole does not consist of a community that can spread gossip and reputations around; and its solidarity in a phase of fight-viewing excitement is ephemeral. The experience of witnessing a fight in their midst may increase the connectedness of everyone present, since they share a common buzz and topic of conversation. These are some mechanisms by which one fight per evening is the usual maximum at a party, even if there is considerable turnover of persons. This awaits testing with better observational data; it may be the case that a high percentage of turnover would allow two fights in the same evening, although I have no instances of this (i.e., two separate fights at the same party, not chained episodes of the sort just discussed). Fights in night clubs and other entertainment venues seem to follow a similar distribution.[29]

The one-fight-per-venue principle applies to other kinds of fights besides carousing. Fights among black high school girls also seem to follow this pattern (Nikki Jones, personal communication, Nov. 2003; see also Jones 2004). One fight at a school (whether between a pair of girls, or two groups) appears to be the maximum per day. These are relatively closed reputational communities, so news of the fight travels widely; this news circulation network, and the assembling and post-assembly activities of the audience, works to fill up attention space with one fight at a time, which is to say in one dramatic episode. It is worth investigating whether fights in such settings also take up a longer period of attention, lasting several days or a week; especially when there are recriminations and threats or retaliations, a single chain of fights—or just the chain of drama surrounding a fight—may squeeze out other possible fights.

In closer detail, we can see how one fight preempts another. A brawl in a Los Angeles high school between black and Hispanic students, involving 100 out of 2,400 students in the school, is set off when two black girls are fighting in the lunch room, and a Hispanic group pelts them and calls them names (*Los Angeles Times*, April 15, 2005). The fight inside one ethnic group stops and is superceded by a bigger fight along ethnic lines. We also see here what happens when a fight which is staged and limited in front of an audience—two black girls carrying out their own drama for their own reputational community—is interrupted by outsiders. The black high school community—or at least its violent fraction—is affronted en masse because its own ritual boundaries have been violated. It is likely also that the Hispanic cluster who first intervened—part of an 80 percent majority in this school—began jeering at the black fighters in a mood of scorn and perhaps amusement, for preempting their own attention space.[30] In effect this began as a struggle over who was to control the dramatic attention space of the lunchroom.

Ethnographic detail from a student report shows the obverse case, where one side in the larger confrontation, by breaking up into fighting among themselves, can preempt a between-group fight. A teenage party is winding down late in the evening. A group of older students attempt to crash the party, but they are confronted across the front lawn by a little knot of five younger students, with the girls standing apprehensively in the background. The defensive group huddles and decides they want to use the pocket knife that one of them carries; but he does not want to give it up. The largest boy in his group argues with him angrily, then chokes him by the neck until he temporarily loses consciousness. Both groups of antagonists then disperse, the older leaving, the younger moving to the backyard without the knife. The mini-fight inside the home team takes up the entire attention space, defusing the larger confrontation.

In sum, I propose that a law of small numbers governs fights in carousing situations, perhaps in violent situations generally. This resembles the law of small numbers in an intellectual attention space, which limits the number of notable positions to between three and six (which is to say, topics of intellectual disagreement divide the core networks into that number of recognized positions or factions) (Collins 1998). A general theory of attention spaces has been scarcely developed; it is clear from comparing intellectual attention spaces and carousing fight attention spaces that they differ considerably in the precise form of their law of small numbers: three to six factions among intellectuals in a given specialty, but one fight (i.e., two factions) in a fight zone. I will pursue the analogy at greater length in chapter 11. The point I wish to emphasize here is that the structure of the field limits the amount of emotional energy individuals within it feel. The fight itself benefits (if that is the right word) from the audience's limited but concentrated focus of attention; but the same focus de-energizes other possible fights.

And all this happens regardless of how drunk the persons present are. One might expect, in the abstract, that if drinking increases the chance of violence, assembling a large number of drunks in one place would give rise to many fights, simultaneously or successively. But such fighting of everyone-against-everyone, a free-for-all in the classic imagery, is virtually unknown in real life (as we have noted already in chapter 1); later in the companion volume, I will argue that one-fight-at-a-time is typical on most scales of violence on up through war, and constrains how it can happen. Heavy drinking does not shift the law of small numbers. Indeed, if drunken persons are highly susceptible to simple emotional moods, we would expect them to conform to the pattern especially strongly.[31]

This is the key to explaining the paradox that intoxication seldom causes violence. This is so even in just those places where the cult of anti-nomian excitement in the form of violence is strongest. Even a concerted effort at making carousing venues into potential fight scenes—the messages sent by demeanor, testiness about trivial deference, a cult of heavy drinking, the narrative culture of talking about fights—does not make fights come off anywhere nearly as often as the cultural façade would suggest. The carousing culture, including its drunken version, is chiefly engaged in staging an atmosphere of exciting violence rather than the thing itself. When it does happen, one fight per venue is enough to satisfy the dramatics of the occasion.

Fighting as Action and Fun

So far, we have seen that the audience sometimes regards fighting as fun; when do the fighters regard it as fun? By no means all cases in carousing venues are of this sort; many seem motivated more by lack of fun, by frustration or exclusion.

An unusual ethnographic study that gives an inside perspective on groups who do seek out fights is the research of Curtis Jackson-Jacobs (2003; Jackson-Jacobs and Garot 2003). The subject is a loose-knit group of about eighty-five young men (and a few women) in their late teens and twenties who attend weekend parties and bars in a big Arizona city. Many of them come from suburban upper-middle-class backgrounds, some are educated in universities and professional schools; but many are school drop-outs or have checkered educational careers. The group as a whole is alienated from middle-class respectability, and are ashamed of their white, affluent class background, which they regard as "un-hip and un-cool"; experiences in the unrespectable world of jail, rehab centers, and unemployment offices give them pride, a kind of reverse social climbing. They choose to live in poor ethnic neighborhoods, avoiding conventional collegiate scenes. It is these houses—small single-story dwellings with un-kempt yards inside a chain-link fence—that are the venues for weekend parties and for seeking fights.

The parties are relatively anonymous, since most people arrive by hearing about them through several network links of acquaintances; peak crowds ranged from thirty to one hundred or more. The fight-seeking group used these scenes to attempt to provoke fights:

> You know how sometimes you bump into someone at a bar kinda hard, but you try to make it seem like it's not clear whether you meant to hurt him or were just trying to get by? I did that to this guy. And a couple steps later I turned around and he was looking back at me. So I gave him this "come on outside" kind of smile. He never came out though. (Jackson-Jacobs and Garot 2003)

Staring, making hostile jokes, and provoking quarrels were other ways to stir things up. Fights might be one-on-one, but more frequently whole groups jumped in. Unusually, in this fight-seeking group, individuals would seek out bigger opponents, or provoke a fight with a larger group. In one instance, a man with two companions picked a fight with a group of twelve, who rolled on him, and on his friends who eventually joined in. Members fought for the sake of fighting rather than for the sake of winning; an honorable beating was a cause for considerable bragging. They sought out opponents who fit categories that made them fearful and dramatic opponents: "big guys," "black guys," "gangsters," "bikers," "skinheads," and "athletes" (Jackson-Jacobs 2003).

Here we see a very different pattern than fighting in gangs or in the lower-class black street code: these persons fight to keep up a reputation, to intimidate others; as we shall see in chapter 9, street code performances are mostly bluster, designed to keep off challenges; when fights occur, weaker or at least suitable opponents are chosen if possible, and the concern is to win. The Arizona fight-seeking group, for all their downwardly oriented stance, maintains a version of upper-middle-class reflexivity and inwardness of values, by setting up dramatic situations in which they lose physically, but claim a moral victory. In all their activities they emphasize an underdog theme; in contrast, gang members promote themselves as an invincible elite (with considerable pretence, of course). The upper-middle-class fight-seekers who brag about their defeats and bodily injuries resemble German dueling fraternity members, for whom the point of the duel is not to win but to acquire honorable scars from the opponent's sword.

The fight-seeking culture of this group is sustained largely by what Jackson-Jacobs calls "narrative gratifications." They do much talking about fights, speculating as to whether a fight will happen at upcoming parties; after a fight actually occurs, they spend great lengths of time recounting it. In one instance, the group gathered the day after a fight—in which the chief protagonist was stomped by a group of opponents and ended up covered in blood—and spent the next thirty-six hours talking about it. The narrating is a central feature of the party scenes themselves. In the midst of a noisy party with the sounds of rap or punk music reverberating, members laugh boisterously while telling exaggerated stories of their fights, sometimes acting them out in pantomime complete with blows and grimaces. One could say they fight for the sake of the narrative that it allows them to perform. And indeed, narratives about fights are much more common than the fights themselves.

The narrative is also part of the micro-sequencing that leads up to fights. The places where stories about fighting are told are often the same scenes where the fights take place. What makes up the "scene," the action, is a combination of semi-anonymous party crowds, drinking and story-telling, and the tension/excitement of checking out strangers, sometimes culminating in challenging them, and in fighting. The loud rap and punk music is another part of the total package of stage-setting; the narrating, rhythms, bodily posturing, and the punctuation with fights are all part of the same staged event.

But this is Goffmanian stage-setting in the sense of show and pretence. Fights are not easy to start, even in these settings; indeed, quite possibly because the stagey narrative and the scene of omnipresent, impersonal bluster takes the center of attention, establishing an equilibrium point in itself. The methods for starting a fight are standard and easy to enact—bumping, aggressive eye contact, vocal challenges—and the crowded conditions makes potential encounters ubiquitous. Nevertheless, fights do not happen every night that members go out looking for one; over a period of time, this makes them frustrated, and hence adds to their euphoria when they manage to pull one off. Why are fights rare, despite the ostensible convergence of all party features on facilitating them? One reason is that a fight occurs only by mutual consent: the other side has to see the challenging gesture and react to it in the appropriate way. These gestures are sometimes subtle, with an effort to keep them from being blatant; much of the time they are not picked up, perhaps deliberately ignored. The gesturing isn't enough; there must be an emotional dynamic that energizes some persons to go further. Despite the appearance of a field of abundant opportunities, the most common outcome is nothing.

There is also the pattern, rather typical in violent groups of all sorts, that the fight-seeking group is stratified. Some are particularly aggressive; others follow and join in; still others stay in the background. These latter tag along with their friends at party venues where violence is a possibility; but these individuals rarely have fought—perhaps only one or two incidents in their lives; generally they have gotten embroiled merely by staying on the scene when a fight breaks out, since in these settings anyone who does not flee may be regarded as a fair target. The group as a whole, including its hardest fighters, does not take them to task, or put any obligation on them to fight (this is the role that Jackson-Jacobs took as an observer). How do they continue to be acceptable members of the group? Apparently it is because they are part of the narrative component; they are interested audiences for fight-stories, and they circulate the culture capital of the group, spreading the reputations of its leading members, and keeping up an ethos of antinomian action that is the group's hallmark. The fight narrative is the leading ritual of the group; occasional fights are needed in order to feed materials into the narrative ritual, but constant fights are unnecessary. Too many fights might well overwhelm the group's narrative consciousness; there is likely a "law of small numbers" operating in this attention space as well.[32]

Fighting for fun also existed in nineteenth-century Ireland (Conley 1999). On festive occasions such as fairs and markets, large-scale brawls often broke out, usually between extended family groups. There was a recognized ritual for challenging to a fight: a man would wheel around in the crowd, sometimes calling out names: "Here is Connors and Delahanty. Is there any Madden will come before us?" Taking off one's coat was a further sign of willingness to fight. Fights were tolerated and indeed supported by the community, as long as the proper rituals were followed. Weapons had to be confined to fists, sticks, and stones; knives were considered unfair and their use was heavily punished by authorities. But homicides were rarely punished if the victim had engaged in fighting gestures or words; even bystander deaths and injuries (including children) were lightly punished or excused, since the prevailing attitude was that being in the presence of fights meant assuming unavoidable risks; and children were often involved in fights, too, with no clear boundary drawn between older and younger ones. Irish recreational brawling suggests a form of proto-athletics, in places where formal team sports had not yet been organized. It is a way of staging one's own excitement, using some of the same dramatic resources that elsewhere would become developed as organized sports, and various forms of staged fighting by its fans.

MOCK FIGHTS AND MOSH PITS

The clearest cases of fighting for fun are mock fights: fights that are explicitly playful, like children's rough-housing, or the playful arm-punching or imitation boxing-style sparring that young men engage in on occasions of ebullience. These mock fights are often accompanied by laughter, joking, or squeals of delight; although this may occur more on one side than another, and one side can have much more fun. Usually there is a more-or-less clear boundary between fun and when the fight turns serious— that is, when it is no longer fun. This suggests that "real" fighting has a distinctive quality, easily recognized; no doubt this is the arousal of confrontational tension/fear, which poses a challenge to get through and calls for a different emotional orientation in doing so.

Sometimes play-fighting disguises itself as serious. This occurs chiefly in settings where antinomian displays are prestigious, and fighting has cachet as entertainment; while at the same time there are inhibitions against embracing all-out violence. A good example is the mosh pit.[33]

This is an area of varying size opened up by an audience standing in front of a band, for a small number of slam-dancers or moshers—usually on the order of twenty out of an audience of three hundred, although the figures can run larger or smaller. Slam-dancing (almost always by males) consists of running into the other dancers, pushing and flailing, bouncing like bumper-cars off each other and the human wall of spectators. A pit forms spontaneously when two or three people begin to crash into each other to the beat of the music; others give them space and form a circle around them. It is pretend-fighting; demeanors are tough and angry-looking, not laughing and humorous. Nevertheless, there are tacit understandings: no hitting too hard, no fists, no kicking; when someone falls down, the others quickly pick him up. The edge of the surrounding crowd participates in the same way, good-naturedly absorbing bodily impacts and steering out-of-control dancers back into the pit. The human circle around the mosh pit is an integral part of it, focusing attention, cheering the dancers, and moving to the rhythm of the music. One observer noted that the mosh pit depends on the circle, and disintegrates if one side of the pit is left open; in one instance, when a block of spectators walked away to get beer, the slam-dancing ceased.[34]

The central feature of slam-dancing is coordinating the pseudo-violence with the musical beat. Thus moshing stops between songs. The dancing usually occurs during the "mosh" part of a song, when the music is especially harsh, loud, and violent-sounding. It is when the moshers do not keep the beat that it turns into serious fighting. The pit collectively defends itself against this turn of events. An observer recounted an instance in which a "preppie" outsider (i.e., wearing clothes associated with that form of high school status group) entered a concert mosh pit, and immediately distinguished himself by not slamming to the beat, and appeared to be trying to hurt others. The other moshers maintained the beat, while the lead mosher came and forcibly removed the violator. In small mosh pits, a leader or rule-enforcer tends to emerge spontaneously; this is not one of the initiators of the pit, nor the most violent dancer, but typically the biggest male; he usually dances more slowly than the others (although still keeping the beat), and takes it upon himself to keep smaller moshers from getting trampled, and helps the fallen to their feet or ushers them out of the pit.[35]

Conditions that sustain the pit are visible when the pit breaks down. Pits are easier to sustain when they are relatively small (about eight feet in diameter); in large crowds they may grow to fifteen feet in diameter or more, but these are more likely to break down into serious violence. This may be the result of large pits occurring in very large concerts; but if the proximate feature that sustains the mosh pit is its tight integration with the surrounding audience, it follows that the circle has the strongest sense of its unity and its role in sustaining the moshing when it is compact enough so that its members can see each other and move together in the same rhythm. Other ways in which mosh pits break down are when outsiders intervene, whether these be police or external groups with a preexisting (and hence rival) social identity, such as skinhead gangs. These fit the pattern described earlier as boundary exclusion violence at the edges of a carousing zone. On the whole, however, security guards, although they may arrest trouble-makers in the crowd, leave the mosh pit alone. It works best—and indeed only exists—when it is self-regulating.

Slam-dancing is the rare instance of a free-for-all, each participant striking out in all directions; this in itself is an indicator that it is only play-fighting, like a water-fight or snowball fight. When it escalates into real fighting, it turns into the standard two-sided mode. Participants are clearly aware of the boundaries. Real fights do occur around mosh pits from time to time; there are several instances in student reports. In one case, two large gangs of skinheads attend a punk concert; they gather at opposite sides of the mosh pit, and eventually invade the floor, meeting at the middle for a two-sided fight; the moshers, who are apprehensive about this menace, stop slam-dancing and flee the area. In another case, a small posse of fight-seeking toughs attend a punk concert; they join the slam-dancing, but more roughly, using their fists. But the moshers refuse to fight with them; frustrated, two of the posse have a fist-fight with each other. Such fights are clearly separate from the slam-dancing. In some instances, the band stops playing when fighting happens.

In effect, moshing is a ritual of solidarity, featuring all the interaction ritual ingredients: bodily assembly, rhythmic entrainment in a mutual focus of attention, building to high levels of collective effervescence. The patterned violence of slamming body against body under shared control generates a high level of entrainment—not merely by getting into the same micro-rhythm, as in most IRs, but by bodily touching; a female musician gives her opinion that it is "an excuse for men to touch each other." Normally the entrainment of prolonged body touching is sexual; in slam-dancing, any sexual connotation is consciously negated by the violent tone, similar to the forearm bashes, mock punches, and butt-slaps that express solidarity among athletes.

Moshers do get hurt; many leave the pit with bruises, scratches, and cuts, which they show off proudly—one asked his girlfriend if she thought it made him look tough. Websites exist where moshers post their pit injuries, to compare them with others. It would be more accurate to say that injuries are badges of membership. Moshers regard themselves as an elite group, and some describe fellow moshers as "family," although most of those in the pit at any one time are anonymous to each other.[36] Moshers are clearly distinguished from other types of youths; they are not athletes, nor particularly muscular, although some may be big; nor do they usually belong to factions such as skinheads, who flaunt violence as a general demeanor in all situations. Their identity is usually around the music itself, chiefly punk, that includes as well a clothing style: this is the group that began (in the late 1970s) the fad of body piercing, along with hair dyed in bright colors and cut into mohawks and other extreme styles, and the wearing of steel-studded leather straps and similar items. It is a cultural movement of disaffected middle-class youth; originating in part as one of the counter-cultures in high schools that were mobilized in the late decades of the twentieth century in opposition to the jocks-cheerleaders-and-preppies who dominated high school sociability (Milner 2004). Its rebellion has been successful insofar as it creates a separate enclave, with its alternate cultural standard of prestige, and its gatherings where members emanate their own collective effervescence. It is a youth culture segment that showily rejects middle-class respectability, without going all the way to lower-class gang-style street culture. Hence its central ritual is carefully controlled pseudo-violence, distinguished from respectable and violent groups alike.

In conclusion, let us put this development in historical context. The surrounding audience focuses their attention upon the moshers, who become the Durkheimian sacred object at the center of the group's attention space. This is one of a series of shifts in the center of attention in public entertainment events. Before the 1950s or 1960s, bands existed primarily so that male/female couples could dance to them. Dancers paid more attention to each other, and secondarily to who else was on the dance floor, than to the band; in the dance etiquette that prevailed until the rock n'roll revolution of the 1950s, there was a status hierarchy as to who was dancing and who was not (low status "wall-flowers"), and who would cut in on whom (marking the most popular dance partners). Even quite famous bands of the swing band era were treated merely as hired help who made the dancing possible, receiving their attention mainly in polite applause at the end of each dance tune.[37]

As bands rose in status during the 1960s, couples dancing died out. Audiences clustered around the stage to get as close to famous bands as possible; or attended huge outdoor concerts where most sat on the ground or in distant seats. At most, a minority of individuals might stand and dance alone in their place, dancing consisting almost entirely of body swaying and arm movements, but without moving from place to place (which necessarily makes dancers pay attention to each other in order to avoid collisions). These solo dancers were not the centers of attention for the audience, and they all danced facing the band. (In contrast, during the jitterbug era of the 1940s, especially good dance couples would be given the entire floor, while the audience gathered around them and applauded.) Although records of popular bands were sold from the 1920s onward, it was in the 1960s and thereafter that bands and their star musicians became known above all as media figures, dominating their audiences in money, honor, and in the situational attention space.

Slam-dancers and mosh pits, appearing around 1980, revived dancing at concerts as a primary center of attention. They used the appearance of violence as a sure-fire attention-getter, trumping the bands' rise to centrality. As we have seen throughout this book, violence is the most powerful way to focus attention of human beings; whether one favors it or opposes it, one cannot ignore violence in one's immediate vicinity. That slam-dancing is only pseudo-violence does not alter this fact; indeed, violence in general is chiefly dramatic show, and bluster is a major part of all violent confrontations. Mosh pits are a brilliant tactical invention, since they nicely calculate the level of violence for optimum effect in creating group solidarity, extending it to the immediate ring of audience, and using it to recapture the center of attention away from the band.

Moshing is also part of another status revolt, within high-school status rankings (described by Milner [2004]; and discussed in chapter 5 regarding bullying). One side-effect of the rise of popular musicians to media stars, and the displacement of couples dancing by musical performance watching, was to make music concerts into an alternative gathering place to school athletic events, and to school dances and parties. These latter were the arenas dominated by the traditional school elites, the jocks and popular party-goers and stars of the dating market. As popular music consumption became the central identifying point of youth cultures, it also came to support greater pluralism in student status hierarchies; punk and other alternative culture groups acquired their own venues where they could generate their own collective effervescence, dominating in their own emotional attention spaces. Moshers became the leading edge of punk culture, the attention-getters within their chief cultural rituals and gathering places. Not surprisingly, there is strong antagonism between moshers and jocks, their chief counterparts in the use of controlled violence in the conventional youth culture.[38]

These are sophisticated developments. We might call it the revolt of the audience in an era of entertainers' domination. It is a differentiation of sophisticated in-groups claiming elite status within youth culture, and within popular entertainment culture generally. In the following chapter, we will see similar developments in the realm of sports.

CHAPTER 8

Sports Violence

IN A NATIONAL BASKETBALL ASSOCIATION game in 1997, Dennis Rodman deliberately kicked a cameraman in the groin while stumbling off the court struggling for a rebound under the basket. The kick occurred during a tense moment in the game,with the score tied 71–71 between the defending champion Chicago Bulls and the Minnesota Timberwolves, who had just rallied to make up an eleven-point deficit on their home court. Play was stopped for seven minutes while the cameraman was taken off on a stretcher. The delay cost the Timberwolves their momentum; the Bulls pulled ahead again to win 112–102, for their eighth win in a row. Rodman was known as a defensive specialist, and the violence broke out as he made an extreme effort to break up a scoring spree by the other team. Rodman was backed up in comments by players and coaches on his team after the game; although hitting a helpless bystander was a blatant violation of sportsmanship, teammates accused the cameraman of faking the injury. "When you're that close to the game, you've got to be willing to get out of the way," said Bulls star Scottie Pippen. "This is our court" (*San Diego Union*, Jan. 16, 1997). In one sense the fight was extraneous to the game, since there was no confrontation between opposing players. But like player violence it happened at the most likely point in the action, and it became the turning-point of the game.

There are at least three different kinds of sports violence. First, what causes players to fight with each other during a game? This is best answered by asking *when* in a game do fights break out? We shall see that just what produces maximal drama in the game is also what produces player violence. Second, what explains spectator violence? Spectators become engrossed in the same dramatic time-flow of events, hence there is a close relation between spectator-versus-player violence and player-versus-player violence. Third is off-site violence by spectators or fans: when do they fight against each other, or against inanimate objects or the police? An extreme extension of off-site violence is sports hooligan violence, which becomes totally disconnected from the rhythms of the game; yet even here, the dramatic structure of what happens in the arena helps explain violence outside it.

My method throughout this chapter, wherever possible, is direct observation of the details of action. The emphasis is not on the background characteristics of players or fans, but on the actual flow of events in the emotions of lived time. I draw on my own observations of games, largely from television, and from interviewing experienced fans of particular kinds of sports. My generalizations draw also on a news clipping file of incidents of sports violence over the years 1997–2004, and on photographs of those incidents. Sports in recent years is the best recorded of all forms of action, and thus it is possible to see the time sequence of conflict better here than in most other kinds of violence.

SPORTS AS DRAMATICALLY CONTRIVED CONFLICTS

Sports are deliberately contrived for producing exciting and entertaining contests. What happens during a game is spontaneous and unpredictable in details. But the kinds of things that can happen are structured by procedures selected in advance. A game is the most highly staged of all conflicts; the conflict form itself has been chosen because of the drama it produces. Rules have been formulated and reformulated to channel the action in particular pathways; these conscious choices are usually made to promote more dramatic action in the game. The height of the pitcher's mound is lowered and the strike zone reduced to bring more hitting in baseball games; football games introduce forward passes; basketball games add 3-point shots and narrow the zone in which defenders can stand to block the basket.[1] Sports are real life, and this makes them engrossing; but real life at its most deliberately and artificially organized and controlled. It is larger than life, conflict in its purified forms, better focused and therefore more dramatically satisfying than in ordinary events.

At the center of sports is its emotional appeal. Spectators follow the action above all for the experience of dramatic moments: the surge to go ahead in the scoring; the defensive rally to fend off an attack; the drama of catching up after having fallen behind; the last-minute triumph. One's favorite does not always prevail, of course; on average, half the games will be lost. But even a losing effort can be dramatically satisfying, enough to keep spectators coming back for more, if there are enough dramatic moments along the way. The basic elements of drama are simple and repetitive, but they can be varied in many ways. Particular sports have their own patterns in the timing of dramatic moments; baseball with its long rallies of a sequence of players getting on base, building tension that may or may not go over the brink into scoring runs; soccer with its long continuous pressure and sudden release in a rare goal; the intermediate targets in American football with its 4 downs to go 10 yards and another chance to keep moving the ball toward the goal line; the series of nerve-wracking time-outs near the end of a close basketball game as teams struggle for a crucial shot, block, or steal.

A literary narrative depends on plot tension; archetypally a protagonist has a problem, launches out on a search to solve it, encounters obstacles, acquires help, goes through setbacks and deceptions, and finally meets the chief obstacle head on (classically delineated in Propp 1928/1968; cf. Elias and Dunning 1986). In adventures, romances, and comedies, the hero finally wins; in more complex dramas, there may be a tragic failure, losing the external goal but gaining a moral victory by having fought well, making a heroic sacrifice, or by gaining inner insight. Sports rarely have the most complex of these dramatic resolutions, but they are propelled by the basic shape of dramatic narrative.

To enjoy the game fully, one needs to go through these moments of suspense in real time; merely to watch taped replays or to read about the outcome in the news is to miss most of the emotional experience. Without the tension buildup, there is little of the surging joy of triumph, and the letdown of failure is the price people willingly pay for the chance of having those moments. Moreover, the emotional experience is a collective one; it is the reverberated sounds and mutually entrained gestures of the crowd that makes it fun to be in the stands watching one's team's rally—even if it doesn't ultimately come off—and that makes the moments of triumph an experience for lifetime memories. That is why spectators will pack a stadium for an eagerly anticipated game, even though their seats may be poor, and on the whole they would have a better view on TV. What the fan experiences is not the sights of the game itself so much as the dramatic sequence of emotions, amplified by the presence of a like-minded crowd.

There are additional sources of excitement besides the short-run tensions of the game action. Anticipation and tension can build up from a series of games or matches, and from the standing of teams in a league playing for the season championship or from their position in a tournament. In some sports (chiefly American ones), secondary goals are elaborated by record-keeping, so that individual players can win batting or scoring championships and get their names in the record books in various ways, apart from whether the team wins or loses.[2] A game may also feature some extraordinary moments of skill display—a shortstop making a spectacular fielding play, a basketball player's flying dunk—but these are unpredictable, not framed by a buildup of prior tension; they are enjoyable for the crowd but off to the side of the drama of conflict. There are also the dramatic aspects of individual player's histories: newcomers and aging veterans; injuries and recoveries; players moving from team to team and recasting old rivalries; quarrels with teammates, coaches, and officials. Knowledgeable fans participate in an ongoing serial melodrama, a real-life soap opera; this material makes both for a continuous flow of news copy and for conversational capital for sociable ties among fans. This is why long familiarity with the stories of the players makes the experience of a sports event much thicker in meanings than it does for an outsider, who will likely find the same events uninteresting. For this reason, fans often find sports in other countries boring.

Spectators attend for the collective effervescence, the flow of dramatic emotions building up tension into group energy and solidarity. Players enact these emotional surges in a more complex way. In team sports, they share collective emotions with their teammates, and successful performance depends on emotional resonances that keep the team coordinated as well as energetic; these two features together are colloquially referred to as "momentum" or "chemistry" (Adler 1984). Players also are involved in an emotional interaction with their opponents, whether in individual contests or team sports. Play consists in a contest of skill and effort, but most importantly in moment-by-moment challenges as to who will become emotionally dominant. It is a struggle over emotional energy (EE) in the technical sense of interaction ritual theory; the player or team who gains EE wins at the point where the opponent loses EE. These are the emotional turning points of a game.

These three kinds of emotional dynamics—collective effervescence in buildups of dramatic tension in the audience; the degree of emotional resonance within a team; EE contests between opponents—make up the background for outbursts of sports violence.[3]

GAME DYNAMICS AND PLAYER VIOLENCE

When does violence happen? Below I will try to pin down the moments during the game when it is most likely. Consider here a broader comparison: what are the features of sports that makes violence more frequent, and (not necessarily correlated) more severe?

Some violence is part of the game itself. Boxers hit each other; American football players block and tackle with as much force as possible; ice hockey players body check. Injuries frequently happen within the rules of the game. We reserve the term "sports violence" for violence that happens outside the rules; typically it brings play to a stop. There are overlaps, and some violence on the field of play is quasi-recognized by the rules; there are penalties for fouls, unnecessary roughness, and illicit hits. These make up a continuum from legitimate player force, to fouls, to game-interrupting fights; emotional escalation goes up the continuum.

Sports may be divided into three main types: staged combats, in which there is both offense and defense situations; parallel contests, in which competitors strive to outdo each other toward a goal; and skill exhibitions, where competitors win by impressing a panel of judges. Sports violence is most frequent in staged combats, or rather in a subset of them. Considering why this is so will show us that the structure of the encounter is much more important than dispositional and background explanations that are often invoked to account for sports violence.

Masculinity is often put forward as an explanation of violence, whether in the form of a cultural code of aggression and dominance, or in the physiology of testosterone and bulked-up muscles. But among the most muscular and masculine-looking of athletes are track-and-field performers in shot put, discus, and hammer throw; yet fights are almost unheard of at such competitions. This is also the case with weight-lifters, the sport with the greatest emphasis upon sheer muscles. These are parallel competitions, with no direct confrontation of offense and defense; the form of the encounter, however tense and competitive, does not promote the dramatic form of violent confrontation.[4] Still further from such confrontations are contests of skill exhibition, such as gymnasts; male gymnasts are very muscular but the structure of their encounters are non-confrontational. This is a reason why men who engage in similar exhibitions (whether they are organized as competitive sports, such as ice dancing, or are considered musical entertainment, such as ballet) tend to be regarded as not very masculine, even though they display a very high level of strength and body coordination.

Sports with both offense and defense situations are especially dramatic, in that they tend to build up tensions through a series of episodes, and allow for both sudden and creeping reversals of dominance. Players attempt both to execute their offense, and to block their opponents. There is the tension and drama of fending off threats and thwarting the juggernaut; and the emotional triumph of finally breaking through a strong defense; there can be bitter emotions over having one's skill disrupted and team flow broken down. The clash of offense and defense through a series of such episodes is most likely to produce emotional turning points.

Sports that take the form of staged combats have the most frequent violence, but this in itself is not enough. The sports that are closest to real fights are boxing and wrestling. But these rarely lead to extracurricular fighting; as we have seen in chapter 6 in the case of the Holyfield/Tyson ear-biting incident, severe escalation of violence beyond the rules tends to disrupt the fight entirely. Fighting is so completely incorporated into the sport itself that there is no way to make a dramatic statement by escalating the fighting. In other sports, player fights are ways of showing that the mock-fight that constitutes the game has now escalated into a real fight; the dramatic form of boxing, which pretends to be a real fight, precludes this, or at any rate leaves little dramatic resources for framing one's dispute and one's anger as above and beyond the normal.[5]

Figure 8.1 Masculine athlete in unviolent sport: pole-vault champion (2004). Reuters.

Wrestling is even more extreme in avoiding extra curricular violence.[6] Skilled wrestlers operate at close range, where more violent moves of kicking and punching are virtually impossible to mount with any force; the standard wrestling moves involve taking down the opponent to the ground and then leveraging the other into a defenseless position on his back. Even relatively unskilled wrestlers generally know how to tie up the opponent and to stall; such a match tends to turn into a muscular endurance contest. The dramatic form here is rather simple, and instead of building up to peak moments of tension, tends to wind down into a gradual establishment of dominance, or near-stalemate. Highly skilled wrestlers can make sudden attacks and escapes; but the momentary result of each such move is generally to make the opponent more harmless. Thus wrestling, as the form of sport fighting that involves the most direct and prolonged muscle-on-muscle confrontation, is caged by its very form into confining fighting to the main lines of the event.

Player violence is most frequent in offensive/defensive combats organized as teams rather than individuals, even though the fights themselves are generally between individuals. This fits the general pattern that violence depends upon group support. There are two main features that

Figure 8.2 Boxers' pre-fight stare-down (2001). AP/World Wide Photos.

predict violence: the extent to which violent moves, efforts, or threats are incorporated into the game action itself; and the extent to which players are protected from being hurt.

Systematic data on player violence is comparatively rare.[7] In the absence of other direct observational counts of fights during games, I offer the following from my own checking of news reports and televised games, and from questioning experienced fans: Hockey fights occur at a rate of about one per game (in professional hockey). Football players' fights occur once or twice per weekend (totaling about fifteen games) in the professional season, but more concentrated in tense games near the end of the season.[8] Baseball fights occur about once a week, out of ninety professional games. Basketball fights are rare, below 1 percent of the games.[9] Soccer player fights appear to be very rare.

How is this ordering to be explained?

In some games, direct bodily impedance of opponents is the main form of action. In American football, violence is the normal play itself, the bodily collisions of tackling, blocking, and running through tacklers. Hockey involves body checking, and slamming speeding skaters into the boards; basketball includes a certain amount of pushing and grappling for position, as well as the possibility of charging or blocking in the movement of players on the way to the basket or in scrambling for the ball. Baseball has some legitimate forms of running into or blocking a player, notably in close plays at home plate between the catcher applying a tag and an oncoming runner. It seems obvious that normal playing violence would carry over into angry fights, which stop the play of the game, or that the tensions and frustrations of normal playing violence break out in extracurricular violence. Nevertheless, although body contact sports of this kind are the main locus of player violence, this is not enough to explain either the frequency with which different kinds of sports have violence, or the particular moments when violence breaks out.

Games with impedance of the opponent's scoring efforts structurally promote fights. Games without impedance thus almost never have fights. But impedance may arise obliquely in the same locations where it is formally absent. Golf is a parallel contest in which the players, small numbers of whom are playing together on the same hole, are not physically separated but are very peaceful. Fights do sometimes happen on golf courses; the only ones I have personally witnessed, heard, or read about, have occurred not between golfers who are competing with each other, but in non-tournament situations where golfers become angry at those in front of them for slow play; they will sometimes try to hit the slow players with a ball, or physically confront them. This is an instance of impedance, which occurs in the context of a game but separate from the actual competition itself. This shows that golfers are generally peaceful, not because they are more polite and upper-middle-class than other athletes, but because the dramatic structure of tensions in the game is not organized to produce confrontations with one's competitors.

Similarly, tennis players, although in a sport traditionally connected with the polite upper classes, are not above angry outbursts (and among female as well as male players). Tennis is a form of offensive-defensive combat, with players directly impeding each other's scoring efforts. But the players are physically separated by a net, and the form of the action is to keep the ball away from the opponent rather than forcefully hitting at him or her. The tension of sudden efforts and reversals of movement and the dramatic failures in losing a point can lead to emotional outbursts; but these are directed at referees rather than opponents (Baltzell 1995). Anger is not enough to produce a fight.

Rules have been manipulated so as to take into account violence that gets out of hand. In football, there are penalties for unnecessary roughness; clipping or hitting a player from behind or in vulnerable parts like the knees; hitting especially vulnerable or non-violent players such as the quarterback; impeding a pass receiver or pass defender who has not yet caught the ball; and so forth. These penalties in varying degrees affect the possibility of winning the game; however, since both teams tend to commit penalties (and penalties for violent play are treated in the same way as penalties for other violations such as off-sides), there is a tendency for penalties to balance out among both teams, and there is no overwhelming incentive for players to avoid violence penalties. Similarly, in hockey there are a variety of penalties including those for forms of violence that are beyond the rules: high-sticking, hooking the opponent with one's stick, as well as especially violent body checks. More serious fighting is itself penalized as a normal, expectable violation that occurs frequently in the course of a game. The penalties (sitting for a certain number of minutes in the penalty box) affect the chances of winning, but are incorporated into both offensive and defensive strategies ("power plays" when the other side is short-handed because of penalties, but also tactics for killing a power play).[10] In basketball, rough play is penalized by penalty shots; given the high rate of scoring, these do not usually give enough points in any one occasion to make a big difference in winning the game, although they might do so in the aggregate or at crucial moments. Penalties are so frequent on both sides that they are normalized and incorporated into the flow and tactics of the game; the game includes a range of play that is, strictly speaking, illegal but expectable, another arena of risk and competition that good players and teams must be proficient at. A penumbra of controlled violence surrounds the main play of the game. Penalties allow for a form of protected violence, kept within bounds that are implicitly understood by everyone involved; penalties are ways of making violence possible, overcoming confrontational tension/fear by socially organizing the violence in a limited form.

The influence of penalty regimes can be seen by comparing games that have quite severe penalties. Soccer is normally a low-scoring game, because of the presence of a goalie (as compared to games with an open goal and prohibitions on goal-tending) and off-sides rules that favor the defense. Rather draconian rules against tackling by body contact set up unimpeded penalty kicks on goal that often decide a game; moreover, since players who are sent off the field for penalties cannot be replaced, the offending team is very disadvantaged by playing short-handed. Severe penalties of this sort deter borderline violence within the game; and this sets an atmosphere in which extracurricular fights are rare.

Nevertheless, institutionalization of frequent mild penalties does not itself predict very well the level of player violence. Hockey, football, and basketball all have penalty structures that normalize violence beyond the rules; but hockey has very frequent fights, football moderately frequent, and basketball very infrequent fights among players. In addition, baseball, which does not have much in the way of a normalizing penalty structure for rough play (but instead a comparatively severe rule on fighting—expulsion from the game, sometimes with fines and suspension from future games—in this last respect similar to soccer), also has rather frequent fights of a distinctive kind. Another condition for fighting must be invoked.

This is the extent to which players are protected from being hurt if a fight breaks out.

Hockey players wear heavy padding, including helmets and gloves; although they carry sticks, which can operate as weapons, these are virtually never used in a fight itself, although hooking or high-sticking might be a provocation to a fight. Typically in a hockey fight players drop their sticks and pummel each other with gloves on. The equipment operates both to protect them against attacks and to limit the damage they can do to each other during a fight.[11] Moreover, the fighters are usually soon surrounded by other players, who scuffle and push but generally limit the space in which fighters can maneuver, constricting what good blows can be gotten off. Fighters on skates do not have good footing and are not in a position to carry out an effective boxing match.

Football players are heavily padded and wear helmets with face-guards. Football players fairly often get into fist fights, but these do little damage, since the fist is a poor weapon against such protection; thus fights are less damaging than what can be normally done during play, where most injuries occur.[12] The most dangerous weapon carried by a football player is his helmet, which is used as an effective striking weapon for spearing an opponent with a full-body lunge. But this can be done only while a play is going on. There is also a certain amount of punching, even biting and gouging in pile-ups, out of sight of the referees and the audience.[13] But although some players have reputations playing dirty behind-the-scenes, this appears to be a self-contained arena that does not spill over into other kinds of more publicly visible and therefore more dramatic violence. It is minor violence compared to the ordinary violence of the game.

Basketball is played without protective equipment. When rare fights among players break out, they usually take the form of posturing and gesturing, and solid punches are rarely thrown. Thus one of the two most protected games (hockey) has the most fights, the least protected (basketball) has the fewest among combat sports. Other unprotected games, like soccer, also have low violence, although we have seen multiple reasons for why player violence is kept low.[14]

Football, by my estimate, has somewhat fewer fights than hockey, although still at the medium-high end of the range. Both sports are approximately equally protected from physical injury by equipment, and both regularize violent violations under penalty rules (although one could argue that hockey fights are more regularized). But football players have more opportunity to fight, legitimately, in the course of play itself; rough checking is only part of the game of hockey, but blocking, tackling, or breaking tackles happens for almost all players on every play in football. The vast majority of football injuries happen during play, not during fights; if a player is angry enough to want to injure an opponent, the most effective way to do so is to continue with the game. Football has the most room for legitimately demonstrative violence during the course of the game; although there are perhaps the greatest abundance of game situations from which violence could overflow, it is more dramatically satisfying to carry out the strongest violence within the rules.

The pattern is as follows: the more protected the participants, the more frequent the fight. Hockey players, like football players in an extracurricular scuffle, are in the position of children scuffling with each other near adults who can break it up; they are bigger and stronger, but the damage they can do is limited both by their padding and their social surroundings. It is the same pattern that appears in the contrast between German student duelists in the *Mensur*, literally measuring each other's mettle for a fight while padded from waist to neck, in protective goggles and using shallow unpointed swords; and, on the other hand, French duelists with much less body protection but keeping their distance in sword and pistol fights; the German students hack away energetically and at length to produce a few honorable scars; the French make their duels a display of bluster but statistically manage to avoid most injuries. Hockey and football players closely resemble the bundled-up German students playing a prolonged game of mild punishment; most other players of confrontational games resemble French duelists.

Comparison with baseball shows that protection can be social rather than physical.[15] Baseball is not a body contact sport (with a few exceptions), so one might expect a low level of fights on that score. And its players are generally unprotected by equipment; they wear gloves on defense, but these are usually discarded during a fight. Batters wear helmets, although these do not protect the face, and sometimes elbow and shin

Figure 8.3 Limiting the scuffle by use of protective equipment (July 2004). Reuters.

guards, but these have little relevance to fights. Only the catcher, with chestguard, shin guards, and face mask, is heavily protected (against his own pitcher, chiefly).[16]

Almost all baseball fights begin after a pitcher hits a batter with a pitch; in the following inning (usually), the opposing pitcher retaliates by hitting a batter on the opposing team, who then angrily shouts at, insults, or attacks the pitcher with his fists. The rest of both teams then run onto the field, including the reserve players. Usually there is little violence; other members of both teams grab each other, and may wrestle the most excited fighters to the ground, where pummeling with fists is little effective.

There is more of a mêlée in a baseball fight than in other sports fights; basketball fights have few mêlées but more of an individual face-off;[17] football and hockey fights are generally restricted to those already on the field and usually just to those closest to the action. This difference in team participation results from the fact that baseball pitcher-retaliation fights are an explicit code (although forbidden by the formal rules, very similar to dueling in relation to formal law); all members of the team are expected to make at least a token show of solidarity.[18] Bench players will indicate that they ran onto the field because everybody else did, and they felt expected to do so too; while on the field, much of the action consisted in a mixture of grabbing opposing players—as a hostile gesture, but also as a defensive move to keep them from grabbing and knocking down one's own players—and grabbing one's own players to restrain them from getting further into the fight, ostensibly to avoid penalties for fighting.

Leaving aside the ostensible motivations and justifications, the microsociological process of a baseball fight is that a few angry principals carry out a ritual retaliation and honor defense; other players who are closely connected to them join in with some degree of anger, but also to restrain them; other players bodily mass together, as if one huge ritual of body contact, mixing solidarity and hostility. Players are rarely hurt during such mêlées; and the most dangerous weapon—the batter's bat—is virtually never used in such a fight, but is always discarded just before the fight begins.[19] In general, baseball lies in an anomalous position among other games in degree of danger; getting struck by a pitch can sometimes cause death or crippling injury, and there are some other rough plays in base-running (especially when a catcher blocks a runner at home plate; also when a runner breaks up a double play at second base by upending the fielder), but the level of bodily hitting is much more intermittent than in football or hockey. Rough base-running plays rarely lead to fights, in comparison to a hit by pitch, nor are they retaliated for by hitting by pitch. Partly this is because close base-running plays happen only occasionally and at unpredictable times, whereas the pitcher can at any time deliberately throw at a batter, just as a duel can be scheduled at will. Highly motivated violence needs to be dramatic violence; and dramatic staging takes tension buildup to an appropriate, well-anticipated moment.

Here again the exception or historical variant helps confirm the rule. Base-running was much more violent in the period before 1920, when attention shifted to the home run and hence to the hitter-pitcher confrontation. Prior to a rule change in 1897, stolen bases included extra bases taken on a teammate's hit. In the next two years, the new stolen base record was established at seventy-seven for the season. In the seven-year period between 1909 and 1915, heated competition built up among half a dozen players who came near to breaking the record, several of whom successively raised the record to 81 (Eddie Collins), 83 (Ty Cobb), 88 (Clyde Milan), and finally 96 (Cobb again) (Thorn et al. 2001: 543, 547). It was during this time that Cobb acquired the reputation for sharpening

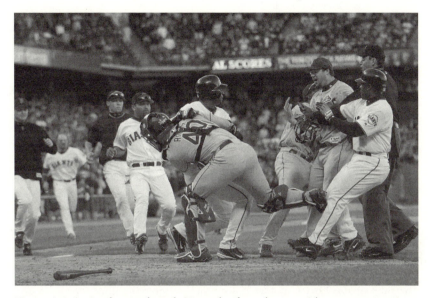

Figure 8.4 A ritual team brawl. Note the few players with angry expressions (chiefly the pitcher) and the discarded bat (2004). AP/World Wide Photos.

his spikes to bloody defensive players with his violent high slides. The reputation was in part bluster, an image and strategy of intimidation; Cobb also perfected techniques of guile and timing by carefully observing the moves of opposing pitchers. Rival base-stealers developed similar strategies and techniques. After this period of competition, the record remained stable until 1962; base-stealing was no longer an object of rapt attention; the yearly totals of Cobb and the other contenders dropped off considerably, and fights centering on base-running virtually disappeared.[20]

A thought-experiment will illustrate the theory to this point. Soccer is a game with very low extracurricular fighting, for a head-to-head mutual impedance sport of offense versus defense. But soccer could be changed into a high-fight game, similar to hockey or American football, by making two modifications: players wearing more padding (such as light-weight synthetic body armor) so they are less vulnerable to being hurt; and changing the penalty structure so that rough play does not count so much in the dramatic action of winning or losing the game. This could be done by adopting football- or hockey-type penalty rules, in which rough players are sent off for only short periods (thereby lessening the amount of time that the team would have to play short-handed), or allowing substitutions if players are ejected from the game. This mental exercise should show that it is these kinds of structural features that determine on-field player violence, rather than something intrinsic to the ethos of particular games.

Winning by Practical Skills for Producing Emotional Energy Dominance

Sports as staged combats are unusually prolonged face-to-face struggles, compared to the usual brevity of real-life fights. Techniques of winning a game are applied on each play; they are a matter of establishing dominance over the person right in front of you—momentarily physically, and in a longer time-frame emotionally. Football linemen charge ahead while defenders push back; winning this contest happens in surges of momentum as one team imposes its will on the other. The struggle is over emotional energy (EE) dominance, just as it is in the climax of military battles, where the winning side becomes energized into a frenzied attack while the other side gets caught in confusion and paralyzing passivity; just as it is in armed robberies where the robber tries to get the jump on a victim. The difference in sport, apart from the restrictions on violence, is that the struggle for dominance is usually stretched out and visibly displayed for the sake of spectators. Where holdup artists seize the jump suddenly and soldiers go into an outburst of forward panic after a period of tension, athletes often go through prolonged efforts yielding temporary and partial dominance at best, occasionally building up to spectacular and decisive momentum-swings.

EE is collective in several senses. It spreads through the team, who become high or low on EE as a unit. More precisely, some segments of the team may have more collectively shared emotion than other players; teams vary in emotional cohesiveness, both high and low; and it varies over time. The inner history of each game played is the sequence of emotional coordination and its level. Collective emotion can be both good and bad: collective confidence and initiative, or collective depression or frustration; at the low end, this turns into quarreling among teammates.[21]

There is simultaneously a reciprocal interaction with opponents so that one side gains EE at the expense of the other side losing it. It is often noted at such moments that the defense is getting tired out, allegedly from being on the field a long time; but this cannot be simply physical tiredness, since the opposing offense is on the field for the same amount of time. The physical tiredness is a manifestation of losing EE; the bodies of the yielding defenders are losing their emotional charge. Another way to say it is that they are being emotionally beaten in a fight, perhaps all the more so because the fight is restricted rather than all-out violence. Sports tactics aim to destroy the opponent emotionally rather than physically.

Players' techniques for blocking and fighting through blocks, for knocking the other player down, for causing him to miss a catch or a running man, are what wins the game as well as the little segments within it. These are techniques of a violent contest in two senses: both to control the opposing player physically so that the play can be executed or stymied; and to establish EE dominance, charging oneself up further and taking away the other's EE.[22]

Such conflicts can spill over rather naturally from violence-within-the-rules into extracurricular violence or player fighting in the sense we are using the term here. In football, the most effective violence happens within normal play, and hence fights are largely expressions of the emotional dominance that has already been established. In other sports, notably baseball, fights can be dramatic high points and turning points of the game.

In baseball, the chief head-to-head battle is between pitcher and batter. Part of this struggle is a guessing game: the batter tries to anticipate what kind of pitch will be thrown, its speed and location, while the pitcher varies his pitch selection to try to make the batter guess wrong.[23] There is also an aspect of sheer physical control of the batter: a pitcher with overpowering speed can freeze a batter's swing, or make him look awkward in trying to catch up with it. What makes pitch speed overpowering is not purely a matter of how high over 90 mph it is thrown; it is often a matter of the rhythms built up through a series of pitches; especially in strike-outs, a pitcher makes the batter fall into his dominant rhythm.

Sports commentators conventionally use terms like "the pitcher is in his rhythm" when he is making an effective series of pitches for a strike-out, and also getting one batter after another for a series of outs. This raises an issue: if the pitcher establishes a rhythm, why doesn't the batter know what pitch is coming, and adjust to it? Nevertheless, he plays the passive role. There are parallels in other areas (discussed in Collins 2004: 122–24). In swimming and other races, habitually winning competitors establish a pace that the others must adjust to. If we think of the race through the technical details of interaction ritual theory, the dominant person is the one who makes him/herself the focus of attention—the winner focuses on the goal, the loser focuses on the winner. Chambliss (1989) emphasizes especially the cognitive interpretations made by winner and losers. There is also an emotional aspect, which he refers to as "the mundanity of excellence"—the winner is calmer and more detached, focusing on performing the micro-detailed techniques that s/he has confidence will bring victory; the loser has more anxiety, feeling that there is a mysterious power that superior athletes have that s/he does not share. The winner's technique includes, perhaps above all, methods for setting the rhythm and making the other competitors adapt to it.

There is further evidence in another area of micro-sociology: the fine-grained rhythms of conversational speech. In high-solidarity interaction, conversationalists fall into the same temporal rhythm. In some interactions, there is a struggle over who sets the conversational rhythm; tape-recorded data shows instances both of the struggle at these moments and of the emergence of one speaker as dominant over the other, who gives in and lets the other set the rhythm (Collins 2004). This is analogous to the pitcher who achieves rhythmic dominance over a batter.

There are also more complicated, reflexive ways of pitching, disrupting the batter's swing by change-ups that are slower than they appear; as well as curves thrown in various directions as they cross the plate. Pitching is partly deception; partly sheer physical dominance through speed; and partly a form of explicit intimidation. Pitchers throw inside, both to catch the inner corner of the plate (especially if a batter has a weakness there) and to back the player up, making it more difficult for him to hit the next pitch on the outside. The brush-back pitch, thrown directly at the batter so he has to jump or fall away to avoid being hit, is a standard technique for all these purposes. On top of this, it also can have an intimidating effect, changing EE dominance between that batter and that pitcher.[24]

Batters are in a Goffmanian face contest with the pitcher; to let oneself appear intimidated is to give an advantage to the pitcher, and controlling one's external expression may be an attempt at controlling one's interior emotions as well. A batter who has been brushed back, knocked down, or hit by a pitch may become angry precisely because he feels a bit of fear that he cannot control; it is better to mask this by anger, to keep up a dramatic front by making a gesture (usually ineffective) of intimidating the pitcher in return.[25]

Aggressive pitching is largely a form of bluster rather than actual violence, although occasionally batters do get hurt; it is the threat of violence more than its actual occurrence; its success comes when it gives EE dominance, with physical dominance coming in its train in the form of a batter's poor performance. Baseball fights almost always start when the batter escalates in reply to the pitcher's bluster. But in fact the pitcher is usually just as angry as the batter, sometimes more so (see the facial expressions and gestures in figure 8.4), showing that fear of getting hurt is not essential to the anger.

Escalation does not happen all the time. As usual, we run astray by sampling on the dependent variable. Although it is true that most baseball fights start because of pitchers' conflicts with batters, if we count incidents of bean-balls, we find they are much more frequent than fights. In an eight-day period, for example, there were sixty-four incidents of hit by pitch in 105 games, but only two fights (forty-two games had at least one HBP, and twenty-two games had multiple incidents); that is, 40 percent of games had an incident, but only 3 percent of these resulted in a fight (calculated from *San Diego Union-Tribune* and *Los Angeles Times*, Aug.

25–Sept. 3, 2004). It takes additional dramatic elements to turn an incident into a fight.

In hockey, most of the action consists in passing and disrupting passing, and in fighting for the loose puck. Such fights are especially vehement in the corners behind the goal; defensemen consider these their special turf, and incursions by the offense have to be especially aggressive, both to have a chance of winning the practical fight over the puck and to meet the high level of emotional confrontation. One hockey player explained:

> I know a lot of times a guy will go into the corner. That's where you find out if the guy is going to come back at you or challenge you or anything. You see what he can take. [Interviewer question: So the corners are important?] Sure, you go in and really rap him hard with the elbow and let him have it in the head maybe and the next time you won't have any problems with the guy. Maybe he'll come in the corner but not as hard as he did the first time, he's taking a chance of getting another elbow in the mouth. Maybe you get a penalty, but you take him out of the play, that's a good penalty. . . . I'll give 'em an elbow and, you know, hit guys dirty. Now I wouldn't hit a guy in the head with a stick, but you get 'em solid with a good check. This is your job, and you watch, he won't come back into the corner too quick.
>
> The guy you've got to worry about is the guy who turns around and really hits you back, bang, right in the nose, and the guy who keeps going into the corner to dig it out. The next time you're thinking, he's got you going. You've got to respect him because you know he'll take it and give it back. He doesn't back away. (Faulkner 1976: 98–99)

The borderline between normal play and fouls is itself part of players' consciousness of the game. Players distinguish between good fouls and stupid fouls; good fouls not only serve a purpose in the game, but also are precisely the fouls that are delivered most aggressively and send the message of domination. "Cheap shots" are looked down upon because they are not violent enough. The hockey player elaborates:

> To intimidate a guy you've got to rap him, cheap penalties are no good really, a hooking penalty is a cheap penalty, tripping, holding is a cheap penalty. A good penalty is charging provided you hit the guy and he *knows* he's been hit. If you trip the guy, it won't hurt him, it doesn't even bother him, he won't care. Tripping is really stupid, the only time you'll trip a guy is if he gets behind you or if you miss the puck and hit his feet. These are stupid because you haven't really done *your* job. This means the guy's beaten you and you have to slow him down so you can hook him or hold him. If you can intimidate him he won't get in this position in the first place. (Faulkner 1976: 99)

The course of a game, as well as longer stretches of players' careers, depends on the cumulative effect of these contests for emotional dominance. "It's a known fact that there are certain guys on certain teams that if you nail 'em once or twice, if you show 'em you're going to take charge, well, they can't take the hitting and so they've got to respect you. They'll be looking, so you can kill their game" (Faulkner 1976: 99).

This is not simply a matter of masculine identity; in hockey testing the opponent's aggressiveness is a key part of the game. Lack of aggressiveness makes one perform badly, and will be taken advantage of by opponents in normal play. The hockey player continues,

> I know we've got a couple of guys on our team, well you know he's scared. He's just scared. You can tell him not to worry that if anything happens don't worry about it, the guys will back you up. But this guy is just scared, you'll make a pass to him and he'll let the pass go off his stick, he'll make a stupid play, he'll move away from the trouble. Last week we got the puck out to him across the blue line and their defensemen came in to take him out of the play and our guy just let the puck go off his stick. So this guy on the other team got it and went in to make a shot on net. Now damn, that's really bad. My defense partner and myself were on the bench and he said, "Look at that goddamned chicken." And you just look at that type of thing and it makes you mad. This guy better change his attitude or everybody will tell him. (Faulkner 1976: 101)

Faulkner notes that the experience of being called upon by others to protect them seems to increase a player's sense of confidence in his own skills. Ritualistic fights give EE to the entire sports performance. Fighting is not just encapsulated as separate activity, or expression of masculinity apart from the process of winning the game:

> If the other team knows that when one of your players is in trouble the whole team will back him up, then we *all* have confidence. This is why some teams are feared, like with S., everyone is there. Someone will put a stick in to stop a punch, if a guy is trying to throw a sucker punch from behind. As a team they're tougher because they back each other up all the way. You never let your teammates get beat because it can swing a whole game around. A guy works your teammate over pretty bad, that gives the rest of them a lift and if we don't go out and challenge him and straighten him out we're *dead*. (Faulkner 1976: 105)

Violence in hockey acts as a high-intensity interaction ritual, riveting collective attention and producing emotional entrainment. It is a common cliché to complain that fights in hockey are more important than the game; this is not strictly true (since goal scoring and saves are the apex of the game), but fights are often the moments that are most successful in stirring up collective energy. This can be the result of entrainment both among teammates and between them and fans.

Another player reports,

> The first thing that comes into my head is the cheering every time somebody gets hit into the boards and a fight breaks out; everyone stands up and cheers that kind of thing, and when they see blood. A lot of fans came to see that and they got bored if there wasn't some kind of violence going on. In my personal conversations with them and how they react to the game, it was enough for me to see that they wanted to see that violence thing, and it does promote it. I mean, when the crowd is behind you and cheer when you knock people into the boards I'm not going to lie, it gets you fired up and want to make you do more banging of guys into the boards, and lots of times, if it takes that to get the team fired up, then that's what you're going to do. It always helps to get the fans behind you they definitely have a role in promoting violence in the sport. (Pappas, McHenry, and Catlett 2004: 302)

Violent techniques are just part of the techniques of a hockey team; some players specialize as scorers, and these (along with goalies) seem to be rarely involved in fights, or even in rough play.[26] Other players are known as the "heavies," and these in turn fall into subtypes. Some are regarded as "policemen," who intimidate opponents, respond to their aggression, and readily join in fights to back up embattled teammates. Some of them regard their role as protecting the fast-skating and slick stick-handling scorers. A "good policeman" is oriented to the game, and avoids penalties in crucial situations. Others, who fight too recklessly, earn the reputation as "goons"; they are disliked by opponents for hits beyond the normal level of intimidation, but also by teammates for involving them in more group fights than necessary. This division of labor shows again that hockey violence comes not simply from a generalized commitment to masculinity, or even to producing violence for the fans; but rather from particular techniques concentrated at particular places in the game (cf. Pappas et al. 2004; Weinstein, Smith, and Wiesenthal 1995; Smith 1979). Every team needs one or two "policemen," but it is not necessary for every player to be one.[27] Even more than scorers, goalies are treated as high-skill specialists who are not expected to fight. If they are hit in front of the goal by encroaching opponents, their defensemen gather around protectively, and may fight on their behalf. In rare instances, when a full-scale mêlée occurs between teams, the two goalies will square off at center ice, against each other, trading token punches. Thus even in an all-out fight, the specialized organization of the teams in terms of violence is maintained.

The Timing of Player Violence: Loser-Frustration Fights and Turning-Point Fights

Now we are concerned, not with normally violent or intimidating game action but the points at which it turns into specifically bracketed fights. When do fights in this sense happen during a game?

One type of player fight arises from frustration. Frustrated fighting occurs late in a game. This happens most noticeably in football, around just the time when one team recognizes that it has lost the possibility of winning the game. The fight is a way of staving off admitting being dominated; it is a last gasp of resistance, at the last moment when the players are still struggling hard. Such frustration fights are usually ineffective as violence (as football fights normally are), and never seem to turn the momentum around.[28]

A second type of player violence changes the emotional situation so dramatically that it determines the outcome of the game. Turning-point fights occur after the tension of the contest has been going on for some time, and thus usually in the last third or quarter of the game.

August 10, 2001: A big bench-clearing brawl in baseball game. This one is unusual because the initiator is really angry, a batter who throws his batting helmet at the pitcher; wrestles him to the ground, and punches him while he is on the ground; as both benches rush the field, other players trade punches too, and the instigator keeps pursuing the pitcher, tackles him again near homeplate as he is trying to get away, again punching him on the ground. The manager of the team on receiving side of the helmet-throwing calls it "the most vicious thing I've ever seen." The brawl stops play for 12 minutes, and the instigator plus one coach on each side are thrown out of game. The fight is unusual in the amount of punches thrown, although there is also the usual milling around, pushing each other at arms length, and angry shouting (*Los Angeles Times*, Aug. 11, 2001).

The immediate lead-up to the fight: Mike Sweeney, Kansas City Royals' first baseman and clean-up hitter, complains that the Detroit Tiger's pitcher, Jeff Weaver, is leaving the white resin bag on top of the mound so that it distracts the hitter's vision. Upon his second complaint to the umpire, the pitcher says something, quoted by Sweeney afterward in an interview: "He said, 'You (expletive expletive), (expletive) you. [i.e., something like 'You fucking asshole, fuck you.'] For me, I wish it never happened, but in the same breath, he called me out." Weaver is 6 ft. 5, a big macho guy. Sweeney is the clean-up hitter, a fairly big muscular guy, too (6 ft. 1, over 200 pounds). Sweeney had a reputation as mild-mannered, according to press reports—so it's not personality. Instead there is the build-up of tension in several kinds of interaction ritual chains.

First are the long-term frustrations and expectations. Both teams, earlier highly regarded, are having very bad seasons, at the point in mid-August where it's clear that they are just fighting to stay out of the cellar. KC is in last place in the American League central division, nineteen and a half games back; Detroit is just ahead of them in fourth place, fifteen and a half games back. But Detroit is sliding; KC has been gaining ground on them and sees a chance of catching up in this head-to-head series, of which this is the first game. Moreover, KC is playing at home, with the crowd of 22,000 behind them.

Second, the tension builds up in the game. It started badly for KC: Detroit jumped ahead in top of the first inning, the first four batters all hitting singles and scoring two runs. KC comes back with one run in bottom of first, which Sweeney drove in with a sacrifice fly; but thereafter the Detroit pitcher settles down and allows no hits and no walks in the next four and two-thirds innings. KC pitching settles down, too, allowing no more runs. So when Sweeney comes to bat in the bottom of the sixth, the game is tense: they've been one run back for five innings (over an hour). Finally after two outs, the Royals get a base-runner on with a double, putting a man in scoring position. Sweeney feels all the pressure on him to tie the game; he also has the expectation—the EE—to do so. Both in long-run EE: he is leading the team in RBIs (82), and in batting average (.311). And his short-term IR chain is up: he drove in the team's only run with a sacrifice in his first at bat. But he still doesn't have a hit for the game. Weaver, on the other hand, is Detroit's best pitcher (at this point, 10 W 10 L); he's been cruising since the first inning, until giving up a double with two outs. It's crunch time for him, too. He apparently tries to upset the batter by playing with the resin bag; and deliberately taunts him when Sweeney complains.

Then comes the fight, unusually prolonged anger on the part of the batter, and prolonged chasing and punching of the pitcher (although punching someone while both are on ground, in wrestling position, isn't very dangerous). Note that the pitcher, although he provoked the fight by taunting, and is the bigger man with a more macho reputation, is passive; tries to get away; is wrestled to the ground several times; doesn't hit back.

Third, a switch occurs in EE dominance. After the fight, Sweeney is ejected from the game; the pitcher stays in. But Sweeney has won the fight, making the pitcher back down, manhandling him and emotionally dominating him during the fight. The angrier person, charged up with EE, wins the fight. Then the pitcher's performance breaks down: Weaver walks the next batter (having walked no one in the game up to that point); then he gives up a single, which scores a run and ties the game (losing his potential victory); then he throws a wild pitch to next batter, which advances the runners to second and third; then he hits the batter with a pitch, loading the bases.

Then the entire team's EE gives way. Weaver is taken out for a reliever, who gets the next batter to hit a routine fly ball; but the Detroit center fielder bobbles it for an error, allowing three runs to score. The reliever walks the next batter; the following batter hits a double to drive in two more runs. This momentum swing results in six runs scoring, all after the fight (when Detroit needed only to get one out, but failed to do so for six straight batters, only two of whom got hits). During all this, from the fight onward, the home crowd has been roaring (and had been building up spirit since the double just before Sweeney came up). After the crowd settles down, Detroit comes back for one run in the top of the seventh, but the rest of the game is routine, and KC wins, 7 to 3. In the following two days, KC continues on a roll and defeats Detroit twice to sweep the series.

Winning the turning-point fight is crucial for winning the game; both are about establishing emotional dominance. Conversely, fights may break out when the game is on the line, but if the fight is a stalemate, the momentum is not broken.

An example from football: Of four NFL first-round playoff games televised on January 5, 2003, only one had fights during game. This was the hardest-fought game (two others were blowouts; the third had one momentum swing as the trailing team came from behind to win).

San Francisco 49ers versus New York Giants. First quarter swings back and forth, each scoring two touchdowns, 14–14. Second quarter and most of third quarter dominance swings to Giants, who open up a 38–14 lead—scoring on four consecutive drives while SF could neither stop them on defense nor move on offense. Giants control momentum for a total of fourteen minutes playing time, but it seems much longer in real time since it also includes the half-time break. Then momentum swings again: SF mounts two drives, scoring touchdowns and two-point conversions, while Giants can't move the ball; the score is cut to 38–30. Then SF drives again, but can only kick a field goal as the defense stiffens, leaving the score 38–33 with under eight minutes to go. SF has now dominated for eleven minutes until stopped. During these three drives, the Giants defense looks very tired, panting, out of breath, while SF performs a no-huddle fast-paced offense. Of course, both opposing offense and defense participate in same number of plays and make just as much physical effort; the apparent tiredness is an emotional let-down, a loss of EE.

Having finally broken the 49ers' momentum, the Giants move the ball for five minutes but cannot score. SF gets the ball back with three minutes to go, and mounts a drive. During this last drive, only one NY player—

defensive safety Shaun Williams—hustles to make plays, and temporarily saves a touchdown. Then SF scores on a pass, to go ahead 39–38; star receiver Terrell Owens, a very tall, dominant receiver, known for showing off while celebrating his touchdowns, taunts the Giants safety, who punches him furiously. Both players are called for fouls; this is especially irrational for the Giants, since they will get the ball back on the kickoff, and a fifteen-yard penalty on their opponent would move them close to field goal range. But the penalties offset, so there is no effect.

SF tries for a two-point conversion, which if successful would give them a three-point lead, so that a Giants' field goal would do no more than tie them. But the Giants intercept the pass, and try to run the ball back out (which is against the rules, since the defense can't advance on an extra point try). Owens comes over and hits the Giants ball carrier (a defensive back) out of bounds—another flagrant foul; but the Giants retaliate, in fact, twice: another of the Giants defensive backs hits Owens; plus the same Giants safety who got the previous foul (Shaun Williams) punches a big SF lineman (a hundred pounds bigger than himself) who had intervened in the first fight. The same set of players can't stop fighting with each other. So again it's off-setting fouls—again SF gives the other side a penalty break, but the other side can't take advantage of it because of retaliation. Giants then move the ball down the field rapidly; another brief fight breaks out; then Giants try for a field goal, which they miss as time runs out. 49ers win.

What we see is an extremely hard-fought game; momentum swings very strongly first to Giants, then to SF; the most effective defensive player in trying to break the momentum swing starts a fight in response to boasting by the SF performance leader after he finally scores to take the lead; then the SF star angrily attacks after their insurance play has been foiled, and the NY defensive leader counter-attacks. The individuals with the highest EE and most personal dominance initiate the fighting and keep it going with retaliation. The fighters are those who have put in the most effort to shift the momentum swings of the game.[29] But no one wins these fights. The fights do not change the momentum, but only confirm it. The team in EE decline also fades out in their last-ditch effort to win.

Tension can build up over a series of games, compounded out of team rivalries, the pressures of elimination tournaments, and accumulating incidents of in-game intimidation.[30] The fights that result can become the dramatic centerpiece of the action. This is most notable in professional baseball and basketball playoff series, where teams and their fans store up emotional memories of previous confrontations, and winning or losing a fight tends to determine the following sequence of action on the field, for a whole series of games.[31]

Figure 8.5 Male and female players display identical gestures of domination (2004). Left: AP/World Wide Photos. Right: © McClatchy-Tribune Information Services. All Rights Reserved. Reprinted with permission.

Turning points can also occur in the kinds of non-contact sports that involve no fights but emotional tests of dominance. In the Wimbledon tennis championship in 2004, Maria Sharapova battled the prior champion Serena Williams in a exchange of twenty-one volleys at break point in her first service game of the second set (having won the first set already). Finally, Sharapova hit a forehand deep in the corner, and Williams slipped and fell. Sharapova gave Williams a hard stare and pumped her fist, while Williams lay on the ground, an expression of agony on her face. Sharapova went on to ace the next serve and to take the rest of the match easily (*San Diego Union-Tribune*, July 4, 2004). The loser is beaten both physically and emotionally, at the turning point, while the winner goes on from that point demonstrably and self-consciously full of confidence. Battles for dominance are not gender-specific, but are shaped by the dramatic sequence of the game. We see this also in photos of women pitchers in softball games making the same gestures that men pitchers do after recording a crucial strike-out: jaw thrust forward, fist punching the air.

Basketball fights often happen in a climax of frustration when a team blows a lead and loses momentum. This may take the form of especially rough play rather than a frame-breaking fight. In the final game of the

2004 NBA Eastern Conference championship, the Indiana Pacers had led by fourteen points in the first half, but the Detroit Pistons slowly caught up and tied the score with just under four minutes to play. The Pacers' best defender, Ron Artest, then knocked down the Pistons' best scorer, Richard Hamilton—a much smaller man—with a forearm shiver to the jaw. Hamilton picked himself up, made the two penalty shots, and his team never trailed again, going on to win the series (and eventually the NBA championship). The team that won the fight physically did not win it dramatically, and was emotionally knocked out of the game (*Los Angeles Times*, June 2, 2004).

Further light is cast on the dynamics of player fights by asking when they do *not* occur. After all, only a minority of games have frustrated game-losing violence, or turning-point violence, although most games have a point at which a team becomes aware it has lost. I have argued for the structural principle of one fight per venue or dramatic sequence. The same pattern of filling the emotional attention space predicts when fights will not happen. After the buildup to a dramatic climax, further fights become emotionally superfluous. Based on this principle, I predicted successfully that after the dramatic American League championship series between the Yankees and the Red Sox in 2004, coming to an emotional climax in the sixth-game collision between Yankees star Alex Rodriquez and Red Sox pitcher Bronson Arroyo,[32] there would be no further fights, either in the remaining seventh game or in the following World Series.

SPECTATORS' GAME-DEPENDENT VIOLENCE

Spectator violence takes several forms: fans can invade the field, or throw things at the players from a distance; players might fight with spectators, although this is rarer; and fans can fight with each other during the game.

This last form of fan-on-fan violence has not been much studied.[33] Some stadiums are known for sections of the stands where fights are common; for instance, the cheap, upper-level seats of Philadelphia's old Veterans Stadium (demolished in 2004) were known as places where rowdy young men threw things and engaged in fisticuffs, especially against fans of an opposing team who ventured into the area. It is unclear how such fights relate to the rhythm of the game action. Stadiums known for rowdy fans of this kind are chiefly in the big cities of the Northeast (notably Boston, New York, and Philadelphia, and especially in professional football and baseball games); West Coast fans of the same sports are much less violent, and also do much less rough cheering and jeering. A pattern consistent with my observations is that fans at the rowdy stadiums are much more likely to consist in groups of young men, whereas West Coast and Midwestern crowds have a higher proportion of women and family groups. This is the same pattern that has been suggested to account for the difference in violence between North American hockey and football spectators (predominantly middle-class, college-educated, and almost half female), as compared to European soccer matches (whose fans are largely working-class males between ages seventeen and twenty) (Roberts and Benjamin 2000). It is not clear when and how often spectators get into small-scale fights unrelated to team partisanship—possibly very little, if team-identity sides preempt the violent attention space.

Most of what is known about spectator violence concerns large-scale crowd disturbances. One study, which listed all the episodes of collective violence at games reported in Toronto newspapers during one year, found that of the twenty-seven incidents of crowd violence, 74 percent were ignited by player violence (Smith 1978). For example, during a Hockey Association Junior game, a cross-checking incident sparked a fight that eventually included most players from both teams, several hundred spectators, and twenty city policemen. In a professional hockey game between Buffalo and Cleveland, players brawled, touching off a paroxysm of chair-throwing by spectators, whereupon players, sticks flailing, went into the stands to fight with the fans. In a Toronto soccer game between Yugoslavia Zagreb and the Greek All-Stars, many of the 13,000 spectators invaded the field after eighteen minutes of the second half. The score was tied 1–1 at the time. The Yugoslav goalkeeper tripped a Greek player as he was racing for the goal. The referee awarded a penalty kick and the goalkeeper protested. There was a shoving match and then fans raced to the field. The spectators started kicking at the players (note that fans mirrored the players' actions) who returned the blows. This fight is framed by ethnic divisions between both players and rival fans. But it also happened at the turning point of the game, since the penalty kick might well have resulted in victory or defeat: at a tense moment, with the score tied, more than halfway through the game. The players broke the framework of the game by fighting with the referee, whereupon the fans joined. The battle ended only with massive police intervention.

Fans are subject to the same rhythms of dramatic tension as players; indeed, it is chiefly to experience these tensions and to express their emotions collectively, thereby transforming them into the additional feeling of collective effervescence and group solidarity, that fans are attracted to attending a game in person. Thus it is not surprising that fans get into fights at about the same moments that players get into fights.[34] This is also true across different sports: psychological testing has shown that fans' belligerence increases after (and presumably during) football and hockey games, but not after attending gymnastics or swimming meets (Goldstein and Arms, 1971; Arms, Russell, and Sandilands 1979). Fans go with the emotional flow of the episodes contrived by the particular kind of game. Dramatically appropriate violence is that which is an extension of the game action; fans become aggressive only where the violence is perceived as intentional (Zillman, Bryant, and Sapolsky 1979); when an injury is seen as accidental, fans are not aggressive, and may even shift frames to applaud an injured opposing player.

When players and fans directly fight each other, one or the other must intrude into the other's space. A mass of fans sometimes invades the playing field, although often they are more intent on disrupting the game and bringing it to an end—either in victory or in disgust—or attacking the officials. When just one or two isolated fans invade the field, however, the players are likely to meet them with violence (for which they receive the general support of the fans [see note 11 in chapter 6]).

Players are the violent elite compared to the fans, and most of the serious player-versus-fan violence occurs when players attack, most typically by invading the stands in response to jeering. But jeering is a fairly normal occurrence, indeed part of the appeal of being a fan where hostile displays can be made with impunity and even with crowd support; and so the times when players respond with violence must intersect with some special tension on the part of the players. In chapter 3, we saw Ty Cobb invading the stands during the tension of his record-seeking hitting and base-stealing season. In other instances, the tension comes from the special dramatics of the team contest.[35]

Teams "have a history with each other" because of the dramatic incidents of conflict they have been through; and this history is well known to the fans, indeed celebrated by them as part of the appeal of attending an upcoming game. Fans are drama-seekers; whether the drama happens to be violent or not is somewhat incidental. Earlier we met a key bit of history between the Indiana Pacers and the Detroit Pistons in the on-floor violence that was the turning point of the Eastern Conference championship. The next time the two teams met during the following season, the Pacers made up for their defeat by leading all the way in a blowout. Ron Artest, the Pacers player who had delivered the climactic (and counterproductive) blow in the championship game, also started the subsequent brawl when he delivered a hard foul on the Pistons' biggest player just at the end of the game; with forty-five seconds to go and a fifteen-point lead, the foul was pointless except to punctuate the sense of payback. The Pistons player apparently took it as an insult, and shoved Artest in the head, leading to a little mêlée of players from both teams on the floor. Artest, as if taunting the rivals, lay down on the scorer's table by the sidelines—invading the officials' turf, but also showing off his safe haven as his irate victim was held back from attacking him. Then—since the game was being played in Detroit's home arena—the Detroit fans got into the act, in keeping with the typical pattern of fan fighting entrained from player fighting. In the midst of noisy jeering, one fan, apparently tempted by the seeming passive posture of Artest lying on the table, dumped a cup of iced drink on him. Artest now jumped into the stands, along with a supporting teammate, and exchanged punches with two fans; the fight spilled back onto the floor, and Artest punched a fan wearing a Pistons jersey (i.e., acting out his fantasy identification) who accosted him, and was tackled by another fan who in turn was punched by another teammate. The brawl ended with the Pacers players retreating from the floor, pelted by the fans who remained in the safety of the stands. The remainder of the game was called off (*Philadelphia Inquirer*, Nov. 21, 2004).

The fight received great attention in the media, and was universally condemned as especially shocking; several Pacers players received lengthy suspensions from the league. But in fact every element in the fight fits the general patterns of sports violence. Efforts by the most vociferous fans to take part in, as closely as possible, the dramatic conflict are what brought about the player's retaliatory violence, in this case and in all other cases of player-fan violence known to me. Nevertheless, the universal reaction of officials and commentators points up a fundamental structure of sports dramas: they are performances for the benefit of spectators who wish to indulge their emotional experience of protected fantasy conflict. The borderline between spectators' turf and players' turf is the framework of the whole display; players' violence, both within and without the rules of the game, is to be confined to each other; spectators' for the most part fantasy violence against players is indulged to a degree; but the real violence of the players—who, after all, are much better at it than anyone else—must be kept inside the arena and not directed at the spectators.

The structure of involvement is different for players than for spectators, so it is not surprising that their style of fighting is quite different. Player fights generally have the form of symmetrical fair fights; two players scuffle or trade punches, two teams mill around on the field. But spectator violence tends to be extremely one-sided, attacking the weak: local fans pelting or pummeling a small number of visiting fans, or attacking the visiting team, or sometimes attacking the security forces if the latter are outnumbered.

Players' fights are very much like staged fair fights, similar to those of duelists. Keeping the fight balanced between both sides is part of the ethos of being an elite. Spectators, however, are not elite; they act like riot crowds in attacking the weak, vastly outnumbering the opposing team when they jeer and sometimes physically attack. Fans and players are both emotionally and symbolically involved in the same conflict; but they operate on two quite different status levels: fans as shameless and ignominiously tribalistic partisans;[36] players as heroes in evenly matched contests under honorific traditions. Fans in their moments of enthusiasm abase themselves before the players like the most primitive religious fanatics in the presence of their cult objects. Fans also act like would-be carousers on the outskirts of a well-publicized party. Players react to fans' incursions of their turf, like an elite repelling boundary incursions by plebeians. Just as aristocrats, who settle their own disputes by the honor code, but peremptorily beat an offending lower-status person with a stick, athletes mete out degrading punishments to those who intrude on their terrain. We shall see some consequences of this disparity in status between players and fans in the creation of more sophisticated forms of fans' violence.

Offsite Fans' Violence: Celebration and Defeat Riots

Most of the violence that happens in a sports arena is related to the rhythms of confrontation on the field. There are three main kinds of fan violence that happen independently, over and above the drama of game events. The most extreme disconnect is football hooligan violence, which I will leave for the end. There are also several forms of spectator violence that begin at the stadium or in connection with game events, but spill over into offsite violence and develop an independent course of their own. These include political violence and celebration and defeat riots.

Political violence at games is mobilized in part by extraneous conflicts, for which the game presents an opportunity to confront a national or ethnic opponent up close instead of at a remote distance. But the buildup of contention around the game itself can also make political rivalries stronger and more salient than they usually are.

For instance, a soccer game was held in Sarajevo in 2002 between Bosnia and Yugoslavia, for the first time since they had fought a war, in 1992, which was notorious for ethnic cleansing atrocities. The game was held in the Bosnian capital, where the home crowd consisted of about ten thousand Bosnians, plus supporters of the Yugoslav team, a group of about three hundred made up mostly of local Bosnian Serbs. Bosnian fans stamped their feet during the Yugoslav anthem; Yugoslav supporters responded by mooning during the Bosnian anthem. Several hundred police kept the two groups apart. A chanting contest followed, with the Yugoslav supporters chanting "This is Serbia," and "Karadzik, Karadzik," the name of the most wanted war-crimes suspect. Bosnian fans responded by chanting "*Allah-u-akbar*," the traditional Islamic war-cry "God is great." The Yugoslav team went on to win the game 2–0. Police protected the Yugoslav fans as they left the stadium; whereupon abut two hundred Bosnian fans attacked the police outside the stadium; six fans and nineteen officers were injured, and eight fans were arrested (*San Diego Union-Tribune*, Aug. 23, 2002).

Here the pretend-combat of the game operated to recall and reinvigorate earlier political violence. Sports riots with political and nationalist themes can also hinge upon game events. During the 2002 World Cup, Russian soccer fans, who were watching the game with Japan on a big screen in a central Moscow square, rioted after Japan scored the one goal of the game. Russia had won their previous game, and were originally much more highly regarded that Japan, so expectations were dashed. About eight thousand fans, mostly teenagers and young men, ran through the streets chanting "Forward, Russia!" some of them wrapped in the Russian tricolor flag. They broke shop windows over an area of a mile, jumped up and down on cars, smashing their windows, and overturned about a dozen of them; seven cars were set on fire. Five Japanese classical music students, who were attending a nearby musical competition, were attacked by the fans. The rioters also threw bottles and fought among themselves as well as with police; one man was killed, and about fifty were hospitalized, including twenty police (*San Diego Union-Tribune*, June 10, 2002). In this case, the timing of the opponent's score sets off the violence, which spreads quite far, hitting both Japanese and other targets.

The 2002 Moscow riot is both a political riot and a defeat riot, the counterpart to a victory celebration riot. As we will see, celebration riots can be just as destructive as defeat riots; and celebration riots are much more frequent. Losing a game is generally emotionally deflating, and the crowd lacks the ebullience and the traditional rituals (such as tearing down goal posts), which can segue from a victory celebration into a destructive riot. Defeat riots require an additional mechanism. One clue is that defeat riots seem to be more common in international competition than domestically, and where sports rivalries are highly politicized. Defeat riots depend more on features extraneous to the game, since the emotional flow of the game itself will generally de-energize the defeated and energize the victors.

Victory-celebration violence is a version of carousing.[37] The fans' celebration is an extension of the celebrating that players themselves do after an emotional victory. Both players and fans engage in solidarity behaviors—yelling together, hugging, jumping around to let off adrenalin—and in antinomian rituals that mark the specialness of the occasion. Winning football teams celebrate by pouring a barrel of liquid on their coach; this is a version of playful violence and authority role reversal, which the coach is expected to take in good humor. A championship team in American professional sports generally opens bottles of champagne in the locker room, which they do not drink but pour over each other. This is similar to a wild party, but with rather restricted destruction.

Fans have a different set of options; they rarely can get close to the players to express bodily solidarity with them; instead, they storm the basketball court or invade the field. The traditional football victory ritual was to tear down the goal posts at the end of the game. (This began with college games at the turn of the twentieth century, when goal posts were made of wood; the metal goal posts of recent decades has made this more difficult, although it is sometimes attempted). Fans are attracted into the center of the interaction ritual, where they make contact with physical objects imbued with magical significance: tearing up pieces of the turf, the basketball floor, or the chairs to take home as souvenirs is a way of acquiring a sacred object and appropriating its *mana*. Victory celebration violence combines the potlatch, as in a memorably wild party, with the attempt at getting into the center of the action.

But fans are not part of the elite at the center; and they are often prevented from getting even these tokens of symbolic contact. In recent years, stadium officials employ large numbers of security guards and police in an effort to keep fans off the field at all times. This is one reason why victory celebrations expand away from traditional potlatch-like limited destruction at the sporting site, and into full-scale riots offsite. This implies that offsite riots increase as field security goes up; the hypothesis is testable both over time and between events that have different levels of security.

In the following example, the victorious team is away from home, and the celebration riot takes place at the home campus. Detail on the time-sequence of violence and social control moves are especially useful here:

In April 2003, the University of Minnesota hockey team was playing in Buffalo, N.Y., for its second straight championship. Back in Minneapolis, beer kegs were set out on fraternity lawns in anticipation of a celebration in public space. When news of the victory came at 8:30 p.m., people started pouring out of fraternities, sororities, and apartments, growing to a crowd of about a thousand people. Within twenty minutes, a bonfire was started in a street intersection (i.e., in a safe spot, away from buildings) with a mattress, a park bench, and trash receptacle. Firefighters quickly doused the blaze—which is to say, they put out the celebration. Fans then set fires in four other locations, in garbage cans and dumpsters—again, burning trash. At the street corner where the original fire had been set, a traffic signal was broken off, and someone hung on the crossbeam over the street, rocking it, trying to bring it down. A police officer said the crowd was "cheering them on like it was some sort of sports contest"—that is, a continuation of the game experience.

Police were outnumbered one thousand to two at this point. The crowd was heaving beer bottles at them, and they retreated to their squad cars. Eventually almost two hundred officers were called in. Both sides escalated. Motorists caught in the crowd were having their cars pummeled. Fire engines were now having trouble getting to the fires that were being ignited at nearly every intersection.

Two rows of fifteen officers, standing shoulder to shoulder and side-walk to sidewalk, walked down the street to confront the crowd. Over a loudspeaker, an officer ordered the crowd to disperse. Students were slow to respond. "Getting out in the middle of the street doesn't happen that often," a sophomore woman told a reporter. "What's wrong with that?"

The crowd remained unruly. People threw bottles, and some threw lighted kindling at the police. Police began macing the crowd, which backed off, splitting up and heading in three directions. It took about fifteen minutes for police to clear the intersection, and then firefighters drove in to put out the fire. Police stayed to hold the intersection.

In the meantime, smaller crowds were setting new fires at other intersections. More police squads were brought in and cleared the intersections one by one. Around 10:30 p.m., police advanced on a crowd of about three hundred to four hundred. The crowd was shrinking, though enthusiastic. "People were chanting 'U-S-A! U-S-A!' " a witness said; someone yelled, "It's just like Baghdad!" Here they borrowed slogans from international sports events, notably the memory of the U.S. upset victory over the USSR in Olympic hockey in 1980; and the recent victory of U.S. forces in Iraq in March 2003. As I will argue later, all sorts of emotionally memorable symbols are pressed into service in the immediate moment.

A crowd of youths cheered as they flipped over a car in a parking lot. Someone set some newspaper racks on fire, along with a dumpster, and then the overturned car. Many of the people in the crowd were on cell phones, talking about what they were seeing. A witness heard someone say, "Man, you got to see this, it's incredible!" Narrative gratification blends with the action itself.

Elsewhere, a parking lot booth was burning and someone had opened a fire hydrant, flooding the street. Police used launchers to fire chemical spray into the crowd, driving a considerable portion of the crowd to run from the area.

About 11 p.m, some in the crowd tried to kick in the doors of the university Sports Pavilion. A fire blazed in a trash receptacle. Some fans even tried to light the bushes. The police used mace again, and the crowd ran off.

Shortly before midnight, a fire truck was pelted with bottles, shattering the windshield. The last fires were put out around 1 a.m.; the riot had been going on for five hours. A total of sixty-five fires had been set in the university neighborhood, cars were overturned and burned, one store looted, windows smashed, and street signs torn down. In keeping with the celebratory mood, the looting took place at a liquor store. By the time police got there, the windows had been smashed and the looters had fled; someone had thrown a bike rack through the window. Bystanders said looters were coming out with cases of beer on their heads. "They pretty much cleaned out the vodka," said the store-owner. "Cheap stuff, expensive stuff, they weren't choosy" (*Minneapolis Star-Tribune*, April 20, 2003).

The riot ended when the fires stopped; there were a long sequence of fires building from the original few, spreading over a wider area as police forces grew stronger and more aggressive. The activity of the riot, besides the ebullient shouting of the crowd (which seemed to peak within the first two hours), consisted chiefly in finding new places to set fires. Most of these followed the same pattern, burning trash and construction waste. There was no attempt to burn buildings (although some were menaced by fires later in the evening when the police had driven the fans out of the open spaces of the street intersections). The fires were the main vehicle for keeping the moral holiday going. We find the usual pattern of a relatively small proportion of activists: peak crowds reached about one thousand out of some thirty-nine thousand students at the university campus, and some of those present were spectators rather than participants.

To a considerable extent, celebration riots attacking authority happen because of a lack of traditional potlatch-like festive destruction in a restricted setting, like old-fashioned goal-post smashing and bonfires. This lack of an institutionalized venue for moderately destructive moral holiday is one ingredient. It combines with heightened attention through the mass media on the team's own celebration. Such riots resemble boundary-exclusion fights that occur at parties; blocking enthusiasts from getting into a prestigious carousing scene generates anger combined with ebullience, the formula for an energetic brawl.

OFFSITE VIOLENCE AS SOPHISTICATED TECHNIQUE: SOCCER HOOLIGANS

The offsite violence of English and European football hooligans is a special case, the most sophisticated form of sports violence.[38] I call it "sophisticated" because it is deliberately contrived for the sake of having a good time in the excitement of fighting. Hooligan violence usually gets organized in conjunction with a soccer match, especially when fans are traveling away from home to another city, or better yet, another country. But the violence does not depend upon the events of the game in any way; it can happen the day before the game, or any time around the period when fans are assembled; the game itself serves only to get them mobilized and bring them together. Football hooligans consciously seek the emotional thrills of a fight, with all the legitimating overtones and symbolic resonance that a sports contest provides; but they emancipate themselves from the fate of the team. They avoid the downer of losing a big game, or the uncertainty of a big victory celebration. Instead, they deliberately and regularly schedule violence, under their own control; and they accumulate organizational tactics by which a satisfying fight can be carried out. As noted, fans are unequal to players; the latter are the elite, while the spectators follow them emotionally; fans get their collective effervescence as the players develop the dramatic conflict of the game. When players fight their honorific duels and vendettas, fans follow along with vicarious excitement, or attempt to join the violence but do so in the much less honorable fashion of attacking the weak. Sports are contrived to generate moments of emotional entrainment and collective solidarity among the fans; hooligan violence is contrived to provide the entrainment and solidarity of fights, without being subordinate to the players. This violence emulates the combat structure of the game, with the hooligans raised into heroes in their own right, usurping the place of the athletes.

Soccer hooligans are often explained as manifestations of class consciousness and hostility in highly class-stratified British society. But hooligans are not from the poorest part of the working class, but often from its elite segment;[39] and some members of football firms are white-collar workers or small-business owners, attracted by the energy and excitement (Buford 1993: 31, 118, 216; Dunning et al. 1988); they find the temporary status of elite in the world of fans to be superior to the duller pleasures of middle-class life. Hooligan violence is a case where deprivation does not explain violence, but the positive attractions of violence do; and this in turn depends on situational conditions that can be manipulated by those who have accumulated the requisite techniques.

What are these techniques? First, a capacity to maneuver through streets and public areas, both to avoid the police and to meet the enemy in a favorable place and circumstances. These techniques are like an army unit maneuvering in units of company (200) or even battalion (1,000) or regimental size (in exceptional crowds of 4,000). But organization is virtually ad hoc. There is no formal chain of command, and no clubhouses, treasuries, elections, or written records; there are some informal bases such as pubs (with pub-owners prominent among the most active hooligans), and a few quasi-illicit businesses in travel arrangements and ticket touting provide logistics, and also some of the leaders.[40] There are informal leaders in the core firms of supporters of a particular soccer team; these are well-known individuals, often flamboyantly dressed, who are in the center of the action when hooligan violence is shaping up or under way. Buford (1993: 29–30, 81–93, 119–20), a participant-observer with the Manchester United supporters and other English hooligans for five years during the 1980s, found that each leader had his personal following, a little firm of as many as thirty or forty, mostly youths ages fifteen and sixteen or even younger, eager to prove themselves; these started many fights, and acted as sub-lieutenants. Such a leader would jog through the streets of an Italian city, showing the way to several hundred supporters, evading the massed Italian police who were set out to restrain the English invaders, surrounded by half a dozen youths who conveyed orders to split up or regroup, until finally the crowd of supporters found suitable victims—a frightened group of Italian fans (not fighters but families) on buses, or small groups of Italian youths on an empty street. A leader at times would tell supporters when the time was or was not right for action, "helping the police, directing traffic, or pushing away supporters who were blocking the streets and reprimanding those who had broken bottles or were behaving in disorderly fashion" (Buford 1993: 68).

Experienced hooligans also have widely distributed tactical knowledge apart from such leaders: how to take the speed of a trotting walk-run, when the action is not yet begun but is being watchfully anticipated and sought out; when to group together and move as a phalanx; when to spread out. When police met them in strong formations, hooligans would drop back into civilized demeanor, slipping through police lines, "not walking too fast, everyone maintaining the I-am-on-my-own-and-not-about-to-start-trouble look" (Buford 1993: 198; also 92–93). Since this could happen immediately after a riot, police were not necessarily taken in, but their own inclination to avoid further confrontation generally motivated them to go along with this Goffmanian performance. Hooligans are sophisticated about the confrontational tension/fear of police, and deliberately take advantage of it. They know the authorities will not use much force on them, if not caught in the midst of a riot, and they turn violence on and off with considerable care.

Temporary leaders can also emerge out of the situation; individuals who take the initiative in spreading the word—a march up the street to take place at 6 p.m., pass it on—or who are the first to step off the sidewalk in the eyes of the waiting police lines, expecting others to follow (which sometimes happens and sometimes not—in which case the would-be leader looks around nervously and then steps back into the crowd trying to look inconspicuous) (Buford 1993: 282–89). Leaders facilitate the maneuvering of the crowd, but the crowd mood is crucial in empowering leaders, for shorter or longer periods of time.

Tactics and stratagems were used not only against the police but also against opposing firms. When Man U's rival West Ham was known to be arriving on a train for a match, a plan was hatched to burst through the station entrance at just the right moment and attack the West Ham firm as it came off the train.

There were a thousand people, milling around "casually," hands in their pockets, looking at the ground. The idea was to look like you were *not* a member of a crowd, that you just happened to find yourself on High Street—at the time that a thousand other people happened to have done the same. . . . Another minute and the supporters drifted into the middle of the street. There was still the studied casual look, but it couldn't be maintained. As the clusters of people came together, a crowd was being formed, and as it was in the middle of the High Street, it was conspicuous and intrusive. . . . The crowd was starting to move; it had started off in the direction of the station. It proceeded in a measured way, nothing frantic, at the pace of a steady walk. I could see the confidence felt then by everyone, believing now that they were actually going to pull this thing off. The pace accelerated—gradually. It increased a little more. Someone started to chant, "Kill, kill, kill." The chant was whispered at first, as though it were being said reluctantly. Then it was picked up by the others. The pace quickened to a jog, and then a faster jog, and then a run. An old woman was knocked over, and two shopping bags of food spilled on to the pavement. There were still no police. Halfway up the ramp, the group was going at full spring: a thousand people, running hard, chanting loudly: "KILL, KILL, KILL." (Buford 1993: 121–23)

In this instance, the Man U firm had been outmaneuvered; police with dogs were inside the station, waiting to catch the firm in full formation; and the West Ham firm, disembarking their train at just that moment, had the satisfaction of following police through the local crowd, which was in full flight. This was regarded as a humiliating defeat by the Manchester firm, described as allowing their rivals to "take the city."

Sometimes a firm carries out a successful maneuver: Man U's firm circling through the streets of London, guided by one of their leaders with his little lieutenants, being followed by Chelsea supporters, but then looping back upon them to take them from the rear (Buford 1993: 201–3). Sometimes an "aggro" was arranged by cell phone calls among opposing leaders, finding a meeting ground out of sight of police mobilized to prevent just that (especially among Belgian hooligans: Van Limbergen et al. 1989). A chief characteristic of hooligan violence is the extent to which it is premeditated—not only anticipated but planned, although with a degree of improvisation on the fly. One researcher refers to it as "violence by appointment" (Johnstone 2000).

Another set of sophisticated techniques involves knowing what the supporters can get away with. Traveling together on a train or bus to an away match, supporters vandalize the cars, throw bottles out of windows, taunt and threaten any respectable middle-class persons who are trapped in with them (Buford 1993: 13–15, 62–66). Police are usually concerned to speed them through, get them out of their own area, and hence do not intervene in this sort of vandalism and rowdiness. Firms know the advantages of appearing in numbers, overwhelming ticket-takers and food servers. The term "on the jib" was used by Manchester United supporters to refer to traveling in this fashion without paying, taking food in restaurants and then leaving; some veteran supporters refer to themselves as "inter-city jibbers." Hundreds of lads would mob a food stand at a train station, filling their pockets with food and drink for the trip; the very chaos of the scene—from the point of the view of the overwhelmed attendant—was exploited, as the lads threw food through the air, "amid chants of 'Food fight! Food fight!'—they split up, some going to the left, others to the right, everybody disappearing" (Buford 1993: 64). They make the trip for free, it appears, not because they cannot afford it—Buford documents that most supporters have jobs and considerable money—but out of the fun of jibbing for its own sake.[41] It is a minor form of crowd violence, a version of a moral holiday but deliberately contrived by a group that has made a tradition and a technique of doing so.

Elias and Dunning (1986) describe football violence as motivated by a "quest for excitement" in unexciting, pacified societies that have undergone the civilizing process of recent centuries.[42] The explanation is too wide for its target. Staged excitement is the aim of virtually all institutions of modern sports; but deliberately orchestrated offsite violence takes both the deliberation and the excitement to a higher pitch.

Group leaders are both tactical leaders and excitement leaders:

Sammy then turned and started running backward. He appeared to be measuring the group, taking in its size. The energy, he said, still running backward, speaking to no one in particular, the energy is very high. He was alert, vital, moving constantly, looking in all directions. He was holding out his hands, with his fingers outstretched. Feel the energy, he said. . . .

Everybody crossed the street, decisively, without a word being spoken. A chant broke out—"United, United, United"—and Sammy waved his hands up and down, as if trying to bat down the flames of a fire, urging people to be quiet. A little later there was another one-word chant. This time it was "England." They couldn't help themselves. They wanted so badly to act like normal football supporters—they wanted to sing and behave rudely and carry on doing the same rude things that they had been doing all day long—and they had to be reminded that they couldn't. . . .

At one moment, a cluster of police came rushing toward us, and Sammy, having spotted them, whispered a new command, hissing that we were to disperse, and the members of the group split up—some crossing the street, some carrying on down the center of it, some falling behind—until they got past the policemen, whereupon Sammy turned around, running backward again, and ordered everyone to regroup: and the little ones, like trained dogs, herded the members of the group back together. . . .

Sammy must have been leading his group around the stadium, hoping to find Italian supporters along the way. When he turned to run backward, he must have been watching the effect his group of two hundred walk-running Frankensteins was having on the Italian lads, who spotted the English rushing by and started following them, curious, attracted by the prospect of a fight or simply by the charisma of the group itself, unable to resist tagging along to see what might happen. And then Sammy, having judged the moment to be right, suddenly stopped, and abandoning all pretence of invisibility, shouted: "Stop." Everyone stopped. "Turn." Everyone turned. (Buford 1993: 81–85)

What followed was a mêlée. In the usual pattern of crowd fights, it broke up into little clusters of unequal forces; Buford watched a young Italian boy, isolated, knocked down and then kicked repeatedly by a group of English hooligans that grew in size from two to six to eight, rushing in on the easy target.

Sammy was transported. He was snapping his fingers and jogging in place, his legs pumping up and down, and he was repeating the phrase, It's going off, it's going off. Everyone around him was excited. . . . There was an intense energy about it; it was impossible not to feel some of the thrill. Somebody near me said he was happy. He said that he was very, very happy, that he could not remember ever being so happy. (Buford 1993: 87–88)

A few moments later the group caught up with an Italian family, a man with his wife and two sons attempting to get into their car and escape. The English hooligans hit the Italian man across the face with a heavy metal bar, knocking him to the ground; others trampled him, sometimes stopping in their forward rush to kick him.

The emotional high comes from the power of the crowd, having created a moral holiday, thereby controlling the space immediately around it. This sense of power is not necessarily violent; it occurs in the sheer logistics of movement as a consciously united group:

The group crossed a street, a major intersection. It had long abandoned the pretence of invisibility and had reverted to the arrogant identity of the violent crowd, walking, without hesitation, straight into the congested traffic, across the hoods of cars, knowing they would stop. (Buford 1993: 89)

And another occasion, this time in London, as Manchester supporters leave their gathering place:

The pub is evacuated, glass breaking as pints of beer are simply dropped, and a crush of people instantaneously fills up the small street outside, a preposterous number in a preposterous hurry—no one wanting to be left behind—and then turns into the main Euston Road, spreading out, curb to curb, blocking traffic in both directions, everyone organized and united and feeling the high energy and jubilant authority of suddenly being a crowd.

They avoid the Underground at Euston Station (too many police) and march to the next one, Euston Square, entering it as one—placards, posters, stools being picked up and swept along en route, no barricade or turnstile as an impediment—everyone chanting now, the group's euphoria building, no one buying a ticket, no one being stopped or challenged. (Buford 1993: 194)

They have successfully gone through the tipping point, feeling the energy and jubilation. The violence they produce, it should be noted, is ecstatic only when it occurs in the context of the mobilized crowd; individual fights that they may be in at other times have none of the same panache.

The experience of going through the barrier into a moral holiday, a moral holiday controlled by the hooligans themselves with their sophisticated tactics, is the apex experience.

A crowd is forming, and the effect is of something coming alive. I can see more people joining up, attracted by the familiar, powerful magnetism of numbers, but they don't seem like additions: they don't seem to come from the outside, but from within the crowd itself. You can feel it growing. . . . We are free, the faces are saying. We have got past the police, the faces believe. We cannot be stopped now. . . . The pace picks up. I can feel the pressure to go faster, an implicit imperative, coming from no one in particular, coming from everyone, a shared instinct for the heat and the strength of feeling, knowing that the faster the group goes the more coherent it becomes, the more powerful, the more intense the sensations. The casual stroll becomes a brisk walk and then a jog. Everyone is jogging in formation, tightly compressed, silent.

I am enjoying this [the respectable upper-middle-class observer reports]. I am excited by it. Something is going to happen: the crowd has an appetite, and the appetite will have to be fed; there is a craving for release. A crowd, already so committed, is not going to disperse easily. It has momentum, unstoppable momentum. (Buford 1993: 199–200)

The experience is like the surge of drug intoxication, especially the high moment when a drug hits the blood stream and the consciousness:

This is the way they talk about it. They talk about the crack, the buzz, and the fix. They talk about having to have it, of being unable to forget it when they do, of not wanting to forget it—ever. They talk about being sustained by it, telling and retelling what happened and what it felt like. They talk about it with the pride of the privileged, of those who have had, seen, felt, been through something that other people have not. They talk about it in the way that another generation talked about drugs or drink or both, except that they also use both drugs and drink. One lad, a publican, talks about it as though it were a chemical thing or a hormonal spray or some kind of intoxicating gas—once it's in the air, once an act of violence has been committed, other acts will follow inevitably. . . . I realized later that I was on a druggy high, in a state of adrenaline euphoria. And for the first time I am able to understand the words they use to describe it. That crowd violence was their drug. (Buford 1993: 204–05)

Drug users often describe the peak pleasure as the moment they inject themselves with heroin, the inhaling of the cocaine or the smoke of marijuana (Becker 1953, 1967; Weinberg 1997). Here I want to emphasize that the most exhilarating moment for the hooligan crowd is when it crosses a threshold and explodes into the moral holiday zone they have created. They consciously focus on the violence, but much of this comes later, after the zone is established. A close look shows that violence to which is attributed this kind of drug-intoxicating quality is embedded in a larger social process. The violence is at the peak of collective attention, but it is largely a symbol of the wider process of antinomian collective effervescence, and the distinctive solidarity of a group that has mastered the technique of deliberately creating moral holidays.

The group, when it takes over a public space, is rude and obnoxious. This is deliberate antinomianism, aimed at shocking bystanders, and includes drinking and pissing in public squares, shouting and chanting (Buford 1993: 52). Swigging on wines bottles all day long before a match may be not so much an effort to get drunk, as drunkenness is the price they pay for keeping up a gesture of public rowdiness, while the violence is not yet arranged to go off.

The actual violence of the hooligans mostly takes the form of attacking the weak.[43] Buford's specific examples all have the pattern of a larger group of hooligans beating at length on an isolated victim; sometimes these are opposing toughs, sometimes mere tokens of the opposing side (such as the family supporters of Italian teams). The sophisticated maneuvering of the firms is aimed at creating just such a tactical advantage. When sizable numbers of opposing firms meet (which happens chiefly when the English firms invade each other's home turf at the time of a game), they usually confine themselves to ritual taunts and bottle-throwing from a distance, but back away from a full-scale fight. Another participant observer notes,

Figure 8.6 Soccer hooligans gang up on isolated fans of opposing team (Munich, 2001). AP/World Wide Photos.

What almost always happens in football hooliganism is that the bigger firm wins—and the other one runs away; and significantly, it is allowed to run away (thereby minimising injuries). However, this fact, although constantly recognized, is then also constantly concealed so that each group can take maximum honor from each incident of violence. The bigger group conceals the fact of its numerical superiority from itself in its remembrance of the fight, while the smaller group can emphasize exactly the mismatch so as to take honor even from a defeat. Thus, there is an ideal which is constantly evaded in practice and one of the reasons is that a fight between two serious, evenly matched firms would result in extremely serious injury. I am not saying that such fights never happen—they do—but more often fights are quickly resolved by the numerically advantaged firm "running" the other one. The brute fact of the effectiveness of numbers is recognised but also conveniently effaced in action. And the ideal of the numerically outnumbered honorable firm defeating their equals is always drawn upon. (Anthony King, personal communication, Nov. 2000)[44]

In reality the fighting, although very much the center of attention as firms maneuver for when "It's going to go off," and as they discuss events afterward, is a relatively small part of their activities. King sums up:

Although the highpoint of the hooligan's existence, fighting itself constitutes a negligible length of time in the lives of these fans. For all the
discussions of violence, confrontations like the fight in the Velodrome
(a brief brawl in the Marseille stadium) are almost invariably quick and
indecisive. By contrast, discussions of fights are lengthy. The imbalance
between the time spent actually fighting and the time spent talking
about it suggests that the conventional analytic orientation to hooliganism might be inverted. (King 2001: 570)

The chief ritual of the hooligans is gathering in pubs, where they build
solidarity and good cheer narrating past fights. Peripheral members of the
group, those not actually present at a fight, become carriers of the collective memory of the group; the narration also affirms the stratification of
their own ranks between storied individuals (often not distinguished from
the storytellers) and audiences. Expeditions abroad are especially valued,
but only if there has been a notable incident. Having been there makes
one a celebrity (Buford 1993: 113–14). Violence is a valuable commodity
to the group, but only because it can be narrated in the context of the
group: in fact, doubly situated, in the content of the narrative as a high
point in the life of the firm; and also in the ritual of its telling and retelling,
which brings the supporters together as a larger entity than the core activists. Narratives of violence are the crucial cultural capital that circulates
in the firm. As King argues, the firm exists in the consciousness of its
members as an ongoing construction of collective memory. Its narratives
have a mythical quality; only the high points are singled out, and these are
skewed to make one's side look heroic, suppressing the tactical realities of
the one-sided assaults on easy victims and the furtive escapes from
stronger forces. Like the party-fighters described by Jackson-Jacobs
(2003) this fighting is chiefly for the sake of the narrative gratification.

A little violence goes a long way. The little incident in Marseille was
enough to make the whole trip meaningful for the English fans; and violence as drama is a nicely available resource, since it can almost always
be produced in sufficient amounts, and thus is more reliably available
than football victories.

The Dramatic Local Construction of Antagonistic Identities

I have been arguing that the situational techniques of the hooligan groups
are the key to their behavior, and the source of its attraction. A widespread
line of explanation, to the contrary, emphasizes features of the cultural
background: a culture of aggressive masculinity, grounded in the machismo of patriarchal societies; nationalism; regionalism (e.g., Dunning

et al. 2002). There is abundant evidence to support these descriptions. Hooligans themselves, a highly vocal group, craft their challenges and insults in just these idioms. They sing and chant patriotic songs and insult foreign nationalities. On an individual level, a favorite put-down is to call a man a "cunt" (Buford 1993: 281).

Nevertheless, the insults are highly situational. An example:

On a bus arriving for a match in Italy, the supporters chant "England" over and over again.

> Another, more sophisticated [song] was based on the tune of "The Battle Hymn of the Republic." Its words were:
>
> Glory, glory, Man United
> Glory, glory, Man United
> Glory, glory, Man United
> Your troops are marching on! on! on!

Each "on" was grunted a bit more emphatically than the one before, accompanied by a gesture involving the familiar upturned two fingers. There was an especially simple tune, "Fuck the Pope"—simple because the words consisted exclusively of the following: *Fuck the Pope. . . .*

> [One man] . . . had reversed himself into a position in which the opened window by his seat was filled by his suddenly exposed and very large buttocks—his trousers, this time, deliberately gathered around his knees, the cheeks of his buttocks clasped firmly in each hand and spread apart. Just behind him a fellow was urinating through his window. People were standing on the seats, jerking their fists up and down, while screaming profanities at pedestrians, police, children—any and all Italians. (Buford 1993: 43)

In short, a gamut of ritual obscenities, shaped to the situation at hand, escalated out of team cheers and patriotic chants.

National songs and chants are brought out when the English are traveling abroad, omitted when they are challenging a rival team at home.[45] Despite the use of sexist epithets to insult men they do not like, the hooligans of the 1980s were ardent admirers of Margaret Thatcher and the queen—presumably because these could be used to assert English solidarity and superiority, and to put down respectable educated liberals and leftists; although in Italy they chant *Fuck the Pope!* at home they defend the Catholic church, out of hostility to the Anglican establishment (Buford 1993: 95). The pattern is much like that analyzed by Katz (1999) in his study of freeway road rage: curses are brought to one's lips because they fit the particular target one is confronting at the moment; they need not be based on deeply held beliefs, and the repertoire can be inconsistent and contradictory from occasion to occasion.

Curses and insults are drawn from a larger cultural repertoire, but it is the situation that gives them life. The impression of nationalism, sexism, or other prejudice is more staged effect than cause; it is the collective techniques of constructing moral holidays that makes such insults a useful part of the repertoire, and brings them to the forefront.

We can be more specific. Narrative gratification is the key experience, to which fighting is a necessary but limited ingredient. And narrative blends over into vocal action of the kind illustrated above (chanting "fuck the Pope!" blends over into telling stories about how we "fucked the Italians," a narrative in large part about vocal action). It is easy to get the impression that the content of what they say at these moments is the motive for why they say it. This confuses speech act and content. To avoid falling into this trap (natural enough in ordinary discourse, and in ordinary political talk, which is its extension), let us look at the micro-interactional circumstances of vocal action of this kind.

The group engages in vehement chanting at particular times, as a ritual of both solidarity and verbal aggression. Buford's observational detail suggests a pattern when chanting and singing happen, and when not. These happen when the supporters throw off their cover and announce themselves as a crowd in action; but before the violence has "gone off." But when the hooligans are actually fighting—six to eight of them kicking a lone Italian boy on the ground—no one says anything; there is only the sound of the kicks, softly muted thuds or gritty crunches, depending on which part of the body was hit (Buford 1993: 84–86). This speechlessness may well indicate a return of confrontational tension, showing that the ebullience is not in the fighting itself but in the verbal ritual that surrounds it before and after.

King (2003; esp. chap. 11, "Racism in the New Europe") makes a useful distinction between organic and instrumental racism. The former is deep-seated, preexisting in the larger society. Instrumental racism is often apparent in the chants of fans in football matches. For example, Italian fans call black players on foreign teams African monkeys and taunt them by throwing bananas on the pitch. Spanish fans who had chanted racist epithets at black players on a visiting English team were not, according to King, committed racists but defended themselves as merely joking and using a verbal tactic to upset their opponents. Racial insults are even generalized as a way to insult opponents of the same race who are supporters of rival teams. North Italian fans insult white fans from the south by yelling that Africa begins at Rome; Liverpool fans chant "I'd rather be a Paki [Pakistanian] than a Scouse [nickname for rival fans]." In these verbal tactics they draw upon a background convention of racial hierarchy, which their instrumental behavior unconsciously reinforces.

I suggest a stronger thesis: the experiences and practices of being a football fan create or at least expand the amount of racial antagonism in the larger society. Not only is racial taunting a tactic for distracting opposing players; the culture of fans is an accumulated repertoire of techniques for taking part in the drama of the game, and adding an independent drama on their own initiative by mock-conflicts enacted in jeering opponents. The main attraction of any sports event is the opportunity to take part in moments of collective emotional experience in a conflict motif, without most of the dangers and costs of real conflict. Racial taunting is one of those techniques.

The argument can be stated in a thought-experiment: if football were abolished, the amount of racism would decline.[46] There are independent, preexisting sources for racial/ethnic antagonisms in society; but these may well be minor (judging from the marginality and weakness of right-wing movements in earlier decades). The expansion of football popularity in Europe, and its repertoire of game-based fan expressions of mock-conflict, has expanded the amount of racial antagonism, spilling over outside the grounds as well. The link from inside-grounds expressive chanting to violence beyond the game sites is made by groups of football hooligans or their imitators, seeking to expand the solidarity and drama of the game into a similar experience they can use in other spheres of life.

An issue not yet answered in the comparative sociology of sports is why the growing popularity of soccer football has fostered racial taunting, whereas in American mass spectator sports racial taunting is virtually nonexistent. There is a well-developed tradition of mock-jeering during and around games, and some stadiums have traditions of fighting with opposing fans. But racial jeers are widely taboo; team solidarity is the precise limit of antagonisms. (I can't imagine an American fan, even a very violent one, yelling something like "I'd rather be a nigger than a Yankees fan.") An explanation may be that American sports have been the leading edge of racial integration, from the time of the first black baseball players in white leagues in the 1940s, through the time of the 1960s civil rights struggles, and continue to uphold that role very self-consciously. In American football and basketball, the majority of the players have been black since the time these sports came to dominate mass media popularity in the 1960s. Taunting of black players who integrated baseball lasted only during the first few years and was widely condemned. It was not taken as a mode of jeering the opposing team, and thus as an ambiguously joking form of instrumental racism, but as straightforward racial antagonism unconnected to fan loyalties. Whether or not sports have entwined with larger social movements such as civil rights may explain the international divergence; although it is also related to differences in the way fans are organized. American teams lack hooligan firms; such firms are a crucial link, the lack of which keeps the potential for fans' opponent-taunting rituals from generalizing to larger social conflicts and spilling over outside the sports grounds into movements in the larger society.

REVOLT OF THE AUDIENCE IN THE ERA OF ENTERTAINERS' DOMINATION

Consider the history of hooliganism as a history of techniques for sports-like ebullience and collective effervescence, progressively emancipated from the game itself.

Violence at soccer games goes back to the early twentieth century and even earlier. It has been found worldwide; some of the most violent riots have occurred far outside the orbit of British hooligans, such as in the Soviet Union in 1982, when sixty-nine were killed, or in Lima, Peru, in 1964 when about three hundred were killed and five hundred injured at a match against Argentina (Dunning 1999: 132). A war was set off in 1969, when Honduras expelled several hundred thousand Salvadoran peasants who had immigrated in recent decades; the flashpoint was a soccer game between the two countries, ending in a riot that turned into a five-day war in which two thousand died (Kapuscinski 1992). But our analytical criterion is not just the number of casualties; this does not tell us what kind of social pattern was operative. The Honduras/El Salvador soccer war was not hooligan violence, but the kind of political violence that we have examined in a previous section, where celebration and defeat riots were convenient mechanisms for mobilizing conflicts extraneous to the game itself. It may be the case that such riots (and wars) are especially likely to happen in authoritarian societies where sports is virtually the only mobilizing arena available. Its contrast is what we are concerned with here, the development of sports violence in democratic societies via the social organization of hooligan firms, deliberately using their technology for creating moral holidays: culminating in "riot on demand" emancipated from the game itself. Most of the early violence was spontaneous and unsophisticated fan behavior of the sort we have already examined: on-field incursions, and spill-overs of game emotions into off-field celebration and defeat riots.

Soccer leagues began in England in the 1860s, and like other sports, were a province of the upper and middle classes; by the late 1880s soccer had professionalized and acquired an audience of working-class men. Crowd sizes grew and with them incidents of crowd violence. Most of these incidents took place in the grounds (i.e., the stadiums); since there were minimal barriers between the spectator area and the playing area, chiefly these were mass incursions onto the field of play.[47]

An accidental feature of the configuration of British stadiums may have been crucial in developing the special kind of appeal of crowd enthusiasm and fan violence. In the classic period of soccer violence, spectators— especially those who were the rough supporters—were crowded into sloped terraces at the stadium. Early terraces were merely earthen mounds; later they became made of concrete, with bench-like seats. However, no one sat down; both because the custom was to stand, and because, with the growth of hooliganism, police would pack as many people as possible into one of these terraces, surrounded by chain-link fences and other barriers, and lock them in. The strategy was to keep the hooligans (and especially supporters of the visiting team) segregated from the rest of the crowd, and to usher them in and out of the stadium at an opportune moment when they could not confront locals. This strategy had several unintended consequences. In inhibiting ritualistic onsite violence, it contributed to the development of strategies for generating offsite violence, separated from the game—the technical innovation of English hooligans for constructing moral holidays on demand.

Another consequence was to increase the solidarity and the emotional entrainment of the crowds in the terraces. These locked-in cages were colloquially referred to as "pens" and "pits"; inside them, people were pressed together, palpably swaying their bodies in rhythm in a high intensity interaction ritual:

> It is not uncommon, in any sport, to see spectators behaving in a way that would be uncharacteristic of them in any other context: embracing, shouting, swearing, kissing, dancing in jubilation. It is the thrill of the sport, and expressing the thrill is as important as witnessing it. But there is no sport in which the act of being a spectator is as *constantly* physical as watching a game of English football on the terraces. . . . You could feel, and you had no choice but to feel, every important moment of play—through the crowd. A shot on goal was a felt experience. With each effort, the crowd audibly drew in its breath, and then, after another athletic save, exhaled with equal exaggeration. And each time the people around me expanded, their rib cages noticeably inflating, and we were pressed more closely together. They had tensed up— their arm muscles flexed slightly and their bodies stiffened, or they might stretch their necks forward, trying to determine in the strange, shadowless electronic night-light if this shot was the shot that would result in a goal. You could feel the anticipation of the crowd on all sides of your body as a series of sensations. (Buford 1993: 164–66)

Not everyone in the terraces was a hooligan; this was an elite minority of activists, who were most likely to be massed in their own terrace when traveling to an away game, especially on the Continent. But the experience of the terraces was the historical breeding-grounds of the collective solidarity experience; raised to an unusual pitch—compared to other sports spectator experience—it was then further transformed when taken as the goal, the experience to be contrived offsite by the sophisticated techniques of maneuver that grew up in the 1960s.

We have virtually experimental confirmation of the importance of these local configurations in creating crowd experience, by seeing what happened when they changed. During the 1990s, English stadiums changed over to American-style area seating: separate seats, with arm-rests (which also served as body separators), were introduced where economically possible. Whereas classically police would herd spectators in hurriedly, and fans could often avoid ticket takers, or paid cash at the gate without receiving a ticket to a specific seat, policies were enforced to make all entrants have a paper ticket, paid in advance, with a numbered seat. Games were increasingly marketed to respectable family audiences (Buford 1993: 250–52; Anthony King, personal communication, Nov. 2000). Cruder forms of single-seater stadiums, however, continue to exist; King (2001) describes a fairly traditional cage-like terrace in Marseille, where the seats were numbered but the fans ignored them and stood all over.

This is part of the puzzle. Early particularities of the experience in British stadiums created a distinctive kind of crowd emotional buzz, which later became emancipated from the stadium and the game. An intermediate step occurred in the 1960s, when police attempted to reduce fighting among rival fans inside the stadium by segregating them in different terraces. This had the unintended effect of increasing the violence, in several ways: First, by generating greater homogeneity and solidarity within the most rabid fans in a terrace, indeed all the more so that they were locked in during the game. Second, by creating territorial targets, so that fans could try to storm the seating area of opposing fans, before or during the game. The fans were becoming more like an auxiliary "B-team" to the on-field players' "A-team"; they had their own goal to invade, not by kicking a soccer ball into it, but by physically intruding with their massed bodies or by throwing missiles into it. And third, stricter police measures motivated fans to take their confrontations outside the grounds. This pattern of escalation and counter-escalation in the tactics between police and fans turning into better-organized hooligan firms has been noted by English sociologists and others (Dunning et al. 1988; Van Limbergen et al. 1989); it parallels, but in a much more drastic way, the pattern I have noted above in which American security forces preventing onsite victory celebrations tend to displace them into more violent celebrations outside.

One more pathway toward the sophisticated techniques of soccer hooligans came in the area of transportation. The earliest instances of fighting around soccer games at the turn of the twentieth century involved groups of fans who traveled collectively to games in so-called brake clubs in hired motor transport (Dunning et al. 1988: 115, 140, 167–79). The first outbreaks of what look like modern soccer hooligans were reports in the 1950s of fans wrecking trains. The chief venues for fights between fans began to be train stations. By the late 1960s and into the 1970s, the full apparatus of techniques was in place: jibbing; coordinated traveling designed to evade the police; organization involving leaflets distributed before hand announcing fights to be held at particular matches. As police took notice and massed their own forces at appropriate times and places, hooligans shifted increasingly to seek fights by incursions into the home territories of rival fans. The territory had now expanded, not just from taking the visiting "end" of the stadium, but "taking the manor," intruding into the town itself, and "running" the opponents where they could be maneuvered into a position of weakness.

English-style soccer hooliganism is a social technology, invented to emancipate stadium excitement from the game itself. The technology spread to the Continent (notably Holland and Germany) and elsewhere. Belgian hard-core hooligans deliberately imported English techniques in the 1980s, going so far as to visit England for the purpose of observing and bringing back their most sophisticated refinements, as well as borrowing English songs and slogans (Van Limbergen et al. 1989).

The purpose of these techniques was twofold: First and most obviously, the experience of the "buzz," the excitement of collective solidarity and dramatic tension and release that are the technical achievement of modern sports, but transformed into a portable technique that can be used on demand, away from the game itself. Second, the raising of the status of the fans to co-equals with the players, and indeed perhaps even beyond them—the soccer team might lose or perform in a mediocre way, but the firm could "take the manor" or repel its rivals, in either case arriving at a higher level of narrative gratification than the team itself, and displacing it from the center of ritual attention. Fans, we have seen in previous sections, have a rather ignominious existence, if viewed with any degree of objectivity—though of course all the conditions of the fan experience collaborate to make them lack any vantage point outside themselves to see what they look like. They are subservient to the players in the most groveling way, dependent upon them for their emotional well-being and rhythms of attention; in the most intense moments of fanhood, as we see in the previous photos, they are bodily controlled, rapt, in single-minded worship of their sacred objects.

The invention of the social technologies of hooligan groups emancipated fans from this subservience. Not only did it give them back their autonomy in time and space, but it raised their honor in the realm of conflict, in a profound way. Fans in the throes of the game experience are reduced to the most primitive level of tribal morality: they have no honor, attacking the weak in the weight of numbers, tens of thousands massed in a stadium raising their voices and inclining their bodies in mock warfare against the visiting team of a dozen or so.[48] Players, in contrast, are heroes; they fight equally matched teams. Hooligans cut themselves loose from the fan-player hierarchical relationship, and enter into the horizontal relationship of hero-gang versus hero-gang. Of course there is much sham and illusion in this; in reality, they seek out fights only where they have a large advantage in numbers, and retreat or refuse battle when the odds are anything close to even. But their narrative rituals cover all this up; in their ritual subjectivity, they are heroes.[49] The B-team displaces the A-team.

Of course this is not strictly true in all respects. Hooligan gangs have emancipated the drama of conflict, as far as their subjective and emotional participation in it is concerned, from the events and personalities of the game itself. But they have not emancipated themselves from their teams as far as the organization of their fighting in time and space. They still organize these activities around the schedules of matches between opposing teams; these are the occasions on which they will make incursions into rival turf, or defend their own. They remain parasitical on the formal league organization. This is inescapable, insofar as the hooligan firms are based on a loose and informal organization; it is this organization that makes it possible to construct their chief techniques, blending in and out of normal crowds, evading police authorities. They can get along without formal structure, without permanent headquarters, treasuries, officers, and all the rest, the social movement organization that even the loosest political movement needs, because they can rely upon the league scheduling to provide the most basic coordination. The scheduling of football matches serves as a convenient way of bringing the group together, so that it can practice its techniques.

Social techniques for creating violence are historically situated, rising and falling, changing along the way. They are part of a wider range of techniques that constitutes modern popular culture. Ultimately it is not sheer physical violence that is sought, but the collective excitement. Modern sports are the ongoing development of ritual technology for blending Durkheimian solidarity with the dramatic tension of contrived plot lines on the field of action, with just enough open-endedness to keep up the emotional edge. Sports hooligans further manipulate the social focus of attention so as to make oneself into the hero stratum of the show.

Here we may note a parallel between the concluding topics of this chapter and chapter 7. There I noted the invention of the mosh pit at popular concerts was a way of taking back the center of attention from the band; a counter-move by the audience from its position of passivity and subservience to the star musical performers, into the center of the emotional attention space. This too is what English soccer hooligans invented with their social technology of moving the game spectator experience out of the stands and into a sphere which they themselves could control, turning the ebb and flow of dramatic moments of the game into "riot on demand."[50]

In the long-term view, moshers and soccer hooligans display the same evolution of social techniques. Both are forms of the revolt of the audience in an era of mass commercial entertainment. I am not suggesting that they are here to stay, certainly not in their present forms. They bear some resemblance, nevertheless, to the futuristic dystopias envisioned by writers and filmmakers of the mid-twentieth century: roving gangs of violent thrill-seekers like those that populated *Blade Runner*, *Clockwork Orange*, and *Barbarella*, descendents of the futuristic fears of Aldous Huxley and others. What all this suggests is that mere material comfort does not give rise to social peace; the advance of technologies of leisure consumption have brought predominance of the entertainment economy, and with it an increasing recognition of the arts of how to contrive experiences for their own sake.

We have become more sophisticated, more reflexive, capable of at least tacitly recognizing when a form of behavior is embedded in another, as a distinctive realm of artificial reality. Social centers of attention are always a form of stratification in their own right; in the past fifty years, they have become increasingly matters of situational stratification, severed from other forms of economic and political stratification, and from long-standing hierarchies of social respectability; sheer situational status severed from class and power. But they are not severed from their own immediate social base: the organizational conditions of micro-interaction, the means of dominance of the immediate attention space. Musical entertainment, especially of the noisy and heavily rhythmic kind, together with the drama of athletic events, have become the chief organized technologies for compelling social attention. By standing in the spotlight broadcast by these technologies, the stars of entertainment (including sports-as-entertainment) have become the situational dominants wherever they appear, attracting attention from everyone exposed to them. Remarkably, even as this new form of status stratification has appeared, new social technologies have developed around their periphery; the very fans who are most subservient to them because most engrossed in them, have created means of status revolt, taking back the center of attention. Historically ephemeral as these may be, they point toward a larger trend.

Contriving drama in games leads to further inventions contriving drama in offsite violence; just as the techniques of loud rhythmic musical entrainment have led to side-inventions of actions that speak louder than music in the pseudo-violence of the mosh pit. This suggests that more social technologies of excitement may be invented in the future, with or without admixtures of violence.

There is both good news and bad news in this. The good news is that there is nothing primordial about the things that people fight about. They are not long-lasting or deep-rooted social identities and antagonisms; the strength of such identities are products of just how intense the ritual technology is that situationally produces them. The bad news is that we are capable of creating new causes for violence, however ephemeral they may be. Perhaps the silver lining here is a fact that we have seen over and again in this book: most violence is bluff and bluster, much show and display compared to actual substance. The social technology of the staged event may preserve us yet, however much it may scare us.

PART III

Dynamics and Structure of Violent Situations

CHAPTER 9

How Fights Start, or Not

TO THIS POINT, I have discussed how people fight; I have not yet answered the question of why they fight. I have purposely avoided giving emphasis or priority to this question. Answers generally have been theories about prime motives, postulating one or another basic interest or overriding concern: for honor, for material gain, for the group, for power, for masculine identity, to propagate one's genes, to satisfy cultural imperatives. As an analytical strategy, this seems to me the wrong way to explain who fights whom, when, and how.

First, whatever the motive or interest that individuals or groups might have for fighting, the overriding empirical reality is that most of the time they do not fight. They pretend to get along; they compromise; they put up a peaceful façade and maneuver behind the scenes; they bluff, bluster, insult, and gossip, more often at a distance than to their opponent's face. When they do actually come to violence, the determining conditions are overwhelmingly in their short-term interaction. A theory of motives for fighting explains little, because having motives is a long way from actually committing violence on their behalf.

Second, inferring motives is often a dubious business. Freudian, Marxian, and other such theories are notorious for interpreting whatever happens in terms of their chosen motive. Let us reverse the gestalt; begin with the situational process. Motives tend to emerge as the conflict heats up; once the situation has escalated, the persons involved start to form an idea of what they are fighting about. In deeply entraining violence, the perpetrators often have little clear idea of why they keep on doing what they are doing. The fighting and the motive become structured and articulated simultaneously as part of the same process. If we follow participants over time, what they say tends to wander and shift. Motives are a category of folk cognition used by participants for explaining events to themselves, and by outsiders such as news reporters, lawyers, and officials for the purpose of settling on a public account of why an incident of violence happened; it is part of the process of closure, of socially defining past reality in order to declare it finished. Multiple, shifting accounts of what the conflict is about are part of the texture of the action itself, not something that stands behind it and guides it like a puppeteer pulling the strings (see Fuchs 2001 for a general formulation).

In the preceding chapters, I cut in at the point where a conflict is already well advanced, on the brink of violence, and then watched how it plays itself out. In this chapter, I will pursue this further back, looking explicitly at the early stages of conflict, with an eye to what keeps the interaction stuck there, as well as what makes it—exceptionally—move down into the tunnel of violence.

NORMAL LIMITED ACRIMONY: GRIPING, WHINING, ARGUING, QUARRELING

Let us begin with situations of regularized acrimony: the small-scale griping and quarreling of everyday life. There is a folk theory that minor quarreling builds up, festers, and accumulates until it finally explodes.[1] The folk theory is grossly unrepresentative of what normally happens. After violence breaks out, it is often possible to put together a narrative that retrospectively attributes the violence to this gradual buildup of festering, boiling, heating tension/pressure; but most of the time quarreling is normal, regularized, limited. Most of the time it stays on the near side of the invisible wall, the barrier of tension/fear that makes violence difficult to carry out. The folk theory assumes that violence is easy, and that all it takes is a sufficient buildup of steam to blow the top off. We have seen, to the contrary, that violence is socially difficult, and it is much more common to carry out social rituals that pretend to fight but confine it to conventionalized gesturing.

This gesturing takes two forms. One is verbal acrimony; the second is blustering and boasting. Verbal acrimony is the polite middle-class form of face-to-face conflict; it ranges from calm through edgy and sarcastic (i.e., sending hostile messages in the paralinguistic channel) up through vehement emotional outbursts. But even these outbursts—loud shouting matches, stomping out, announcing the breaking off of a relationship—are not in themselves violent. We have no survey of the incidence of various kinds of quarrels, but it seems a fair estimate that, in the first place, only a minority of quarrels lead to high degrees of anger; and in the second place, only a minority of angry quarrels lead further into violence. What I shall examine is what kinds of interactional dynamics tend to keep most quarrels normalized and limited; and what are the special circumstances that take some of them over the ultimate limit into actual violence.[2]

The other type of gesturing that acts as a substitute for violence is boast and bluster. Again, speaking very schematically, this is the opposite of polite middle-class quarreling; its archetype is masculine, indeed macho, working-class/lower-class youth; or historically, the realm of warriors, specialists in fighting. It might seem obvious that boasting leads to violence because it is part of the culture of those who habitually fight. But this is ignoring the dirty little secret of violence—the barrier of tension/fear that makes fighting incompetent when it happens, and produces much more gesture than real fight. Thus instead of defining the macho culture as a culture of violence, it is more accurate, and more revealing, to think of it as a culture of boasting and making claims about violence. The culture of machismo, of the tough guys, the action scene, is mainly the activity of staging an impression of violence, rather than the violence itself.

This sets up our analytical problem. The world of boasting and bluster is a repetitive set of situations; much of the time these have their own equilibrium, staying within their own limits, but sometimes they spill over those limits. Much of the time the tough guys carry out their rituals, telling stories about violence, boasting about themselves in aggressive ways, playing aggressive verbal and nonverbal games with each other. Some of the time this make-believe violence escalates, spills over, and become real violence. Under what conditions does this happen? The intermediate step is the zone of bluster: making threatening gestures, especially the mixture of verbal and paralinguistic gestures in cursing and insulting. This might seem to be the imminent brink of violence, and indeed it can be an actual accompaniment of violence. But bluster is also a common way of staying at the brink, or just back from the brink: and many would-be fights peter out because an equilibrium is established in the ritual of blustering at one another.

The ritual staging of belligerence is a Goffmanian frontstage, whose backstage is the feeling of using the performance as a substitute for violence. The staging process sets up a distinction between insiders and outsiders, those who understand that staging is being done, and those who are taken in by the staging; the simplest version is the stratification between the tough guys with their bluster and those who are intimidated by it. This staging is what Elijah Anderson calls the "code of the street."

The baseline for the normal limited acrimony of everyday interaction is described by Goffman (1967) as "face-work," a ritual process of orderly accommodating to one another. Individuals try to maintain their own face, their claim to be what they put themselves forward as being (at least in that situation), and they help others do the same. Conversational interaction and other aspects of face-to-face encounters are a cooperative game, in which each allows the other to maintain their illusion of being the idealized person that they display for the occasion. Participants claim to be various things: relatively high in social status, morally proper, a sophisticated insider, on friendly terms with the person they are talking to, good-humored and at-ease with the situation, or just plain competent social interactants. Whatever it is they are claiming, they tend to avoid ways in which these claims break down, both on their own part and on the part of the other; they use and permit vague claims and half-truths, overlook lapses, and act tactfully so that blatant contradictions and pretenses are papered over as smoothly as possible. Where a blatant failure comes to the surface and is explicitly acknowledged, ritual repairs are usually set in motion, so that excuses are made and accepted; rather than drawing out these embarrassing moments, everyone generally tries to get past them as quickly as possible so as to resume the smooth surface of appearances.

Goffman's analysis is drawn from the polite middle and upper classes of British and American society around the mid-twentieth century, and it is not clear just how far it applies, historically, cross-culturally, and across categories of age, social class, and ethnicity. At any rate, we may say that it is a standard for "being on one's good behavior" for these other groups in contemporary Western societies, and apparently more widely.[3] We may take it as a baseline against which to ask the question: given ritual constraints that severely limit acrimony, how does conflict arise and become expressed in situations subject to these kinds of accommodative pressures? Goffman himself suggests two pathways.

First, playing within the rules of the polite game, one can engage in "aggressive use of face work." Recognizing others' tendency to accept apologies, one may see what offenses one can get away with; given others' attempts not to hurt feelings, one may pointedly act hurt and provoke attempts at remedy (drawing this out at length is sometimes referred to as "guilt tripping"). Criticism of other persons, and especially of their situational claims to be more than they can prove to be, can be slyly made by indirect allusions, while keeping up a nonverbal aura of politeness and friendliness. "Points made by allusion to social-class status are sometimes called snubs; those made by allusions to moral respectability are sometimes called digs; in either case one deals with a capacity at what is sometimes called 'bitchiness'" (Goffman 1967: 25). The aggressive game can become two-sided, when the victim of a put-down manages to mount a clever and apposite comeback; this has the additional effect of showing that the verbal aggressor was not as good at the interactional game as he or she claimed to be, thus blowing a hole in this person's situational self-presentation, and not just setting the game back at even but awarding extra points to the counter-attacker. As Goffman notes, these games work best when there is an audience, which in effect acts as referee and score-keeper—all surreptitiously behind the pose of polite civility.

The second pathway to conflict is where ritual repairs are incompetently carried out or not accepted. The game is basically cooperative, and that requires the willingness of everyone to accept tactful remedies for offenses. Perfunctory apologies and excuses are usually taken at face value, but if the person who feels offended does not accept them, the only alternative is to "make a scene." This means to insist explicitly on the offense and demand a remedial action that is more humiliating than it would have been if it had been allowed to be carried out tacitly. But in doing so the offended person is breaking the conventional surface of politeness and tact, revealing oneself as not a good interactant; and thus however much the interactional whistle-blower may have been seen as in the right as to the underlying offense, he or she becomes situationally in the wrong over their remedy for it. The balance of forces shifts a bit toward the offender, who may feel emboldened to resist further ritual humiliation; the offended person now has few alternatives but an angry and perhaps violent outburst, or to withdraw from the encounter "in a huff." In polite adult middle-class encounters, the loss of face from escalating to physical violence is severe;[4] hence the main retaliation that most people are willing to risk are angry withdrawals and breaking off relationships. An accomplished player of the game of aggressive facework (in Goffman's day called a needler) may play on the perceived emotional breaking point of his or her interlocutors, pushing opponents into an outburst that destroys their reputation.

In settings where polite Goffmanian ritual order holds sway, expressing anger is generally rather far from actual fighting, and sometimes antithetical to it. In administrative politics, a seemingly friendly, affable demeanor is *de rigueur* in all situations, above all in conflictual ones. A standard tactic of lawyers and debaters is to try to get their opponent angry, and then to use the fact that they are angry as a proof that their arguments are emotional rather than rational and not worth listening to. Persons who get caught in this tactic tend to become still further enraged, because it takes their own commitment, the fact that they strongly believe in what they are saying, and twists it into a weapon against themselves. The lawyer's trick is to bring about a breakdown in situational self-presentation as a competent interactant, and use that to focus attention away from the substance of what is being argued. Such legal or other institutional gatherings, of course, are ultra-polite, front-stage situations where all turns for utterances are strictly controlled by a formal protocol; if violence occurs, it is a scandalous breach that calls for severe punishment and more or less de facto loss of one's case. This limitation on use of violence is extreme but otherwise typical of interactions in the part of society that claims "proper" or polite status.

The baseline of social interaction is accommodative. Researchers in conversation analysis, performing detailed examination of conversations recorded in natural settings, conclude that conversation has a preference for agreement (Heritage 1984; Boden 1990); it is demonstrably easier for an audience to cheer than to boo (Clayman 1993). How, then, is normal acrimony carried out? We will examine four kinds, in roughly ascending order of intensity.

1. *Griping* is the type of negative conversation carried out about third parties, persons who are not present. This is a practice of complaining, telling horror stories or sardonic accounts of what other persons have done. Here is a case where verbal aggression does not necessarily or generally lead to conflict, let alone violence.

Griping can be a form of entertainment, filling up the conversation with things to talk about, which have a certain amount of dramatic interest. We see this in the sequence of topics in middle-class social gatherings such as dinner parties. Usually the conversation at the beginning is affable, good-humored expressions of interest in the other persons present, setting the tone of the encounter as a festive occasion. Later shop-talk tends to take over, sometimes counteracted by recognition that this is excluding people, and thus interspersed by general topics of shared conversation such as food, restaurants, travels, and entertainment. Usually late in the sequence, the talk settles onto politics (if those present are on the same side of the spectrum), which mostly takes the form of stereotyped complaints about the stupidity and outrageousness of the behavior of opposing politicians. Political talk usually winds down the evening, because it is an easy filler, drawing on shared emotions and not requiring much thought, since participants are satisfied to repeat well-known formulas of abuse of the rival political party as applied to the details of the news. Political griping is an easy way of keeping up the conversational ritual, especially when participants at a social gathering do not really like each other very much or do not have much conversational resources to share that are festive or fun. (A testable hypothesis: the more enjoyable the party, the less time people spend talking about politics or other forms of complaining.) This kind of complaining about generalized targets does not produce much personal solidarity, since it remains frontstage and invokes no very tight ties among the persons who share in the complaining. In contrast, gossip and especially malicious gossip can be highly entertaining, since it casts the gossiper in the light of an insider and witticist, and the hearer as privileged audience; this is especially the case where the gossip takes places within and about a elite group such as high society or literary circles (Capote 1986; Arthur 2002: 159–85).

Third-party complaints that are about personal targets—one's boss or employees; one's organization; one's acquaintances and friends—are implicitly backstage; the fact that complaints are not intended to be heard by their targets implies a sense of intimacy among those who carry out the conversation. This is a variant on the principle that conflict with outsiders generates solidarity in the group. Hence it is possible to play up conflicts, or even to manufacture them, in order to increase one's local solidarity; this can be one of the situationally arising motives for creating malicious gossip. Here again the conflict is not so much a preexisting motivational force as a social construction.

2. *Whining* is a term for complaining in the second person, within the immediate interaction itself. This is low-key complaining, designed to stay within limits so that it does not threaten the interaction. It easily becomes chronic mild conflict, as opposed to acute conflict, which is rarer. Whining has an emotional tone of mild, whimpering pain; it is an expression (indeed a staging) of weakness. A whiner does not threaten to escalate to anger or violent attack, but leaves this to the interlocutor; and in fact whining tends to provoke some kind of attack, since, as we have seen, attacking the weak is the most common dynamic of fighting. Whining is repetitive and thus frustrating and annoying to the person whined at, which is one explanation of why the whinee may eventually escalate a counter-attack.

   These counter-attacks are usually mild, feeding into the cycle that keeps the whining going. The whiner may count on being attacked; consciously or more likely unconsciously, whining is a move to break up the situation and to make oneself the center of attention. It is a version of an underhanded Goffmanian ploy to make the other abandon the normal flow of staged interaction; "to get their goat" by repeating small, relatively unobtrusive moves until they retaliate with an angry blowup, making them bear the onus of having destroyed the situation. Small children often play this out with their parents.[5]

3. A higher stage of normal acrimony is *arguing*, explicit verbal conflict. It may be explicitly encapsulated to a particular topic, and thus can be carried on relatively good-naturedly; people "agree to disagree." Some arguing is deliberately staged as a standard form of entertainment; casual or convivial gatherings among males are often filled with debating about the merits of sports teams, the relative greatness of athletes, and the like.

4. Arguing can escalate into serious *quarreling*: verbal argument that is seriously meant, usually concerning the relationship of the arguers themselves. Verbal markers like "You always . . . " or "Why do you always . . . " stake a claim on a level of generality, which explicitly rules out framing the dispute as encapsulated and situational. Quarreling is generally repetitive; it is usually a version of a protected, limited fight, with tacit agreements on what kinds of tactics may be

used. Typically these are various kinds of Goffmanian aggressive face-work, sometimes culminating in angry blowups; insofar as the cycle repeats itself, each blowup is handled, sooner or later, with a Goffmanian ritual repair (apologies, reconciliations, or just a tacit agreement to ignore what happened and return to normally staged interaction).[6] Repetitive quarreling is a domestic version of a hockey game, in which violations and punishments have become incorporated into the expected flow of the game.

The typical pattern is for persons to be nicer to strangers in conversations than to family members. Burchler, Weiss, and Vincent (1975) demonstrated this by comparing conversations in a medical waiting room. The strength of commitment to the social bond, or the security of an institutionalized relationship, allows minor conflicts routinely and repetitively enacted (Coser 1956). Quarreling is not necessarily a matter of building up resentments; repetitive quarreling is not so much "pent-up" but flows rather freely just because it is not very costly. Quarreling does not necessarily involve deep disagreements or jealousies; it can be part of the expectable, routinized flow, a way of filling up conversation and avoiding boring moments.[7] In relationships that have a stable balance of power, domestic quarreling is the equivalent of encapsulated arguments about sports, but raised to a higher level of emotion and carried out for higher stakes, thus making it a more exciting game. Thus quarreling is a central activity—indeed, *the* central activity, in "love/hate" relationships, which generally have a self-conscious image as especially dramatic and "tempestuous."

Analyzing video recordings of martial counseling sessions and other conversations among couples, Scheff and Retzinger (1991; Retzinger 1991) show the detailed sequence of moves in repetitive quarrels among couples. They find micro-interactional patterns that break the normal flow and coordination of interactional solidarity. This ongoing level of tension Scheff (1990) describes as the emotion of shame, a negative feeling about one's self that comes from not having one's sense of self validated in the interaction. What Scheff calls shame can be regarded, in terms of interaction ritual theory, as broken attunement, a failed interaction ritual. Shame that is not acknowledged, brought into overt social consciousness, and repaired by restoring the interaction, Scheff terms "bypassed shame"; it can be banished from consciousness, by an internal loop of being ashamed of being ashamed. Its manifestations still exist, however, evidenced in fine-grained patterns of tension in postures and speech. The accumulated tension of shame, especially as intensified by shame about shame, becomes transformed into rage when it finally bursts out in verbal action. Shamed persons continue to break inter-actional attunement in subtle or not-so-subtle ways, using Goffman-ian aggressive face work. This in turn generates further shame on the part of the other. The quarrel goes on as a retaliatory cycle of shaming each other, complemented by internal cycles within each participant of repressing or bypassing recognition of shame and let-ting it build up into rage.

Although marital disputes and similar ongoing quarrels among intimates (close friends, or parents and children) go through this pat-tern of repeated quarrels, punctuated by outbursts of anger, they tend to stabilize at that level: angry outbursts are as hostile as it gets, without escalating further into violence, and after an outburst the mood subsides again into a normal routine of partial attunement and disruptive disattunement. The point I want to emphasize is that the mechanisms in Scheff's theory that explain the repetitive quarreling do not explain those occasions when violence happens; most of the time violence does not occur, and it takes special situational features for that to happen. This is what we are seeking in this chapter.

Escalating quarrels is one way to get to the brink of violence. Anticlimactically, I break off the sequence here. We must retrace our steps, to take account of one other path that leads to this point.

BOASTING AND BLUSTERING

Boasting is generally outside polite middle-class conversational ritual. Not that something of the sort doesn't take place there in a surreptitious form; the polite manner is to get other people to do your boasting for you, so that one can gracefully demur and display one's modesty.[8] Straightforward crowing and pride about one's accomplishments is gener-ally kept to private, backstage situations, a kind of shameful display of egotism that is allowed in front of intimates; parents provide such an audience for the pridefulness of their children. But even in these situa-tions, boasting is supposed to be limited to pride and joy in actual accom-plishments, not generalized claims about oneself or specific put-downs of rivals as grossly inferior. Here again the polite Goffmanian style provides a baseline against which we see what is involved in social milieux where boasting is overt.

Boasting is characteristic of masculine company, and of youth; in con-temporary times, more typically in the lower classes than the middle and higher; but historically, prominent in warrior societies such as the Vikings, where stereotyped boasting ritual was a part of festive entertainment as well as a preliminary to battles (Bailey and Ivanova 1998; Einarsson 1934;

Robinson 1912). Even in these groups, boasting is situational; it occurs on appropriate occasions but not every minute of the day. Whereas boasting sometimes escalates into violence, middle-class Goffmanian politeness is organized in such a way as to avoid any overt moves toward fighting—indeed, boasting may have become taboo in polite society precisely for this reason.

Boasting comes in two forms: as a general assertion of one's status in the world, and boasting in the face of an immediate rival. The latter is more obviously a challenge and a provocation; but in their effect on the interaction there may be little difference between the two. It is a question for research whether impersonal boasting or personal boasting is more likely to lead to violence. To say "I am the greatest" is not so different from saying "I am greater than you," since the latter statement is implied in the former, although the former is less direct and the challenge is thereby easier to overlook. More importantly, the manner of boasting is much the same: a strongly expressed claim for being the center of attention, and thus to dominate the attention of others. A generalized claim may be controverted by someone present, whether sarcastically or bluntly, just out of the feeling that the boaster is making too much of himself as a matter of conversation, not because the hearer thinks the statement is untrue.

But much boasting takes place in a tone of ebullient good humor. It often is a staple of carousing situations, festive gatherings of a masculine group, especially in the context surrounding real or mock-contests such as athletic events. Boasting is part of the entertainment. Individual boasting, too, may be accepted in good spirit, as a display of verbal facility, amusing hyperbole and impromptu figures of speech, above all when there is an audience present. Here assertive boasting shows the same structure as Goffmanian aggressive use of facework in polite middle-class conversation, where topping a subtly aggressive remark is recognized as a form of verbal artistry. But there is a major difference in the consequences if the loser in a boasting contest does not take it in good grace: whereas the polite conversationalist has to accept being topped, or can try for no more than further verbal digs, the loser in a boasting match can take it as a serious challenge to his dignity and retaliate by escalating to violence.

A contest of boasting shades over into insults, which may still be taken as entertaining and in good humor if they are cleverly worded.[9] Past a certain borderline, insults and boasts turn into bluster. Instead of generalized and hypothetical, verbal struggle over dominating the attention space threatens to turn into a violent struggle. The person who escalates to violence always wins at least a momentary victory: he successfully claims attention and generally wipes away all other topics of conversation. This victory may be short-lived and its costs (whether physical or social) may be severe; but it is an incentive that many will take in an otherwise losing situation.

Bluster is the final step before violence. It is an expression of pointed threat, anger directed at an immediate opponent. It may be the first step in the fight, a move to intimidate, to force the opponent to waver, to gain an advantage, an opportunity in which to strike. But bluster also can be a move that forestalls and substitutes for violence. It is an attempt to scare the enemy so that he will back down and back away from fighting; and a staged presentation of oneself, that makes one look braver and more competent at fighting than one actually is.

This is most apparent in military combat, where a good deal of the fighting situation consists in posturing (Grossman 1995), firing more for the sake of the noise than seriously aiming at the enemy. S.L.A. Marshall (1947) emphasizes that soldiers keep up morale and solidarity in their own group by shouting loudly back and forth; yelling can also be directed at the enemy to frighten them. Traditional societies have their traditional battle cries, from the yelping and imitation of animal sounds in tribal combat to the ululations or long rhythmic trilling cries by which Arab women encourage fighters.[10] Vocal intimidation was effectively practiced by Japanese troops in jungle warfare in World War II; the whooping "rebel yell" was a tactic of Confederate armies in Civil War battles where the armies were often hidden from each other in the woods. Ulysses S. Grant (1885/1990: 55–56) describes an incident in Texas during the Mexican war: traveling with a few riders through a region of tall grass, he was disturbed by the noise of what seemed to be a large group of wolves ready to attack; it turned out to be only two wolves, who became silenced and turned tail as they were finally approached. The essence of bluster is to magnify the size of a threat from a safe distance.

As we have seen, the sound of shattering glass makes a dramatic impression. But it is chiefly used as a form of bluster. British victim surveys show that although 10 percent of alcohol-related assaults involved threatening someone with a bottle or glass, in virtually none of these incidents was someone actually hit with it (Budd 2003: 17).

The aggressive use of bluster is sometimes found in situations of racial or class intimidation: This can be observed on the streets of large cities like Philadelphia, on the fringes of white middle-class areas; such examples are analyzed in Anderson (1990). The following incident is from my own observations:

> A roughly dressed black man is moving restlessly back and forth on the sidewalk outside a convenience store, shouting and cursing loudly, scaring most passersby into crossing to the other side of the street or making a wide berth around him. But the situation is stable since it

goes on for many minutes without any further move toward violence. Police reports included no incidents in that area that afternoon.

In another observation, the line of confrontation is class rather than racial:

A white homeless man is standing on the sidewalk across from Rittenhouse Square, shaking his fist and cursing toward the square; but not crossing the street. This is a square in the midst of the upper-middle class residential district, frequently patrolled by police and strictly prohibiting panhandlers, although they can be found on adjacent commercial streets. There is a display of palpable unease on the part of beggars who approach this forbidden zone; it is apparently not just a matter of fear of the police if they enter more deeply into these alien zones, but is a case similar to that of tribal warfare in which the bravest warriors will only briefly cross the enemy line, then turn and run back, as if stretching a rubber band. As a spontaneous experiment, I crossed the street directly at the corner where the homeless man was cursing and gesturing and walked slowly up to him—in what I believe was an expressionless manner, but without indicating fear or intimidation. (We were both of about equal size: somewhere in the range of 6 ft. tall, nearly 200 pounds; his age could have been in the 40s, probably ten or fifteen years younger than myself at that time.) As I got near him (and without ever making eye contact), he stopped cursing and gesturing; it was bluster, not an actual invitation to a fight.

Quite possibly the man was mentally ill; but that does not alter the analysis; even mentally ill persons shape their behavior by interacting in situations.

What determines whether bluster leads onward to violence, and when is it taken as a sufficient display of one's situational presence so that it is no longer necessary to fight? The issue can be examined in depth in the case of the "code of the street" in black inner-city poverty areas.

THE CODE OF THE STREET: INSTITUTIONALIZED BLUSTER AND THREAT

According to Elijah Anderson (1999), the street code arises because of the lack of reliable police protection, together with the feeling that the police are prejudiced against everyone in the ghetto and are as likely to arrest the complaining party as the perpetrator. Accordingly, each individual tries to demonstrate his ability to take care of himself, to provide his own protection by displaying his willingness to use violence. This propensity is reinforced by long-standing conditions of poverty and racial discrimination that foster an alienated and distrustful attitude toward mainstream white society.

Nevertheless, as Anderson indicates, a majority of people in these essentially unpoliced areas want to lead normal lives, with regular jobs, family responsibilities, and community respectability. In the local idiom, most people are "decent," only a minority are hard-core "street," alienated from mainstream values and committed to an oppositional way of life. But for self-protection, most "decent" people will "go for street" when the situation seems to call for it: "I can get ignorant too." Idiomatically, "knowing what time it is" is a way of expressing the ability to code-switch, knowing in what situations it is useful to switch from decent to street styles. Hard-core street persons, too, on occasion may switch back to the "decent" code; for example, this sometimes happens if a street individual is alone in the presence of a large group of men of the decent type, who are respected, among other reasons, because they have also demonstrated their ability to code-switch in the opposite direction (Anderson 1978).

The code of the street is a Goffmanian staged presentation of self, albeit a version that sharply inverts one aspect of the Goffmanian facework that I have emphasized so far, the maintenance of a front of civility and accommodation. For the most part, the street code is frontstage, the decent self is backstage. Some persons, however, become entirely committed to the code-staging, caught up in it so that there seems to be no other self. There are instances of being caught up in a frontstage self in many other realms of social life besides street-oriented individuals; for example, it is characteristic of upper-middle and upper-class persons who prefer their staged public persona, since it is a situation in which they get power and deference; in contrast, working-class persons tend to prefer their backstage self, since they get more emotional gratification in being free from formal situations in which they are subordinated (Rubin 1976; Collins 2004: 112–15). In an analytical sense, the committed street-oriented individuals are similar to upper-middle-class workaholics, or to socialite "social butterflies," in that all of them prefer their frontstage selves, since this is where they get the most deference, and the most emotional energy.

This is not to say that people who identify strongly with their frontstage selves, and who keep up a virtually nonstop performance of the street self, do not have to engage in staging work. For some individuals, the street code is a superficial self, performed part-time and with varying degrees of distaste and unwillingness; for others it has become so attractive, or has cut off alternative performances so that it is all that one has, and it is performed with considerable commitment (Anderson 1999: 105). Nevertheless, for persons all along the continuum of commitment, it is still a performance for an audience, and hence must deal with the usual Goffmanian difficulties and techniques of social performance. In the case of the performance of a violent self, one of those difficulties is how to surmount the normal condition of tension/fear in violent confrontations; the street code is especially theatrical, stagey, because this especially strong difficulty has to be overcome.

Let us now examine the several components of how the street code is staged.

First, the code involves presenting oneself with a distinctive visual appearance through clothing style, grooming, and accessories. The typical style of the 1990s, for males, included baggy pants, or pants worn exaggeratedly low on the hips, untied sneakers, and ball caps turned around backward.[11] These are items of antinomian self-presentation. They take their meaning because they pointedly reverse conventional styles of demeanor; they are membership markers of a group flouting the symbols of the conventional group and thereby signaling a defiant attitude toward its values. They are membership markers in a counter-culture, an expression of rejection of white mainstream society. They also imply a symbolic rejection of "decent" black society for adhering to white lifestyle, referred to as "going for white."[12]

Another component of bodily demeanor, however, is not antinomian at all, but a display of status claims. This is expressed by wearing expensive athletic suits and shoes, and prestigious brandname items. There is a subtle message here as well; in an area of pervasive poverty, wearing expensive clothes—and even more so, jewelry—implies you have overcome poverty by "street" means; ostentatious wealth comes most often from the drug business, but single items of clothing such as jackets can be stolen from others, and a "decent" person wearing such an item may be attacked for that reason. Thus there is an element of visual boasting in wearing such clothes.

A second element of the code is a style of talk. Part of this is a specialized vocabulary and idiom, parallel to that of any group that marks itself off as distinctive. Equally important is the paralinguistic style, not what is said but how one talks. The street style is generally loud and accompanied by exaggerated gestures. The emphasis is on vocally taking the initiative and thus taking command of the situation. This leads to verbal sparring, with an emphasis of quick repartée, not letting another person's verbal move go unchallenged. Some of the speech action includes verbal aggressiveness: teasing, joking, and boasting. This is a continuum of challenge, ranging from playful humor up to explicit hostile boasts and insults. The middle of this continuum includes what black athletes refer to as "trash talking."

These forms of talking make up an ongoing claim to dominate the interactional space, or at least to keep up with the level of challenge and avoid being dominated. In Goffmanian terms, an aggressive talking style is a frontstage presentation of self; in Anderson's analysis, it is an attempt to avoid violence by boasting and bluster, projecting an image of confidence in one's ability to fight well.

Notice an additional implication of verbal staging of the street code. Some violence is avoided, not by deterrence but by showing membership. The display of symbols shows that one belongs to the group—in this case, the group that adheres to the code. They are marks of solidarity; and this in itself sometimes inhibits violence. Anderson gives an example (personal communication, Oct. 2002):

> In a racially mixed middle-class area on the edge of the poverty zone, an integrated group was having a street party for local families, and the end of the street was blocked off to cars. A car carrying two drug-dealers, displaying the street style, drove their car past the barrier and proceeded slowly up the street, apparently looking for an address; by their actions and postures they were expressing contempt and mild hostility toward the middle-class scene they had penetrated. Most of the local people shrank from any confrontation. However, one black man, a resident of the block, approached the drug dealers and spoke to them, using the idiom of the street code. His message was scolding, telling them they shouldn't be disrupting the family-oriented block party with their car; the drug dealers took the rebuke, not by escalating into a fight, but backing down apologetically.

In Anderson's analysis, the local resident was able to establish membership with the drug dealers by speaking in the street code; but he modulated his message so that the content of what he said did not lead to an escalation of insults and a struggle over control of the situation, but to redefining the situation as one in which aggressive action was inappropriate. The verbal part of the street code is made up of both messages of solidarity and specific messages about dominance and threat; invoking the first can reduce chances of violence, while invoking the latter increases them.

There is also a subtle, tacit form of membership being tested in talk. It is a test as to whether one recognizes what kind of game is being played at that moment. The insider can tell the difference between what is a serious threat, and what is staged front or bluster; when insults are an entertaining game, and when they are a challenge to dominate or being dominated. Thus, if the game is played well by all persons present, membership is confirmed and violence is avoided. There is also the danger that the test will not be passed; the game of entertaining insults may go badly, either because one person fails to keep up with the repartée and is made to look like an easy victim, or an interloper, or both—thus making him a target for violence; or because the person who fails in the verbal game refuses to take verbal defeat and escalates to violence on his own initiative.[13] The verbal ritual has an equilibrium point at which it inhibits violence, but it is a dangerous game that can move to violence if it fails.

The third aspect of the street code is to present oneself as explicitly willing to use violence; in its strongest form, it is a performance of the threat here-and-now. This may be very direct; at the first sign of challenge, one immediately goes on the offensive. Anderson (1999: 80–84) gives an example of a fifteen-year-old, Tyree, who has moved into a new neighborhood; as an outsider, he is accosted by the local group of teenagers and beaten up (since they outnumber him twenty to one). To get some respect back, the next time he sees one of this group alone, Tyree immediately attacks him. Both fights are limited and ritualistic; when the group first encounters Tyree, whom they regard as an interloper in the neighborhood, they "roll on him," with most of the group rotating so everyone can get in a punch. This is distinguished from "messing someone up," causing serious injury that would send the victim to the hospital. Similarly, Tyree retaliates against an individual group member by punching him a few times and bloodying his nose. The fight ends with a verbal acknowledgment and quasi boast: "You got me that time, but I'll be back!" To which Tyree responds with a boast: "Yeah, you and yo' mama" (Anderson 1999: 84).

There are both stronger and milder versions of the display of willingness to use violence. The actual damage intended can be more serious, including the use of weapons. Or the display may merely take the form of showing signs of being tough: building up one's muscles so that one looks imposing; putting on a threatening demeanor; displaying weapons; blustering and cursing directed either at someone in particular, or just at the general environment. A good deal of this is Goffmanian staging; it is not so much a way of looking for a fight as of getting dominance over the situation, and thus situational respect, without actually having to fight. But the same devices that can be used to avoid fighting can also, if taken the wrong way, lead to escalation into actual violence.

In what ways, then, does displaying the street code control and limit violence, and when does it cause violence? We might expect that staging the street code limits violence; in Anderson's argument, it is usually a pretense of violence and a display of one's capacity to protect oneself, designed to deter violence. Displaying the code also indicates membership, so that there is no cause to fight someone as an outsider. An additional consideration comes from our general analysis of violence: tension and fear are the common human feelings in hostile confrontations, making the actual performance of violence difficult. Thus the street code, as a socially institutionalized way of presenting a show of aggressiveness, might be expected to stabilize behavior at just that point where it stops short of actual violence. But this also means that the street code, as a graduated continuum of degrees of aggressiveness and threat, also allows for a considerable amount of mild violence; it falls under the general pattern that socially limited and controlled violence allows violence to go on longer and more chronically than violence in situations where it is not channeled by mild and protected forms.

Consider now four different kinds of fighting in the inner-city ghetto, ranging from relatively limited and controlled, to serious and out of control:

Gang fights. Especially among teenagers, these fights are chronic but limited in several respects. Gang fights are directed against members of other gangs, or against other young males of the same age as the gang members, who are regarded as interlopers in the neighborhood or territory. Teen gangs typically do not attack adults; Anderson (1999: 83) indicates that older women in the neighborhood may regard it as safe because the groups of youths are not hostile to them, and even protect them. By the same token, children below the gang age are not attacked, although they may fight each other. Fighting is thus segregated by age group; and generally also by gender.

In part this is because fighting has a ritualistic significance as tests of membership and group boundaries. Entering into a gang typically involves fighting as an initiation rite. Anderson's account of Tyree's experience shows him going through a series of fights of this sort: first a rough "introduction" ritual of being rolled on by the whole gang, making everyone formally aware of each other; then some small individual fights as Tyree tries to establish respect; finally he is allowed a full-fledged, formal test of entry, in which he explicitly negotiates to fight one of the group while the others watch (Anderson 1999: 85–87). He is required to fight an older and bigger youth, six inches taller and forty pounds heavier, for about twenty minutes; as expected by everyone, he loses the fight, but he gains respect by continuing to scrap and by inflicting some damage on his stronger opponent. As the result of this fight, he is taken into the gang.

Fights of this sort are limited in several respects. Except where an outsider is "rolled on" by the entire group, these are set up as one-on-one fights with others staying out. And there are rough guidelines or rules as to what kind of blows are allowed and disallowed; these are fights with fists, not with weapons; scratching and biting may be allowed, but not eye gouging or blows to the genitals. Once an individual is a member of the gang, he may continue to have fights, including with his close friends and allies, over particular annoyances and incidents of disrespect; these are supposed to be fair fights, with rules such as "no hitting in the face," "you got to use just your hands," and "no double-teaming" (Anderson 1999: 89–90). Anderson describes a fight of this sort that goes on for about twenty minutes; this is far longer than intense, unlimited fights, and it is made possible because the fighters limit the amount of serious fighting included in it: "Malik and Tyree dance and spar, huffing and puffing, dodging and feinting. To the onlooker, it appears to be a game, for real blows seem hardly to be exchanged." Inadvertent violations of the agreed-upon rules, such as a slap to the face, are quickly followed by an apology, to avert a rapid escalation to more serious violence. Successfully performing this kind of ritual, Anderson points out, strengthens the personal bonds of those who have gone through it; they have shown they can settle their differences, display their toughness, and keep the fighting at a ritual-istic equilibrium.

This kind of ritualistic fighting that limits the damage done appears to be most characteristic of gangs that are institutionalized as relatively enduring groups. But there are also ad hoc groups of allies that may get mobilized in particular situations to protect one of their members. Rela-tives, neighbors, and friends may rally around, especially on their front porch or in front of their house, to protect one of their own from a threat (Anderson 1999: 41–42). These ad hoc groups may well be more danger-ous and unlimited in their violence, when they happen to use it, than gangs that have institutionalized the methods and occasions of fighting. An example took place in summer 2002 in the Chicago South Side when a van driven by a drunken driver accidentally ran into a family group partying on their doorstep (*Los Angeles Times*, Aug. 2–5, 2002). A twenty-six-year-old woman was caught under the van and badly injured, along with two other women. Three relatives of the trapped woman, all men in their forties, along with four younger men and teenagers, pulled the two occupants of the van out and stomped and kicked them repeat-edly, as well as beating them with a concrete block. Both victims of the attack died. The case attracted considerable media attention, in part be-cause news stories described a crowd of about one hundred onlookers who watched the attack but did not intervene to stop it. This outsider viewpoint fails to catch the dynamics of the situation: in the context of the street code, the violent intrusion by the van into the family group was taken as an assault to be met by a group counter-attack; the women hit by the van were avenged by their relatives and friends, who no doubt felt at the moment that their group's reputation was at stake, as well as the life of one of their family. The counter-attack also has the character of a forward panic, as the situation of sudden shock is turned into one where overwhelming advantage is on one side; clearly the counter-attackers be-come entrained in their own repetitive motions, engaging in overkill, with one man (a forty-four-year-old brother of the victim) described as stomp-ing and kicking both victims "until he was out of breath." The unre-strained violence of a forward panic is always shocking to everyone ob-serving from a distance. The analytical point, however, is that the unrestrained violence is more characteristic of groups that lack ritualized procedures for carrying out routine violence. This comparison brings out ways in which the chronic violence of gangs, with all its ritualized procedures, is generally more restrained than the violence of those situationally mobilized groups that we are prone to call "mobs."

Individual fights over reputation. Such fights arise where the street code of aggressive gesture and attempts at situational dominance brings about escalation rather than equilibrium. The code is essentially posturing, but it carries the danger that the posturing will not be accepted; it is a type of Goffmanian performance problem where the performer fails to find the signs from the audience that his performance is being accepted. Hence the various minor ways in which being "dissed," disrespected, can lead to fights. In many such fights, it is not necessary to win the fight; all one has to show is that one is willing to fight, to inflict and, if necessary, take some physical damage. This restores or establishes membership in a community of tough guys. Such fights are often tacitly limited, in ways like those in which gang fights are limited, to reestablishing ritual equilibrium in the mutual self-presentation of bluster that makes up the street code.

Adherents of the code may also attack those who are perceived as cultural outsiders, as "straight." Here again the immediate rationale tends to be a matter of feeling disrespected; a person who is doing well in school, who dresses in a conventional way rejecting the local style, and thereby identifying with the middle class, may end up being attacked, and the attacker or attackers will justify their action as morally proper as "who does he think he is," or "that will show him for going for white" (Anderson 1999: 93–95, 100–103). Girls are attacked by other girls, with similar rationale, if they are taken as presenting themselves as superior in school achievement, or just because they are prettier (in which case the violence may try to disfigure them by scratching or by pulling out their hair).[14] Such attacks have a hidden underside beyond the overt rationale of claiming to feel disrespected. As we have seen, fighting is not easy to mobilize, and one way in which to build up the confidence to fight is to choose an easy victim; individuals who are conventional, not displaying the gestures and signs of the street code, are taken as easy targets.

As noted, we should not take too literally the claim that fights in the poverty zone occur because of lack of respect.[15] The claim to have been "dissed" is a justification, a situational ideology. Some persons aggressively seek out occasions to be touchy over disrespect; the same person, in other situations, lets a gesture or action go by, in good Goffmanian fashion, to keep up the flow of the situation. The difference often has to do with whether there is an appropriate target present, someone who is weak enough to be safely attacked, or someone who is an appropriate reputation-builder when one is on a campaign to increase one's respect.

Respect is not a question of one's generalized status before an abstract conception of Society, but in the eyes of particular persons who are regarded as significant; making one's way into a gang makes one touchy about disrespect from certain persons but not others, whose opinions do not count. Fighting for respect is really fighting for reputation: the former way of putting it makes it sound more legitimate than the latter.

Individuals who code-switch, putting on a front of the street code, run a danger when going up against someone who is much more hard-core street. Anderson (personal communication, Nov. 2002; for context see Anderson 1978) gives an example from field research in Chicago in the 1970s:

> Two men are involved in a dice game outside a liquor store; one of them, TJ, is a "regular" (in Anderson 1999 his orientation would be called "decent"); the other, Stick, is a "hoodlum" (in Anderson's later terminology, hard-core street). The two get into an argument over who won the point. TJ, who is already venturing into the region of the street code by playing dice with a hoodlum, slaps Stick's face. Then, as if realizing what he has done, he turns and runs. Stick is furious to have been slapped by a "regular." He shouts at the crowd: "He stole me!" Stick chases after TJ, cuts his face with a knife; then still angry, he steals TJ's wallet, and finally burns it, as if mere injury and robbery are not enough to exorcise the insult. He acts as if he has been violated in his status as a hoodlum, and must engage in a ritual of ostentatious destructiveness to get his status back. The victim makes it easy to do so, turning the situation into attacking the weak.

Yet another type of attack is related in a round-about way to maneuvering for respect in the local hierarchy. As we have seen, part of the visual display of membership involves wearing expensive, locally fashionable clothes. Someone who is too poor to afford these items will not only *feel* disrespected but will *be* disrespected by their own immediate peers, who may jeer at them for their poor clothes. Persons who happen to be wearing prestigious clothes or athletic shoes, but who are situationally weak— because they are not part of the street culture and its gang alliances—are prime targets for stealing their clothes or intimidating them into giving them up (by "loaning" them). What is going on here is a Goffmanian backstage activity, getting the materials together with which to present one's frontstage. This too generates a limited amount of violence.

So far I have been listing kinds of fights that involve efforts to maintain membership, to be part of the group on a par with others. Some individuals aim higher than this; they want not just to hold their own but to dominate others and be recognized as one of the dominants, the true tough guys. The reasons why a particular individual will take this path may well be more emergent than predispositional, arising from a chain of opportunities that opens up in that direction. An individual who finds success in situational intimidation by word and gesture, and in the fights that sometimes ensue, will feel attracted to try for greater success in that direction. In terms of interaction ritual theory, they find their payoffs in emotional energy are greatest in these kinds of situations, and thus are attracted by a species of emotional magnetism toward situations in which their emotional energy continues to rise. This may also have an effect of burning their bridges back to the "decent" world; what starts out as a situational defensiveness of performing the street code, can shift over into a deeper personal commitment. Because they are outstandingly successful in the interactions enacting the street code, they are not just "going for street" but feel that they *are* street—they want all situations to be street situations, because these are the situations in which they shine.

To do so involves reputation-building. This is a matter of going up the hierarchy, starting with average or minimal membership, and proceeding onward to higher levels of reputation for toughness. Ambitiously seeking reputation necessarily involves having more fights, although this does not mean fighting all the time. At the lower ranks, one picks easy targets: outsiders to the street code, or newcomers to the locale who are being hazed and initiated into the group. The targets, however, cannot be too easy. Males do not get reputation by attacking females; cross-gender fights do happen, but these typically take place in private, in the home, in relationships where sexual property or household authority is being enforced. But these carry no weight in the hierarchy of the street. Similarly, although females do not dominate the street group, they can have a parallel hierarchy; girls will fight other girls, adult women fight other women; when muggings take place, older women in the black community are generally exempt from attacks by males, but may get mugged by gangs of girls. Thus the status hierarchy of toughness limits violence in another respect: only persons in a particular status are normally targets for violence by particular attackers.

Getting into the higher levels of the hierarchy involves taking on persons who are themselves known to be extremely tough: because they are especially ready to fight, because they win their fights, and because they are willing to escalate the amount of violence by using weapons. In moving up the hierarchy, one may try to establish a reputation for being someone whom it is dangerous to cross in any respect, someone who can be set off into a high level of violence by very minor provocations. Thus one may build a reputation—whether as a conscious strategy, or by inadvertently drifting down this pathway—by acting "crazy."[16] This has the effect that many people will defer to him, giving him the victory in the bluster and threat of ordinary street code interaction. The man with a reputation as "crazy" does not necessarily have to act crazy very often, once he has established the reputation, since most people, especially those only mildly committed or embedded in the street code, will defer to him.

Clearly, the hierarchy of dominance within the street world promotes violence, at a higher level of incidence and destructiveness than the ground-level of mere membership, getting by as sufficiently tough to be accepted. Yet even within the higher rungs of the reputational hierarchy, the code still operates situationally. A deft enactment of the code may head off violence and still bring reputation, as we see in the following example (Anderson 2001, personal communication):

> A man with a reputation as a killer is sitting in a night spot at a table with a sexy-looking woman, with whom he has an intense relationship. He gets up to go to the toilet; in the meantime a second man, also with a reputation as a killer, sits down and starts talking to the woman. The first tough guy returns and demands, in a threatening way, to know what's going on. The second tough guy stands and says, "I didn't think she was your kind of woman." First tough guy pushes open his jacket so that everyone can see the butt of his gun; and says: "I'm letting you live—for now." He then roughly grabs the woman by the arm, says "come on bitch, we're getting out of here," and leaves.

The encounter is a deliberate challenge, and each man escalates it at each move. They have both shown they are tough, courageous, willing to fight; but they also show that they are good at verbal repartée. Tough guy number two gets credit for his blatant move and putdown of someone with a very high reputation for dangerousness; tough guy number one counters with a dramatic move that both escalates and equilibrates the situation. Further evidence that this is the case comes from the aftermath; months later, the two men still had not fought. The story of their encounter circulated widely; the fact that they have carried it off enhances both their reputations. They were not faking it; their prior reputations prove that they could have killed someone. But they also had keenly judged on a tacit level just what they could do, that would be both provocative and satisfactory to their audience. In this case, the confrontation is so dramatically appropriate, so fitting as a *coup de théâtre*, that any further fighting would be an anticlimax. To keep up a high level of reputation, one must take on others at a high level; the top level tough guys need each other, to be at the top. The code allows them a repertoire by which they can express this; as a dramatic gesture, the insults and threats can work even better than actual violence.

Drug business violence and stickups. Connected to the street code are two other forms of violence. These are serious, often deadly, and not regarded as entertaining. They do not attract enthusiastic audiences, and typically are carried out in as much privacy as possible. Drug business violence occurs because the activities of an illegal business are not regulated by law, and there is no way to take disputes to settlement by the official forms of lawsuits and court enforcement. Violence occurs in several forms of the self-regulation of business: turf wars, competition for customers in a particular location; deals gone bad, which is to say transactions in which one party or the other was dissatisfied with the quality or delivery of goods or payment; enforcement of discipline in a business hierarchy, such as higher level distributors making sure that lower level dealers pass along the money they have collected, or that they do not steal drugs they have been consigned (Anderson 1999: 114–19).

Drug business violence is in a sense within the code, as a form of intimidation in the absence of legitimate state authority to settle disputes. Drug violence occurs in a quasi-predictable way, as part of the operation of an illegal organization. Stickups, however, threaten unpredictably. Armed robbers operate alone, or at most in small groups of two or three (one of these may be a woman who acts mainly as lookout or driver); robberies are more clandestine than other forms of violence, involve more deception and planning, and sharing out the loot among participants; all these are reasons to keep the number of robbers small. This also means that robbers have much less social support; they are not looked up to, even within the street community, the way successful drug dealers are.

The two forms of illegal activity tend to clash; the best targets for robbers, inside the poverty community, are drug dealers, since they have the most money. And the robbery of a dealer, especially after he has sold his drugs but before he has paid off his supplier, creates ramifications up the chain. The dealer who has been robbed and cannot pay now will be subject to violent sanction from those to whom he owes money, and so on throughout the circuit of drug cash (although probably with diminishing effects higher up as the amount of money missing because of any one stickup becomes proportionately less). Armed robbers in one sense might be thought of as the toughest of the tough, predators who prey upon the other elite of the street code, the drug dealers. But robbers are not accorded reputation in the same sense; the common term for them, "stickup boys" (Anderson 1999: 130, 81), indicates contempt, given that the term "boy" is avoided in the black community for its historical connotations of racist condescension.

In a sense, both drug business violence and stickups are encouraged by the street code, since it socially legitimates and celebrates an antinomian attitude, and provides techniques of situational self-assertion and intimidation. Drug violence and stickups can use the code display as a device for getting compliance; victims who know the code can recognize the warning signs early and give up their valuables, heading off further violence (Anderson 1999: 126–28). These are instrumental uses of the code on the part of the aggressors, going considerably beyond the merely defensive Goffmanian front that "decent" people put on, or the membership ritual violence involved in youth gangs.[17] The drug business is not merely group membership, but an alternative status hierarchy; as in all hierarchies, there is relatively less room as one ascends, and hence more prospects for using the code violently to make one's way, or even just to fend off rivals. Stickups, however, push the code to its edge, and even outside the bounds of the community. Even in a community organized on an antinomian stance against the straight world, it is possible to go too far. To do so is to risk isolation and loss of status.

In general, then, the street code is institutionalized bluster, and at a lesser degree of confrontation, institutionalized boasting. It stabilizes interaction at a level that is almost violent, by polite middle-class Goffmanian standards. Sometimes it goes over the edge, but in a relatively limited way, considering that the stance is to project a great deal of potential violence. The street code is a strong example of how bluster can substitute for violence. At the same time, as a form of Goffmanian staging that stays at the edge, there are occasions in which the staging is done badly, or done too well, and what starts as a dramatic show becomes the real thing.

Pathways into the Tunnel of Violence

Return now from the special case of the street code to the more general model of situational confrontation and contingencies of escalation. In previous chapters, I used the metaphor of a tunnel of violence; in those contexts, this was chiefly the situation that I called "forward panic," in which tension and fear suddenly turn into one-sided weakness, creating an emotional vacuum into which the now-victorious side rushes. The ensuing frenzy of repetitive attack, atrocity, and overkill is like a tunnel into which the aggressors have fallen, entrained by their own emotional resonance with the reciprocal emotions and gestures of the fallen, strength egged on by weakness. Eventually the perpetrators emerge from the tunnel, sometimes not recognizing themselves in what they had done while they were inside it.

Let us now generalize the application of the metaphor. All situations of violence in full-bore rhythm are like being in a tunnel; at this point the dynamics of the fight have taken over, the actors caught up in them until the fight winds down of its own accord. The forward panic type of asymmetrical entrainment of the momentarily dominant and the passive defeated is the most spectacular version, the deep pit inside the tunnel of violence. But there are other kinds of things that can happen in the tunnel besides the strong pummeling the weak; violence can be briefer and more restrained; given enough social support, the tunnel may contain a fair fight, with the wall of spectators almost literally providing the tunnel. And there can be ways in which the tunnel stretches out in time, from one situation to another, as in a serial killing, where what happens inside is no longer the concentrated tensions and entrainments of hot emotional rush but an emotional zone that is more rarified, cooler yet outside the emotional atmosphere of everyday experience.

What I want to concentrate on here is not what happens inside the tunnel, but the process of entry and exit. A forward panic, which we have seen so often in military and police violence, is one pathway into the tunnel of frenzied violence. It has the specific character of built-up tension and release by the sudden weakness of one side. But there are other pathways which lead up to the brink of the tunnel, and sometimes over it; the resulting stay in the tunnel may not be very long, and it may not have much of the character of one-sided piling on; the tunnel itself can become frightening, or at least repelling, and soon pops its inhabitants back outside.

There are long pathways and short pathways into the tunnel. As I have emphasized throughout, the short pathways are crucial; even the long pathways toward violence generally have to cross through one of the short pathways to get there. Let us leave the long pathways for another place and focus in on the details of situational process.[18] A confrontation is under way; when will it turn violent, and when will it stabilize or recede? In the ordinary acrimony of everyday life, such situations form two main types of pathways: quarreling that becomes heated argument; and the more ebullient pathway of boasting leading to insult and bluster. Let us take these in turn.

One micro-interactional feature of arguments as they become heated is that they violate the turn-taking ritual of normal talk. Ordinary, high-solidarity talk is finely attuned in the rhythm of alternating turns to speak; one speaker monitors the other's speaking rhythm (and bodily movements) so as to come in at the end of the other's utterance, keeping up a flow that is very much like singing together (Sacks et al. 1974; see further evidence and analysis in Collins 2004). High-solidarity talk has "no gap, no overlap"; it avoids embarrassing pauses, as well as clashes over who has the floor, that is, the attention of the audience as the speaker of the moment. Escalated arguments involve clashes, not just in what is said, but the micro-interactional procedure of conversing; speakers try to talk over the other, refuse to give the other a chance to talk, or attempt to break into their utterances (see transcripts in Schegloff [1992], and analyses in Grimshaw [1990]).

In heated argument, cognitive disagreement becomes supplemented, and eventually overwhelmed, by an increasingly physical struggle to control the speaking and hearing situation itself. Arguments become louder because loudness is a move to control the conversational space, and escalates as each talker increases his or her loudness against the other. Utterances become sharp, staccato, and emphatic, shaped for their dramatic effectiveness in being heard; hence the cognitive content of arguments tends to degenerate into slogans, stereotyped expressions, and cursing—not because this is all that the speaker necessarily believes or wants to convey, but because the process of staging one's point of view is reduced to the effectiveness of the most dramatic appeals for attention. Angry talking is an emergent interactional process, not a matter of individual intentions; people often find themselves raising their voices and speaking in a nastier tone than they intended, and even against their conscious determination not to get into a dispute.

The very difficulty of navigating the narrowing dramaturgical constraints of the situation can sometimes lead to snatching a form of victory from the jaws of defeat. A speaker in an argument who can combine some remnant of intelligent expression of their point with a pithy and dramatic way of expressing it will likely carry off a dramatic victory, especially if there is a wider audience to appreciate it. Episodes of angry argument thus may come to an end because a dramatically appropriate closing is found, bringing the episode to a climax without further escalation to violence.

More frequently, it comes to an end because one or both participants withdraws "in a huff," which is to say with a dramatic show of anger and contempt for the entire scene of argument. Usually there is tacit agreement that the other will be allowed this "huff" posture, instead of pursuing him or her to continue the argument. A third possibility is that the argument stays stuck at a repetitive level, and eventually falls apart out of a feeling of boredom. I will say more on this later, since this is a key moment as to whether verbal conflicts will escalate to violence. The fourth pathway is for the argument to turn into violence; this is often a micro-escalation growing directly out of the turn-taking struggle, the attempt to talk over the other person. The struggle to get the floor becomes increasingly loud, emotionally intense; muscles strain in the effort to get oneself heard, and to make the other one cede a place to be heard; and this strain goes over the top, into a blow.

Blustering, too, can follow the same four micro-pathways flowing into or away from the tunnel of violence. Someone may lose to a perfectly delivered insult, victory being decided by an appreciative audience. Someone may break off the encounter, leaving the scene; this is similar to leaving an argument in a huff, except that a huff implies the moral onus is on the one who broke up the normal scene of civility and the normal ties of social relationship; whereas the person who leaves a scene of bluster has given in to just what the blusterer usually intends: it is a victory of the situation dominator over the situationally dominated. Third is stabilization through repetition, which we now proceed to illustrate. Fourth is further escalation into violence, which comes about through failure of the other three paths.

At first experience, all bluster seems alike: coarse, frightening, ugly, uncouth. We must focus in quite carefully on its micro-patterns if we are to see how blustering may stabilize and eventually de-escalate without a fight. As noted, bluster can grow out of an entertaining or carousing situation of boasting and playful self-assertion. At the stage of bluster, insults are no longer meant to be humorous. The emphasis on being witty disappears. Insults tend to become stereotyped, and are repeated over and over. This means that if blustering goes on long enough, it becomes boring; it loses interest. Audiences fade away (an example of this is in my own behavior and that of other observers of the Somerville street fight described in chapter 2); eventually the performers themselves no longer find much energy in their confrontation, and let it lapse into mutters.

An example from a student report:

> Two teenage boys outside a high school, in an area where students await rides to take them home, start shouting at each other. They approach to arm's length and shove at each other, back and forth. This goes on for several minutes, while other students watch anxiously from a safe distance. (That is to say, there is no high-solidarity crowd egging them on, but a scattered collection of individuals watching apprehensively.) Eventually the two boys back away from each other, and go off in opposite directions.

Likely there are many more confrontations of this kind than of full-scale fights. Another example (from a southern California police report):

> During the middle of a school day, a gang of black teenagers enters the grounds of a high school (not their own school), and sends a girl inside to call out a particular boy they are seeking. He comes out, followed by his supporters. The two groups stand at a distance, flashing gang hand-signs at each other. A girl, standing to the rear of the invading group, holds a backpack with guns in it; from time to time some of the boys open the bag to reveal the guns. On the other side, gang members raise their shirts to reveal pistols tucked in their waistbands. The action is all on the level of taunting, showing signs of gang membership as a form of invading someone else's turf, and making threatening gestures; no fight occurs, and eventually a school janitor

intervenes, and calls a patrolman. Although the gang members are armed, they do not fight it out with the janitor or the patrolman, but flee; these are outsiders, not part of the show they are enacting, hence not socially appropriate targets.

Confrontations between equals, we may expect, tend to stabilize at the level of bluster. On the level of micro-detail, the longer the insulting and shoving goes on, the less likely a fight is to actually take place (I owe this observation to Luke Anderson). Conversely, it is when there is a rapid escalation through the blustering phase that fights happen. This may be described in terms of the dynamics of emotions in the situation: not the emotions of the separate individuals, but the emotional pattern of interaction in which they are entrained. Quarreling or boasting are ways of asserting dominance in the attention space of the immediate situation. These verbal actions escalate to the extent that they are resisted; both sides need to put more energy into contesting the conversational turns and drawing the attention of the gathering to their self-assertion. The stage of bluster is where this turns into an explicit threat of force, challenging the other to back down. The put-up-or-shut-up phase is reached in one micro-move; if the challenge is accepted, then the fight happens.[19] Striking the first blow is just one more escalation in the degree of energy already put into dominating the situation. If the blustering continues beyond the first move, it is already a tacit sign that the participants don't really want to fight; and they have available to themselves a tactic of continuing to bluster until it becomes boring, letting the conflict wind down.

The content of insults is not very significant, compared to these situational dynamics. Naïve outsiders, reading accounts of fights that are set off by an insulting mention of the person's mother, may regard this as an indication of the sacredness of the mother in lower-class black culture. But there are numerous instances in which an insulting reference to someone's mother is not taken as grounds for escalation, since the situation is not right for it. (An example is given above on p. 352 from Anderson 1999: 84). Depending on circumstances, any verbal utterance can be taken as a provocation to violence, or as humorous, or as a humdrum utterance to be disregarded.[20]

On the level of micro-detail, there is similarity between the escalation of quarreling and of blustering. Heated quarrels break the turn-taking rhythm, with participants attempting to talk over each other, resulting in a contest of loudness; but the content becomes repetitive, and if the intensity can be stabilized, the boring character of what is said eventually leads to emotional de-escalation and a path away from fighting. Insults, too, can become repetitive and boring and thereby de-escalating; but that depends upon the absence of paralinguistic escalation. Thus we may expect

Figure 9.1 Angry confrontation, momentarily stabilized by repetitious gesturing (Jerusalem, October 2000). Reuters.

that insult contests remain encapsulated in a level of ritual equality as long as they respect the turn-taking rule; each allows the other a speaking turn in which to utter one's insult, where if both try to insult at the same time, talking over the other, in effect trying to shout the other down and out of the verbal interaction space, the fight will turn violent.

Evidence for several of these processes can be found in the well-documented quarrels among literary figures (Arthur 2002). For the most part these are carried out in print, denigrating each other's work and sometimes personal character; sometimes they are circulated in dense personal networks of writers and their followers. Most such quarrels develop among writers who are aiming for the same literary niche; as Truman Capote suggested to Gore Vidal in 1945 when both were bursting into reputation in the New York literary scene, there is room for only one *enfant terrible* at a time (Arthur 2002: 160). Particularly bitter quarrels grow up where one of the writers has been a protégé of the other, learning a style and being introduced into the heart of the literary establishment from an already-situated mentor; then the protégé grows up, acquires his own reputation, and eclipses the mentor. In such cases, professional jealousy over exploiting the same stylistic niche is compounded by a sense of betrayal, on one side, and the need to break away into an autonomous literary personality on the other. In such competitive fields, breaks are inevitable, and they become manifested at the micro-level in quarrels, whether at close range, or more likely in print, since that is where literary reputations live.

Most such quarrels stay merely verbal. Occasionally they escalate to violence. The process may be observed in the quarrel between Theodore Dreiser and Sinclair Lewis, which came to a head in 1931. During the 1910s, Lewis had been something of a protégé of Dreiser. The older man had written the first great American naturalistic novel, *Sister Carrie*, in 1900, but it had been withdrawn from publication because of moralistic censorship; Dreiser subsequently made a living editing conventional ladies' magazines, the same milieu in which Lewis got his start in publishing, and where they became acquainted. Dreiser's reputation gradually built up among elite intellectuals, and younger writers like Lewis took him as a model for naturalistic exposés of ordinary American life. In the 1920s, Lewis published a series of best-selling novels, exposing small-town life in *Main Street* (1920) and making *Babbitt* (1922) a household word for shallow boosterism; eventually Dreiser published his long-awaited masterpiece, *An American Tragedy* (1925), which did well with the intellectuals but not with the public. Now Lewis was in a position to patronize his old patron, offering to promote his book, and extending aid to him on a European trip. Dreiser took all this as his due, attempting to seduce Lewis's wife (a newspaper foreign correspondent), and blithely plagiarizing her writings for his own book on travels in the Soviet Union.

In 1930, the Nobel Prize for literature was expected to be given to an American; Dreiser was the leading candidate of the intellectuals, but Lewis won. Publicly Lewis continued to offer homage to Dreiser as his greater predecessor. Privately their relationship rankled. It burst into the open at a banquet of New York intellectuals in 1931. Dreiser, as usual the prima donna, arrived late; waiting for him, the others indulged in heavy drinking. When the speech-making began, Lewis briefly announced that he did not wish to speak in the presence of a man who had plagiarized his wife and had been telling others privately that Dreiser did not deserve the Nobel Prize.

After dinner, Dreiser called Lewis aside into a private room, berated him for his statement, and demanded that he "say it again or take it back" (Arthur 2002: 68–69). Lewis said it again, and Dreiser slapped him across the face. "And I asked him if he wanted to say it again. He said it again. So I smacked him again. And I said, 'Do you want to say it again?' At this point a third man entered the room, to hear Lewis say 'Theodore, you are a liar and a thief.' The third man grabbed Lewis and suggested that Dreiser leave. Lewis said again, 'I still say you are a liar and a thief.' 'Do you want me to hit you again?' Dreiser demanded. 'If you do, I'll turn the other cheek.' Dreiser said, 'Aw, Lewis, you shit!' The third man was pushing Dreiser through the door when he turned and shouted, 'I'll meet you any time, anywhere. This thing isn't settled!' Lewis followed, muttering something. Dreiser said, 'Lewis, why don't you peddle your papers somewhere else?'"

The scene is Goffmanian. Lewis has been maintaining a publicly staged performance of respect for his old mentor, while backstage he has been complaining about his behavior. He finally lets his backstage opinions out in a public gathering, a shocking break in frame. The occasion for the frame break is nevertheless highly appropriate: it is a gathering of all those most closely interested in the reputational struggle, a gathering of their literary peers; and it is a festive, carousing occasion, with the iconoclasm of a drinking party during Prohibition; and there is a kind of professional investment in iconoclasm, since this generation of writers get their fame in the movement of naturalism, displaying the sordid side of life. Lewis himself has a reputation as an iconoclastic speaker, and he does not disappoint.

Dreiser seeks a ritual repair, retiring first into private; but his blunt demand for an apology is also an escalation, leaving no way out. Lewis now can save face only by repeating his charge, and Dreiser retaliates with a ritualistic slap in the face. If this had been eighty years earlier, it might have led to a duel; but these men are self-conscious modernists. In fact their fight settles into a standoff, repeating the same words and actions. Finally a third party intervenes, and grabs Lewis, who turns out to be not steamed up for a fight but "limp and unresisting" (Arthur 2002: 69). Dreiser, on his way out, formulaically offers a further challenge to meet again, but the fight mood peters out into an exchange of banal insults. In the event, they had found a way to avoid any further fighting. Dreiser was pleased with the publicity that followed the fight; Lewis, who was already basking in public controversy because of his iconoclastic books, took the incident in stride and went back to making statements of admiration for Dreiser's work.

Why didn't the fight escalate? At the time, Dreiser was sixty-one years-old, but at 6 feet 1 inch and over 200 pounds, he was bigger and stronger than the tall, slender Lewis (age forty-six); this helps explain Dreiser's willingness to escalate to a blow—although not a very serious one—and with Lewis keeping his response merely verbal. The standard devices for avoiding escalation are used: repeating the same words and gestures; letting third parties break it up; making vague challenges for further confrontations. Both men save face; nothing much happens; the uproar of publicity leaves everything as it was privately, if not on the Goffmanian frontstage.

We have seen a number of ways that pathways up to the brink of the tunnel go no further, and turn back. When do participants take the fourth path, into violence itself? The theory developed in this book is that confrontations bring tension and fear, which inhibits effective violence; emotional tension gets released into violent attack only where there is a weak victim, or where the conflict is hedged round with social supports to make it a staged fight fought within socially enforced limits. Thus bluster is likely to lead onward to a fight in one of these two circumstances: First, *if* one side feels much stronger than the other, at least at that moment, the stronger launches an attack. The bluster itself may provide the test of who is weaker; wavering or cringing in the face of bluster, or retreating from it, is one thing that can trigger an attack.[21] Second, *if* there is a highly interested audience, witnessing the buildup of boast and bluster, the scene is set for a fight, and the principals may not be able to back out of it if they wished. The influence of the audience is all the more powerful when at least one of the individuals in the confrontation is well known personally to the audience; this gives the actor a stake in maintaining or losing his reputation, putting costs of backing away from the fight in any manner except one that is dramatically pleasing to the audience. Thus we would expect confrontations without audiences, or ones in which the audiences themselves are anonymous, to have the least likelihood of escalating to sustained violence.[22]

Much of the time these conditions are lacking. The contestants are too evenly matched, or feel only slight edges, not enough to give them confidence in carrying on to an open and prolonged break. Recall the conclusions of chapter 2, that the reluctance to fight found so widely in military combat is not just fear of being hurt, but a generalized social tension arising from nonsolidary interaction. There is an underlying apprehension of being the loser in a situational contest, that is, of losing something more than bodily pains. It is not just a matter of fighting or not fighting, but of looking well in the process of doing it.

This interactional touchiness, which most of the time keeps us from going very far from the conventional flow of reciprocated gestures in micro-interaction, is also the source of just those slights that we take from other people's micro-behaviors and that arouse us to at least threaten an escalated conflict. People come to the brink of violence because of breaks in the flow of micro-interaction; these are Goffmanian violations, broadly speaking, although the specific contents of what people take as interactional failures ranges far beyond those middle-class conventions of mid-twentieth-century politeness that Goffman first wrote about. What leads up to the brink is not the content of the quarrel or the nature of the insult, but the fine-grained micro-details of how the confrontation is managed from the point at which it has become a conscious matter of dispute. Thus it also sometimes happens—indeed, may well happen most of the time— that antagonists find ways of altering the rhythm and focus of their hostile back-and-forth; perhaps not using the standard Goffmanian ritual repairs, but on a tacit paralinguistic level, settle themselves back into a situational equilibrium. Even after the Goffmanian challenge and apology, or the polite overlooking, have failed to work, there are processes of micro-de-escalation through repetition, loss of cognitive content, and deflation of anger into boredom.

The other condition for proceeding to violence is the audience encouraging or even enforcing a fight. But this condition, too, is often lacking; audiences are frequently very uneasy in the near presence of threatened violence—heated quarrels and bluster; they usually do not have the courage to intervene but they shrink away where they can, not supporting but abhorring the prospect of a fight. To be sure, blusterers may stage their action just for the sake of cowing an audience, but this is collusion, a form of limited violence rather than all-out attack, not a descent into the tunnel but a faking of it for the sake of the impression.

We are used to spectacular stories of violence, and among these are accounts of crowds that egg on individuals to fight. But such audiences have special conditions: they are found particularly where both the larger community and particular antagonists are in fairly dense networks of relationships, so that individuals are known by name and have reputations to be made, defended, or lost. This is one of the structural features of the inner-city neighborhoods where the code of the street is found. There is a similar pattern of the goldfish bowl of audience and individual reputation in high schools and in prisons, which is to say, in total institutions stratified between an underclass of inmates or compulsory pupils, and a staff that has formal charge of them. Here the fighting that the underclass engages in among themselves operates not just for private purposes, but as an act of rebellion against the authorities who prohibit it. Here is not only a reputational goldfish bowl, but an antinomian status system in which one gains some reputation by fighting even if one loses. But these are complex and special circumstances, not found everywhere. On the whole, the distribution of conditions that foster escalation from everyday conflict into violence are relatively rare.

Most of the time, people find ways to confine violence, to back down from the brink. Short-term micro-situational conditions can trigger violence, but it is not usually a hair-trigger. Much more often, the micro-situational trigger misfires.

CHAPTER 10

The Violent Few

VIOLENCE ALWAYS surges up in the form of a small proportion of people who are actively violent, and an even smaller proportion who are competently violent. Surrounding them usually is a larger number of the emotionally involved. Sometimes these are ostensibly part of the same team, the same rioters, the same military or police force, the same gang, the same fans or carousers, a larger group that we can call the nominally violent. Sometimes there are further layers of audience, supportive or merely curious, and finally accidental bystanders. And there can be layers of opponents and victims on the other side, possibly with their own supporters, back rows, and so forth. All these together make up a social scene, a structure pervaded with confrontational emotions; the violent few are those who use this emotional field to their advantage.

SMALL NUMBERS OF THE ACTIVELY AND COMPETENTLY VIOLENT

Let us briefly review the data of the previous chapters.

The starting point was the finding that in World War II only 15 to 25 percent of frontline troops were doing all or most of the firing in battle; and this is consistent with photographic evidence for most twentieth-century wars. In some previous historical periods, with better organizational control in massed infantry formations, the proportion firing was higher, although competence in hitting their targets was low; in ancient and tribal war, on the other hand, the active fighters were often very few. After the Korean war, Western armies changed their training methods to ensure a higher rate of fire, but competence in firing remained low, as measured by the level of wasted ammunition. Data from the Vietnam war shows infantry troops divided into three categories: a small proportion (around 10 percent) who almost never fired; about 45 percent who sometimes fired, sometimes not; and another 45 percent who virtually always fired. The proportions of high-firers were higher among volunteers, lower among draftees; among less enthusiastic troops only about one-quarter were in the high-firing group—not so different from S.L.A. Marshall's findings. Even after the training reforms, there remain a highly aggressive minority and a mass of ordinary soldiers doing just enough to maintain participation. And the most actively violent are not necessarily good at hitting the enemy; the competently violent are a smaller fraction still.

For police violence, we can distinguish several levels of violence: routine force to subdue suspects; high levels of force including those that are called "excessive"; and shootings. Nationally, about 0.2 to 0.3 percent of all police shoot anyone during a year, about one-third fatally (Fyfe 1988; Geller 1986).[1] Shootings as well as other kinds of police violence are more common in big cities with high levels of crime and gang activity. In the Los Angeles Police Department, 7.8 percent of all officers had ever been involved in shooting; 0.2 percent had fired in three or more shootings (Christopher 1991: 36–40). Use of routine force was fairly widespread; 70 percent of the LAPD had been involved in at least one use-of-force report, generally involving physical tactics to restrain and take suspects into custody. This is "normal" and "legitimate" force, but it is concentrated: the top 5 percent of officers produced 20 percent of the force incidents; the top 10 percent of the cops produced 33 percent of the incidents. Similarly, reports alleging use of excessive force or improper tactics involved 21 percent of the police.[2] This highly violent elite contained further stratification: 2.2 percent of the entire LAPD had four or more such allegations in their records; 0.5 percent had six or more. This last group, the "cowboy cops" of the department, were also more active in routine force; they averaged thirteen force reports of all kinds, as compared to 4.2 force reports for all the officers who had used any kind of force. This was about once a year for the average cop who used any force at all, somewhat less than that for the entire police force; whereas the "cowboys" had about three or four incidents per year. The cowboys were also more violent when it happened; 58 percent of their force reports alleged excessive force, whereas for the average force-using cop, the proportion of excessive force allegations was 14 percent.

Other researchers estimate similar patterns. Toch (1980) indicated that a small number of the Oakland police force produced most of the police violence. Bas van Stokkom, studying Dutch police in Amsterdam, states that a small proportion of officers were named in the majority of citizen complaints about rough or aggressive behavior (personal communication, Sept. 2004; see also van Stokkom [2004]; and chapter 14 in Geller and Toch [1996]).

On the other side of the law, violence is also concentrated. Cohort studies following up all young males from birth have found a high-crime segment of 15 percent at most that committed as much as 84 percent of the violent crime (Wolfgang et al. 1972; Collins 1977). Not all crime is violent, of course, but it follows a similar pattern in which 6 to 8 percent of male juveniles and young adults commit 60 to 70 percent of all crimes in their age group.[3]

Studies of prisoners display a fractal repetition of the larger pattern, a criminal elite within the population of criminal activists. Blumstein et al. (1986) found a pyramid of criminals serving time for armed robbery and burglary:[4] the bottom 50 percent committed five crimes or less per year (once every ten weeks or less); the top 10 percent robbed or burglarized more than once a week; the top 5 percent committed 300 or more crimes per year, or almost every day. At the apex was a small group characterized as "violent predators," who committed about three crimes every two days (Chaiken and Chaiken 1982). Another prison study found 25 percent were career criminals, who committed 60 percent of the robberies, burglaries, and auto thefts (Peterson et al. 1980). A study that followed juvenile offenders up to their thirties described three tiers: (1) a career criminal elite of about 3 percent, who sustained a high rate of crime throughout; (2) a criminal middle class, so to speak, comprising another 26 percent who kept up an intermediate level of crime; and (3) a majority of less committed criminals (71 percent) who dropped out of crime over the years (Laub et al. 1998). In these studies, the more committed and active criminals are also the most violent ones. Persistent violence marks off an elite within the larger criminal milieu.

Criminal populations are a subset, nested inside the larger population. Putting the two kinds of research together, we see that 25 to 40 percent of criminals commit (or at least are convicted for) the large majority of serious crimes; multiplying these figures by the 20 to 40 percent of the male population who are arrested (Farrington 2001; Blumstein et al. 1986; Wolfgang et al. 1972; Polk et al. 1981; Wikstrom 1985), we can infer that 5 to 15 percent of all males commit most of the serious crime.[5] The outer limits of the criminal population is the largest proportion of persons who have any kind of brush with the law (again we count only males). In a different kind of study, relying on questionnaire self-reports rather than police records, and asking about criminal activity whether or not it had been caught, 36 percent of black teens and 25 percent of white teens said they had committed one or more violent offenses (Elliott 1994).

Coming at this from another angle, the proportions of their age groups who belong to gangs is in fact much lower than the popular image. Nationally, there were about 730,000 gang members in 2003; this would be 11.5 percent of black and Hispanic males ages 15 to 24, a maximum estimate since some gangs are of other ethnicities.[6] For historical comparison, in 1920s Chicago, about 10 percent of boys ages ten to twenty-four were in gangs; of the immigrant population, about 13 percent.[7] Some of these numbers in particular ethnic communities are quite high (30 percent of southern California blacks and Hispanics in the early 2000s; 40 percent of Italians in Chicago in the 1920s), although never reaching a majority even of the male youth group. Some of the earlier gangs were only mildly delinquent; not heavily armed, and engaged in relatively little violence. Contemporary gangs do more killing; but sheer membership in a gang does not itself mean that most gang members perform much violence most of the time. There were about 16,500 murders in 2003; if half of these were done by gangs, only one out of eighty-eight gang members (1.1 percent) would commit a murder during the year. Gangs typically use fighting as a rite of passage; and there are sometimes fights to change one's position in the pecking order (Anderson 1999; Jankowski 1991). No good data exists on how often gang members fight; but it appears to be specialized within the gang itself.[8] Thus, even within an ostentatiously violent milieu, only a few percent are in the murderous elite.

Even the outer limits of the quasi-criminal population is not a majority in any of these studies; it gets nearest to it in samples of working-class communities, or in the American black population in the late twentieth-century. The violent segment comprising all degrees of activism and competence is surrounded by 60 to 80 percent of the male population who commit no more than trivial violations of the law.

To pinpoint the violent elite within the total population, we can use the figure of the top 10 percent of prisoners who were exceedingly active in violent crimes, or the 3 percent of persistent career criminals from their juvenile years onward; that gives us an estimate of somewhere between 0.6 to 1.2 percent of all males at the low end, and 2 to 4 percent at the high end, who are specialists in persistent violence. The low figure is around the same proportion as competent killers on the official side of the law: military snipers, or ace pilots. The high figure is somewhere around the level for violent police.

For the other types of violence in this book, only some allow us to estimate the proportion of perpetrators. In schools, bullies vary from 7 to 17 percent of the boys, 2 to 5 percent of girls (data in chap. 5, pp. 160–61, 173). Staged fights among heroes are necessarily limited to an elite. In aristocratic societies, the military aristocracy, usually marked out with privileged markers such as wearing swords, was around 2 to 5 percent of the population (Lenski 1966). The rate of dueling from the early seventeenth through the nineteenth centuries in various European countries peaked at 200–300 per year, with more typical figures around twenty duels or less; the peak would be only one per 60,000 of the adult male population, and even in particularly honor-prone groups such as German officers, the rate of ten to seventy-five duels per year involved at most 0.8 percent of the total officer corps.[9] Within the dueling group, there was a tiny elite of chronic duelists, some of whom fought several dozen times.

For carousers, we have seen in chapter 7 that at most 10.3 percent of binge drinkers are involved in a simple assault during the year, and 3.3

percent in a serious assault. It may well be that the best party fighters are light drinkers or abstainers, but ethnographies suggest that these fighters are an even rarer group of specialists. Among athletes, the widest participation in fighting is among baseball players, since the entire team is obligated by custom to come out on the field during a confrontation; but few take an active part in actual fighting; judging from suspensions and fines for fighting, the serious fighters are rarely more than two or three of a twenty-five-man team plus the ten-man coaching staff (i.e., 10 percent maximum). In American football, a maximum of 5 to 10 percent of players from a forty-five-man squad might fight during a game. In basketball the proportion is lower, in hockey higher, although the latter sport explicitly has one or two "enforcers" on the squad, or about 6 to 12 percent of the team. A soccer team similarly may have one enforcer among the defensive players (9 percent of the players on the field).

Exceptions to small numbers. The one area in which the pattern does not hold involves children. As we have seen in chapter 5, p. 187, 80 percent of small children attack their siblings; 85 to 95 percent of parents physically punish their small children, and 50 percent their teenagers (judging from victimization rates). On the other hand, the types of domestic violence that take place between adults are within the normal range of small numbers: common couple violence occurs in 16 percent of couples per year; more extreme abuse in 6 percent. The former is generally two-sided scuffling between partners of both sexes; the latter is overwhelmingly a proportion of males.

Notice, too, that small children are frequently but not competently violent, thus preserving the small numbers pattern in another respect. This fits with another exceptional pattern. As I have noted in chapter seven, adults and older teenagers almost always confine themselves to one fight per venue, with the rest forming an audience or joining one of the sides. But children may have multiple fights going on at the same time or in brief succession, as in an unruly classroom,[10] without the continuity between the line-ups that characterizes sequential adult fights and makes them continuations of a single ongoing dispute. Altogether, children are a lot less limited by the usual adult restrictions on violence; some researchers regard this as primal violence that is eventually socialized out of most children as they grow up, leaving the violent few as the unsocialized few (Tremblay et al. 2004). But this way of looking at it overlooks the point that competent violence is a matter of interactional techniques that are developed over time. Kids do not start out as skilled snipers, ace pilots, hitmen, or cowboy cops. What children develop as they grow up, I suggest, is greater sensitivity to the larger group around them. For many people this inhibits violence—more precisely, it de-energizes it—while for others it provides a niche that increases violence, and especially high-activity and high-competence violence.

Confrontation Leaders and Action-Seekers: Police

To explain how some persons are actively violent, and even fewer are competently violent, we need to grasp the implications of the point that violent incidents are rare. Our best data concern the police.

Observational reports of ride-along researchers enable us to sample situations where police violence might happen. In high-crime big-city neighborhoods, police use force in 5 to 8 percent of their encounters with suspected offenders; most of the time this consisted in grabbing and restraining; excessive force was used less than 2 percent of the time. When arrests were made, police used force 22 percent of the time. Figures were even lower in low-action suburbs, small towns, and rural areas (Friedrich 1980; Sherman 1980; Black 1980; Reiss 1971; Bayley and Garofalo 1989; Worden 1996; Garner et al. 1996; Alpert and Dunham 2004).

These are low numbers. Our image of violence is based on the most dramatic instances; as we have seen throughout this book, violence is not an easy or automatic process, and it takes a lot to trigger it. Police violence in this respect is like other kinds of violence. Whenever we are able to look across a range of situations and avoid sampling on the dependent variable, we find that most of the time most people avoid violence.

Why is police violence infrequent? Most of the time people defer and comply with the police, even when being arrested. Force is most likely to occur when the suspect threatens or attacks the officer (or is perceived as doing such), or attempts to flee; it also occurs when persons answer back with verbal abuse or disobey officers' commands (Friedrich 1980). Physical resistance is by far the most likely factor to lead to police violence. Holding resistance constant, the suspect's demeanor—the degree of insolence versus compliance or deference to the police—further determines violence.[11]

The situational nature of police violence is underscored by the fact that a variety of background and attitudinal differences among police are uncorrelated with who is high or low in violence. Ride-along data and administrative reports showed no relation with the officer's race, education, prior military service, or civil service test ratings; nor was there a difference in attitudes toward their role as police (Friedrich 1980; Croft 1985; Worden 1996; Gellen and Toch 1996). The Christopher Commission found high-violence officers had positive performance evaluations. Toch (1980) found the chief personality characteristic of violence-prone cops is that they are extroverts, energetic, even "forthcoming, intelligent, and charming."

This is similar to military patterns. In the wake of S.L.A. Marshall's findings, a number of studies tried to distinguish the best fighters from the rest (notably Robert Egbert's research in Korea, summarized in

Glenn 2000a: 139). The most active fighters were more dominant, physically bigger and heavier, more proactive ("doers"); other soldiers preferred to be around them, both for sociability and during combat. This is consistent with a picture of elite fighters getting much social support, as the center of group attention; getting emotional energy also from dominating others (non-violently as well as violently). Active firers also tested as more intelligent and as having more military knowledge; like action-oriented cops, they are strongly committed to the professional lore of their job. Highly rated combat soldiers, far from being afraid of injury, were relatively confident that they would not be hurt; like the ace fighter pilots we consider later, they expected to be successful in combat, to prevail over the enemy (Clum and Mahan 1971; consistent with Stouffer et al. vol. 2, 1949). This confidence is the emotional energy specific to the interactional field of fighting.

The pattern hangs together in another way as well. The most violent police receive good administrative reports; they are well-liked by other cops. This is not only because they are often high-energy extroverts (although that appears to be true too); they are the informal leaders of the police. This fits a basic principle of small-group research: the popular members of the group are those who most closely express its values and are best at what the group is attempting to do (Homans 1950). Studies of police routine show that an officer always attempts to assert control of the situation, from the outset of any encounter with suspects and, indeed, ordinary citizens in general (Rubinstein 1973). Alpert and Dunham (2004) call it an "authority maintenance ritual."

In their interactional lore, to be a good cop is to be in charge of the situation; if necessary to err on the side of aggressiveness rather than to let the other side establish situational dominance. All the more so where police deal with suspects who challenge their control. As these situations edge into the zone of violent confrontation, police are in the same general condition as we have analyzed throughout this book: they have to deal with confrontational tension/fear. It is not surprising that only a small percentage of police are violent, since it is generally the case that only a small number of persons overcome confrontational tension/fear. Like being a good soldier, being a good cop is tested in combat-like confrontation, although for police these confrontations are at much closer range than for most soldiers, and in much smaller groups, without as much organizational backup and compulsion to keep them performing. Police who are good at this, like the soldiers who fire their weapons most often and aggressively and take the lead in combat, are looked up to by the other cops, or troops.

There are some indications that police who are older (in their thirties and forties rather than twenties) and have higher rank and more experience are the most violent (Alpert and Dunham 2004: 70, 81, 84). This is not youthful ebullience, but appears to be part of the style of those who are most committed to the profession. Alpert and Dunham (2004) provide data from use-of-force reports that show the sequence of moves made by police and suspects in response to each other. As an encounter begins, police expect to receive deference for their mere presence and verbal commands. If suspects resist these early moves verbally, by hostile stares or expressions, or more seriously by attempts to evade searches and hand-cuffing or by running away, police counter-escalate through their own increasingly aggressive tactics. They raise their voices; grab, push, shove, and twist arms; at a higher level they subdue the suspect with choke holds, fists, and kicks. Suspects can escalate too, with increasingly activeness and aggressiveness, up to the level where they brandish guns or other weapons, or attempt to run the officer over with a car. Police counter-escalate still further, with clubs, tasers, stun guns, and finally with deadly force. Alpert and Dunham's chief finding is that the level of escalation on both sides (what they call the Force Factor) is reciprocal and closely correlated; cops and suspects are rarely more than one force level away from what the other side has just done. Most violent encounters take three to five reciprocated pairs of moves (Alpert and Dunham 2004: 94): the fact that a suspect was calm and cooperative in the first round does not preclude an escalation later, and suspects who used guns or other weapons are more likely to do it in the second or third round. The oldest and most experienced cops tended to deal with resisting suspects by either the lowest or highest levels of force. Where younger officers more often used medium levels of force, the older ones stayed longer at the level of merely verbal commands and forceful demeanor; or else they jumped to high levels of force such as intermediate and deadly weapons (Alpert and Dunham 2004: 141, 165). Their technique was less to scuffle with suspects, but rather to talk them down or to use the overwhelming advantage of their powers.

The inner culture of the police comes from the centrality of confrontations in their work. Police (at least in the big-city police forces heavily studied by sociologists) do not like to associate with outsiders in their leisure time, and are suspicious of them as well as of their own departmental superiors (Westley 1970; Skolnick 1966). We can interpret this to mean that officers are used to dominating everyone they encounter, and hence they avoid off-duty situations where this is not possible. This ongoing self-segregation of the police from those whom they patrol keeps up a degree of polarization and cultural isolation.

In part this effort to assert control at every point in the encounter flows from the fact that the police are a small minority in most situations; they are like a tiny military patrol in the midst of a large number of potential enemies; hence their effort to establish situational dominance from the outset, to avoid showing weakness, which could leave them vulnerable to being overwhelmed. This is the special tension of police work.

The police ideal is to dominate in every phase of confrontation. But in fact only a small number of them reach high levels of violence with any frequency. Maintaining authority is the baseline of police violence, but it does not explain why some officers are so much more extreme about this than others. The violent minority of police, the "cowboy cops," are not only those who react violently when threat or defiance comes their way. They are action-seekers; they volunteer for the most dangerous and exciting activities, such as drug busts and raids to serve arrest warrants.[12] Some officers repeatedly find that violent confrontations come their way; they find themselves in situations where suspects flee or threaten them; sometimes they are shot at or hit by suspects. These risks do not come entirely at random; to volunteer to take the lead as point man in entering a home in search of a suspect is not only to expect danger but to seek it out.

Klinger's (2004) interviews with police on their experiences in shootings cast light on why, although shootings are rare events, a small subset of officers tend to be repeatedly involved in them. These are the officers who volunteer for dangerous duty, or who move toward the scene of action wherever possible. One officer during a career of some twenty years had been in two dozen dangerous encounters, having worked both in narcotics and on hundreds of SWAT missions.[13] He remarked, "I liked to chase people when they ran. I always kind of got a kick out of it, just to see if I could catch them" (Klinger 2004: 184).[14]

Another officer described taking the lead in entering an attic where a home-invasion robber was hiding:

I know [the SWAT team leader] was a little bit nervous about sending Paul and me up into that attic. But I wasn't worried. When I first heard the guy wasn't gonna give up, that he planned to take a couple of us with him, I figured it wasn't going to be any different than any other barricaded-subject call-up. Just same ole, same ole. In fact, I was looking forward to going in to find him. It's a hunt-or-be-hunted type of deal. You need to think of what he's doing, think like he's thinking, listen carefully, and pay attention to your nose. A lot of times when we go into a room where suspects are hiding, I can smell these guys. Their adrenalin's going, they're sweating, so if you're paying attention, you can smell 'em. . . . You gotta think of all the potential hiding places. . . . So my mind was not on fear at all. That was the last thing in it. It was on all my training, all my intuition, just doing my job and thinking, "Where is this son of a bitch? Where's he at?" (Klinger 2004: 199–200)

The search ended with the officer and his two partners shooting twenty-one rounds into a man hidden in a roll of insulation.

The most proactive police are not necessarily seeking violence, but they are seeking action, and they think positively about using violence if it comes to that. They are self-consciously an elite who regard themselves as better at their job than other police. Another officer quotes a colleague who told him, " 'I'm gonna tell you this off the record 'cuz I don't want to see you dismayed by this job, but don't expect out of your peers what you expect out of yourself.' . . . . Then once I got in the academy, I saw that there were people in my class who didn't really have a grasp on reality, who had no idea what they were getting themselves into. Then we also had people who got into it for paychecks. . . . There were several other people who thought the way I did, so there was a group of us that were really serious, really intense" (Klinger 2004: 50). Both the elite and the non-elite cops know who each other are. In the LAPD at the time of the Christopher Commission, the most action-oriented police on the special squads were famed throughout the force. Police psychologists distinguish two categories: "The first group may be thought of as slackers by their peers because they purposely avoid hot situations; the second group is thought of as adrenalin junkies because they race from hot call to hot call" (Artwohl and Christensen 1997: 127).[15]

One off-duty policeman was paged by the SWAT team to the scene where a woman had called police after her boyfriend had beaten her (Klinger 2004: 147–52). He recollected,

> I already had the information that he'd fired at officers, and I was kind of confused about why they were letting this guy walk around with a rifle after he's already shot at some patrol cops. I was wondering, "Why aren't they shooting?" . . . The atmosphere at the scene was very strange. There were police cars all over the place, with their emergency lights on, so many that I had to stop about three hundred yards down the street from where the gunman was. Police officers were all over the place, the news media was already there, and there must have been fifty spectators standing around where I pulled my car up. . . .

The officer found a patrolman with a semi-automatic assault rifle (the civilian version of the military's M-16), but the latter told him he didn't know how to use it.

> He told me, "I can't figure out how to work the sights on this gun." I said, "Jesus Christ!" and told him and the other officers they were too close, that we needed to move the perimeter back and let the snipers contain the situation. I looked up, and the guy was standing right where Jeff [another SWAT member] told me he had a clear view, and I couldn't understand why he wasn't shooting. . . .
>   I still hadn't heard a shot, so I decided to drop this guy. . . . Before I pulled the trigger, I started wondering about my decision again. I said

to myself, "Pete, maybe you're missing something here, because no one else is shooting, You just told Jeff to drop the guy, but he didn't. Maybe I'm missing something here. Don't shoot so quickly." . . . I told the guy to give up, but he just stood right there and didn't fucking move. As I was aiming my gun at him, I was thinking all kinds of stuff. . . . When I stopped myself from shooting him the first time, I started going through my mental check list. . . . "What justification do I have to shoot him when fifty other cops are standing around and they're not?"

The officer's thoughts then turn to technical matters, comparing what kind of gun he has with the suspect's weapon, and deciding whether to leave it on full automatic or shift to semi-automatic. He calculates the distance at which his weapon is sighted, and decides to aim a few inches above the suspect's belly button since his bullet should hit four-to-six inches higher than his point of aim.

The suspect begins cursing at the officers, demanding they turn their spotlights off of him and threatening to kill someone if they do not. The officers turn the lights off. Apparently this is the double sticking point for the SWAT officer; the suspect has demonstrated his dominance over the situation, the most basic affront to the police; in addition, he begins to wrap his rifle sling around his hand, as if preparing it for firing. "When I saw him do that, I said to myself, 'This has gone far enough.'"

The officer then shot what he believed was a burst of four or five rounds; in fact nine rounds hit the suspect. He then advances, even though correct policy was to be cautious: "I started walking up on him as soon as he hit the ground. I probably should have stayed behind the cover of the patrol car for a little longer and evaluating things before moving up, but I didn't. . . . At that point, I realized that I had killed him and I said to myself, 'Pete, you've been involved in another shooting' " (Klinger 2004: 147–52).

This officer provides a good portrait of the violent few among the police. He self-consciously takes charge in a potentially violent situation. He has the strongest emphasis on his arms and technique; he is in the small group that assiduously spends time preparing at the shooting range, concerned about their weapons, even practicing martial arts. He is also the most mentally attuned to potential violence, frequently repeating statistics and stories about cops who have been shot, and mentally asserting that it will not happen to him because he will be better than his opponent.[16] He regards himself as more conscious of the ever-present danger than other, less-prepared police. But he deals with danger not by avoiding it, but by seeking it out.[17] Such cops are a prototype for the violent elite in other arenas as well.

Who Wins?

We come now to the elite of the elite: not only the most actively violent but the truly competently violent. I will argue that their competence is not just a matter of having the best eyesight or the quickest reflexes, but a social competence in domination. That means the techniques of the violent elite are above all in their distinctive micro-situational tactics for overcoming confrontational tension/fear.

Military Snipers: Concealed and Absorbed in Technique

The sniper is chiefly a phenomenon of twentieth-century wars. Until mid-nineteenth century, smooth-bore muzzle-loading muskets were too inaccurate and too cumbersome in reloading to be used with any effectiveness except in massed ranks. Their accurate range of aimed fire was one hundred yards, and battles were often fought out as close as thirty yards or less (Pegler 2001: 5; Griffith 1989: 146–50). By 1900, industrial improvements brought spiral-grooved rifles with percussion-fired breech-loaded cartridges to all the major armies; these rifles could reach targets at one thousand or even two thousand yards, but only with telescopes could shooters see much of the target beyond three hundred yards. Troops became divided into a mass of infantry with relatively poor aim operating at close ranges, and a small number of snipers.

The proportion of snipers has always been relatively small, on the order of 1 percent or less of infantry troops, with highs of slightly over 2 percent (Pegler 2001). Why these numbers are so small can be considered in several ways. Snipers needed specialized equipment (scopes, special rifles, and ammunition), which armies are not generally eager to provide, in part because of complicating logistics problems, in part because of expense. Perhaps more importantly, officers (as well as regular troops) looked askance at snipers, considering them not quite palatable kinds of fighters, even though their superior effectiveness was well known. Whatever the mix of practical, organizational, and ideological reasons, different armies all converged on approximately the same proportions of snipers.

The effectiveness of snipers tends to be heroized by looking at the very top of the distribution. The all-time top sniper totals—over 500 and 400 kills, respectively—were set by two Finnish snipers during the Russian invasion of Finland in 1939–1940, virtually invisible wearing winter white camouflage and moving on skis inside Russian lines. The top World War I sniper was a Canadian credited with 376 kills on the western front. In World War II, the top two German snipers each had over 300 kills, both on the eastern front; the top Russian was a woman who had 309.

Other top snipers in particular armies were lower; the top American sniper in Vietnam had 113. In general anything over forty kills has been considered noteworthy (Pegler 2001: 31, 57; 2004: 139–40, 167, 176–78; Grossman 1995: 109).

The rate for average snipers was quite a bit lower. In World War I, the elite South African sharpshooters unit of twenty-four men (recruited from big-game hunters) killed 125 Germans each on the average; spread over two and a half years, this was four per month. Other sniper units in various armies averaged between one kill per month and one per three months. The entire contingent of Russian women snipers killed an average of eight each during the length of World War II (calculated from Pegler 2001: 24, 29; 2004: 140–42, 178; Keegan 1997: 162–63). The very peak-killing snipers—300–500 kills—are the top one or two individuals in an entire army of millions of troops; even those with a hundred kills are a handful at most. Their kill totals are similar to those of the very top ace pilots. These peak totals depend upon several conditions beyond the sheer motivation and ability of the killer; also necessary is a prolonged period of combat with many accessible targets.

A better way than total kills for assessing the skill of this killing elite is their firing accuracy. It is sometimes asserted that a sniper averages one kill per 1.3 rounds fired, compared to 7,000 rounds of small arms fire for ordinary infantry in World War I and 25,000 rounds in Vietnam (Hay 1974); and military sniper schools in recent decades adopt the doctrine of one shot, one kill. This is an ideal that has evolved historically, with the improvement of equipment, especially of highly accurate scopes. Again the narratives concentrate on the successes: one sniper in Vietnam hit fourteen enemy sentries in fourteen shots; an Australian (a former kangaroo hunter) in New Guinea shot twelve advancing Japanese with twelve shots within fifteen minutes—a case where the targets were unusually exposed, at relatively close range. Only occasionally does a combat narrative tell of misses: an American, going into his initial sniping action in the Pacific in World War II, hit two of five shots. A U.S. sniper in Vietnam reported attempting a difficult shot at 1,300 meters, missing five times, hitting on the sixth. In Northern Ireland, two British snipers fired at an IRA ambush at 1,200 yards, hitting ten of eighty-three shots (Pegler 2001: 48; 2004: 28, 211, 224, 286).

What the "one shot, one kill" ideal implies is optimum conditions: the ability to hit a person in the head at 400 yards, and in the body at 600 to 800 yards. The ideal has risen with the equipment. In World War I, accuracy of fire in trench warfare was rarely more than 300 to 400 yards, and most hits were under 200 yards. In World War II, improved scopes were theoretically accurate to 800 yards, but most snipers operated within 400 yards, and even the best rarely hit beyond 600 yards, though occasional hits were celebrated out to 1,000 yards (Pegler 2001: 22–31). High-tech equipment at the end of the century brought occasional record-setting hits at 1,500 meters or even farther in the 1991 Gulf war and the 2002 Afghanistan war. But the one-shot standard is an ideal for a very elite group operating within what are considered appropriate ranges out to 600 meters, with high magnification scopes.

There are numerous limitations and obstacles that are not held against the ideal. Weapons sometimes malfunction, or become fouled from use, dirt, and moisture. Scopes fog up. Wind conditions blow shots off course; heat mirages, especially in deserts, make distance estimation inaccurate; extreme cold changes ballistics. Jungle or heavily wooded terrain cuts down the range of visibility. Thus high-accuracy as well as high-kill totals depend on relatively optimum conditions, especially open terrain, crop fields, or damaged buildings providing hiding posts as well as allowing snipers to get within moderate distances of enemy fixed positions. Hence the greatest opportunities for snipers were in trench warfare, and in relatively static urban battles such as the eastern front in World War II.

Success as a sniper depends on more techniques than shooting accuracy. Snipers often take up positions in no-man's-land or near the enemy lines; this requires finding or constructing suitable hiding places, and camouflaging themselves thoroughly against tiny tell-tale signs of movement, breath, smoke, or glints of light from guns and equipment. Like most successful violence, snipers make most of their kills against temporarily defenseless or oblivious targets, shooting primarily at officers, artillery, and machine-gun operators. Because of their sudden and clandestine attacks, snipers are the most feared and hated of enemies. When captured, they are almost without exception executed on the spot; although this is in violation of the rules of war, the act of sniping itself tends to be regarded as itself at least a violation in spirit (Pegler 2004: 17–20, 239).[18] In contrast, artillery troops, who cause the most casualties, are regarded with no special animosity.

Snipers tend to be disliked even by their fellow troops, or at least are regarded with uneasiness. A British sniper officer in World War I noted that infantrymen did not like to mingle with the snipers "for there was something about them that set them apart from ordinary men and made the soldiers uncomfortable" (quoted in Pegler 2004: 20–21). World War II soldiers sometimes jeered at them. U.S. snipers in Vietnam were met with the comment, "Here comes Murder Incorporated." The attitude continued even with the high-tech feats of late-twentieth-century snipers; the sniper section of a British battalion in the late 1980s was known as "the Leper Colony" (Pegler 2004: 21–23). In part the lack of solidarity came from the distinctiveness and privileges of snipers; generally they were free of ordinary duties and fatigues; they had unusual freedom to move about and choose their own time and place of action; they tended to wear idiosyncratic uniforms, made even more bizarre by their predilection for extreme forms of camouflage. But most of all they were emotionally distant; generally less sociable, more reserved than other troops; and their cool absorption in their craft gave them the reputation of cold-blooded killers.

Not only were troops cool or hostile to snipers. Traditional officers at the beginnings of the world wars were initially unconvinced of the need of snipers, and sniper forces were built up only with reluctance. Officers too regarded snipers as outside the normal tactics and mode of honor of battle, where troops faced each other with at least a certain degree of danger to themselves in return for their attempting to take the lives of the enemy. As it turned out, snipers tended to take high casualties too; but the mode of confrontation—shooting from the most extreme concealment possible, avoiding the moment of confrontation with an equally dangerous enemy—felt like a violation of military honor. It is not surprising that sniper training and weaponry, hastily improvised after the beginning of each war, was speedily shut down at each war's end.

Sniping is indeed a cool and calculating business. Successful snipers are patient and slow; working their way forward or backward into the proper vantage point and place of concealment, usually taking very few shots a day. In part this was a safety precaution, to avoid giving away the location of their hiding place; but the clandestine approach is also an offensive move, waiting to find an accessible target and to take the best possible shot at him. This is why high numbers of kills per day by a sniper are rare; most snipers wait for a month or more for their kill. But some snipers do score much higher than others, even on the same front; these ultra-elite killers are not only clandestine but also aggressive in seeking out targets. The average sniper, on the other hand, has plenty of opportunities to pass up shots, ostensibly for technical reasons.

Snipers are selected not merely because they are good shots, although that is generally what gets them initially into sniper training. One estimate is that 25 percent wash out as unsuitable. Furthermore, the top marksmen on shooting ranges are not always successful in sniping live targets in combat situations, where it is necessary to find one's own target and approach within shooting range. In this respect they are like ace fighter pilots, who see potential targets where others do not. The difference between good shots and snipers is often described as a matter of temperament; hotheads, confrontational and belligerent persons do not make good snipers (Pegler 2004: 121, 121, 243, 303).

How then do they do it? Snipers, although isolated from other troops, are not without social support; most operate in two- or three-person teams, although some operate solo. Usually one acts as telescopic spotter for the primary sniper; a third may carry conventional automatic weapons and act as a guard. In effect this makes sniping a group-operated weapon, the type that S.L.A. Marshall (1947) found had the highest firing level.

Like all violence, sniping must overcome confrontational tension/fear. The sniper has the special advantage of shooting at the longest distance of any small arms. Usually the target is at 300 to 400 yards. At this distance one can pick out the legs of a standing man, but the head is barely visible on the torso. At 150 yards—very close distance for a sniper—the line of people's eyes are visible; at eighty yards the face is clearly visible, and the eyes are distinct points. Farther out, at 600 yards, colors of clothing are not distinguishable except for white; at 800 to 1,000 yards a body of troops is visible as a low line.[19] This means that snipers fire at distances at which the usual signs of face-to-face confrontation, including the opponent's emotional expressions, are not visible.

Snipers generally use scopes, with magnification of between 3 and 10, and this usually makes the face visible, if not the eyes. But even with the scope, the interactional psychology is different than normal; there is no reciprocity, since the enemy does not see the sniper's face or eyes, or indeed see the sniper at all. The basic features of social interaction—the tendency to become entrained in a common focus of attention and a shared mood—are lacking. Firing with a scope brings out, like a controlled experiment, the interactional details that normally make the confrontation difficult. It is not just seeing the other's eyes that makes for interactional entrainment, but mutual recognition that both see each other's eyes.

The core of the sniper's technique, even more than shooting ability, is invisibility. Snipers use concealment not merely as a defense against retaliation, but as an offensive weapon; it is a way of making the interaction asymmetrical. Thus the key item in the sniper's social identity is one's ability at concealment and camouflage. In this respect they are similar to professional hitmen, and to terrorists. It is this emphasis on concealment that gives them a reputation of being "cowardly" or at least not quite honorable, from the point of view of other soldiers.

In addition, the sniper's attention is not on the confrontation in the same way that individuals in a fight or battle are caught up in the conflict. Instead of a contest of wills, hostilities, and fears, with its urges to action in flight or fight, the sniper sets his own time frame, slowly and patiently waiting for an opportunity. Whatever tension he has tends to be swallowed up in focusing upon the technical details of getting the proper distance, wind speed, elevation, and other factors affecting the shot; instead of focusing on the enemy as a human being or even as an opponent, he or she focuses on adjusting his or her sights. Snipers describe their own experience chiefly in terms of recalling the technical details from training school, and applying their techniques with as much care as possible. This obsession with one's own technique removes the situation from the emo-

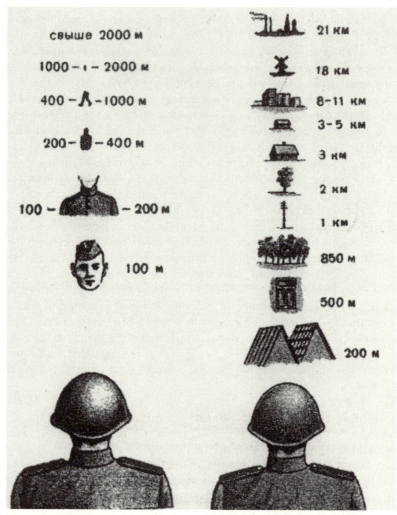

Figure 10.1 Visibility of targets at various distances: 1942 Soviet sniping manual.

tions of killing, into a quiet zone where it is almost entirely depersonalized. Pegler (2004: 316) quotes a British sniper in Iraq in 2003: "I knew I only had one shot and had to get the angle exactly right. It was hot and wind was blowing strongly and steadily from left to right as we crept up to a vantage point about 860 meters from the target. I saw I had a clear shot at my man . . . his head and chest were exposed. My training then took over and I got into the perfect sniping position. I was concentrating so hard that I didn't have time to think about him as a person or the fact that I was just about to kill him. He was just a distant shape magnified ten times in the telescopic lens."

Snipers' deliberation is the opposite end of the continuum from face confrontations at close range. As the following example shows, violence can be completely neutralized when fighters come into confrontation so abruptly that there is no preparation on either side for the killing mode: In the 1944 campaign in the dense *bocage* hedgerows of Normandy, "one astonished GI walked around a bend into an equally amazed German. Neither had the ability to shoot and they could have reached out and touched one another. The GI yelled 'Shoo! Get the hell out of here!' and the German took off" (quoted in Pegler 2004: 253).

A similar situation is described by a policeman, in this case compounded by the diminished hearing that comes in the heat of violent confrontation:

> My partner and I had chased a bank robber into an empty lot over-grown with trees and bushes. Stan ran toward a long hedge as I ran alongside it in the other direction to cut off the suspect when he got flushed out. When I rounded the corner, I heard the shot. It wasn't a loud bang, like at the range. It was just a little pop. In fact, I remember thinking as I pushed through the limbs of a huge tree that it couldn't be a shot, it had to be something else. Then I came face to face with the suspect. He had been pushing through the tree branches too, coming toward me, his pistol pointed right at my face. We both froze.
>
> Although we couldn't have stood there for more than a second, I remember the moment very clearly. We were about five or six feet apart and his face looked as surprised as mine probably did. I remember he had a tie-died T-shirt on and he was big and bushy-haired. Then we backed away from each other and the branches fell back and blocked my view. (Artwohl and Christensen 1997: 40–41)

It turned out that the policeman's partner had indeed been shot; nevertheless, the robber was too startled to pull the trigger again in the sudden close-up confrontation. Minutes later, the two had another confrontation, now from thirty yards away; this time both pointed their guns, and the cop got his shot off first.[20]

It is situations of this sort that snipers' interactional technique is designed to avoid. Their skill at avoidance, while aggressively seeking out targets, is what determines their success.

Fighter Pilot Aces: Aggressively Imposing Momentum

Some of the strongest evidence for the concentration of effective violence in a small elite is the distribution of fighter pilots. World War I invented the category of the fighter ace, a pilot who shot down five or more enemy aircraft. Fighter pilot performance became a topic of avid record-keeping.

Among American fighter pilots, less than 1 percent became aces from World War I through the Korean war; but they typically accounted for between 37 and 68 percent of the enemy aircraft destroyed (EAD) in air-to-air fighting. The majority of pilots had no kills at all.[21] The result came from a combination of pilots firing inaccurately—the low competence pattern—or not firing at all—Marshall's low firing ratio. In the Korean war, half of American fighter pilots "never fired their guns, and of those who had fired, only 10 percent had ever hit anything" (Bourke 1999: 62). Top pilots were not merely good shooters but those who were the most aggressive in seeking out enemy targets.[22]

Similarly in other air forces. In the British Royal Air Force in World War II, 5 percent of the pilots accounted for 60 percent of the air victories; those credited with ten or more victories made up 0.2 percent of the military pilots. Japanese pilots in World War II who had twenty or more kills were well below 0.5 percent of all pilots. In the Soviet air force, at most 0.3 percent had twenty or more victories. The criterion for what was counted as an ace varied in different air forces, depending on how high the kill records reached.[23]

In a class by themselves were World War II German pilots. The top two pilots had over 300 kills; another thirteen had 200 plus (www.au.af.mil/au/awc/awcgate/aces/aces.htm). As we will see, these extremely high numbers were due to special conditions on the eastern front.

We have no information comparable to that of snipers on the firing accuracy of pilots, but we can get some averages of planes shot down per sortie, or per month in combat. The highest success rates were for top German aces in World War II. Otto Kittel flew 583 missions and shot down 267 planes, a ratio of 46 percent of his missions. Other top pilots with over 200 kills had success ratios from 22 to 44 percent of their sorties. Erich Hartmann, the top ace of all World War II pilots with 352 kills, also had the most missions—over 1,400—for a success rate of about 25 percent.[24] A top Japanese pilot, Saburo Sakai, had 64 kills in about 200 combat missions, or 32 percent (Caidin et al. 2004). Even under the most favorable conditions, the batting average for fighter pilots is like that of baseball hitters, with anything above .400 as epoch-making.

In other theaters of operation, peak success levels were lower. Major Richard Bong, flying in the Pacific in World War II, broke the U.S. record with twenty-eight kills in 142 missions, a ratio of one kill per five sorties or 20 percent of the time (Gurney 1958: 113). The top RAF ace in World War II (J. E. Johnson) had thirty-eight kills over fifty-four months combat flying, averaging about one kill per month (*Daily Telegraph*, Feb. 1, 2001). In World War I, the top ace was the German Manfred von Richtho-fen with eighty kills in twenty months (about 1 per week); the top U.S.

ace, Eddie Rickenbacker, had twenty-four kills in somewhat over a year (about two per month) (Gilbert 1994: 290–91, 415; Gurney 1965).[25]

As a baseline for average pilots, U.S. Navy fighters in World War II flew 146,465 sorties, a ratio of 6.3 percent per enemy aircraft destroyed in aerial combat.[26] We can also calculate the accuracy of an air force in reverse, since the losses of one side are the successes of the other side. In the European theater in World War II, the RAF flew 1,695,000 fighter plane sorties and lost 0.6 percent per sortie; American fighters lost 0.8 percent per sortie (Keegan 1997: 139). Given that some of the losses were to anti-aircraft ground fire, we can estimate the chance of a German pilot shooting down the planes that were his targets in any particular sortie would be 1 percent or less in air-to-air combat. And this was arguably the top air force in the war. The Luftwaffe got most of its air victories against the inferior Soviet air force. This shows in the aggregate what I argue later on the individual level: one good air force against another good air force results in a relatively low kill level.

Unlike snipers, aces were given wide publicity in the news media and covered with honors in the military community. During World War I, enemy pilots recognized each other's aces. When von Richthofen, the top German ace, was finally shot down in 1917, he was buried with full military honors behind the British lines; and British pilots dropped wreaths on the funeral inside German lines for another famous German ace (Gurney 1965: 65, 75). In World War II, both Japanese and German forces knew the names of American aces and treated them honorably as prisoners of war, a fate very unlike that of snipers who were hated in all armies and were generally executed immediately when captured.

Fighter pilots quickly became regarded as the ideal heroic warrior. There was great enthusiasm among civilian pilots to join in both of the world wars, beginning as volunteers for the French and British air forces before the United States officially declared war. In the regular military, fighter pilots disliked administrative desk jobs, and sometimes violated regulations to sneak out and fly. Their motivation for joining was not political or patriotic, but chiefly getting into the center of heroic action. Pilots in World War I and up through the 1930s were often stunt pilots or racing car drivers, who made their living by public exhibitions. World War I units were called "flying circuses" with some justification. Combats, which took place at altitudes below a few thousand feet, were sometimes announced and scheduled with ground audiences assembled. Far from seeking disguise, some pilots painted their planes in bright colors; von Richthofen's squadron was bright red (hence his nickname the "Red Baron"). By World War II, American pilots had evolved a ritual upon returning to base, performing one barrel roll before landing for each enemy plane shot down. The equivalent in the Luftwaffe was to

Figure 10.2 American pilots in World War I with flying top hat emblem.

waggle the plane's wings the requisite number of times (Gurney 1958; www.acepilots.com/index.html#top). This was acrobatic showing-off in the same vein as the acrobatic flying tactics that were regarded as the key to combat victory.

Why were aces highly honored for killing in single combat while snipers were generally reviled? Both shot their targets from approximately the same distance—in World War II, usually within 300 yards; from the slower-moving small planes of World War I, even closer. But whereas snipers took their time to set up a shot with good visibility through a telescope, fighter pilots maneuvered to catch their enemy briefly from rear or side angle; though fighters sometimes could see the enemy pilot they never confronted face to face (since two planes flying toward each other would pass at very high speeds). Fighters regarded the plane as the object of the "kill," not the pilot; enemy pilots were allowed to eject and were not shot at while parachuting.[27] And pilots who dueled skillfully might be locked together for minutes as they flew loops and dives to evade the other on their tail—hence the term "dogfight." This would have produced a strong and somewhat playful if antagonistic entrainment between the enemies.

These interactional structures turned aerial combat into the equivalent of a limited fight among members of an honorific elite. The title of "ace" was closely guarded to exclude those who were not fully elite; in World War II, gunners on bomber crews sometimes shot down enough enemy planes to qualify as aces, but with very few exceptions they were not granted the title. Bomber gunners were enlisted men, not officers, whereas virtually all pilots were given the rank of commissioned officer, which carried the connotation of "gentleman."[28] The obverse case, which proves the general rule, is the fact that Japanese pilots had no system of "aces" (Mersky 1993). Pilots were mostly low-ranking enlisted men. No official records were kept nor awards given; at best a very high-performing Geki-tsui-O ("shoot-down king") might be posthumously promoted to officer status. The best pilots were navy petty officers, who spotted enemy planes in the sky and signaled attack, leaving their nominally superior officers to follow. It is likely that complaints from embarrassed officers were the reason for the order given in 1943 forbidding keeping individual records, although the official reason was to promote teamwork. Nevertheless, Japanese pilots kept individual logs, and their fighter planes had "score-boards" painted on their tails and fuselages, a form of local bragging. The top three Japanese pilots apparently had records of eighty, seventy, and sixty kills each.

The honorific and sport-like ethos of fighter battles is shown in the proliferating social construction of records. Aerial combats began as ancillary to other military activities, but they soon became glorified in themselves. In World War I, small planes were used for battlefield reconnaissance (supplementing balloons, which had been used since the mid-nineteenth century). Enemy balloons were an initial target for fighters, but they did not become counted toward ace totals; balloons were protected by anti-aircraft ground fire rather than their own guns, and as stationary targets they lacked the dramatics of combat among planes of a similar type. Thus evolved the so-called dogfight among rival reconnaissance planes, largely as an end in itself, and with huge surrounding publicity. Some pilots became so obsessed with getting proper credit for their kills that they would land immediately at the nearest balloon observer and present blank forms for a certifying signature (Gurney 1958: 34). In World War II, American planes added gun cameras to record the event.

In World War II, fighter pilots were used for more substantive tasks: providing protection for bombers over enemy territory; attacking enemy bombers; in naval combat, attacking enemy ships and especially carriers; attacking harbors; defending air bases; occasionally providing combat ground support against positions and troop movements. Some venues (such as battles over harbors important in military logistics) became regular meeting places for fighter dogfights, and hence places where ace totals were racked up. But most of these targets were excluded from ace totals and other records; the honorific ideal was to shoot down another fighter plane who had an equal chance of shooting down yours. Enemy bombers destroyed in the air were generally included in the record totals, but other targets were not. There were no honorific records for destroying enemy ships, even though this was the biggest contribution of fighter planes to winning the Pacific war. It was controversial whether to count as EAD planes that were destroyed on the ground (i.e., while at their bases); such statistics were kept separately (and made up a substantial proportion of enemy aircraft destroyed), but generally were not counted toward "ace" totals. The deciding issue was not the amount of danger; strafing planes on the ground usually exposed the attacker to heavy anti-aircraft fire, and such fire in general accounted for the largest proportion of planes lost.[29] But this lacked the dramatic structure of the duel and the mythology of man-to-man fight.

The official justification of honoring fighter pilots was that they saved lives of other troops, especially those of bomber crews. But this utilitarian argument did not explain the dynamics of honors given and the way records were created. As the number of aces rose in the massive airforces of World War II, there was a proliferation of various kinds of records. In the American and British militaries, becoming an ace with five kills remained the primary honor. Pilots also became honored for the highest number of kills in each combat theater. Squadrons vied for the title of the most total kills. Individuals were celebrated for achieving the first kill in a combat theater; becoming the first ace in the theater; achieving the first jet kill. Records were established and progressively raised for the largest number of kills in one combat sortie. These records were taken seriously not only by the pilots themselves but by the military organization, which established "victory boards" to verify and preserve records. Pilots who established significant records (such as breaking the record for kills in a particular combat theater) were generally pulled out of combat and assigned to training and public relations duties.[30] This was a ceremonial, not a rational utilitarian move, since it meant taking the demonstrably best pilots out of combat where they could have the most effect. Top aces had become human treasures, too important to risk in mere mundane combat. The Luftwaffe, which had pioneered records in World War I, had a different problem of record inflation. So many enemy planes were shot down on the Russian front that standards had to be drastically raised. Early in the war, twenty-five or fifty victories were rewarded with the King's Cross. By late 1943, Erich Hartmann needed 148 for the medal. Eventually his totals rose so high (to 352) that medals were piled on medals, and special new awards were created for him and his high-performing peers.[31]

Dogfights give us unusually detailed information on the process by which an air battle was won. Particular air squadrons as well as entire air corps had high or low patterns of performance, showing it was not just a matter of individual pilots' qualities. In World War I, there were notable flying units in all armies; in World War II, German, American, and British

Figure 10.3 Ace scoreboards: The pilot is not a Nazi, but an American ace showing off his victories with symbols of the planes he has shot down (1945).

units were especially victorious. Five main factors are responsible for a high level of victories.

1. Sometimes military forces had superior planes over their local opponents. German planes were greatly superior to Soviet planes, although not to American and British planes. Planes might be superior in speed, maximal altitude, range from base, diving ability, or all-around maneuverability; some were better built and able to survive enemy fire. But success was not straight technological determinism. Planes were often better in some features and weaker in others. Japanese planes, for example, were highly maneuverable, and their pilots were often better at acrobatic battle tactics; nevertheless, they tended to lose heavily to American pilots,[32] since the Japanese emphasized highly coordinated group maneuvers and engaged in less

Figure 10.4 Korean war pilots show off their squadron's collective scoreboard of enemy kills.

improvisation. Pilots and their commanders learned to play to the strong points of their planes, designing tactics that masked their weak points against enemy planes.

2. Sheer abundance of targets and length of time in combat determined the upper limit on ace records set by different air forces.[33] The Luftwaffe had at least 627 pilots with twenty or more kills; the Soviets fifty-three pilots, the U.S. thirty-one, United Kingdom twenty-six, Japan twenty-five. These figures reflected the sheer masses of planes on the eastern front. German pilots not only had better planes and better training, but their bases were near the front where they could fly as often as two or three sorties a day (Overy 1995: 212–20). Russian planes were used in huge numbers (17,800 in the offensives of summer 1944), largely as flying artillery in massive tank battles. This left them vulnerable to the superior air-to-air capabilities of the Luftwaffe. We should note also that several air forces had no policy of rotating pilots out of combat except when wounded; German, Soviet, and Japanese had a "fly 'til you die" policy of almost

continuous service. Thus the highest scoring Japanese pilot (eighty kills), Tetsuzo Iwamoto, began flying in the China war in 1938 and continued through 1945. His total of eighty kills was far above the level of the top U.S. pilot in the Pacific (forty kills), among other reasons because there were many more U.S. planes for the Japanese to shoot at than vice versa (Mersky 1993; Sakaida 1985; Okumiya et al. 1973).

3. Ace pilots might be those with particularly good flying skills. This was very much on display in World War I, as fighters chased each other at low altitudes and close range, making rapid turns, rolls, and dives. Sometimes a kill could be made by drawing one's opponent (especially one who had gotten a dangerous position on one's tail) to follow into a dive that pulled out just before hitting the ground, while luring the less skilled opponent into a crash; this was like a game of "chicken" played by car racers. But many dogfights among skilled pilots ended with no kill; they continued evasive maneuvers until one side exhausted their ammunition (because most shots missed) or fuel and had to go home. On the whole, most kills were made by ace pilots against inferior opponents. Hence the higher level of German success against the Soviet air force, which pushed pilots into combat with inadequate flight training (Overy 1980).

4. Contrary to the ideology of heroic individual combat, aerial combat victories were often the result of teamwork. In World War I, tactics were developed such as the "Lufbery circle," in which a group of planes circled, each covering the vulnerable space behind the next. In World War II, a defensive pattern over air bases or supporting massive bombing raids was "thatching," a criss-cross pattern of layers allowing no unprotected air space in which enemy fighters could intrude. Teamwork was also stressed at the level of small-group formations: pilots always flew in pairs of wingmen giving mutual support; one or more planes were assigned to fly above and behind as lookout and cover for the others; squadrons assigned lead and backup roles. The top World War I German ace, von Richthofen, was killed, not by any of the Western aces, but by an otherwise unknown Canadian pilot who was flying top cover and caught von Richthofen unawares while he was chasing an isolated British plane away from the main battle groups (Gurney 1965: 75). In contrast with the relatively isolated position of snipers, pilots had intense social support on the battlefield, as well as at their home base before and after combat; this emotional support made aerial killing a joyous event, and shaped the status distinction between aces and snipers as popular and unpopular killer elites, respectively.

More complex tactics were used by squadrons, such as sending isolated planes to lure or decoy the enemy, while the main force hid above in cloud cover or in the direction of the glare of the sun. These tactics led to guessing games on both sides; bluffs might be used to disguise a weakness. The overall effect of these complexities was to make pilots less aggressive; and less confident or energized pilots could use tactics to avoid serious combat. A distinctive feature of the aces and record-setters was their willingness to forego these kinds of relatively safe tactics and also to take advantage psychologically of those who relied on them.

5. The most important factor in winning was the local structure of the aerial confrontation itself—the momentary situation in the sky. Most aces made their kills in short bursts of action, often with multiple victims. Some aces got most of their kills in one day. Moreover, several pilots from the same squadron would have a victorious day at the same time; one force would come out of combat without their planes even being hit, while the enemy side would suffer numerous planes downed. These one-sided battles resemble the decisive land battles, in which one army disintegrated organizationally and then suffered huge casualties that the other side inflicted with impunity. Big aerial victories resemble forward panics, or at least a situation in which one side has all the momentum and the other side is passive. Gurney (1958), the specialist who studied the record most extensively, concluded that aces were the most aggressive pilots, and that they dominated where the enemy was most defensive. Momentum versus passivity was the key, even where the attacking force was outnumbered. This is plausible because fighter pilots and bomber gunners, like other fighters, tend to miss their targets far more often than they hit them; the advantages of aggressiveness (and in exacerbating the corresponding disadvantages of passiveness) made one side better able to zero in psychologically on their targets, while the other side became less able to defend or even to take evasive action.

Top aces all gave much the same account of their winning style:

Attack! Never be on the defensive. Shoot the enemy down before he can shoot you down. You are better than he is, but don't give him a chance. He may get in a lucky shot but you're invincible. Move toward any dot in the sky that remotely resembles an airplane. Move to attack, with switches on and the sight ready. If it's not a ship or if it's a friendly one you'll be ready anyway, and your arrogant luck will last longer. (Gurney 1958: 136)

Another ace, with twenty-seven kills, said:

> If I were to pick out the most valuable personal traits of a fighter pilot, aggressiveness would rate high on the list. Time and again, I have seen aggressive action, even from a disadvantageous position, completely rout a powerful Nip formation. And conversely, have seen flights lose their advantage through hesitation. Obviously, aggression can be carried to the point of foolhardiness. However, this sort of action is never so foolish as poking around looking for an ideal setup and ending up being jumped yourself. (Gurney 1958: 118)

According to another, with twenty-two kills:

> Another characteristic of the younger [Japanese] pilots is their lack of alertness. In many instances we have engaged enemy fighters and they made no effort to evade our initial attack, evidently because they didn't see us. . . . In order to effectively attack the Jap, *you must see him first.* . . . You cannot wait to decide what he is going to do; you must plan your attack as you go into action. If your attack is sudden and aggressive, the enemy will be at a disadvantage regardless of his numbers and position. Don't wait; attack immediately and pick your targets with the intent to destroy. (Gurney 1958: 119)

The second highest American ace, with thirty-eight kills, noted "Aggressiveness is the key to success. . . . The enemy on the defensive gives you the advantage, as he is trying to evade you, and not to shoot you down. . . . *Go in close, and then when you think you are too close, go in closer.* At minimum range your shots count and there is less chance of missing your target" (Gurney 1958: 116).

Getting in close was a technique for overcoming the normal incompetence of firing caused by confrontational tension; the best pilots got so close that they could not miss. As we will see, professional hitmen use the same technique.

German aces had similar tactics. Hartmann had discovered a blind spot in the Russian anti-tank fighter-bombers, which he exploited by diving low and coming up underneath them with his superior speed; he preferred to get in very close, less than 100 yards, before firing a burst about 1.5 seconds long before his speed carried him past. Although the Soviet planes were armored and carried rear-gunners, this tactic aimed at the vulnerable oil radiator underneath. His method was always to wait "until the enemy aircraft filled the windscreen"—not shying away by taking a hasty shot at the first opportunity (www.acepilots.com/index.html#top; Toliver and Constable 1971; Sims 1972).

These were techniques that developed with time, not from sheer instinct or talent. Gerhard Barkhorn, the second-ranking ace with 301 kills, had no kills at all in his first 120 sorties, which included the Battle of Britain in September 1940. Hartmann, the record-holder, had only two kills in his first five months, but eventually sustained a peak rate of twenty-six kills per month.[34]

Winning techniques involved getting into the flow of very fast-moving situations. Most aerial battles were extremely short; some shorter than one minute, others lasting seven minutes, or fifteen. Exceptional circumstances might last as long as an hour, as when seven U.S. fighters followed a convoy of forty Japanese bomber escorts who took a passively defensive formation; the smaller pack of aggressive American planes harried them along the edges, picking off those who wavered or straggled outside their supporting formation; the American commander alone made nine kills, setting a new single engagement record (Gurney 1958: 77–78). Aces established their reputations in one-sided battles.

Nevertheless, it virtually never happened that all of the enemy's planes were destroyed in an air battle. Even in very one-sided victories, the losses of the defeated were limited. This happens because there are relatively few highly energized aggressors in the situation; a handful of pilots racking up their ace totals, battening on the mass availability of enemy planes; but the majority of pilots of the victorious side continued to have no kills. The defeated side might be psychologically beaten, unable to defend themselves and fleeing the scene of battle, but the concentration of attackers in a small violent elite allowed many of them to escape. This is another aspect of the situational law of small numbers in effective violence. Because of the incompetence of most violence, combat is survivable by many, or even a majority. This is what allows wars to go on; indeed, what sustains the practice of violence generally.

All indications are that aces' kills were chiefly the weaker pilots on the other side—less experienced, less skilled at maneuvering, above all lacking in emotional energy. Once again, we see the fighters with high emotional energy battening on the weak. This fits with the attitudes expressed by ace pilots prior to battle: they did not expect to be killed; there was none of the leaving of last-minute messages for loved ones, the earmarking of mementos to be sent home in case of death, although these rituals were common among ground forces before a major attack, and among bomber crews before a raid over a heavily defended target (Gurney 1958: 135–36). Top fighter pilots believed they would win in combat, and that they would die only as the result of accident. As we have seen, accidents are relatively frequent in military flying (and 9 percent of top aces died that way, sometimes after the end of war: calculated from Gurney 1958: 259–69); but this was a ritual dividing line between mundane and sacred/honorific forms of danger; amidst the latter, aces believed themselves surrounded by a magic halo that kept them safe and victorious. Top fighter pilots constructed a social enclave in which they were confidently empowered, although it had borders that they were usually careful to stay within.

In the Zone versus the Glaze of Combat: Micro-situational Techniques of Interactional Dominance

The second-by-second phenomenology of being in a violent confrontation is a distortion of normal consciousness. For some antagonists, the distortions of their stream of consciousness are favorable, enabling them to dominate; for other persons, the distortions are disabling. Common distortions are tunnel vision and time-slowing. One becomes hyperconcentrated, focusing intensely on the point of danger, defocusing everything else as irrelevant.

One of a pair of cops describes a barricaded hostage-taker coming out from cover:

> When he started toward us, it was almost like it was in slow motion, and everything went into a tight focus. . . . When he made his move, my whole body tensed up. I don't remember having any feeling from my chest down. Everything was focused forward to watch and react to my target. Talk about an adrenaline rush! Everything tightened up, and all my senses were directed forward at the man running at us with a gun. My vision was focused on his torso and the gun. I couldn't tell you what his left hand was doing. I have no idea. I was watching the gun. The gun was coming down in front of his chest area, and that's when I did my first shots.
>
> I didn't hear a thing, not one thing. Alan [his partner] fired one round when I shot my first pair, but I didn't hear him shoot. He shot two more rounds when I fired the second time, but I didn't hear any of those rounds, either. We stopped shooting when he [the suspect] hit the floor and slid into me. Then I was on my feet standing over the guy. I don't even remember pushing myself up. All I know is the next thing I knew I was standing on two feet looking down at the guy. I don't know how I got there, whether I pushed up with my hands, or whether I pulled my knees up underneath. I don't know, but once I was up, I was hearing things again, because I could hear brass [discarded shells] clinking on the tile floor. Time had also returned to normal by then, because it had slowed down during the shooting. That started as soon as he started toward us. Even though I knew he was running at us, it looked like he was moving in slow motion. Damnedest thing I ever saw. (Klinger 2004: 155)

Although a gun going off in an enclosed space can be painfully loud, it is very common for police to hear the sounds of their own gun as only a distant, muffled noise; often they do not hear the sounds of others' guns around them at all. This is tunnel vision in the auditory sense. Whether this heightened focus is good or bad for the combatant remains to be seen. It strengthens one's attention to the most relevant point, good in a situation that is not too complex and where the danger does not shift around. In some instances, though, this narrowed focus also means that one cop loses track of what the others are doing; in the following cases they get unconsciously entrained in each other's fire, resulting in over-firing or hitting the wrong target:

At the end of a car chase of an escaping bank robber, three cops approach:

Tony scrambled out of his car with his shotgun. In the second or two that it took him to get out and move within 10 feet of the suspect's door, the holdup man was out and moving slowly toward the rear fender. He held a Beretta along his thigh. "The guy was looking at someone I couldn't see [later determined to be another officer just out of Tony's sight] and the guy kept repeating in a demanding tone, "Just do it, just do it." Then he looked at me and started backing up toward his open door. He brought his gun up to his head. Again he said, "Just do it."

Tony was standing between six and nine feet from the suspect. "I wasn't thinking in terms of cover. I knew that we were here until some-one shoots. I repeatedly told the guy that it was over." Due to Tony's tunnel vision, he was not aware that Officer Greggor was to his left, pointing a shotgun at the man, and another officer was to the left of Greggor, pointing his handgun.

If the suspect heard Tony's order, he didn't show it. Witnesses later said that the suspect swung his Beretta toward Tony, but Tony only remembers the man's elbow dropping and his wrest bending. Tony fired.

"I saw the pellets hit, but on his right side," Tony says. "Since I was standing in front of him, I couldn't understand how my shot hit him in the side. I looked down and saw that the spent shell hadn't fully ejected, so I shook it out and pumped another round in."

Tony had not heard Greggor's shotgun explode or the other officer fire his handgun. "My tunnel vision made everything smaller," Tony says. "You could have been standing right next to me and I wouldn't have seen you." It was Greggor's shotgun pellets that struck the suspect in his right side. Tony's pellets center punched the suspect's abdomen, though Tony had only seen Greggor's hits.

Figure 10.5 Police shootout at close range (1997). AP/World Wide Photos.

After the shooting Tony has an overwhelming adrenaline rush. "I went to the car phone and punched in my home number. I got the recorder but I knew my boys were home, probably still sleeping. I screamed for someone to pick it up and I kept screaming until it awoke my boys downstairs. When they answered, I screamed at them what had just happened and that I wanted to see them." (Artwohl and Christensen 1997: 144–45)

In this case, the officer performs his part even though he has no sense of what his partners are doing or that they are even there. Luckily for them they are lined up in such a way that they cannot hit each other with cross-fire; tunnel vision of this sort is doubtless responsible for many friendly fire hits. In another case, the same combination results in a hostage being hit:

I charged up the stairs, Clancy and Thompson on my right. We moved down the narrow, dark hall, which was barely illuminated by the filtered light from a downstairs hallway, and into Jeremy's [the twelve-year-old hostage] room. We could make out North [the hostage-taker] seated on the edge of the bed, holding Jeremy between his legs in a one-arm choke hold. The boy was completely shielding North's body, and the way he was holding the knife at the boy's throat made it look as if the knife was sticking in his neck.

With his arm up and wrapped around the little boy's neck like a chicken wing, I had a perfect shot. I decided to do it. My eyes, already straining in the dim light, zoomed right in on his flannel shirt, like I was looking through binoculars. I double tapped twice [fired two rounds, paused, fired two more] into his chest. As bizarre as it sounds, I could actually see the rounds going in. I could see his shirt flap around and I could see the rounds going into his chest. Then when I pulled back, I could hear other shots going off. This confused me because I thought I was the only one firing. But my partners were also shooting, round after round.

When I looked at the bed, North was riddled with holes. But Jeremy was slumped over, too. (Artwohl and Christensen 1997: 105–6)

The hostage-taker was dead; the little boy died a few hours later in the hospital.

Most police in shootouts had diminished sound and tunnel vision—88 percent and 82 percent, respectively. Smaller proportions—65 percent and 63 percent, respectively—experienced heightened visual clarity and time slowing (Artwohl and Christensen 1997: 49). The latter phenomena are conducive to a higher level of competent performance. Shootings, in fact, tend to go very fast, a few seconds at most. Time seems to slow down when the shooter perceives a great deal of detail, seeing the scene with special sharpness. In real time, violent action is moving very fast; it appears slow because the perceiver is taking so much in. One's brain is not necessarily moving faster, but one establishes a clear gestalt of what is going on; everything is comprehended because it all falls into its place in the image. In one's subjective sensibilities, the situation has a clear form.

In the following instance, a cop is executing an arrest warrant on a man who had been selling sawed-off shotguns to an undercover officer:

As I stepped through the doorway and into the bedroom, my attention was drawn to some commotion in this bathroom that was to my left, but I caught some movement in my peripheral vision off to my right. As I shifted my attention that way, I saw this guy pulling a shotgun down off this wall rack and turning to his right, toward me. The bedroom was only about eight by nine feet—we're talking real small—so he was only maybe two yards from me. When I first saw him, the barrel of the shotgun was pointed up at about a forty-five-degree angle. As the guy completed his turn, he lowered the barrel and brought the stock up to his shoulder, so that the shotgun was pointed right at me.

As I was watching the shotgun come around on me, my mind went into this mode of incredibly clear thinking, just like it did in my first shooting. I know I could get shot. I knew it would probably hurt like crap because I was really close to it and it was a 12-gauge, but I wasn't scared. It was weird—just real clear, cold, calculating thinking. I knew that the possibility existed for me to get shot and die, and I knew I needed to protect myself from that, but I wasn't scared.

I was focused on the gun, and the first thing I saw on it was the adjustable choke mounted on the end of the barrel. I said to myself, *Look at that action.* So I followed the barrel down to the action, and that's when I saw that it was a Remington. I actually thought, *That's a Remington 1100.* Then I said to myself, *See where his finger is on the trigger.* So I went to his hand. I saw the finger on the trigger, and I thought, *This is going to hurt like hell, but you gotta keep going.* So I was thinking that I was going to shoot, but I was also thinking, *Sidestep the barrel and try to give yourself some more time.* So I started to sidestep as I brought my gun up. Then I thought, *Here we go again,* looked through the sights of my MP-5, and fired.

As I started to pull the trigger, I was thinking, *How do I need to shoot this guy?* It was really weird. I wanted to keep the rounds on center mass, and I'd trained to fire two-round bursts, but this guy had a friggin' shotgun at point-blank range on me. I was thinking, *Do I just need to hose him till he goes down, or do I need to give him two-shot burst, two-shot burst, two-shot burst?* I knew I couldn't control the MP-5 on full auto—especially trying to move sideways—and I was worried about misses because of the other officers on the scene. So all that was going through my mind as I started pulling the trigger, and I thought, *No auto. Two-shot bursts.* I ended up firing two two-shot bursts, and the guy went down in a heap onto a pile of clothes on the floor. He didn't get a shot off. . . .

Bill—the team leader—stepped in behind me. He looked at the kid and me. I told him, "I still got guys behind me!" because my back was now to the bathroom door, where I heard the people when I first stepped into the bedroom. I could still hear them moving around in there, and I thought, *God, do they have guns too?* Bill was standing there, looking at me, so I yelled at him, "Behind me, behind me!" Then he turned, went into the bathroom, stepped in there, and got the two people who were in there. (Klinger 2004: 164–65)

Unlike the other cases just quoted, this officer is completely aware of who else is on the scene, both his fellow officers whom he wants to protect from the possibility of full automatic fire getting out of control, and the suspects in the bathroom behind his back. He has a full gestalt of the scene, both in space and in time, as we see in the detail with which he focuses on his opponent's gun and his own firing procedure.

This kind of time-slowing, with the formation of a comprehensive gestalt of the scene, appears to be characteristic of the most competent members of the violent elite. It exists among professional hitmen (e.g., Fisher 2002: 61) and among armed robbers: "I felt detached when I went in . . . switched off . . . very cold," one said. Another: "During the robbery, I was calm. I had tunnel vision. I had heightened awareness of the surroundings and intense concentration" (Morrison and O'Donnell 1994: 68). Apparently ace fighter pilots are like this as well. The small number of highly competent combat firing soldiers also appear to have this quality.

Time-slowing has been reported most extensively in athletes at the peak of their performance. This too is an arena of fast-moving, antagonistic confrontation. Baseball hitters in the midst of a hitting streak say they can pick up the trajectory of the ball right out of the pitcher's hand, and watch the rotation of an incoming pitch; some say the ball looks bigger. Instead of reacting in a rush to what the pitcher is doing, they see it in a pattern, hold themselves back, and strike at the proper moment. The competent quarterback is the one for whom the action slows down in front of him and he sees the movements of pass receivers, defensive backs, and oncoming pass rushers as patterned gestalts that he recognizes and manipulates.[35]

Athletes refer to this state of mind at the peak of performance as being "in the zone." The violent elite are those who are in the zone in their own arenas of action. What it takes to get in the zone differs from one type of violence to another; the ace pilot operates within a fast-moving gestalt in multiple dimensions of space that resembles to some degree the actions of the football quarterback, but these do not appear to be transferable.[36] The police officer in a point-blank shoot-out has a different zone of high competence, the sniper yet a different one.

In contrast to being in the zone—the experience of the most competent military elite—most soldiers in combat are in an emotional and perceptual state nearer the other end of the spectrum. Clausewitz spoke of the fog of war; others have written about the "glaze of combat" (Glenn 2000a). Especially at the peak of violence, and when there is movement away from fixed positions, everything is confusing; people move in a blur; it is unclear where the enemy is, or where he is moving, or how many there are and which direction is the greatest threat at the moment. There is a morass of bits of information, but no clear perception; the average soldier cannot form it into a clear gestalt.

The glaze of combat is the experience of confrontational tension, raised to a high degree at the moment of actual violence. As we have seen throughout the book, most people are debilitated in one degree or another by confrontational tension; only a few under favorable social circumstances overcome it enough to perform active violence, and fewer still are truly competent. Some completely freeze up; others passively follow whatever activists are nearby; some become caught up in frenzied hot participation; a few perform coolly and effectively. Within the same group in a violent confrontation, people are partitioned into these various roles.

Winning out in a violent confrontation is not merely being in the zone; it is being in the zone in relation to others who are not in the zone. We may call it being cool in the midst of other people's hot emotions. These hot emotions include anger, but there are others: they could also be fear, excitement, and joyful ebullience. The center of the struggle is this interactional process. The violent elite are those who have perfected cool techniques for taking advantage of targets who are caught in the glaze of combat. But it is not always merely attacking the preexisting weak. The struggle in violent micro-interaction is to push one's opponent into the glaze of combat, while settling oneself into possession of the zone.

One way of doing this is manipulating victims' emotions. The violent elite practice techniques for getting the other person off guard. Armed robbers attempt to "get the jump" on the victim by striking at the moment they are just locking a door, or coming from light into dark or vice versa (see chapter 5). Assassins (political as well as professional) often strike when the victim has just come into a room;[37] this not only minimizes confrontation and the tension that arises from it, but also frames the situation psychologically as one in which the victim can form no gestalt of what is the scene and what is happening; he is caught up in the momentum established by the attacker. This is what the skilled baseball pitcher does, when he freezes the batter with an unanticipated strike.

A technique used in more complicated situations depends on being able to form a gestalt of who are the weakest and strongest targets on one's opponent's side, and using this to throw them into confusion. Some very top snipers used this technique when they had lost their cover and a large number of troops were advancing rapidly on the sniper's position. A German sniper on the Russian front would stand and shoot at the rear wave of the advancing troops, not at those in the front row. These were the most easily terrified soldiers, and when they were hit, their screams caused the others to abort the attack. In another instance, "[H]e waited until three or four attacking waves had begun to advance, then he started to put as many rounds as possible into the stomachs of the last wave. The startling cries of the wounded and the fact that the attack was being demoralised from the rear unnerved the front ranks. The attacks started to falter. That was the moment he started to take the front rank into his reticle [crosshairs]. Enemies nearer than 50 meters were hit with head or heart shots—men further back were shot in the trunk to create as many wounded as possible."[38] The tactic of this German sniper is remarkably similar to the most famous American war hero's performance in 1918, Sergeant Alvin York, who successfully sniped at a line of machine-gunners at 300 yards. He was spotted and charged by a squad of German infantry; York calmly shot all ten, starting with the one in the rear, reloading and killing the leader when he was only ten yards away (Pegler 2004: 145).

The attacking Germans were not able to shoot him while they were on the run; they were in a hot frenzy, compounded perhaps by fear and anger, made worse by the cool technique of their opponent who deliberately built up their emotional weakness.

Yet another manipulation in the heat of conflict consists in goading the opponent into a display of anger, and then using his frenzy against him. This is often done in insult contests among tough youth, where a weak fighter is goaded into attacking a strong and cool one; much the same technique was used by sword duelists good at evading charges and making counter-attacks. It is similar to the military tactic on the larger scale of luring a headlong attack, then hitting it from the flank with reserves held in hiding. Here the manipulation of opponent's emotions blends with staying cool in the midst of hot emotions, except that it has an added level of self-conscious technique. Football teams deliberately design plays for when their opponents are over-charged with adrenalin, in the expectation that a defense will over-pursue and become vulnerable to a deceptive play that cuts back in the other direction.

Conflict dominance is not just a matter of having practiced a technique so well that one has permanently learned it; it is not like riding a bicycle, which one never forgets even if out of practice. Every conflict is a struggle between who will be in the zone, and who will be in the glaze of combat. We can see this fluctuation, sometimes even within a few seconds. Even competent soldiers may fluctuate between moments of emotionally over-charged wild firing and calm competence. In one incident on Guadalcanal in 1942, as a Japanese attacker began to run away, the U.S. Marine sergeant "was nervous. He fired several shots, working his bolt fast and missed. He inserted another clip of cartridges and fired one of them. But then the Jap had sunk down into cover again. It was a little disappointing—but only for the moment. He started to get up again . . . when Sgt Angus, now quite calm, took careful aim and let one shot go. The Jap sank as if the ground had been jerked out from under him. It was a neat shot—about 200 yards" (2004: 217). Notice that of a small group, probably squad size, only one was shooting, the others watching their leader shoot. This is the usual stratification of emotional energy in combat. But the leader is first hot, active but incompetent; then he switches to cool and effective. The key appears to be the short break in the action, when the Japanese soldier withdraws into cover; this enables the sergeant to establish a new gestalt: probably, the enemy afraid and himself in command.

Performing coolly in the midst of opponents' glaze of combat is always relative to what is going on in the immediate situation. This accounts for why a team may be beaten badly in a championship game.[39] To get to the championship the team must have performed extremely well through the season; in other words, it had shown many times that it could perform in the zone while putting their opponents into a glaze. But this capacity to form a gestalt in which they control their confused opponents is brittle; it is a social construction that can rapidly shift.[40] A team that relies most strongly on its superiority in putting opponents at an emotional disadvantage (as compared to grinding out relatively narrow victories) may be especially vulnerable, when they lose their edge, to falling badly into the glaze themselves.

Sports are artificial social constructions in just the respect that they channel the most highly competent competitors into eventually matching up against each other. In real-life violence, such matchups are generally avoided. Even so, competence that depends on being in the zone while others are in the glaze of combat is an intrinsically relative thing. This is one of the reasons why there is a ceiling on how many persons at any one time can be in the violent elite.

We should not draw an absolute distinction between hot and cold techniques as far as their effectiveness in winning a confrontation. True, there is probably a correlation between cool techniques and highly competent violence—those best able to hit their targets, make their kill, win the fight or the game. Those who engage in hot violence are more likely to be the actively violent than the competently violent, the middle-ranking rather than the highest, the soldiers who fire often but don't hit anything, the noisy activists in a rioting crowd.

But it would not be the right formula to claim that victory always consists in cool violence prevailing over hot violence. There are two main complications. First, some fights and battles hinge on accidents: falling down, traffic jams of bodies or vehicles, lucky or unlucky hits, friendly fire; incompetent violence is often unpredictable when many small incidents are compounded and concatenated. And second, there are successful forms of hot violence. The most spectacular is a forward panic, which is a winning rush upon a suddenly defenseless enemy whose organization has crumbled. It may well be that most battles and large-scale fights are won by these sorts of conditions and not by coolly executed techniques. On a smaller scale, individual or very small group fights are sometimes won by whoever musters the most sheer physical energy; in simple situations without room to maneuver, the stronger and most energized by anger, enthusiasm, or desperation may overwhelm a cooler opponent.

We lack good information on how often fights take these various forms. I would hypothesize that the most frequent situation in which hot violence prevails is when the actively violent segment attacks the merely nominally violent; hot violence is dominant when it attacks not cool violence but the other end of the continuum, those who are deeply caught in confrontational tension/fear. Thus the ability to muster anger, bluster, ebullience, and frenzied exertion will dominate a matchup

Figure 10.6 Winning by emotional dominance: faces of basketball rebounders (2006). © McClatchy-Tribune Information Services. All Rights Reserved. Reprinted with permission.

against the emotionally weak, those who are rendered passive by their hot emotions, especially fear.

Some persons operate mainly in emotionally hot scenes, such as angry bar fights or gang turf street corner fights. Here, the fight is between two (or more) hot fighters; I conjecture that the winner is the relatively coolest, the one most able to slow down subjective time and formulate a gestalt of the entire situation. The key to winning may still be in knowing when to throw a punch or bull rush an opponent, rather than to maneuver for an opportunity or take careful aim. It is always an interactional playing field, whatever the particular emotions present. The victor pushes the loser into the glaze of combat. Sometimes the emotional dominants do not have to push their opponents far, since they are already deep in confrontational tension/fear; at others times both sides may start out in the zone and have to push the other one out of it—failure to do so would, of course, bring a stalemate, which is one way that fights stop. Victory consists in manipulating the glaze of combat to one's advantage. Winners don't have to be deeply in the zone, just more in the zone than losers.

THE 9/11 COCKPIT FIGHT

As an appendix, consider the fight that took place in the cockpit of United Airlines flight 93 on September 11, 2001. An audio recording gives the micro-sequence of sounds made by the four al-Qaeda hijackers, who intended to crash the jet into the Pentagon, and some of the thirty-three passengers who rushed the cockpit. Words in italics are spoken by the hijackers in English; words in bold italics are translated from Arabic. Other words are presumably the passengers' (text in *Philadelphia Inquirer*, April 13, 2006, p. A10).

9.58.50	SOUNDS OF GRUNTING AND SHOUTING (first attempt to break down the door)
9.58.55	In the cockpit.
9.58.57	In the cockpit.
9.58.57	***They want to get in here. Hold, hold from the inside. Hold from the inside. Hold.***
9.59.04	*Hold the door.*
9.59.09	*Stop him.*
9.59.11	*Sit down.*
9.59.13	*Sit down.*
9.59.15	*Sit down.*
9.59.17	***What?***
9.59.18	***There are some guys. All those guys.***
9.59.20	Let's get them.
9.59.25	*Sit down. . . .*
9.59.30	LOUD CRASH (sounds of metal against metal, glass breaking, plastic cracking. Passengers apparently use service cart to ram cockpit door. Second attempt.)

UNINTELLIGIBLE SHOUTING.

9.59.42	***Trust in Allah, and in him.***

9.59.45	*Sit down.*
10.00.06	*There is nothing.*
10.00.07	*Is that it? Shall we finish it off?*
10.00.08	*No. Not yet.*
10.00.09	*When they all come, we finish it off.*
10.00.11	*There is nothing.*
10.00.13	(unintelligible shouting)
10.00.14	*Ahh.*
10.00.15	*I'm injured.*
10.00.16	(unintelligible shouting)
10.00.21	*Ahh.*
10.00.22	**Oh Allah. Oh Allah. Oh Gracious.**
10.00.25	In the cockpit. If we don't, we die.
10.00.26	LOUD CRASH of metal, glass, and plastic rammed together hard (another assault with the service cart. Third attempt.)
10.00.29	*Up, down. Up, down.* (Hijacker pilot pushes steering yoke forward and back, in attempt to throw passengers to floor. Plane's stall alarm sounds briefly.)
10.00.29	In the cockpit.
10.00.33	The cockpit.
10.00.37	*Up, down. Saeed, up, down.*
10.00.42	Roll it. . . .
10.00.59	*Allah is the greatest. Allah is the greatest.*
10.01.01	(unintelligible)
10.01.08	*Is that it? I mean, shall we pull it down?*
10.01.09	*Yes, put it in, and pull it down.*
10.01.10	CACOPHONY OF NEW VOICES SHOUTING (unintelligible)
10.01.11	*Saeed.*
10.01.12	*. . . engine . . .*
10.01.13	(unintelligible)
10.01.16	*Cut off the oxygen.*
10.01.18	*Cut off the oxygen. Cut off the oxygen. Cut off the oxygen.*
10.00.41	*Up, down. Up, down.*
10.00.41	*What?*
10.00.42	*Up, down.*
10.01.59	*Shut them off.*
10.02.03	*Shut them off.*
10.02.14	Go.
10.02.14	Go.
10.02.15	Move.
10.02.16	Move.

10.02.17	Turn it up.
10.02.18	*Down, down.*
10.02.23	*Pull it down. Pull it down.*
10.02.25	*Down. Push, push, push, push, push.*
10.02.33	*Hey. Hey. Give it to me. Give it to me.*
10.02.35	*Give it to me. Give it to me. Give it to me.*
10.02.37	*Give it to me. Give it to me. Give it to me.*
10.02.40	(unintelligible)
10.03.02	*Allah is the greatest.*
10.03.03	*Allah is the greatest.*
10.03.04	*Allah is the greatest.*
10.03.06	*Allah is the greatest.*
10.03.06	*Allah is the greatest.*
10.03.07	No.
10.03.09	*Allah is the greatest. Allah is the greatest.*
10.03.09	*Allah is the greatest. Allah is the greatest.* **PLANE ROLLS BELLY UP, CRASHES.**

In the four minutes and twenty seconds from the first assault on the door until the plane crashes, there are many repetitive utterances. Confrontational tension and fear are palpable, especially on the side of the hijackers, no doubt because they are more clearly recorded. That is one source of the repetitiveness; but it is also a way of dealing with confrontational tension/fear.

The attacking passengers are hard to hear on the tape, but they repeat the phrase "the cockpit" five times, twice in a two-second interval as they mount their first attack. They chant it again three times in the eight seconds starting at 10.00.25 just before they mount their third and last effort to smash down the cockpit door: "In the cockpit. If we don't, we die." These are rhythmic repetitions, getting themselves together for the group effort. There are other exhortations—"Let's get them." "Roll it."—but even these tend to be repeated in pairs in a second or less: "Go." "Go." "Move." "Move."

The hijackers defending the cockpit make three kinds of utterances, also very repetitive. First, they tell the passengers, in English over the speaker system, to "Sit down." This continues the strategy that they had used thirty minutes earlier, upon taking over the plane, of calming the passengers by pretending to land them somewhere as hostages. But this strategic talk turns into an incantation: repeated every two seconds starting at 9.59.11; the last effort is at 9.59.45, even after the second attempt to break down the door, this time with a loud and apparently frightening crash of a metal cart, when it is clear that the strategy isn't working.

Second, the hijackers shout instructions to each other, mostly in Arabic—to hold the door, whether to "finish it off" (presumably by crashing the plane), to jolt the plane's tail up and down to throw the passengers on the floor, to cut off the oxygen. But these instructions are very repetitive too: "Up, down" is repeated eight times; "Cut off the oxygen" is repeated four times in two seconds. "Give it to me" is repeated eight times in four seconds. Practical discourse is becoming an emotional incantation, too.

Third, formulaic religious phrases. These start at tense moments, and become more repetitive as the crisis intensifies. "Trust in Allah, and in him" is uttered just after the second assault on the door (the frightening crash of the cart). "Oh Allah. Oh Allah. Oh Gracious" is heard just as the attackers rush the door for the third time. "Allah is the greatest" is repeated nine times, in different voices, in the last seven seconds before the final crash.

Conflict talk in general is highly repetitive. As we have seen in chapter 9, heated arguments consist not in trying to communicate with one's opponent but in trying to talk him down, ignoring turn-taking and not allowing the opponent the floor. Since at this point in the argument the content doesn't matter—no one is listening to what their opponent is saying—loud repetition is the best way to hold the floor. Verbal repetitiveness carries over in actual violence. It becomes an emotional technique, aimed not at the opponent but at building one's own energy and solidarity, an incantation of self-entrainment. In the 9/11 cockpit fight, both sides use this crude emotional technique: it is a struggle of opposing self-entrainments.

CHAPTER 11

Violence as Dominance in Emotional Attention Space

WE NOW REACH A PARADOX. If only a small number out of a nominally engaged fighting force do all the violence, why not get rid of the rest? Why not pare down the army, the gang, or other confrontational organization, to those who are actively violent, or better yet, the small minority who are competently violent? Why not have an air force consisting only of aces, or any army only of snipers and other elite troops? Such arrangements are virtually impossible, for structural reasons. Violence is not generated by isolated individuals but by an entire emotional attention space.

WHAT DOES THE REST OF THE CROWD DO?

The best way to approach this is to examine crowds during riots. Using visual evidence, we can see both the small numbers pattern of those who are violent, and the way they relate to the larger crowd.

My generalizations draw on news photo clippings collected between 1989 and 2005, along with published photo collections (Crespo 2002; Allen 2000), plus a smaller number of video recordings from television newscasts. In principle, video clips might seem preferable; but they are generally no longer than three to five seconds of continuous action. Hence there is relatively little difference between videos and still photos. Raw video footage is drastically edited by news directors to show the high points of the story. In reality, the minute-by-minute action of a demonstration is highly repetitive. When it turns into actual fighting—a riot—the action becomes very spread out, and most of what one sees during continuous observation is people standing around, some running across open spaces, plus usually more stationary or slowly moving formations of security forces. Moments of violence in a riot are scattered in time and space, punctuating scenes that are mostly boring for outside observers, although exciting, frightening, or frustrating for participants. Most people who are present are merely nominally violent. This surprisingly undramatic character of raw videos of riots becomes clear when one views actual footage of a riot and speaks with camera operators about their experience. [1] To make a sustained, continuously dramatic video of violent mass confrontation, one would need a large number of camera operators posted in different locations, and do considerable editing and cutting pieces together. The result would distort the reality of the riot precisely in privileging the violent moments and eliding the empty spaces and drawn-out times. Violence is stratified in time and space just as it is in participation; these features are part of the same social process.

These visual scenes fall into four categories: *standoffs*, when opposing groups confront each other but violence has not yet begun; *attacks; retreats;* and *victories*, when one side at least locally dominates the other. These types differ greatly in how densely the crowd is assembled. Standoffs are generally dense; it is virtually only these that give the expected picture of a mob, a large emotionally aroused group acting in concert.[2] It is because the group remains unviolent that it is able to keep up its high level of coordination.

When actual fighting breaks out, in attacks and retreats, the scene breaks up. Riots are quite a lot like S.L.A. Marshall's description of the empty battlefield, except that the opponents are visible, not hidden from sight. The difference in confrontational distance is because the weapons used are rocks and slingshots, sticks, as well as fists and feet, rather than guns, for the most part; tear gas and smoke canisters can create a very literal equivalent of the fog of war. The distances between the enemy forces are not hundreds of yards or more as in military combat, but a few feet out to a few dozen yards for the frontline activists; 50 to 150 yards for nominal participants and observers a safe distance behind; and a midgroup in between. The split between the violent few and the rest of the crowd is often clearly marked out in space, all the more so as the level of violence increases.

In a typical *attack* scene (see figure 11.1), we see three Palestinian boys, young teenagers, in a city street throwing rocks at Israeli soldiers while another one is picking up rocks, as two more boys run toward them from about twenty feet back. In the middle distance about fifty yards back, a clump of seven others hold their ground or move cautiously forward. Still farther up the street, at about 150 yards, another thirty watch at a safe distance, while two are visible running up the street away from the action. The visible activists are four out of forty-five, around 10 percent; at least two-thirds of the crowd keep maximal distance (June 5, 2003, Agence France-Presse photo).

In a photo of a soccer riot in Moscow (see figure 11.2), after the Russian team had lost to Japan in a televised match, we see a cluster of eight young men kicking at a car, while one jumps up and down on the roof; on the other side of the square are eighty spectators, most of them on the sidewalk against a building eighty yards away. Again the active attackers make up about 10 percent of the crowd (June 10, 2002, Associated Press).

Figure 11.1. Multiple layers of a riot: front line, near supporters, middle, back (Palestine, 2003). Musa Al-Shaer/Getty Images.

Another photo (not shown) shows a Palestinian young man in an open field hurling a smoking tear gas canister back at Israeli soldiers; he is surrounded by three others nearby, while fifteen onlookers are against a row of trees in the background, and three others retreat from the foreground (Dec. 28, 2003 Reuters photo). About one-fourth are momentarily in the front line, though only one person is currently active.

Shifting the scene to Northern Ireland, a cluster of seven Protestant mid-teenagers confront a British soldier; the one in front is throwing a rock, while the other six stand in two rows behind him, several with hands in pockets, or looking away from the action. It is a scene of desultory violence, and their faces look more bored than engrossed. In many of these scenes we see the same territorial markers; only the lone rock-thrower has stepped off the sidewalk into the street; the others are safely in the non-confrontational zone of the sidewalk, except for one youth who gingerly stands at the rear of the group, with one foot in the street, the other on the curb (Sept. 10, 2001, Peter Morrison/Associated Press photo, not shown here). Similarly, in a refugee camp in the Gaza Strip, we see one youth dragging a burning tire into the middle of the street; about twenty spectators are visible 150 yards down the street, while nearby on the sidewalk are four apparent supporters, one of whom is just stepping off the curb (Oct. 1, 2004, Adel Hana/AP photo, not shown here).

Figure 11.2. Ultra-activist, front cluster, plus background onlookers. Soccer riot in Russia (2002). AP/World Wide Photos.

Altogether about 20 percent of those visible are activists, although at the moment their activism consists in providing physical companionship to the one individual who is actually doing something.

We might question whether there is a methodological bias in these photos. Isn't it possible that most of violent activists are out of the picture frame, somewhere else in the crowd? But surely the news editors picked the most violent photos they could find. The look of real violence, unlike the contrived violence of movies, is disappointingly undramatic, precisely because it is so intermittent and spread out. Perhaps the stop-action, instantaneous nature of a still photo shows us only the particular individuals who are violent at that moment; maybe others are violent at other moments. This is undoubtedly so to a degree; but that degree is small. Longer video clips do not show any great alternation of personnel stepping up regularly to take each other's places in the front of the action. There are also identity markers in the heat of the action that correlate with how violent an individual's participation is. I have already noted the significance of stepping into the street versus staying on the sidewalk.[3]

Another marker, which has become common in demonstrations in Europe and America since around 2000, is wearing bandanas, headscarves, hoods, ski masks, balaclavas, or other masks to cover the head or face. In an Associated Press photo (July 21, 2001; not shown here) of a demonstration against a world economic summit in Genoa, Italy, we see two young men in the middle of the street throwing rocks; behind them, near

Figure 11.3. Single demonstrator confronts police line while crowd remains unfocused (Genoa, July 2001). AP/World Wide Photos.

a row of burning trash bins, are three more who are crouching, perhaps briefly breaking the action. Back on the sidewalk ten yards away, thirty people are visible, filling the space against the building. (No doubt there are more outside the picture frame.) All five activists in the foreground are masked; few of those in the background are masked. Figure 11.3 shows the same demonstration (July 21, 2001, Associated Press) while still in the standoff phase. A phalanx of police in helmets and plastic shields confront a crowd, of whom 150 are visible in the photo frame, standing about ten rows deep on a sidewalk backed up to the wall. Most of the crowd are turned sideways or away from the police line; only three young men in the front row are directly staring at the police. One of them has stepped forward into the open space of about ten feet and gestures with his middle finger toward the police. A notable detail: although most of the crowd are wearing helmets (motorcycle or construction type), the lone taunter is the only one wearing a gas mask as well (clear plastic visor with a canister breathing filter); although one of his hands, resting on his hip, is bare, the hand with which he makes the traditional gesture is wearing a shiny metallic glove. Even in a standoff, there is a division between a small number of confrontational activists, and the mass of the crowd; we see this in their position in space, their postures, and their symbolic accoutrements.[4]

In a photo (May 2, 1992, Associated Press) of a demonstration in Berlin, one young man is in the act of throwing a stone; he is in full combat gear, wearing hood and face mask. A few yards back, another man wears a bandana mask and appears to be stepping forward toward the action.

Still farther back, two men in hoods have their bandanas on but pulled down from their faces, as if not currently in mask-action. Two more wear hoods only, and at the moment are mere onlookers, as are another six heads visible in the crowd. The thirteen persons in the picture divide into the different layers of the riot participation, from the one currently violent activist out of the total thirteen down through the varying degrees of symbolic aggression expressed by their accoutrements. They are an expression in demeanor (in Goffman's precise sense) of the layers of the crowd found in the spatial zones as in figure 11.1.[5]

Closeup photos manifestly show only a small segment of a larger scene. Presumably they have been chosen, by photographers and editors, to illustrate the peak of the action. But even here this peak of action often consists of just one individual being violent in the midst of others who are not. Some of these show an individual sling-thrower winding up; an individual rioter breaking a store window; occasionally we get a picture of a protestor with yards of space around him, heaving a rock at police lines, while a couple of figures are spread out haphazardly behind him. (Again in this instance, we see the rock-thrower alone in the street beyond the curb, the others on the sidewalk. [*London Daily Mail*, May 2, 2001, p. 7, not shown here]). In a labor clash in Spain, we see one man in balaclava and face-mask firing a slingshot, while in the background another seven stand in casual poses, leaning on railings or standing around ten to twenty yards away (Sept. 22, 2004, Ramon Espinosa/Associated Press, not shown here).

At most, we see little groups of the actively violent: two young Palestinians climbing twenty feet up a wall to protest an Israeli barrier in the West Bank, the foreground area of perhaps 800 square yards is empty except for a single youth waving a flag (Dec. 28, 2003, Agence Presse-France photo, not shown here). We get a closeup of four Palestinians releasing their slingshots in unison. (*The [London] Times*, Oct. 14, 2000, p. 6, not shown here). It is very rare to get a photo where everyone visible is violent at the same time, or even a majority. Five Palestinians crouch on the parapet of a wall, three actively throwing rocks or holding them in readiness, another two resting (Oct. 7, 2000; Reuters photo, not shown here). In a Reuters photo (Oct. 29, 2002, not shown here) depicting Israeli settlers throwing stones at Palestinian homes, in fact only one of thirteen persons visible is actually throwing a stone. What are the others doing there? I suggest they are setting an atmosphere and providing support; their pretense of violence—simply being there in the front line of the confrontation zone—is emotionally necessary so that some can be the few who are violent.

In Shanghai, three young Chinese men are throwing rocks at the Japanese consulate, while eleven others are visible three rows deep in the background (April 17, 2005, China Photos/Getty Images, not shown). Here

Figure 11.4 (*four-photo sequence*) Lone demonstrator, energized by small group of supporters, runs forward to taunt police and is shot (Gothenburg, Sweden, 2001).

we can see the facial expressions; the rock-throwers' faces look tense, teeth or lips clenched in the moment of muscular effort; two others in the backup group have their mouths open in yells of encouragement; but several of the others look down or away from the action.[6] What is displayed is the tension of confrontation on the part of the actively violent; others supply their presence as a nearby mass of bodies in solidarity with them, along with a noisy atmosphere and emotional focus.

In the following we see that a cheering cluster of activists energizes a lone individual to go forward into extremely dangerous provocation. A sequence of photos (figures 11.4A, B, C, D) shows a demonstrator being shot by police at the European Union summit in Gothenburg, Sweden (news reports in *The Independent*, June 17, 2001, p. 1; *Sunday Telegraph*, June 17, 2001, p. 3; ITN photos). Wearing a hooded jacket and waving a wooden club, he approaches within about twenty yards of a group of six helmeted police who have been separated from the main force. The taunter sees a policeman take aim with a gun, then turns and runs. The sequence of photos shows mostly empty pavement; just the few police on a broad avenue, and a sole supporting demonstrator nearby as the taunter is hit and falls to the pavement, perhaps forty yards away from the police. There had been a large, peaceful march of many thousands in a festival atmosphere. Later in the day, techno music from a van was suddenly turned up to a deafening level. Police pushed a group of a hundred or so demonstrators into a park; a smaller group in masks appeared from a side street and cut off a small group of police, pelting them with cobblestones and downing one cop with a hit to the head. According to the camera-man's report, the demonstrators in balaclavas cheered, then screamed when the police opened fire with eight shots at the lone taunter who dared to approach within twenty yards of the police. The episode resembles the filmed tribal warfare described in chapter 2, consisting more in taunting and episodic hits than in sustained fighting, with the most active few rush-ing briefly toward enemy lines, then running away. But here we see a telling additional detail: an intermediate-size cluster near the front line, whose cheering gives emotional support to the few who take the confron-tation still closer to the enemy.

Retreats show much the same division between the small number of activists and the rest of the crowd. When a crowd runs away, in the face of police tear gas, concussion grenades, shooting, baton charge, or just plain forward-moving threat, photos typically show a part of the crowd that is not panicked because they are already at a safe distance of 150 yards or more, or off on a sidewalk backed up against the buildings. In the middle distance, there is a rush with backs turned; generally there are a few defiant ones, retreating but facing the oncoming forces. Sometimes three or four out of a hundred stop at fifty yards or so to turn and throw rocks at the attackers (as we see in figure 11.5). In places where such emblems of militancy are worn, we see hoods and masks on the defiant few at the tail of the retreat. They are the boldest and most belligerent. This is not to say they are unceasingly brave; we see this in the photo sequence (figure 11.4) of the Swedish demonstrator who shifts from taunt-ing to a terrified expression as he tries to flee a gun aimed at him.

Next, a few words on *victories*. Fighting usually disassembles a crowd; a victory tends to reunite it. Just how large a number reunite varies nearly inversely with how close their victory celebration is to the fighting itself. On the borderline of a victory gathering is a forward panic type of attack; we have seen photos of these in chapter 3, where a group of attackers has gotten the upper hand, having isolated or knocked down a single victim. As in the Rodney King beating tape, most of the beating may be carried

Figure 11.5 Crowd of protesters run from police; three rock-throwers remain forward (Jerusalem, 2002). AP/World Wide Photos.

out by perhaps 20 percent of the group, while the others provide emotional and vocal support.[7] The lion's share of the emotional energy goes to those at the forefront of the attack; an anthropologist witness to an African street mob attacking a market thief notes that the bulk of the crowd waits their turn to come up and give a not particularly enthusiastic kick to the fallen body (Igor Kopytof, personal communication, Feb. 2002). But the rest of the crowd does at least pull together, sharing solidarity in the sheer massing of bodies—just what is absent in the moments of attacks and retreats when the issue is not yet settled.

The mutually supportive relation between violence leaders and the crowd is illustrated in photos from the Palestinian *intifada*, with its ongoing round of reciprocal killings and atrocities. Four Israeli soldiers called to duty with their unit in Ramallah unknowingly drove into the aftermath of a funeral procession for a seventeen-year-old boy killed by Israeli soldiers (*The [London] Times*, Oct. 13, 2000, photos AFP). Young men in the procession had been shouting *Allah-u-akbar* (God is great), tearing their shirts, and cursing the Israelis as killers of children; older men joined in religious chants. When the soldiers' car was spotted, it was set afire with petrol bombs. Palestinian police rescued them and took them to a police station; a lynch mob of several hundred swarmed the walls and broke through barricades, injuring a dozen policemen. A photo (figure 11.6) taken minutes later, shows a young man leaning out the second-floor window of the station, his mouth open in an exultant yell, holding up his bloodied palms for the crowd to see. The blood-stained hands of two other men are also thrust into view in the window. In the crowd below, the picture silhouettes seven men, part of a larger throng, almost all turned toward the window with arms extended to clap or with clenched fists. Moments later bodies of two dead Israelis are thrown from the window. A second photo (not shown) shows a densely packed crowd of fifty men, the inner circle kicking at the body; a man two rows back brandishes a knife pointed at where the body lays. Most are jostling forward to attack the body, or at least get a close look at it; three men, however, have turned their backs and are leaving the center of the circle—apparently they have seen or kicked enough. Their jaws are set grimly, differing from the eager or angry expressions on the visible faces of men who have not yet reached the center of the circle. There is one woman in the picture; she pulls her shawl over her head and turns away from the body—apparently she had come to look, perhaps as a relative of some prior victim. This is a case in which the emotional connections among the larger group and its sub-segments—the funeral marchers, the attackers of the car and police station, the lynchers who complete the murders—are acted out very clearly. The violent few show off their killing, and receive acclaim for it; they go on to send down the bodies as further ways of establishing a physical connection with the next-most ring of participants. The bloody hands and victims' bodies are like symbolic tokens, establishing connection among the different layers of the mob.

Some victories take the form of a violent celebration ritual, attacking the body of a dead enemy. We see this in a video of the battle in Mogadishu, Somalia, in 1992 between American forces taking part in a U.N. rescue mission and supporters of a local warlord; an American helicopter has been shot down, one of the pilots is dead and his body is stripped and dragged through the streets while several members of a crowd of people—most young men and boys—kick at it (KR Video 1997). In Fallujah, Iraq, four Americans in a private security firm were ambushed by Iraqi insurgents and burned to death when the crowd set their vehicles on fire (April 1, 2004 A.P. photos, not shown). Another photo (figure 11.7) shows the charred bodies hoisted on ropes and hung from the girders of a bridge over the Euphrates River. Of twelve men visible in the photo foreground, six wave their arms in the air exultingly. Another climbs a bridge girder with his shoe in hand to strike the dead body, a gesture of extreme insult in Arab culture. Earlier, a ten-year-old boy was seen grinding his heel into a burned head. In both these instances, there is widespread participation, a higher level than in actual fighting. There are also a few whom we may

Figure 11.6 Ritual solidarity gestures between violent front line and supporters. Palestinian youth displays blood on his hands after lynching of Israeli soldiers (October 2000).

Figure 11.7 Ritual desecration of enemy in victory celebration. Charred corpses of American civilians hung from a bridge in Fallujah, Iraq (April 2004). AP/World Wide Photos.

call demonstrative extremists, who go beyond others in symbolic violence over a fallen enemy.

Probably a more common form of victory celebration at the end of a violent clash are attacks on non-human targets. After the fall of the Serbian nationalist leader Milošević, the group of activists who invaded the parliament building threw computers from the windows onto the square, to the cheers of some of the crowd below. A photo (not shown) depicts the state TV building, the chief symbol of Milošević's power, burning. The news report says that the crowd is stoning the building. What we actually see are three men within twenty to thirty yards of the building, two of them throwing rocks at the broken windows while flames billow up. The panorama of the picture is perhaps one hundred yards long, an expanse almost empty of people. Another hundred yards off to the side, we see two bystanders, looking in other directions while going about their business ([London] *Daily Mail*, Oct. 6, 2000, p. 3; also *The Guardian*, Oct. 6, 2000, pp. 1–5; *Daily Telegraph*, Oct. 6, 2000, pp. 1–3). Out of the 400,000 demonstrators in downtown Belgrade that day, it appears that only a tiny number took part in the symbolic destruction.

Are the demonstrative extremists the same as the violent few, the most active fighters, the ones who actually carry out the killing and beating at the peak of confrontation? Data is lacking, since we can rarely track individuals from the moment of the fight to the expressive actions that take place afterward. But there are some clues to suggest that they are not the same. Demonstrative extremists—the ones who kick the dead bodies, hit them with a shoe, and so forth—are often much younger than the fighters; these actions seem most commonly carried out by children. It may well be that demonstrative extremists are not at all competent fighters, but emerge from the crowd after the violence is safely over. Nor is it useful to regard them as expressing the emotions of the crowd (much less as expressive leaders). It is dangerous to assume that we know what are the "real" feelings of the crowd, apart from what is expressed by particular persons; it is misleading to fall into the rhetoric that the crowd has an emotion (such as righteous anger, vengeance, etc.) that they express in action. But in fact, as I have tried to show throughout, violent confrontations generate their own situational emotions, above all tension and fear; and we see this on the faces and in the body language of most of the crowd during these events. The demonstrative extremists are not expressing an emotion that we can safely infer, on the basis of the evidence, as generally existing in the crowd; they are another specialized minority (different as well from the minority of violent activists) who have found their own emotional niche in the context of the crowd. And in fact the bulk of the crowd does not usually follow them, even when it is safe to do so because there is no opponent present but only a dead body or a captured building; the demonstrative extremists are usually separate from the rest of the crowd.

Some evidence bearing on this point comes from photos of lynchings in the American South and West in the period 1870–1935 (Allen 2000). Most of these photos—and the ones that are most revealing on this point—were taken several hours in the aftermath of the actual violence, or the following day. Individuals offering acts of gratuitous insult to dead bodies are safely disconnected from the actual commission of the violence. In a photo (Allen 2000: plate 93, not shown here) we see two white men standing beside the body of a black man hung from a tree, one poking the body with a stick, the other punching it. In the background are four other white men looking on. In another photo (Allen 2000: plate 25, not shown) a young man leans nonchalantly with his eyes closed against the post from which the charred body of a black man, lynched the previous night, is hanging; the nineteen other faces visible in the crowd are somber. This is the usual pattern in all the photos: a few are the demonstrative extremists; most of the others are somber, serious, awed, or uncomfortable in the presence of death.

Our first reaction may well be to interpret the gestures of the demonstrative extremists as expressions of the racism shared by the crowd (or the entire society). But this would be to ignore what we actually see: a small number of individuals (I have selected the worst instances available in the photo collection) stand out from the crowd in their actions and bodily expressions.[8]

But the mood of demonstrative extremists in the aftermath contrasts with the emotions that are displayed during the actual lynching itself. In a rare set of photos, we see a lynching while it is going on: a black man showing the welts of whipping on his back stands in a wagon shortly before he is hung; his executioners stare at his face with hard, hostile stares (Allen 2000: plates 42 and 43; not shown here). There is no clowning, no expression of joy; these are the frontline activist few, engaged in an angry, domineering stare-down. A violent confrontation itself is tense; even when one side has the upper hand (the usual formula for successful violence) it is compelling, focused into the business at hand, unable to ironicize it.

Thus the demonstrative extremists, operating safely in the aftermath, show something else: an attempt to raise themselves from the bulk of the crowd, the back line of merely nominal supporters of the violence, and to raise their status by closer connection with the violent action that had galvanized the attention of the group. By putting themselves close to the dead body, engaging in gratuitous acts of insult upon it, they put themselves closer to the center of the attention space.[9] The most blatant expression of joy among Allen's (2000) lynching photos is in plate 97 (not shown), which shows two well-dressed young men grinning (rather mirthlessly) at the camera while viewing a black body being burned. This was not in the heat of the action, however, but in the aftermath; the victim, accused of molesting a white girl, had already been hung from a lamppost and riddled with bullets. These cheery demonstrative extremists are probably proud of themselves for standing so close to the workman in grimy overalls who is tending the fire; everyone else in the photo is farther away, and the twenty-nine other visible faces range from somber to apprehensive. Demonstrative extremists are showing off, according to the mores of the violent attention space, claiming a higher level of stratification although they cannot rank with the violent perpetrators themselves.

Finally, let us return to the standoff photos. Here the crowd is densely packed; exhibiting their strength and resolve in numbers (as Tilly 2003 emphasizes), they are also supporting each other emotionally. But even in these photos, there is usually some differentiation visible in gestures and expressions. The front line of demonstrators, pressed against police lines—in Cairo, Ayodhya (India), Madrid, Kiev—lean over a barricade, reach their arms out in thrusting gestures, or hold their hands in the air; it is the faces in the front that include the few most likely to be shouting, taunting, or engaged in stare-downs with their opponents (March 3, 2002 Agence-France Presse; Oct. 31, 1990, Associated Press; March 10, 2001,

European Pressphoto Agency). Often visible off to the side of the barricade where it comes up against a building, there is the familiar crowd of bystanders on a sidewalk or raised sill, backs against the wall, observing silently with mouths closed and without gestures. In a photo (not shown) taken in Kiev as rioters attempt to force out the Ukrainian president, out of a visible crowd segment of thirty faces, there is just one highly expressive person, gritting his teeth and wielding a stick in the front row as he tries to reach across to the security forces, whose own sticks are raised threateningly in the air (*Daily Telegraph*, March 10, 2001, p. 20). Eventually the crowd (totaling 5,000) and police clashed with sticks and truncheons; at the photo moment, however, we see a tiny proportion pushing for a confrontation that is yet to come.

A few confrontations remain relatively well organized even in the fighting phase. These are chiefly in South Korea. A photo example (not shown) depicts a line of Korean protestors, wearing gas masks and armed with long staves, striking out at a police line of shields; both sides are phalanx-like (Nov. 14, 2004 Ahn Young-Joon/Associated Press). Ten staves are visible, all roughly at the same angle; it is not clear how many demonstrators actually make it to the front lines, as their ranks appear to be only one or two deep, and the preceding rally was attended by 20,000. Such battles may well be ceremonial, following established formulas that limit how much harm actually is inflicted.[10]

More usually, standoffs are differentiated, with a few demonstrative extremists in the front line, while the rest are fairly restrained. The tiny number of individuals acting on their own in taunting the enemy, become energized by acquiring self-confidence in the midst of a crowd; but they are not the crowd's leaders, and generally much of the time they are regarded with amusement, scorn, or distaste by the rest of the crowd, who think of them as "crazies" or (in the British term) "nutters." When they go into action alone, contrasting in demeanor and behavior with those around them, they fail to bring the rest of the crowd along with them. What they lack is a small cluster of supporters who mediate between them and the crowd; it is this mediating group that sets off a ripple of joining in an attack.

An occasional photo enables us to analyze the moment at which a crowd goes onto the offensive. In an anti-government demonstration in Ankara, Turkey (April 12, 2001, EPA photo), we see 230 men in the photo frame (out of some 70,000 who had marched earlier in the day) (see figures 11.8). In the foreground is a cluster of eight men, a little separated from the rest of the crowd. Two are throwing sticks, expressions of muscular effort on their lower faces and jaws. Flanking the two stick-throwers to left and right, and in the row just behind them, are six other men, all staring intently in the same direction, their brows drawn together and

Figure 11.8 Violent cluster in demonstration. Two men throw missiles while immediate companions provide emotional focus (Ankara, Turkey, 2001).

wrinkled over the nose in the facial cues of anger (Ekman and Friesen 1975: 95–97); several have teeth clenched, the others have their mouths open in an apparent shout. The militant cluster contrasts with the rest of the crowd; a large proportion of the others are looking in other directions, some turned away entirely from the front; only six others (out of 200 visible) have their mouths opened and appear to be yelling.[11]

The militant cluster may well be those who started the violent part of the confrontation, at least in that vicinity. Only 1 percent of those visible are doing anything violent; with their supporters, they make up about 5 percent of the visible segment—who are also approximately those who are visible to each other in the attention space comprising that part of the crowd. The outburst is generated in three layers, rather than a two-layer transmission between the initiators of violence and the bulk of the crowd. The crowd's confrontational emotion does not simply well up into violence by the foremost activists. The key emotional surge comes first through their immediate clique of supporters; as if their job is to act as an emotional intensifier, ramping up the expression of anger and willful effort in a wave of sound that will propel the bodies of those throwing missiles from the midst of their cluster.[12]

Like most individual confrontations, it is likely that most crowds that threaten violence do not actually carry it out. Our research is largely confined to sampling on the dependent variable. Occasionally we have an ethnographic account of a riot that aborts. A sociologist doing development research in highland Peru in 2005 describes such an instance (Rae Lesser Blumberg, personal communication, July 2005). A group of protestors march around the town plaza, shouting angry slogans against a judge who ruled against them in a land dispute. The procession is headed by two men carrying a coffin marked with a death's head and the judge's name. Behind them are several dozen men and women, some carrying signs. The men with the coffin try to lead the procession up the steps into the government offices. But a woman wants to continue around the square. The procession splits; the coffin-carriers lose initiative, their emotional energy. A micro-detail that hampers the would-be violence leaders is that they have their hands on an empty coffin, so that they cannot actually start the attack themselves without putting the coffin down; their symbolic action doesn't easily allow room for violent action. Furthermore the crowd's chanting is raggedy, lacking strong rhythmic coordination; strong ritual solidarity is not being generated. Within a couple of hours, the demonstration has dissipated.

This fits the finding of table 6.1 (in chapter 6) that the attitude of the audience toward an incipient fight determines the severity of the fight and whether it will abort. The exception, documented in table 6.2, is that if the group that wanted to fight was larger than five or more, it could ignore an ambivalent crowd; in effect, groups of this size provide their own audience support. Hence the importance of militant clusters of moderate size; it is when these clusters are formed within a larger crowd, that the ambivalence of the crowd and its normal antipathy to actual violence is overcome. The crowd splits up, and the small groups go into action. This is the dispersion in space that we see in the attack photos, and in the little clusters of four or five activists who seek down an ever smaller fragment of the enemy to pile on with unequal numbers (as we have seen in the photos in chapter 3).

In sum, what does the rest of the crowd do that the violent few need for their action? Every segment or layer of the crowd contributes something. The most *actively and competently violent* get their immediate emotional support from a little cluster around them. Some of the *support cluster* are also violent, but it appears that they spend much, or perhaps all, of their time making noise and providing emotional support. They are emotion providers for the apex of the violent few who go into action against the enemy; this is so even in the cases of standoffs where the action is so far merely provocative gestures. Then comes the *middle mass of the crowd*, like-minded as to goals, somewhat less emotionally energized, less confident, unable to take the initiative. This nominally violent majority gives a sense to the leading edge that others will back them up, give a weight of numbers that will help overawe the enemy once the momentum is flowing. Finally, even the *back rows*—those who watch from a safe distance, hugging the sidewalks—provide something.[13] It is perhaps just on the level of the buzz that one gets from being in a crowd on a big city street, or an unfocused stream of concert-goers or sports spectators on their way to the upcoming event. Even the most cowardly and non-committal part of a crowd provides something: the attention space. Though all they do is look, they look all in the same direction, with wavering interest as it may be; when something exciting happens, their eyes are riveted on the event.[14] Bringing up the rear are individual *demonstrative extremists*, who usually appear after the violence is over; it is unclear what segment of the crowd they emerged from before then.

Sometimes the support of the crowd for the militant few is explicit and conscious. In a demonstration by death penalty protesters, when some of the group were about to commit civil disobedience and be arrested—the nonviolent equivalent of the activist violent few—the other demonstrators intensified their emotional support. "People in crowd whispered to each other: 'Yell and you'll help keep them focused.' And the crowd got louder [as protesters were arrested]" (Summers-Effler 2004).

The apex of the event is the actions of the violent few. The basis of their emotional energy—their confidence, enthusiasm, initiative, their non-passivity—is the successive layers of helpers, co-participants, and spectators around them. The layers of the crowd are like a giant cone, quasi-visible in their arrangement in space, and almost literally making up a giant sound chamber that intensifies noise toward the center; these layers of human attention shape the energy that makes possible the confrontation at its focal point.[15] The crowd in the standoff phase provides the tension buildup. If circumstances (usually some sign of weakness on the opposing side) release this into action, it is now small clusters who are energized into violence. These violent few could not be launched without the prior concentration of emotional attention by the crowd.

Violence without Audiences: Professional Killers and Clandestine Violence

Since I have argued that violence is energized by appropriating the center of attention in an emotionally aroused group, I must deal with the apparent exception: highly competent solitary violence, without audiences. The best evidence comes from professional contract killers.[16]

The most typical technique is a clandestine quick-hit. The killer waits in his car for the victim to arrive at some habitual spot, preferably on a dark street without passersby; he then rapidly approaches and shoots as soon as the victim is getting in or out of his car. Or the victim is lured to a meeting place, and is shot as soon as he enters the door. Or he answers the front door and is immediately shot. Professional killers prefer to get the victim isolated, and also prefer to work alone. This is a way to minimize witnesses and reduce chances that information will get to the police either from bystanders or from accomplices who might become snitches. More importantly, it is a way of keeping every procedure in the hitman's own hands. This enables him to be absorbed in his own techniques and emotional manipulations, avoiding side-entanglements that might diminish the cool self-absorption that is the key to his success.

These kinds of hits require considerable planning. The hitman must be given information about the victim's routines, or he acquires it himself by tailing and staking-out; often he takes pains to corroborate information from his employers. He may spend days in choosing possible sites, working out the details, and testing his equipment. There is often a long period of clandestine activity, what the law and the media refer to as cold-blooded calculation. It is precisely the technical details that allow the emotional detachment; the hitman is absorbed in a series of small tasks that he carries out in scrupulous detail. His mind is not on the victim as a human being, nor on the emotional aspects of the coming confrontation. Some hitmen prefer not to know what the victim allegedly did, what was the offense or reason for the hit; it is purely a technical matter, not involving their own emotional relationships.[17]

Some executions are less well planned, generally because the victim is wary or hard to find. Professionally networked criminals who know there is a contract out may find a sudden opportunity when they are notified that the victim is in a particular place, such as a restaurant, or that his car has been sighted outside a gambling spot. But the actual technique is usually the same, waiting for him to come out alone, getting very close to him unseen, and firing immediately when in range. If the victim cannot be isolated, a different tactic may be used. With information as to where the victim is seated in a restaurant, the hitman enters, approaches suddenly, and fires immediately; or he may make his way to the bathroom (if it is to the rear of the target) and upon returning shoot him in the back of the head. One hitman commented that although he would normally use a silencer, so the shot made an innocuous "pfftt," for a hit in a restaurant full of people he would use a large, loud pistol. The explosion would send these potential witnesses diving for cover; it would also create confusion in which it was easy to escape (Fisher 2002: 57). He also played on the psychological pattern that having many witnesses would result in a wide variety of descriptions, making him impossible to identify.

Professional killers, as if aware of the difficulties of firing accurately, prefer to operate at extreme close range, often three feet or less. This closeness makes for a severe challenge to overcome confrontational tension; which is one reason why professional killers prefer to fire into the back of the head when possible. Even more importantly, the suddenness of the attack minimizes any interactional entrainment. The killer suddenly confronts the victim; there is no opportunity to speak or even to exchange expressions. The quick-hit is not only a way of getting the jump on the victim, making him momentarily incapable to resisting; it is also a way of avoiding the micro-interactional problems the hitman might have with his own emotions.[18] In sum, both the clandestine phase of preparation, and the suddenness of the attack, serve to overcome confrontational tension/fear.

Some professional contract killings, nevertheless, do involve prolonged confrontations with the victim. The victim may be forced into a car and driven to a remote location to be killed; or lured to a supposed meeting, surrounded by a carload of companions who turn out to be his executioners. How do killers overcome confrontational tension in these cases? Their chief technique appears to be to try to keep the victim calm, to lull him into believing he may not be killed. This subterfuge is not just a way of keeping the victim under control; it is also a way of keeping the killer calm, upholding the pretense for himself as well that he is not about to kill someone. The pretense that there is no violence in the offing is a Goffmanian frontstage, but one that is emotionally contrived for the sake of the performer as well as the victim. When the killing finally happens, it is abrupt, following as much as possible the pattern of clandestine normalcy suddenly broken by a brief episode of violence.[19]

A second factor comes into play here; in most instances of prolonged confrontation where interactional detail is available, we find a group of abductors surrounding a single victim. The killers get group support, thus departing from the problem of solitary violence that I have been concerned with here. This is even more clearly the case in the rare instances where contract killers torture a victim before killing him; this is usually done in order to send a message, express revenge, or terrify an opposing group. Torturing builds confrontational tension to its height, whereas his usual techniques minimize it in a tiny window in time. It appears that torture is virtually always carried out by groups, and the group emotional dynamic is at the center of the process.[20]

The techniques of being a successful hitman are psychological and interactional. Hence, professional killers are often of medium size or even smaller, and not necessarily very strong.[21] This is not simply because they always use guns; all of them began as dominant fighters. Such fights took place among youthful compatriots, in protecting one's turf in criminal businesses, or in prison; all the hitmen in my sources were proud of their reputations for never backing away from a fight, and doing whatever necessary to win. Some started by building a repertoire of dirty fighting tactics; or by psychological tricks such as smiling and acting deceptively passive until launching a sudden assault (Mujstain and Capeci 1993). "Joey," who started his underworld career as a fifteen-year-old numbers runner on a street corner in New York City, responded to three bigger youths who demanded a percentage of his take, by going into a nearby store, getting a baseball bat, and, without saying a word, launching a sudden attack that broke many bones (Fisher 2002: 11). "Mad Dog Sullivan" perfected the technique of digging a thumb into the corner of an opponent's eye socket and popping out his eye (Hoffman and Headley 1992: 276). In the normal rounds of hand fighting among a community of tough guys, these individuals developed psychological techniques and interactional tactics that put everyone else on the defensive. They became specialists in taking the violent initiative, and with such suddenness, determination, and ruthlessness that others gave way to them.

Hitmen make themselves experts in emotion management, both their own and others'. There are two aspects of this, short-run and medium-run. In micro-situational confrontation, the hitman is cool in execution. He is acutely aware of the victim's emotions; if he has to confront him face to face, he notices signs of fear—eyes, glistening sweat, trembling hands. Concentrating on these technical details, he averts entrainment, the usual barrier of confrontational tension. Tony the Greek, a good observer of prison gang fights in the heat of the action, comments on the distinctive smell of tension and fear coming from their massed bodies (Hoffman and Headley 1992: 125, 133) (remarkably similar to the SWAT officer quoted in chapter 10, p. 378).[22]

For the most part, the hitman tries to get the jump on his victim, avoiding confrontation entirely; but this is not always possible, and sometimes a hitman contracts to take out a very difficult opponent, even another experienced hitman. "Joey" sizes up the relative degree of toughness of his opponent; one who is merely in the business of intimidation, talking roughly and making a show, or using muscle against weaker victims, is not what Joey considers much of an opponent, even if the latter is wary and has a gun. "I wasn't really worried. As long as I was quick he would never get to use it. People who don't normally handle guns are reluctant to shoot at all. And if you've never killed a man you're really going to take some time to think about it before pulling the trigger. I knew that no matter how scared Squillante was, when he saw it was me approaching the car, he would hesitate for a slight moment. . . . While he was thinking about it I would kill him." It turns out that although his victim is pointing a gun at him, he acts like he is in a daze. Joey calms him with his smooth manner and talks him into driving to another spot; when Joey finally pulls his own gun, the victim freezes up completely (Fisher 2003: 169–70, 193, 199).

Figure 11.9 Contract Killers. Above: "Mad Dog" Sullivan, in chains, facing murder charges (1982). AP/World Wide Photos. Right: Joey Gallo, trigger man in killing of Mafia boss Albert Anastasia (1957). AP/World Wide Photos.

The hitman is not without emotions, but he manages them. Waiting in ambush as the time approaches for a killing, Joey feels excitement and a sense of power building up: "The adrenaline just flowed right through my whole body, putting me in a super-sensitive state. I was attuned to everything. . . . I could hear sounds the average person can't hear and that ordinarily I couldn't hear. There is a point at which thinking ceases and movement and reaction begins. I was building toward that point" (Fisher 2003: 179). After a glitch delays the hit, he notes, "I had lost the killing emotion, I was relaxing. Now, as we got closer to the restaurant, I started letting it build up inside me." He stares at a spot on the victim's head that will be his target; checks on his silencer, and looks for a dark place to park the car. Just before he fires, he says, " 'So long, Joe,' and the words sounded tremendously loud" (Fisher 2003: 199). This heightened auditory "tunnel" is the same phenomenon documented in chapter 10 by police shooters, who vividly notice a tiny detail at the moment of confrontation.

Some hitmen feel fear, especially when it is a dangerous hit against another professional. This is chiefly fear of failure, and fear of a difficult confrontation. Tony the Greek explains, "I had reached the top of my profession as a contract killer . . . receiving respect from the crime families; and bone-deep I was afraid of losing it all, a guaranteed denouement if only once I hesitated, lost my nerve, or just plain fucked up. Every time I went on a job I had to psyche myself up, whip my mind and guts into an internal frenzy." He is familiar with the emotional sequence, and uses it to work up fear of enemy into anger at enemy, giving himself momentum to move forward. Just before the attack he uses internal dialogue to tell himself: "*You have the advantage. . . . You got the offense, Greek. Take him. Calm and fast*" (Hoffman and Headley 1992: 9–10).

Another technique is allowing a small amount of fear from the immediate situation into one's consciousness, then using it to provoke anger against the source of fear. "Joey" recalls that early in his career, he went through an inner dialogue in which he portrayed the man he had taken a contract to kill, as just as liable to kill him if their positions were reversed (Fisher 2002). This is also an extremely common pattern for police who are involved in shootings; in most of the cases in Artwohl and Christensen (1997) and Klinger (2004) where subjective detail is given, the officer tells himself that his target has threatened to kill other officers or civilians (see the incidents quoted in chapter 10, pages 378–80). This is virtually a constant in police shoot-outs in recent decades; the shooter has a belief (whatever its source may be) that his opponent has vowed to "take some others with him" as he goes down. This may well be emotional self-manipulation, not merely to put the officer morally in the right but to call up a burst of anger, which impels him into action. In effect this is inoculating oneself with a controlled dose of hot frenzy in an otherwise cool technical approach.

Some hitmen use anger as a tool. Joey Gallo, a Mafia "muscle" intimidator and hitman, practiced making frightening faces in the mirror; when he beat up someone, he worked himself into a frenzy of hate that made the beating prolonged and vicious. "Joey," in contrast, declares he had lost the capacity to hate during the course of his career (perhaps because of his specialization in clandestine hits and lures). "Mad Dog" Sullivan got his nickname from his style of working up extreme rage in his face at the moment he attacked his victim; ordinarily he was polite, soft-spoken, and could manipulate people calmly. He would deliberately recall humiliating childhood events to get himself into the mood for a paid killing. His meticulous technique followed up shooting by cutting the throat to make sure his victim was dead, since bullets are sometimes ineffective; since he forced himself into a particularly gruesome form of confrontation, which other cool killers avoid, he needed to draw on additional emotional force to carry through his routine to its conclusion. (Fisher 2002: 198; Hoffman and Headley 1992: 97, 275).[23]

The emotional coolness of the hitman also shows up in the immediate aftermath of a killing. Having kept his adrenalin arousal within a controlled range, he has no need to work it off in boisterous and wild behavior (unlike Lt. Caputo, in chapter 3). Nor does he engage in recriminations; he can go home and get a good night's sleep,[24] comfortably pretending to his wife that everything is routine; or dress to attend a wedding reception. In part this is because he follows a psychologically self-supportive post-killing routine. He is absorbed in technical matters: breaking apart his gun and silencer, disposing of the pieces where they cannot be found (e.g., Fisher 2003: 206); even disposing of the dead body (if that is the plan) fills his attention with routine skilled activity that transitions him emotionally back to normalcy.

How a body is disposed of is regarded by the public as further evidence of the morally disgusting or deranged character of professional killers. Nevertheless, if one approaches this as part of the sociology of work— just the attitude that such killers take—this is merely a matter of technical considerations. A killer may leave the body exposed, especially when it is intended to send a message—threatening others, publicizing punishment for organizational malfeasance, or demonstrating that a particular mob boss is dead. Alternatively, as a rational plan to minimize risk of detection, the body may be disposed of. Through accumulated experience, killers have found that burying a body under a construction site will usually lead to detection because of the smell if the body is not decomposed with lime; similarly a body dumped in a river will float to the surface if the lungs are not punctured. Some of the gruesome aspects of the post-killing routine come from sophistication about these processes. The DeMeo crew, which worked in Brooklyn during the 1970s and 1980s, killing between seventy-five and two hundred victims, developed a technique of cutting bodies to pieces and disposing of them separately (Mustain and Capeci 1993: 222–23). They evolved refined techniques such as the gunman wrapping himself in a towel to avoid blood splashing from the original hit; stabbing the heart repeatedly to keep it from pumping blood and thus making a mess to be cleaned up; and waiting for almost an hour for the blood to congeal before dismembering the body, again to minimize mess. Two of the members of the six-man crew happened to have been trained as butchers, which gave them the initial approach (for another example of a butcher-turned-hitman who dismembered his bodies, see Hoffman and Headley 1992: 240). All these techniques gave them a rather horrific reputation, which made them a standout even within the Mafia families to which they were loosely affiliated. But I would argue there were no new and special emotions involved in their post-killing behavior; all this work seemed to keep them methodical and calm, paralleling other successful, high-volume hitmen. The DeMeo crew was unusual chiefly because it did all their killing as a group activity, unlike the other hitmen who preferred when possible to work alone. It is likely that this group support is what made it possible for them to maintain their cold professional attitude in the gruesome work of dismembering bodies, whereas the more individualistic hitmen preferred to leave their victims exposed, or to have others carry out the disposing. "Joey," who carried out thirty-five contract killings on his own, said that he did not like funerals or dead bodies (Fisher 2003: 8).

The hitman's most important long-term emotion is pride. Sometimes this involves a degree of exhilaration; but not the wild celebrations found in many other kinds of violence, such as military carousing and sports violence. For some hitmen, this is a feeling of mild but controlled excitement, both from the adventure of the killing episode and from the sense of dominance. This is straightforward instance of building up emotional energy through dominance over EE-losing victims. "Joey" states, "Once you've experienced how quick and easy it is [to kill someone], then there is absolutely nothing to it. . . . You begin to think of yourself in a different way. You feel you are somehow protected, that nothing can ever go wrong, that you are a very special person. This is a wonderful feeling if you know how to use it" (Fisher 2003: 34). He goes on to explain that this self-confidence, which applies to the moment of the killing itself, should not undermine his commitment to planning and preparing every detail beforehand. Hitmen appear to be attracted to their calling, not merely because of the money, but because of the action and status. "Joey," who is the most self-controlled of the hitmen in my collection, comments that legitimate business is boring to him, and even his normal criminal activities (chiefly gambling, loansharking, and their enforcement) are too routine without the occasional hit (Fisher 2002: 48, 106; similarly, Hoffman and Headley 1992: 214).

Above all, hitmen have pride in their technique, especially in their clandestine skills. My informant, like "Joey" (Fisher 2002: 70), went on at length about the ability to lead a double life: to live as an apparently average citizen with a job and family, while hiding away large amounts of illegally made funds. He told stories of the heroes of his profession, assassins who could penetrate any security by their use of disguise, and who could walk away from a hit by tricking guards with their aplomb. We may call this the attraction of clandestine excitement.[25] Similarly, some armed robbers with a high identification with their trade described a split between their normal lives resembling that of the most clandestine contract killers: "Outside, I'm a quiet man, a good neighbor. . . . There are different rules of engagement when I'm at work. I'm never involved in violence outside a work context. However, at work, I've always been very violent." Another said, "[armed robbery] is no big deal. It's just like going out to do a day's work and coming home in the evening to the wife and kids" (Morrison and O'Donnell 1994: 68).

My informant, when asked how someone might carry out a killing in a restaurant, told me he would put his pistol with a silencer under a napkin, get up to go the bathroom, walk around behind my chair, shoot me in the back of the head, and then just keep on walking normally, not looking back, right out the door. Stealth, normal appearances, and aplomb in keeping up the front: this was the chief source of professional pride. Hence the personalities of hitmen, although varied, show some common traits. They are hardworking, conscientious, and meticulous about details, at least as these apply to their profession. Some of them are quiet and restrained, even somewhat puritanical; others spend their free time in the action-seeking hedonism of underworld life, variously involved in gambling, drugs, and commercial sex. My collection of hitmen were intelligent and articulate;[26] in this respect they resemble the most violent police, described earlier. They are good at what they are doing, having risen to the top of a very competitive profession.

To pull the argument together: I have argued that the basic process by which a violent elite is constructed is by drawing on the emotional support of the surrounding group. How is this done, if the violent elite operates alone? Part of the answer is that these killers have mastered techniques of clandestine preparations and post-killing coverups that take up their attention and avoid dwelling on the confrontation; that they generally act suddenly to minimize the confrontational moment; and that consciousness of their micro-interactional skills give them confidence and coolness even in those occasions when confrontation with a victim is prolonged.

There is also a larger social condition in the background. Contract killers have a reputation in the criminal community. In part, this is their reputation for efficiency and reliability; it also has a moral dimension, strange as this may sound from the point of view of conventional morality. Both "Joey" and Tony the Greek make a point of emphasizing that they are completely honest in carrying out contracts. If they take the money, they will carry through the killing. Since their job is frequently to police criminal businessmen's employees or clients who are stealing from their bosses or evading debts, the hitman needs a reputation as someone who operates strictly within the rules of the criminal business. In addition, he takes pride in keeping up his reputation for never informing to the police; in return, he expects to be backed up with legal and illegal help if he gets caught. Such a hitman has a good professional reputation, which brings him not only much contract work, but also respect. He is thus an elite in several respects compounded. He is the toughest of the tough, holding out against the police and rival tough guys. He is also the most skilled in the hierarchy of violence; not just nominally or actively but competently violent.[27]

Although the hitman usually operates out of sight and without immediate social support, there is a community in the background in which he is known and respected. His name is not widely known, but is more in the nature of special knowledge among the cognoscenti. This generates a special kind of reputational pride, possible only in a community structured by hierarchic layers of secrecy and prestige. Hitmen acquire their greatest eminence, and with it their greatest degree of specialization and skill, when crime is highly organized as an underground government.[28] Although he lacks the institutionalized prestige of organized crime families with their rankings of bosses and underbosses, he is free of their obligations (such as being on call, and passing along a percentage of his take). He is more prestigious than mere "muscle," and than ordinary mafia soldiers, even though the latter do occasional killings. His first killing has given him a reputation; as he is approached for more jobs, and subsequently more difficult ones, his performance has brought him to the top of the status hierarchy. He represents, so to speak, the prestige of pure violent competence and its accompanying professional standards, unalloyed by the other duties defining other criminal roles.

"I had become that most envied criminal, a cold-blooded hit man, and daily I saw my newfound status reflected in the deferent, fearful eyes of others." Tony the Greek defines himself in contrast to lesser forms of violence: "I'm not referring to bullies, dim-witted, slow-footed behemoths able to scare the shit out of some elder loan-shark victim, but guys who won't back down from anybody. Who won't run away during a shootout. Panic driving a getaway car. Who can kill and get away with it" (Hoffman and Headley 1992: 51, 91; see also 13, 103. "Joey" describes similar experiences and attitudes in Fisher 2002: 48–49. See also Dietz 1983: 77).

They also look down with scorn on mere amateur killers, "the hysterically angry ones shooting their wives and like that" as well as ordinary hoodlums (Fisher 2003: 33). There is a further hierarchy among professional hitmen. Those who work for organized crime generally will not take contracts from "civilians," unconnected citizens who want to kill a spouse or collect insurance money (Hoffman and Headley 1992: 194; Fisher 2002: 50–52). Joey and Tony explain their rationale: civilians are too unreliable, too easily intimidated by the police, likely to incriminate their contractees. These kinds of jobs are taken by low-end professional killers; they get paid less: on the order of $5,000 for low end, compared to $20,000 or more at the high end, depending on the importance of the person to be killed; in contrast, mere "muscle" might go on salary, or be paid $250 for an episode). Here the money symbolizes rank, as much as it pays for higher-quality service. Differences in rank are paralleled by differences in density of social structure. Low-end hitmen, like unaffiliated criminals generally, make social connections in a random, hit-or-miss fashion; they have much less access to good information about their victim's behavior, and their contacts easily become informants for the police (e.g., Magida 2003). The core networks of organized crime have much more dense surveillance of each other; this makes it possible both to find a good hitman when one wants his services, and it makes him more efficient in carrying out his tasks (since he is generally killing persons with known routines in crime businesses). The hitman is a reputational elite, in a milieu acutely tuned to monitoring each other. In this larger sense, although the elite hitman kills alone, he is operating in a social community whose respect he cares about. His elite identity is very much a part of his personal consciousness as he goes about his clandestine work.[29]

Confrontation-Minimizing Terrorist Tactics

If we classify violent actors by their methods and not by their motivations and ideologies, we find that a prominent variety of terrorists resemble professional hitmen. There is a particularly close fit with suicide bombers, who maintain a clandestine approach all the way up to the instant of their attack; like hitmen, they use a pretense of normalcy to penetrate defenses and get very close to their victims, so that the attack is highly reliable and does not miss its target as so often happens given the normal incompetence of most violence. Both use the tactic of sudden, confrontation-minimizing attacks on unaware victims. The tactic not only makes for effective violence; it also gives psychological support to the killer. In deceiving others, one also deceives oneself; the clandestine killer does not approach as if it were a confrontation, in a mood of anger and tension, but in a mood of routine nothing-unusual-is-happening-here. The professional killer is just an ordinary passerby, the terrorist is just a subway rider or a shopper with a bag—until the last moment when the gun is pulled out, the bomb is left behind, or the detonator is pressed. Confrontation is minimized not just by the clandestine approach, but by confining violence to a tiny window in time. The hitman ideally shoots the victim in the back of the head as soon as he gets out of his car; if all goes well, there is not even a moment of eye contact. Suicide bombers carry this psychological advantage to the extreme, since they never have a moment when they confront another person in open recognition of antagonism. This is a specialized tactic for circumventing the barrier of confrontational tension and fear that all violence must surmount; and a particularly useful tactic for a sole attacker, acting alone and thus without the support or pressure of an audience that gives most violent individuals their emotional energy at the moment of attack.

There is, of course, a much wider variety of terrorists as the term is commonly used, even confining it to oppositional or insurgent terrorists and excluding shock methods used by state authorities targeting non-combatants.[30] Although all of them have a period of clandestine preparation and approach to the target, they differ in how much confrontation takes place once the attack is sprung: at one end of the continuum are prolonged confrontations such as hijacking, hostage-taking, and kidnapping, especially if they involve intimidation and torture. These confrontational tactics are virtually always carried out by small groups acting in concert, not only because they need the manpower, but also because they use group emotional solidarity to overcome confrontational tension; they cannot rely on the deception-plus-self-deception that no violence is going on here. Suicide bombings are at the extreme opposite of the continuum, psychologically the easiest to carry out as far as confrontational tension is concerned since there is not even a need to concern oneself with facing an audience while making an escape afterward. Also at this end of the continuum are remote-detonated bombs and booby-traps (like the roadside devices causing a large percentage of casualties in Iraq from 2004 onward [www: iCasualties.org]), although they are less reliable if there is no human actor on the spot making sure the weapon is right on its target.[31]

Also near the confrontation-minimizing end are many targeted assassinations, in which a particular individual is sought out—rather than an accidental collection of civilians from the target group; they often use the tactic of clandestine approach and sudden confrontation-minimizing attack; these latter are virtually identical with hitman tactics.[32]

Most research on terrorists has concentrated on their ideologies and motives, and more recently on their networks and organizational structures of recruitment, training, and support (Sageman 2004; Gambetta 2005; Pape 2005; Davis 2003; Stern 2003; Geifman 1993). Relatively little is known on the micro-interactional dynamics of how terrorists manage to confront their victims. But no matter how ideologically committed would-be terrorists are, and how strong their support network, they cannot be successful if they cannot overcome confrontational tension/fear.

Consider this question: what goes through the minds of clandestine terrorists in the moments leading up to the attack? Would we expect their internal dialogue to be something like: "*Allah-u-akbar*! Death to the infidels! Revenge on the Jews who destroyed my refugee camp/killed my brother/etc."? On micro-interactional grounds, I suggest that this kind of internal dialogue would make it difficult to keep up the pretense of normalcy that makes the clandestine approach successful. Internal dialogue of this sort would tend to work up emotions that would leak into one's facial expression, postures, and movements; it would not only make it harder to avoid detection, but also harder to keep oneself ready for the task ahead. Instead, taking a clue from what we know of the mental processes of hitmen, I suggest that the terrorist's thoughts focus on keeping oneself calm and normalized.

Some micro-evidence bearing on this point are photographs of suicide bombers, together with witness accounts and bits of dialogue. First, two photos of female suicide bombers in the Palestinian *intifada*. One photo is taken from an ideological video made shortly before the attack (April 22, 2002, Reuters, not shown here); her face is completely smooth, expressionless; no vertical wrinkles between the eyebrows nor tense eyelids and hard-staring eyes expressing anger; no center-forehead wrinkles, raised eyebrows, and gasping mouth of fear (cf. Ekman and Friesen 1975: 63, 95–96); no hard-set mouth of determination and effort such as we see in the previous riot photos above (e.g., figure 11.8). Her confrontational stance is expressed entirely in her costume—head-scarf, checkered shawl—and in the Quran that she holds in her hand—a costume that she did not wear during the attack. The second photo (figure 11.10) is an eighteen-year-old woman in Western dress, a portrait made for her family shortly before she died; again her face is completely bland, not smiling, but showing no signs of anger, fear, or determination; like the other woman, poker-faced (March 30, 2002, Associated Press).

Their last hours are doubly clandestine, hiding their intent not only from enemy authorities but also from their own families and acquaintances. The eighteen-year-old talks with her fiancée the evening before about finishing high school and getting married in the summer. The next morning on her way to meet the driver who would take her to the Israeli

Figure 11.10 Suicide bomber poses for photo shortly before attack. Her emotionless face is part of the clandestine, confrontation-avoiding approach (March 2002). AP/World Wide Photos.

supermarket where she would detonate her bomb, she passes a female classmate, says "Hi," and keeps on walking. The driver says she made chitchat with him in the car, looking calm with the bomb in a shoulder bag at her feet. Five minutes before letting her out of the car, the driver asked if she wanted to back out; she said no, she was not afraid, that she wanted to kill people, that she was ready to die. Five minutes later her bomb had killed herself, a young Israeli woman, and a security guard (*Los Angeles Times*, June 12, 2002).

A third woman bomber, interviewed by a reporter before her attack, says that "you don't think about the explosive belt or about your body being ripped to pieces" (*USA Today*, April 22, 2002, p. A1). The reporter says she seems nervous about the interview, but exchanges giggling pleasantries with two Palestinian women who greet her as she enters the room; in contrast, her escort is a grim-faced male bodyguard. The women bombers seem calmer, more normalized, than the ideologists who will not actually carry out the non-confrontational attack. Terrorist organizations select their operatives on the basis of calm and mature personalities, rejecting many applicants both in the *intifada* and in such organizations as the al-Qaeda training camps (Sageman 2004).

Not all clandestine-attack terrorists make it all the way through; some unknown proportion drop out at the last minute. The aforementioned Palestinian driver tells of delivering a twenty-year-old woman to the vicinity of a crowded pedestrian mall; fifteen minutes later she used her handheld radio to tell the driver to come pick her up, begging and pleading, "I want to go back home. Get me" (*Los Angeles Times*, June 12, 2002). What shift in her emotions and interior dialogue could have brought this about? Could it be that her thoughts drifted to her home instead of staying on the normal routine of pretending to be a shopper?[33]

Another set of photos of clandestine terrorists in action are from security cameras in the London bombings of London subway cars and buses in July 2005. One photo (figure 11.11) shows all four bombers in the July 7 plot as they enter a train station on their way to London, carrying their bombs in backpacks (July 17, 2005, Scotland Yard). The four men are within a few feet of each other, but they give off no Goffmanian tie signs of being together; they make no eye contact and have no common focus of attention, eyes looking down or away from one another as if withdrawn into themselves. Looking at each other would remind them of their mission and add a layer of communicative action that belies their clandestine approach; not so much that they are concerned at this point in giving themselves away to outsiders (there are no other people in the photo and the attack is still an hour away) but because they need to concentrate on their own sense of normalcy, the emotional self-deception necessary for their own calm. It is harder for a group to be clandestine when acting in concert than for an individual, since any communications among them also carry a penumbra of their hidden agenda.[34]

Closeups of three of the men, made later after they have split up, show very slight emotion, none of it expressing anger or determination. One

Figure 11.11 Four suicide bombers beginning their mission. They do not look at each other, and show no tie-signs, as if absorbed into themselves. Photo taken ninety minutes before bombing of London underground (July 2005). AP/World Wide Photos.

man has a tight-mouth smile, not the spontaneous smile that makes crow's-feet wrinkles at the outer corners of the eyes; another has a slight eyebrow raise and central brow-furrow, a slight expression of fear, his lower face expressionless, his eyes perhaps vacant; a third man's face is completely blank (July 20, 2005, Scotland Yard, not shown, cf. Ekman and Friesen 1975: 112, 63). Six more individual photos show another set of four men who failed in a similar subway-and-bus coordinated bombing two weeks later, when their bombs smoldered rather than exploded (July 23, 2005, Scotland Yard). The faces of three of them look bland, unexpressive, their brows unfurrowed; their mouths closed, looking perhaps a little sad. None looks at the other passengers visible in the train or bus cars, but they all look down at the floor or up at the top of the wall (see figure 11.12). The fourth, going down the passageway with his backpack on his back, looks back over his shoulder, as if apprehensive (his brow and forehead hidden by a cap). This fourth individual was spoken to by a passenger just after he had been knocked down by the abortive explosion; he was described as looking confused, dazed, shaken, but then he jumped down onto the tracks and ran. A later photo of him on a vacant bus, having made his escape, shows his face again expressionless, his eyelids half-shut, a slight furrow (fear?) across his forehead. One of the others is photographed running up a vacant subway corridor after the failed attack, mouth shut or nearly so, face still unexpressive. Altogether, the photos are consistent with the interpretation that their cognitive tactic is to be withdrawn into themselves, not thinking of anything except the narrowest practical exigencies. Depression, a little leakage of fear—these are not surprising for persons going into a deadly confrontation while avoiding all thought of it. Even after the attacks fail, they appear very low in affect, relying more on clandestine expressionlessness than on strong emotions of aggressiveness and exertion.

In one case the suicide bomber expresses anger, but it is an exception that proves the rule. A young man gathers a crowd at an Iraqi army recruiting station by making a loud speech, angrily denouncing unemployment and corruption; he then sets off a bomb that kills himself and twenty-two listeners and injures forty-three (*Los Angeles Times*, July 11, 2005). Here the bomber is using the expression of anger for instrumental purposes, to mask his true target and to bring his victims up close to kill them more reliably. His underlying motivation may well be anger, but it is masked by another layer of anger put on as a performance. His backstage anger is hidden by a performance of frontstage anger.[35]

In the great majority of clandestine attacks, on the contrary, backstage anger is sealed off a long way back in time; as the attack approaches, such terrorists prepare themselves by closing down their emotions, numbing themselves, using a near trance-like blandness as their tactic and their psychological defense.[36] Witnesses of suicide bombers just before their attacks have often remarked on their dazed or trance-like appearance (Merari 1998; Gambetta 2005: 275, citing a conference presentation by Merari). It is the technique of emotional self-control that is the key to the success of confrontation-minimizing clandestine attacks.[37]

In an important sense, the history of terrorist attacks, since the first round of bombings in the 1880s, has depended upon the creation and diffusion of confrontation-minimizing techniques of attack.[38] What has been adopted is not just the technology of how to make bombs and detonators but a micro-interactional technology. It is a social technology that has made it possible for ideologically motivated terrorism to be carried out by middle-class women and men without backgrounds in ordinary boisterous or criminal violence. As a generalization, the more clandestine and confrontation-avoiding the technique of violence, the more its practitioners are from the respectable middle class, and indeed from its non-boisterous, well-behaved sector.[39] Terrorist bombing is, so to speak, the violence of the meek.

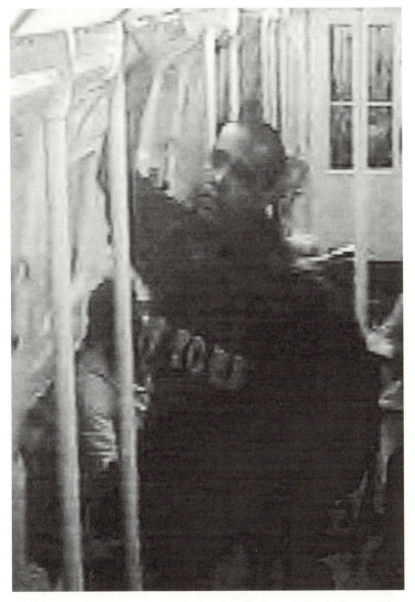

Figure 11.12 Suicide bomber escaping after a failed attack. He looks away from other subway passengers, gazing expressionlessly at the top of the wall (London, July 2005). AP/World Wide Photos.

Violent Niches in Confrontational Attention Space

Wherever we turn, in every kind of violence, there is a small number of persons who produce most of the violence. We could conceive this as a collection of individual processes. The violent few are those who have acquired the techniques for being violent in particular kinds of situations. I have demonstrated that successful violence is more in the style of dealing with other people in a confrontation than in handling weapons per se; above all in dealing with one's own emotions and taking advantage of other people's emotions, both supporters and victims. Why can't everyone learn these techniques, and become part of the violent elite? This is the approach of combat psychologists (Grossman 2004) and the aim of military and police trainers, to turn non-fighters into fighters. The same would apply to every other kind of violence: if the techniques became well enough known, presumably everyone who wanted to could become a hitman, a terrorist, and so forth.

I am arguing that this is not possible. These interactional techniques unquestionably exist, and can be understood, taught, and acquired. They are not simply innate predispositions; a primal genetic capacity to be angry or aggressive is a long way from being competently violent, especially given the wide range of specialized types of violent interaction we have examined. But the limit on the numbers of those actively violent, and especially on those who are competently violent, is so widespread across different kinds of situations that we must conclude we are dealing with a feature of interactional structure, not a feature of individuals. As sociologists, we turn the gestalt around: what appears as the mysterious fact that some individuals have interactional techniques that others do not have, can be seen as the way in which social interaction works. There is a process by which the violence of the majority is limited, and this is the same process by which the violence of a small number is generated. The emotional arousal of the group in a confrontational situation flows from some parts of the group to others. The collective effervescence of mutual entrainment is differentiated into an array of emotional qualities and intensities: some persons are relatively passive, feeling more tension and fear, more reliant on others in the group to set the tone and take action; others become more pumped with initiative, confidence, and enthusiasm. The latter are a relatively small number because they are the beneficiaries of a focus mechanism, whereby the emotional power of the group becomes embodied in them.

This is not a metaphor. What I am arguing can be seen directly as we closely examine the micro-interactional features of violent interactions, including their surrounding onlookers.

Violence is an interactional accomplishment in a situation structured by emotion. The most pervasive emotion in situations of violent threat is confrontational tension/fear. As we have seen throughout the book, violence is difficult, not easy; whatever the background conditions may be—the motives, grievances, hotheaded feelings, material incentives, or cultural ideals—most of the time violent situations abort; there is bluster, threat, and confrontation, but most of the time participants back away with symbolic gestures or at most with brief, untidy and incompetent violence. For violence to happen, the situation must present a way for at least some participants to circumvent confrontational tension/fear.

Such pathways can be grouped into two main types: hot emotional violence and cool technical violence. Usually hot violence comes from the emotional flow of an assembly whose attention has become sharply focused, whether as companions, audience, or antagonists. The most typical hot emotion is anger; but there are other emotional varieties and blends: it might be a buildup of tension and fear suddenly transformed into a forward panic; it could also be enthusiastic and ebullient emotion of the kind found in carousing, entertainment, and athletic situations. These are all hot, high levels of adrenalin arousal, cycled through the assembly of human bodies. It is worth repeating that the mere presence of hot emotion is not enough for successful violence to occur; the hot emotion needs to be configured in such a way across the group so that confrontational tension/fear is overcome.

In another category are the varieties of cool technical violence. Here, the violent activists perform techniques by which they manage their own emotions and take advantage of the emotional weaknesses of their opponents. And since these categories are ideal types, we can find combinations of hot and cold techniques in particular kinds of violence.

Our problem is to explain why violence is limited to a small number of activists and competent elites, first for hot violence, then for cold technical violence. The first is straightforward. Group-located hot-emotion violence is a massive interaction ritual, in which the assembly becomes emotionally unified by focusing on a single confrontation; and this provides the feelings of excitement and solidarity that energize a smaller segment of fighters. The transition to violence is easiest when the crowd itself is not fighting anyone, but acting only as supportive spectator, as in sports and convivial or celebratory audiences who treat fights as entertainment. Similarly with staged fights among hero-elites: the latter have the peculiarity, as in many species of duels, that the fighters themselves may not have hot emotions, but they are forced into fighting by the emotional pressure of the crowd, and by pride in maintaining their standing. These kinds of spectators-surrounding-fighters arrangements commonly take the form of a unified ring of spectators who help the fighters overcome confrontational tension/fear; the emotional support flows inward to the few at the center.

The problem of overcoming confrontational tension/fear is harder when the larger group itself becomes a participant in the violence—even if this is only nominal participation, not really doing much, but nevertheless taking up a stance of confronting a real opponent who might engage them. Sometimes the crowd has an easy opportunity, as when an authority-free zone is created, and the crowd can engage in rioting against inert physical emblems of the other side, such as by looting and burning. Here, too, we have seen that the crowd is stratified into looting leaders, preexisting gangs or clusters, and, gradually over time, a larger amateurish mass of participation-seekers drawn by the emotional atmosphere; yet even the latter reaches only about 10 to 15 percent of the community who could take part. Similarly in celebration rituals over the dead body of an opponent; the situation is safe from real confrontation, but the desecrators of bodies are few, and even in these situations there is a tiny apex of the group who become demonstrative extremists, like those climbing the girders of the bridge at Fallujah to hit the bodies that are hanging there with the sole of a shoe. Even the activist crowd is unequally energized, with the mass confining themselves to gestures.

The most widely shared participation is when an entire group goes into a forward panic. Here the energy comes from tension/fear of a standoff or chase, suddenly released when the group finds it has a weak enemy who has given up the confrontation. We have seen this in the climax of military battles, in police chases, and in the typical pattern of ethnic/communal violence. In these cases, the group is so strongly energized because it uses confrontational tension/fear as its source of arousal; tension and fear are easy emotions to arouse, unlike anger in the face of a real opponent. This route is, so to speak, the most natural way of dealing with a violent confrontation. The tension/fear phase of the conflict, becoming intensified while it remains drawn-out, serves to draw the group together emotionally as long as they maintain a tight social organization among themselves, rather than breaking off into pieces going in different directions. If the enemy suddenly shows a collapse of resistance, the emotionally energized and unified group goes into an uncontrollable attack, a frenzy of piling on and overkill.

A forward panic might seem to be an exception to the small numbers of violent activists, and the still smaller number of the violently competent in the sense of successfully destroying the enemy. We lack detailed enough descriptions to know just how widespread is the participation in a forward panic violence. In police chases, where we have recordings, a small proportion of the officers present—rarely above 20 percent except in very small groups—act out the forward panic, as if on behalf of the larger group. In military forward panics, we have less detail; apparently every-one rushes forward, and large numbers may take part in killing the fallen or cowering enemy (like the battlefield at Agincourt) or torching civilian huts (as in Vietnam). But it is unclear how many in this situation were effective killers and arsonists, and how many merely rushed around, per-haps adding their emotional support to the scene by yelling. Similarly for ethnic massacres when rioters break in on demoralized victims. The hot, frenzied emotion of group activists appears to be widely shared; but those who do the actual breaking in and killing may be different persons from those who engage in ritual destruction, while others may merely express vocal support.[40]

If hot violence is produced by the crowd acting as a large focused inter-action ritual, cool technical violence is a cluster of practices that at first glance appear to be individual. A brief list would include (1) staying cool in the midst of other people's hot emotions: being "in the zone" while opponents are in the glaze of combat; (2) self-absorbed focus on the tech-nicalities of one's weapons and procedures (e.g., snipers); (3) emotional self-manipulation techniques (e.g., making oneself angry by recalling past insults); (4) manipulating victims' emotions; (5) clandestine, confronta-tion-minimizing tactics; (6) victim-finding techniques, such as those prac-ticed by muggers and armed robbers, in more extreme forms by serial killers and serial rapists; (7) victim-training techniques, including the long-term relationship between bullies and their victims, and the form of domestic abuse that I have called "terroristic torture regimes." In sum, there is a bag of techniques that make up the competence of cool technical specialists in violence. The theoretical puzzle applies to all of them: why is it that the practitioners of these techniques are always a small number of the nominally violent combatants, in every arena of conflict?

In the case of hot frenzied forms of violence, we have already answered the question: the violent elite generally depend on the emotional support of a group and the narrowing focus of emotional attention as the group distributes violent energy to only a few persons. In the case of the cool techniques, however, we might ask, Why can't everyone learn these tech-niques? Individuals could be trained to practice breathing techniques to keep their adrenalin in a middle range, and overlearn their firing responses on a range so that it becomes automatic in a confrontation (Grossman 2004); they could learn to shut out the human aspect of their targets by focusing on calibrating their aim, to keyhole their violence by confronta-tion minimizing, or to practice techniques of emotion management on themselves and their victims. Since this is a thought experiment, imagine psychology courses in colleges, or month-long commercial training semi-nars, in which instead of anger-management or touchy-feely emotional expression there are studies and drills in how to become an accomplished gun-fighter, armed robber, clandestine confrontation-minimizing killer, victim-finder, and so on. The thought-experiment forces us to ask, Is there an upper limit to how many people could become violent experts?[41]

My argument is that there is an upper limit to such numbers. Even if more people had the opportunities to learn these techniques, the fluctuation would stay within a range; the ceiling would still be around 10 percent or less of any given group of the nominally violent becoming competently violent. I will give first a theoretical analogy, and then propose mechanisms. The analogy comes from the world of intellectuals. Throughout world history the number of notable philosophers, in any generation when there is any intellectual action that achieves importance in historical memory, has almost always between three and six (Collins 1998). This "law of small numbers" divides up niches in the attention space that makes up the intellectual community. If there are too many intellectuals claiming to create important new philosophies, some of them fail to find a niche; they attract few followers, and their historical memory dies out.

Both intellectual and violent attention spaces are structured by conflict. Creativity in the intellectual world consists of saying something new; that means not only negating what was done in the past but also negating the positions of rivals who are also struggling to gain recognition. Creativity is driven by conflict; creativity occurs simultaneously in different parts of the field, never in a single isolated upheaval against the past but in rival reformulations of dominant conceptions of knowledge. The most creative intellectuals are puzzle finders, raising points to argue about, not just puzzle-solvers. Star intellectuals, like the violent elite, make their reputations by stirring up trouble. Instead of backing away from it, as most people do from violent confrontations, they seek it out, as we have seen with career criminals and hooligans as well as ace pilots and cowboy cops.

Creativity is energized by the attention space. This is stratification of emotional energy, not merely possession of superior cultural capital. In intellectual networks the eminent thinkers of one generation tend to breed the future eminents of the next generation. But star teachers have many students, and those who become the most creative do not initially differ from many others around them in the cultural capital that they receive from their teachers and mentors. But some use their inherited cultural capital more aggressively than others. They become what I have called "energy stars," a personality pattern that emerges as those who have acquired a successfully exploitable niche in the field throw themselves obsessively into their work; they turn out a huge volume of publications, often far more than the segment they become famous for. Subjectively, these intellectual leaders are more self-reliant, able to operate in longer periods of isolation from companions, absorbed in their own work. But they are by no means isolated from their community. They begin their careers in the core of social networks of the already highly competent; they struggle against the most competent rivals of their own generation; they are aware of their position in the larger attention space of the audience that hears and reads their work.

What creative intellectuals get from their predecessors is not just a stock of culture, but also techniques of how to think, how to make effective arguments against opponents, how to sense the opportunities for when to create a new theory or a new style. What protégés have acquired is their mentors' techniques for winning battles in the struggle to control the attention space, even if they apply these techniques to new situations, and forge new techniques going beyond the older ones. Creative intellectuals have internalized a sense of the surrounding intellectual world and its lines of loyalties and conflicts; they can think more rapidly than their competitors and put together combinations of ideas that will appeal to audiences. This apparently intuitive grasp of the field comes from having deeply internalized the ideas and techniques of thinking that mark membership in various intellectual factions. Their thinking is without laboriousness and self-consciousness, because their very process of thinking carries with it a sense of the social position that they occupy in relation to others in the intellectual field. Instead of arguing with other persons, or with abstract ideas, they argue with both simultaneously; their thinking consists in making coalitions in the mind while picking battles in the mind. And these coalitions and battle-lines confidently translate into on-going centers of concern in the intellectual community. The creative elite has an automatic, overlearned sense of positions in the field, both as to who their supporters are, as well as their rivals.

The violent elite, too, start out in the same place as many others with the same cultural background or milieu. Instead of seeing their background as a disability for making a career according to mainstream middle-class values, we could view it as cultural capital favoring success in violent and criminal careers. But those who become the violent elite are not the only ones who come from poverty, tough neighborhoods, broken families, and so forth. Because we so often sample on the dependent variable, doing our research on those who become the violent elite, we miss how many in the same background have failed to make a success at violence. Just as notable intellectuals started out in networks that give them high cultural capital, the stars of violence started out in networks where they inherited a high level of the culture of violence. The question is why some of those who start with this cultural inheritance win out over others to become the elite; they do not simply inherit violence, but must outcompete others similarly situated.[42]

A second point of analogy is that for the violent elite, too, it takes emotional energy to build on one's cultural capital rather than passively accepting it. In the biographies of hitmen we see this emotional energy[43] building up as they begin to make their way in the crime world as young teenagers. They win out over rivals who threaten to move in on their slice of the crime business, small as it is at that point; we see one picking up a baseball bat to repel those who want to horn in on his numbers racket; another hustling to build up his muscles by overloading himself with boxes in his delivery job (Fisher 2002; Mustain and Capeci 1993: 30). Although in one sense the violent elite of the criminal world are lazy—they want a short-cut to success, they scorn the routine of ordinary jobs—they are nevertheless a very hard-working group. The crime business operator has to make his daily rounds, picking up his money, checking on who might be cheating, putting in an appearance to make sure others know he's there, applying threat or muscle when needed. Even their off hours in the carousing or gambling scene are in a sense obligatory; they have to be around to keep their hand in. Keeping up one's reputation is a full-time job.[44] Thus although there may be an ideology of "work is for suckers," within the milieu of "wiseguys" and their analogues, it is the lazier who lose out to the energetic and committed. Instead of seeing these as individual characteristics, we should grasp the pattern as a social distribution of emotional energy.

The same is true in other areas of violence. The crime world may be the most mutually cut-throat; but there are indications of the same pattern for the violent elite among soldiers, pilots, police, and others. Ace pilots hate desk jobs; their biographies are full of incidents where they sneak out against orders with the intention to fly. Everywhere, the most successful in their brands of violence are also the most energetic and committed.

Third, there is an analogue to the intellectual stars in their higher level of self-reliance, self-directedness, and willingness to go through long periods of isolation. This is clearly illustrated by hitmen, enduring long hours of staking out their victims, charting their movements, waiting for an opening. Military snipers are the violent exemplars of quiet patience par excellence. Burglars and armed robbers often operate alone, the most dedicated of them many hundreds of times; operating alone does not bother them, and apparently feels comfortable, even a source of strength. Not to say that the violent elite are isolates all the time; they also may check in on the usual action scenes and keep their presence known among their peers. But this is analogous to intellectuals; they may spend long hours alone writing, but also keep contact with their professional network. Self-motivation in isolation is highest among the violent elite, those who are best at the cool techniques of violence; the less competent layer of the actively violent, practicing hot violence in the midst of groups, have much less of this self-reliant character.

A fourth point of analogy is the network pattern. Eminent intellectuals emerge from networks where the action previously has been, and reorganize the network for the new round of action in the present. For intellectuals, this dependence upon the network has both a vertical and a horizontal aspect: the stars of the new generation tend to have teachers and mentors of the creative stars of the last generation; and the new stars tend to start out in clusters who strike out in a new direction together.[45]

To give just one example: youthful clusters making their career moves together appear to be common in gangs, where they make up the more serious criminal crews, in contrast to others who are in the gang merely for protection or excitement. The former often graduate to a higher level through a stint in prison, a place that tests and winnows the youthfully defiant into those who are genuinely good at violence and committed to it; this takes place through fights to establish the pecking order in prison, which create cliques at the top of the local violence hierarchy; and these cliques then go on to more serious—more competent—violence when they are released. Tony the Greek describes how network ties concatenate into clusters in prison: since he knew Irish hoods from the West Side of New York, he was taken into a tough Irish prison gang during his first stint in prison, at age twenty. He describes the prison "class system": " 'good guys' didn't rat and could take care of themselves in a fight; 'bad guys' weren't violent and didn't know anybody. The good guys had free rein to beat up and extort the bad guys" (Hoffman and Headley 1992: 45). At this point in his life, Tony had been a drug dealer and muscleman; soon after being released from prison he performed his first contract killing. He killed a pimp on behalf of a prostitute he sold heroin to; since she was under the auspices of a Mafia family captain, Tony came to be known in the Genovese family and received further contracts, which he successfully carried out, launching his career. Jankowski (1991) similarly describes Hispanic and black prison gangs that support and strengthen the gang identities of individuals in prison; what needs to be added here is a winnowing process, whereby some persons gravitate into the apex of the network, while others are peripheralized by their lesser competence or commitment to fighting.

Similarly for emergent networks. Participating in the business side of crime gives the opportunity to meet persons who help take one's violence to a higher level. Auto theft is low-level, usually nonviolent crime, but when it becomes regularized and repetitive by connecting to chop-shops for stolen parts, an auto thief may meet armed criminals, and these in turn may connect to a Mafia acquaintance, and eventually form a crew of contract killers (Mustain and Capeci 1993). This kind of analysis poses many empirical and analytical problems; it is not merely a matter of making the network contacts but also winnowing them; only a few who have connections with chop-shops go on to join a hitman crew.

How to theorize this winnowing process is a crucial problem for the sociology of violent networks.

Experts in one kind of violent confrontation are not necessarily good at other kinds. That is because violent techniques are in specialized niches; you cannot take the whole niche with you just because you have the technique, since this would mean bringing along the same built-up relationships of turf-claiming that existed in one's previous field. Some hitmen had combat experience, but played it safe at the front (Fisher 2002: 12); and Mafia soldiers disparaged combat veterans, apparently out of a feeling that a different attitude toward violence is involved (Mustain and Capeci 1993: 22). Both Tony the Greek and Joey Gallo were notoriously tough musclemen and hitmen, but when riots broke out in their respective prisons, neither was in the violent forefront of the fighting; both operated coolly in the heat of the riot, Tony becoming a negotiator with the guards, Joey rescuing a captured guard and turning him over, to curry favor for his own release (Hoffman and Headley 1992: 150–56). To ironicize about their apparent cowardice in these situations would be to impose outsiders' values upon them; both remained detached and took individual advantage of the heated situation, which was how they had made their careers.

For the intellectual world, the network structure tends to reproduce the pattern of a small number of stars; both because only a few lineages and clusters are generated at the center of action, and because those at the center de-energize and exclude other competitors. Analogously, network patterns centering around the violent elite would promote a small-numbers pattern for each type of violence.

We come now to the micro-mechanisms by which a small number of individuals make themselves the elite, while others who start out with similar ambitions and opportunities drop by the wayside. The creative elite builds up emotional energy specific to a particular branch of the intellectual field—philosophers, mathematicians, sociologists, painters, etc.—whatever constitutes itself as a self-enclosed attention space. Within this space, there is competition over a small number of niches, positions that can receive recognition. Emotional energy in its general form is the sense of enthusiasm, confidence, and initiative; in the case of abstract verbal intellectuals, they work with ideas that feel successful (feel like great ideas). They enjoy using their intellectual techniques and renew their energy by using them, because those techniques are part of their positions in the field; in using their techniques they are enacting their sense of interaction with the audience they have internalized. In terms of the model of thinking I have described in Collins (2004: chap. 5), these intellectuals are engaged in internal interaction rituals, loops of emotional self-entrainment that give them both confidence in what they are doing and a sense of their identity in the field of their competitors and supporters.

As Chambliss (1989) finds for swimming races, winners are those who have acquired minute techniques that they believe give themselves an edge over competitors; there is a positive feedback loop because they identify with these techniques and enjoy practicing them. Their dedication to practicing not only deepens their skills; the very exercise of their skills puts them into a special social space, a relationship of eliteness in relation to the rest of the field, even when they are ostensibly alone and the opponents are merely implicit. Practitioners of such techniques find themselves in a cocoon of self-confidence that Chambliss calls the "mundanity of excellence," a cool attitude that opponents mystify to their own detriment. Small marginal differences in performance become magnified as winners become further energized, while losers become de-energized. Similarly, some cops practice shooting on the range religiously, and constantly remind themselves of scenarios in which they may face a life-or-death shootout (Klinger 2004: 37–38, 42, 85; Artwohl and Christensen 1997: 64, 150); while others play down both preparation and confrontation. Although we know less about this for other kinds of violence, some soldiers embrace their weapons training and look for opportunities to use it; others slough it off, some sooner, some later depending on their chains of encounters both with enemies and with compatriots who are more strongly or weakly committed than themselves. Similarly again, to be an accomplished ghetto street fighter or armed robber, it is not enough simply to be in the milieu of violence; some who start out in this arena hone their violent skills at every opportunity, while others settle for occasional token encounters that are just enough to keep up their reputation. High-frequency robbers and burglars (like those who commit a crime more than once a day) are always keeping their hand in and their skills up; those who are not very good at burglary or robbery risk it less often, and are sooner to drop out. What Anderson calls the code of the street is a skilled performance for some, mere window-dressing for others; it is the former who "go for street," their identities and energies taken over by their performance because it is the most successful thing they do.

The emotional energy of the intellectual elite is continuously being rebuilt by a positive spiral. Being more energized than others enables them to create forefront positions before others do; they get more acclaim, which in turn feeds their self-image, their confidence, and their flow of energy to get still further work done. The same positive loops generally flow on the material side as well, with greater ease of access to publications, research equipment, money, and jobs that give them the time to devote to their intellectual work, and so on.

Similar loops flow in a negative direction for those who begin to lag behind the energy leaders. They fail to get recognition; they find themselves too late and become disappointed in their expectations. Material supports fall away as well; some would-be intellectuals find they cannot make a living at their vocation, just as some would-be criminals find their life of crime brings in too little income. As the distance between themselves and the leaders palpably widens in the reputational field, would-be elites face a choice point: to continue to strive for recognition as a leader while getting shunted to the side; or to give up their claim for eminence, and settle for being a follower of someone else's position. Some lose their enthusiasm and their identity entirely, and drop out of the field. This model of the intellectual world explains why eminence in violence too is limited to a small number, simultaneously by processes that take place in the emergent elite and in the emergently failing non-elite.

There is not only a process of emergence but also of submergence; and the two are reciprocals of each other for persons in different positions within the same attention space. The same holds for the emergence of a violent elite and the submergence of those who try and fail. It is not simply a matter of the elite having learned particular kinds of high-performance techniques. They have learned these techniques in the midst of competition with others; their enthusiasm for using their techniques, and engaging in the practice that sustains them, comes from the recognition they get from a surrounding community.

Recognition from the larger community, like the acclaim that goes to a famous intellectual, has its counterpart in communities like the world of organized crime, where a few individuals get the respect of being a hitman, others famed for lesser degrees of toughness. In legitimate arenas like the military, there is enormous institutionalized acclaim for such individuals as fighter aces; and of course athletics is organized centrally around publicizing such relative standings. In all these arenas, the ones who are at the top are energized (and receive that much more subjective sense of high-status identity from concentrating on their techniques), while those who fail to crack the attention space after a period of trying become demoralized, and their techniques deteriorate.[46]

Similar for recognition that comes from one's immediate cluster of supporters. The cluster of cops on the SWAT team, or otherwise in the forefront of action-seekers, may start out composed entirely of those who are energized for confrontations. Nevertheless, in any particular encounter, a certain few will work at the point of attack and get the brunt of the action. They become both even further action-trained, while others fall into a habit of relying on them. Similarly in military combat, the initially gung-ho eventually find that emotionally they are content to let someone else do it. We lack good detailed evidence of this sort for criminal groups; but it appears that in the world of gangs, it is those who are seeking admission into the gang, and to move up in its hierarchy of prestige, who are most likely to be involved in fights (Jankowsky 1991). Once they have proven themselves, many rest on their reputations. The upper limits of the law of small numbers asserts itself, winnowing out even those who have initially staked their career trajectories and their idealized self-images on the model of the violent elite.

The emotional energy and the techniques of the violent elite are both built up and worn down by being tested. In any violent confrontation, there is a winner and a loser; or else there is a standoff. Of these three alternatives, the only one that certainly maintains one's upward spiral of emotional energy as a violent elite is winning. It might seem that once you have acquired the techniques of cool violence, you own them as a personal possession. But there is evidence that this is not the case. In one instance, a highly reputed hitman was hired to kill another such hitman. Catching his rival off guard by approaching in disguise, then pretending to be a street robber, Tony the Greek gets the jump on him with a concealed weapon; he then proceeds to use his normal tactics of taking him for a ride to a place where he can conveniently shoot him and dispose of the body (Hoffman and Headley 1992: 9–14). The rival hitman, who presumably has some of the same techniques, recognizes what is being done, but is unable to do anything about it. He proceeds to give in emotionally, falling for the tactics of being calmed down by a deception that neither hitman really believes in; he shows unwonted moments of fear, as he bargains and pleads for his life; having lost emotional control, he even shits in his pants—like many policemen and soldiers under fire (Hoffman and Headley 1992: 9–14, and for another instance, 105–7; cf. Grossman 2004). Even violent techniques that make one a member of the elite can be de-energized and de-learned.

Mere standoffs among elites probably do not run down their emotional energy and their confidence in techniques as much; but likely they are not good for them. A likely hypothesis is that violent elites who are not winning are losing their edge.

In most fields of violence, the elite build up their standing by attacking weaker victims; their skill is in seeing and attacking their opponents' vulnerabilities, not their strengths. Thus the violent elite generally avoid going up against each other. This runs contrary to mythology of the *Iliad* type, and to the long tradition of fictional violence. In the real world of all-out violence, an expansion in the number of persons who had elite violent skills, as individuals, would at some point lead to an increase in confrontations among members of this elite group. By my argument, and by the precedents cited here, such confrontations would de-energize and de-skill some of that elite.

Sports are an artificial social world in just this respect, since they engineer tournament-like winnowing structures where the most skilled competitors have to face each other. Sports are a form of limited violence, with plenty of crowd and team support to overcome confrontational tension. In athletics of head-to-head competition, those with skills of the "cool in the midst of hot frenzy" kind nevertheless go through peaks and slumps. Athletes and coaches have become very conscious of techniques, and use sports psychology both in the form of accumulated lore and high-tech professionalism, but without eliminating these kinds of streaks. Trends over time in performance in offense-versus-defense sports imply that the thought experiment I described earlier, where everyone could learn the techniques of the most highly competent violent elite, would not lead to any drastic rise in the ceiling for the law of small numbers.

The techniques by which the intellectual elite dominate their rivals are techniques which give an internalized sense of the field. Similarly for the techniques of the small numbers who successfully practice cool violence. The technique works because it gives one a sense of positions in the field of combat: in sizing up one's opponent, not only as an individual but also in terms of all the layers of the opposition, judging, without having to think about it, who is hot and who is cool, who is bluster and who serious, who is frontline, supportive cluster, or backline follower. Similarly the dominator's technique extends to a clear sense of one's own side, who is a strong or weak supporter and how well he or she is doing. Ace pilots often brag about not losing a wingman; though they are the stars they also understand the value of teamwork; they are like the star quarterback who knows where everyone is on both sides of the field.

That the technique is internalized means that it is fast; rather than self-conscious, the violent elite do not have to stop and think. (In the same way, the intellectual elite do not have to stop and think about how to think; they go ahead and make their move before someone else thinks of it.) Lacking a micro-sociological vocabulary, we tend to describe such behavior as intuitive or natural, but it is socially acquired; we have seen how fighter pilots may go through a long period of mediocrity before they click into high gear as aces. The winning gunfighter, whether cop, duelist, or criminal, is not just quicker on the draw (or the quicker swordsman of samurai lore) but is socially faster in getting the jump, making decisions without deliberation, getting more quickly into the zone. This speed is always relative to that of someone else; one's quickness, naturalness, intuitiveness in adapting to the speed of violent action is always a matter of being faster than one's rivals. Thus it is a technique that is always on the edge, always being tested; it is not a quality of the individual, an immutable possession, but an interactional relationship. The winnowing effect of a chain of violent encounters is always to build up some and wear down others; it is a specialized kind of interaction ritual chain, in which the emotional energy of some has built up in the confidence and initiative to move faster than anyone else. As in interaction ritual chains, the matchup is always a possible tipping point; the violent elite have to stay at the dominant edge, or their technique goes backward.

I have been attempting to show why a law of small numbers applies not just to hot violence, which typically depends upon audience effects, but also to cool violent techniques, which appear to belong to individuals. It is easy to explain why in one type of situation the hot-heads are the violent few: they get their emotional energy to overcome confrontational tension by the support of the rest of the group. We have seen a version of the law of small numbers operating within the immediate structure of the confrontational attention space: when there is violence, it almost always takes the form of one fight per venue. When carousers fight, one antagonism imposes its structure upon the attention space, defocusing and de-energizing other conflicts; the audience is mesmerized into a single focus of attention while the fight is going on, and tends to buzz with narrations in the aftermath, which take up the emotional attention for the time being. This is a micro-version of the law of small numbers; there is an analogous pattern on the larger level, spread out over time, as we tally up the number of cowboy cops who dominate violent incidents over a period of years; or ace pilots, hitmen, hyper-active armed robbers, and on through most other forms of violence.

The analogy to eminent intellectuals shows us a law of small numbers that restricts the number of the elite over a long period of time, an entire generation. Something similar happens for each generation in each arena of violence.[47] The violent elite build up their cool techniques during a period of apprenticeship or tryout that implicitly or explicitly brings them into competition with the existing hierarchy of violent practitioners, until they reach a period when they dominate all rivals. Why is it that only a few can do this during any one expanse of time? In essence, their techniques boil down to devices for keeping oneself from being affected by the glaze of combat that is around them, and for taking advantage of the other side's confrontational tension. Their techniques are cool precisely because they are designed to keep one from being affected by the hot emotions of combat; they batten on opponents' emotional states, not just on the confrontational tension and fear that makes most people incompetent, but also on the hot anger and confrontational courage or bravado that can also be manipulated by a cool opponent.

Only a small proportion of persons can have these cool techniques. I state this as an empirical pattern, based on the evidence to date. We can explain it as an emotional dynamic of the structure of confrontational attention spaces. The cool techniques of violent domination are social on every level: In the immediate confrontation, they consist in a way to swiftly and unself-consciously perceive the emotional positions and trajectories of everyone around one and manipulate these to one's advantage. But only a few can do so, because success in exercising these techniques de-energizes the techniques of one's less successful rivals. In the chain of confrontations that make up each violent individual's life, the successful become more and more identified with their techniques; but this also makes them hyper-sensitive to their successes and failures, liable to be displaced if they fail—not merely in the sense that losing a fight may cost one's life, but that merely failing to dominate, or backing away from a confrontation may cost one's edge. Moreover, if it is true that the violent elite tend to be in the center of reputational networks, their own interaction ritual chains of fights plus their narrative aftermaths intertwine throughout a community of talk; the elite's confidence in their techniques is not only built up through the fame of their successes but can also be run down not just through their failures but even through a shifting of community attention elsewhere. The rise of some other tough guy, some other ace, some other cop promoted to point man in the SWAT team can have the effect of taking away some of the emotional edge that powers the elite. So it is in the realm of intellectuals, a community hyper-dependent upon communicating about where the intellectual action is and whose ideas are hot. If the analogy holds, the long-term law of small numbers that governs the distribution of eminence in the field of creativity also explains why even the possessors of cool violent technique are never more than a few.

CHAPTER 12

Epilogue: Practical Conclusions

THIS BOOK IS PRIMARILY an effort at sociological understanding. But a few practical implications suggest themselves.

It is remarkable how many different kinds of violence there are. The book began with combat infantry and police violence, and ended with hitmen, ace pilots, and clandestine terrorists, with stops in between at bullies, gang initiations, and mosh pits, among others. I count at least thirty types of violence in the book. And there are many kinds of violence not treated in this volume, including rape (which comes in various kinds), torture, holocaust, serial killings, and school rampages. This means that no single practical recommendation can work for everything.

Practical recommendations should not be addressed just to government agencies or legislators. This top-down approach, common in policy studies, may not be where the greatest value in sociology lies. This book is focused on the micro-level of interaction, the here-and-now that we all inhabit when we wake up in the morning. Its insights ought to be useful to us as real people living our lives as they actually happen, rather than in the rhetoric of official speakers on formal occasions.

The job of a serious sociologist is not to be simple-minded. This is rather the opposite of the technique of electoral politicians and speakers for ideological movements, who generally sway public attention to the degree that they can simplify issues down to a rhetorical slogan. No slogan on the order of "zero tolerance" or "hugs not drugs" will come close to dealing with the issues of violence. This is true also for goals that are good in themselves, such as eliminating poverty and racial prejudice. If poverty were eliminated (which seems very unlikely under present circumstances), a great many kinds of violence would still exist; the background condition of poverty is not what causes carousing violence, forward panics, sports violence, or contract killings, to mention just a few. There has been a real reduction in racial prejudice in recent decades, but that has not reduced many forms of violence. We need to think truly outside the box, and that means outside the clichés on all sides of the political spectrum. Our own side's clichés are always hardest to recognize as such.

I put forward these suggestions without dogmatism, since most programs of action have unforeseen and unintended consequences. Often these side-effects can be quite negative, especially when programs are instituted by bureaucratic organizations, both public and private, since macro-institutions have their own momentum. I hope that advice on the micro-level is less likely to lead astray, but we need to keep alert to such possibilities.

1. When encountering the police, be aware of their potential to go into a forward panic. It is your task to reduce their confrontational tension. If you find this a loss of personal dignity, remind yourself that you are taking charge of the situation emotionally by calming people down. Be especially aware of the problem as the numbers of police on the scene goes up.

2. Similarly as advice to police officers and officials: Awareness of patrol officers' potential for forward panics in tense situations may help counteract them. Be aware that the more officers called to the scene, the greater the chance of a forward panic or other kinds of police violence, quite apart from what the suspect does. Be aware that communications in these situations are prone to rumors, which build the potential for violence. Many police officers already know how to defuse potentially violent encounters; police forces should spread the knowledge of how they do it.

3. The same awareness of forward panics should be explicitly recognized by military combat troops and officers. The public and the media should also try to understand the dynamics of emotions under the pressures of confrontational tension in a combat zone. Instead of being vindictive and self-righteous about forward panic atrocities, we would do better to recognize the dynamics of forward panics and develop a program to deal with them.

4. Advice again to us ordinary people: Learn how to deal with bluster, including one's own. Focus on how to make blustering among antagonists an equal-sided ritual, rather than escalating by trying to top the other. Potential fights wind down when the blustering becomes repetitive and boring; that's what you should try to achieve.

5. Learn some sensitivity to the inner-city black code of the street. Try to distinguish between posturing that is done defensively and for effect, and the kinds of challenges where someone is seriously looking for a fight. According to Elijah Anderson, most street code performances are the former. This kind of sensitivity on the part of whites and others should have important effects in reducing racial tension.

6. A rather speculative proposal: inner-city violence could be reduced if the practice of defending a group's honor (or "respect") were

replaced by the practice of *one-on-one* fair fights. Even duels with pistols would be better than gang drive-bys and street fights, with their potential for bystander hits and chains of future retribution. Maybe duels could be turned into boxing matches or something like them; even ostensibly very violent one-on-one fighting rituals are better than vendettas. Remember, the history of dueling was a movement toward self-limiting forms.

7. This would not take care of drug business violence, which is built into the necessity of defending one's territory and policing malfeasance in dealers' supply chains. The answer here is straightforward: legalize drugs. I have no expectation that in our political climate this is likely to happen. But it is clear to social scientists that a market for illegal commodities, which cannot enforce its contracts by law courts, creates its own underground system of enforcement. Those of us who uphold drug prohibition are indirectly responsible for murders in the drug business.

8. Learn how not to be a victim; recognize the techniques that bullies, domestic abusers, muggers, and street thugs try to use on you. This is easier said than done; but it is not a matter of your physical size, but your emotional energy and interactional style.

   An example from Elijah Anderson: He is pumping gas late at night at a crime-ridden spot in the ghetto, when a young black man suddenly walks up and asks if he has the time. "Instinctively I looked him in the eye and said, 'What's up, buddy?' as though I expected an answer. There was silence. Then I said, 'I ain't got no watch, man.' Experience on the streets had taught me that one ruse muggers use is to ask the intended victim a question that distracts him, getting him to drop his guard and setting him up for the mugging. By saying 'What's up, buddy?' I gave him pause and made him rethink his intentions. In a stickup or a mugging, timing is crucial. My body language, my tone of voice, and my words, all taken together in that instant, may have thrown him off, possibly averting an attempted stickup. . . . The rules of the street say that a strange black male does not approach another black male around midnight on a Saturday night and ask for the time" (*Streetwise*, 1990: 173).[1]

   This is careful micro-analysis. A naïve outsider might think that if a robber has superior force, he is going to carry out the robbery no matter what the victim does. Not so; even the habitually violent choose their time and circumstances; they attempt to establish the emotional momentum, get the jump on the other by timing their approach, setting the dominance in the interaction before the violent phase. Being "streetwise" is being tuned in to these rhythms and using them for defense.

Not being a victim does not mean you have to escalate and counter-attack; there is a subtle way of doing this that leaves the situation stable, emotionally flat. After all, most situational violence does not come off. Our aim is to keep it that way.

9. A tip from the military psychologist Dave Grossman (2004): if you are in a situation where tension is rising, you can feel it in your breathing and your heart rate. Adrenalin is pumping, which can go in the direction of either fear, anger, or self-conflicting mixtures. These emotions are dangerous, to yourself or to other people. You will deal better with the situation if you can bring your heart rate down. This can be done by breathing in while you count four seconds, holding your breath for four seconds, then breathing out for four seconds, holding your breath for four seconds, and so on. The key is not just to take a deep breath, but to establish the four-part rhythm slowing down all parts of the breathing cycle.

10. Be aware of the influence that audiences have on whether a fight will become serious, mild, or abort. As an audience, we have great influence on fights that happen in our presence, at least if the number of antagonists is below about five on a side. The crowd has a big effect in providing the emotional support to overcome confrontational tension; if we don't provide it, fights tend to peter out. That doesn't mean everybody will be happy, but we can keep violence to a relatively innocuous level.

A theme runs through my suggestions. Eradicating violence entirely is unrealistic. Trying to make every one adhere to an idealistic code of good manners is not going to work; more likely it will divide people into those who follow it and those who defy it. Given the antinomian trend of popular youth culture, many will take the latter direction. But it is possible to reduce the intensity of some kinds of violence, to replace serious violence with relatively mild and ritualistic forms.

There is no single remedy for the ills of violence. Different mechanisms of violence need to be headed off in different ways. This seems discouraging. But there have been some successes within this vast field. Running amok was a traditional form of honorable suicide in Indonesia, where a man would suddenly go into a frenzy of slashing at everyone around him with his machete until he was finally cut down (Blacker and Tupin 1977; Westermeyer 1973). Amoks in traditional Indonesian society were eradicated when the authorities stopped killing them at the climax of their killing frenzy. Instead, they were sentenced to life in prison and not allowed to die. Since running amok was an honorable form of suicide, this eliminated the purpose. One case was solved. Would that the rest were as easy.

Notes

1. See summaries in chapters 4 and 10.

2. I am concerned here chiefly with the violence of individuals and small groups. A different kind of violence, as in war or genocide, is structured by large-scale organizations, and can produce much higher numbers of persons killed and injured, in actions that can go on for much longer periods of time. But even here, the individuals involved are not violent all the time and in all contexts; at other times they generally are surprisingly different from the way they act in the midst of their violent routines.

3. During 2004, between fifty-three and fifty-six journalists and media workers were killed, the highest number since 1994 during the ethnic violence in former Yugoslavia (*San Diego Union Tribune*, Jan. 8, 2005). A considerable proportion of these were photographers and video camera operators.

4. I first began to get an inkling of the micro-sociology of violence when I asked a Vietnam vet, during the late 1960s, what the war was actually like. He was very reluctant to talk about it. Finally, when I persisted, he said that it was not at all what you think. Men were burrowing into the ground, shitting in their pants, crying like children—not at all the heroic image; nor the vicious destructive image held by the anti-war movement that I was active in at the time.

5. Even in communities where fighting is common, and most individuals present an image of themselves as tough, they do not jump in on the action when two tough guys threaten to fight. See the incident of armed black men (from Anderson 1999) described in chapter 9. The crowd was attentive, but rather hushed, watching the confrontation.

6. An example is reported in the *Philadelphia Inquirer*, Feb. 2, 2005, under the headline: "Phillies prospect injured. Cole Hamels, thought by many in the organization to be its best young pitcher, broke his throwing hand in a fight near a Florida bar." My ethnographic materials include numerous examples.

7. Fighting among children is not simply a matter of masculine culture. At young ages, when girls are about as strong as boys, little girls often engage in hitting, biting, and kicking at about the same rate as boys—varying by about 5 percent at most, and sometimes slightly exceeding boys (Tremblay 2004). And by strategically picking situations where parents are present, a little girl can get away with fighting her male siblings, even in attacking them, thus turning the boys-don't-pick-on-girls ideology to their own advantage, since the boy is the one who typically gets punished for retaliating. I have observed this repeatedly among small children in domestic situations.

8. In my collection of twenty-two photos of faces of bank robbers and other hold-up men in action (mostly from security cameras), none is smiling; their expressions range from tight-lipped concentration and tension to fear. In eighty-nine observations of fights from student reports and my own observations, in only three cases are the fighters in good humor: one where a pair of pre-adolescent boys bully a smaller boy by throwing a beach ball at him; and two instances where post-game fans, young black males, on a crowded bus harass middle-class white college students. Good-humored fighters thus appear only in situations of very limited violence, more accurately bluster, by groups with overwhelming advantage over their targets.

9. Bourgois (1995), Willis (1977). For a critical debate over these perspectives, see Wacquant (2002), Anderson (2002), Duneier (2002), and Newman (2002). Resistance theory gives few clues as to how violence would vary. Resistance violence is ascribed only to class and racial subalterns; but those subordinated by gender and sexual preference do not display resistance violence to any significant extent (more in the case of battered women killing their batterers than in the case of homosexuals striking back); women and homosexuals are chiefly victims of violence, whereas class and racial minorities are perpetrators of resistance violence. Obviously a theory of mobilization of grievance into violence is called for; but this is a level of specificity on which resistance theory does not proceed.

10. At a conference where I presented a piece of the present theory, one audience member rose during the question period to dispute why I had considered merely physical violence, and not symbolic violence. He asserted that he himself had been a victim of symbolic violence, in the previous session, when he did not get called on in the question period. There is a micro-sociology of who does or does not get to speak in a group meeting, and at what point in the sequence of speakers (Gibson 2001, 2005); even on this level, to invoke "symbolic violence" as an explanation of what happens is merely to make a rhetorical complaint, not to provide an explanatory mechanism. The fact that sophisticated intellectuals can believe that what they call symbolic violence is at all close to physical violence, shows how unaccustomed most intellectuals are to thinking in micro-sociological terms, and what little familiarity we have with real violence.

11. Tremblay, Nagin et al. (2004) argue that violence is the result of interaction between innate predisposition and social interactions in the family; the innate propensity tends to become socially repressed, since aggressive behavior is highest among young children and declines thereafter, except for a minority who go on to become criminals. But small children's violence, as seen in micro-situational detail, is very limited and to an extent indulged by parents and other children; it is often a mode of making social contact and getting attention. This is consistent with Tremblay's (2004) finding that violence of small boys and girls is more frequent if there are siblings present in the home. Small children's violence fits the pattern of protected and staged violence for an audience, which I describe in chapter 6. The situational conditions of early childhood interactions determine this violence as well as that of adults. In Tremblay's (2004) data, child violence peaks at about thirty months old, not earlier; it is constructed during the social development of the first three years. This is the period of "the terrible twos" related to the formation of an autonomous self through greater internalization of social im-

agery and audience viewpoint; in symbolic interactionist terms, the formation of "me" and "other" rather than expression of sheer primal "I" (Collins 2004: 79–81, 204–5).

12. I will consider the dynamics of warfare in greater detail in later chapters; and in a following volume, which will deal with macro-dimensions of conflict. Modern armies, too, are relatively poor performers in face-to-face combat, but they have improved their killing abilities in several ways: by organizational devices for keeping troops on the battlefield; by technologies for killing at long distance, where confrontational tension is lower because one cannot see the enemy's face; and by weapons of such highly destructive power that a small amount of competence may produce at least some casualties. We have become more deadly in battle, not because of greater individual ferociousness but because we have found social and technological ways around confrontational tension/fear. See Grossman (2004: 192–218).

13. Elias (1939/1978). In effect, Elias historicized Freud, presenting evidence that rough manners of all kinds (such as spitting, nose-blowing, and touching food with one's fingers) were gradually tamed, beginning with the rise of court societies in sixteenth-century Europe, which brought independent warriors under control of a centralizing state. Elias argues that aggression was regarded as a pleasure, alike in combat and in torturing, mutilating, and killing helpless victims. But this does not mean that violence was easy to perform in the micro-situational conditions of politically fragmented medieval societies, or in prior periods of history. We cannot assume, like Freud (1920/1953) in the period of his death-instinct theory, that there exists a primal reservoir of aggressiveness, once upon a time unrepressed, that is kept down only to the extent that there are social controls on it, and that pops out when controls are off. To the contrary, I will attempt to show that violence is always socially constructed; the history of violence is the history of social techniques for constructing particular kinds of violence. Accordingly, recent historical increases in violence are not the result of "decivilizing" but are the construction of new kinds of social techniques of violence; for example, in chapter 8, I argue that football hooligan violence, as it emerged during the 1950s to 1970s, was the creation of a sophisticated technique.

14. For example, I used to work at home in California in an upstairs study, with the windows open in good weather; every afternoon the children in the house just behind the hedge some twenty feet away would come out to play with their babysitter. Their repetitive patterns of whining used to annoy me, until I realized that there was a distinctive vocal pattern, which I could follow with stopwatch and notebook. This bit of data finds its way into chapter 9. And being in the researcher mode was a lot better for my own peace of mind.

CHAPTER 2
CONFRONTATIONAL TENSION AND INCOMPETENT VIOLENCE

1. Keeley (1996) is concerned to controvert the interpretation that casualties in tribal warfare are low. What he demonstrates, however, is that casualties in full-scale battles are generally low; but since such battles may be very frequent,

the aggregate number of deaths over a period of years can be quite much higher than the battle deaths of large-scale modern societies when averaged across their bigger populations and relatively infrequent wars. Keeley overrides the distinction between micro- and macro-sociological levels; on the micro-level, his data are consistent with the pattern given here.

2. Marshall's method of firsthand, total reporting did not ask each soldier: "Did you fire your gun or not?" Marshall's estimate of 15 to 25 percent was of the soldiers who stood out in his interviews as having carried on the bulk of the activity of the battle. He was concerned with the top end of the distribution, not the bottom end. Thus it is not clear from his report that the remaining 75 to 85 percent were uniformly frozen in fear or inactivity. He himself noted they often did things to help the most active firers; by Marshall's criterion, some of them might have fired occasionally. Later I use Glenn's (2000b) Vietnam data, and my own analysis of combat photos to reconstruct a more nuanced picture.

3. In a battle in the Ardennes, during the crucial Battle of the Bulge, December 1944, Marshall describes a battalion in which the number firing at the enemy was "between 25 and 30 per cent. Even so, it had as high an efficiency of fire as any unit which I have ever known." Marshall praises this unit, which won all its battles, with these words: "I doubt there has ever been a finer fighting unit in the Army of the United States" (1947: 73–74).

4. These figures are for heavy continuous action in World War II, and estimates for trench warfare in World War I. In many other wars, the actual time spent in combat might be rather intermittent (Holmes 1985: 75–76).

5. Glenn's data comprised two samples: infantry troops (mostly enlisted men) and officers at the combat level of platoon and company commanders. The response rate for the surveys was 52 percent of the troops, 70 percent of the officer sample. About half of the troop sample who replied were non-commissioned or commissioned officers; only 30 percent were combat riflemen or other weapons-handling troops. More than half of the troops sample were volunteers, not draftees (although the combat troops in the Vietnam war generally were highly skewed toward draftees). Virtually all those troops who had served additional combat tours in Vietnam beyond the one-year rotation—about one-fifth of those who responded to the survey—had enlisted as volunteers (Glenn 2000b: 7). Volunteers had higher self-reported firing rates than draftees. Of the volunteers, 57 percent were in the high firing group, compared to 41 percent of the draftees in this sample (calculated from Glenn 2000b: 164).

6. This is not without problems. What are presented as war photos are for the most part not actually photos of soldiers confronting their enemy at the moment of violence. In eleven collections of war photos or illustrated histories of wars, the number of photos showing troops in combat ranges from 5 to 44 percent, with a median of 22 percent. We will call this category (A), but more frequently war photos show (B) soldiers awaiting combat, or moving into the combat zone, or wounded and dead in the aftermath of battle; (C) soldiers in rear areas, including troops and supply vehicles on the road, and in hospitals and prisoner areas; (D) top military leaders and politicians, and scenes of recruiting and training. There are hazy boundaries between (A) and (B), such as when soldiers are on patrol. And some combat photos show warfare at a distance: planes dropping bombs, or

artillery firing. I confine my analysis to category (A), further limited to infantry engaged with small arms, including machine guns and man-portable rockets (and sometimes with knives, machetes, and rocks), while omitting artillery and mortar crews. The photos are grouped into three collections: an extensive collection of Vietnam (the most heavily photographed of all wars)—104 photos (Daugherty and Mattson 2001; all other twentieth-century wars—seventy-two photos (Arnold-Forster 2001; Beevor 1999; Bowden 2000; Gilbert 1994; Holmes 1985; Howe 2002; Keegan 1976, 1993; Marinovich and Silva 2000); and photos of the conventional phase of the 2003 Iraq war—seventeen photos (Murray and Scales 2003). Since it is not always clear whether a particular soldier is firing, I have given them the benefit of a doubt and present maximal percentages. Each set of photos is subdivided into *all photos*, and those in which *at least one combatant is firing* (or using a weapon). The latter category guarantees that it is indeed possible to fire, giving maximal chances that other soldiers will fire also.

It is possible, of course, that soldiers who are not firing at the moment the photo is taken are firing at other moments. But see my discussion in chapter 11 of the similar problem of the small numbers of active participants in riot photos and their constancy over time. Embedded reporters and TV camera operators in the 2003 Iraq war showed mostly military vehicles rolling across the desert but only occasional snippets of behavior under fire, which did not contradict the SLAM pattern. Ultimately it may be possible to use video from unmanned battlefield drones (UAVs) for continuous data on soldiers in combat, similar to cameras now mounted in police cars.

7. McNeill 1995; Speidel 2002. When Roman armies were defeated by Germans, on the other hand, it was usually because they were marching in densely wooded areas, where their formations were broken—as in the famous battle of the Teutoburger Wald in A.D. 9

8. "The majority of the active firers used several weapons; if the machine gun went out, they picked up a rifle; when they ran out of rifle ammunition, they used grenades" (Marshall 1947: 56).

9. Preston 2000: 399; Chadwick 2006. The Zulus lacked firearms, and inflicted only seventeen deaths with their spears. The Zulus thus also had a low level of effectiveness—only one out of 175 attackers killed anyone—although they did have high solidarity in keeping up the attack; this was due among others reasons to the adoption of European-style phalanx formation, which they found very effective against unorganized native African fighters. Ineffectiveness of hand weapons was historically typical; in a battle in the Roman civil wars in 48 B.C., thirty thousand arrows were collected, which wounded 1,500 men (a ratio of one per two hundred arrows), and killed less than twenty (Caesar 1998: 105 [*Civil War*, Vol. 3: 52]).

10. British army experiments have used laser pulses to simulate historical battles of the nineteenth and early twentieth centuries; these have shown that the potential firing accuracy of the weapons was always much higher than the casualty rates actually found in those battles (Grossman 1995: 16).

11. It has been argued that very recent, twenty-first century warfare, with the advent of precision-guided weapons, has changed all this. Long-distance weapons are claimed to be becoming infallible; by implication, emotions of confrontation

become irrelevant to the outcome. I discuss such weapons in the following section. It should be noted that the claim applies only to large-scale military combat, not to the other forms of violence discussed in this book. And the photo evidence on the 2003 Iraq war does not show infantry firing rates different from previous wars.

12. In another variant, troops empty their guns at an enemy who has already been defeated, or even killed. Shalit (1988: 141–42) gives an example of Israeli troops overwhelming an Egyptian position in a 1973 commando raid: surprise was achieved and firing was almost completely one-sided, continuing so heavily that the dead were riddled with bullets. He comments that "firing is a very effective method of relieving tension and fear, and is often engaged in even when there is no need for it. . . . One often fires not so much to destroy and conquer the enemy as to overcome and control one's own fear." Shalit concludes from his observations that 100 percent of well-trained troops usually fired, overcoming the SLAM problem. The mechanism here is similar to what in chapter 3 I analyze as "forward panic."

13. "You began by firing by platoons, and perhaps two or three would get off orderly volleys. But then would follow a general blazing away—the usual rolling fire when everybody blasted off as soon as he had loaded, when ranks and files became intermingled, when the first rank was incapable of kneeling, even if it wanted to" (quoted in Holmes 1985: 172–73). This was Frederick the Great's army, considered the most disciplined of the eighteenth century.

14. Friendly fire casualties of this sort happen in mass demonstrations as well. In the overthrow of the Yugoslav dictator Milošević in October 2000, the turning point came when workers brought a bulldozer to break through police lines. A girl in the crowd was killed by being accidentally run over (*The Guardian*, Oct. 6, 2000, p. 1).

15. Murray and Scales 2003: 269–77. The experience of the U.S. bombings in Afghanistan in 2001–02, continued to include incidents of bystander hits. The air war in Afghanistan was described by the Pentagon as the most accurate ever, with 75 to 80 percent of bombs and missiles hitting their targets. Nevertheless, some of these air bombardments caused "fratricide" of coalition troops, estimated at 35 percent of coalition casualties; and several thousand Afghani civilians were killed (Burgess 2002). There were similar results with NATO bombing in Serbia in 1999; among the famous mishaps was the bombing of the Chinese embassy in Belgrade, under conditions of haste and bureaucratic complexity where out-of-date information was fed to operational forces. During the Israeli bombardment of Hezbollah missile sites in Lebanon in 2006, a U.N. post was repeatedly hit and U.N. observers killed even though they had phoned Israeli officials and identified themselves. The information did not make it up the Israeli military hierarchy to where targets were chosen (*Los Angeles Times*, July 28, 2006, A11, A13).

16. Casualties of American/Canadian/European forces in the Afghanistan war Oct. 2001 through April 18, 2002: total forty-one deaths; fifteen by hostile fire, seven by friendly fire, nineteen by traffic accidents (chiefly aircraft) and non-combat accidents (*USA Today*, April 19, 2002). Total enemy-caused combat deaths 37 percent; non-enemy-caused deaths 63 percent. This is much higher than Keegan's estimate for 15 to 25 percent in the world wars. In the Iraq war from March 2003

through mid-November 2005, 227 of the 2,083 U.S. military deaths (11 percent) were from non-combat-related incidents (*USA Today*, Nov. 21, 2005).

17. On the repetitive structure of scandals, see Thompson (2000). On the structure of friendly fire accidents, see Snook (2000). The underlying explanation is Perrow's (1984) theory of normal accidents: the combination of complexity and non-linear interdependence among many components of a system—technological and/or human—makes it statistically likely that unforeseen combinations of small anomalies will concatenate into periodic disasters. The accidents are caused by the structure of the interactional system, although our cultural ritual always seeks out specific individuals to blame.

18. This includes the ritualistic posting of yellow do-not-enter tapes around areas of a crime scene, or even of a traffic accident—part of the self-importance of those involved in a conflict situation, vis-à-vis all those not so privileged as to be involved. For instance, a Los Angeles freeway was closed in both directions for seven hours, causing an enormous traffic pile-up, while police investigated a car in which a man had been shot to death (*Los Angeles Times*, Dec. 23, 2002).

19. During World War II, over 50 percent of American troops in the European theater were never under enemy fire; in Vietnam, around 70 percent (Holmes 1985: 76).

20. Emotions are categorized following the methods of Ekman and Friesen (1975); see also Ekman (1985). I have expanded the collection to include prisoner interrogations and executions, and wounded soldiers and medics in the combat zone. Multiple coding of emotion-blends brings the total above 100 percent.

21. My collection of news photographs includes one in which a man displays almost the identical expression of rage as the peace demonstrator in Daugherty and Mattson (2001): jaw thrust forward, mouth opened hard and square, neck and face muscles contorted. In this case, the angry man is the father of a murdered woman, confronting the convicted murderer in court; the murderer sits impassively and the rest of the audience looks uneasy (*San Diego Union Tribune*, March 7, 1992, A1). In general, angry faces are much more common in photos of peaceful demonstrations than of situations of violence.

22. Napoleon was explicit about his tactics during the French Revolution in 1795 in dispersing a Parisian crowd attacking the seat of Revolutionary government: "I made the troops fire ball at first because to a mob who are ignorant of firearms, it is the worst possible policy to start out by firing blanks. For the populace, hearing a great noise, are a little frightened after the first discharge but, looking around them and seeing nobody killed or wounded, they pluck up their spirits, begin immediately to despise you, become twice as insolent, and rush on fearlessly, and it becomes necessary to kill ten times the number that would have been killed if ball had been used in the first place" (quoted in Markham 1963: 29–30). A former district magistrate in India reports his experience that when police were given orders to avoid firing at ethnic rioters except as a last resort, the crowds generally acted in a more threatening manner to the police, and tended to panic them into wild firing. In contrast, where police were authorized to fire as they deemed necessary, their demeanor tended to scare off the rioters, and incidents of actual firing were very low (S. K. Menon, personal communication, Feb. 2002). The same pattern is reported in Belgium in the late 1980s, where police forces

controlling soccer crowds were given the option of wearing more casual uniforms (short sleeves) to provide a friendly atmosphere, or militaristic paraphernalia including helmets and shields. The police in casual dress reported feeling vulnerable to missiles thrown by hooligans; these police produced more violence than those in intimidating gear (Van Limbergen, Colaers, and Walgrave 1989). Lode Walgrave, Catholic University of Leuven (personal communication, Sept. 2004), provided detail on this point.

23. Both the firing ratio and the accuracy level appear to be much higher than for soldiers or police; although in 105 of 151 incidents more than one person had a gun, and in 79 of 107 times when a gun was fired there could have been several people firing; hence the firing ratio and accuracy level could be much lower. When respondents fired, they claimed to have hit their opponents 51 percent of the time; when opponents fired, respondents were hit 13 percent of the time (calculated from Wilkinson 2003: 129–30, 216). Respondents reportedly outhit their opponents by 3.8 to 1. There may well be some egotistical bias in their recollections; but it also may indicate that these ultra tough guys were chiefly picking their fights when they had the advantage over their opponents. As we shall see (in chapter 6), gangs as well as solo hoodlums attempt to avoid violent situations in which they do not have the upper hand from the outset. Wilkinson reports (181) that whichever side initiated the fight (shot first) was more likely to injure the other side.

24. Marshall 1947: 44–48 stresses this point. "The common scene in open warfare is landscape: the total absence of moving things is the surest sign that one has reached the line of danger. . . . On the battlefield it is only when the fire impasse has been at last broken that military forces have that appearance of continuity of strength in line which the uninitiated mistake for the reality of a victorious tactical formation when they see it on the motion-picture screen" (89).

25. In a survey of attempted violence, 80 percent of American children between ages three and eighteen who had siblings admitted trying to hurt their brother or sister during the year; almost half had kicked, punched, or bitten a sibling; 40 percent had hit one with a hard object; and one-sixth had beaten one up (Gelles 1977). But the rate of injuries from being struck reported in emergency departments for ages five to fourteen is 3.1 percent (2.7 percent for ages zero to four); even if we attributed all such injuries to siblings and if we assumed only one violent incident per child per year, the proportion of sibling attacks that resulted in effective violence is very small. Calculated from "Overall struck by/against nonfatal injuries and rates, 2001," National Center for Injury Prevention and Control (at www.cdc.gov/ncipc/wisqars).

26. A characteristic instance is a medic who went forward under severe fire to treat a wounded soldier who was obviously about to die. The medic's explanation: "When someone hollers for a medic, if you're a medic you run toward the shout" (Miller 2000: 42).

27. For instance, in a security camera photo of a holdup at an ATM, the gunman holds a pistol at the back of the victim's neck, who has his head bowed; the gunman's face is tense. There is no eye contact (Oct. 4, 1991, AP distribution of Maitland, Florida, police photo).

28. From interviews with Philadelphia police officers. In another instance, U.N. forces in Srebrenica, Yugoslavia, in July 1995 became emotionally dominated by Serbian paramilitaries, and thereby failed to prevent a massacre of 7,000

Bosnian prisoners. The Dutch commander of the U.N. troops, who backed down in a face-to-face confrontation with the Serbian commander, was incapacitated for several days thereafter with severe diarrhea (Klusemann 2006).

29. Similarly in the case of audiences of political speeches, applause lasts much longer than booing; and booing is harder to get going, and harder to sustain, since mass participation drops out more easily (Clayman 1993).

CHAPTER 3
FORWARD PANIC

1. A similar case of LAPD officers beating a car thief at the end of a footchase, videoed by a news helicopter, is shown in a sequence of photographs in the *Los Angeles Times*, July 24, 2004.

2. But not, apparently, a completely innocent and passive person: he was vocally aggressive, at least until the fight started; he had worked in dangerous manual labor; he also had a certain amount of prominence in local political circles, as protégé of a local sheriff (Stump 1994: 206). This type of individual seems characteristic of the rough politics as well as the rough spectator atmosphere of baseball at this time.

3. The feat of hitting .400 two years in a row was matched only once, by Rogers Hornsby in 1924–25. The pressure of batting over .400 is probably the highest experienced in sustaining any baseball record, since it requires getting two or more hits every day of the season (allowing for occasional hitless days), making virtually every at-bat crucial, without any letdown.

4. I owe this observation to Robert Lien, a sociologist who has studied emotions in high-challenge sports.

5. The debilitating effect of an adrenalin rush that is not allowed to culminate in a fight is shown in the following incident. In a game at Yankee Stadium in 1923, Ty Cobb was managing the Detroit Tigers against a pitcher, Carl Mays, who had killed a man, Ray Chapman, by hitting him with a fastball. Cobb instructed his batter to fall down at the first close pitch and writhe around, whereupon Cobb walked to the mound. The batter recalled, "I thought he intended to jump all over Mays. But to my surprise he only said, 'Now, Mr. Mays, you should be more careful where you throw. Remember Chapman?' Cobb walked back to the plate, shaking his head. Mays was actually trembling . . . he was so unnerved that he couldn't get anybody out. We scored five runs off him to beat New York easily" (Stump 1994: 351). Cobb's reputation as the most violent man in baseball had the pitcher keyed up for a severe fight; when it did not happen, his body was shaking with undischarged adrenalin. The incident also indicates that an extremely aggressive person like Ty Cobb was not simply at the mercy of raging impulses; like some other persons who make a career out of aggressiveness—such as Mafia enforcers—he could let himself go into the tunnel of violent emotion, but he could also recognize other persons' anticipations of his behavior and play on their expectations to his own advantage.

6. One sees a similar version among athletes in sports victory celebrations, combining expressions of elation with a kind of symbolic or truncated gesture of anger: a home-run hitter circling the bases pumping his fist; a pitcher celebrating a

strikeout at a crucial moment with a gesture like a boxer's punch. Compare figures 8.5A and B in chapter 8 of pitchers' pumping fists and protruding lower jaws.

7. See Collins (2004: 205–11) and Katz (1999, esp. 18–83 and 229–73) for analyses of rhythmic self–entrainment; these includes private forms of magic-like incantation such as cursing and forms of crying.

8. We are inclined to take this kind of laughter during a forward panic atrocity as further evidence of the extreme moral depravity of the perpetrators. But this is our folk psychology, and it reverses the actual order of causality; the hysterical laughter is an expression of uncontrollable self-entrainment.

9. A similar incident was substantiated by the U.S. Army's investigative Vietnam War Crimes Working Group for an infantry attack on villages in the Que Son Valley in September 1969, killing animals along with civilians and children while burning homes in a sweep for guerrillas. Documents summarized in *Los Angeles Times*, Aug. 6, 2006, p. A9.

10. Just what proportion participated with what degree of enthusiasm is difficult to estimate from available evidence. As we have seen in the SLAM ratio of firing in combat, and as we will see more extensively in chapter 10, a small proportion of the group carries out most of the violence in virtually all collective actions; where victims are completely helpless, however, many others follow the violence leaders.

11. The term was coined by William James, then imported into sociology by Martin (1920).

12. The example of John Rabe, the Nazi Party member who attempted to stop the killing at Nanking, and even wrote letters of protest to his Nazi superiors in Germany, asking for their political intervention with the Japanese (Chang 1997: 109–21), shows again the situational character of atrocities. The Nazis, for all their own atrocities, were not atrocious in all situations; where they were not caught up in their own dynamics of killing, they might take the stance of outside observers shocked by such violence.

13. In this respect it is similar to the milder phenomenon of carousing zones, discussed in chapter 7.

14. A variant of the responsibility-from-above theme is that official policy has inadvertent consequences leading to atrocity. Gibson (1986) is chiefly concerned to show that in the Vietnam war, the emphasis by the U.S. military command upon a high level of enemy body counts, in order to calculate the progress of a war of attrition, was responsible for loose definitions of combatants and the killing of civilians. This explanation fits classic organizational theory of unintended consequences of purposive action, and is very likely true. Nevertheless killing of civilians did not occur in every possible encounter, but in particular situations; many of these had the emotional dynamics of forward panics, although the proportion is hard to establish.

15. Thus mass rapes are typically the result of a forward panic which opens the way for a moral holiday. Conversely, moral holidays may occur independently of forward panics, as we see in chapter 7.

16. This passivity is situational, not a constant. A Jewish militant assassinated a German diplomat in Paris in 1938; in 1943, the Warsaw ghetto carried out two military uprisings. Passivity was specific to the deportations and death camps,

where the whole interactional atmosphere was rigged to produce not just physical but emotional dominance by the Nazis.

17. When artillery, machine guns, or other lethal distance weapons became available, as in the Napoleonic wars, the American Civil War, and the world wars, lengthy battles involving assaults on dug-in defensive positions produced higher casualties. In the Civil War, casualties in major battles ranged from 6 to 12 percent at the low end to 25 to 29 percent at the high end. Under these circumstances, the heavy casualties were usually taken by the attacker, unless there was a sudden breakdown and panic retreat, such as Union forces underwent at Chickamauga and Confederate forces at Chattanooga in 1863. See Griffith (1986: 46; 1989).

18. Caesar (*Civil War*, 197) explicitly chose a similar target for attack in a lengthy marching battle during his African campaign: "He gave the signal when the enemy had begun to throw their weapons perfunctorily and carelessly, and suddenly launched his cohorts of foot and squadrons of horse at them. In an instant they drove the enemy effortlessly from the field."

19. There continue to be instances, even with modern mechanized warfare, where a local rout concatenates to demoralize and disorganize an entire army. These include the Italian army's disastrous retreat from Caporetto in 1917, and the French army's response to the German blitzkrieg in 1940. The main features of a forward panic attack are reproduced on the macro level when one side succeeds in paralyzing their opponents by imposing emotional momentum on them. In the Gulf war of February 1991, Iraqi forces went into a panic retreat of vehicles streaming back along the highway from Kuwait into Iraq. American pilots strafed them unmercifully, causing thousands of casualties in an air-power version of a forward panic, with the pilots reporting back in a mood of elation at the "turkey shoot." In the conventional phase of the March–April 2003 Iraq war, U.S. attack so disorganized the Iraqi army that it melted away, with few units giving concerted resistance. Similar to small-scale forward panics, losses of winners and losers were hugely disproportionate: Germans in 1940 losing 1 per 150 of their troops, the French having virtually their entire army taken prisoner; in the Gulf War, the United States losing 1 per 3,000 troops, in the Iraq invasion 1 per 1,400; Iraqi losses in each war disintegrated armies of hundreds of thousands (Biddle 2004; Lowry 2003; Murray and Scales 2003; www.icasualties.org/oif). The situational nature of such disparities is indicated by the fact that U.S. losses were proportionately much higher during the phase of guerrilla war that followed during the occupation of Iraq, when forces on both sides fought without organizational breakdown.

20. The vestibule was five feet wide by seven feet deep. Two of the officers led the firing, shooting sixteen bullets each; the other two were caught up in the contagion, firing an additional nine bullets between them. (*New York Post*, Feb. 9–13, 1999; *USA Today*, Feb. 28, 2000; www.courttv.com/archive/national/diallo).

21. In the following I draw heavily on Horowitz (2001), a study of 150 cases of ethnic violence, almost all since World War II, chiefly in Asia, Africa, and the former Soviet Union, with the largest number of cases from Hindu-Muslim riots in India.

22. Horowitz (2001: 80). These are especially prominent in ethnic riots in South Asia and Africa; not in American race riots. But racial lynchings often have a similar process of rumor exaggeration about ritualistic offenses, which in turn

are paid back by corresponding ritual mutilations (Senechal de la Roche 2001; Allen 2000). Since the initial rumor is generally false, the imagery of mutilation circulated during that period is more a matter of creating an image, foreshadowing or planning what will be done to the victim.

23. One such case occurred in Gujarat (western India) during February 27 to March 2, 2002: Muslims firebombed two railroad cars full of Hindu demonstrators passing through the area on their way to a sacred site in central India contested between Muslims and Hindus, killing fifty-eight. In the ensuing three days of attacks by Hindus on Muslim villages, several thousand villagers were trapped and burned to death, while firefighters were blocked from entering the area (*Human Rights Watch* 14, no. 3 [April 2002]; available at http://hrw.org/reports/2002/india/).

24. Horowitz (2001: 74): "Once the riot becomes intense, any disposition the targets may have felt to resist and counterattack will almost certainly disappear. In the relatively few cases of significant early resistance, there are reports of victims who then became 'pathetically passive and allowed themselves to be slaughtered like sheep.'"

25. Nor are targets picked because of maximal cultural distance. Nearby comparisons are easier to make than distant ones, and thus nearby ethnic targets often are relatively similar in culture to their attackers (Horowitz 2001: 187–93).

26. On occasion, a smaller ethnic group may attack a larger one. Horowitz (2001: 393) refers to these as instances of "desperation demography," where one group is becoming outnumbered by the more rapid breeding or in-migration of their rival group. But in these instances, too, there is always local superiority of numbers: attacking in just those neighborhoods where the balance of power is favorable, and targeting more civilized, middle-class groups who are averse to using violence. More "advanced," educated, urbanized and middle-class ethnic groups rarely riot against groups less "advanced" on these indices, although they sometimes may be recruitment bases for guerrilla or terrorist movements (Horowitz 2001: 180).

27. Thus Horowitz (2001) points out how much care a riot-preparing group may put into choosing its targets, avoiding false positives, members of the wrong ethnic group who might get mistaken for the appropriate victims. This may be regarded as a form of calculating rationality, fighting with just the targeted ethnic group, and avoiding raising further enemies and having to fight more than one enemy at a time.

28. In Petersburg, after the first confrontation, a small number of rebellious soldiers in the demonstration fired back, and government troops eventually retreated; each side sustained about the same number of killed and wounded (Trotsky 1930).

29. Buford (1990: 303–8) describes what it is like being the victim of a police attack in just these circumstances. As a journalist accompanying a large group of British football hooligans during the World Cup match in Sardinia, he finds himself in the pathway of Italian police on their way to counter-attack a large group of hooligans who have just rampaged through the city. Buford decides to detach himself from the crowd and to crouch in a defensive posture with his hands guarding his head, hoping that the police will just give him a passing blow on their way

to attacking the main group. Instead he unknowingly has taken the most vulnerable victim position, attracting three policemen who beat him at length while he is lying on the ground trying to cover up vulnerable parts of his body; this seems to goad the police into a mini-contest to try to tear his hands and arms away so that they can hit him more painfully.

30. Generalizations in this section, and in chapter 11, are based on my collection of four hundred photos of crowd violence from 1989 through 2005 in the Americas, Europe, the Middle East, Africa, and Asia. The reader may find many of the photos cited in this book by date in the online image archives of the following: APImages.com; pictures.Reuters.com; procorbis.com; GettyImages.com.

31. We may add yet a fourth factor leading to the prolonged beating of King: the officer who initially led the car chase and first attempted to arrest King was a woman. King's demeanor when he finally left his car to surrender in the first moments of the arrest was not so much threatening as insolent. The woman highway patrol officer testified that he grabbled his buttock and shook it at her. King was not taking the arrest seriously, and even was expressing a sexual innuendo at the woman officer. At least this was how the other officers present took the gesture. The woman officer, having trouble subduing King, drew her pistol; whereupon the LAPD sergeant on the scene told her to get back and that he and his men were taking over the arrest (testimony on Court TV video "The Rodney King Case," 1992). King rushed the officer who tried to handcuff him, knocking him down, whereupon a second officer hit him across the face with a baton, and the beating was on. All this fits a pattern that is common in fights generally, although more usually in carousing, barroom and nightclub scenes: men are more likely to fight in the presence of women (Grazian 2003: 21; personal communication, 2004). This does not mean that they are fighting over the women; my ethnographic collection of student reports indicates that men without dates pick fights with other men without dates. This may be regarded as a particular kind of bystander effect: women onlookers, even if they are entirely passive, tend to make men more contentious toward each other, and to blow up confrontations into violent ones. In a sense, King and the policemen who took over the arrest from the woman officer were all showing off in front of her. Thus, on the micro level, the tension continued to escalate even after the end of the car chase.

32. A similar sequence in West Virginia in 1901 ended in a lynching. It began when a small-town police chief chased a black man fleeing from arrest for a street disturbance; in the ensuing tussle, the black shot the cop with his own revolver, then jumped through a window and was pursued by a crowd of five hundred who had gathered watching the fight; after a half-mile chase, the fugitive was beaten and hung from a tree (Allen 2000: 193).

CHAPTER 4
ATTACKING THE WEAK: I. DOMESTIC ABUSE

1. Maxfield and Widom (1996). This was an unusually thorough follow-up study of abuse victims through age thirty-two, by which time most crimes are committed. Similarly for other criminal arrests for nonviolent violations: excluding traffic

violations: the abused and neglected group had a rate of 49 percent, but the control group was 38 percent—a ratio again of 1.3 to 1. Undetected crimes and violence would no doubt make these figures higher, but the ratio between the two groups seems likely to be the same.

2. Kaufman and Ziegler (1993) give 30 percent as best estimate for intergenerational transmission of severe abuse, in retrospective studies; that is, sampling on the dependent variable, 70 percent of abusers did not report being abused. Sampling on the independent variable in a longitudinal study, Egeland (1993: 203) found a 40 percent transmission rate; this, however, is an examination of the consequences of being abused, and does not capture the entire population of those who abuse others. Furthermore, these are families with multiple sources of stress; in the larger population where risk factors are lower, the transmission percentage might well be lower. In any case, these figures are much higher than estimates of the rate of child abuse in the population, about 2 to 4 percent (Straus and Gelles 1986). The experience of being abused has some causal effect on subsequently abusing others. If we expand the definition of being abused to all forms of corporal punishment, this becomes a very weak predictor, since there are many more persons who were subjected to corporal punishment of non-extreme forms (around 90 percent) than those who go on to carry out extreme abuse of the following generation. Johnson and Ferraro (2000), summarizing the change in scholarly opinion in the 1990s, note that most of the studies of the 1980s that made popular the "cycle of abuse" explanation were from clinical data lacking control groups and relied on retrospective data.

3. Similarly for transmission of spousal violence to the next generation by example; Johnson and Ferraro (2000: 958) note that "even among the group of men whose parents were two standard deviations above average in level of partner violence, 80 percent of adult sons had not even once in the last 12 months committed any acts of severe violence on their partners."

4. Compare the common ineffectiveness of peace-keeping forces in situations of ethno-national conflict. Local fighters quickly recognize that the altruistic commitment of U.N. troops and other neutral parties makes the threat of using violence against them implausible; thus not only are they not inhibited from continuing to attack their local enemies, but they also typically steal aid supplies and blackmail peacekeepers into trading subservience for any show of cooperation (Oberschall and Seidman 2005; Kaldor 1999).

5. Daly and Wilson (1988) argue that stepfathers and other non-relatives are much more likely to harm children of their sexual partner, whereas biological fathers are not, because of a genetic propensity to maximize the propagation of one's own genes. Nevertheless, any such genetic theory must provide a mechanism by which this differential propensity to violence against children operates. It would have to be something that operates through differential perception of struggle with an attention-seeking, crying child. A purely sociological explanation is that for (many, if not all) birth fathers, there have been successful interaction rituals between mother and father with the baby in the focus of attention; the baby becomes a sacred object, an emblem of their relationship and their identity as a family. The lack of this symbolic bond of respect for the baby (however much it may be strained by other processes) is a key difference that explains why non-

parents commit more violence against partners' children. This could be tested: biological fathers who had no ritual contact with the mother and child around time of child-bearing would act like non-fathers in their propensity to abuse.

6. By the same token, parental ideology does make a difference for the amount of corporal punishment used on teenagers; perhaps because parents have more of a range of control resources to choose from (Straus and Donnelly 2001: 208). About 50 percent of teenagers are hit by parents in any given year (Dietz 2000; Straus 1994).

7. Daly and Wilson (1988: 37–94). The evolutionary psychology argument is that mothers kill their children when they assess they do not have a good chance to raise them to maturity. It is dubious that mothers who commit infanticide make this kind of rationalistic judgment; often they are reacting to their own stigma of an unwanted or socially illegitimate birth (Kertzer 1993).

8. The use of corporal punishment in schools was notorious in some traditional Catholic schools, where nuns used disciplinary methods bordering on torture, such as making children sit on hot radiators. Nuns have also sometimes inflicted brutal punishments upon novices in nunneries. The exalted nature of authority in such organizations, and their greater traditionalism, are responsible for nuns using more violence than other modern teachers. My point here is that there is nothing intrinsically male about it; where women have extreme control over others, they also use violence.

9. Mothers who have more children are more likely to use corporal punishment, and to commit child abuse (Eamon and Zuehl 2001). This is understandable in that women in this situation are more absorbed in child-rearing, more socially isolated, and have less resources to devote to controlling each child; violence is the cheapest and most rapidly applied control in the immediate situation. But it also means that women who on the face of it are most "maternal" are also those who are most violent toward their children. Structurally, this is the same pattern as German forces using more brutality in rounding up Holocaust victims to transport to concentration camps (and killing more by a factor of four to one) when there was a lower ratio of guards to prisoners (Browning 1992: 95); or of prison guards who are isolated from the outside world and are heavily outnumbered by their prisoners (Haney, Banks, and Zimbardo 1983).

10. Or her, as in the case of abuse of small children, like the babysitter who held the child's hand in scalding water.

CHAPTER 5
ATTACKING THE WEAK: II. BULLYING, MUGGING, AND HOLDUPS

1. Olweus (1993: 14), however, in Scandinavian data found much lower crossover, with 17 percent of victims also acting as bullies; these bullies/victims were 1.6 percent of all children.

2. Students were twice as likely to be bullied at elementary school than on their way to or from school; in high school, three times as likely (Olweus 1993: 21). The school is the bullies' field of action; and high school is an especially intense field, although as noted, the bullying becomes more verbal and less physical. Ol-

weus (1993: 15–16) found that there are many more victims than bullies in the earliest grades; by the time they have reached secondary school, there are more bullies than victims. This implies a shift from individualized bullying to collective bullying.

3. Since much assault in prison, as well as elsewhere, is not bullying in the strict sense of the term (an ongoing exploitative dominance relationship; not simply the experience of being beaten up in a fight), there is a serious methodological problem of separating out bullying when trying to measure its extent in prisons, and to gauge whether it is stable, intransitive, or passed on by cyclical reversal to others.

4. In one study, 56 percent of youth offenders and 26 percent of adult inmates were called insulting names within the past month; but only 20 percent of the serious assaults during that month involved insults. Moreover, 70 percent of the youth and 80 percent of the adult prisoners were not assaulted during the month, indicating that most incidents of insult don't escalate (Edgar and O'Donnell 1998: 640). Similarly, Ireland (2002) found that insults are much more frequent than fights.

5. Homophobic language is often used by students in the popular crowd to denigrate members of music bands and drama groups, which are mid-ranking "alternative" cultures in American high schools (Milner 2004: chap. 4 and n. 62). Milner judges that most students do not seriously believe these accusations, but only use them to justify scorning the position of certain individuals in the school status system. Kimmel and Mahler (2003) note that in the mass killings in schools in the 1990s, most of the shooters had been called homosexual, but none of them actually was. The killers were weak victims of collective bullying: either small and skinny, or badly overweight, with complexion problems, and far from the school ideal of the athlete and sexual market stars; it was this low-status position in the school hierarchy that gave some local sense for branding them as homosexual.

6. Gaughan, Cerio, and Myers (2001) found in a national opinion survey that blacks regarded bullying as a less serious problem than whites.

7. Franzoi et al. (1994) used five categories: popular, controversial, average, neglected, and rejected. The last are those most explicitly bullied, at least by reputational jeering and pointed exclusion.

8. The crucial feature affecting likelihood of killing is whether the victim is hooded, not the killer (Grossman 1995: 128). On a less lethal level, this is the same pattern as in the humiliation by U.S. military guards of hooded prisoners at the Abu Ghraib prison in 2004 (Mestrovic 2006).

9. Muggers may be gang members, but the gang as a whole is generally an umbrella organization for a variety of criminal activities, and mugging is usually carried out by small groups temporarily detaching themselves from the gang (Jankowski 1991). The vast majority of muggers (98 percent) are male; about 20 percent of their victims are female; the victims of female muggers are almost always female (Pratt 1980).

10. Goffman analyzes this structure formally in *Strategic Interaction* (1969) as a hierarchy of clandestine moves in deception and uncovering it. An example is in the Choderlos de Laclos novel, *Liaisons Dangereuses*: the seducer of a young ingénue makes his first move by offering to deliver her letters from her lover,

against the wishes of her mother; she agrees and gives him a key to her bedroom; when the seducer shows up in her bed, he prevents her from calling for aid by asking how she will explain it to her mother that she has given him the key.

11. In the sympathetic public atmosphere of the late twentieth and early twenty-first centuries, racial minorities sometimes play this drama in street encounters for its own sake, without money payoffs. Duneier (1999: 188–216) describes in close detail, with both conversational recordings and photographs, how an aggressive poor black man can dominate the sidewalk in a white upper-middle-class Manhattan neighborhood, making persistent sexual advances to young white women who act embarrassed about fending them off. Here the payoff is nothing more than situational dominance itself, through having mastered a technique of face confrontation. The very fact that the polite white middle-class style is what Goffman calls "civil disattention," is made into a source of weakness by the black man who gives it the interpretation of racist rejection. He thereby gets to control the situation and to expand his emotional energy, at the expense of the other's EE loss.

12. Katz (1988). Just such an event was described to me by a young Chicano male who had been held up while working in a liquor store.

13. Such robbers were particularly nervous in the moments immediately before the robbery, as they tried to bring themselves to the point of making the attempt: "I was thinking, 'Will I do it? . . . Can I do it?'" Another: "It's the initial . . . enormity of what you're doing. Once you get over that, everything becomes easier" (Morrison and O'Donnell 1994: 74).

14. The black nationalist Eldridge Cleaver (1968: 33), in a famous passage, describes how he became a rapist: "To refine my technique and *modus operandi,* I started out by practicing on black girls in the ghetto . . . and when I considered myself smooth enough, I crossed the tracks and sought out white prey." He does not say what those techniques were that he perfected. Cleaver was a big muscular man, so the techniques he developed were not simply a matter of raw force. One of my students, who also had associated with Cleaver (some ten years after he had written the above), reported that he taught how to look at the everyday details of the urban scene like a hunter looking for prey, noting attractive women's habitual routines, and finding ways to catch them off guard.

15. An example: A homosexual army sergeant engages in giving fellatio to a fellow soldier (who is not primarily homosexual himself, and never reciprocates). Their relationship becomes obsessive as they fall into the practice of seeking out situations in which they are in danger of being caught by other soldiers nearby; both of them explicitly recognize a major part of the thrill comes from the risks they are taking (Scott 2001).

CHAPTER 6
STAGING FAIR FIGHTS

1. These fights are highly idealized, in the crucial sense of my analysis: virtually every fight is described as brief and deadly, usually settled in one blow by the winning hero; in fights where both heroes are especially important, the fight is

slightly prolonged by parrying a preliminary blow by the other side. There are virtually no misses; everyone is competent and accurate. The only exceptions occur in single combats: the counter-hero sometimes misses—but very closely—with his weapon; or a hero's armor—which is one of the ritual foci of attention, and a prime object of victorious spoils-taking—just staves off a deadly hit. Homer vividly describes wounds and death-agony, and this gives a ring of brutal authenticity; but this is the kind of blood-and-gore authenticity that war stories have always had, diverting attention from the unrealistic idealization of military bravery and competence that goes with it.

2. They put themselves forward with some trepidation, since Hector is regarded as ranking superior to virtually all of them; only Achilles, the top Greek fighter, is considered better, but he is sulking in the camp, refusing to fight because of a quarrel he has had with the Greek paramount king over possession of women captives. There is a clear rank ordering among heroes. Menelaos and Paris, who fought the opening duel, are considered rather low on the list, and Menelaos is prohibited from representing the Greeks against Hector for this reason. In this social arena, not only are all reputations clearly known among both friend and foe, but they are strictly ranked by fighting prowess. The sequence of single combats that make up the plot of the *Iliad* resembles a heavy-weight boxing tournament: starting with lower-ranking fighters, and ending with the top two.

3. This is explicitly described as a stroke of good luck, since Aias along with Diomedes are considered the top heroes currently available: that is, they are numbers two and three, below Achilles, in the Greek top ten.

4. Such organization is superior to the single-combat style in two senses: superior in winning battles by force, killing the others; and superior in dominating the emotional focus of the situation. Romans did *not* have a code of honor encompassing dueling or vendettas; because their army was organized in this distinctly different fashion; and because in domestic politics, dominant households assembled huge blocs of property and power by the use of political connections and organized force (MacMullen 1974). No Roman would risk himself in a duel, when he could use his money and influence to buy votes, or his agents to assassinate opponents; if both antagonists were strong, they raised large armies (by money, by repute for generalship and therefore by chances of winning, and to an extent by kin ties and patronage). Roman honor focused chiefly on an honorable death, especially suicide when one was defeated in battle or in politics. Individual courage was a last refuge against being paraded in a degrading way in a conqueror's triumphal train, not a display of one's own fighting prowess. Something like a duel existed but only in the gladiatorial shows and in their training schools; but gladiators were not Roman citizens, but an inferior class providing entertainment. Romans did not fight duels but civil wars. Neither vendetta nor duel are to be explained simply as "ancient Mediterranean" traditions, since the most famous Mediterraneans of them all practiced neither.

5. The rampages by Homeric heroes through the opposing army are secondary in the narrative to their single combats, but the rampages may be regarded both as demonstration of their capacity to act like a "berserker"—carried away in a frenzy of attack—and as a way of building up their reputation in the course of the narrative, so that their eventual single combats are given proper weight.

6. In laboratory experiments with small groups, the presence of an audience has been found to produce escalation in an exchange of insults, with more escalation when egged on by a troublemaker, and less escalation when advised by a peacemaker (Felson 1994: 33–34). These are one-on-one conflicts, which remain short of violence, at the level of what I would call bluster; in real-life violence, and with sizable audiences, as we see the effects are even more palpable.

7. Assaults peak statistically on Friday and Saturday nights, and in carousing zones (Budd 2003: table 6). What has not been measured is whether fights are more frequent per capita present in those venues.

8. Fukuzawa was in fact generally a courageous man, who risked assassination many times during his career, as a leading Westernizer during the political struggles over the opening of Japan. Five or six years earlier than this incident, when he was a student in Osaka, he and his classmates would start mock fights in the midst of crowds on summer evenings, just for the fun of frightening bystanders, who were from the lower-ranking merchant class (1981: 66). In each case the interactional situation promoted, controlled, or demobilized the violence.

9. My collection of violent confrontations were almost entirely without guns; in only one case was a gun present, and it was only shown, not drawn; the audience was neutral, and the fight aborted. It is possible that audience effects are less important in a heavily armed, lower-class milieu. Wilkinson's (2003) study of violent young black and Hispanic males does not directly address the effect of various stances taken by the audience. Her data does show that if fights take place without weapons, 26 percent of them are squashed or abort before they become serious, and only 14 percent lead to an ongoing expectation that the fight would be resumed at another time. If guns are used, only 8.5 percent aborted, and 40 percent were ongoing; these figures rise to 10 percent and 48 percent if successful holdups are excluded (calculated from Wilkinson, 205). Thus fights with guns (even if the guns are not fired or no one is hit) are harder to abort, and are more likely to promote an ongoing conflict. It is unclear how much this is affected by the patterns of street fighting in East Coast cities; in West Coast gangs, drive-by shootings are the most prominent form of gun use, and these are usually brief and quasi-abortive (Sanders 1994). There are also numerous incidents where rival gangs taunt each other in a school yard or playground by lifting their shirts to show guns tucked in their waist-bands, but do not engage in firing (from court files). In Wilkinson's data, guns were present in 78 percent of the crew-on-crew confrontations (fifty-nine of seventy-six) and were fired in 36 percent of the scenarios where they were present (twenty-one of fifty-nine) (calculated from Wilkinson, pp. 130, 188). As we shall see, in the case of dueling, guns per se do not exclude powerful audience effects.

10. Bystanders generally stay out of staged fair fights, as well as most other fights, unless they are strongly tied to one of the fighters and are antagonists of the group represented by his opponent (as in a football firm or ethnic group). Researchers (e.g., Tilly 2003) have placed so much emphasis on the activation of collective identities in group fights that they overlook this pattern, which is probably much more frequent. There need to be special conditions, even when group identities exist, to mobilize the audience up to the level where they overcome confrontational tension/fear and actually fight.

11. Compare incidents in Chicago in September 2002 and April 2003. In each case one or two rowdy fans invaded the baseball field and attacked, respectively, a fifty-four-year-old coach and an umpire. The attacks appeared to be motivated by drunken ebullience, and a stated desire to get into the center of attention by getting on television. My point here is the social reaction: in both instances players from both teams rushed the invaders and beat them before they were taken away by police; the crowds strongly booed the invasion, and cheered for the players who retaliated against them. The intruding fans were taking attention away from the primary contest; it was this frame-breaking that called forth a widely shared reaction of moralistic punishment.

12. The earliest schools in ancient Greece were for training cohorts of upper-class youth in games and gymnastics that prepared for various kinds of combat; such schools predated by several centuries schools for literacy and verbal skills (Marrou 1964; Collins 2000).

13. There are other rituals as well, such as a sequence of fighting moves (*kata*) performed against an imaginary enemy, which can be interpreted as reenactments of famous fights in the past by masters of the lineage. Sources for the observations in these paragraphs include Draeger (1974) and five years of my own experience in three different martial arts schools, as well as observations of such schools attended by my children.

14. The staging that is pervasive in such schools presents their technique as much deadlier and more effective than it actually is; in real life, trained martial artists too rarely live up to the ideal touted in the schools. I once asked my karate teacher what to do if there were someone with a gun; his reply: "Run like hell." As if to illustrate the point, the world-champion Thai-style kick-boxer, Alex Gong, was shot to death on a San Francisco street when he chased a driver who had crashed into his parked car (*San Diego Union*, August 5, 2003).

15. Hence boxing schools in the black inner-city ghetto provide a haven from the violent code of the street, not a weapon to use in it (Wacquant 2004).

16. In hundreds of hours in karate schools, witnessing hundreds of matches, I have never seen a fight that spilled over the stopping point—the fighters might get angry during a match, and try to hit harder, but they did not keep on hitting after the master called the round to an end, nor fail to bow to the other. Members of karate schools could have grudges against each other, but they usually expressed them not by fighting but by use of etiquette. This was especially likely when a lower-ranking fighter bested a higher-ranking fighter in a match (e.g., a green belt beating a red belt). Retaliation usually took the form of the higher-ranking fighter later ordering the lower-ranking one to mop the floor or perform some other menial task.

17. The sport of boxing emerged in eighteenth- and nineteenth-century England from rural and lower-class bouts sponsored and attended by the upper-class "sporting set," as a form of staged excitement and gambling. It was these aristocrats who codified the rules, including eventually the wearing of padded gloves. Bare-knuckle fights lasting unlimited rounds until one fighter was unable to continue were largely supplanted by the 1880s. The pastime in the 1920s was epitomized by Hemingway, who routinely engaged in practice sparring—of which

he was very proud—but never fought in a public competition (Dunning 1999: 55–60; Callaghan 1963).

18. A student report describes an incident in the early 2000s in which a group of Korean-American students got involved in a fist-fight over who was going to escort a girl. Although one of the participants in the fight was trained in the martial arts, he did not use any of its techniques. This fits a ritual separation of spheres: idealized fighting at school, low-level brawling outside.

19. Hamlet's duel is in fact a school-like fencing match, consisting of a series of rounds with supposedly baited (blunted) foils. It starts with a courtier, acting as go-between, who delivers the challenge; but in this case it takes the form of a bet, made by the king, who is sponsoring the contest: new French dueling swords, wagered against a more traditional prize, war horses. The duel as a purely private grudge match to the death, enacted under etiquette, is not yet depicted in Shakespeare.

20. In this respect, the duel was a considerable change from the medieval practice of trial by combat; the older practice was an official one, legal when granted by the king, and such combat would take place in the presence of the assembled authorities. Duels were for purely private grievances, indeed rather trivial ones in contrast to the property and vengeance claims that made up the medieval judicial combat; and duels were fought in secret, as far as official society was concerned. Trial by combat could be granted to any free man; dueling was monopolized by the aristocracy as a mark of status.

21. McAleer (1994: 75, 93–94, 114, 224); Nye (1993: 185). German duels generally were punished by the authorities, including special army courts, only when there were deaths; hence the high range of estimates is for duels without fatalities.

22. In France during the 1880s, about one-third of duels were settled before they were fought (Nye 1993: 186).

23. Even today, the effective range of a .45 caliber military pistol is officially set at eighty-three feet (U.S. Air Force 2006: 50)—that is, twenty-seven paces. Most police shootings take place at ten feet or less, and as we have seen, misses are frequent.

24. Compare the early chapters of Tolstoi's *War and Peace*, which includes a scene of carousing army officers drinking, gambling, and showing off by dares such as draining a bottle of rum while perched suicidally on an upper-floor window sill. This was published in 1867, based upon Tolstoi's military experiences before and during the Crimean War of 1854–55.

25. And indeed there was a distinctive "backwoods" style among poor white farmers and laborers that prevailed in the South before the dueling style percolated down from the upper classes (Gorn 1985). These "rough-and-tumble" fights were no-holds-barred, allowing eye-gouging as well as hair-pulling and maiming; their boisterousness appears to have been in deliberate contrast to the emotionally restrained, polite manners of upper-class duelists. In the eighteenth and early nineteenth centuries, the upper classes regarded poor whites as beneath their dignity to duel with. As democratization proceeded, the two styles came closer together.

26. Not that the pacified nineteenth-century elite had no insults and disputes, but it was in the process of developing an etiquette that included sanctions such as "cutting" an offender (in a purely metaphorical sense) by refusing polite ges-

tures of recognition in public, as well as an array of institutions such as private clubs from which an offender could be blackballed (Baltzell 1958; Cannadine 1990).

27. The most famous gunfighter of the late 1870s, Billy the Kid, worked for one of the rival syndicates of property owners during the so-called Lincoln County war in the New Mexico territory. He became famous because of widespread newspaper coverage of the conflict, with its rival claims to organize law-enforcement in remote areas of the territory, and its connections to wider political factions (Kooistra 1989). Gunfighters were generally hired mercenaries, but also robbers, professional gamblers, and thus part of an "action crowd" similar to urban criminal milieux. They resemble eighteenth-century British highwaymen, similarly preying on newly founded long-distance transport services such as stagecoach lines. The growth of popular culture heroizing pistol-wielding plebeian highwaymen must have been part of the process that lowered the status of gentlemen's pistol duels; these largely disappeared from British society by the 1820s.

28. We are used to thinking in terms of an evolutionary sequence between tribal organization and early states, but there is often an intermediate formation that is neither (Weber 1922/1968: 365–66; Borkenau 1981; Collins 1986: 267–97; Grinin 2003). It arises not only when tribes have begun to amalgamate, but as warriors leave their clan identities behind to join marauding groups. Examples are the Viking bands; many of the German coalitions outside the Roman Empire; Greek instances reflected in mythology include the Argonauts, a band of heroes who join together for a distant voyage in search of booty; and the ad hoc army that besieges Troy.

29. Hero-warriors of this type must be distinguished from famous bandits, who may also have the idealized reputation as brave, daring, and invincible fighters. The structures under which these appear are where a state breaks down (as in weak phases of Chinese dynasties), or where a state penetrates into tribal or local village areas enough to motivate formation of bands of resisters (hence "bandits"); the state lacks sufficient administrative structure to rule, while the bandits lack organizational capacity to supplant the state (Eberhard 1977; Hobsbawm 2000). The key is that aristocratic heroes fight one another under an honor code; bandits do not fight horizontally but vertically, against stronger organized forces from above. This gives bandit-heroes their reputation as romantic individualists, miraculously defying authority and evading capture; aristocratic heroes do neither.

30. Another deliberately contrived modern tribe-like structure is the athletic team: thus teams engage in vendetta-like patterns of violence (e.g., bean-ball wars in baseball), and their fans engage in corporate vengeance upon each other. This idea will be developed in chapter 8.

31. An intermediate form exists where the belligerents suggest or demand that the other "step outside"; this is a naming of time and place, but it happens immediately and without the mediation of seconds, in contrast to formal duels. This degree of scheduling is almost always confined to fist fights; indeed, if the challenge is agreed upon to step outside, it is implied that the fight will be limited in that respect. Thus staged fair fights from the twentieth century (or, for England

and America, since the mid-nineteenth century) onward have become almost exclusively fist fights.

32. An apparent exception: In the fights described by Fox (1977), given earlier, the principals were the subject of much community gossip and treated as celebrities. This helps highlight by contrast the distinctive features of fights in anonymous urban venues: the Irish west coast island community had an extensive network linking virtually everyone and thereby making a shared public object out of everyone's reputation; and this network was instrumental in keeping the fights organized as fair, and in limiting their escalation.

33. My collection of student reports includes cases like the following: A dense crowd is exiting a train in New York City's Penn Station, bumping and jostling (late November 2001). A black woman, moving rapidly and wearing a headset, is bumped by a white woman, causing her to drop her CD player. The black woman calls out, "Oh shit! Watch where you're going!" The white woman gives an exasperated sigh, pauses briefly and begins to rush off. The black woman is angered by the lack of acknowledgment, and yells "Hey, pick it up! Pick up my CD, bitch! You, BITCH!" The white woman glances back and continues to walk away. The black woman shouts "YOU WHITE FUCKING BITCH!" and kicks her in the back—a little clearing having formed in the crowd as other passengers shied away. A white male bystander picks up her CD player and hands it to her; the black woman takes it roughly and storms away. The dispute does not become very escalated, because one side (the white woman) simply refuses to stay and fight, not so much forfeiting honor as not recognizing the situation as one involving honor.

34. Sanders (1994: 148) notes that among Mexican-American gangs, "[O]ne can always save face by noting the inopportune nature of the situation and claim retaliation at a later date when the situation lends itself better to retaliation." Wilkinson (2003: 137, 141, 144, 151, 154–55, 169) gives numerous instances where a confrontation ends because one or both sides run away from a gun. In one instance, an armed crew invaded another's neighborhood to take revenge for the robbery of one of their girlfriends, but after a brief shootout in which no one was hit, they left and never returned (Wilkinson 2003: 156–57).

35. In chapter 10, I give evidence that the proportion of gang members among young males in a community is usually around 10 percent at most. Alice Goffman (personal communication, Oct. 2005) confirms that the violent drug dealers she studied would admit only a small proportion of would-be recruits into their ranks; failure to be admitted into the criminal elite is an important reason why others in the community pursue low-paying straight jobs.

36. In an incident described in footnote 11, one of the two males who invaded the field and attacked a coach, when asked why he did it, answered, "He flipped us off." If true, this could have occurred in response to the fan's heckling. Moreover, the older of the two had made cell phone calls telling friends to watch the game on TV because something involving themselves was going to happen. Sanders (1994: 147) notes that although gang members use the rhetoric of retaliation to account for how fights start, "there are too many instances of gangs instigating violence for this to be true."

37. These are in contrast to the names chosen by middle-class white gangs, who play upon an ironic counter-culture stance as outcasts ("the Losers"). Similarly with counter-culture youth groups generally (Milner 2004); they do not go looking for respect, but for disrespect, ironically mocking standards of respectability and popularity.

38. A member of the San Diego Police Department Gang Unit told me in the summer of 2004 of an agreement established among members of the Mexican Mafia—a kind of honorary inter-gang association of Chicanos who had been in prison and were regarded as especially tough. After a drive-by shooting in which a small child had been killed, the relative of one of the Mexican Mafia members, he gathered the heads of gangs together and got them to agree that one foot must be on the ground (rather than both feet in the car) while shooting. The rule was presumably designed to make firing more careful. The rule was generally adhered to by Chicano gangs, but was ignored by black gangs. White and Asian gangs, on the other hand, did not practice drive-bys. Motorcycle gangs were mostly white, and confined their rivalries to each other. Each ethnic group was segregated by violent techniques and targets; each constituted its own audience and field of reputation.

39. This is based on my collection of cases; in duels the audience does not cheer, but it takes an extremely active part in organizing the duel, and is crucial for whether the duel will come off or not.

40. In my collection of cases, of the twenty-six serious fights, only five came about without scheduling at least some major aspect of the situation; all the others (81 percent) were either announced and scheduled as fights, demonstrations, or confrontations (eight), or developed in the midst of scheduled carousing situations (street festivals, parties, games: eleven); or in crowded school assemblies (two). In contrast, of forty mild or brief fights, twenty-two (55 percent) similarly were in scheduled situations; of twenty-three abortive fights, seven (30 percent) were in scheduled situations.

Putting the matter the other way around: of fifty conflicts arising in scheduled situations, twenty-one (42 percent) produced serious fights, whereas in thirty-nine non-scheduled situations there were five serious fights (13 percent); in scheduled situations, fights aborted only 14 percent of the time (seven cases), whereas in non-scheduled situations, they aborted 41 percent of the time (sixteen), with the remaining 46 percent (eighteen) cases) being mild fights.

41. In the seventeen instances in my data where the audience cheered the fight, eight of these were one-on-one fights; the others took the form of attacking the weak. All were in scheduled situations.

42. Hamlet, for example, cannot decide how to take revenge—vendetta style—and refuses an opportunity for unfair advantage in killing the king when he catches him alone and unarmed. In the end he engages in a ritual duel, is fatally wounded because his opponent cheats, and finally encompasses his revenge by killing all those who are implicated in the trespass of dueling rules. At almost every point, Hamlet shows his moral superiority by following the rules of fair fights; the exception is when he kills an eavesdropper by stabbing him through the wall-hanging, but even this is a punishment for deception, and of a lower-ranking person.

43. Jankowski (1991) stresses this interpretation: what I see as incompetence he sees as deliberate cultivation of a terroristic image, which is good for business if one is attempting to sell protection or create monopolies of illegal enterprise. The two explanations are not mutually exclusive; I argue only that the incompetence is pervasive and generic, even if gangs take advantage of it for their own purposes.

44. Wilkinson's data (2003, recalculated from pp. 182 and 188) shows that one-on-one fights are most likely to be carried out with no weapons (51 percent, 60 of 118) and only 28 percent of them involved guns (33 of 118); in all other kinds of fights (ganging up on one victim; and crew-on-crew) only 20 percent (33 of 162) were without weapons, and 68 percent (110 of 162) involved guns. Guns are least likely to be used in fights among friends (32 percent, 11 of 34) or acquaintances (38 percent, 33 of 86) and most likely among rivals (66 percent, 35 of 63), and intermediate among strangers (52 percent, 67 of 130). The concept of a fair fight exists in these groups and instances are given throughout Wilkinson's interviews, although there are no explicit figures on fair fights.

45. This discussion refers primarily to violence within and between Mafia organizations, which is where most of the killings take place. Mob violence is more overt and public when it is used against victims in the outside world whom it wants to shake down, subject to taxation and protection payments; this is to a considerable extent put on as an intimidating show. But it is businesslike in its purposes, to establish and keep up a regular flow of income.

46. One reason why Mafia has had a relatively strong, self-reproducing organization is that it recruits from real families. Lower-class gangs, in contrast, often recruit from broken families, and are unable to use family ties much as a basis of organization. This is more true of black gangs than Hispanic gangs (Horowitz 1983).

47. Another reason for the romanticization of the Mafia is suggested by its historical timing: popular sentimentalized films about Mafia families, like *The Godfather*, began in the 1970s. This was just the time that the Mafia began to be displaced as a major force in organized crime; Jamaican and Hispanic syndicates took over the wholesale drug business; in the 1990s, old standbys of extortion and organized prostitution became dominated by Russian and other ex-Soviet crime business. The widespread legalization of gambling also cut into a traditional area of criminal protection. It is a much more localized and less culturally threatening Mafia that is the real-life basis for romanticization in the late twentieth and early twenty-first centuries.

CHAPTER 7
VIOLENCE AS FUN AND ENTERTAINMENT

1. This last perception is not strictly accurate. In large and prolonged riots, most arrests are for looting. In the 1992 Los Angeles (Rodney King) riot, arrests totaled 9,500; in the 1977 New York City blackout, 3,000 arrests; in the 1965 Watts (L.A.) riot, 3,900 arrests (Halle and Rafter 2003: 341–42). But in the mood of the moral holiday, few think of this contingency, and in fact their chances of

being singled out from other perpetrators is relatively low. The prevailing feeling is of membership in a collective entity that is temporarily impervious to outside authority.

2. Breaking glass has a dramatic and symbolic quality that is used in many situations; it seems to be a favorite of the semi-violent, those who make a show of contentiousness but are wary of following through into full-scale fighting. In chapter 2, we saw a fight that began when someone threw bottles from the trash into the street, but that quickly petered out; in chapter 8, we will meet English football hooligans who mark their departure from a pub by simply dropping their beer glasses onto the floor. Riotous celebrations in eastern Europe (e.g., New Year's eve in Prague) chiefly revolve around bottle-throwing in public squares, leaving a spectacular litter of broken shards. In 2004, British pubs began experimenting with a law replacing glass beer mugs with plastic ones; preliminary results indicate that these have reduced the amount of violence (Meredith Rossner, personal communication, Sept. 2004).

3. Burning an enemy's property, in contrast, is a very different tactic. There is a long history of arson as a weapon: in uprisings against landowners; as a punishment for failure to pay taxes (used in states with low organizational capacity); in a literal "scorched earth" policy for putting down guerrillas; as a terroristic display by a conquering army to compel later surrenders (Goudsblom 1992: 118, 160, 184).

4. Hannerz (1969: 173) noted that in the Washington, D.C., riot in 1968, there were some incursions into the predominantly white downtown shopping area, looting some clothing stores, but virtually no fires were set there; the fires were almost all in the ghetto, along its main shopping streets; which is to say, the local gathering places.

5. Similarly with the rioting by North African immigrants in France from October 27 to mid-November 2005, which went on for about twenty days. It consisted especially in nocturnal car burnings (plus burning public buildings and stoning transport vehicles and police), beginning in one Paris suburb, spreading to other working-class immigrant suburbs on days four through six, then to distant cities beginning days seven through eight, while the violence petered out around Paris. Destruction built progressively to a peak at days ten through twelve, the time of maximum geographical spread, then steadily declined. In most cities, the maximal duration of violence was five to seven consecutive days. The overall level of violence across France declined as participating areas reached this time-limit of active involvement, and fewer new locations were added (calculated from timeline and statistics in en.wikipedia.org/wiki/ 2005_Paris_suburb_riots).

6. Spilerman (1976), in a study of racial disturbances in 170 American cities between 1961 and 1968, found that few cities had repeated disturbances; most of these were small in destructiveness and short in duration. The bulk of the riots were concentrated in the latter part of the 1961–68 period, especially in the weeks following the Martin Luther King assassination in April 1968. In the immediate aftermath of that heavily publicized event, cities experiencing a first outbreak had more severe violence and destruction (i.e., more looting and arson) than cities that were veterans of previous riots. In the remaining months of 1968, the more riot-experienced cities had a decline in severity. Myers (2000) found that riots in

smaller places (i.e., cities with smaller black populations and black neighborhoods) were shorter and less severe in every respect.

7. Tilly (2003) summarizes a wide range of evidence in the generalization that looting (which he regards as opportunism) occurs on the fringes of virtually all forms of collective violence; that is, away from the central focus of attention or chain of command. In my view, this happens because violence destroys most forms of authority except its own, and where rebels lack a military command structure, the situation turns into a moral holiday.

8. The contrast with looting following natural disasters such as hurricanes and floods shows that absence of authority is not a sufficient cause; it must be a breakdown of authority against which the crowd regards itself as collectively in rebellion. In natural disasters, looters are a tiny number compared to as many as 20 percent of a population who loot in a civil disturbance. Disaster looters are usually solitary individuals, strangers to the area, working secretively, and are almost universally disapproved; whereas civic looters are local residents who do their looting in groups, openly and in an atmosphere of social support (Quarantelli and Dynes 1970).

9. There had been, however, a prior history of racial protest uprisings in the same black and Hispanic poverty areas of the city thirteen years before.

10. Eighty-two percent of those arrested in the first hour had records of previous arrest; this dropped to 67 percent of those arrested in the second wave, and to 55 percent of those arrested in early morning and daylight hours.

11. In news photos of the 1992 L.A. riot, 16 percent of the looters visible are women (calculated from Los Angeles Times, May 1–2, May 12, 1992). Women made up 7 percent of those arrested in the NYC blackout riot (Curvin and Porter 1979: 86).

12. The most detailed description is in Compton Mackenzie's autobiographical Sinister Street (1913) book 3; the scene is satirized in Max Beerbohm, Zuleika Dobson (1912), and Evelyn Waugh, Decline and Fall (1928); it is treated seriously in Waugh, Brideshead Revisited (1945).

13. Famously wild parties are indexed by the degree of spectacular destruction. At one celebrated football weekend at Princeton (still storied in the early 1960s, but probably dating from the 1930s) the crowd of students managed to overturn the local railroad cars from the tracks. Drunken Dartmouth students were remembered for going off a ski jump in a baby carriage.

14. This occurs most typically where one's living quarters and surroundings are temporary; what one smashes up is not one's core, identity-giving property, but things one has the use of by virtue of one's status as privileged sojourner. The worst kind of such destruction is the middle-class parents' nightmare: leaving their home in the hands of youthful children, who give a house party that ends up leaving the house completely trashed. Such parties tend to expand through remote network connections, acquaintances of acquaintances, as word of mouth lets it be known that there is available, in effect, a free zone. Eventually the majority of the party-goers have no connection with the hosts and no sense of responsibility; and at the same time early bits of careless trashiness (spilling, leaving debris around) send a message that further destruction is acceptable or even at some point expected. If the parents' absence is prolonged, the house may be badly de-

stroyed. Structurally similar opportunities can result in similar outcomes: youth gangs in the 1920s, enticed into a local Chicago settlement house by its recreation room (and the indulgent attitude of the settlement workers), vandalized the pool table and the play equipment, made bonfires out of playing cards, and left no part of the rooms undefaced (Thrasher 1927/1960: 78).

15. The Detroit riot of July 1967, which resulted in massive casualties, began when police attempted to raid an after-hours drinking and gambling club in the heart of the black area. The police raid could hardly have been more ill-timed: at peak hours on a Saturday night, the high point of a carousing weekend. After a failed attempt to get into the club at 10 p.m., which served only to alert the denizens of the club, police returned in greater force at 4 a.m. This time they succeeded in shutting down the club, but a crowd gathered and pelted the officers as they loaded arrestees into paddy wagons. Faced with this counter-escalation, the police withdrew, setting off a full-scale moral holiday of looting and arson (Kerner Commission 1968: 84–87).

16. Gould (2003) argues that violence is caused not by inequality but by horizontal relations and by adjacent positions in a status hierarchy that is inconsistent or unstable.

17. Indeed, in the literal dictionary sense, "carousing" means "a noisy, lively drinking party" (Oxford Concise Dictionary). I am using "carousing," however, in a wider sense, of emotional ebullience in a socially constructed situation of moral holiday. The archetype of a wild party is the North American Indian potlatch. But potlatches (at least until very late in their history) were carried out without alcohol (see sources cited in earlier discussion). There is an emotional intoxication as well as a physical one; the thread of my argument throughout is that the emotional dynamics of group situations are the key determinant of when violence does or does not come off.

18. Other social psychological and cultural mechanisms connecting alcohol and violence have been proposed by MacAndrew and Edgerton (1969), Lithman (1979), Bogg and Ray (1990), Lang (1983), Gantner and Taylor (1992), Pihl, Peterson, and Lau (1993), Taylor (1983), Room (2001), Room and Mäkelä 1996.

19. It is not clear how much looting in riots is accompanied by drunkenness. Descriptions of the kind given so far in this chapter show that the emotional mood of the moral holiday is an emotional intoxication of its own, and stories of drinking do not figure prominently. Liquor stores are looted where possible, but it appears that the serious looters do not do very much drinking, since it impairs their ability to make away with the loot. In the 2002 Ohio State football victory riot, none of the persons arrested (generally those who were most active in destruction or in confronting the police) was intoxicated, according to police reports (Vider 2004: 146). This supports the point that those who are most effective or militant in violence are the soberest ones, although they are supported by a cheering crowd (of which they are only a small percent), many of whom are drunk.

20. They get drunk more often, so they also have more chances to get into fights. There are about one-fourth as many heavy drinkers as occasional binge drinkers, but they drink at least five times as often. The average American binger gets drunk about twelve times a year; heavy drinkers are binging around sixty

times a year, totaling 720 million binges; although it seems surprising, their chances of getting into fights per binge are slightly lower than occasional bingers.

21. Chapter 6 presented evidence that attitude of the crowd has a strong effect; in the above incident outside the fraternity house, the crowd of spectators looks forward to a fight, although the immediate friends of the fighters do not seem enthusiastic.

22. A member of the U.S. Olympic team in tae kwon do karate was asked by a reporter if he ever used his skills on the street. He said he had one time. "You know how guys can get after you . . . they're drunk or whatnot. Things happen." But the fight ended quickly. "I think that's the worst time for someone to really try and attempt to get in a fight. When they're drunk, they don't have much balance to begin with. It's not much of a fight" (*San Diego Union-Tribune*, Aug. 28, 2004). Police also find drunks the easiest kinds of belligerent offenders to subdue; they are more likely to receive the minimal amount of force than sober suspects; and they put up the least violent resistance to the arresting officers, usually confining themselves to verbal bluster and passive resistance (Alpert and Dunham 2004: 67, 81, 164).

23. Intoxicated suspects were least likely to be encountered by police investigating property crimes (12 percent) and most likely when called for domestic cases (48 percent) (Alpert and Dunham 2004: 73). This fits the pattern that domestic abuse, as we have seen, is largely attacking the weak; alcohol is most often involved in violence when the violence is already easy to perform, not when it is difficult. In the British Crime Survey, victims 17 percent of the time thought their muggers were drunk (Budd 2003: Table 1.1).

24. The whole sequence shows how difficult it is be successfully violent. In an earlier encounter, the protagonist carried a gun but had been smoking marijuana and failed in shooting his opponent; subsequently they had also had a fist fight, a one-sided knife-fight (the protagonist was the aggressor in all of these fights), and finally a two-sided gunfight in which both had missed (Wilkinson 2003: 212–13). He is finally successful when he loads up all possible advantages: getting his opponent outnumbered, disguising himself, sneaking up from behind, as well as being sober versus drunk.

25. Thus what anthropologists (e.g., Marshall 1983) call "pseudo-intoxication"—pretending to be drunk—may be the ideal tactic if one really wants to do well in a fight. But it appears what usually happens is not necessarily violence, but just offensive behavior and blustering. And the pseudo-intoxicated in these studies are generally taking advantage of more sober people, not drunker ones.

26. According to some of my informants, straight-edgers generally confine their fights to the punk scene. They differentiate themselves by marking XXX on their forearms, and also (at least in particular periods during the past twenty-five years that punk culture has been in existence) by all-black clothing rather than the chains, mohawks, and colorful hair of what might be called "mainstream punk" style. Other informants say that straight-edgers also fight jocks and skinheads; the latter are their particular enemies, since skinheads tend to hang around punk concerts but differ radically in political ideology (right- versus left-wing). Still other informants say that straight-edgers do not fight, but take part only in mosh pits (which I discuss shortly), which they regard as expressing anger in a

righteous manner against the larger social system. My sources on straight-edgers include a female punk musician; a former straight-edger from the early 1980s; and a half-dozen persons of university student age. Straight-edgers are also described in "underground" punk magazines. See also Milner (2004: 42, 248) on straight-edgers in the high-school status system.

The relations of straight-edgers to other sub-groups suggests a process of building internal rankings inside the alienated youth subculture. There is a parallel here to my analysis of English soccer hooligans, in the following chapter: hooligans are also a sophisticated development of fighting (although in the realm of collective maneuvers, not a sobriety advantage over opponents); and they are similar in elaborating an internal hierarchy within the larger category of sports fans. Among Belgian soccer hooligans in the late 1980s, the hard-core fighters avoided alcohol and drugs in order to have a clear-headed advantage during confrontations with their rivals; in other respects they consciously emulated the tactics of English hooligans (Van Limbergen et al. 1989). There is also an old tradition of mugging or "rolling" drunks (Shaw 1930/1966), but this was not carried out by members of a carousing scene, and had little prestige. During the twentieth century, it appears that the sophistication of techniques of recreational fighting has evolved along with local prestige standards.

27. Of eighty-nine cases, seventy-eight were isolated single incidents (including both fights and abortive fights); in six cases where incidents were chained together, the second incident included all or some of the antagonists of the first incident (four of these second incidents aborted); in five cases there were two or more entirely separate fights in the same gathering (6 percent of the total). A total of thirty-eight of all incidents were in carousing or entertainment venues; of these thirty were single incidents; four were chained repetitions; four involved separate fights (11 percent of the total).

28. These included two individual fights witnessed by one observer in the Mardi Gras crowd, followed by a riot; multiple fights and riots seen by another Mardi Gras observer a different year; two separate incidents of prolonged harassment in a post–NBA All Star game crowd, taking place in separate buses; an individual fight off to the side of a mosh pit, followed by an unrelated battle between two groups of skinheads invading the floor (I do not count the moshing itself as a fight). One instance took place in a non-entertainment situation: a large political demonstration, with 2,300 demonstrators and 700 police; the violence took the form, typical of crowd violence, of breaking up both sides into small groups of unequal size, with the clusters beating isolated members of the opposing crowd.

29. Some instances are documented in California court cases, where a bar is sued for injuries caused during fights, in which several fights break out in the same bar. In one case, the crowd engages in several fights just outside the bar at closing time (a version of end-resisting violence).

30. In this respect they are not so different from the high school popular groups who dominate a lunchroom scene—in white middle-class schools as well—and who jeer at intruders, as well as engage in food fights and other pelting as a form of fun. See Milner (2004) and discussion in chapter 5. Only the degree of escalation differs.

31. Chapter 1 noted that violations of the rule of one-fight-at-a-time can occur in playful group water fights, snowball fights, or food fights; but these stay multi-sided only as long as they are light-hearted and unserious. In the following section we examine mosh pits. In all these apparent exceptions, the rule holds: fights that threaten what is understood as real violence make the situation highly polarized, for audience as well as participants, producing a simple bipolar structure.

32. Jackson-Jacobs describes the euphoria of these party-fighters, after a successful fight, as connected above all to the awareness that they finally managed to pull off a fight. "And even though I got beat up, I was kind of happy we got in a fight. Just because it's kinda good to do that once in a while so you don't forget . . . what it's like to get in a fight" (Jackson-Jacobs 2003). It is instructive to contrast this with soldiers after combat. Soldiers are almost never euphoric when they have been beaten. Indeed, soldiers are often not euphoric even after they have won, especially if it has been a long battle. There is of course plenty of ritual narrative about military combat; but tough talk and story-telling occur mainly among soldiers in the rear areas, whereas the frontline soldiers are contemptuous of this talk (as we have seen in chapter 2). Why are the narrative rituals so disjoined from the actual experience in combat? One reason is the large amount of mythology surrounding combat; the extent of fear and incompetence in combat being very high, there is an elaborate defense against explicitly recognizing it. And also, especially in modern armies where the tooth-to-tail ratio is high, there are large numbers of troops in intermediate areas who can have an audience of troops even farther from the front; Goffmanian staging of toughness in the form of bragging and combat stories seems mostly designed for the most naïve audiences; it wouldn't fly with the frontline soldiers who know better what combat is like. Frontline soldiers do not construct narratives about how brave they are, and war stories are taken as marks of not really being part of the combat group. The narrative emphasis of party-fighters shows how far their staged experiences are from the realities of combat.

33. The following is based on five student reports, and interviews with a punk band musician.

34. Apparently only one mosh pit at a time can be sustained. In some concerts, smaller pits may be initiated off to the side of the main pit, but these disintegrate quickly. This is probably because the pit needs the active support of the crowd, but the crowd can sustain only one violent focus of attention at a time. The pattern supports the point that one fight per venue takes up the attention space.

35. This resembles the instrumental leader, as distinguished from the expressive leader, in small groups of all sorts (Bales 1950). Here it is notable that the biggest male does not use his size advantage to be more violent than others; since too much violence actually threatens the existence of the group, the way to lead the group is to use his size as protector and tacit rule-enforcer.

36. In this respect moshers are distinguished from gangs, which have dense ties of mutual acquaintance, and which tend to be ethnically homogeneous. Here moshers betray their middle-class orientation, more individualistic and more cosmopolitan than lower-class gangs. Several participant-observers commented on the mosh pit as a true melting pot, held together in its own self-created solidarity.

37. From my own experience: in 1960 I attended a dance at Princeton during the Harvard football weekend. In the field house, three bands were playing simultaneously: Count Basie; Jerry Lee Lewis; and, off in a side room, the Coasters. These were top-rank stars from the swing and rock 'n' roll eras. Not only did the bands have to compete against each other for attention; the audience spent more of their time dancing than clustering around the respective stages.

38. We have seen this in the foregoing discussion of straight-edgers, who are very active participants in moshing.

CHAPTER 8
SPORTS VIOLENCE

1. The early history of sports is full of rule changes that sometimes dramatically reshape the action (Thorn, Palmer, and Gershman 2002: 79–103). Numerous changes have been made in recent decades as well; for example, professional football changes penalty rules to protect quarterbacks and pass receivers, in order to encourage more dramatic pass plays.

2. These side-contests provide a way in which interest is kept up, over and above the main outcome—but they don't seem to figure in precipitation of sports violence. American games have particularly complex dramatic formats. One might call this an American tradition of inventions of social technologies for sports entertainment. In older sports contests, of the racing or track-and-field variety, there is also some emphasis on record-breaking; but this does not usually change the dramatic structure of the contest: setting the world record in the 100-meter dash necessarily involves winning the race and cannot be a side-show to it.

3. Sports violence has been approached by social sciences as part of the larger question of why spectators find violence appealing to watch. Theories are reviewed in Goldstein (1998), who concludes that there is no well-substantiated theory of the attractions of violent entertainment. McCauley (1998) notes that existing psychological theories fail to explain why viewing fictional or contrived violence is sometimes appealing but watching real violence (as in experiments with realistic films of slaughterhouses or violent injuries) is not. The difference, of course, is the dramatic plot tension.

4. Some parallel contests in practical reality have an element of defense as well as offense. In races, runners may block each other; occasionally they get tangled up and fall down; and a common way that a very fast runner will lose a race is because he or she gets trapped in a pack and cannot get to the front. These patterns occur chiefly in middle-distance racing, where runners are not confined to separate lanes, and there is not enough time for the pack to thin out. Such events can lead to bitter defeats and sometimes prolonged hard feelings: the most famous incident was among two women racers in the 1984 Olympic 1,500 meters, when the American Mary Decker Slaney was tripped by the South African Zola Budd, knocking both of the famous stars out of the race; Slaney was hostile to Budd for years thereafter. But blocking during races almost never leads to fights. Races can indeed be severely contested; African marathoners, for whom prize money is a very important consideration if they are poor, are known to throw their water bottles at

opponents' refreshment tables in order to slow them down; but fights do not appear to result. The structure of the action itself precludes it: to take time out from a race in order to fight is to lose the race.

There are, however, instances of auto-race pit crews who fight. In a NASCAR race at Chicago, Kasey Kahne was leading the race when he was spun out by the car driven by Tony Stewart; Kahne crashed into the wall (but was not seriously injured) and Stewart went on to win (*Los Angeles Times*, July 14, 2004). Kahne's pit crew went to Stewart's pit, where a heated discussion turned into a shoving match, which was finally broken up by officials. This fight took place not among the drivers but their assistants, who do not race; and it was instigated by the team that was out of the race. For them the issue of losing time in the race did not arise.

5. Boxing is unusual among virtually all sports, including the most confrontational ones, in that there are fairly frequent pre-game fights. Fights in other sports typically happen late in the game when dramatic tension has built up. In professional boxing matches, however, it is common for the fighters to appear at a ceremonial weighing-in, where they pose for the press, and are photographed face to face (see figure 8.2.). The ritualized stare-downs and trash talking that may occur on these occasions sometimes escalate into brief fights; but these are almost always confined to shoving, sometimes knocking over furniture, and usually involve scuffles with the entourage of the opposing fighter. The pattern is ceremonial bluster; fists are rarely used. Some of it is deliberately hyped to stir up interest in the commercially staged fight. All this fits the pattern of fighting as audience-oriented entertainment. Even where fighters are genuinely hostile, pre-fight violence is very restrained, keeping the focus on the scheduled violence. In other kinds of sports, although individuals or teams may sometimes bluster at each other in the days before the game, this is usually discouraged by coaches and the players themselves in order not to stir up their opponents. As we shall see, football games have the highest amount of pre-game scuffles (other than boxing weigh-ins); coaches do not object to this, since it is a way of establishing aggressive dominance in the immediate situation, whereas mere talk during the preceding days of practice are regarded as aiding the other team's emotional preparation.

6. That is, real sport wrestling as practiced in school or amateur federation matches. In contrast, professional wrestling, which has little to do with the rules and techniques of sport wrestling, is heavily staged to give an impression of all-out violence, and includes regular occurrences of wrestlers fighting their opponents outside the ring, persisting in blatantly illegal weapons and techniques of attack. This is staged and rehearsed; in my opinion, a serious amateur wrestler would be able to tie up a professional exhibition wrestler very easily by applying standard take-down and immobilization moves. Sumo wrestlers also seem never to fight outside the prescribed moment. They do spend considerable time in posturing and stamping just before taking their starting positions for the match; this has an element of attempting to disrupt the opponent's concentration, especially by standing up and walking away from the ring for a few seconds with a gesture of contempt. The honorific nature of these moves is shown by the fact that higher-ranking sumo wrestlers are officially given more time for these preliminary rituals; and these gestures are often cheered by spectators for their theatrical quality (from

my observations and explanatory pamphlets at the Tokyo sumo arena, May 2005).

7. One study asked high school athletic directors in North Carolina to estimate the frequency of verbal and physical intimidation, as well as outright violence in three sports (Shields 1999). Violence was judged highest in football (hockey was not included in these schools); soccer had a level of verbal intimidation slightly above football (this seems surprising, but it may be because bluster was the only weapon available, given strong restrictions on actual violence). Basketball was moderate in verbal and physical intimidation, and almost as low as soccer in violence. Intimidation builds up in a sequence: verbal intimidation explained 45 percent of the variance in physical intimidation (i.e., shoving and grappling); and physical intimidation in turn explained 42 percent of the variance in physical violence. These figures must be taken with a grain of salt; they are not based on actual counts of incidents in games, but on summary statements of athletic directors as to their impressions of the overall amount of the various kinds of intimidation and violence.

8. High school athletic directors also indicated that intimidation and violence occurred more often in playoff games than in regular games (Shields 1999).

9. During the eleven NBA seasons between 1987 and 1997, there were six playoff games that had fights serious enough to result in suspensions by the league. In three of these games, one player was suspended for throwing a punch (i.e., without significant retaliation); three of the games involved brawls, but only two players took a major part in each, while others were penalized for coming onto the floor during the fight (*San Diego Union-Tribune*, May 16, 1997). There are about eighty playoff games per season, so about 0.7 percent of playoff games have fights. I estimate that the frequency of fights is lower during the regular season. Sociological researchers who study amateur and school basketball teams confirm that fighting is very infrequent (Reuben A. Buford, personal communication, Aug. 2005); Scott Brooks (personal communication, 2003) reports that inner-city basketball players do not have to fight for reputation, even though it is required of other young black males. Wilkinson (2003) collected instances of fights among black and Hispanic hoodlums; although they play various recreational sports including basketball, the only fights they mention as arising in connection with games occur in football.

10. Thus hockey penalties vary from two minutes for ordinary rule violations; four minutes for excessively rough play; if players go on fighting for more than the ten or twenty seconds it usually takes the referees to separate them, they may be ejected from the game. But since both fighters are usually ejected, and substitutes are allowed, this does not much favor one team or the other.

11. The most serious injuries in hockey violence come not from fights when the game action has stopped, but from vicious hits in the course of the game itself: like when a player blind-sides an opponent skating up the ice away from the puck, in retaliation for an earlier confrontation.

12. In National Football League games during 1980–88 there were sixty-five serious injuries per team per year, or about three per team for each game played (*Los Angeles Times*, Jan. 24, 1997). Almost 10 percent of the team roster is injured each week. Football was an especially violent game at the turn of the twentieth

century; in 1905, eighteen players were killed in college games (professional foot-ball was not yet in existence) (Rudolph 1962: 373–93). Injuries were historically high in part because players' protective gear was not very effective: relatively thin leather helmets and body pads, compared to the heavy plastic and foam-padding that developed after 1950, and the military flak jackets and face visors that came to be used late in the twentieth century. Prior to the adoption of the hard-shell helmet in the late 1940s, tackling and blocking were done with the shoulder, like a boxer slipping punches rather than straight-on blows (Underwood 1979: 93–109). Thus although football players are bigger and stronger than in the early days, there are fewer fatal injuries. With improved training techniques, weight-lifting, steroids, and other body-building measures, contemporary football players doubtless hit much harder than early players, demonstrating the importance of protective padding in allowing a much higher level of controlled violence. Fatali-ties now almost all occur during the rigors of training.

13. Players try to get the ball away from opponents at the bottom of the pile by biting, eye-gouging, clawing, and jabbing vulnerable parts of the body including testicles (player interviews in *Sport Illustrated*, Jan. 31, 2005: 38–39). One player said, "The ball generally changes hands only once. You have trouble breathing in the pile, let alone having enough room for the ball to be moving around. There's usually one thief able to take it away from somebody, and that's the end of it." This is dirty play outside the rules, invisible and uncontrolled by referees, who judge who has the ball only when the bodies are finally unpiled. But these hidden fights are self-contained, and do not lead to further fighting once the players are back on their feet.

14. Injuries in soccer games, worldwide at all levels from youth leagues to pro-fessionals, are on the order of two to three injuries per match (twenty-two players) for male players, half that for females. These are mostly contusions, strains, and sprains to the legs; fractures or concussions were much rarer. Injuries that result in missing a subsequent match are about one per match at the professional level (Junge et al. 2004). These are much lighter than American football injuries, which are reported only if they substantially affect the chances of playing the following week's game.

15. At the end of chapter 2, under the heading "Fear of What?" I argued that soldiers and other serious fighters are less concerned with physical injury to them-selves than with the confrontational tension of threatening another human being in face-to-face contact. Confrontational tension/fear is chiefly about disruption of the basic entrainment of human interactions, a symbolic/emotional hurt. In the case of athletes, the specific tension is above all of losing one's aplomb, one's self-direction, in a publicly visible scene where one is in the center of attention.

16. These protections do sometimes figure in baseball fights. In several photos one can see catchers in a fight with an opposing team player (e.g., Red Sox catcher Jason Varitek, intervening to get between arch-rival New York Yankee slugger Alex Rodriguez and the Boston pitcher who just hit him with a pitch; see figure 8.3). In both cases the fight takes the usual form of a shoving match; in both we see the catcher, still wearing chest-protector and face-mask, shoving the oppo-nent's jaw and face backward and upward with both arms extended. The catcher is not only protected against effective retaliation, but since his fist is still inside his

catcher's mitt while shoving into the opponent's face, he is not doing much damage. See also *Los Angeles Times*, July 29, 2002.

17. This seems also to be true of pickup games. One student ethnography describes how contention built up between two players over several days; when the fight finally broke out, other players stood around and watched.

18. A player recalls his first day in the majors: "We had two bench-clearing brawls. I just came out of the dugout with everyone else. I didn't know what to do. It was my first day. I was nervous already" (*San Diego Union-Tribune*, Aug. 13, 2001; see also Adler 1984).

19. Baseball bats are, however, sometimes used as weapons in street fights and in holdups (e.g., Felson 1994: 32; Morrison and O'Donnell 1994, Fisher 2002).

20. Although Cobb has been retrospectively labeled a "psychopath," the historical circumstances of competition are a better explanation of his behavior than attributing it to a personality essence. Baseball created his personality.

21. Teams that are being beaten not only lose emotional dominance, but lose their cohesion. An interviewer asked Eric Dickerson (record-holder for most rushing yards in a season), "How could you tell when a defense was cracking?" He replied, "What you'd have is, you'd have a team bickering. That's when you knew you'd got them. You'd have them, 'Why don't you guys make a tackle up front!' Then, 'Why don't you make a tackle in the back!'" (*Los Angeles Times*, Dec. 27, 2003).

22. It is important here to distinguish between short-run and long-run flows of EE. In the prior statement of my theory of interaction ritual chains (Collins 2004), I noted that EE tends to be cumulative, both in positive and in negative directions. As individuals move from one encounter to the next, those who come to an encounter with high EE will dominate someone who comes in with low EE, and this repeats throughout the chain. A series of repeated encounters among the same persons will stabilize their EE ranking relative to each other. In sporting contests, such a pattern would make for boring and predictable games, lacking in drama. Even if teams were initially matched for levels of prior success, whoever broke out on top would dominate the rest of the way. Game rules are contrived to prevent this. There must be opportunities for players to get back the EE (also known as momentum) that they have lost. Hence games leave a role for chance (e.g., lucky or unlucky bounces of a ball); and for large ramifications of very small differences in performance: a difference of a fraction of an inch in a pitch can make the difference between a strikeout, foul ball, or home run. This is yet another respect in which games are artificial. Ordinary life is far less fair, less balanced; bullies keep on bullying monotonously, and their victims rarely turn the tables. In sports, techniques of dramatic production have been developed over the years to present something more dramatically satisfying.

23. It is notable in this regard that batters and pitchers rarely look at each other's eyes, or even faces. They seem to be attempting to maximize the trickiness of the guessing game by assuming the demeanor of poker players. Another aspect of the situation is that players take direct looks as hostile gestures; eye contact triggers a fight as much as verbal insult. In one instance, a fight began during the batting practice period before a major league baseball game, when a player from one team approached a rival player to apologize for an incident that had happened

in the previous game. The rival took the effort to make eye contact as a challenge, starting off a brawl that lasted four minutes (*San Diego Union-Tribune*, July 28, 2004). This is paralleled by my observation of a near-fight in a long line waiting to clear airport security (in August 2006): one man warned another with whom he was quarreling about cutting in line: "Don't get in my face." The offender backed away from eye contact and the fight aborted.

24. Some pitchers, such as Roger Clemens, or historically Bob Gibson, are known for their intimidating manner; these are pitchers who have set strikeout and ERA records, although other record-setting pitchers did not have the same confrontational style. Intimidation is one technique among others.

25. Some batters take the other tack and make it part of their technique to stand close to the plate, even to risk getting hit often as a way of getting on base and of disrupting the pitcher's pattern. Thus the same players lead the league yearly in being hit by pitch. A hypothesis in keeping with my observations is that such batters do not become angry when they are hit by a pitch, nor become involved as principals in brawls. Just as there are pitchers who rely on deception and those who emphasize overt domination, there are batters who rely more on cool-headed technique and others who rely on energy surges. (Recent examples of the former would include Barry Bonds, Ichiro Suzuki, and Tony Gwynn; of the latter, Manny Ramirez.) It is the latter who we would expect to start more fights. Similarly, we would expect pitchers who try to overpower batters are more likely to get into fights than pitchers who rely on deception and fine placement. Thus a fight would be most likely where a power pitcher faces a batter who relies on sheer muscular dominance or sheer emotional intensity.

26. Wayne Gretsky, the all-time scoring leader in professional hockey, had a reputation among opponents as a "sneaky" player, deft and surprising in his moves to the goal rather than confrontational.

27. There are limits on how many such players a team needs. A headline and lead in a story about the Philadelphia Flyers read, "Fedoruk in a fight for enforcer's job. But the Flyers might not be able to keep two tough guys" (*Philadelphia Inquirer*, Sept. 28, 2001).

28. According to my informants among knowledgeable fans, fights in hockey are especially likely after a team has clearly lost the game. The losing players start these fights, as if to show they still have a presence on the ice, even though they can no longer win the game.

29. In chapter 7, I suggested the principle that "one fight per venue" fills the emotional attention space. There can be multiple fights in a game, as in the present example. But these are all part of the same drama between two opposing sides; just like some fights in carousing venues, they are a series of chained fights with an overlapping cast of principal and supporting characters.

30. I have offered the generalization that turning point fights usually occur in the latter part of a game. But where games take place in a series of repeated rivalries, fights in pre-game warm-ups sometimes set the tone for the game. In the final football game of the regular season in 2002, the Pittsburgh Steelers, attempting to clinch the AFC northern division championship, were in the home stadium of the Tampa Bay Buccaneers, who had already clinched their division. Tampa defensive star tackle Warren Sapp—a huge man known for his mouthy outbursts—was

prancing and exhorting the crowd during the pre-game warm-ups; Pittsburgh's huge running back, Jerome Bettis (known as "the bus" for his size), bumped and shoved Sapp. "Last year they walked all over us during warmups," Bettis said, "and we wanted to let them know we were going to bully them in their own house." Several players from each team pushed and shoved each other. When the game started, the Steelers jumped to a 14–0 lead within the first four minutes, then held on to win 17–7. Pittsburgh dominated time of possession; Sapp ended up with no tackles, assists, or sacks, shut out by the Pittsburgh offensive line (*San Diego Union-Tribune* and *Los Angeles Times*, Dec. 24, 2002).

31. An example is the 2003 American League championship series between the New York Yankees and the Boston Red Sox (*Los Angeles Times*, Oct. 10–13, 2003). The Red Sox, who had not won a world series in eighty-five years, were heavily hyped as having their best chance in years. After splitting the first two games at Yankee Stadium, during which both teams repeatedly threw knock-down pitches at each other, the Red Sox returned home to a pivotal game with each team's best pitcher on the mound, Pedro Martinez and Roger Clemens. In the top of the fourth, as the Yankees rallied to overcome a Red Sox lead, 4–2, Martinez angrily threatened to hit the Yankees batters in the head, and the Yankees yelled back at him.

In the bottom of the inning, Clemens took the mound for the Yankees; he had been warned by the umpires that any retaliation would result in being thrown out of the game; teammates said the veins were popping out of his neck from the tension as he attempted to keep his emotions under control. The next batter was the star Red Sox slugger, Manny Ramirez, who had driven in the first run of the game in the first. Clemens threw a pitch high, but not inside; although the pitch was not near his head, Ramirez reacted as if it were, and stepped toward the mound, waving the bat in his hand—the dangerous weapon that batters almost never use in a fight. (The bat-waving was bluster; it was never used.) Both teams ran onto the field in a mêlée that lasted for fifteen minutes. Immediately after play resumed, Manny Ramirez struck out flailing at the first pitch Clemens threw, even though it was far outside the strike zone. Ramirez was emotionally out of control in the entire fight sequence, and failed to get a hit the rest of the game. The Red Sox went flat after the fight, and ended up losing the game 4–3. The Yankees took the offensive in another fight at the end of the game, beating and kicking a stadium groundskeeper rooting for the home team. After this emotional climax, there were no more fights in the remaining games. The teams alternated close victories, and the Red Sox again failed to make the World Series.

32. This was the same duo who started a brawl between the two teams the previous July (shown in figure 8.3 discussed above in note 16). The July fight was widely taken to represent the dramatic rivalry between these two teams, both competing to post the best record in the American League, and reprising their fight at the end of the previous season. After the July fight, the entire Red Sox team went on a victorious surge that eventually took them into the playoffs and the showdown with their hated rivals.

33. Police records for stadium disturbances do not usually distinguish among assaults, public drunkenness, and other misbehaviors; and mere numbers of arrests, citations, and ejections from particular games give little sense of what spe-

cifically happened and in what context. Figures occasionally compiled by newspapers show no clear pattern or trend (*San Diego Union-Tribune*, Oct. 31, 2004).

34. In Smith's (1978) data, in only 10 percent of the sixty-eight incidents of serious sports violence was there crowd violence unrelated to player fights or near-fights on the field.

35. In September 2004 in Oakland, during a tight race between the two teams for a playoff berth, a player on the visiting Texas Rangers threw a chair into the stands at a persistent heckler sitting near the bullpen; the result was a bystander hit, breaking the nose of the woman sitting next to the heckler. The entire Rangers team congregated at the bullpen to back up their player, showing the usual solidarity of teams in fights (*USA Today*, Sept. 15, 2004).

36. Consider the ritual of catching a foul ball (or indeed a home run) hit into the stands. This is treated as a matter of great importance by the fans, and the one who catches it momentarily becomes a hero in the immediate vicinity. The baseball is treated as a sacred object, a connection from the peripheral realm of the stands to the heart of the collective attention space on the field. It is enough to get the ball any way one can, whether it is rolling around or even handed over by a field attendant; but there is special prestige in making a real catch on the fly. This is one way in which a fan can momentarily rise above his/her status, genuinely emulating one of the acts of the players. This always brings applause by the other fans. The phenomenon is similar to collecting autographs, another form of subservient contact with spectator idols for tokens of connection. The utilitarian-minded will say that baseballs are sometimes worth a great deal of money on the sports memorabilia market, as in the case of record-setting home runs. But this does not explain why ordinary baseballs are also treated with ritual respect; nor indeed why record-setting balls have such a market value. The more famous balls are intensifications of the ritual value of ordinary ones.

37. For a detailed analysis of celebrating riots, see forthcoming book by Jerry M. Lewis.

38. In this section I am using the term "football" in the European sense (i.e., "soccer"); clubs of violent fans or "supporters" can also be referred to as "firms," using the British term. The term originated in the London criminal underworld, after a "mafia-like gang that ran its criminal affairs in a corporate manner. In the 1970s, the term was appropriated by gangs of violent football supporters" (Buford 1993: 316). Subsequently, a "firm" might refer to small groups who stick together and take an active part in fights (what Americans would now call a "posse"); or it might be used loosely to refer to all the supporters of a soccer team who engage in deliberate fighting tactics. Supporters are a larger group than hooligans or firms.

39. This is the same pattern as seen in the historical mobilization of the working class in labor movements. The degree of mobilization does not depend on the amount of economic grievance, but on resources for mobilization. The height of soccer hooligan violence, the 1980s, was a period of relative prosperity.

40. Buford (1993: 29, 213) describes most of the prominent leaders as flashing expensive clothes, cars, and other wealth. Some of them are professional criminals such as thieves and counterfeiters (confirmed by Anthony King, personal communication, Nov. 2000). Football violence, however, is not an ordinary criminal ac-

tivity for them, since it is more costly than profitable; Buford's leaders behave as if they are enjoying themselves immensely. For this section generally, see also Dunning et al. (1988, 2002); Dunning (1999); King (2001); Johnston (2000); Marsh, Rosser and Harré (1978); Van Limbergen et al. (1989).

41. Something very like jibbing is found in higher social classes, chiefly among children, although it is usually very small-scale. Scott Fitzgerald in *This Side of Paradise* describes a small group of Princeton undergraduates in the years before World War I making an extended spree in Atlantic City without any money, by jauntily ordering food in restaurants and then leaving without paying, having learned the Goffmanian lesson of the strength of maintaining normal appearances.

42. In Elias and Dunning's (1986) pioneering formulation, sports became organized from the eighteenth century onward to allow for a pleasurable tension that is lacking in modern life. The civilizing process, the argument runs, causes repression of natural impulses—in effect, the Freudian argument that repression is the price we pay for civilization; sport allows a safe parallel universe of fantasy conflicts in which these tensions can be expressed that previously would have come out in violence. In addition to releasing tensions, sports create a pleasurable tension and excitement that is in demand in proportion to the monotony that spectators experience in everyday life.

There are two weaknesses in this argument. One is that premodern violence was not so easy and untrammeled; confrontational tension/fear has existed throughout history, and violence was not a pleasurable expression of natural impulses but the same kind of ignominious attacking of the weak, or an honorific limited and staged fighting, as we have seen in this book. What sport expresses does not exist as natural unrepressed violence anywhere. Second, premodern sports also created pleasurable tension, ranging from tribal games, ancient Olympics, Byzantine chariot-races, to medieval jousts and popular games. As Elias and Dunning (1986) themselves document in the case of medieval English folk football, the chief difference from modern times was that the games of the lower classes had little formal organization; there were no referees or codified rules, and participation drew in entire communities rather than specializing among the most skilled, encouraging large and unspecified numbers of players who might be variously on horse and on foot, of all ages and sizes, using sticks, hands, or feet; thus serious injuries or deaths were common. What has changed is the growth of formal, specialized organization that has controlled some aspects of violence but encouraged others, in the interest of creating the most dramatic experiences of entertainment, those that sustain long and complex plot tension. Upper-class sports had more such organization throughout ancient and medieval times, since they had the resources to contain confrontational tension/fear and simultaneously convey high status by staging fights among equals who followed stylized rules. The main historical shift has been the growth of wealth and leisure among all social classes, and an ongoing expansion of the life-cycle period of schooling; these have created more opportunity and time to fill, time that would previously have been taken up for most people with the drudgery of work. It is doubtful that the amount of monotony has shifted much throughout history. What is displaced into sports by modernity is not an allegedly uninhibited premodern violence, but the former pervasiveness of work. The distinctive forms of sports violence are not a civilizational substitution but an ongoing civilizational creation.

43. This is also shown in a Reuters photo (Feb. 16, 1995), "English fans attack an Irish fan outside match at Dublin." It shows a three-on-one cluster (see pictures.Reuters.com).

44. A number of examples of this pattern were related to me during 2000–01 by English field researchers Anthony King and Eric Dunning. Buford (1993: 93–95) gives one example: After having rampaged through an Italian city after the soccer match, the English supporters gathered in a bar during the evening; their animated talk concerned not the game itself, which Manchester United had lost, but their own victory, and "how the Italians had 'shat themselves.' There was a sense of closure to the evening, an end-of-a-good-day's-work atmosphere." Outside in the square, several thousand Italians had gathered, seeking revenge on the two hundred English inside. The English did not venture out, but waited until police arrived to escort them away. Notice that the Italians outside, although enjoying great advantage in numbers, did not attempt to invade the bar. Bluster and confrontational tension/fear are found among hooligans and their opponents, as elsewhere. In the earlier literature on football hooligans, emphasis was on their development of deliberate tactics and organization to evade police countermeasures; what needs to be added is that they are also sophisticated in overcoming the perennial problem of all fighting, confrontational tension and fear—in this case by elaborate techniques for holding off attacks until they get their opponents in weak moments.

45. King (2001). In Germany, an English supporter goes around shouting "*Heil Hitler!*" because it is an appropriate way to upset the Dutch supporters whom England is facing in a tournament (Buford 1993: 228). Van Limbergen et al. (1989: 11) sum up the ideological self-presentation of Belgian hooligans: "They pretend to be racist, sexist, and regionalist. Their ideas are simplistic and antidemocratic. This ideology is rather badly developed and not well thought out. They only chant specific slogans to provoke."

46. It is often claimed that meeting on a playing field is a substitute for international violence and a way to bring enemies together; but such meetings also tend to stir up, indeed to create, national animosities. Sipes (1973) concluded from a comparison of premodern societies that those with warlike games were also those that more frequently attacked other societies. This does not directly address the issue of international (or in this case, inter-tribal) competitions; no doubt there are multiple causes, since a degree of peace and international contacts are necessary for international sports to take place; given that, what are the further effects of sports? The ancient Greek Olympic games were held in a region where inter-city fighting was endemic, and the struggle for honor in the games was given a chauvinistic interpretation.

47. Dunning et al. (1988). American baseball games were historically similar in some of these respects; in the early 1900s, crowds in the outfield stood and were separated from the field only by ropes. A famous game in New York in 1908 hinged on the fact that the crowd surged onto the field as the home team scored the ostensible winning run in the ninth inning; but a runner named Merkle had not touched base (hence this was known as the "Merkle boner"), and the visiting

Cubs chased down the ball in the crowd, touched the base, and had the Giants called out for the inning and their run nullified. The game was replayed at the end of the season with the pennant at stake, before an unprecedented overflow crowd; this game was several times interrupted by fans invading the field. When the Giants lost, there was a post-game riot in the stadium.

48. During the American League championship series between Boston and New York in October 2004, the Yankees fans greeted Red Sox pitcher Pedro Martinez with a child-like refrain. He had said to the press, after losing several games to the Yankees, that the Yankees were like his daddy; the fans chanted this over and over in a sing-song voice, "Who's your dad-dy, Who's your dad-dy," up-and-down a musical minor third exactly in the tune of preschool children jeering at an outcast of the group (traditionally "Nya-nya, nanny-goat.").

49. "They see themselves as the true heart of the club; most of the players are just mercenaries" (Anthony King, personal communication, Nov. 2004). "The real match was not inside the stadium; it was here in the streets outside it. This is where you found the crowd, the press, the television cameras, the audience" (Buford 1993: 215).

50. There are of course significant differences; moshers practice pseudo-violence, and are ideological poles apart from the soccer hooligans (and from skinheads, their nearest American counterpart).

CHAPTER 9
HOW FIGHTS START, OR NOT

1. Lakoff's (1987) analysis of common idioms for talking about anger goes so far as to claim that the folk theory is an accurate induction from experience, that this is how violence is actually caused, although he offers no evidence beyond the linguistic expressions themselves.

2. For this reason, it is important to maintain a distinction between real physical violence and other kinds of aggressiveness. Social activists and official control agencies dealing with various kinds of violence and abuse try to expand the definition and the scope of their problem, by subsuming verbal aggression and emotional outbursts as forms of "abuse," "harassment," or "bullying," and prescribing "anger management" programs as a cure-all for violent and non-violent aggressiveness alike. But that badly muddies the causal pathways: it is not possible to explain real violence by the model of normal, institutionalized acrimony; in crucial respects their causal patterns are antithetical. Anderson (1999: 97) describes a group of black inner-city youths watching a video on conflict resolution as an alternative to fighting; their reaction is to dismiss it as unrealistic, in the context where they perceive violence could be headed off or at least contained only by putting on a show of pretended anger and other posturings of the street code.

3. Non-Western societies often have even more stringent standards of protecting one's own face and saving others' face; Goffman (1967: 15–17) includes some comparisons to classic Chinese manners; see also Bond (1991) for contem-

porary Chinese and Ikegami (2005) for Japanese manners. Interactional practices in these cultural regions appear to be ultra-Goffmanian.

4. For instance, a punch thrown by one professor at another, during the course of a political argument, resulted in a lawsuit, and in the professor, despite his considerable eminence in his field, being unable to get another appointment in an American university; and eventually in the abolition of the department itself by the university administration. (These events took place around 1970.)

5. Two supporting observations: (a) Late in the afternoon, I would be at home (during a period when I was writing at home) with my two children, a boy and girl at ages between four and eight, waiting for their mother to come home from work. We are carrying on a playful conversation. The mother comes in the door; the children greet her with excited shrieks and hugs. She reciprocates warmly for a few minutes, then sits down to tell me about her day. At this point the children start up a whining tone of voice, sometimes also squabbling with each other. Eventually she loses her temper, bursts out with a complaint about being received like this when she comes home, and retires to another part of the house. Examining this situation in terms of attention: the children begin by being in the center of adult attention for a half hour or so, while also anticipating the moment when they will see their mother. After that peak of excitement, they become relegated to the background while the adults fall into the flow of a conversation between themselves. The children's whining eventually restores attention to them briefly and negatively; but at any rate, the offending conversation among adults ends also. This seems to restore equilibrium for the children, since after this event they stop whining and go back to their normal moods.

(b) Over a period of many months, I had the opportunity every afternoon to hear two small children in a neighboring house, ages two to three and four to five, come out to play in their backyard, which was behind a hedge about twenty feet away from the study in which I was writing with windows open to the warm southern California air. The children were accompanied by a babysitter. The smaller child, within a few minutes after entering the yard, would begin to cry. Her voice modulated in intensity, from annoyed-sounding whimpering, up to strong crying; typically this started in a dispute with the older child (possibly over possession of a toy), but also this happened if the babysitter's voice was not heard for a few minutes, indicating that her attention was elsewhere. Inevitably the babysitter's voice would reply, upon which the child's crying would modulate down, sometimes quite abruptly. These episodes would repeat when the babysitter's voice withdrew, until finally she would give up and take the children into the house. This scenario was repeated each day almost without fail. Small children do not simply cry spontaneously because of pain and distress, but can use crying as a move in response to the social situation. Small children have little resources for power over others, but crying is one resource they have, and they sometimes use it in tyrannical manner (cf. Katz 1999: 229–73).

6. An example from a student report: At the end of a family gathering in a restaurant, a dispute breaks out over who picks up the check. The widowed mother takes it as an affront that one of her married daughters tries to pay for everyone, stating that she seems to think that she (the mother) can't afford to pay for her own children. The siblings take sides with one or another of the principals;

their siblings' spouses maintain an embarrassed silence, as if tacitly taking advantage of their more distant relationship to stay out of the quarrel. The scene culminates in an angry shouting match in the parking lot, with car doors slamming as they drive away, the two disputing groups in separate cars. This is a Goffmanian face dispute, in which neither side backs down. Nevertheless, despite the blowup, the family group is committed to periodic reunions, which they go on having; they handle the dispute by never mentioning it again, going on with normally staged encounters as if nothing had happened. Black (1998) generalized, on the basis of comparing anthropological evidence, that groups built on intimate and relatively egalitarian relationships tend to smother quarrels rather than resolving them.

7. Among male acquaintances, stirring up a quarrel is often a way of enlivening a boring encounter, a milder version of the frustrated carousing pathway to violence described in chapter 7. This hypothesis can be tested by the situations and emotional sequence in which such quarrels arise. Typically this occurs in sociable situations, and is all the more likely in carousing situations where participants consciously expect a level of excitement, "action," out of the ordinary. Middle-class men generally confine the dispute on the level of an emotionally heated verbal exchange; working-class men, especially young men, are more likely to threaten violence, if not always to carry it out. Couples also quarrel in such situations; survey evidence shows entertainment is the second most common occasion for marital quarrels, after disputes over money (Blood and Wolfe 1960: 241).

8. An institutionalized form is the testimonial dinner or awards ceremony. A series of speakers take the floor, holding the group's attention to tell the recipient how wonderful he or she is; the recipient in turn thanks the others by telling them how wonderful *they* are. The higher social classes thus manage to avoid first-person boastfulness, while putting on a fine example of Mauss's (1925) ritualistic gift-exchange.

9. Labov 1972. A comparable custom in some middle-class professions is a "roast," a banquet at which the honored guest is the target for joking put-downs. A "roast" is a strictly controlled middle-class version of boisterous masculine ritual conflict. The custom emerged in the 1970s, perhaps as part of the emulation of lower-class manners that went on at that time. It is not part of the politer or more traditional part of the middle and upper classes; it does not exist for instance in academic circles, nor in high society. Women may be integrated into these occasions but the provenance is distinctly male.

10. A recording of the former may be heard in the bird-like cries in tribal battles in New Guinea in the film *Dead Birds* (see chap. 2 above); of the latter, during the urban uprising in 1958, in the documentary *The Battle of Algiers*. For a study of ululation see Jacobs (2004).

11. Anderson 1999: 112. The street code is more sharply marked in male clothing and body demeanor styles than in female styles. Males are the core members in the group marked by the street code; although females participate, usually as followers, or in a derivative way. Lynn Green (2001), studying the sex lives of working-class black teenage girls, notes that their daily lives are dominated by their boyfriends' activities if they hang around with them, and that the girls feel they have to break with them if they want to concentrate on their schoolwork or just to follow interests of their own.

12. This conflict helps explain the appeal of Muslim or African outfits for black males: they represent a way to express rejection of white mainstream membership, but at the same time to express commitment to a disciplined, middle-class lifestyle. They are a militant version of the "decent" culture of the black ghetto. The role of African and Muslim clothing is often misperceived by whites, who see it as a hostile form of reverse racism. What they miss is the commitment to conventional middle-class behavior that is expressed by these same symbols. Far from being an ally of the street culture, it is an alternative to it. For the emergence of this style, see Lincoln (1994).

13. Being topped in trash-talking does not necessarily lead to violence, however. There is typically an audience present, and the verbal ritual is usually carried out with the audience in mind. A person in the position of having been verbally put down might take the stance of the audience, joining in laughter and acknowledging it as a good joke. This is a situational displacement of self to another part of the group; and since the group also conveys membership in the street scene, such a move can temporarily defuse violence.

14. Jones (2004). In the late 1990s, black teenage girls wearing Muslim-style robes and headcoverings were targets for fighting in Philadelphia high schools, attacked by girls who claim to feel put down by the Muslims who publicly criticize their sexual behavior and drug use. The Muslim clothing is an extreme rejection of street clothing styles, above all in female dress including long robes, headcoverings, and veils; and is associated with a message overtly attacking the street culture as morally inferior. These fights are similar to those in which street-oriented males attack those students who are visibly members of the "decent" culture, on the rationale that these are claiming to be "better than us."

15. Another piece of evidence against seeing disrespect as the motive for violence is the fact that the street style is widely adopted, in one degree or another, by white youths, including affluent ones (Anderson 1999: 124). Far from being a reaction against disrespect, among these white youth it is a claim for high status in the youth scene. One can see this in the situational way in which they put on their gang-like clothes and manners in carousing situations such as party weekends, and put them off when they return to the utilitarian routine of school and work.

16. Anderson (1999: 73). This pattern is common in criminal organizations such as the Mafia, especially among those playing the role of the enforcer. A number of these gangsters have nicknames such as "Crazy Joe." They were able to rise through the ranks to a position of eminence by acquiring the reputation for going into a frenzy of violence, committing extremely vicious acts of overkill or gratuitous cruelty to those whom they are attempting to intimidate (for instance in loan-sharking enforcement or extortion rackets, or in fighting with rival gangsters). Some evidence that this is a deliberate performance in building a reputation comes from the pattern that these acts of violent frenzy typically happen early in the gangster's career; later, after he has risen to a commanding rank in the organization, he may act quite routinely with little or no personal violence, which he can now delegate to others. Thus Sam "Mooney" (1930s slang for "crazy") Giancana, and Tony "Joe Batters" Accardo (for taking a bat to a victim's head) both rose to be competent heads of the Chicago mob, positions that they held in

sequence during the years from 1950 to 1966 (*Chicago Sun Times*, August 18, 2002).

17. On the other hand, attempting to avoid being a "chump," an apparently easy victim of a stickup, is a major motive for decent people putting on the street code (Anderson 1999: 131).

18. I will deal with long tunnels of violence in a companion volume on time-dynamics of violence, including also its long-term macro dimensions.

19. The dueling code provided a different way of dealing with this point. Making a challenge to a duel, and accepting it, brought the immediate confrontation to an end; the actual violence was postponed to another time. The stage of bluster and insult was ended with the setting of the duel. Issuing a dueling challenge solved the Goffmanian problem of "making a scene" by giving a polite method of being offended, which preserved everyone's face, at the cost of risking physical casualties later.

20. In a different historical setting, Francis Bacon (1225/1963, *Essays*, chap. 62) advised that common insults may be used in quarrels without making deep enemies, but that insults which hit home at an individual's particular weakness will not be forgiven. It is a problem for empirical investigation whether generalized insults ("asshole," "stupid shit," etc.) are less likely to give rise to violence than insults especially tailored to the individual.

21. The "he stole me" incident described by Anderson (described in the previous section of this chapter) gives an example of this dynamic.

22. Thus one reason the Dreiser-Lewis fight ends so easily is that it takes place in private. In addition, the one-man audience who intrudes, while not anonymous, acts not to encourage the fight but to break it up.

CHAPTER 10
THE VIOLENT FEW

1. Information on the distribution of violence-prone individuals within police forces is difficult to get. Police unions guard the confidentiality of such records, and departments are concerned over lawsuits. The best statistics are from the Christopher Commission, which investigated the Los Angeles Police Department after the scandal of the Rodney King case; its data covers the period from 1986 to early 1991.

2. "Improper tactics" generally means highly aggressive or reckless behavior in dealing with suspects, a lesser administrative charge than excessive force, which is criminally actionable. "Excessive" or "improper" force in the internal records of a police department does not usually mean that these officers were charged or convicted of violations, or even administratively punished.

3. Tracy, Wolfgang, and Figlio 1990; Shannon et al. 1988; Piquero, Farrington, and Blumstein 2003; Piquero 2000; Piquero and Buka 2002; Polk et al. 1981; Nevares, Wolfgang and Tracy 1990; Moffitt and Caspi 2001; Farrington 2001; Wikstrom 1985; Pulkinnen 1988; Guttridge et al. 1983. These studies cover numerous American cities and other parts of the world.

4. Burglaries are sometimes unviolent, but they are among the more adventurous and nervy crimes, and may lead to confrontations with victims, and hence to assaults and rapes.

5. These calculations confirm the findings of cohort studies. The concentration of crime among female prisoners is similar to that among males (English and Mande 1992). Their crimes, however, are generally less violent than men's.

6. Calculated from Department of Justice, National Youth Gang Center; FBI Uniform Crime Reports; U.S. Census; and information provided by the San Diego Police Department gang unit.

7. Calculated from Thrasher 1927/1963: 130–32, 282–83.

8. We do know that murders committed by persons under age eighteen are only 5.2 percent of all murders; and in the black population, victims ages thirteen to nineteen are only 12.9 percent of all black murder victims, and most of these are in the ages seventeen to nineteen group. (Where information is known, 92 percent of all black murder victims are killed by other blacks.) In contrast, 53.2 percent of black murder victims are ages twenty to thirty-four. Altogether, this implies that the substantial proportion of gang members below age twenty, and especially those below age eighteen, commit very few of the murders even in gang neighborhoods (calculations from FBI Uniform Crime Reports 2003, Violent Crime, tables 2.4, 2.6, and 2.7).

9. Sources from chapter 6 pp. 214–15; and calculations from McEvedy and Jones 1978; Gilbert 1970: 11; Cambridge Modern History 11: 409, 579; Klusemann 2002. The Prussian, subsequently German army ranged from 500,000 in 1870 to 790,000 million in 1913; one estimate shows the proportion of officers at 2 percent.

10. Several teachers have reported that multiple fights among different children sometimes happened in the same class period; these involved sixth-, seventh- and eighth-grade classrooms in urban poverty area schools (Mollie Rubin, personal communication, Nov. 2004; Patricia Maloney, Oct. 2005). Milner's research (2004: 105) describes one occasion in a big, racially mixed (but predominantly white middle-class) high school when two fights broke out within ten minutes of each other during the lunch period; the first fight was all-white, the second black-on-black. There were many hundreds of students in the lunch area, and most of them ignored the fights, especially the fight in the other racial group; all of which suggests that the school had segregated attention spaces. The only description I have encountered where adults had several fights simultaneously in the same attention space is from Riker's Island prison in New York City, where an inmate describes three fights going on as he walked down the cell block, each pair of individuals fighters surrounded by a circle of spectators "watching the battle of their choice" (Hoffman and Headley 1992: 45). Yet the observer, a professional killer, seemed to regard this as very unusual, and an indication of how extremely tough this prison population was. The crucial factor may be that these multiple (but in fact limited, one-on-one) fights were a way the inmates as a whole could defy the guards, much as multiple fights in a classroom are a way of running the teacher ragged. The authority that is defied may be the key element in these attention spaces.

11. Worden 1996. Controlling for both resistance and demeanor, race of suspect also determines the likelihood of police violence, with blacks receiving more violence. Race is the weakest factor; overall in the raw data, blacks are more likely to be beaten by police but most of this violence is explained by race-neutral factors; blacks are more likely than other races to resist the police, and to show a hostile rather than compliant demeanor. There is a large gap here between the empirical data and public perception. Racism is the most frequently asserted explanation of police violence. But being a racist does not make it easy to commit violence, and situational conditions are still necessary—and indeed operate also without racism.

12. Peter Moskos (personal communication, April 2005) reported, on the basis of his participant observation study in a big-city police force, that officers with a reputation for being involved in a lot of violence tended to be on specialty units such as drug squads or gang squads. Similarly, officers self-select to get on SWAT (special weapons and tactics) teams, which specialize in violent confrontations.

13. He fired his gun in three of these encounters, illustrating that even in the most dangerous situations police shoot only a small proportion of the time. A study of four big-city police departments found that police fired in only a "fraction" of the situations where law and policy would allow it (Scharf and Binder 1983). Klinger (2004: 58) interprets such instances as reasonable restraint. Micro-interactional detail, however, supports the point that those who shoot are those who are most energized in such confrontations. The prevalence of non-firing can also be interpreted as confrontational tension/fear, and as fitting the normal pattern of small numbers of violent activists.

14. A similar remark about enjoying the "cat and mouse" game of car chases was made to me by a police officer in a ride-along in 2004 in which his squad car was cooperating with the narcotics squad in setting up a drug sting. This officer was a member of an elite special unit, the gang squad. The arrest, however, was completely without violence; the suspects gave themselves up passively when they were finally pulled over.

15. In Peter Moskos's study, which focused on police who were most interested in easy jobs and extra pay opportunities, being involved in shootings was regarded as a way of getting into trouble with the administration (personal communication, April 2005). Conversely, officers who want easy duty attempt to serve on midnight shifts, since there is relatively little action especially after 3 a.m.

16. An officer who had been involved in three deadly shootings describes his emotions at the end of one shoot-out: "I was feeling this tremendous exhilaration. It was a real rush and I'd never felt anything like it. Hey, he tried to kill me, but I killed him first. Fuck him. Then when the ambulance people started working on him, I remember thinking I didn't want them to save him" (Artwohl and Christensen 1997: 164). This officer volunteered for a frontline position on SWAT team search entries; his wife had temporarily dissuaded him from taking a lead position, but he was soon back again (171).

17. About sixty-five police were murdered on duty annually during the 1990s, the great majority of them with firearms. Over a ten-year span, several thousands survived being shot, and tens of thousands were assaulted ("Law enforcement officers killed and assaulted," 2000, FBI Uniform Crime Reports; Geller and Scott

1992). These figures show that police in fact were winning most of their encounters; they outkilled suspects at a rate of about 10-to-15 to 1, and outshot them about 10-to-1. High-violence officers mentally portray themselves in a high level of danger, but implicitly they are committed to a very high degree of dominance even in this area.

18. Hence snipers whose locations are known draw heavy fire, even from artillery or planes. More effectively, snipers are countered by bringing in opposing snipers, who use their own insider lore in the arts of concealment to locate their opponent, and their firing skill to dispatch him/her with a well-placed shot. Static fronts with trench warfare and abundant skilled snipers on both sides tend to produce sniper-counter-sniper contests, which are costly on both sides. Sniper-versus-sniper is a war among elites. In the criminal world, the toughest guys do not go usually up against the other toughest guys. The high attrition of the sniper-on-sniper pattern, reaching 90 to 100 percent in the world wars (Pegler 2001: 58; 2004: 140–42) suggests what would happen if they did.

19. A comparison of the visibility of human bodies, buildings, and various natural objects at varying distances is given in a 1942 Soviet sniping chart (see figure 10.1). Similar specifications are given in the 1865 U.S. Army handbook (Kautz 1865/2001: 241–43). Kautz notes that at twenty-five to thirty yards one can see the white of the eye; hence the famous order in eighteenth-century warfare, when guns were very unreliable, "wait until you see the whites of their eyes."

20. Another example is given by Ardant du Picq (1903/1999: 8) from the Crimean War. Two small groups of soldiers, without officers, suddenly encountered each other around a piece of broken ground at a distance of ten paces. Forgetting their guns, both sides threw rocks at each other while retreating. Finally, when an additional troop coming in from the flank set one side into full flight, the other side recovered their composure and fired at the fleeing enemy. Du Picq put this at the outset of his treatise on combat to show the importance of surprise in successful violence, which is to say getting the jump on the enemy and imposing one's emotional momentum upon him. Whoever is surprised is unable to defend oneself. When both sides are surprised, both are incapacitated from serious violence.

21. In World War I, there were about 1,050 American pilots; they shot down about 780–850 enemy planes, or a little less than one per pilot. Aces made up about 8 percent of the pilots—an unusually high figure—and shot down a similarly high 68 percent of EAD. There were about 1,200 aces in World War II, when total fighter pilots numbered about 125–135,000, making the aces just under 1 percent. Super-aces with ten or more kills were 0.1 percent (calculated from Gurney 1958: 83, 158–63, 187–207, 226–27, 254, 256–65, 270–72; Keegan 1997: 139; Dyer 1985).

22. In World War II, it is estimated that even the best pilots fired in only about one third of their sorties (Toliver and Constable 1997: 348).

23. Calculated from www.au.af.mil/au/awc/awcgate/ aces/aces.html; Shore and Williams 1994: 10; Overy 1980: 143–44; Mersky 1993; Boyd 1977.

24. www.acepilots.com/german/ ger_aces.html; Toliver and Constable 1997: 348–49. Hartmann had over 800 aerial combats, so his success rate was approximately 44 percent of combat episodes, although it is impossible to say how many enemy planes he actually encountered. The number of sorties is always higher

than the number of actual combats, but the latter information is rarely available, and so we are left with the rough ratios of kills per sortie.

25. Record-keeping of this kind is exceedingly nationalistic, and conventional publicity often gives a distorted picture. The top French and British aces, respectively, had seventy-five and seventy-three kills. Altogether, eight French, more than fifteen British, and more than twenty German pilots exceeded Rickenbacker's American total (Gurney 1965: 173–75). Part of the disparity is due to the fact that these countries were in combat somewhat over twice as long as the American flyers; aerial combat began in July 1915 and became common in 1916.

26. Calculated from Gurney 1958: 270–71. This 6.3 percent figure is a maximum possible average; an unknown (but probably much smaller) proportion of EAD were shot down by bomber pilots. Moreover, since navy and marine aces accounted for about 40 percent of the EAD, the success rate for the remaining pilots was around 4 percent.

27. As a show of bravado, however, American pilots in World War I did not wear parachutes, although they were used by non-heroic balloon crews (Gurney 1958: 23).

28. Thus the all-time record for kills in one combat episode was credited at the time to Lieutenant Paul Lipscomb for shooting down seven Japanese planes on January 11, 1945. Sergeant Arthur Benko had also shot down seven Japanese planes on Oct. 2, 1943, but he was a bomber gunner and was not recognized as a record-holder (Gurney 1958: 121, 140).

29. In World War II, 68 percent of U.S. Navy planes lost to enemy action were to anti-aircraft fire; in Korea, the comparable figure for all allied planes was 86 percent (Gurney 1958: 273).

30. For example, when Richard Bong in 1943 broke Rickenbacker's old World War I record of twenty-six total kills, he was pulled out of combat and returned to the United States. He eventually managed to finagle an assignment as a noncombatant gunnery instructor in the Pacific theater; by bending the rules, he accompanied his students into combat and raised his total to forty kills, which still stands as the all-time record for an American pilot. Seven months before the end of the war, the top commander again removed Bong from the combat zone and returned him to home duty (Gurney 1958: 113). Since Bong's record of twenty-eight had been superceded by several other pilots who reached totals as high as thirty-eight, he had a strong incentive to return to combat.

31. www.acepilots.com/index.html#top There was nothing like this proliferation of records among rifle snipers. In the army that placed the greatest emphasis on snipers, the Soviet during World War II, top snipers with record kills were sometimes also retired from combat and paraded as heroes on the homefront; this was notably the case with women snipers, treated as emblems of all-out mobilization for the war effort (Pegler 2004: 177).

32. U.S. Navy pilots shot down Japanese planes in World War II at a ratio of 10.2 to 1 for American losses. The ratio grew during the war: from 3.1 to 1 in 1941–42, to 21.6 to 1 in 1945, as the quality of Japanese planes and pilots fell (Gurney 1958: 82). Hence the tendency for American kill records to escalate in the last year of the Pacific war, but not to anything like that extent in the European war.

33. For this reason, the ace total has dropped in every war since World War II. The United States had very few "double aces" with ten or more kills in Korea. The Chinese kept their bases to the north of the Yalu River, past the diplomatic border of peninsular war; American jets would fly several hundred miles from the battlefront in the south, attempting to provoke the MIGs to come out and meet them. These battles took place in a corridor eight miles high colloquially called "MIG alley" (by American pilots; it is unknown what the Chinese pilots called it). American jets prevailed in combat by a ratio of fourteen kills to one (Gurney 1958: 210); nevertheless, the Chinese continued to meet them; the confrontation must have been highly honorific on both sides. Jet fighter dogfights had virtually nothing to do with the rest of the war, becoming again an enclave almost as restricted as in World War I. In Vietnam there were only two aces, each with the minimum five kills. The smaller North Vietnamese air force had a least two aces, the top shooting down thirteen American planes, benefiting from an abundance of enemy targets (Toliver and Constable 1997: 322–32).

34. www.acepilots.com/german/ger_aces.html Another slow starter was Otto Kittel, who eventually reached 267 kills (fourth highest on the list). He had seventeen kills in his first six months on the Russian front (three per month); in the next fourteen months, another twenty-two (less than two per month). Thereupon he hit his stride, averaging nine to ten kills per month for two full years. Hartmann got his first kill in his second month in combat (November 1942), but his second took three months more. In subsequent months his tactics began to crystallize: he had twenty-three kills by his ninth month (now at five kills per month). Then his kills accelerated, hitting his peak rate—twenty-six per month—at about one year's experience.

35. Tiger Woods explained his ability to hit golf shots at crucial moments: "When I am in that moment when my concentration is the highest . . . I see things more clearly. It's like it's magic" (*Philadelphia Inquirer*, March 1, 2006 E2).

36. See note 46 in chapter 11.

37. E.g., the assassination of the French Catholic leader, the Duke de Guise, during the religious wars in 1588, was carried out by inviting him to an audience with the Protestant king, then having guards attack him as soon as he entered the antechamber, giving him and his retinue no chance to draw their swords (*Cambridge Modern History* 3:45).

38. Pegler (2004: 195, 199). In situations like this, the elite sniper might have twenty hits in a few minutes, but he did not count them as part of his record. He did not consider this to be true sniping, showing that he made a clear distinction among his various techniques.

39. Two famous instances: the Oakland Raiders lost the Superbowl in 2003 to the Tampa Bay Buccaneers by 48–21, and were completely overwhelmed on both offense and defense from almost the outset of the game, trailing at one point 34–3. In the 1940 professional football championship, the Washington Redskins, led by their record-setting quarterback Sammy Baugh, were beaten 73–0 by the Chicago Bears.

40. Notoriously, star college quarterbacks often turn out not to be good professionals; and others who come from a mediocre background sometimes train themselves to excellent performance at the rhythm of the professional game. The speed,

complexity, and deceptiveness of the professional game is at a different level and requires forming a new kind of gestalt.

CHAPTER 11
VIOLENCE AS DOMINANCE IN EMOTIONAL ATTENTION SPACE

1. As I have done in the case of the demonstrations at the Democratic National Convention in Los Angeles in 2000. Their observations fit with my memories of participating in campus demonstrations and riots in 1964–68. I have also examined a raw video of the 2002 Mardi Gras celebration in the four-block carousing zone of South Street in Philadelphia. Violent encounters between police and crowd members, or fights in the crowd, are visible in ten incidents, ranging from five to eighty seconds long; altogether the violent action totals four minutes and twenty seconds out of a video four hours long.

2. Demonstrations, such as rallies or marches without directly confronting an opposition, also have closely assembled, relatively unified crowds (McPhail 1991). I omit demonstrations from my analysis unless there are photos of violence that develops around them.

3. A photo (not shown) of a Buenos Aires protest shows a group of unemployed workers retreating before seven oncoming police; all seventeen protestors on the sidewalk are huddled in postures of fear against the wall (except for two cameramen who attempt to hold their ground); the police attacks are concentrated on a cluster of nine who are in the street. The five nearest the police are brandishing or have just dropped sticks that they apparently were using as weapons; two have tripped to the ground, and one still fights with the point man in the police wedge. Fighting or confronting authority is quite literally in the street (June 28, 2002 AP photo). Buford (1993: 283–85) describes the moments at the beginning of a soccer hooligan riot that hinge upon whether the first man who steps from the sidewalk into the street will be followed by others; when this collective threshold is finally crossed, the crowd becomes confident and joyous with their sense of achievement; they have "taken the street" in the face of authorities who also regard this as a threshold.

4. Figure 3.7 shows another part of the same massive demonstration; once again, we see a small number of rock-throwers (in this case, two) out in front of the crowd.

5. One might argue a purely rationalistic explanation of wearing masks: they are a way to avoid being identified by the police for one's violent acts. Nevertheless, this does not accord with the fact that the same persons pull their bandanas up or down on their faces, depending on whether they are stepping into action or not, since they could be identified by continuous observation. There are also accoutrements that do not cover the face, such as hoods; in some fight contexts, the marker is taking off one's shirt (as in figure 3.9; see also fight narration in chap. 7, p. 267). A similar photo (Crespo 2002: 8) shows a lone paint bomb–thrower at a demonstration at the 2000 Republican convention in Philadelphia; unlike the rest of the visible crowd, he wears a bandana and head covering, and

is shirtless—a combination of all the violent action emblems. We might propose that face masks are utilitarian protection against tear gas; if so, only a few participants at a time seem to have that concern.

6. In figure 2.4 (chap. 2) of Palestinian boys throwing stones toward an Israeli tank, of the twelve persons visible, eight are turned from action, not doing anything; of another boy we see only his face expressing fear. One boy is winding up to throw a rock, two others right next to him are crouching with rocks in their hands; while five others crouch behind them (one cowering by a wall), and four are sitting against the forward wall with backs turned to the enemy.

7. In figure 3.4, two of the twenty men visible beat the market thief; in an EPA photo (Oct. 1, 2000, *Daily Telegraph*, p. 2; not shown here), four men beat a Serbian riot policeman while six others are visible in the background looking in various directions; in a Reuters photo (May 1, 1992; not shown here), three black men kick one white man during the Rodney King riots in Atlanta, while seven other black persons are visible at various distances in the background. Figure 3.5 is the only one that shows everyone in the photo on the victorious side (a total of thirteen) either beating the fallen motorcyclist, or rushing to join the beating or at least to be close at hand while it happens. In this last case, the victim was killed.

8. Of fifty photos in which crowds are visible, five show individuals expressing some degree of joy; as a percentage of the total crowd faces in this subset of photos, it is well below 10 percent.

9. Of course, this is what the entire crowd of onlookers also do, but at a greater distance. In some instances, onlookers in these photos (Allen 2000: plate 32 and pp. 176, 194) clutch pieces of clothing torn from the victim's body and distributed in the crowd. We are so appalled by the racism of many of these photos (although twenty-three out of eight-seven victims of lynchings in Allen's collection are white, typically following murders or in cattle wars in the West) that we tend to overlook the sociological point that lynch mobs, like violent crowds generally, feel they are morally in the right, and that they are vindicating an injustice—the alleged murder or rape that precipitated the lynching. Hence their ritualized behavior in putting themselves near the victim's body is a way of expressing solidarity with the communal enterprise. This is the same as what we see in the *intifada*, Mogadishu, and Iraq photos discussed earlier. See also Senechal de la Roche (2001).

10. Mann (1993: 635, 674), notes a similar pattern of ceremonial labor/police confrontations in pre–World War I Germany, with few injuries; it is not clear how the ranks of demonstrators behaved on the micro-level.

11. Some are carrying signs or flags, but these are mostly ten rows back in the crowd. This is a different kind of protest display, quite distinct from violence. Note that in figure 3.7 the flag-waver is turned toward his own side, not toward the enemy. A hypothesis: those in a sports crowd with flags and banners are not those who take the lead in intrusions onto the field or other spectator violence.

12. The militant cluster is not entirely supported by everyone close to them; just behind the stick-throwers, one man cowers down with his hands protectively over his head. The only other expression of fear that I see in the crowd is the face of a man two rows back, behind one of the group's yelling supporters. In the

immediate vicinity, a tipping-point has been reached; the majority of those nearby throw themselves headlong into the path of violence, either in act or emotional expression, but a minority reacts with fear and withdrawal. Their fear is apparently of their compatriots, not of the enemy; it is not a fear of physical danger so much as it is the fear of violent confrontation coming to its peak. We may predict that these men will now retreat, leaving the field to the small clusters of militants as the crowd breaks up into violence.

13. In communal violence in India, men do the actual killing and burning, but some of the women, forming the back of the crowd, may use tactics of nonviolent resistance, lying in the streets to prevent fire engines from getting in, and thus making possible more death and destruction (Horowitz 2001; Human Rights Watch 2002). This is borderline violent activism, secondary in initiative to the main action, and far enough away in space so that these "nonviolent" women do not have to see their ethnic enemies being burned. Again, this kind of participation may be stratified; we don't know what proportion of women and other backup spectators took part in blocking the fire engines.

14. Recall evidence cited in chapter 3 that bigger crowds produce more frequent lynchings and other violence, and larger numbers of police and onlookers present at an arrest increases the chances of police violence—even though only a small proportion of the group takes part in the violence.

15. Data on several riots give some dimensions of different layers of the cone. In the 1965 Watts riot in Los Angeles, 5 to 10 percent of adult black males in the ghetto said that they participated in the riot, and another 33 to 40 percent had pro-riot attitudes (Ransford 1968). Another resident survey found 15 percent active in the riot, plus another 31 percent of "close spectators" (Inbert and Sprague 1980: 2–3). In the 1967 Detroit riot, 11 percent said they were participants, and 20 to 25 percent were spectators (Kerner Commission 1968: 73). These were among the most serious and violent race riots of the 1960s. For carousing and celebration riots, a campus athletic victory riot involved 3 percent of the 30,000 students on campus; many of these were spectators, and the crowd that kept up the celebratory vandalism dwindled to about 300, or 1 percent (see sources in chap. 8). In another campus football victory riot at Ohio State in 2002, between 4,000 and 6,000 students took part (8 to 12 percent of the total student body); most of them stood watching while a smaller group flipped over cars and set dumpsters and couches on fire; seventy were arrested (about 1.2 to 1.8 percent of the crowd (Vider 2004). In the 1999 Woodstock riot at the end of a massive concert, out of a crowd of 155,000, about 200–500 (about 0.1 to 0.3 percent) actively took part in looting and vandalizing; while several thousand (about 1–3 percent of the crowd) cheered them on. There were forty arrests, comprising 10 or 20 percent of the hard-core rioters (Vider 2004). Of the 97 percent or more who were bystanders, most simply watched, their mood bemused, cowed, or frightened.

16. The following is based on micro-situational detail culled from Fisher (2002, 2003); Hoffman and Headley (1992); Mustain and Capeci (1993); Dietz (1983); Anastasia (2004). These are chiefly based on autobiographical accounts by career hitmen or their associates. I draw also on a four-hour interview with a

reputed hitman; he apparently had worked for organized crime rather than lower-paid and lower-status contract killing for "civilians." We did not discuss particular killings but rather techniques of violent procedure and interaction. Most of the information here concerns high-level American hitmen working between 1950 and 1990. Female contract killers exist, but the only ones I have heard of are in the lower tier. In the following examples, I refer to the victims as well as the killers as male, since this is the case in every example in the sources, with exceptions noted.

17. A contract killer in Detroit quoted in Dietz (1983: 79) said, "We're not his judges, just his executioners." The rationalization was offered both by "Joey" (the pseudonymous hitman in Fisher 2002, 2003) and by "Tony the Greek" Frankos (in Hoffman and Headley 1992) that their victims were very bad guys; since they were usually in organized crime, this may well have been true. My interviewee spontaneously made the same statement. He also commented that although he was a patriotic American and if possible would take revenge for the 9/11 attacks, strictly as a technical matter, he had to admire the careful clandestine tactics of the hijackers.

18. Professional hitters usually fire three bullets or less. These professional killings differ from the forward panic overkill often found in military, police, and domestic killings.

19. In one instance, very unusual because the victim was a female, two young men in the DeMeo crew were assigned to kill the nineteen-year-old, beautiful girlfriend of a mob associate. Both the couple were privy to mob activities and were considered liable to inform to the police. While the boyfriend was being shot with a silencer inside the gang's clubhouse, one killer flirted with the girl through one car window, while the other leaned through the opposite window, then shot her abruptly (Mustain and Capeci 1993: 152–53).

20. For an example, see Hoffman and Headley (1992: 105–7). I examine the social structure of torture in Collins (1974) and more extensively in a companion volume to this one; see also Einolf 2005. The chief exception to everything I have been arguing here is the serial killer, who usually works alone, and sometimes engages in torture before murder. This type of violence is the rarest of all. Serial killers resemble hitmen in the clandestine planning and the development of technique; but they work only for themselves, and become much more emotionally involved with their victims, while hitmen avoid any occasions for emotional interaction. There are several different types of serial killers, specialized by their methods of finding victims and their violent techniques. The serial killers with the longest strings of victims, however, are generally those who use non-confrontational techniques, such as poisoning medical patients or taking them off life support (Hickey 2002). This again reinforces the point that non-confrontational violence is easiest.

21. "Tony the Greek" was medium height, 160 lbs; "Joey" was a little under average height, though strongly built; Harvey Rosenberg, a.k.a "Chris DeMeo" was 5 ft. 5 inches and moderate in build; Roy DeMeo was pudgy and unathletic though strong. Joey Gallo, who killed mob boss Albert Anastasia in his barber

chair in 1957, and who later launched a war on another gang faction, was 5 ft. 7 inches and thin. Joe "Mad Dog" Sulllivan (who had over 100 hits and was regarded by Tony the Greek as the best in the profession) was 5 ft. 11 inches, 180 lbs. (Hoffman and Headley 1992: xxii, 92, 96, 133, 154, 236; Fisher 2002: vii–viii, 198; Mustain and Capeci 1993: 28–37). Tony also did debt collecting for loan sharks, sometimes accompanied by a 300-pound man who frightened and beat their victims, and mentions several other enforcers in the 245 to 300 pound range. Hired "muscle" of this sort, however, is distinct from contract killers per se; they specialize in intermediate degrees of physical intimidation, but crime business wants continually paying customers and working employees, not dead ones. "Almost anyone in the business is capable of running muscle," says "Joey." "Strength is not that important, although the tougher an individual looks the less often he has to prove how tough he is. But almost anybody is capable of swinging a baseball bat or an iron pipe" (Fisher 2002: 82).

22. "Joey" similarly describes cornering his victim in a revenge killing: "I could smell the fear. If you've ever wondered why an animal attacks someone who's afraid of him, it's because the fear just pours out of him and creates an odor. I saw it. I smelled it" (Fisher 2002: 68).

23. This is a version of working up anger to motivate oneself in a fight. Athletes such as boxers, as well as team coaches in contact sports, look for anything their opponent did or said that can be construed as insults or slights, to work up anger for an upcoming match. Specialists in violence thus may hoard memories of previous humiliation or deliberately nurse a grudge. Their "chip on the shoulder" should not be taken simply as mere unconscious repression or bypassed shame that comes out as rage. Not to deny that Scheff's (1994) model can operate in a straightforward manner; but there are also complex versions of emotion self-management, in which one deliberately uses past emotions as a resource to get an advantage in a present confrontation.

24. This may seem morally cold; but it is the same kind of reaction as that of the German ace pilot Erich Hartmann, who shoots down several Russian planes on a 3 a.m. sortie and returns to nap before going out to shoot down several more at 6 a.m. (www.acepilots.com; cf. Fisher 2002: 56, 63).

25. Similarly, most people are not good liars, since they do not know how to control their paralinguistic expressions that give away the fact they are lying. But those few who are good liars also tend to give off tiny facial cues that Ekman (1985: 76–79) calls "duping delight"—joy in getting away with it.

26. Fisher (2002: x; Hoffman xxv–xxvii). I found my informant to be thoughtful and clear-spoken, more serious and less boisterous than the usual masculine bar-room company.

27. Tony the Greek's closest friend was Mad Dog Sullivan, pairing two of the top contract killers in the New York underworld (Hoffman and Headley 1992: 263–64): an example of friendship homogamy by professional rank.

28. To avoid a common misunderstanding, it should be emphasized that organized crime is not a unified bureaucracy, but a combination of several loose organizational forms. The overarching structure is a federation or peace pact among

armed groups operating to limit jurisdictional disputes and to monopolize territories. On another level are organized crime businesses routinely providing illegal commodities and services such as drugs, gambling, loan-sharking and auto chop-shops; these are not carried out by the crime families but by individuals who operate under their umbrella of protection. American Mafia families, strictly speaking, have been illegal governments, organized by what Weber would call patrimonialism, over and above a collection of illegal businesses.

29. It follows from this argument that low-end hitmen are less competent; because they are not in a tight reputational network, they receive less emotional support.

30. Goodwin (2006) defines terrorism as attack on complicitous civilians in the effort to undermine their support for military or political authorities, or to rally one's side for an insurgency; the latter aim would include keeping up one's own morale by a spectacular if localized victory. Guerrilla warfare resembles terrorism in its clandestine preparation and in fading back into the civilian population after an attack. But guerrillas attack military targets, terrorists civilian ones; they differ also in that guerrilla tactics, once the moment of confrontation with the enemy occurs, are typically prolonged (at least for minutes or hours, compared to terrorist attacks taking place in seconds), and the emotional support for the confrontation is the normal military one of small groups in action together. Their different means of overcoming confrontational tension/fear makes it likely that they have different kinds of recruitment methods and organizational structures at the operational level.

31. We have no estimate of how often remote-operated or time bombs fail, compared to suicide bombers. A spectacular example of failure was the plot to kill Hitler in July 1944, which likely would have succeeded if the German officer who carried the bomb had made a suicide attack instead of leaving the bomb behind and exiting the bunker before it detonated. Estimates are that suicide bombings are ten to fifteen times as effective as other terrorist attacks; worldwide from 1980 to 2001, suicide bombings made up 3 percent of terrorist attacks but caused 48 percent of the deaths (Pape 2005; Ricolfi 2005).

32. An early modern example from the religious wars in France shows the details of avoiding confrontation: On July 28, 1589, the Protestant king of France was about to attack Paris, an anti-Protestant stronghold. A Catholic monk, pretending to present a letter to the king, went to the house where he was staying in the suburbs. While the king was reading the letter, the monk kneeling before him in the customary posture of a religious supplicant reached up and stabbed him in the belly. The piece of paper was between them; the attack was made literally without face confrontation (*Cambridge Modern History* 3:5, 47).

33. An estimated 5 to 10 percent of Palestinian suicide missions fail (Ricolfi 2005: 79).

34. The parallel case, as we have seen earlier, is the professional hitman who prefers to work alone, avoiding distractions that accomplices would make in his self-absorption.

35. There are some analogies to this kind of complex emotion-work among professional hitmen. One created an image of himself in public (within the criminal world) by pretending to be angry and out of control, as way of lulling his targets into thinking that he lacked the cool technique to be a real danger (described in the interview noted in note 16 in this chapter). Also in the routine crime business of extortion or debt-collection by intimidation, professional "muscle" may pretend to be angry, or work themselves into anger, for the calculated effect of getting the victim to pay off.

36. The mother of a nineteen-year-old Lebanese woman who belonged to an underground resistance cell and became a suicide bomber, retrospectively recalls: "We used to be watching TV with the neighbours and some issue about the [Israeli] occupation [of Lebanon] would come up and I would be having a heated discussion with my neighbour over it. But Loula wouldn't say anything. She'd just look at us and smile. Now we know she was working on something bigger" (Davis 2003: 79). Calming oneself for clandestine violence appears to involve a long-term technique of emotional self-control. The self-advice in the death note left by Mohammad Atta, a leader of the 9/11 attacks, similarly did not focus on grievances but on calming himself, avoiding to appear nervous, and repeating God's name in inner dialogue (Davis 2003: 87); the last not only has religious significance but also is a method for self-concentration.

37. An alternative interpretation of videos presenting *intifada* suicide bombers is that these are commitment mechanisms, devices by which these individuals are required to make a public display of their intentions so that they cannot back out (Gambetta 2005: 276, citing Merari 2005). But this does not explain why their emotional expressions are calm rather than fervent; and in fact videos of suicide bombers in action show the same expressions as the publicity videos.

38. Ricolfi (2005) notes that air hijackings, the most prominent technique of terrorist organizations in the 1950s through 1970s, were replaced in the 1980s by the diffusion of suicide bombings. Both are high-visibility techniques for publicizing a political cause; but whereas hijackings are merely a form of blackmail, suicide bombings carry a claim to martyrdom, at least for some audiences. I would add: the recruitment base for suicide bombings, once the technique became known, was much wider, because it is a confrontation-minimizing technique. Hijackings are at the opposite end of the spectrum, a confrontation-prolonging technique.

39. Pape (2005) finds little evidence of criminal background among suicide terrorists; see also Sageman (2004). Indeed, the threatening bluster of a confrontational criminal style of interaction would make it extremely difficult to carry out a clandestine suicide mission. A perhaps rather typical suicide bomber (who killed sixteen and wounded 130 Israelis—including small children—in a Jerusalem pizzeria in August 2001) is described as a shy, "mild-mannered youth, who had never been in a fight, not even with his brothers" (Davis 2003: 106).

40. In the Peterloo massacre near Manchester in 1819, a cavalry troop (perhaps 200 men) rode into a crowd of enthusiastic election-reform supporters, slashing with their sabers; although a horrific scene, the twelve deaths and forty wounded and otherwise injured (such as by trampling) out of 50,000 imply that not every soldier was effectively violent (*Cambridge Modern History* 10: 581).

An eyewitness noted that a portion of the troop confined themselves to cutting down the placards at the speaker's stand, thus performing only symbolic and nominal violence (Lewis 2001: 358–60). The attack began when the magistrates, frightened by precedents of violence in France and elsewhere, and by the crowd's own cheers of "Liberty or Death!" and similar rhetorical extremes, ordered the troops to attack.

41. To underline a point that may be bothering the reader: I am not asking, why don't most people become professional hitmen, or cowboy cops, etc. The simple answer would be that most people don't want to because they have a moral objection. But, in fact, people can find an opportunity to be violent on any side of the law or conception of morality, and many forms of violence carry their own moral codes that their practitioners believe are highly honorable. I am asking: why is it that most people who are in a particular situation of conflict—soldiers, police, mobs who have mobilized to fight what they conceive to be a morally appropriate enemy, members of the criminal population—do not become part of the small minority of actively violent, and the even smaller minority of the competently violent? I am arguing that it is not simply a question of motivation; even if most people in the general population do not want to become one of these types of violent elites, the number who do is undoubtedly larger than the number who succeed at it. Social limits on the possibility to acquire and practice the technique, not people's background motivation to be violent, are the key determinants.

42. Jankowski (1991) calls gang members defiant individualists, not group conformists. Hence they are not simply explained by belonging to a group culture; they are attempting to be standouts in that culture. The analogy to intellectuals would be the distinctions between those who are happy to read others' books, or write books imitating others, and those who write original books; all of them are in the intellectual subculture, but the easier versions of conforming to the culture do not bring eminence in it.

43. To repeat: in interaction ritual theory, emotional energy is defined as initiative, confidence and enthusiasm in a particular kind of interactional practice.

44. Jankowski (1991) notes that gang members get little sleep; the inference he draws is that they are often irritable and erratic as a result, but it is also evidence of how hard they have to work, and how dangerous it is to take a break.

45. How far this analogy applies to the violent elite is a question at the frontier of our knowledge of careers in violence. There is a wide range of types of violence in this book; some types may be more embedded than other types in network ties to successfully violent persons. There are suggestions that network ties are important for careers in Mafia-type organized crime, and for terrorists; are they important also for ace pilots, cowboy cops, or armed robbers? And since there are two kinds of network to be explored, working this out would be an extensive research project. Network origins (intergenerational) and network emergence (horizontal) may have different weights for different kinds of violence. Are the violent elite mentored by, or benefit from, close role-modeling from ties to predecessors in the violent elite? Do new generations of the violent elite start out as an ambitious cluster feeding off of each other's energy and determination to reach the violent elite together?

46. Ted Williams, the most cool-headed and technical of all the great baseball hitters, flew thirty-nine combat missions as a fighter pilot, but never shot down an enemy plane. Williams set a record in a gunnery competition when he was in training, but this not did carry over into the actual conditions of combat. After his drastically lowered position in the field of fighter pilots became apparent in Korea (after his first eight or ten missions), he began to be sick, dogged by persistent colds that resisted medical treatment—quite possibly psychosomatic reactions to the positional strain. But his health recovered quickly when he was discharged, and he returned to his usual high-performance level in baseball (www.tedwilliams.com; Thorn et al. 2001).

47. The length of an active generation is shorter for violence than for intellectuals; it also seems to vary among different kinds of violence: for youth gangs, ten years or less; for pilot aces perhaps only a couple of years; and so on. Burnout among police who have been involved in shootings may indicate the limits of generational succession among this particular violent elite. The problem awaits investigation.

EPILOGUE
PRACTICAL CONCLUSIONS

1. Anderson emphasizes (in a personal communication, 2006) he kept one hand in his pocket during the encounter, leaving an ambiguous impression whether he had a gun.

References

Abbott, Andrew, and Emanuel Gaziano. 1995. "Transition and Tradition: Departmental Faculty in the Era of the Second Chicago School." In *A Second Chicago School?*, edited by Gary Alan Fine. Chicago: University of Chicago Press.

Abbott, Andrew. 2001. *Chaos of Disciplines*. Chicago: University of Chicago Press.

Adler, Peter. 1984. *Momentum*. Beverly Hills: Sage.

Allen, James. 2000. *Without Sanctuary. Lynching Photography in America*. Twin Palms, Fla.: Twin Palms.

Alpert, Geoffrey P., and Roger G. Dunham. 1990. *Police Pursuit Driving*. New York: Greenwood.

———. 2004. *Understanding Police Use of Force*. New York: Cambridge University Press.

Anastasia, George. 2004. *Blood and Honor. Inside the Scarfo Mob—The Mafia's Most Violent Family*. Philadelphia: Camino.

Anderson, David C. 1998. "Curriculum, Culture and Community: The Challenge of School Violence." *Youth Violence*, edited by Michael Tonry and Mark H. Moore. Chicago: University of Chicago Press.

Anderson, David L. 1998. *Facing My Lai: Moving beyond the Massacre*. Lawrence, Kans.: University of Kansas Press.

Anderson, Elijah. 1978. *A Place on the Corner*. Chicago: University of Chicago Press.

———. 1990. *Streetwise. Race, Class and Change in an Urban Community*. Chicago: University of Chicago Press.

———. 1999. *Code of the Street. Decency, Violence, and the Moral Life of the Inner City*. New York: Norton.

———. 2002. "The Ideologically Driven Critique." *American Journal of Sociology* 107: 1533–50.

Archer, Dane, and Rosemary Gartner. 1984. *Violence and Crime in Cross-national Perspective*. New Haven, Conn.: Yale University Press.

Ardant du Picq, Charles. 1903/1999. *Études sur le combat*. Paris: Éditions Ivrea, translated edition. *Battle Studies: Ancient and Modern Battles*. New York: Macmillan, 1921.

Arms, Robert L., Gordon W. Russell, and Mark Sandilands. 1979. "Effects on the Hostility of Spectators of Viewing Aggressive Sports." *Social Psychology Quarterly* 43: 275–79.

Arnold-Forster, Mark. 2001. *The World at War*. London: Random House.

Arthur, Anthony. 2002. *Literary Feuds*. New York: St. Martin's.

Artwohl, Alexis, and Loren W. Christensen. 1997. *Deadly Force Encounters*. Boulder, Colo.: Paladin.

Asbury, Herbert. 1928. *The Gangs of New York: An Informal History of the Underworld*. New York: Knopf.

Athens, Lonnie H. 1980. *Violent Criminal Acts and Actors: A Symbolic Interactionist Study*. Boston: Routledge.

——. 1989. *The Creation of Dangerous Violent Criminals*. Boston: Routledge.

Baca, Lee, and William J. Bratton. 2004. "Gang Capital's Police Needs Reinforcements." *Los Angeles Times*, October 29.

Bachman, R., and L. Saltzman, 1995. *Violence against Women*. Washington, D.C.: U.S. Dept. of Justice.

Bailey, James, and Tatyana Ivanova. 1998. *An Anthology of Russian Folk Epics*. Armonk, N.Y.: M. E. Sharpe.

Baldassare, Mark, ed. 1994. *The Los Angeles Riots*. Boulder, Colo.: Westview.

Bales, Robert Freed. 1950. *Interaction Process Analysis*. Cambridge, Mass.: Addison-Wesley.

Baltzell, E. Digby. 1958. *An American Business Aristocracy*. New York: Macmillan.

——. 1995. *Sporting Gentlemen*. New York: Free Press.

Barnett, Arnold, Alfred Blumstein, and David P. Farrington. 1987. "Probabilistic Models of Youthful Careers." *Criminology* 25:83–107.

——. 1989. "A Prospective Test of a Criminal Career Model." *Criminology* 27: 373–88.

Bartov, Omer. 1991. *Hitler's Army*. New York: Oxford University Press.

Bayley, David H., and James Garofalo. 1989. "The Management of Violence by Police Patrol Officers." *Criminology* 27:1–27.

Becker, Howard S. 1953. "Becoming a Marijuana User." *American Journal of Sociology* 59: 235–52.

——. 1967. "History, Culture, and Subjective Experience: An Explanation on the Social Bases of Drug-induced Experience." *Journal of Health and Social Behavior* 8: 163–76.

Beevor, Anthony. 1999. *The Spanish Civil War*. London: Cassell.

Berkowitz, L. 1989. "Frustration-Aggression Hypothesis: Examination and Reformulation." *Psychological Bulletin* 106: 59–73.

Berndt, Thomas J., and Thomas N. Bulleit. 1985. "Effects of Sibling Relationships on Preschoolers' Behavior at Home and at School." *Developmental Psychology* 21: 761–67.

Berscheid, Ellen. 1985. "Interpersonal Attraction." In *Handbook of Social Psychology*, edited by Gardner Lindzey and Elliot Aronson. New York: Random House.

Besag, Valerie E. 1989. *Bullies and Victims in Schools*. Philadelphia: Open University Press.

Biddle, Stephen. 2004. *Military Power: Explaining Victory and Defeat in Modern Battle*. Princeton: Princeton University Press.

Bilton, Michael, and Kevin Sim. 1992. *Four Hours in My Lai*. New York: Viking.

Bishop, S. J., and B. J. Leadbeater. 1999. "Maternal Social Support Patterns and Child Maltreatment: Comparison of Maltreating and Nonmaltreating Mothers." *American Journal of Orthopsychiatry*, no. 2:69, 172–81.

Black, Donald. 1980. *The Manners and Customs of the Police*. San Diego: Academic Press.

———. 1998. *The Social Structure of Right and Wrong*. San Diego: Academic Press.

Blacker, Kay, and Joe Tupin. 1977. "Hysteria and Hysterical Structures: Developmental and Social Theories." In *The Hysterical Personality*, edited by Mardi J. Horowitz. New York: J. Aronson.

Blau, Peter M. 1964. *Exchange and Power in Social Life*. New York: Wiley.

Bloch, Marc. 1961. *Feudal Society*. Chicago: University of Chicago Press.

Block, R. 1977. *Violent Crime*. Lexington, Mass.: Lexington.

Blood, Robert O., and Donald M. Wolfe. 1960. *Husbands and Wives*. New York: Free Press.

Blumstein, Alfred, Jacqueline Cohen, Jeffrey A. Roth, and Christy A. Visher. 1986. *Criminal Careers and "Career Criminals."* Vol. 2. Washington, D.C.: National Academy Press.

Boden, Deidre. 1990. "The World as It Happens: Ethnomethodology and Conversation Analysis." In *Frontiers of Social Theory*, edited by George Ritzer. New York: Columbia University Press.

Bogg, Richard A., and Janet M. Ray. 1990. "Male Drinking and Drunkenness in Middletown." *Advances in Alcohol and Substance Abuse* 9: 13–29.

Bond, Michael Harris. 1991. *Beyond the Chinese Face: Insights from Psychology*. New York: Oxford University Press.

Borkenau, Franz. 1981. *End and Beginning: On the Generations of Cultures and the Origins of the West*. New York: Columbia University Press.

Boulton, Michael J., and Peter K. Smith. 1994. "Bully/Victim Problems in Middle-School Children: Stability, Self-Perceived Competence, Peer Perceptions, and Peer Acceptance." *British Journal of Developmental Psychology* 12: 315–29.

Bourdieu, Pierre. 1972/1977. *Outline of the Theory of Practice*. New York: Cambridge University Press.

Bourgois, Philippe. 1995. *In Search of Respect: Selling Crack in El Barrio*. New York: Cambridge University Press.

Bourke, Joanna. 1999. *An Intimate History of Killing: Face-to-Face Killing in Twentieth-Century Warfare*. New York: Basic Books.

Bourque, Linda B., Judith M. Siegel, Megumi Kano, and Michele M. Wood. 2006. "Morbidity and Mortality Associated with Disasters." In *Handbook of Disaster Research*, edited by Havidan Rodriquez, E. L. Quarentelli, and Russell R. Dynes. New York: Springer.

Bowden, Mark. 2000. *Black Hawk Down: A Story of Modern War*. New York: Penguin.

Boyd, Alexander. 1977. *The Soviet Air Force since 1918*. New York: Stein and Day.

Brondsted, Johannes. 1965. *The Vikings*. Baltimore, Md.: Penguin.

Browning, Christopher R. 1992. *Ordinary Men: Reserve Police Battalion 101 and the Final Solution in Poland*. New York: HarperCollins.

Budd, Tracey. 2003. "Alcohol-related Assault: Findings from the British Crime Survey." Home Office Report 35/03. Available at www.homeoffice.gov.uk/rds/bcs1/html.

Buford, Bill. 1993. *Among the Thugs*. New York: Random House.

Burchler, Gary, Robert Weiss, and John Vincent. 1975. "Multidimensional Analysis of Social Reinforcement Exchanged between Mutually Distressed and Nondistressed Spouse and Stranger Dyads." *Journal of Personality and Social Psychology* 31: 348–60.

Burgess, Mark. 2002. "The Afghan Campaign One Year On." *The Defense Monitor* 21, No. 8 (September 2002): 1–3. Washington, D.C.: Center for Defense Information.

Caesar, Julius. ca. 48–44 B.C./ 1998. *The Civil War. With the Anonymous Alexandrian, African, and Spanish Wars.* Oxford: Oxford University Press.

Caidin, Martin, Saburo Sakai, and Fred Saito. 2004. *Samurai!* New York: I Books.

Callaghan, Morley. 1963. *That Summer in Paris: Memories of Tangled Friendships with Hemingway, Fitzgerald, and Some Others.* New York: Coward-McCann.

Cambridge Modern History. 1907–1909. Cambridge: New York: Cambridge University Press.

Cameron, Euan. 1991. *The European Reformation.* Oxford: Oxford University Press.

Cannadine, David. 1990. *The Decline and Fall of the British Aristocracy.* New Haven, Conn.: Yale University Press.

Capote, Truman. 1986. *Answered Prayers.* London: Penguin.

Caputo, Philip. 1977. *A Rumor of War.* New York: Ballantine.

Carter, Hugh, and Paul C. Glick. 1976. *Marriage and Divorce: A Social and Economic Study.* Cambridge, Mass.: Harvard University Press.

Cazenave, N. and M. A. Straus. 1979. "Race, Class, Network Embeddedness, and Family Violence: A Search for Potent Support Systems." *Journal of Comparative Family Studies* 10: 280–99.

Chadwick, G. W. 2006. "The Anglo-Zulu War of 1879: Isandlwana and Rorke's Drift." *South African Military History Society Military History Journal.* Vol. 4.

Chagnon, Napoleon. 1968. *Yanomano: The Fierce People.* New York: Holt.

Chaiken, Jan M., and Marcia R. Chaiken. 1982. *Varieties of Criminal Behavior.* Santa Monica, Calif.: Rand Corporation.

Chambers Biographical Dictionary. 1984. Edinburgh: Chambers.

Chambliss, Daniel F. 1989. "The Mundanity of Excellence." *Sociological Theory* 7: 70–86.

Chang, Iris. 1997. *The Rape of Nanking.* New York: Basic Books.

Cherlin, Andrew. 1992. *Marriage, Divorce, Remarriage.* Cambridge, Mass.: Harvard University Press.

Christopher, Warren, ed. 1991. *Report of the Independent Commission on the Los Angeles Police Department.* Los Angeles: Diane Publishing.

Clayman, Stephen E. 1993. "Booing: The Anatomy of a Disaffiliative Response." *American Sociological Review* 58: 110–30.

Cleaver, Eldridge. 1968. *Soul on Ice.* New York: Random House.

Clum, George A., and Jack L. Mahan. 1971. "Attitudes Predictive of Marine Combat Effectiveness." *Journal of Social Psychology* 83: 53–62.

Cohen, Lawrence E., and Marcus Felson. 1979. "Social Change and Crime Rate Trends: A Routine Activities Approach." *American Sociological Review* 44: 588–605.

Collins, James J. 1977. *Offender Careers and Restraint: Probabilities and Policy Implications*. Washington, D.C.: Law Enforcement Assistance Administration, U.S. Department of Justice.

Collins, Randall. 1974. "Three Faces of Cruelty: Towards a Comparative Sociology of Violence." *Theory and Society* 1: 415–40.

———. 1986. *Weberian Sociological Theory*. New York: Cambridge University Press.

———. 1998. *The Sociology of Philosophies. A Global Theory of Intellectual Change*. Cambridge, Mass.: Harvard University Press.

———. 2000. "Comparative and Historical Patterns of Education." Pp. 213–39 in *Handbook of the Sociology of Education*, edited by Maureen T. Hallinan. New York: Kluwer Academic/Plenum Publishers, 213–39.

———. 2004. *Interaction Ritual Chains*. Princeton: Princeton University Press.

———. 2004a. 2004. "Rituals of Solidarity and Security in the Wake of Terrorist Attack." *Sociological Theory* 22: 53–87.

Conley, Carolyn. 1999. "The Agreeable Recreation of Fighting." *Journal of Social History* 33: 57–72.

Connolly, Irene, and Mona O'Moore. 2003. "Personality and Family Relations of Children Who Bully." *Personality and Individual Differences* 35: 559–67.

Coser, Lewis. 1956. *The Functions of Social Conflict*. New York: Free Press.

Coward, Martin. 2004. "Urbicide in Bosnia." In *Cities, War and Terrorism: Towards an Urban Geopolitics*, edited by Stephen Graham. Oxford: Blackwell.

Crespo, Al. 2002. *Protest in the Land of Plenty*. New York: Center Lane Press.

Croft, Elizabeth Benz. 1985. "Police Use of Force: An Empirical Analysis." Ph.D. diss., State University of New York, Albany. *Dissertation Abstracts International* 46:2449A.

Curvin, Robert, and Bruce Porter. 1979. *Blackout Looting! New York City, July 13, 1977*. New York: Gardner.

Daly, Martin, and Margo Wilson. 1988. *Homicide*. New York: Aldine de Gruyter.

Daugherty, Leo J., and Gregory Louis Mattson. 2001. *Nam: A Photographic History*. New York: Barnes and Noble.

Davis, Allison, B. B. Gardner, and M. R. Gardner. 1941/1965. *Deep South*. Chicago: University of Chicago Press.

Davis, Joyce M. 2003. *Martyrs: Innocence, Vengeance and Despair*. New York: Palgrave Macmillan.

DeKeseredy, W. S. and L. MacLeod. 1997. *Woman Abuse: A Sociological Story*. San Diego: Harcourt Brace.

DeVoe, Jill, Katherine Peter, Phillip Kaufman, Amanda Miller, Margaret Noonan, Thomas Snyder, and Katrina Baum. 2004. "Indicators of School Crime and Safety: 2004." NCES Report: 2005002. U.S. Department of Education, National Center for Education Statistics and Bureau of Justice Statistics.

Dietz, Mary Lorenz. 1983. *Killing for Profit: The Social Organization of Felony Homicide*. Chicago: Nelson Hall.

Dietz, Tracy L. 2000. "Disciplining Children: Characteristics Associated with the Use of Corporal Punishment." *Child Abuse and Neglect* 24: 1529–42.

Divale, William. 1973. *War in Primitive Societies*. Santa Barbara, Calif.: ABC-Clio.

Dobash, R. E., and R. P. Dobash. 1998. "Violent Men and Violent Contexts." Pp. 141–68 in *Rethinking Violence against Women*, edited by R. E. Dobash and R. P. Dobash. Thousand Oaks, Calif.: Sage.

Dobash, R. E., R. P Dobash, K. Cavanagh, and R. Lewis. 1998. "Separate and Intersecting Realities: A Comparison of Men's and Women's Accounts of Violence against Women." *Violence against Women* 4: 382–414.

Dollard, John. 1944. *Fear in Battle*. Washington, D.C.: Arms Press.

Dollard, J., L. Doob, N. Miller, O. Mowrer, and R. Sears. 1939. *Frustration and Aggression*. New Haven, Conn.: Yale University Press.

Dostoevski, Fyodor. 1846/2003. *The Double*. New York: Barnes and Noble Classics.

Draeger, Donn F. 1974. *The Martial Arts and Ways of Japan*. 3 vols. New York and Tokyo: Weatherhill.

Duffell, Nick. 2000. *The Making of Them: The British Attitude to Children and the Boarding School System*. London: Lone Arrow.

Duncan, Renae D. 1999a. "Peer and Sibling Aggression: An Investigation of Intra- and Extra-Familial Bullying." *Journal of Interpersonal Violence* 14, no. 8 (August): 871–86.

———. 1999b. "Maltreatment by Parents and Peers: The Relationship between Child Abuse, Bully Victimization, and Psychological Distress." *Child Maltreatment: Journal of the American Professional Society on the Abuse of Children* 4, no. 1, 45–55.

Duneier, Mitchell. 1999. *Sidewalk*. New York: Farrar, Straus, and Giroux.

———. 2002. "What Kind of Combat Sport Is Sociology?" *American Journal of Sociology* 107: 1551–76.

Dunning, Eric. 1996. "Problems of the Emotions in Sport and Leisure." *Leisure Studies* 15: 185–207.

———. 1999. *Sport Matters*. London: Routledge.

Dunning, Eric, Paul Murphy, and J. Waddington. 1988. *The Roots of Football Hooliganism*. London: Routledge.

Dunning, Eric, Patrick Murphy, Ivan Waddington, and Antonios Astrinakis. 2002. *Fighting Fans: Football Hooliganism as a World Phenomenon*. Dublin: University College Dublin Press.

Durkheim, Emile. 1912/1964. *The Elementary Forms of Religious Life*. New York: Free Press.

Dyer, Gwynne. 1985. *War*. London: Guild.

Dynes, Russell R., and E. L. Quarantelli. 1968. "What Looting in Civil Disturbances Really Means." *Trans-Action* (May): 9–14.

Eamon, M. K., and R. M. Zuehl. 2001. "Maternal Depression and Physical Punishment as Mediators of the Effect of Poverty on Socioemotional Problems of Children in Single-Mother Families." *American Journal of Orthopsychiatry* 71, no. 2: 218–26.

Eberhard, Wolfram. 1977. *A History of China*. Berkeley: University of California Press.

Eder, Donna, Catherine Colleen Evans, and Stephan Parker. 1995. *School Talk: Gender and Adolescent Culture*. New Brunswick, N.J.: Rutgers University Press.

Edgar, Kimmet, and Ian O'Donnell. 1998. "Assault in Prison: The 'Victim's Contribution.' " *British Journal of Criminology* 38: 635–50.

Egeland, B. 1988. "Intergenerational Continuity of Parental Maltreatment of Children." Pp. 87–102 in *Early Prediction and Prevention of Child Abuse*, edited by K. D. Browne, C. Davies, and P. Stratton. New York: John Wiley.

———. 1993. "A History of Abuse Is a Major Risk Factor for Abusing the Next Generation." Pp. 197–208 in *Current Controversies on Family Violence*, edited by R. J. Gelles and D. R. Loseke. Newbury Park, Calif.: Sage.

Einarsson, Stefan. 1934. *Old English Beot and Old Icelandic Heitstrenging*. New York: Modern Language Association of America.

Einolf, Christopher J. 2005. "The Fall and Rise of Torture: A Comparative and Historical Analysis." Paper delivered at Eastern Sociological Society meeting, Washington, D.C.

Ekman, Paul, and Wallace V. Friesen. 1975. *Unmasking the Face*. Englewood Cliffs, N.J.: Prentice Hall.

———. 1978. *The Facial Action Coding System (FACS)*. Palo Alto, Calif.: Consulting Psychologists Press.

Ekman, Paul. 1985. *Telling Lies: Clues to Deceit in the Marketplace, Politics, and Marriage*. New York: Norton.

Elias, Norbert. 1939/1978. *The Civilizing Process*. New York: Pantheon.

Elias, Norbert, and Eric Dunning. 1986. *Quest for Excitement: Sport and Leisure in the Civilizing Process*. Oxford: Blackwell.

Elkin, A. P. 1979. *The Australian Aborigines*. London: Angus and Robertson.

Elliott, Delbert S. 1994. "Serious Violent Offenders: Onset, Developmental Course, and Termination." *Criminology* 32: 1–22.

English, Kim, and Mary J. Mande. 1992. *Measuring Crime Rates of Prisoners*. Washington, D.C.: National Institute of Justice.

Erikson, Kai T. 1976. *Everything in Its Path*. New York: Simon and Schuster.

Espelage, Dorothy L., and Melissa K. Holt. 2001. "Bullying and Victimization during Early Adolescence: Peer Influences and Psychosocial Correlates." *Journal of Emotional Abuse* 2, nos. 2–3: 123–42.

Etzioni, Amitai. 1975. *A Comparative Analysis of Complex Organizations*. New York: Free Press.

Farrell, Michael P. 2001. *Collaborative Circles: Friendship Dynamics and Creative Work*. Chicago: University of Chicago Press.

Farrington, David P. 1993. "Understanding and Preventing Bullying." Pp. 381–458 in *Crime and Justice: A Review of Research*, edited by M. Tonry. Chicago: University of Chicago Press.

———. 2001. "Key Results from the First Forty Years of the Cambridge Study in Delinquent Development." In *Taking Stock of Delinquency: An Overview of Findings from Contemporary Longitudinal Studies*, edited by Terrence P. Thornberry and Marvin D. Krohn. New York: Kluwer/Plenum.

Faulkner, Robert F. 1976. "Making Violence by Doing Work: Selves, Situations, and the World of Professional Hockey." In *Social Problems in Athletics: Essays in the Sociology of Sport*, edited by Daniel M. Landers. Urbana, Ill.: University of Illinois Press.

Fein, Helen. 1979. *Accounting for Genocide*. New York: Free Press.

Felson, Marcus. 1994. *Crime and Everyday Life*. Thousand Oaks, Calif.: Pine Forge.

Finley, M. I. 1973. *The Ancient Economy*. Berkeley: University of California Press.

Fisher, David. 2002. *Joey the Hitman: The Autobiography of a Mafia Killer*. New York: Avalon.

———. 2003. *Hit 29: Based on the Killer's Own Account*. New York: Avalon Publishing.

Fitzgerald, F. Scott. 1934/1951. *Tender Is the Night*. New York: Scribner's.

Fox, Robin. 1977. "The Inherent Rules of Violence." In *Social Rules and Social Behavior*, edited by P. Collett. Oxford: Blackwell.

Franzoi, Stephen I., Mark Davis, and Kristin A. Vasquez-Suson. 1994. "Two Social Worlds: Social Correlates and Stability of Adolescent Status Groups." *Journal of Personality and Social Psychology* 67: 462–73.

Freud, Sigmund. 1920/1953. *Beyond the Pleasure Principle*. London: Hogarth.

Friedrich, Robert J. 1980. "Police Use of Force: Individuals, Situations, and Organizations." *Annals of the American Academy of Political and Social Science* 452 (November): 82–97.

Frijda, Nico H. 1986. *The Emotions*. Cambridge and New York: Cambridge University Press.

Fritzsche, Peter. 1998. *Germans into Nazis*. Cambridge: Harvard University Press.

Fuchs, Stephan. 2001. *Against Essentialism: A Theory of Culture and Society*. Cambridge: Harvard University Press.

Fukuzawa Yukichi. 1981. *The Autobiography of Fukuzawa Yukichi*. Tokyo: Hokoseido.

Fuller, J.F.C. 1970. *The Decisive Battles of the Western World*. Volume 1. London: Paladin.

Fulmer, T., and J. Ashley. 1989. "Clinical Indicators Which Signal Elder Neglect." *Applied Nursing Research Journal* 2: 161–67.

Fulmer, T., and T. O'Malley. 1987. *Inadequate Care of the Elderly: A Healthcare Perspective on Abuse and Neglect*. New York: Springer.

Fyfe, James J. 1988. "Police Use of Deadly Force: Research and Reform." *Justice Quarterly* 5: 165–205.

Gabriel, Richard A. 1986. *Military Psychiatry: A Comparative Perspective*. New York: Greenport.

———. 1987. *No More Heroes: Madness and Psychiatry in War*. New York: Hill and Wang.

Gabriel, Richard, and Karen Metz. 1991. *From Sumer to Rome*. New York: Greenwood.

Gambetta, Diego. 1993. *The Sicilian Mafia*. Cambridge, Mass.: Harvard University Press.

———. 2005. "Can We Make Sense of Suicide Missions?" In *Making Sense of Suicide Missions*, edited by Diego Gambetta. New York: Oxford University Press.

Gantner, A. B., and S. P. Taylor. 1992. "Human Physical Aggression as a Function of Alcohol and Threat of Harm." *Aggressive Behavior* 18: 29–36.

Garbarino, James, and Gwen Gilliam. 1980. *Understanding Abusive Families.* Lexington, Mass.: D. C. Heath.

Garner, Joel, James Buchanan, Tom Schade, and John Hepburn. 1996. "Understanding the Use of Force by and against the Police." In *Research in Brief.* Washington, D.C.: National Institute of Justice.

Garner, Robert, director. 1962. *Dead Birds.* Film of Peabody Museum of Cambridge: Harvard University expedition to Baliem Valley, New Guinea. Carlsbad, Calif.: CRM Films.

Gaughan, E., J. Cerio, and R. Myers. 2001. *Lethal Violence in Schools: A National Survey.* Alfred, N. Y.: Alfred University.

Geifman, Anna. 1993. *Thou Shalt Kill: Revolutionary Terrorism in Russia, 1894–1917.* Princeton: Princeton University Press.

Geller, William A. 1986. *Crime File Deadly Force.* Washington, D.C.: National Institute of Justice.

Geller, William A., and Michael S. Scott. 1992. *Deadly Force: What We Know.* Washington, D.C.: Police Executive Research Forum.

Geller, William A., and Hans Toch, eds. 1996. *Police Violence: Understanding and Controlling Police Abuse of Force.* New Haven, Conn.: Yale University Press.

Gelles, Richard. 1977. "Violence in the American Family." In *Violence and the Family,* edited by J. P. Martin. New York: Wiley.

Gelles, R. J. 1993a. "Through a Sociological Lens: Social Structure and Family Violence." Pp. 31–46 in *Current Controversies on Family Violence,* edited by R. J. Gelles and D. L. Loseke. Newbury Park, Calif.: Sage.

———. 1993b. "Alcohol and Other Drugs Are Not the Cause of Violence." Pp. 182–96 in *Current Controversies on Family Violence,* edited by R. J. Gelles and D. L. Loseke. Newbury Park, Calif.: Sage.

Gelles, R. J., and J. R. Conte. 1990. "Domestic Violence and Sexual Abuse of Children: A Review of Research in the Eighties." *Journal of Marriage and the Family* 52: 1045–58.

Gelles, Richard, and Claire Cornell. 1990. *Intimate Violence in Families.* Beverly Hills, Calif.: Sage.

Gelles, R. J., and M. Straus. 1988. *Intimate Violence: The Causes and Consequences of Abuse in the American Family.* New York: Simon and Schuster.

Gernet, Jacques. 1982. *A History of Chinese Civilization.* Cambridge and New York: Cambridge University Press.

Gibson, David. 2001. "Seizing the Moment: The Problem of Conversational Agency." *Sociological Theory* 19: 250–70.

———. 2005. "Taking Turns and Talking Ties: Network Structure and Conversational Sequences." *American Journal of Sociology* 110: 1561–97.

Gibson, James William. 1986. *The Perfect War: Technowar in Vietnam.* Boston: Atlantic Monthly Press.

Gilbert, Martin. 1970. *Atlas of the First World War.* London: Weidenfeld and Nicolson.

———. 1994. *First World War.* London: HarperCollins.

———. 2000. *A History of the Twentieth Century. Vol. Three: 1952–1999.* New York: HarperCollins.

Giles-Sim, Jean. 1983. *Wife-battering: A Systems Theory Approach.* New York: Guilford.

Gitlin, Todd. 1980. *The Whole World Is Watching: Mass Media in the Making and Unmaking of the New Left.* Berkeley: University of California Press.

Glenn, Russell W. 2000a. "Introduction." In *Men against Fire: The Problem of Battle Comand* by S.L.A. Marshall. Norman, Okla.: University of Oklahoma Press.

———. 2000b. *Reading Athen's Dance Card: Men against Fire in Vietnam.* Annapolis, Md.: Naval Institute Press.

Goffman, Erving. 1961. *Asylums.* New York: Doubleday.

———. 1967. *Interaction Ritual.* New York: Doubleday.

———. 1969. *Strategic Interaction.* Philadelphia: University of Pennsylvania Press.

Goldstein, Jeffrey, ed. 1998. *Why We Watch: The Attractions of Violent Entertainment.* New York: Oxford University Press.

Goldstein, Jeffrey, and Robert L. Arms. 1971. "Effects of Observing Athletic Contests on Hostility." *Sociometry* 34: 83–90.

Goode, William J. 1971. "Force and Violence in the Family." *Journal of Marriage and the Family* 33: 624–36.

Goodwin, Jeff. 2006. "A Theory of Categorical Terrorism." *Social Forces* 84: 2027–46.

Gorn, Elliot. 1985. "Gouge and Bite, Pull Hair and Scratch: The Social Significance of Fighting in the Southern Backcountry." *American Historical Review* 90: 18–43.

Goudsblom, Johan. 1992. *Fire and Civilization.* London: Penguin.

Gould, Roger V. 2003. *Collision of Wills: How Ambiguity about Rank Breeds Conflict.* Chicago: University of Chicago Press.

Grant, Ulysses S. 1885/1990. *Personal Memoirs of U.S. Grant.* New York: Literary Classics of the United States.

Grazian, David. 2003. *Blue Chicago: The Search for Authenticity in Urban Blues Clubs.* Chicago: University of Chicago Press.

Green, Lynn. 2001. "Beyond Risk: Sex, Power and the Urban Girl." Ph.D. diss., University of Pennsylvania.

Griffin, Sean Patrick. 2003. *Philadelphia's "Black Mafia": A Social and Political History.* Boston: Kluwer.

Griffith, Patrick. 1986. *Battle in the Civil War: Generalship and Tactics in America 1861–1865.* New York: Fieldbooks.

———. 1989. *Battle Tactics of the Civil War.* New Haven, Conn.: Yale University Press.

Grimshaw, Allen D., ed. 1990. *Conflict Talk.* New York: Cambridge University Press.

Grinin, Leonid E. 2003. "The Early State and Its Analogues." *Social Evolution and History* 2: 131–76.

Grossman, Dave. 1995. *On Killing: The Psychological Cost of Learning to Kill in War and Society.* Boston: Little, Brown.

———. 2004. *On Combat: The Psychology and Physiology of Deadly Combat in War and Peace.* Belleville, Ill.: PPTC Research Publications.

Gurney, Gene. 1958. *Five Down and Glory.* New York: Random House.

———. 1965. *Flying Aces of World War I.* New York: Random House.

Guttridge, Patricia, William F. Gabrielli, Jr., Sarnoff A. Mednick, and Katherine T. Van Dusen. 1983. "Criminal Violence in a Birth Cohort." In *Prospective Studies of Crime and Delinquency,* edited by Katherine T. Van Dusen, and Sarnoff A. Mednick. Boston: Kluwer-Nijhoff.

Halle, David, and Kevin Rafter. 2003. "Riots in New York and Los Angeles." In *New York and Los Angeles: Politics, Society, and Culture, A Comparative View,* edited by David Halle. Chicago: University of Chicago Press.

Haney, Craig, Curtis Banks, and Philip Zimbardo. 1983. "Interpersonal Dynamics in a Simulated Prison." *International Journal of Criminology and Penology* 1: 69–97.

Hannerz, Ulf. 1969. *Soulside: Inquiries into Ghetto Culture and Community.* New York: Columbia University Press.

Hapgood, Fred. 1979. *Why Males Exist: An Inquiry into the Evolution of Sex.* New York: William Morrow.

Harris, Marvin. 1974. "Primitive War." In *Cows, Pigs, Wars, and Witches: The Riddles of Cultures.* New York: Random House.

Hay, J. H. 1974. *Vietnam Studies: Tactical and Material Innovation.* Washington, D.C.: Department of the Army.

Haynie, Denise L., Tonia Nansel, Patricia Eitel, Aria Davis Crump, Keith Saylor, and Kai Yu. 2001. "Bullies, Victims, and Bully/Victims: Distinct Groups of At-Risk Youth." *Journal of Early Adolescence* 21: 29–49.

Hensley, Thomas R., and Jerry M. Lewis. 1978. *Kent State and May 4th: A Social Science Perspective.* Dubuque, Iowa: Kendall/Hunt.

Henton, J. R., J. Cate, S. Lloyd Koval, and S. Christopher. 1983. "Romance and Violence in Dating Relationships." *Journal of Family Issues* 4: 467–82.

Heritage, John. 1984. *Garfinkel and Ethnomethodology.* Cambridge: Polity.

Hickey, Eric. W. 2002. *Serial Murderers and Their Victims.* Belmont, Calif.: Wadsworth.

Hobsbawm, Eric. 2000. *Bandits.* New York: New Press.

Hoffman, William, and Lake Headley. 1992. *Contract Killer.* New York: Avalon.

Holden, G. W., S. M. Coleman, and K. L. Schmidt. 1995. "Why 3-Year-old Children Get Spanked." *Merrill Palmer Quarterly* 41: 432–52.

Hollon, W. Eugene. 1974. *Frontier Violence.* New York: Oxford University Press.

Holmes, Richard. 1985. *Acts of War: The Behavior of Men in Battle.* New York: Free Press.

Homans, George C. 1950. *The Human Group.* New York: Harcourt, Brace.

Horowitz, Donald L. 2001. *The Deadly Ethnic Riot.* Berkeley: University of California Press.

Horowitz, Helen L. 1987. *Campus Life: Undergraduate Culture from the End of the Eighteenth Century to the Present*. New York: Knopf.

Horowitz, Ruth. 1983. *Honor and the American Dream: Culture and Identity in a Chicano Community*. New Brunswick, N.J.: Rutgers University Press.

Howe, Peter. 2002. *Shooting under Fire: The World of the War Photographers*. New York: Workman.

Hughes, Thomas. 1857/1994. *Tom Brown's School Days*. New York: Penguin.

Human Rights Watch. 1999. *Leave None to Tell the Story: Genocide in Rwanda*. HRW# 1711. Available at http://hrw.org/doc/?t=africa_pub&c=rwanda.

———. 2002. "We Have No Orders to Save You: State Participation and Complicity in Communal Violence in Gujarat." Available at http://hrw.org/reports/2002/india/.

Hutchings, Nancy. 1988. *The Violent Family*. New York: Human Sciences Press.

Ikegami, Eiko. 1995. *The Taming of the Samurai: Honorific Individualism and the Making of Modern Japan*. Cambridge, Mass.: Harvard University Press.

———. 2005. *Bonds of Civility: Aesthetic Networks and the Political Origins of Japanese Culture*. Cambridge and New York: Cambridge University Press.

Inbert, Barbara, and John Sprague. 1980. *The Dynamics of Riots*. Ann Arbor, Mich.: Inter-university Consortius for Political and Social Research.

Ireland, Jane. 2002. "Official Records of Bullying Incidents among Young Offenders: What Can They Tell Us and How Useful Are They?" *Journal of Adolescence* 25: 669–79.

Jackson-Jacobs, Curtis. 2003. "Narrative Gratifications and Risks: How Street Combatants Construct Appealing Defeats in Physical Fights." Paper presented at Annual Meeting of American Sociological Association.

———. 2004. "Taking a Beating: The Narrative Gratifications of Fighting as an Underdog." In *Cultural Criminology*, edited by Jeff Ferrell, Keith J. Hayward, Wayne Morrison, and Mike Presdee. Unleashed. London: Glasshouse.

Jackson-Jacobs, Curtis, and Robert Garot. 2003. " 'Whatchu Lookin' At?' and 'Where You From?' Provoking Fights in a Suburb and an Inner-city." Paper presented at Annual Meeting of American Sociological Association.

Jacobs, Jennifer E. 2004. "Ululation in Levantine Societies: Vocalization as Aesthetic, Affective and Corporeal Practice." *American School of Oriental Research Newsletter* 54 (winter): 19.

Jankowski, Martín Sánchez. 1991. *Islands in the Street: Gangs and American Society*. Berkeley: University of California Press.

Johnson, M. P. 1995. "Patriarchal Terrorism and Common Couple Violence: Two Forms of Violence against Women." *Journal of Marriage and the Family* 57: 283–94.

Johnson, M. P., and K. J. Ferraro. 2000. "Research on Domestic Violence in the 1990s: Making Distinctions." *Journal of Marriage and the Family* 62: 948–53.

Johnston, Lynne. 2000. "Riot by Appointment: An Examination of the Nature and Structure of Seven Hard-Core Football Hooligan Groups." In *The Social Psychology of Crime: Groups, Teams and Networks*, edited by David Canter and Laurence Alison. Aldershot, England: Ashgate.

Jones, Nikki. 2004. " 'It's Not Where You Live, It's How You Live.' How Young Women Negotiate Conflict and Violence in the Inner City." *Annals of the American Academy of Political and Social Science* 595: 49–62.

Jouriles, E. N., and W. D. Norwood. 1995. "Physical Aggression toward Boys and Girls in Families Characterized by the Battering of Women." *Journal of Family Psychology* 9: 69–78.

Junge, Astrid, Jiri Dvorak, Jiri Graf-Baumann, and Lars Peterson. 2004. "Football Injuries during FIFA Tournaments and the Olympic Games, 1998–2001." *American Journal of Sports Medicine* (Jan.–Feb.).

Kaldor, Mary. 1999. *New and Old Wars: Organized Violence in a Global Era.* Cambridge: Polity.

Kaltiala-Heino, Riittakerttu, Matti Rimplela, Paivi Rantanen, and Arja Rimpela. 2000. "Bullying at School—An Indicator of Adolescents at Risk for Mental Disorders." *Journal of Adolescence* 23: 661–74.

Kammer, Reinhard. 1969. *Die Kunst der Bergdämonen: Zen-Lehre und Konfuzianismus in der japanischen Schwertkunst.* Weilheim, Germany: O. W. Barth.

Kan, Sergei. 1986. "The 19th-Century Tlingit Potlatch." *American Ethnologist* 13: 191–12.

Kania, Richard R. E., and Wade C. Mackey. 1977. "Police Violence as a Function of Community Characteristics." *Criminology* 15: 27–48.

Kanter, Rosabeth M. 1977. *Men and Women of the Corporation.* New York: Basic Books.

Kapardis, A. 1988. "One Hundred Convicted Armed Robbers in Melbourne." In *Armed Robbery*, edited by D. Challenger. Canberra: Australian Institute of Criminology.

Kapuscinski, Ryszard. 1992. *The Soccer War.* New York: Vintage.

Katz, Jack. 1988. *Seductions of Crime: Moral and Sensual Attractions of Doing Evil.* New York: Basic Books.

———. 1999. *How Emotions Work.* Chicago: University of Chicago Press.

Kaufman, J., and E. Zigler. 1993. "The Intergenerational Transmission of Abuse Is Overstated." Pp. 209–21 in *Current Controversies on Family Violence*, edited by R. J. Gelles and D. R. Loseke. Newbury Park, Calif.: Sage.

Kautz, August V. 1865/2001. *Customs of Service for Non-commissioned Officers and Soldiers.* Mechanicsburg, Pa.: Stockpole.

Keegan, John. 1976. *The Face of Battle: A Study of Agincourt, Waterloo, and the Somme.* New York: Random House.

———. 1987. *The Mask of Command.* New York: Viking Penguin.

———. 1993. *A History of Warfare.* London: Hutchinson.

———, ed. 1997. *Atlas of the Second World War.* London: HarperCollins.

Keegan, John, and Richard Holmes. 1985. *Soldiers: A History of Men in Battle.* London: Guild.

Keeley, Lawrence H. 1996. *War before Civilization.* Oxford: Oxford University Press.

Kelly, James. 1995. *"That Damn'd Thing Called Honour": Duelling in Ireland 1570–1860.* Cork, Ireland: Cork University Press.

Kelly, John E. 1946. "Shoot, Soldier, Shoot." *Infantry Journal* 58 (January): 47.

Kerner Commission. 1968. *Report of the National Advisory Commission on Civil Disorder.* New York: Bantam.

Kertzer, David I. 1993. *Sacrificed for Honor: Italian Infant Abandonment and the Politics of Reproductive Control.* Boston: Beacon.

Keuls, Eva C. 1985. *The Reign of the Phallus: Sexual Politics in Ancient Athens.* Berkeley: University of California Press.

Kiernan, V. G. 1988. *The Duel in European History: Honour and the Reign of Aristocracy.* Oxford: Oxford University Press.

Kimmel, Michael S. 2002. "'Gender Symmetry' in Domestic Violence." *Violence against Women* 8: 1332–63.

Kimmel, Michael S., and Mathew Mahler. 2003. "Adolescent Masculinity, Homophobia, and Violence: Random School Shootings, 1982–2000." *American Behavioral Scientist,* no. 21.

King, Anthony. 1995. "Outline of a Practical Theory of Football Violence." *Sociology* 29: 635–51.

———. 2001. " Violent Pasts: Collective Memory and Football Hooliganism." *The Sociological Review* 49: 568–85.

———. 2003. *The European Ritual. Football in the New Europe.* Aldershot: Ashgate.

———. 2005. "The Word of Command: Communication and Cohesion in the Military." *Armed Forces and Society* 32: 1–20.

Kiser, Edgar, and Yong Cai. 2003. "War and Bureaucratization in Qin China." *American Sociological Review* 68: 511–39.

Kissel, Hans. 1956. "Panic in Battle." *Military Review* 36: 96–107.

Klewin, Gabriele, Klaus-Jürgen Tillmann, and Gail Weingart. 2003. "Violence in School." In *International Handbook of Violence Research,* edited by Wilhelm Heitmeyer and John Hagan. London: Kluwer.

Klinger, David. 2004. *Into the Kill Zone: A Cop's Eye View of Deadly Force.* San Francisco: Jossey-Bass.

Klusemann, Stefan. 2002. "The German Revolution of 1918 and Contemporary Theories of State Breakdown." M.A. thesis, University of Pennsylvania.

———. 2006. "Micro-situational Antecedants of Violent Atrocity: The Case of Srebrenica." Paper presented at American Sociological Association, Montreal.

Kooistra, Paul. 1989. *Criminals as Heroes.* Bowling Green, Ohio: Bowling Green State University Press.

Kopel, David B., and Paul H. Blackman. 1997. *No More Wacos: What's Wrong with Federal Law Enforcement and How to Fix It.* New York: Prometheus.

KR Video. 1997. "Somalia: Good Intentions, Deadly Results."

Kreps, Gary. 1984. "Sociological Inquiry and Disaster Research." *Annual Review of Sociology* 10: 309–30.

Labov, William. 1972. "Rules for Ritual Insults." In *Studies in Social Interaction,* edited by David Sudnow. New York: Free Press.

Lakoff, George. 1987. *Women, Fire, and Dangerous Things: What Categories Reveal about the Mind.* Chicago: University of Chicago Press.

Lang, A. R. 1983. "Drinking and Disinhibition: Contributions from Psychological Research." In *Alcohol and Disinhibition: Nature and Meaning of the Link,* edited by R. Room, and G. Collins. NIAAA Research Monograph No. 12. Rockville, Md.: U.S. Department of Health and Human Services.

Langtry, J. O. 1958. "Tactical Implications of the Human Factors in Warfare." *Australian Army Journal* 107: 5–24.

Lau, E. E., and J. Kosberg. 1979. "Abuse of the Elderly by Informal Care Providers." *Aging* 299: 10–15.

Laub, John H., Daniel S. Nagin, and Robert J. Sampson. 1998. "Trajectories of Change in Criminal Offending: Good Marriages and the Desistance Process." *American Sociological Review* 63: 225–38.

Leddy, Joanne, and Michael O'Connell. 2002. "The Prevalence, Nature and Psychological Correlates of Bullying in Irish Prisons." *Legal & Criminological Psychology* 7: 131–40.

Lejeune, Robert. 1977. "The Management of a Mugging." *Urban Life* 6, no. 2: 259–87.

Lejeune, R., and N. Alex. 1973. "On Being Mugged: The Event and Its Aftermath." *Life and Culture* 2: 259–87.

Lenski, Gerhard E. 1966. *Power and Privilege: A Theory of Stratification*. New York: McGraw-Hill.

Levine, H. G. 1983. "The Good Creature of God and Demon Rum: Colonial American and 19th-Century Ideas about Alcohol, Crime, and Accidents." In *Alcohol and Disinhibition: Nature and Meaning of the Link*, edited by R. Room and G. Collins. NIAAA Research Monograph No. 12. Rockville, Md.: U.S. Department of Health and Human Services.

Lewis, Jon E. 2001. *Eyewitness Britain*. London: Carroll and Graf.

Lincoln, C. Eric. 1994. *The Black Muslims in America*. 3rd ed. Grand Rapids, Mich.: Eerdmans.

Lithman, Yngve Georg. 1979. "Feeling Good and Getting Smashed: On the Symbolism of Alcohol and Drunkenness among Canadian Indians." *Ethnos* 44: 119–33.

Little, Roger W. 1955. "A Study of the Relationship between Collective Solidarity and Combat Performance." Ph.D. diss., Michigan State University.

Lloyd-Smith, Mel, and John Dwyfor Davies, eds. 1995. *On the Margins: The Educational Experience of "Problem" Pupils*. Staffordshire, England: Trentham Books.

Lowry, Richard S. 2003. *The Gulf War Chronicles: A Military History of the First Iraq War*. New York: iUniverse.

Luckenbill, David F. 1977. "Criminal Homicide as a Situated Transaction." *Social Problems* 25: 176–86.

———. 1981. "Generating Compliance: The Case of Robbery." *Urban Life* 10: 25–46.

MacAndrew, Craig, and Robert B. Edgerton. 1969. *Drunken Comportment: A Social Explanation*. Chicago: Aldine.

Mackenzie, Compton. 1913/1960. *Sinister Street*. Baltimore, Md.: Penguin.

MacMullen, Ramsay. 1974. *Roman Social Relations, 50 B.C. to A.D. 284*. New Haven: Yale University Press.

Magida, Arthur J. 2003. *The Rabbi and the Hit Man*. New York: HarperCollins.

Mann, Leon. 1981. "The Baiting Crowd in Episodes of Threatened Suicide." *Journal of Personality and Social Psychology* 41: 703–9.

Mann, Michael. 1986. *The Sources of Social Power*. Vol. 1. *A History of Power from the Beginning to A.D. 1760*. Cambridge: Cambridge University Press.

———. 1993. *The Sources of Social Power*. Vol II. *The Rise of Classes and Nation-States, 1760–1914*. Cambridge: Cambridge University Press.

———. 2005. *The Dark Side of Democracy: Explaining Ethnic Cleansing*. Cambridge: Cambridge University Press.

Marinovich, Greg, and Joao Silva. 2000. *The Bang-Bang Club: Snapshots from a Hidden War*. New York: Basic Books.

Markham, Felix. 1963. *Napoleon*. New York: New American Library.

Marrou, H. I. 1964. *A History of Education in Antiquity*. New York: New American Library.

Marsh, P., E. Rosser, and R. Harré. 1978. *The Rules of Disorder*. London: Routledge.

Marshall, M. 1983. "Four Hundred Rabbits: An Anthropological View of Ethanol as a Disinhibitor." In *Alcohol and Disinhibition: Nature and Meaning of the Link*, edited by R. Room and G. Collins. NIAAA Research Monograph No. 12. Rockville, Md.: U.S. Department of Health and Human Services.

Marshall, S.L.A. 1947. *Men against Fire: The Problem of Battle Comand*. Norman, Okla.: University of Oklahoma Press. Originally published by William Morrow, New York.

———. 1982. *Island Victory: The Battle of Kwajalein*. Washington, D.C.: Zenger.

Martin, Everett Dean. 1920. *The Behavior of Crowds: A Psychological Study*. New York: Harper.

Mason, Philip. 1976. *A Matter of Honor: An Account of the Indian Army, Its Officers and Men*. Baltimore, Md.: Penguin.

Mastrofski, Steven, Jeffrey Snipes, and Suzanne Supina. 1996. "Compliance on Demand: The Public's Response to Specific Requests." *Journal of Research in Crime and Delinquency* 33: 269–305.

Mauss, Marcel. 1925/1967. *The Gift*. New York: Norton.

Maxfield, Michael G., and Cathy Spatz Widom. 1996. "The Cycle of Violence Revisted Six Years Later." *Archives of Pediatric and Adolescent Medicine* 150: 390–95.

Mazur, Alan, E. Rosa, M. Faupel, J. Heller, R. Leen, and B. Thurman. 1980. "Physiological Aspects of Communication via Mutual Gaze." *American Journal of Sociology* 86: 50–74.

McAleer, Kevin. 1994. *Duelling: The Cult of Honor in Fin-de-Siècle Germany*. Princeton: Princeton University Press.

McCauley, Clark. 1998. "When Screen Violence Is Not Attractive." In *Why We Watch: The Attractions of Violent Entertainment*, edited by Jeffrey Goldstein. New York: Oxford University Press.

McEvedy, Colin, and Richard Jones. 1978. *Atlas of World Population History*. New York: Penguin.

McNeill, William H. 1982. *The Pursuit of Power: Technology, Armed Force, and Society since A.D. 1000*. Chicago: University of Chicago Press.

———. 1995. *Keeping Together in Time: Dance and Drill in Human History.* Cambridge, Mass.: Harvard University Press.

McPhail, Clark. 1991. *The Myth of the Madding Crowd.* New York: Aldine de Gruyter.

Meier, Robert F., and Terance D. Miethe. 1993. "Understanding Theories of Criminal Victimization." Pp. 459–99 in *Crime and Justice: A Review of Research,* edited by M. Tonry. Chicago: University of Chicago Press.

Merari, Ariel. 1998. "The Readiness to Kill and Die: Suicidal Terrorism in the Middle East." In *Origins of Terrorism: Psychologies, Ideologies, Theologies, States of Mind,* edited by Walter Reich. Baltimore, Md.: Johns Hopkins University Press.

———. 2005. "Social Organizational and Psychological Factors in Suicide Terrorism." In *The Root Causes of Terrorism,* edited by T. Bjorgo. London: Routledge.

Mersky, Peter B. 1993. *Time of the Aces: Marine Pilots in the Solomons, 1942–1944.* Washington, D.C.: Marine Corps Historical Center.

Merten, Don E. 1997. "The Meaning of Meanness: Popularity, Competition and Conflict among Junior High School Girls." *Sociology of Education* 70: 175–91.

Mestrovic, Stiepen G. 2006. *The Trials of Abu Ghraib.* Boulder, Colo.: Paradigm.

Meyer, Marshall. 1980. "Police Shootings at Minorities . . ." In *The Police and Violence,* edited by Lawrence W. Sherman. Philadelphia: American Academy of Political and Social Science.

Midgley, Graham. 1996. *University Life in Eighteenth-Century Oxford.* New Haven, Conn.: Yale University Press.

Miller, William Ian. 2000. *The Mystery of Courage.* Cambridge, Mass.: Harvard University Press.

Milner, Murray, Jr. 2004. *Freaks, Geeks and Cool Kids: American Teenagers, Schools and the Culture of Consumption.* New York: Routledge.

Miron, Murray S. 1978. *Hostage.* Upper Saddle River, N.J.: Allyn and Bacon.

Moffitt, Terrie E., and Avshalom Caspi. 2001. "Childhood Predictors Differentiate Life-Course Persistent and Adolescence-Limited Antisocial Pathways, among Males and Females." *Development and Psychopathology* 13: 355–75.

Montagner, Hubert, A. Restoin, D. Rodriguez, V. Ullman, M. Viala, D. Laurent, and D. Godard. 1988. "Social Interactions among Children with Peers and Their Modifications in Relation to Environmental Factors." In *Social Fabrics of the Mind,* edited by Michael R. A. Chance. London: Lawrence Erlbaum.

Moore, Roy E. 1945. "Shoot, Soldier." *Infantry Journal* 56 (December): 21.

Morgan, P. 1983. "Alcohol, Disinhibition, and Domination: A Conceptual Analysis." In *Alcohol and Disinhibition: Nature and Meaning of the Link,* edited by R. Room and G. Collins. NIAAA Research Monograph No. 12. Rockville, Md.: U.S. Department of Health and Human Services.

Morison, Samuel Eliot. 1936. *Three Centuries of Harvard.* Cambridge, Mass.: Harvard University Press.

Morrison, Shona, and Ian O'Donnell. 1994. *Armed Robbery: A Study in London.* University of Oxford Centre for Criminological Research, Occasional Paper No. 15. Oxford: Oxford University Press.

Mullen, Brian. 1986. "Atrocity as a Function of Mob Composition." *Personality and Social Psychology Bulletin* 12: 187–97.

Murphy, Robert F. 1957. "Intergroup Hostility and Social Cohesion." *American Anthropologist* 59: 1018–35.

———. 1959. "Social Structure and Sex Antagonism." *Southwestern Journal of Anthropology* 15: 89–98.

Murray, Williamson, and Robert H. Scales. 2003. *The Iraq War: A Military History.* Cambridge: Belknap.

Mustain, Gene, and Jerry Capeci. 1993. *Murder Machine.* New York: Penguin.

Myers, Daniel J. 1997. "Racial Rioting in the 1960s: An Event History Analysis of Local Conditions." *American Sociological Review* 62: 94–112.

———. 2000. "The Diffusion of Collective Violence: Infectiousness, Susceptibility, and Mass Media Networks." *American Journal of Sociology* 106: 173–208.

Nakane, Chie. 1970. *Japanese Society.* Berkeley: University of California Press.

Nansel, Tonja R., Mary Overpeck, Ramani S. Pilla, W. June Ruan, Bruce Simons-Morton, and Peter Scheidt. 2001. "Bullying Behaviors among U.S. Youth: Prevalence and Association with Psychosocial Adjustment." *Journal of the American Medical Association.* 285, no. 16: 2094–2100.

National Center for Education Statistics. 1995. *The Condition of Education, 1995.* Washington, D.C.: U.S. Dept. of Education.

Ness, Cindy D. 2004. "Why Girls Fight: Female Youth Violence in the Inner City." *Annals of the American Academy of Political and Social Science* 595: 32–48.

Nevares, Dora, Marvin E. Wolfgang, and Paul E. Tracy. 1990. *Delinquency in Puerto Rico: The 1970 Birth Cohort Study.* New York: Greenwood.

Newman, Katherine S. 2002. "No Shame: The View from the Left Bank." *American Journal of Sociology* 107: 1577–99.

Newman, Katherine S., Cybelle Fox, David Harding, Jal Mehta, and Wendy Roth. 2004. *Rampage: The Social Roots of School Shootings.* New York: Basic Books.

Nye, Robert A. 1993. *Masculinity and Male Honor Codes in Modern France.* Oxford: Oxford University Press.

Oberschall, Anthony, and Michael Seidman. 2005. "Food Coercion in Revolution and Civil War." *Comparative Studies in Society and History,* 47: 372–402.

O'Donnell, Ian, and Kimmet Edgar. 1998a. "Routine Vicitimisation in Prisons." *The Howard Journal* 37: 266–79.

———. 1998b. *Bullying in Prisons.* University of Oxford, Centre for Criminological Research. Occasional paper no. 18.

———. 1999. "Fear in Prisons." *The Prison Journal* 79: 90–99.

Okumiya, Masatake, Jiro Horikoshi, and Martin Caidin. 1973. *Zero! The Story of Japan's Air War in the Pacific, 1941–45.* New York: Ballantine.

O'Leary, K. D. 2000. "Are Women Really More Aggressive than Men in Intimate Relationships?" *Psychological Bulletin* 126: 685–89.

Olweus, Dan. 1993. *Bullying at School: What We Know and What We Can Do.* Oxford: Blackwell.

Osgood, D. Wayne, Janet K. Wilson, Patrick M. O'Malley, J. Wilson, Jerald G. Bachman, and Lloyd D. Johnston. 1996. "Routine Activities and Individual Deviant Behavior." *American Sociological Review* 61: 635–55.

Ostvik, Kristina, and Floyed Rudmin. 2001. "Bullying and Hazing among Norwegian Army Soldiers: Two Studies of Prevalence, Context, and Cognition." *Military Psychology* 13: 17–39.

Overy, Richard J. 1980. *The Air War 1939–1945*. New York: Stein and Day.

———. 1995. *Why the Allies Won*. New York: Norton.

Pape, Robert A. 1996. *Bombing to Win: Air Power and Coercion in War*. Ithaca, N.Y.: Cornell University Press.

———. 2005. *Dying to Win: Strategic Logic of Suicide Terrorism*. New York: Random House.

Pappas, Nick T., Patrick C. Mckenry, and Beth Skilken Catlett. 2004. "Athlete Aggression on the Rink and off the Ice: Athlete Violence and Aggression in Hockey and Interpersonal Relationships." *Men and Masculinities* 6, no. 3: 291–312.

Parker, R. N. 1993. "Alcohol and Theories of Homicide." Pp. 113–42 in *Advances in Criminological Theory*, vol. 4, edited by F. Adler, W. Laufer. New Brunswick, N.J.: Transaction.

Parker, R. N., and L. A. Rebhun. 1995. *Alcohol and Homicide: A Deadly Combination of Two American Traditions*. Albany, N.Y.: State University of New York Press.

Parker, Robert Nash. 1993. "Alcohol and Theories of Homicide." Pp. 113–42 in *Advances in Criminological Theory*, vol. 4, edited by F. Adler and W. Laufer. New Brunswick, N.J.: Transaction.

Parker, Robert Nash, and Kathleen Auerhahn. 1998. "Alcohol, Drugs, and Violence." *Annual Review of Sociology* 24: 291–311.

Pegler, Martin. 2001. *The Military Sniper since 1914*. Oxford: Osprey.

———. 2004. *Out of Nowhere: A History of the Military Sniper*. Oxford: Osprey.

Pellegrini, A. D., and Jeffrey D. Long. 2002. "A Longitudinal Study of Bullying, Dominance, and Victimization during the Transition from Primary School through Secondary School." *British Journal of Developmental Psychology* 20: 259–80.

Peltonen, Markku. 2003. *The Duel in Early Modern England*. Cambridge: Cambridge University Press.

Perrow, Charles. 1984. *Normal Accidents*. New York: Basic Books.

Peterson, Mark, Harriet Braiker, and Sue Polich. 1980. *Doing Crime: A Survey of California Inmates*. Santa Monica, Calif.: Rand.

Phillips, David, and Lundie L. Carstensen. 1986. "The Effect of Suicide Stories of Various Demographic Groups, 1968–1985." *Suicide and Life-threatening Behavior* 18: 100–14.

Phillips, L. R. 1983. "Abuse and Neglect of the Frail Elderly at Home: An Exploration of Theoretical Relationships." *Journal of Advanced Nursing* 8: 379–92.

Phillips, Will. 2002. "A High School Fight." Unpublished ms. Department of Sociology, University of Pennsylvania.

Pihl, R. O., J. B. Peterson, and M. A. Lau. 1993. " A Biosocial Model of the Alcohol-Aggression Relationship." *Journal of Studies in Alcohol* (Supplement) 11: 128–39.

Pillemer, Karl. 1993. "The Abused Offspring Are Dependent: Abuse Is Caused by the Deviance and Dependence of Abusive Caregivers." Pp. 237–49 in *Current Controversies on Family Violence*, edited by R. J. Gelles and D. R. Loseke. Newbury Park, Calif.: Sage.

Pillemer, Karl, and David Finkelhor. 1988. "The Prevalence of Elder Abuse." *Gerontologist* 28: 51–57.

Pillemer, K., and J. J. Suitor. 1992. "Violence and Violent Feelings: What Causes Them among Family Caregivers." *Journal of Gerontology* 47, S165-S172.

Pinderhughes, Ellen E., Kenneth A. Dodge, John E. Bates, Gregory S. Pettit, and Arnaldo Zelli. 2000. "Discipline Responses: Influences of Parents' Socioeconomic Status, Ethnicity, Beliefs about Parenting, Stress, and Cognitive Emotional Processes." *Journal of Family Psychology* 14: 380–400.

Piquero, Alex R. 2000. "Assessing the Relationships between Gender, Chronicity, Seriousness, and Offense Skewness in Criminal Offending." *Journal of Criminal Justice* 28: 103–16.

Piquero, Alex R., and Stephen L. Buka. 2002. "Linking Juvenile and Adult Patterns of Criminal Activity in the Providence Cohort of the National Collaborative Perinatal Project." *Journal of Criminal Justice* 30:1–14.

Piquero, Alex R., David P. Farrington, and Alfred Blumstein. 2003. "The Criminal Career Paradigm: Background and Recent Developments." In *Crime and Justice: A Review of Research*, vol. 30, edited by Michael Tonry. Chicago: University of Chicago Press.

Polk, Kenneth, Christine Alder, Gordon Basemore, G. Blake, S. Cordray, G. Coventry, J. Galvin, and M. Temple. 1981. *Becoming Adult: An Analysis of Maturational Development from Age 16 to 30*. Center for Studies of Crime and Delinquency, National Institute of Mental Health. Washington, D.C.: U.S. Department of Health and Human Services.

Pratt, Michael. 1980. *Mugging as a Social Problem*. Boston: Routledge and Kegan Paul.

Preston, Diana. 2000. *The Boxer Rebellion*. New York: Penguin Putnam.

Priest, John M. 1989. *Antietam: The Soldiers' Battle*. Shippensburg, Pa.: White Man.

Prinstein, Mitchell J., and Antonius H. N. Cillessen. 2003. "Forms and Functions of Adolescent Peer Aggression Associated with High Levels of Peer Status." *Merrill-Palmer Quarterly* (Special Issue: Aggression and Adaptive Functioning) 49: 310–42.

Propp, Vladimir. 1928/1968. *Morphology of the Folk Tale*. Austin, Tex.: University of Texas Press.

Pulkkinen, Lea. 1988. "Delinquent Development: Theoretical and Empirical Considerations." In *Studies of Psychosocial Risk: The Power of Longitudinal Data*, edited by Michael Rutter. Cambridge: Cambridge University Press.

Quarantelli, E. L. 1954. "The Nature and Conditions of Panic." *American Journal of Sociology* 60: 267–75.

———. 1980. *Evacuation Behavior and Problems*. Columbus, Ohio: Disaster Research Center, Ohio State University.

Quarantelli, E. L., and Russell Dynes. 1968. "Looting in Civil Disorders: An Index of Social Change." *The American Behavioral Scientist* (April): 7–10.

Quarantelli, E. L., and Russell Dynes. 1970. "Property Norms and Looting: Their Patterns in Community Crises." *Phylon* 31: 168–82.

Radcliffe-Brown, Arthur. 1952. *Structure and Function in Primitive Society.* New York: Free Press.

Ransford, H. Edward. 1968. "Isolation, Powerlessness, and Violence: A Study of Attitudes and Participation in the Watts Riot." *American Journal of Sociology* 73: 581–91.

Reicher, S. 1987. "Crowd Behavior as Social Action." In *Rediscovering the Social Group: A Self-Categorization Theory,* edited by J. C. Turner. Oxford: Basil Blackwell.

Reiss, Albert. 1971. *The Police and Public.* New Haven: Yale University Press.

Retzinger, Suzanne M. 1991. *Violent Emotions: Shame and Rage in Marital Quarrels.* Newbury Park, Calif.: Sage.

Rican, Pavel. 1995. "Sociometric Status of the School Bullies and Their Victims." *Studia Psychologica* 37: 357–64.

Richardson, Anna, Tracey Budd, Renuka Engineer, Annabelle Phillips, Julian Thompson, and Jonathan Nicholls. 2003. "Drinking, Crime and Disorder." Home Office Report 185. Available at www.homeoffice.gov.uk/rds/bcs1.html.

Ricolfi, Luca. 2005. "Palestinians, 1981–2003." In *Making Sense of Suicide Missions,* edited by Diego Gambetta. New York: Oxford University Press.

Ringel, Gail. 1979. "The Kwakiutl Potlatch: History, Economics, and Symbols." *Ethnohistory* 26: 347–62.

Roberts, Julian V., and Cynthia J. Benjamin. 2000. "Spectator Violence in Sports: A North American Perspective." *European Journal on Criminal Policy and Research* 8:163–81.

Robinson, Fred Norris. 1912. "Satirists and Enchanters in Early Irish Literature." In *Studies in the History of Religions,* D. G. Moore Lyons. New York: Macmillan.

Room, R., and K. Mäkelä. 1996. "Typologies of the Cultural Position of Drinking." *Journal of Studies on Alcohol* 61: 475–83.

Room, Robin. 2001. "Intoxication and Bad Behaviour: Understanding Cultural Differences in the Link." *Social Science and Medicine* 53: 189–98.

Ross, Anne. 1970. *Everyday Life of the Pagan Celts.* London: Batsford.

Rowland, David. 1986. "Assessments of Combat Degradation." *Journal of the United Service Institution* 131 (June): 33–43.

Roy, Donald. 1952. "Quota Restriction and Goldbricking in a Machine Shop." *American Journal of Sociology* 57: 427–42.

Rubin, Lillian. 1976. *Worlds of Pain: Life in the Working-Class Family.* New York: Basic Books.

Rubinstein, Jonathan. 1973. *City Police.* New York: Farrar, Straus and Giroux.

Rudolph, Frederick. 1962. *The American College and University.* New York: Knopf.

Sacks, Harvey, Emanuel A. Schegloff, and Gail Jefferson. 1974. "A Simplest Systematics for the Organization of Turn-taking for Conversation." *Language* 50: 696–735.

Sageman, Marc. 2004. *Understanding Terror Networks*. Philadelphia: University of Pennsylvania Press.

Sakaida, Henry. 1985. *Winged Samurai: Saburo Sakai and the Zero Fighter Pilots*. Mesa, Ariz.: Champlin Fighter Museum Publications.

Salmivalli, Christina. 1998. "Intelligent, Attractive, Well-Behaving, Unhappy: The Structure of Adolescents' Self-Concept and Its Relations to Their Social Behavior." *Journal of Research on Adolescence* 8: 333–52.

Salmivalli, Christina, Arja Huttunen, Kirsti M. J. Lagerspetz. 1997. "Peer Networks and Bullying in Schools." *Scandinavian Journal of Psychology* 38: 305–12.

Sanders, William B. 1994. *Gangbangs and Drive-Bys: Grounded Culture and Juvenile Gang Violence*. New York: Aldine de Gruyter.

Scharf, Peter, and Arnold Binder. 1983. *The Badge and the Bullet*. New York: Praeger.

Scheff, Thomas J. 1990. *Micro-sociology: Discourse, Emotion and Social Structure*. Chicago: University of Chicago Press.

———. 1994. *Bloody Revenge: Emotions, Nationalism and War*. Boulder, Colo.: Westview Press.

———. 2006. *Goffman Unbound: A New Paradigm for the Social Sciences*. Boulder, Colo.: Paradigm Publishers.

Scheff, Thomas J., and Suzanne Retzinger. 1991. *Emotions and Violence: Shame and Rage in Destructive Conflicts*. Lexington, Mass.: Lexington Books.

Schegloff, Emanuel. 1992. "Repair after Last Turn: The Last Structurally Provided Defense of Intersubjectivity in Conversation." *American Journal of Sociology* 97.

Schwartz, Michael. 2005. "Terrorism and Guerrilla War in Iraq." Paper delivered at annual meeting of the American Sociological Association.

Scott. 2001. "Semen in a Bullet." In *A Night in the Barracks*, edited by Alex Buchman. New York: Haworth.

Scott, Marvin B., and Stanford Lyman. 1968. "Accounts." *American Sociological Review* 33: 46–62.

Searle, Eleanor. 1988. *Predatory Kinship and the Creation of Norman Power, 840–1066*. Berkeley: University of California Press.

Senechal de la Roche, Roberta. 2001. "Why Is Collective Violence Collective? *Sociological Theory* 19: 126–44.

Shalit, Ben. 1988. *The Psychology of Conflict and Combat*. New York: Praeger.

Shannon, Lyle W., with Judith L. McKim, James P. Curry, and Lawrence J. Haffner. 1988. *Criminal Career Continuity: Its Social Context*. New York: Human Sciences.

Shaw, Clifford R. 1930/1966. *The Jack-roller*. Chicago: University of Chicago Press.

Sherman, Lawrence W., ed. 1980. *The Police and Violence*. Philadelphia: American Academy of Political and Social Science.

Shi Nai'an, and Luo Guanzhong. 1988. *Outlaws of the Marsh*. Beijing: Foreign Languages Press.

Shields, Jr., Edgar W. 1999. "Intimidation and Violence by Males in High School Athletics." *Adolescence*, 34, no. 135: 503–21.

Shils, Edward, and Morris Janowitz. 1948. "Cohersion and Disintegration in the Wehrmacht in World War II." *Public Opinion Quarterly* 12: 280–315.

Shore, Christopher, and Clive Williams. 1994. *Aces High: A Tribute to the Highest Scoring Fighter Pilots of the British and Commonwealth Air Forces in World War II.* London: Grub Street.

Shrum, Wesley M., and John Kilburn. 1996. "Ritual Disrobement at Mardi Gras: Ceremonial Exchange and Moral Order." *Social Forces* 75: 423–58.

Shu Ching (Book of History). 1971. Translated by Clae Waltham. Chicago: Henry Regnery.

Simpson, Anthony. 1988. "Dandelions on the Field of Honor: Dueling, the Middle Classes, and the Law in Nineteenth-Century England." *Criminal Justice History* 9: 137–62.

Sims, Edward. 1972. *The Aces Talk: Fighter Tactics and Strategy, 1914–1970.* New York: Ballantine.

Sipes, Richard G. 1973. "War, Sports, and Aggression: An Empirical Test of Two Rival Theories." *American Anthropologist* 75: 64–86.

Skocpol, Theda. 1979. *States and Social Revolutions.* Cambridge: Cambridge University Press.

Skolnick, Jerome. 1966. *Justice without Trial.* New York: Wiley.

Smallman. Tom. 1995. *Ireland Lonely Planet Guide.* London: Lonely Planet Publications.

Smith, Michael D. 1978. "Precipitants of Crowd Violence." *Sociological Inquiry.* 48: 121–31.

———. 1979. "Towards an Explanation of Hockey Violence: A Reference Other Approach." *Canadian Journal of Sociology,* 4, 105–24.

Smith, Peter K., and Paul Brain. 2000. "Bullying in Schools: Lessons from Two Decades of Research." *Aggressive Behavior* 26: 1–9.

Smoler, Fredric. 1989 "The Secret of the Soldiers Who Wouldn't Shoot." *American Heritage* 40 (March): 36–45.

Snook, Scott. A. 2000. *Friendly Fire: The Accidental Shootdown of U.S. Blackhawks over Northern Iraq.* Princeton: Princeton University Press.

Sommers-Effler, Erika. 2004. "Humble Saints and Moral Heroes: Ritual, Emotion, and Commitment in High-risk Social Movements." Ph.D. diss., University of Pennsylvania.

Speidel, Michael P. 2002. "Berserks: A History of Indo-European 'Mad Warriors.' " *Journal of World History* 13: 253–90.

Spierenburg, Pieter. 1994. "Faces of Violence: Homicide Trends and Cultural Meanings; Amsterdam, 1431–1816." *Journal of Social History* 27: 701–16.

Spilerman, Seymour. 1976. "Structural Characteristics of Cities and Severity of Racial Disorders." *American Sociological Review* 41: 771–93.

Spiller, Roger J. 1988. "S.L.A. Marshall and the Ratio of Fire." *Journal of the United Service Institution* 133 (December): 63–71.

Sprey, Jetse, and Sarah Mathews. 1989. "The Perils of Drawing Policy Implications from Research." In *Elder Abuse: Practice and Policy,* edited by Rachel Filinson and Stanley Ingman. New York: Human Sciences Press.

Stack, Stephen. 2000. "Media Impacts on Suicide: A Quantitative Review of 293 Findings." *Social Science Quarterly* 81: 957–71.

Stark, Rodney. 1996. *The Rise of Christianity*. Princeton: Princeton University Press.

Starr, R. H. Jr. 1988. "Physical Abuse of Children." In *Handbook of Family Violence*, edited by V. B. Van Hasselt, R. L. Morrison, A. S. Bellack, and M. Hersen. New York: Plenum.

Steinmetz, Susan. 1993. "The Abused Elderly Are Dependent." Pp. 222–36 in *Current Controversies on Family Violence*, edited by R. J. Gelles, and D. R. Loseke. Newbury Park, Calif.: Sage.

Stern, Jessica. 2003. *Terror in the Name of God: Why Religious Militants Kill*. New York: HarperCollins.

Stets, Jan E. 1988. *Domestic Violence and Control*. New York: Springer-Verlag.

Stets, J. E. 1992. "Interactive Processes in Dating Aggression: A National Study." *Journal of Marriage and the Family* 54: 165–77.

Stets, J. E., and M. A. Pirog-Good. 1990. "Interpersonal Control and Courtship Aggression." *Journal of Social and Personal Relationships* 7: 371–94.

Stets, J. E., and M. Straus. 1990. "Gender Differences in Reporting Marital Violence." In *Physical Violence in American Families*, edited by Murray Straus and Richard Gelles. New Brunswick, N.J.: Transaction.

Stith, S. M., M. B. Williams, and K. Rosen. 1990. *Violence Hits Home*. New York: Springer.

Stone, Lawrence. 1967. *The Crisis of the Aristocracy, 1558–1641*. New York: Oxford University Press.

Stouffer, Samuel A., Arthur A. Lumsdaine, Marian Harper Lumsdaine, Robin M. Williams Jr., M. Brewster Smith, Irving L. Janis, Shirley A. Star, and Leonard S. Cottrell, Jr. 1949. *The American Soldier*. Vol. 2: *Combat and Its Aftermath*. Princeton: Princeton University Press.

Straus, M. A. 1990. "Social Stress and Marital Violence in a National Sample of American Families." Pp. 181–201 in *Physical Violence in American Families: Risk Factors and Adaptations to Violence in 8,145 Families*, edited by M. A. Straus and R. J. Gelles. New Brunswick, N.J.: Transaction.

Straus, M. A., and Denise Donnelly. 1994. *Beating the Devil out of Them: Corporal Punishment in American Families*. New York: Lexington.

Straus, M. A., and R. J. Gelles. 1986. "Societal Change and Change in Family Violence from 1975 to 1985 as Revealed in Two National Surveys." *Journal of Marriage and the Family* 48: 465–79.

Straus, M. A., R. J. Gelles, and S. K. Steinmetz. 1988. *Behind Closed Doors: Violence in the American Family*. Newbury Park, Calif.: Sage.

Stump, Al. 1994. *Cobb: A Biography*. New York: Workman.

Sugarman, D. B., and G. T. Hotaling. 1989. "Dating Violence: Prevalence, Context, and Risk Markers." In *Violence in Dating Relationships*, edited by M. A. Pirog-Good and J. F. Stets. New York: Praeger.

Summers, Harry G. 1995. *Historical Atlas of the Vietnam War*. Boston: Houghton Mifflin.

Summers-Effler, Erika. 2004. *Humble Saints and Moral Heroes: Ritual and Emotional Commitment in High-risk Social Movements*. Ph.D. diss., University of Pennsylvania.

Sun Tzu. ca. 400–300 B.C./1963. *The Art of War*, translated and edited by Samuel B. Griffith. New York: Oxford University Press.

Swank, R. L., and W. E. Marchand. 1946. "Combat Neuroses: Development of Combat Exhaustion." *Archives of Neurology and Psychology* 55: 236–47.

Taylor, A.J.P. 1971. *The Struggle for Mastery in Europe, 1848–1918*. Oxford: Oxford University Press.

Taylor, S. P. 1983. "Alcohol and Human Physical Aggression." In *Alcohol, Drug Abuse, Aggression*, ed. E. Gottheil, K. A. Druley, T. E. Skoloda, H. M. Waxman. Springfield, Ill.: Thomas.

Terrill, William, and Michael D. Reisig. 2003. "Neighborhood Context and Police Use of Force." *Journal of Research in Crime and Delinquency* 40: 291–321.

Thompson, John B. 2000. *Political Scandal*. Oxford: Blackwell.

Thorman, George. 1980. *Family Violence*. Springfield, Ill.: Charles C. Thomas.

Thorn, John, Pete Palmer, and Michael Gershman. 2001. *Total Baseball: The Official Encyclopedia of Major League Baseball*. Kingston, N.Y.: Total Sports.

Thornhill, Randy, and Craig T. Palmer. 2000. *A Natural History of Rape: Biological Bases of Sexual Coercion*. Cambridge: M.I.T. Press.

Thrasher, Frederick M. 1927/1963. *The Gang: A Study of 1313 Gangs in Chicago*. Chicago: University of Chicago Press.

Thucydides. 400 B.C./1954. *The Peloponnesian War*. London, Penguin.

Tilly. Charles. 2003. *The Politics of Collective Violence*. Cambridge: Cambridge University Press.

Tjaden, P., and N. Thoennes. 2000. *Extent, Nature and Consequences of Intimate Partner Violence*. Washington, D.C.: National Institute of Justice.

Toch, Hans. 1980. "Mobilizing Police Expertise." In *The Police and Violence*, edited by Lawrence W. Sherman. Philadelphia: American Academy of Political and Social Science.

Toliver, Raymond F., and Trevor J. Constable. 1971. *The Blond Knight of Germany*. New York: Ballantine.

Toliver, Raymond F., and Trevor J. Constable. 1997. *Fighter Aces of the U.S.A.* Atglen, Pa.: Schiffer.

Tombstone Epitaph. October 1881. Reprint 1981. Tombstone, Ariz.: The National Tombstone Epitaph.

Tracy, Paul E., Marvin E. Wolfgang, and Robert M. Figlio. 1990. *Delinquency Careers in Two Birth Cohorts*. New York: Plenum.

Tremblay, Richard E. 2004. "The Development of Human Physical Aggression: How Important Is Early Childhood?" Pp. 221–38 in *Social and Moral Development: Emerging Evidence on the Toddler Years*, edited by L. A. Leavitt and D.M.B. Hall. New Brunswick, N.J.: Johnson and Johnson Pediatric Institute.

Tremblay, Richard E., Daniel S. Nagin, Jean R. Séguin, Mark Zocolillo, Philip D. Zelazo, Daniel Pérusse, and Christa Japel. 2004. "Physical Aggression during Early Childhood: Trajectories and Predictors." *Pediatrics* 114: 43–50.

Trotsky, Leon. 1930. *History of the Russian Revolution*. Reprint. New York: Pathfinder.

Turner, J. C. 1999. "Some Current Issues in Research on Social Identity and Self-categorization Theories." In *Social Identity*, edited by N. Ellemers, R. Spears, and B. Doosje. Oxford: Blackwell.

Turse, Nick, and Debora Nelson. 2006. "Civilian Killings Went Unpunished." *Los Angeles Times*, August 6, 2006, pp. A1, A8–9.

Twain, Mark. 1880/1977. *A Tramp Abroad*. New York: Harper and Row.

Umberson, D., K. L. Anderson, K. Williams, and M. D. Chen. 2003. "Relationship Dynamics, Emotion State, and Domestic Violence: A Stress and Masculinities Perspective." *Journal of Marriage and the Family* 65: 233–47.

Umberson, D., K. Williams, and K. Anderson. 2002. "Violent Behavior: A Measure of Emotional Upset?" *Journal of Health and Social Behavior* 43: 189–206.

Underwood, John. 1979. *The Death of an American Game*. Boston: Little, Brown.

United States Congress, Office of Technology Assessment. 1979. *The Effects of Nuclear War*. Washington, D.C.: U.S. Government Printing Office.

U.S. Air Force. 2006. *Airman: The Book*. San Antonio, Tex.: Air Force News Agency.

Van Creveld, Martin. 1977. *Supplying War: Logistics from Wallenstein to Patton*. Cambridge and New York: Cambridge University Press.

Van Limbergen, Kris, Carine Colaers, and Lode Walgrave. 1989. "The Societal and Psycho-sociological Background of Football Hooliganism." *Current Psychology: Research and Reviews*. 1: 4–14.

Venkatesh, Sudhir. 2006. *Off the Books: The Underground Economy of the Urban Poor*. Cambridge: Harvard University Press.

Vider, Stephen. 2004. "Rethinking Crowd Violence: Self-Categorization Theory and the Woodstock 1999 Riot." *Journal for the Theory of Social Behaviour* 34: 141–66.

Wacquant, Loïc. 2002. "Scrutinizing the Street: Poverty, Morality and the Pitfalls of Urban Ethnography." *American Journal of Sociology* 107: 1468–532.

———. 2004. *Body and Soul: Notes of an Apprentice Boxer*. New York: Oxford University Press.

Wagner-Pacifici, Robin. 2000. *Theorizing the Standoff*. Cambridge: Cambridge University Press.

———. 2005. *The Art of Surrender. Decomposing Sovereignty at Conflict's End*. Chicago: University of Chicago Press.

Weber, Max. 1922/1968. *Economy and Society*. New York: Bedminster.

Weinberg, Darin. 1997. "Lindesmith on Addiction: A Critical History of a Classic Theory." *Sociological Theory* 15: 150–61.

Weinstein, Marc D., Michael D. Smith, and David L. Wiesenthal. 1995. "Masculinity and Hockey Violence." *Sex Roles* 33, nos. 11–12: 831–47.

Westermeyer, Joseph. 1973. "On the Epidemicity of Amok Violence." *Archives of General Psychiatry* 28: 873–76.

Westley, William A. 1970. *Violence and the Police: A Sociological Study of Law, Custom and Morality*. Cambridge, Mass.: MIT Press.

Whitcomb, Christopher 2001. *Cold Zero: Inside the FBI Hostage Rescue Team*. New York: Warner Books.

Whiting, Robert. 1999. *Tokyo Underworld*. New York: Random House.

Wikstrom, Per-Olof H. 1985. *Everyday Violence in Contemporary Sweden: Situational and Ecological Aspects*. Stockholm: National Council for Crime Prevention, Sweden, Research Division.

Wilkinson, Deanna L. 2003. *Guns, Violence and Identity among African American and Latino Youth*. New York: LFB Scholarly Publishing.

Willis, Paul. 1977. *Learning to Labor*. New York: Columbia University Press.

Wilson, Edmund. 1952. *The Shores of Light: A Literary Chronicle of the Twenties and Thirties*. New York: Random House.

Wolfgang, Marvin E., Robert M. Figlio, and Thorsten Sellin. 1972. *Delinquency in a Birth Cohort*. Chicago: University of Chicago Press.

Worden, Robert E. 1996. "The Causes of Police Brutality: Theory and Evidence on Police Use of Force." In *Police Violence: Understanding and Controlling Police Abuse of Force*, edited by William A. Geller and Hans Toch. New Haven, Conn.: Yale University Press.

Wyatt-Brown, Bertram. 1982. *Southern Honor: Ethics and Behavior in the Old South*. Oxford: Oxford University Press.

Yoneyama, Shoko, and Asao Naito. 2003. "Problems with the Paradigm: The School as a Factor in Understanding Bullying (with Special Reference to Japan)." *British Journal of Sociology of Education* 24: 315–30.

Zillman, D., J. Bryant, and B. S. Sapolsky. 1979. "The Enjoyment of Watching Sports Contests." In *Sports, Games, and Play*, edited by Jeffrey H. Goldstein. New York: Wiley.

Index